16ª

Sarada Ramakrishna Vivekananda
Associations of Oregon, San Francisco,
New England & Hawaii

# THE AVADHUT

## And His Twenty-Four Teachers In Nature

by Babaji Bob Kindler

Prem Durga Marisela Bracho–*Cover Art and Book Designer*
Mary K. Townsley–*Editor*
Lokelani Cabanlit and Annapurna (Leigh Anne Gurtov)–*Proofreaders*

The publication of this book was made possible by assistance from
the Adelaide and Alexander Hixon Foundation and from donations
from friends and students of the independent SRV Associations.

Printed in the United States of America

Library of Congress Catalogue Card Number: 99-63388

ISBN 1-891893-05-X

# Contents

# Dedication

I dedicate this book to all those who have attempted to
make sense out of this world, whether they have failed or
succeeded, whether they have acquiesced, compromised,
harmonized or transcended, whether they have found the
experience of existence to be lacking, to be satisfactory,
to be bittersweet, or to be ultimately fulfilling.

Victory and salutations to the Blessed Lord and Divine
Mother of the Universe existing above, below, beyond,
throughout and within every shred and fiber
of this boundless creation!

*Babaji Bob Kindler*
Sri Sarada Devi's birthday
New Year's day, 1997

# Introduction

In the Srimad Bhagavatam we find an intriguing testament of the meeting and communion between Sri Krishna and His beloved disciple, Uddhava. Lovingly referred to as the Uddhava Gita, this discourse starts at chapter six and runs through chapter twenty-nine of the eleventh skandha of the Bhagavatam. The level of teaching transmission which Sri Krishna bestows upon Uddhava in this portion of the Bhagavatam is, in content and quality, every bit as rich and profound as that which He gave earlier to another loyal disciple, Arjuna, on the battlefield at Kurukshetra which has become known and revered the world over as the Bhagavad Gita, or "Song Celestial."

Both of these endearing celestial songs, the Bhagavad Gita and the Uddhava Gita, are sonorous duets. Sri Krishna executes the main melody and provides delightful harmony throughout while both Uddhava and Arjuna, in their respective places, add counterpart, essential rhythm and other subtle embellishment which lends each composition additional thematic material and critical movement. The blessed Lord in human form, Sri Krishna is, as well, the adept composer who creates the work and fashions it into a finished masterpiece. This is because He is the world teacher (Jagadguru) who is perfectly suited for the task of dispelling doubts and revealing the lighted pathway to the highest attainment – that of realization of the Atman.

This unborn, undying Self called Atman is the primary subject of Vedanta Philosophy. According to Sri Krishna, who is an authentic authority on the subject, It is all-pervasive, indivisible and eternal. In answer to Uddhava's burning questions about the

Atman, directed to Sri Krishna on the evening of the Lord's destined passage from the human body, the Blessed One relates:

> Controlling thy senses and thy mind,
> behold this universe as spread out in the Self
> and behold the Self as resting in Me, the Supreme Lord.

Thus does Sri Krishna, ever possessed of a consummate and unified understanding, reveal and affirm the intrinsic connection between the manifested universe (Jagat), the spark of divinity realized as the essential portion of each individual being (Atman) and the One who oversees the cosmic functions of the relative universe (Ishvara).

Throughout the Uddhava Gita, the Blessed Lord in human form (Avatar) gives out essential insights in a breathtaking yet systematic manner. About the ultimate teacher He states:

> The Self alone is the teacher of all beings
> and especially of mankind,
> for It conduces to well-being
> through direct perception and inference.

Knowing that the universal Guru exists within each of us, then, is the first and most important step in recovering the pristine and ever-perfect condition that has somehow been lost or overlooked due to ignorant actions committed over interminable periods of time. That the Atman is ever-perfect is also implied, yet it seems as if It can also be covered up or obscured in some fashion. This is due to the limitations of the body/mind mechanism. To remedy this, the Blessed Lord mentions inference, a word which implies the need for both analysis and self-effort — finding out the Truth and implementing Its every tenet into all facets of existence. The Supreme Wisdom of the Atman and knowledge of the spiritual path leading to individual salvation and final liberation are both necessary. The first is realized mainly through the Grace of the Lord while the latter is attained mostly through self-effort and discipline. Regarding the necessity of both Grace and self-effort, Sri Krishna tells Uddhava:

Very often in this world,
beings who have discerned the Truth about the universe
deliver themselves from evil inclinations
through their own exertions.

Personal self-effort is necessary for another reason as well. The universe of name and form, a mutable expression of Reality, is formed from the constituents of nature (Prakriti) and woven with the sticky strands of sattva, rajas and tamas – temporal balance, frenetic activity and incapacitating inertia. These binding elements delude embodied beings by distorting and limiting their awareness. They fasten individualized consciousness to a narrow thought process concerned mostly with selfish considerations which are attended by the dangers of desire and attachment and accompanied by the appearance of detrimental passions such as anger, lust, greed, jealousy and the like. When this mixture is encountered by the average human being identified predominantly with the senses and ego, misapprehension and delusion occur, resulting in disorientation. This, in turn, gives rise to misguided actions which lead to inevitable karmic repercussion. Bondage of all types is the unfortunate outcome. Mankind then enjoys superficially and suffers grievously in repetitious alternating cycles, bereft of the originally intended divine life and forgetting the purpose for human existence

The very fabric of the universe, created by the Lord's enchanting power (Maya), is permeated with binding principles and deceptive appearances. Losing the proper mental facility, living beings fall into the snares of illusion and suffer as a result. Sri Krishna mentions this perplexing predicament as well:

The man of uncontrolled mind
falls into the error that there is a plurality of objects,
and this error leads to merit and demerit.
The differences of action, inaction and evil action
concern only the man who has ideas of merit and demerit.

Obsessed with a "plurality of objects," and thereby losing the awareness of the eternal and indivisible presence of God, man's vision becomes clouded by duality. Forgotten are the words of the great ones who declare that to be free, "thine eye must be single."

To make consciousness unified is the key to escaping all manner of suffering.  In addition to transcending misery, an infinite expanse of spiritual experience awaits the aspiring individual who seeks and finds the valuable keys of harmony and transcendence. Though the universe is full of subtle traps for the avid seeker who desires ultimate freedom – the very condition of body, life and mind being restricting factors – longing for the supreme status of Self-realization drives the aspirant onwards towards attainment of the spiritual goal.  The Blessed Lord desires this ultimate achievement for all living beings as well and loves to sport through human awareness, guiding it through all difficulties.  In the Srimad Bhagavatam He states:

> There are many created cities
> such as those with one, two, three, four, or many legs,
> as well as without legs;
> of these, the human body is My favorite city.

Every living being is a teeming pool of matter, life-force and mental energy.  Each loving human devotee represents a vast metropolis and among all of these Uddhava is certainly one of the Lord's "favorite cities."  With the primal guide, Sri Krishna, as his companion and the intense desire for spiritual emancipation as his driving force, Uddhava is a prime candidate for the boon of God's boundless Grace.  He stands on the brink of liberation and while so doing poses essential questions to his Master, the revered teacher of mankind and Lord of the universe.  Coming to know that Sri Krishna will soon leave the body and disappear from his physical gaze, Uddhava appeals to Him for a similar release in mutual company with the Lord:

> How can we, Thy devotees, give up Thy company
> in lying, sitting, walking, staying, bathing,
> sporting, eating and so on,
> for Thou art dearly beloved of us, nay, our very Self?
> O Keshava, not for half a second
> can I bear to be separated from Thy Lotus Feet.
> Therefore, O Lord, take me also to Thy abode.

The Lord's answer to this poignant plea is significant and forms the foundation upon which the noble way of true spirituality rests. Embarking upon the spiritual path, pursuing it tenaciously, receiving and implementing the teachings pertinent to it and arriving at the goal – all of these, as far as embodied beings are concerned, condense down into one essential imperative – that each being must fully realize his or her inherent nature to be divine and resting completely in that perfect knowledge, continue to abide, in whatever way that God dictates, in that immaculate state under all conditions.  Therefore, Sri Krishna answers profoundly:

> O noble soul, as soon as I leave this world,
> it will be shorn of its well-being
> and will soon be overtaken by the spirit of the Dark Age.
> Thou, too, shouldst not stay here
> after I leave the earth, for, O good soul,
> men will be addicted to evil in the Iron Age.
> Giving up thy attachment for thy kinsmen and friends
> and renouncing everything, roam thou over the world,
> with evenness of vision, fixing the mind wholly in Me.
> Whatever is cognized by the mind, speech, ears and the rest
> – know it all to be a figment of the mind,
> a phantasmagoria, and withal doomed to pass away.

It is after this profound discourse has been delivered that Sri Krishna cites the example of the Avadhut – the free soul who is beyond all dualities, though still abiding in human form as an example for others.  It would seem that He desires for Uddhava to follow this noble way as well.  Knowing that the age of ignorance – a recurring portion of the unending cycle of life in relativity – is upon them, and desiring that Uddhava simultaneously escape the ills of such an age and act as a teacher for other struggling beings, Sri Krishna, the Dvapara Yuga Avatar, directs him along this transcendent pathway.  In doing so, He reveals the ultimate direction for all those who would aspire for absolute perfection.

Sri Krishna is privy to the most profound knowledge.  The Divine Incarnation does not labor under the limited understanding that human beings take recourse to.  For the Avatar, there is no compromise along the path of transcendence. The least bit of clinging to individual existence or longing after terrestrial life is unacceptable. There are some who would criticize the necessity of transcending the universe, citing lack of compassion, escapism and other seemingly valid reasons. These beings prescribe human agency and motivated action as solutions for the ills of the world, assuming that the mind/ego complex engaged in interminable periods of work can somehow do away with pervasive human suffering and misery.

Sri Krishna, on the other hand, knows that all work done in the improper spirit, accomplished by unillumined beings, is both the cause for and the perpetuation of all manner of negativity, and history agrees. In most cases, action is the antithesis of true respite. Few know the secrets of true work and perfect repose and how to combine them. Sri Krishna, the master of Karma Yoga, is aware that the sense of agency in human beings, as long as it remains unripe, only contributes to the problem of human misery rather than assisting in any solution. He is also aware that "ripened" awareness, the mind which has become illumined, immediately perceives the transitory nature of the universe, causing it to simultaneously desist from motivated action (sakama karma) and withdraw into the bliss of the Self. How can one be both uninvolved in action and involved in action yet free from its effects? How can one be a part of the universal process yet simultaneously free and transcendent of it? The Lord explains:

> Beyond the reach of both merit and demerit,
> the illumined being will, like a child,
> desist from prohibited actions,
> though not through a sense of evil,
> and perform enjoined actions,
> though not through an idea that it will conduce to merit.
> Friend to all beings,
> with settled conviction due to knowledge and realization,
> and beholding the universe as consisting of nothing but Me,
> such a one no more comes to grief.

Unlike many others who clamor for more work in the name of service to humanity and who, either consciously or unconsciously, use various altruistic activities for the pursuit of their own oft-concealed personal considerations, Sri Krishna proclaims a way that is based entirely upon the uncompromising and exacting attainment of pure, unadulterated transcendence. His is not an escape from relative existence but a comprehensive understanding that simultaneously perceives the presence of the Atman in all things while retaining the ability to withdraw from the traps and allures of universal projection that snare and bind transmigrating beings. He sees the universe as an expression of Brahman but refuses to acquiesce in the least to the fact that matter, as any given form, is noneternal and that action, in and of itself, ever fails to bring enlightenment, being at best only a preparatory stage involving preliminary purification. In addition, He knows that the condition of true enlightenment does not brook the slightest attachment to name and form and consists of knowing the Atman, the Self of all beings, to be entirely separate from and transcendent of all constituents of the universe, whether they be of physical, material, sensual, vital, mental or intellectual makeup.

Sri Krishna, at the same time, does not deviate in the least from the unified perception that the entire universe, taken as an indivisible whole and being an undeniable expression of Brahman, is permeated by God's presence and is possessed, as it were, of Reality. Like the red-hot iron ball and its heat, the universe shines and radiates the warmth of existence only so long as the fire of Consciousness is associated with it. As soon as Consciousness withdraws, the world loses its essential light and falls away from perception, for there is then nothing left in existence through which to perceive it. Herein lies the secret of the simultaneous reality and unreality of the world, of the coexisting existence and nonexistence of Maya, of the apparent substantiality and nonsubstantiality of the universe.

In order to bring these cosmic dichotomies into focus, and to emphasize both the practicality and benefit of accepting and implementing a spiritual path that sees each – the universe and Brahman – in proper perspective, Sri Krishna begins to tell Uddhava the story of Yadu, a learned prince of the lunar race of kings who is also an ancestor of Sri Krishna. In the Lord's story, Yadu meets the Avadhut who relates to him the teachings he gleaned from observing the actions of twenty-four "teachers" in nature.  It is this story, in part, that has inspired the following book.

It is interesting to note that each of these were accepted as teachers by the Avadhut not in the traditional sense, as perfected or adept instructors giving out teachings which they had previously realized, but as beings who taught by example, themselves experiencing the outcome of life and karma due to their own actions and according to the makeup of their own individual natures.  This situation allows the subtle workings of the Divine Being to be seen in a unique light, reflecting the pertinent lessons which permeate the empirical process and point most emphatically towards the existence of a transcendent witness of all phenomena.  In truth, it can be seen that the Avadhut himself develops and expresses the concentrated and illumined intelligence of such a supremely detached witness, thereby acting as an adept preceptor for those who come into contact with him.  In this way, he is the perfect exemplar, the fulfillment and embodiment in human form of all the qualities and truths that Sri Krishna lovingly relates to his beloved disciple, Uddhava, in the sacred Srimad Bhagavatam.

I have mentioned above that the twenty-four teachers of the Avadhut were nontraditional.  That the Avadhut, Ekanta by name, possesses such a deep spirituality strongly implies contact with gurus of the traditional kind long before he encountered these teachers in nature.  In our story, he has several: a vanaprastin couple, a mountain yogi, a venerable old swami, a baul from Bengal and a few others.  Throughout the book, all of the Paravidya – the wisdom that these human gurus transmitted to him – has been placed in italics so as to call attention to it.  This distinquishes these teachings from the storyline and renders them easy to find for those who are interested in the nondual teachings – the Advaitic essence.  In addition, all of the many poems, songs and scriptural excerpts found in this book, with the exception of a couple of Lex Hixon's lucid poem translations and a few quotes from Swami Vivekananda's poems, have been retranslated by the author.

Readers who are familiar with the lives and teachings of Sri Ramakrishna, Sri Sarada Devi and Swami Vivekananda, who are to me and many others the Divine Trinity of this age, will find many of their teachings and stories throughout the pages of this book.  I therefore acknowledge fully and completely an immense debt of gratitude to them for being my continual source of inspiration throughout this and all previous lifetimes. This tiny recognition sounds hollow indeed considering that I regard the Paramahamsa, His divine consort and His powerful messenger as a complete triple manifestation of Sri Kali, the Divine Mother of the Universe. This being the case, the Kali Avatar has manifested for us in this very age, quite recently, in clear and perfect view of all who have eyes to see. As Swami Vivekananda himself wrote about this unique and incomparable sadguru, Sri Ramakrishna: *"Behold, Sita's beloved has come again to earth!"*

Since God has come before us in this way, it stands to reason that we behold and perceive in Him the divine architect of the blueprint of this infinite universe and also the creator of the wonderful human mechanism with all its exquisite characteristics and subtleties. In the wandering Avadhut, we find a composite of many of the qualities and attributes found in Sri Ramakrishna, Swami Vivekananda and Sri Sarada Devi, my Paramaguru, known lovingly as Holy Mother. Records of their compassionate deeds and salutary virtues have been gathered from all the revealing information that we have been able to compile from their teachings, from eyewitness accounts and from the considerable history that has already been recorded about them.

In writing this book, I have drawn heavily from these SRV ideals (Sarada/Ramakrishna/Vivekananda) as well as from the timeless Vedas and Upanishads, the Avadhuta Gita, the Ashtavakra Samhita, the Vivekachudamani, the Bhagavad Gita and other spiritually based texts. Substantial inspiration has come, too, from over twenty-five years of meditating directly on Sri Ramakrishna and Holy Mother in this lifetime alone, a blessing of unfathomable proportions greatly assisted by profound spiritual instructions from my own monastic and vanaprastin/householder gurus. From such an intense process this book has been born and I offer it at the feet of God in human form. It has a bit of everything in it excluding compromise of the noble spiritual ideal. My intent is that it will inspire others to enter or intensify spiritual life and also inspire parents to instill the perennial wisdom that Ekanta received into the minds of their own children so that future generations will behold godlike men and women by the hundreds, walking the earth and making it a place of divine expression.

# Prologue

It was a blessed and vibrant time, an age replete with all manner of abundance and attended by many auspicious signs. Upon the face of Earth, that radiant loka or divine realm known as Bhur among the lovers of Brahman, there lived a myriad of beings. Some were aware of the Lord's presence in all things, cognizant of His guiding hand in all events and satisfied with a pure and simple life that left them ever content to ply their trades. These dwelled in harmony with one another. Others, driven by passion and desire, had lost touch with nature, their fellow human beings and the radiance of the all-pervasive Reality that, as the ancient scriptures declared, "infilled all things."

With regards to the human context, this mixture of the aware and the unaware, the awakened and the unawakened, the sensitive and the insensitive, was a sign of the times, a sobering usher into a new and darker era. The honored and time-tested spiritual ways of the elders were fast receding, becoming obscured by the advancement of a technological age that threatened to destroy the timeless tenets which had fostered and maintained harmony for so many centuries. Mechanization fell swiftly upon the peoples of these early modern times and the possibilities for wealth and gain that it afforded drew forth from the human mind all manner of ignoble tendencies such as greed, the desire for power, seeking after fame and attachment to lust and lucre.

To further these aims, governments and religious institutions alike, instead of wisely guiding the masses and aiding them in fulfilling the goal of existence, searched for numerous ways to deceive the populace in order to maintain individual and collective control and successfully hoard the things that brought earthly satisfaction and sensual pleasure. Commercialization, then, along with exploitation of the earth's resources and conscious deception of the people, became the normal mode of behavior.

In addition to this and despite signs of well-being and prosperity, the earth's creatures were in constant turmoil, rocking under the repeated expansion and contraction of the six transformations – birth, growth, disease, decay, old age and death. Every world, human, celestial and causal, was subject to these universal laws. No living being existing within the three worlds, whether god, demigod, asura, man or beast, could escape these cosmic imperatives. Therefore, the empirical process wore on, bearing with it the hopes, attachments, possessions and numerous considerations of all embodied beings inhabiting the worlds of name and form.

Across this varied backdrop of terrestrial existence and vying with it for mankind's attentions, moved an occasional enigmatic figure. Bereft of possessions, existing upon whatever came naturally through the Blessed Lord's Grace and seemingly content with life, these beings mysteriously brought a renewed sense of spirituality to the common people and greatly diminished their sufferings brought about by the embodied condition and the impositions of life in the physical universe.

Strange yet wonderful, these holy figures were possessed of many perplexing powers: perplexing because, not only did they refrain from using these forces to benefit themselves, but also because these powers were strangely transparent, for all intents and purposes, nonexistent. This made them not only imperceptible, but also uncovetable. Scarcely understanding the nature of such forces, the simple folk of earth left the operation of these subtle energies to the wise men and women who comprehended and wielded them in such a strangely disinterested and natural fashion.

Many of the ways in which these sublime beings lived and operated appeared, to a great degree, contradictory. For instance, while being extremely aware of all conditions of nature and consciousness, they seemed at the same time to be unconcerned and detached from them. They were extremely meticulous in every detail, yet were observed to be wholly transcendent of any process, whether it be mundane or important, self-motivated or altruistic, secular or spiritual. What is more, they were completely disinterested in the final outcome of any given project or action. Speculation had it, in fact, that these unusual qualities were the source of their subtle yet awesome powers. It was guessed, therefore, that due to a strict adherence to such spiritual mainstays as desirelessness, nonattachment and renunciation among others, that these free and holy individuals were the true masters of the universe and represented, as it were, the will of the Blessed Lord of the Universe made manifest.

These exalted beings fell into many categories of illumined status, all with their own ways and peculiarities: compassionate saints, sages from various schools of wisdom, world-renouncing sannyasins, world-affirming householders, illumined vanaprastins, silent munis, famous and unknown acharyas, adept arhats, naked ascetics, powerful siddhas, wandering yogis, enlightened paramahamsas and holy beings of all religious preferences. Among them, and respected highly by all denominations, lived the Avadhuts, radiant stars in any spiritual firmament. Traditionally, it was known that such a one had renounced the world, though not in the ordinary sense. Belonging to the sixth order of sannyas, they were totally without possessions and wandered the world practicing the most natural type of asceticism. They were without ties or attachments and were completely devoid of unnatural desires.

In all walks of life there are bound to be occasional individuals that transcend even the highest standards, whether sacred or secular. Genius, either worldly or spiritual, sets these above the rest, giving them deeper insight and extensive wisdom. The main character of this story, Ekanta, was of such a unique status. His father, himself a wise and silent knower of Truth, had given the boy his name after observing his quiet and introspective nature. Ekanta, a name which means solitude or seclusion, suited the boy perfectly, for he loved to be alone and naturally sought out uninhabited places even in early life. Ekanta's love for solitary existence was unusual however. Although he would seek seclusion in order to be afforded the time to contemplate subtle internal matters, he did not shun company or feel averse to the ordinary intrusions of the world. He also possessed a special ability to remain outwardly conscious while being absorbed in deep meditation. This double-faceted attribute was utilized in his dealings with the world in general as well. He could perform the functions of thinking, acting and conversing simultaneously while remaining fully centered and focused in the internal Reality. This was possible for him under all conditions of life.

Ekanta's wonderful ability produced in people who came in contact with him the tendency to bare their souls. They sensed in Ekanta, even as a youngster, a being who was completely in touch with the divine Source and ever in communion with that Source. Therefore, even at a young age, people began to seek him out for advice and for the salutary company that he provided. This increase of attention, contrary to popular expectation, did not turn his head whatsoever. Instead, it acted as a force that matured him beyond his years, for now he not only had the ability to withdraw at will from surface existence with all its attendant evils, but he also developed a wonderful sensitivity for the cares, sufferings and considerations of living beings. This made his detachment both mature and effective and without the slightest trace of callousness. From this compassionate condition emerged the further ability to observe the problems of the human mind, analyze them and apply enlightening solutions, with transformative results. As a result, his increasing fame in matters of a psycho/spiritual nature drew increasing numbers of suffering and seeking beings to him.

It was at this juncture that he came in contact with two beings who would change the direction of his life forever. In the forest one day, while pursuing a few hours of peaceful introspection, the boy was driven by peculiar circumstances into the vicinity of a vanaprastin couple, forest dwellers who had renounced common conventionality and who were spending the remainder of their lives in contemplation of the Lord. The couple, man and wife, were radiant with light, wise beyond imagining and well-versed in the sacred scriptures of the ancient Rishis. Except for the boy's formal moral training and the basic teachings afforded him by his mother and father, he had never experienced knowledge of such powerful intensity. Ekanta felt, therefore, that he had found his ordained teachers and wasted no time in offering himself in full prostration, completely, with open heart and self-surrendered mind, at the feet of this divine couple. The two vanaprastins, also recognizing a profound inner connection and perceiving both the impeccable nature of the boy and his ingenious abilities, accepted Ekanta and began training him in spiritual life.

Who can possibly comprehend or describe the intricacies and sublimities contained within the divine relationship between guru and disciple? It is not an ordinary bond, the like of which is common to the denizens of the earth who rely on the advice of family and friends for guidance. Days, weeks and months passed by in the bliss of spiritual transmission. From the nondual texts, filled with undeniable proofs of the all-pervasive presence of Brahman, to the secondary scriptures replete with inspired stories and direct references describing the repeated descent of divinity into the world of name and form, all was revealed to Ekanta in a fashion only faintly imagined in the fondest dreams of sincere spiritual aspirants. In addition, direct observation of the lifestyle and actions of the illumined couple revealed to Ekanta what it was truly like to live a divine life as described by the wise ones of old. What is more, when the teachings of the elders and their exemplary way of life entered as influential impressions into the already awakened and purified awareness of Ekanta's mind, uncommon experiences began to emerge. As a result, his parents and friends began to find him in strange states – sometimes active with amazing energy, at other times deeply introspective and nearly inert, and sometimes laughing and crying in turns.

Due to the increased spiritual maturation of the boy, who had now reached young manhood, it was of little surprise to his family and friends that Ekanta one day announced his desire to leave the village and wander off into the world. Ekanta, possessed of uncommon parents, soon received their blessing and late one night, in order to avoid long good-byes with multitudes of well-wishers, set off into the darkness to fulfill his destiny. Plunging into the woods in the direction of his twin gurus, he soon made out the light of their dhuni fire and came before them. There were no words wasted that evening, for all three – the Guruji, the Mataji and the dedicated disciple – knew that the one, eternal Self in all beings never comes and goes, never departs and never divides. Therefore, when the time for communion was over, Ekanta saluted his revered spiritual teachers with respectful thirteen-point pranams and with tears of love and gratitude welling up in his eyes, withdrew into the deep silence of the surrounding forest.

The wonderful couple watched, equally silent and full of admiration, as the form of their beloved disciple was gradually swallowed up by the darkness.

Minutes passed and perfect quietude reigned. The old couple remained still. Suddenly, an osprey called from a nearby tree. A deer glided agilely through the distant clearing. A python slipped by, visible in the light of the fire. Soon, a huge luna moth shot out of the darkness and danced about the fire, occasionally singeing its wings in the flames. Then, as if on cue, the divine couple turned towards each other. As their shining eyes met, one phrase, uttered in unison and in reverent recognition of their precious student, broke the silence of the forest: "the Avadhut!"

# The Prince and
# the Avadhut

## – Royalty Meets Realized Being

L isten well, friends.  A story is being told about Divinity manifest on earth.  The Avadhut, free and unencumbered by either possessions or misconceptions, and roaming the world to observe the ways of humanity and assist in their spiritual ascension, was once approached by Prince Yadu, the son of a powerful king of the Lunar Race.  Being well-informed in the science of religion, Yadu reverently saluted the holy Avadhut and inquired of him about his unique and salutary lifestyle.

"How wonderful is your demeanor, your simplicity and your disposition, revered one," exclaimed the prince.  "You possess knowledge, intelligence, health and facility – all the coveted qualities through which worldly life can succeed – yet you refrain from self-centered activity and remain calm and balanced under all conditions.

"The entire world, as Shankara has said, is being devoured by disease and deceit as beings exert all effort and energy to

1

achieve earthly success, satisfy desires, amass wealth and attain power. Engaged with these preoccupations, they entirely overlook the Self within and fail to perceive It as the only lasting verity amidst changing circumstances. As a direct result, they suffer the intense heat of the sun of worldliness, unprotected by the cooling shade of the Atman and vulnerable to the effects of lust, greed, anger and other adversities common to terrestrial existence. Therefore, revered sir, kindly reveal to us the secrets of a balanced life and how one can abide in the higher Self without lapses and distractions while remaining free of the dangers and disparities of relative existence."

"Not of myself do I do," answered the Avadhut, "but rather depend upon the Absolute to guide me in all things. This direction from on high proceeds to inform me through an intellect kept pure and clear according to an exacting personal discrimination. This I use to observe all things, all phenomena. As a result, all beings and experiences become my teachers, which are sent to me by my Beloved. Listen to a short list of them, respected Prince.

"The earth, arrowmaker, maiden, moth, elephant, moon, osprey, python, ocean, fish, courtesan, wind, deer, pigeon, sun, bee, brahmara-kita, sky, spider, honey-gatherer, water, snake, fire and the child – these twenty-four teachers added immensely to my understanding of the Universal Form and how It expresses Its infinite, indivisible and formless Essence during extended periods of manifestation. From these expressions of the Almighty, great and small, I have learned some valuable lessons. Since you are so devoted and have prepared yourself according to the words of the guru and the scriptures, I will share these teachings with you."

# Chapter 1

# Teachings from the Earth Mother

THE FIRST GURU —The Earth
THE LESSON —Forbearance

*From Mother Earth, I learned the lesson of forbearance mingled with selfless service. Following Her example, I perform all actions for the sake of others and have dedicated life itself to this Divine purpose. Due to this, I became a disciple of the tree, the mountains and other facets of Mother Vasundhara's realm called Bhur Loka by the ancient ones. This teaching alone formed the foundation upon which I could comprehend a portion of the magnanimity of the Earth Mother. It is to Her that we owe our terrestrial existence and the chance to experience a balanced life in this amazing flow of time and space called the universe.*

The Avadhut stood on a low grassy hill which commanded a sweeping and breathtaking view of the surrounding countryside. It had been quite a few years since he had left his home, parting company with family, friends and teachers to seek out and fulfill his intense inner longing for direct God-vision. He stood quietly in the approaching dusk, his eyes lingering on the interplay of soft hues of light which danced slowly across the changing landscape. Taking a few moments, he tried to recall his age, but this task proved useless and he quickly abandoned the attempt. Indeed, he had almost forgotten his name and had long since lost track of what he looked like. Suddenly he laughed silently to himself, recalling the shock he had experienced upon catching sight of the reflection of his image in a mountain lake some time back. The being staring back at him from out of the still waters was unrecognizable. Time, he thought to himself, what an enigma, what an illusion!

No sooner had these thoughts crossed his mind than the images of his two vanaprastin teachers sprang into his consciousness. The lessons that he had received from the venerable elderly couple could never be effaced from his awareness. He would never forget that moment in time when a particularly profound awakening revealed the nature of time, space and causality — all three — to be transitory and insubstantial concepts of the mind. And the mind itself was revealed to be created of inert matter and filled with innumerable positive and negative impressions, as well as being an instrument designed to calculate, categorize and measure. *"Obsessed with a plurality of objects,"* he recalled, that was how Sri Krishna had described the ordinary mind to the Avadhut's ancient ancestors. The Avadhut could still hear the voice of his teacher in this regard as it transmitted to him the perennial wisdom of the timeless Upanishads:

All is guided by Prajna, or Consciousness.
Those who transcend the world of time, space and causality
do so by realizing the master of Prajna, the Atman,
and having obtained all delights in the world of bliss,
gain immortality – verily, they gain immortality.

A thrill of joy passed over Ekanta's entire being. He was the Avadhut — the solitary one, without company, bereft of possessions, with mind completely devoid of hope for even the next meal or morsel of food — yet the slightest thought of the all-pervasive Atman filled him with a unique satisfaction immeasurable by worldly standards. His twin teachers, the illumined vanaprastin couple, had taught him well. Long ago he had realized that this Atman constituted his entire family. It was his only friend, for it appeared before him as the essence of every being — plant, animal, mineral or human — that came his way or crossed his path. It was also his food, his only true sustenance.

*"Man does not live by bread alone,"* came the inner voice of wisdom, echoing in his mind in the sweet tones of his revered female teacher.

Then, as if both his teachers were present, his Guruji chimed in: *"Man must eat to live, my son, not live to eat."*

It was by teachings such as these, transmitted by those who had mastered the spiritual art of renunciation that the obsession with pleasure — that tendency which enchants the entire world — had been gradually effaced and removed from his mind forever, leaving him free from all attachments.

Ekanta stirred himself from his inspiring reverie. He could not describe how, but there had come a point in time when his mind had lost the tendency to brood over circumstances or waste time in vain mental wanderings and vague imaginations. Under the guidance of his gurus, combined with sincere self-effort, his mind had gradually become a rich field of inspirational thought, like gems waiting to be plucked from the earth and converted into a vast and priceless fortune. Suddenly, his mind began to enter another deep spiritual mood, occurring as quickly as the last had departed. The fond remembrance of his gurus and their teachings had once more brought to the forefront of his consciousness an idea that had been haunting him for weeks. He strongly desired to see his teachers again, but not just in the conventional sense. Over time he had realized, through intense inner contemplation, that his true longing was for the ultimate level of beatific vision — the perception of God in everything, existing everywhere.

At this moment, somewhere within him, and possessed completely of a will independent of any exterior control, arose a power so subtle, so sublime, that he had to struggle to retain normal consciousness. Ordinarily, he would have immediately given in to such a force, since inner experiences were not new to him, but this movement was of a different intensity and vibration, entirely riveting and attended by a simultaneous heightening of all the senses and a great power of detached introspection. After the upsurge of the initial force of this power had subsided a bit, Ekanta opened his eyes and looked around in wonder. Everywhere, on all sides, was the blessed Mother Earth, but instead of seeing only the five elements in their varied combinations of manifestation, Ekanta discovered, much to his surprise and delight, that he could easily behold and decipher the inner significance behind each of these expressions. It was as if Mother Earth had opened up a multitude of Her innermost secrets to him all at once. On all sides he beheld sacred symbols fraught with significance, each bearing a precious teaching pregnant with meaning.

After catching his breath, he proceeded to reorient himself to this fresh perception, this new way of seeing. Since his intelligence was swift and lucid, and no stranger to spiritual experiences, Ekanta understood that, by the grace of the Lord, his powerful longing to perceive divinity in all things was beginning to be realized. Tears of gratitude streamed from the outer corners of his eyes, seeming to explode into space as if they had a life of their own. The entire earth realm was saturated in living bliss, yet all was inexplicably peaceful. Indeed, everything seemed steeped in Consciousness. This was a new experience for Ekanta, for up to this point he had experienced the presence of divinity only in transcendent states of inner absorption, never so vividly and apparently woven in and around the world outside of him. Like a thunderbolt, the teachings of Sri Krishna came rolling into his mind:

*Ihai'kastham jagat krtsnam pashya'dya sacharachara*
*mama dehe gudakesha yac cha'nyad drastum icchasi*

Behold at this moment, O Gudakesha,
a whole host of sentient and insentient beings
and the boundless universe as well,
all as inseparable parts of Me.

*Na tu mam shayase drastum anenai'va svachakshusha*
*divyam dadami te chaksuh pashya me yogam aisvaram*

Strive how you may, beloved one,
you will not perceive this wonder with ordinary senses.
You must receive the divine sight which I now bestow.
Gaze now upon the Master Illusion.

While it was not a human form that Ekanta beheld before him, as was the case when Arjuna heard these thrilling words from the mouth of the Blessed Lord, Sri Krishna, the presence of God was nevertheless palpable. Again, Sri Bhagavan's teachings came to the forefront of his mind:

_Avyaktam vyaktam appannam manyante mam abuddhayah_
_Param bhavam ajananto mama'vyayam anuttamam_

Beings with limited comprehension declare My essence
to be manifest when, in actuality, I am ever unmanifest.
Thus, they do not know My immutable presence
which is ineffable and incomparable.

The Avadhut momentarily pondered the seeming paradox of Reality, with its two basic modes of form and formlessness. Such an incredibly subtle principle, he thought, this transcendent Reality with Its empirical process. He remembered questioning his wisdom teachers about the dilemma of the One and the many. The answer came forth from them:

_"Ever One, appearing as Two, yet manifesting as the many without the slightest sense of separation — this is the Supreme Beloved."_

Satisfied with this comprehensive answer, Ekanta found further verification in the scriptures, recalling the appropriate verse:

Those who acknowledge and realize
that all beings abide eternally in the one Supreme Reality,
expressing apparently and momentarily
as the many through the playful sport of that One,
realize their identity with the Supreme Brahman.

Here, then, before his very eyes, was the opportunity to perceive and understand the essential unity of all things. By the Grace of the Lord, he was now beholding nondual, homogenous Reality, all-pervasive and fully aware, saturating everything while simultaneously remaining pristine, transcendent and untouchable. From his memory emerged an appropriate description: _"The Atman, seated in the heart, pervades everything yet remains untainted and ever pure. It resembles the ether, unaffected by all objects."_

Now he could truly appreciate the teachings given to him by the great Rishis.   Silently, deliberately and with great reverence, Ekanta laid himself face down upon the earth in deep devotion and gratitude.

His heartfelt salutation complete, Ekanta rose to a cross-legged sitting position.   He was now ready to take note of every aspect of the creation, filing it away in the vast repository of his illumined mind.   Immediately, though, before he could begin that process, there arose spontaneously to his lips a prayer and benediction, bubbling up from the depths of his inner being:

*"O Mother Earth, bestower of all good things and perfect expression of the Lord's love and wisdom, you are my teacher. O Vasundhara, especial Goddess who presides over Ishvara's appearance as the world of name and form, who provides sustenance and a home for Him to sport in delightful abandon, fulfill us with all manner of goodness.  O Tulsi Ma, Ganga Ma, Himavat, all ye divinities who make the earth your secret and temporary habitat, transforming it into a living paradise, reveal to me the keys to the mystery of manifestation.   Allow me to behold the many while retaining pure awareness of the One, fill my consciousness with profound thoughts of Thee and permeate me through and through with Thy sweet and benign presence!"*

As if by some hidden signal, this spontaneous prayer acted to prompt his consciousness to the presence of a subtle guide in the creation.   This invisible indicator, though seemingly nondistinct from his own awareness, began to act almost imperceptibly, drawing his attention to a host of appearances spread out before him.

The lay of the land was the first lesson to capture his attention. Gazing at the many variations which complemented the earth's appearance, Ekanta was immediately struck by the far-reaching intelligence of the Creator who had designed such a world.   High elevations, lowlands and intermediary regions, arid climates, wetlands and frozen highlands, all blessed with characteristics suited to the beings dwelling there, graced the earth and gave it immense variety.   Plants, insects, animals and the micro-organisms which accompanied and sustained them, each were given a place in the order of the evolution and were provided with whatever was required for existence.   The entire plan was awesome and immaculate, even decay and death proving crucial and invaluable to its operation.

With heightened senses, Ekanta now became focused on the sounds of the creatures inhabiting the grasses and woodlands around and near him. In the waning light of dusk, insects, fish, fowl, animals and human beings were busy exploring, making habitats and gathering sustenance from Mother Earth. She bore them all upon Her vast body without complaint. She gave them everything, unstintingly and graciously, for the act of giving was intrinsic to Her very nature.

Ekanta marveled at the lesson communicated here. When even the very earth was designed to give away its infinite bounty to all living things in such a manner, was not the act of generosity thereby revealed to be the original intention of the Creator? How then could any living thing, when faced with such graciousness, adopt selfishness as a way of life? Was not the tendency towards self-ishness, with its constituents of calculating, grasping, hoarding, clinging and so forth, not a violation of the intrinsic laws of the universe, demonstrated so obviously by Mother Earth's perpetu-ally open-armed policy?

Bees circled and buried themselves in fragrant flowers which grew in profuse abundance on the slopes of the hill. The nectar gathered there would be stored up for further uses. The pollina-tion process proceeded through this important action and the flowers needed this service as well. Without the give and take required by nature, the creation could not proceed. Ekanta made a mental note to study the amazing species of bees further at another time in the light of his present revelatory state of mind.

From this newly awakened and freshly intensified perspective, the Avadhut marveled at another quality demonstrated by Mother Earth. Her constant sacrifice, accomplished in the spirit of unend-ing service, impervious to every slight or burden imposed upon Her, impressed him immensely. A fresh stream of tears came forth from his eyes every minute as he beheld Her infinite capacity for giving and sacrifice, actuated perpetually with endless patience and unending fortitude. What boundless love She must have for Her creatures in order to bear with all sacrifices so marvelously.

So many of nature's salient qualities were now appearing to Ekanta in such rapid succession that he could barely keep track of them. Suddenly, his attention was drawn to an alien sound rising above the other natural vibrations all around him. Looking down the hill and to his left towards the wooded area below, Ekanta beheld a woodsman setting about the task of cutting a tree on the periphery of the forest. The Earth was sacrificing another part of its precious bounty for the good of its living beings.

As stroke after stroke fell upon the tree's healthy trunk, Ekanta slipped into an introspective mood. Gradually, as his mood deepened, a vision appeared deep within his consciousness. It was as if time folded back in upon itself, revealing a sequence of events that were destined to occur in the near future. As this vision unfolded before him, he saw the woodsman finishing his task, shaving the trunk of branches and splitting a portion of the wood into smaller pieces. He then loaded them on his back in a canvas sling and departed for his distant home.

In rapid succession, another series of events was revealed as Ekanta saw a tiny green bird pick up a seed with its beak and launch itself into the sky. As the bird flew low over the edge of the forest towards its nest, a sparrow hawk attacked from above, seizing the small bird in its talons. The seed fell to earth, landing in fertile soil near a small stream of water. Gradually, over months, the seed sprouted and sent down roots into the ideal soil. More months passed and the little sprout grew into a small sapling. As years streamed by like minutes in the subtle internal condition of Ekanta's vision, a great tree grew and formed, reaching maturity despite many obstacles. Seasons came and went and the tree lived on through droughts, floods, windstorms and other natural events. Birds made nests in its upper reaches, ants and other insects invaded it, animals sheltered from the sun and grazed beneath it while some stripped its leaves for food. Monkeys played in the tree's branches, swinging from limb to limb. Below the surface of the soil, worms and ground-dwelling insects found sustenance and burrowing space due to the powerful movements of the tree's roots, while above on the surface, children came every season to pick its fruits and flowers.

As the tree grew to its full height, its life spanning a hundred years, hawks and other large birds often perched atop it, gaining visual access to regions miles beyond. Squirrels, bear cubs and other animals found safety from predators and camouflage amidst the tree's foliage. Finally, active young boys even built a tree fort on the tree's strong lower boughs. Over time, the tree bore with every act imposed upon it and continued, season to season, to exude life-giving oxygen for the benefit of embodied beings. Finally, the day came when the woodsman approached and unsheathed his sharpened ax. Silently and without complaint, the tree fell in the woods, its life terminated, its lifelong service forgotten.

Before Ekanta could lapse into sorrow due to this sequence of events, his rare inner experience continued on in another vein. Beholding the gradual segmentation of the tree over time into various sized chunks, the Avadhut witnessed the destination and usage for each one. Portions of the tree ended up in the hearths and wood stoves of various homes around the area, providing protection from the cold and heat for cooking meals. In this case, even its embers provided essential functions, as wanderers came to the doors of these households begging for fire for their own needs. Even the remains of these embers were utilized, becoming sacred ash for the arms, bodies and foreheads of wandering ascetics.

In other cases, the tree's wood was fashioned into various objects, useful in many different ways. Planks and boards for construction, shingles for roofing, cabinets for storage, kitchen utensils, toys for children — these and many other uses were found for the wonderful tree. Even the stump, roped and extracted from the earth's surface by a team of mules, was carted home and used as a foundation on which to split the wood of other trees, while the roots and leaves were dried and powdered for use in teas and medicines.

As abruptly as this multifaceted vision began, it ceased, leaving the Avadhut to ruminate over its various lessons. Mother Earth, Her five elements and the many intermingling combinations which were possible — these things occupied Ekanta's mind for a time. Looking up towards the sky, another fascinating element of existence which he wanted to ponder, his eyes caught sight of the distant mountains, some of them snow-capped in glorious majesty. Mother Earth had truly outdone Herself in this regard, adding the element of breathtaking inspiration to an already wonderful creation. The fantastic upheaval of the earth and its various elements, a process resulting in these finely crafted and visually stunning massive images, communicated a tale of unity sprung from diversity, of peaceful repose born from chaos. The long view of evolution, his teachers had told him, was necessary in order to understand, to a minute degree, the cosmic mind of God. An expanded and informed intellect brought deep insights into the realm of possibility and this, in turn, destroyed the tendencies of living beings towards mundane pursuits ending in a wasted life of superficial existence.

Thoughts of his precious human teachers in conjunction with meditation on sacred Mother Earth's majestic mountains directed Ekanta's mind towards the wisdom teachings of devotional songs and scriptures once again. A song he had loved as a boy sprang into his memory. He had first heard it one night around the dhuni fires of the wandering holy men who passed through his village on way to various places of pilgrimage. Ekanta used to adore these beings and spent time serving them and questioning them about the nature of Reality. They, in turn, loved the boy for his clarity of mind and deep commitment to Truth. The pertinent lines of the song were designed to convey the teachings that traditional meditation with eyes closed and the worship of stone images were not adequate for the full realization of Brahman. As Ekanta began to hum the melody of this profound song, the words came flooding back into his consciousness:

> If Lord Shiva, Who is Absolute Reality,
> can be realized by worshipping images of stone,
> then why not adore stone mountains
> ceaselessly, by night and by day?
> If you imagine that Mother's Kali's Wisdom Feet
> can be experienced by sitting with eyes closed,
> then why are all blind persons not illumined sages?

Unique ideas such as these, normally outside of the scope of traditional spiritual transmission, had always attracted Ekanta as a young boy. Due to this interest in the extraordinary and sublime level of teachings from a young age, he had developed his spiritual life and stature to a level rarely attained or even witnessed by citizens of the world. Yet he himself, like a child, remained unaware of the uniqueness of his mind, assuming that everyone, if they be committed to spiritual life, dedicated to the guru and devoted to the Lord, were privy to these insights and realizations.

There had been earlier times, however, while he was wandering in the Himalayas and frequenting pilgrimage sights, when discussions with others had produced a powerful effect. He had witnessed, first hand, the difference between a knower of Brahman and those who merely posture and pretend, and even those who occupy official seats of religious power. His lucid explanation of the scriptures, which proceeded from his natural ability combined with spiritual transmission from illumined teachers, and his ongoing tenaciousness and thirst for spiritual discipline had attracted the attention of many aspirants and wandering holy men. This had proven problematic at times, for certain beings of official capacity had held jealous feelings towards him while others desired to keep constant company with him in order to absorb his deep wisdom. Therefore, he moved from place to place continually, never remaining at one location for long so that ill-wishers, flatterers, would-be disciples or those wanting to use him for various purposes did not gather.

The free life, he thought — simple and pure of intent, unostentatious and fully oriented towards God — this was the answer to all problems inherent in relative existence. *"Flowing water never stagnates,"* his teacher had told him. Thus was the importance of motion — physical, mental and spiritual — brought to bear on his aspiring consciousness. This teaching brought forth memories of a question he had posed to his teachers regarding the immovability of the Atman in contrast to the need or tendency towards action in living beings. How did the realization of the immutable Atman coordinate with an active spiritual life? Were not the two diametrically opposed, the antithesis of one another? Can a living, moving, aspiring human being realize the ever-stationary, all-pervasive Self without renouncing work? Must all movement come to an end to effect this great attainment? Is it possible for still waters to escape stagnation?

At this point, he gave a start. Mother Earth, as it were, began to speak to his heightened awareness of the mountains. Gazing at that wonderful spectacle, he took note of the snowy regions at high elevation. On one not-too-distant peak he could discern the early summer runoff from the melting snow as it began its gradual descent in small streams and rivulets. These individual flows gained momentum and merged with one another, plummeting down the steep slopes to form a series of waterfalls. A few mountain lakes could be seen at lower elevations, fed by this pristine liquid from on high.

New insights began to present themselves in the light of this phenomenon. The mountain taught its lessons well, especially to the one who was willing to listen with patience and observe in silence. This contemplation of the mountains took him inward and back to a day when Yogindra Yogi, an ascetic who lived in the mountains behind his village and whom Ekanta considered as one of his spiritual teachers, had spoken to him concerning the many lessons of nature.

"*Snow,*" came the transmission, as the two gazed in awe at the towering snowcaps above them, "*is simply water in another form. At the highest elevation, Ekanta, it remains stationary without experiencing the impositions of stagnation or impurity. Again, at high altitudes and while melting, it enters an agitated condition and moves furiously through various changes in the terrain while still retaining its natural purity. Finally, and still at lofty elevations, it comes to rest once again in the clear mountain lake, still and free of impurity.*

"*Similarly, the mind,*" the yogi continued, "*when it is poised in the heights of nondual Truth, never fears the intrusions of relativity with its many defects. So long as it remains focused on the heights of spiritual wisdom, it can even plunge into the most intense activity without experiencing any damaging exposure to the vicissitudes of daily life. Resting in the Atman at all times, the mind finds that it possesses the power to explore both modes of existence, action and inaction, without the slightest sense of separation from its natural condition of Peace, Truth and Unity. Therefore, always keep the mind focused on Reality, for both insight and freedom from danger will be the result. As the blessed Lord in human form has often taught us, dear boy, 'Those who perceive action in inaction and inaction in action, they truly see.'*"

Ekanta sighed with deep satisfaction. Yearning for the presence of God never ceases. Restlessness for God, being entirely different than that nervous energy characterized by frenetic activity in the world, is the early stage of an intense inner longing which culminates in a loving relationship with Ishvara and realization of the formless Brahman.  Along the way, this precious movement of awakening consciousness passes through the search for constant communion with the Lord and the many experiences of painful separation due to the apparent withdrawal of His fulfilling presence from the mind and senses.

This train of thought brought Ekanta to remembrance of a saying that his teachers were very fond of.  It was one of many that utilized the sun in a spiritual context as a way of teaching precious truths.  Thinking back, the words of his guru came floating through his mind as if it were yesterday:

*"Longing is like the rosy-red dawn.  After the dawn, out comes the sun.  Spiritual longing is always followed by the vision of God."*

Ekanta leaned back and gazed at the setting sun.  By its late-evening light the distant mountains were being lit up, standing out in stark and beautiful contrast to the darkening sky behind.  A thrill passed through Ekanta's being.  His intelligence, naturally inclined towards spiritual truths, found another wonderful teaching in this spectacle.  The sky, vast and formless, was being apparently modified by the shapes of the mountains in the foreground.  This created what was thought of as the horizon.  The horizon, due to the differing shapes of the many mountains, was giving definition to the sky, lending it the appearance of shape and form.  This appearance was, in fact, an illusion.  The sky cannot solidify, mused Ekanta, cannot be caused to assume form, for it never loses its limitless expansiveness.

In the same sense that the mountains gave definition to the sky, Ekanta pondered, so too the world of name and form with its many limiting adjuncts gave definition to Consciousness.  Without bodies, life-force and various mental vehicles through which conscious Awareness can flow or manifest, Reality remains unknowable and unrecognizable.  So, thought the Avadhut, the universe does, no doubt, limit and obscure the nameless, formless essence called Ultimate Reality, subjecting it, as it were, to apparent division and compartmentalization.  But how else will the Supreme Being express the infinite modes of divine potential inherent in It?  In order to play or sport in the mode of expression, Awareness without boundaries must assume or inhabit various forms.

This phenomena, the static and dynamic modes of Satchit-ananda, Ekanta knew, were the twin moods of Shiva and Shakti, of Mahadeva and Mahamaya. Teachings about this twin mode of Reality were among the first which Ekanta had received from his gurus at an early age. Thinking back, he remembered their words precisely:

*"The blessed Divine Couple, Ekanta, when They want to experience movement and activity, design the appropriate scenario through which to enact Their Divine Play, the Mahalila. If a potter wants to measure and separate out different amounts of an essential liquid, he creates a whole host of various sizes of cups and pots with which to do so. Some of these, like the huge clay vases, have a large capacity and can thereby hold more of the precious liquid, while others, like the clay jugs, will hold less. Small mugs, obviously, will only hold a tiny amount. Thus, according to capacity and by the will of the Creator, all things are fashioned and receive their respective abilities to contain consciousness."*

This particular line of thought and the wonderful memories it brought continued in Ekanta's mind, burgeoning naturally into ruminations about the way the Universal Mother divided and subdivided Her creation. Closing his eyes, he could envision the Mataji standing in front of him giving the teachings patiently and lovingly.

*"As the mountains silently demonstrate,"* she had said, *"standing before us and giving apparent shape to homogenous space, form lends definition to formless essence. Some philosophers are prone to think, Ekanta, that matter and energy are simply transient expressions of Consciousness playing in a dynamic and manifest mode. With all the various forms that appear in relativity, both gross and subtle — earth, stones, plant life, insects, animals, and human bodies, all consisting of the five elements, and subtler elements such as life-force, mind, intelligence, and ego — each is a container or receptacle for a certain amount of conscious Awareness. Battling and arguing about which are real and which are not misses the point. Being expressions of Brahman, all are real, but some, the subtler, are more real than others and Brahman, being the subtlest of all, is*

*pure Reality.  The rest spring from That.*

"*The Universal Mother is the consummate potter then,*" she continued after a pause.  "*The multitudinous forms that she molds hold varying amounts of Her precious liquid called Consciousness.  That liquid, essentially formless, is nothing less than pure Awareness, ever unalterable and indivisible.  It appears mutable and divided due to the projection of countless forms.  This power of projection, the Maya under the control of the supreme will of the Mahashakti, resulting in the limiting or obscuration of Reality by various names, forms and elements which constitute nature, is what Vedanta teachers call vivarta, or false superimposition.  What an intricate framework of illusion the Mother has fashioned here, my boy!*"

"Mataji," the young Ekanta had replied with trepidation, "we are all trapped here then.  I am Consciousness trapped in a body and limited by the mind and ego and its false assumptions.  She has willed this to be so!"

"*No,*" responded the guru, "*you are Her Consciousness, ever free, playfully sporting here amidst various containers.  Never forget these two important distinctions.  She has created this charade-like situation, it is true.  She has apparently modified Consciousness and placed it in different vessels, but the vessels can be modified too, like glass heated and stretched or clay molded and expanded.*"

"*Repeat after me, dear one,*" she said suddenly after a few silent moments had passed.  "*Tattvamasi.*"

Ekanta repeated the phrase.

"*Prajnanam Brahma,*" she articulated slowly.

Ekanta responded again.

"*Ayamatma Brahma,*" came the ancient utterance.

Again the boy replied exactly.

"*Aham Brahmasmi,*" she concluded.

"Aham Brahmasmi," came Ekanta's repetition, softly and reverently.

"Good," she said.  "*Soon, as you learn more of spiritual life, you will know what these four statements mean and you will be free once again.  The Mother loves to sport with limited vehicles, but She loves freedom more.  Those who love Her soon learn this love of freedom and need not accept limitation any more.*

*They will live life under their own conditions, not under the dictates of Maya."*

Recalling the various teachings given by his gurus on the subject of false superimposition, Ekanta remembered one particular day when he had accompanied his guru to the nearby coast of the Indian Ocean. The journey had been full of lessons and laughter. As the day wore on it became late. Gradually, as they were walking, Ekanta became aware of a distant sound. At first he imagined it to be a trick of his ears, but as they continued walking the sound became more audible. Finally, there was no denying that something amazing lay ahead of them just over the rise of the nearby hills.

At this point, his teacher stopped and said, *"We have just experienced the physical manifestation of a subtle spiritual truth. When one hears that sound from a distance, it is certain that the ocean is nearby. Exactly like that, the illumined ones know of a certainty that when the first signs of the sublime sound of Aum, the primal sound, is noticed within their aspiring consciousness, the ocean of Brahman is not far away. By following the sound of the waves, one reaches the ocean."*

Drawing near the ocean at evening time, the two had set their asanas in the sand close to the water, assumed meditation posture and watched the glorious sunset in silence. As the stars emerged from hiding, twinkling brightly, the guru finally spoke.

*"The stars are ever-present and constant, yet they disappear at the approach of daylight. Just so, the Atman, the immortal Self pervading everything, is permanently fixed as the substratum of every mode of existence, yet recedes from human awareness due to the presence of ignorance in the mental sheath. Remove the false superimposition of ignorance and the Light of the Atman will shine through naturally of its own accord. For verily, the powerful light of many suns shining in the night heavens are obliterated by the comparatively inferior light of the earth's sun. Likewise, the vastly superior light of the Atman is obscured in the minds of human beings due to the attachment to earthly pleasures through the lesser lights of the body and senses."*

After a short time had passed in silence, another teaching about vivarta came forth from the blessed teacher.

*"My son, the light which you see radiating from those blaz-*
*ing suns in distant space has taken an interminably long*
*amount of time to reach us, even at the speed of light. In the*
*meantime, some of those suns have exploded and their light has*
*been extinguished for all time. Even these long-lived suns are*
*not eternal then. Therefore, though you see a star shining before*
*you it does not, in reality, exist at all! It is a false appearance,*
*an illusion. Similarly, what we experience with the senses is*
*also essentially nonexistent, having only a temporary appear-*
*ance. What is more, that temporary appearance is also illusory,*
*since everything we experience with eyes, ears, nose etc., is not*
*what it seems. The human eyes see a vast field, for instance,*
*but high overhead the keener eyes of an eagle catch every detail*
*including the movement of its prey. The human nose perceives*
*the aroma of cooked food, but the dog lying on the porch smells*
*food plus additional scents far off in the distance. That same*
*animal hears vibrations far beyond the limits of the human*
*ear. The senses are, therefore, extremely limited and unable to*
*convey to us any substantial rendering of Reality."*

The teacher paused for a moment, then went on. *"Furthermore,*
*the senses can never reveal to us the essence of a thing. We behold*
*the effect, not the cause, when we look at any given object. The*
*eyes see only the sum total of millions of miniature swirling*
*particles which result in the formation of a seemingly solid*
*object. Particles even smaller than these remain unseen to the*
*human faculty, and those are the essential ingredients of the*
*object."* The remainder of the evening and, indeed, his entire boyhood passed under the power of teachings such as these.

The esoteric subject of false superimposition was well-known
to Ekanta. Over time he had come to realize that the problem
of vivarta and the two solutions for it called adhyaropa and
apavada constituted an essential part of the discipline which
characterized a phase of mental discrimination through which
the aspirant passes. When such lessons were thus firmly realized, the apprehension of greater truths naturally progressed.
After perceiving the unreality or ephemeral nature of physical
matter, life-force and mental energy in turn, the aspirant was
then fit to behold the ever-present Atman which permeated all
three and supported, imperceptibly, the three levels or realms of

existence.  The secrets of form and formlessness were then revealed to the illumined mind of the adept.

Ekanta had been well-schooled in this profound level of spiritual life.  He knew that the seeming dichotomy of coexisting form and formlessness was nothing other than the play or Mahalila of the eternal Divine Couple in their static and dynamic twin modes. He worshipped Them and kept company with Them always in body, speech, action, mind, and intelligence.

"You are always talking about the Divine Couple, revered sir," Ekanta said one day.  "Who are They?"

*"They are the Shiva/Shakti or Nitya/Lila of the Tantric and Shaivite schools,* replied the preceptor, *"the Radha/Krishna and Sita/Ram of Vaishnavism, the Purusha/Prakriti of Samkhya Philosophy, the Ishvara/Ishvari of Yoga science, the Turiya/ Vaisvanara-Taijasa-Prajna of the Upanishads, the supreme Brahman/Shakti of Vedanta Philosophy and the Brahman/ Atman/Jivatman-all-in-One, of Advaita Vedanta.  Everywhere They are sporting, Ekanta, yet They are beyond all concepts of form and formlessness.  As Immanent Reality, They are the projected universe of name and form.  As Transcendent Reality, They are the subtle realm of thought and life-force.  As Absolute Reality, They are the eternal, all-pervasive and indivisible Satchitananda, beyond all, yet containing all.  There is no place where They are not found."*

With difficulty Ekanta attempted to bring his mind down from the infinite and transcendent mode to the human and earthly station.  Laughing out loud, he declared, "If God and the universe are one and the same, why is it that whenever I begin to contemplate the former, I tend to forget the latter?"  Though he knew the answer, the sound of the question, voiced audibly, brought comfort and meaning to the moment.  Pausing to drink a few sips of water from his water skin, he felt more present, for this act always grounded him somehow.

Again he turned his attention back towards the sun.  Here was another powerful spiritual symbol, rife with precious teachings. As he began to ponder the golden life-giving orb, another occurrence captured his attention.  A mild wind had sprung up from the south, bringing with it the pleasing aroma of wildflowers.  As Ekanta gazed in the direction of the scent, he beheld a vast field of many-colored flowers just below the hill upon which he rested, which had heretofore been hidden behind him. The entire field with its abundant array of colors was now being swept by the sudden wind, causing a riot of movement resulting in a kaleidoscope of flashing and intermingling colors. It was as if the earth had assumed a form of infinite hues and was coming alive, rising up from slumber.

The Avadhut watched in silent amazement, feeling as if he was the most fortunate being alive. Fragments of some of his favorite poems drifted hypnotically through his mind:

> Thy boundless majesty is expressed imaginatively
> by the verdant earth's beauty in awesome seasonal display.
> Fragrant blossoms are Thy loving thoughts.
> Peaceful waters reflect Thy equanimity.
> Lightning is Thy revelation, the thunderclap Thy decree.
> Unfathomable art Thou, O Blessed One,
> how futile the attempt at comprehending Thee.
> From age to age, Thy Grace is this lover's only hope.

Another beautiful sentiment suddenly entered his mind, communicated to him through a long line of God-loving devotees who had received it from the Source of existence —the Primal Guide Himself: *"Everywhere and at all times, there is a great worship going on."* At this moment, Ekanta understood the very essence of this saying with the full force of his being. The field of flowers was not a coincidence nor merely a creation of nature. It was not even just a beautiful spectacle for the eyes to gaze upon in rapture. It was an exquisite expression of the Divine Mother's creative cosmic mind and an inspiring indication of Her presence and Her boundless love for all beings.

Appreciation at this level of comprehension, Ekanta realized, was not speculative, was not fanciful, was certainly not mere entertainment for the sake of pleasure. This kind of vision commanded nothing less than heartfelt reverence mingled with awe. He remembered the early teachings of his two gurus when they had impressed upon him the difference between the worldly-minded, the struggling, the emancipated and the ever-free. This division, they had told him, was predicated on a difference in degree of sensitivity to things subtle and sublime — things spiritual by nature. Their profound words once again entered his radiant mind, this time via the heart:

*"The worldly-minded are callous, apathetic and indurate — indifferent and unresponsive to spiritual matters. The struggling are taken up with individual concerns such as freedom from suffering and attainment of mastery over mind and matter and are therefore gradually possessed of an increasing amount of respect for the Supreme Being. The emancipated and the ever-free, however, have had their respect transformed into reverence, for they know that nothing happens except by the unalterable will of the Divine Couple — the Supreme Being — and pondering this knowledge has transformed them and filled them with awe and wonder."*

At this moment, looking on as witness to the movement of hundreds of wildflowers as they swayed to and fro and became motionless in turns, Ekanta beheld nothing less than the Divine Couple in another of their many love-filled expressions. Like the mountains giving definition to the sky, or like the wind giving life and motion to the field, the blessed Lord and Divine Mother of the Universe verily interacted and sported interminably before his eyes, ever lost and steeped in static contemplation and bliss-filled ecstasy in turns. In a sense, Their wonderful sport was like a window frame, Ekanta thought, which outlines and draws attention to the vast blue expanse beyond, representing the transcendent Absolute. Transported into a similar ecstasy and savoring this experience with deep appreciation and refined emotion, Ekanta looked on, waiting for more profound lessons to be revealed.

Despite motion and nonmotion, mutability and immutability, a deep sense of intense calm permeated everything. Everywhere he looked, he saw nothing but the divine drama of blissful expression, at times static and subtle, at other times vigorous and thrilling to behold. The plummeting mountain waterfall merging with the still mountain lake, the arcing ax of the busy woodsman plunging deep into the motionless old tree, the mobile bees joyfully penetrating stationary honey-filled flowers, even the way the brilliant light from the sun was gradually surrendering to the softly falling shadows of dusk — it was a rapture of continual divine communion, an all-pervasive and perpetually ongoing experience of union and separation.

In a sense, the Avadhut surmised, it was all feigned, for underlying everything, he knew, was an invariable and uniform Omnipresence, the Supreme Witness of all phenomena Who was silently watching with unimaginable powers of penetration.

*"This is the Ultimate Guide,"* his guru had told him, *"the salutary and proverbial Guru, the Unseen Seer, the Unmoved Mover, the marvelous purveyor of pure revelation who is the Fount of Love, the Home of Peace, the Abode of Blessedness, the Essence of Truth and the Source of all existence. Knowing that One is to know all, for pervasiveness is Its nature and It penetrates all levels of existence from the transcendent nondual on through to the multifarious creation. Even Maya, my boy, the perplexing power of delusion-producing ignorance, is only a limited power of the representative of the Absolute called Ishvara, God within the universe."*

The ever-pleasing thought of Ishvara brought Ekanta's mind full circle back to the field of flowers. Only the blessed Lord, entering into the universe as Living Awareness, could cause such overwhelming beauty. The Avadhut laughed with a combination of pity and disbelief. People who refused to believe in an Omnipotent Creator were not only the world's most unfortunate living beings, they also labored under the heaviest imposition of all — the unripe individual ego — the binding sense of I, me and mine. Ekanta immediately recollected several teachings which came to him from guru and scripture:

*"The creation itself is proof of God's existence,"* echoed his mind's memory.

At another time, when approaching his teacher to find a Sanskrit word for nonbeliever, the retort came back:

*"There is no word in Sanskrit for an atheist or an agnostic, Ekanta. The nearest equivalent translates as 'those of deluded intellect.' The Upanishads call these 'nonentities.'"*

Ekanta perked up. A newcomer had entered his field of vision. Upon inspection he noticed that it was a young girl who had entered the field of flowers and was already in possession of a few handfuls of them. A few notes from her song were already audible, blown towards his hearing by the soft winds that caressed the landscape. Such simple happiness filled Ekanta with indescribable joy, as if he was party to the same pure experience that the girl was enjoying. With childlike abandon, the girl suddenly flung the collected flowers in the air and ran into the surrounding woods, her laughter diminishing as she disappeared from sight.

Instantly, teachings about nonattachment entered his mind, particularly with regard to a child's freedom from the three gunas — sattva, rajas and tamas — the binding modes of nature. Words of the Avatar, gleaned from the few existing books at his teacher's forest ashram, came to mind.

*"You may have noticed a young child's behavior, how such a one is quite detached from possessions. A child may cry and yell at the suggestion that he give his candy to an uncle or nephew, but the next instant he will give it away without consideration to a complete stranger! Though the three gunas are present in the child, there is no lasting attachment to any one of them. Such is the state of a holy being as well, but there is a world of difference between the childish and the childlike."* As his own teachers had put it: *"Be infinite, not infantile."*

The sun was now resting, as it were, on the distant mountain tops. It is a fine illusion, thought Ekanta, for the sun appears to have come to rest upon the earth. It reminded him of the story of the child who, seeing the moon shining through the branches of a tree at night, imagined it to be an ornament hanging on its branches and just sitting there for the taking. As the sun fell lower on the horizon, it seemed to be losing its shape from the bottom up, as if the earth were slowly absorbing it. The legend of Rahu flashed in the Avadhut's mind, a mythological creature to whom simple-minded people attributed the gradual consumption of the sun during eclipses and of the moon over its monthly cycle. Bite by bite, the moon thus vanished slowly from sight, a little every night until all was devoured. Thankfully, another moon periodically came along to take its place.

Soon, as the Avadhut watched, the sun was completely "devoured." Actually, as he had learned in the Vedangas — the six limbs of secondary teaching in Vedanta science — the rotation of the earth and its movement through space had obliterated the sun's presence for approximately another twelve hours. To contemplate that another part of the earth on which he sat was receiving the full light and warmth of the sun, activated Ekanta's spiritually-oriented imagination. Light and darkness, daytime and evening—these dualities were precious and revealing, both terrestrially and spiritually. In this elevated state of mind Ekanta wondered what nightfall would bring.

The sunset was glorious, enhanced by the earth's many charms and attributes. Beholding the sun's descent, Ekanta quoted out loud from the Kathopanishad, most of which he had by memory:

> It is the Supreme Being that causes the sun to rise and set.
> The gods originate from and merge in It.
> None can transcend That, for all is verily contained within It.

Gradually, darkness prevailed, save only for the faint glimmer of the distant stars. The earth slept soundly, yet all around Ekanta was a palpable and ever-awake presence. Another sloka from the Kathopanishad came forth spontaneously from the Avadhut's lips:

> While others rest in sleep,
> the Primal Purusha continues to function in full wakefulness,
> fashioning an infinite world of objects and experiences.
> Everything springs from It and also rests in It.
> Nothing transcends It.

As Ekanta waited, poised in deep silence amidst the darkness, he gradually became aware that creatures were still moving about. This reminded him of another ancient teaching from the scriptures:

> What is morning to the average being
> is night to the Atman-cognizing muni,
> and what humans consider as nighttime
> is the clear light of day to the illumined.

How true this is, thought Ekanta, though difficult to understand at first. How often he had watched the citizens of the earth labor under error and delusion, despite the well-intentioned teachings and correcting influences of the enlightened ones and the words of the scriptures. Paying heed only to their own limited egos and turning a deaf ear to all wise counsel, worldly people only placed more and more obstacles in the way of their own path. The words of the Avatar quickly came into his mind:

> The camel loves to eat thorny bushes,
> and even though its gums bleed profusely,
> it continues in its folly.

At the edge of the forest, Ekanta could make out some subtle movements. A flock of deer had emerged from the wooded area and were grazing in the meadow below. Occasionally they would frolic quietly in the semi-darkness but were ever on the alert for danger. When, all of a sudden, they became alarmed at some imagined noise or hidden presence, they disappeared like shadows into the forest. Their ultra-sensitivity impressed Ekanta and he found himself wishing that human beings would be as sensitive to Truth and ever on guard for any danger that would cover or obscure it.

Nearby, an owl began its evening song, sending out its mono-syllable mantra every few minutes. This reminded him of a well-known devotional song to the Universal Mother:

> All sounds you hear are prayers and praises,
> arising spontaneously as the whole universe worships Her.

With this teaching in mind, Ekanta fell into a deep meditation, prompted further by the lulling yet vibrant sounds of the crickets all around him. Their constant drone reminded him of the tamboura which accompanied the inspiring devotional music he had heard throughout his life. To Ekanta's heightened sense of hearing, they were chanting ancient and primal scriptures, encoded in a language unknown to ears bereft of the ability to perceive deeper meanings.

Over the constant tone of these tiny musicians of nature, the eternal subtle sound of Om gradually revealed itself to the Avadhut's internally sensitized awareness. This primal sound of creation, the soundless sound, transcendent of all manifestation yet saturating everything as the initial vibration of the cosmos was, to the enlightened, the voice of the Atman. It represented the all-pervasiveness of sacred Divinity and heralded the subtle spiritual experiences received in deepest contemplation on Absolute Reality. Ekanta welcomed the advent of this holy sound with all his being and was soon plunged in deep absorption and lost to the outer world.

At first light, the Avadhut emerged from his deep meditation. Better than sleep, the superconscious state refreshed and healed the body/mind mechanism like no other thing available to mankind. Perfect repose in the Atman, effected in part by meditation on Reality, kept the body healthy, the life-force vibrant and the mind free of impurities and other impediments. Ekanta's first thoughts this morning, springing from his well-intentioned and compassionate nature, were that all beings would rediscover the ancient and time-honored method called meditation and teach it to their children from a very young age. Thus would many of the vicissitudes of life be greatly diminished.

Personal delusion, Ekanta knew from experience, would be gradually attenuated and done away with completely by creating the habit of deep introspection. Fear of death, too, would disappear from the human mind through the practice of meditation guided by an illumined teacher. Finally, even the superimpositions over consciousness caused by the inherent circumstances in nature due to the cosmic laws would be overcome. Birth, disease and old age could then be overcome as the art of transcendence was mastered. With both of these problems — personal delusion and universal superimposition — overcome, mankind could again live in harmony and in balance with the earth.

The sun was appearing from beyond the eastern horizon. As the brilliant golden orb began its ascent into the morning sky, Ekanta reverently initiated his morning routine, performing the powerful "Salute to the Sun" taught to him by his precious spiritual teachers. His mind was still in a lofty condition. He felt fully involved in all of life yet also supremely detached from everything. Witness Consciousness, he thought; I am no stranger to that condition. The wonder of it, he knew, was that all states of consciousness and all beings and their experiences are fully contained in it. Some whom he had met had tried to describe it as a void, as a state negating all others. The Avadhut had seen that these beings were as yet immature in their outlook and understanding — that they had not yet experienced, first hand, the bliss of the formless Brahman and Its all-embracing, all-containing inclusiveness.

The thought of the Absolute vaulted Ekanta's mind into heights of subtle bliss. Through the waves of this sublime experience wafted the nectar-like words of the great Advaita Vedanta teacher, Shankaracharya:

*Vacha vaktum ashakyam eva manasa mantum nava shakyate*
*Sva'anand'amrita–pura–purita–parabrahm'ambhuder vaibhavam*
*Ambho–rasi–vishirna–varsika–shila–bhavam bhajan me mano*
*Yasy'amsh'amsha–lave vilinam adhun'anand atmana nirvrtam*

The awesome majesty of the ocean of the Supreme Brahman,
replete with the swell of the nectar-like bliss of the Atman,
is virtually beyond the scope of words to express
and outside of the mind's capacity to comprehend,
in an infinitesimal portion of which,
my mind melted and became fully absorbed,
like a hailstone falling into a boundless ocean,
and now rests eternally in static equipoise and subtle bliss.

The Avadhut gave a deep sigh. Focusing his mind and senses on the external world, he lowered himself into sitting position. The wonders of the morning spread out before him on all sides. The hum of the insects awakening from nocturnal sleep reminded him of the previous evening's meditation on the sacred sound Om. The cloudless sky seemed to be an adequate representation of the formless Brahman, still and sublime, without boundaries and full of Consciousness. The vast green mantle which lay before him, dotted here and there with earthy browns and various other hues, seemed like a canvas upon which the Lord had just painted a fresh masterpiece. Off in the distance, nestled between forest and field and bordered on one side by a stream of water, was a cabin. A thin stream of smoke issued from its chimney, an indication that living beings inside were attending to the morning activities and preparing the breakfast meal.

The thought of food reminded Ekanta that he had not taken nourishment for the body for several days. Bidding farewell to the sacred and ideal spot where he had spent so many wonderful hours and received such sublime insights and realizations, he gathered his few belongings and headed down the high hill in the direction of the green forest. Reaching the bottom, he turned and saluted the holy spot upon which he had spent the enthralling evening. "Bhagavata, Bhakta, Bhagavan," he whispered to himself, indicating that the Lord, the scriptures, and the devotee are all one. Finishing this sacred act, he turned and plunged into the forest.

The Avadhut had an eye for detail while in the forest. He had a sense of reverence for all living things and he was also practical, for he had to gather food that sprang naturally from the earth. Knowing what was edible and what was not comprised an important part of survival for his particular lifestyle.

Moving quietly and easily through the foliage and undergrowth, it was not long before he came upon several types of berries, growing wild and untouched amidst fern and creepers. His happiness increased in proportion with his hunger as he drew near and observed that the berries were newly ripened and of a large variety. Folding his hands in prayer, the Avadhut stood, still and silent, a solitary figure deep inside the forest reaches. Quietly, he spoke the words of Lord Krishna from the Bhagavad Gita:

> The Blessed Lord provides the food.
> The Blessed Lord is the article on which the food is offered.
> The Blessed Lord is the one who partakes of the food.
> The Blessed Lord is the food.
> The Blessed Lord is in all, is everything, is everywhere.
> Those who behold the Lord in this manner reach the highest
> level of realization.

Having uttered this profound prayer, the Avadhut slowly and methodically began to gather the berries in a small cloth. As he worked his way around the berry patch, he came upon a mature tree with it branches laden with nuts. These, too, were reverently sampled so that when his cloth was brimming full, he had a veritable feast. A container of fresh water, pulled from a small rivulet in a nearby hillock, made his repast complete. Having eaten his fill of the bounteous fruits of nature, Ekanta lay his sleeping cloth down under a tree on a smooth patch of short grasses and was soon enjoying a short nap. Before falling into peaceful slumber, he mentally recited a few lines from a favorite devotional song to the Divine Mother of the Universe:

> Consider the act of lying down to sleep
> as devoted offering of your body and mind to Her.
> Allow your dreams to become radiant meditations
> on the Cosmic Mother.
> As you wander through the countryside or city,
> feel that you are moving through Mother Kali.
> O wandering poet, whatever food or drink you receive,
> offer as oblation in the sacrificial fire of your body,
> and meditate intensely on Her encompassing Reality.

As these thoughts receded from his consciousness, Ekanta slipped into deep and profound sleep.

Awakening in a refreshed state and with mind clear and alert, Ekanta sat up to meditate. The forest was now in a different mood than when he had fallen asleep. It was some time after midafternoon and a hush had fallen on all activity. The strange peace, as if everything living was temporarily napping, lent a languid air to the atmosphere, but it was nonetheless interpenetrated by anticipation. Then, as if by some secret signal, hidden birds in the surrounding trees suddenly burst into a rash of chatter. Each seemed intent on outdoing the other in volume and outright obnoxiousness. Ekanta smiled and added his own boisterous laughter to the obstreperous din pressing in on all sides around him. After about twenty seconds of this cacaphony, it all stopped as suddenly as it began with the diminishing calls of a few stragglers trickling out at the end.

Ekanta's laughter came about due to his recollection of an experience he had undergone while wandering through the holy city of Benares on pilgrimage. The birds and their competitive squawking had reminded him of it. While wandering the holy city, Ekanta had stopped along one of the streets at a convenient place and was resting in the shade. It was near dusk and soon, soothing to his ears, came the sounds of worship emanating from the temples and mosques. The Muslim call to prayer, soulful and reminiscent of the Almighty Father, mingled with the sublime sounds of Hindu arati and both were overlaid with additional sacred sounds issuing from Buddhist and Jain temples.

It was not long before another kind of sound made itself known. Out of a nearby household came the angry sounds of two women clashing in argument. It was anyone's guess what was the cause of such fighting, but Ekanta had never heard the like of it before. No sooner did the first woman finish her tirade than the next would pick up instantly right after her, bathing her in a barrage of defamation which set the mind reeling and put one's teeth on edge. The verbal bombardment thus continued on interminably, each trying to intimidate the other, and no slight or insult was too low or considered unworthy enough for the achieving of this aim. People stopped their activities and turned an ear in the general direction of the fight. It was inconceivable that such language could issue forth from the mouth of any human being, especially from those known as the 'fair sex.' Slanderous oaths, the kind of which Ekanta had never heard or ever heard since, seemed to roll easily and freely off the tongues of these two senseless beings. He wondered, after a time, if they would eventually come to blows.

Finally, a well-intentioned man had attempted to intercede. Ekanta thought that this would bring the misunderstanding to a timely and much desired end. Ignoring this unwanted interruption of their private verbal war, the two women continued their mutual denigration of one another in callous fashion, disregarding for the most part the unfortunate man's presence, who then became party to a few of their callous insinuations. Whenever it seemed that the fight would reach a conclusion or even come to a standoff, fresh waves of abuse recurred due to additional irritation raised by a particularly disturbing insult. Ekanta listened in disbelief. How could the human voice could withstand such extreme levels of throat-rending volume? That people could be capable of such horrible vilification was beyond comprehension.

In due time, after a seemingly endless and shocking interval of this outright tirade, a precious moment of silence occurred. The sudden quietude was both welcome and unexpected, but it was made all the more surprising by the abruptness of the moment. It was at this critical split second that a crow — that indisputable king of raucous bickering, whose very existence is spent in delving into and consorting with filthy and disgusting things, and which no manner of foul sound, sight or smell could ever ruffle — meekly ejaculated a weak and stunned "caw." It was this tiny incident, in contrast to the horrific haranguement that had previously ensued, which had caused Ekanta's tumultuous laughter, both then and now. To observe the absolute bewilderment of the inimitable crow, heretofore peerless and incomparable in the art of vicious debate, and to witness its shocked disbelief at the utter depravity which humans could descend to, was more than he could bear. His mirth at the incident had lasted all evening and was even now returning to visit him once again, years later.

The experience was not without significant and sobering lessons. Since ignorant and evil beings inhabit this world, he thought, all those who would strive for higher consciousness must pay heed and take precautions. A certain amount of protection would always be necessary in order to insure one's physical and mental safety against these ego-oriented forces. Now, mulling over this experience from the past, Ekanta heard the words of his teachers speaking to him across time once again.

*"Perhaps you have noticed, my boy, that God has created trees that produce sweet fruit and others that bear sour fruit. Both are necessary in this world, and it is admitted by those who know that the sour fruit is often more nourishing than the sweet. Therefore, never shun what is difficult, for challenging experiences build character and strength, whereas pleasures possess little lasting value and often create desires and further attachments."*

Ekanta had remained curious and somewhat unconvinced.

"If the world is so created as to include the painful and pleasurable, and the creation is fraught with these imperfections then the Creator too must have faults," he stated.

*"The wise think otherwise, my dear,"* said the guru. *"The snake, for instance, certainly contains poison within it, but it is not affected thereby. Similarly, the Supreme Being may utilize contrasting dualities — even negativity — for His purpose in the creation, but He is never subject to them or affected by them."*

Ekanta knew that the best web of defense against extremes and negativities was the supremely natural one of keeping holy company and fixing the mind upon God at all times. Negative impressions in the subconscious mind would thereby not receive any activating energy through which to manifest and, that being the case, would soon wither and die away for good. He remembered one of his teacher's lesson on the subject:

*"Meditating upon God and keeping holy company affords the*

*subconscious mind no opportunity to spawn negative repercussions. If the conscious mind remains idle it invites all manner of trouble in the form of surfacing samskaras which, if left unchecked, turn the mind from a natural fertile landscape of divine preoccupation into a stagnant swamp of pain-bearing obstructions."*

Traveling the world and observing the way in which people lived and dealt with each other, Ekanta had learned firsthand of the wayward tendencies prevalent in the Kali Yuga. He was no longer naive but neither had he become jaded or pessimistic. He had been trained to see God everywhere but had also escaped the traps of a strictly moral outlook which categorizes all things into neat little packages of good and bad and right and wrong, regardless of the differences in cultures and human perspectives. His was not the outlook of a moralist who attaches to or obsesses over an ethical code of behavior that remains inflexible in every instance. His was the position of absolute freedom, never caught in the moral dilemmas of worldly considerations in the first place and far beyond the limitations of puritanical morality and judgmental righteousness. This was the way of the Avadhut, of the Paramahamsa, of the devotee of the Lord of the Universe.

Mother Earth reminded him of these lessons every day of his existence, and revering Her immensely, he paid heed with the full capacity of his being. Glancing at the nearby bushes, he saw a spider spinning its web. That sticky material would soon entrap its unsuspecting victims and the spider would then suck the life-energy out of those unfortunate creatures.

*"The ego is the sticky substance within the human consciousness,"* his teacher had declared to him one day, *"and all manner of detrimental impositions will linger there, wreaking havoc in the divine kingdom of the mind. If your mind is clear, free from all inhibitions, attachments and desires, no foreign or alien substances can gain a foothold there. Where there is no ego, there is no point of purchase for negativities. They simply pass by, like smoke carried through a screen by the wind, and disappear harmlessly."*

Learning this lesson had freed him early in life. It was no wonder that he had such great reverence for his illumined spiritual teachers.

Once, traveling farther than usual, Ekanta had penetrated deeply into the southern coastal regions of India. In the humid sectors of that part of the country, baked by the warm tropical sun and periodically deluged with heavy precipitation that nurtured lush rain forests, he had seen many curious sights. One day, as he sat near a rather large body of water, watching water fowl feed, he saw a long stilt-legged bird (a stork or an egret) suddenly buckle as if cut in half. The commotion that ensued revealed the hidden danger in the form of a young crocodile who lay in wait for its supper, completely devouring the poor bird with a few snaps of its powerful jaws. Drawing nearer, the Avadhut noted several gray-colored protuberances on the surface of the water which appeared to be rocks jutting above the surface. As he watched carefully, he noticed that they occasionally and almost imperceptibly moved. He then concluded that a host of these large predators lurked there in secret, just below the surface and well-camouflaged, waiting for their victims to draw near.

The pertinent teaching was ready and evident to his mind. The Avatar transmission, so ingrained into his memory by his concerned teachers, now brought the full force of this lesson home through the life-and-death drama of nature. Came the teaching:

Hidden in the reservoir of the mind, six alligators lie waiting
— anger, lust, greed, envy, pride and avarice.
Before entering those inviting waters,
carefully apply the turmeric paste
of discrimination and dispassion
which acts as a repellent to all such dangers
lurking in relativity.
Then swim and bathe at your own leisure,
eternally free of fear and happy.

Thinking compassionately about suffering humanity, Ekanta had, over time, adopted a policy whereby he took every opportunity that naturally presented itself to inform the citizens of the world about these powerful teachings. He was loath to force such teachings on those who would not listen, but even in these cases he sometimes acted, putting his own well-being in jeopardy for the sake of others. This kind of action most often amounted to a sacrifice, bringing some painful repercussion in its train. His guru had given him a story in this regard in order to strengthen his resolve and expand his compassion.

*"The sage, my boy, reaches in again and again to save the drowning scorpion from a watery death, receiving a painful sting every time. When a bystander asks him why he does not just let the venomous insect drown, the sage answers, 'It is its nature to sting, but it is in my nature to save.'"*

Besides evil beings, Ekanta thought, there were many miserable people in the world as well. These people suffered unnecessarily, even though beneficial aid was right within their grasp most of the time. The hard part was getting them to acknowledge and receive it. Mother Nature had an apt scenario for this unfortunate phenomenon as well. Once, during Ekanta's travels, he had seen cows being herded to slaughter by Muslim herders. This sight, an unnerving spectacle for most every Hindu, was almost too much for the peace-loving Avadhut to bear. He had forced himself to see the process through to the end though, not only as a test for the practice of freeing himself from aversion, but also that he would have the precise and proper information on file in his mind for use at a later date.

The meek and helpless cows, being herded to their death in such brutal fashion, put him in mind of the masses of human beings who suffer needlessly every moment of their existence, heedless of the powerful and practical steps they could take to avert such misery. The teachings of the Avatar had again entered his mind while he stood there looking out over the fields:

The cow cries "hamba," which means "I."
That is why it suffers.
It is yoked to the plough, forced to work in rain and sun,
and finally killed by the butcher.
Shoes are made from its hide and also drums
which are mercilessly beaten.
Even then its sufferings are not over.
Strings are made from its entrails for the bows
used in carding cotton.
At this point, it sings "tuhu," meaning "thou,"
and its troubles are over.

The ego, thought Ekanta, the sense of individuality in its unripe and unsurrendered form, is the cause of all suffering. If beings gave themselves to the Lord of the Universe and accepted the teachings of eternal nondual Truth without question, their sufferings would rapidly diminish and soon come to an end. Their unwillingness to do this in this day and age was due, in part, to their inadvertence and inability to perform sacrifice for the good of all beings. Only by adopting the attitude of *"Not I, but Thou,"* could the ego be squelched and selfless service to humanity — the ancient way of good will and balance — be restored to the empirical process, the march of events in relativity, once again.

Ekanta had been taught the importance of yajna, sacrifice, by both his parents and his spiritual teachers. His father's words came often into his mind in this regard:

"Sacrifice, my son, in the original scheme of things and according to the ancients, is of five kinds: Deva yajna, which demands fealty and offerings to the gods and goddesses who represent the cosmic functions prevalent in the universe; Rishi yajna, which involves reverence for the world teachers and the guru and the following and spreading of their teachings; Pitru yajna, which proceeds through respect for your parents, loved ones and ancestors and making offerings in honor of the fond memory of the departed; Nara yajna, having to do with compassion for and loving service of human beings as manifestations of God in human form, and Bhuta yajna which includes concern and caring for animals, plants, insects and the blessed land upon which we live and which has been given to us in sacred trust and for our own benefit."

*"If the cosmic plan is followed,"* declared his teacher one day, *"the upset balance of the planet will gradually and naturally right itself, for the gods and goddesses will be pleased, beings in the heaven realms and the netherworlds will prosper and be fulfilled and all beings on earth — men, women, children, animals, insects, plants and minerals — will be seen as manifestations of one indivisible and absolute Reality."*

Asking how this could truly be accomplished, given the extremely deteriorated condition of the world and the stunted spirituality of its peoples, Ekanta had received the answer in the form of Lord Krishna's teachings:

*"The boon of material sustenance in the form of food proceeds*

*from rain falling from the skies. That liquid nourishment from the heavens is granted due to sacrifice performed in the proper spirit. Right sacrifice is accomplished by striving in selfless works. Selfless works arise from knowledge of the scriptures. This precious knowledge comes direct from the imperishable Brahman who is its source. Supreme Wisdom is thus facilitated greatly by means of sacrifice."*

Great care had been taken by Ekanta's gurus that he was not fashioned into a mere philanthropist. Altruistic works for the good of the earth and its beings were not the end-all and be-all of human existence according to Vedanta science. If they were, insisted his teachers, the presence of God would be unnecessary and the will of human beings would be enough to create of the world a paradise free from all imperfections and disparities. Charitable works had never been enough to transform the world and, if the truth be known, had often contributed to the further confusion and frustration of all good intentions due to the pervasive sense of agency and ownership prevalent in human nature.

*"The true crux of the matter,"* said the Mataji one day, *"rests in the fact that all work, all creation, all thought and action in the universe is born from and accomplished solely by the Supreme Being. This ultimate and pervasive Intelligence, the detached witness of the empirical process and author of its universal scope, is the only force capable of directing the multifarious aspects and the infinite intermingling of energies playing throughout the boundless universe. It alone remains ever free from the desire for acknowledgement and the seeking after selfish gain, as well as the fear of repercussion or retribution. In short, it is free from cause and effect. Only the Transcendent One can control and oversee the vast sea of pressing imperatives which constitute the manifestation and operation of the infinite universe."*

Inspired by this remembrance, Ekanta began to sing the lines of a famous devotional song which transmitted this ultimate teaching:

O Mother of the Universe, everything occurs
due to Thy insistent and irresistible bidding.
Without doubt, Thou art the singular
and most powerful Will in the Universe!

Actions and their outcome, enacted and coveted
by countless living beings,
are really perpetrated and brought to fruition by Thee.
Puppetlike beings seem to move and act,
but You pull the strings.
Nothing occurs without Thy sanctifying permission!

The massive elephant becomes a weakling in the tar pit,
while the crippled wanderer prevails
over steep mountain passes.
Some, there are, who reap the bounteous rewards
granted by Thy inexhaustible Grace,
while others weep and wail,
caught in the inscrutable chains of Maya.

I am the warrior, but You wield my weapons.
I fashion the dwelling, but You reside within.
I enter the battlefield on the shining chariot,
but it is You who control horses, reins and charioteer.
Thy will is absolute, may your blessings be forthcoming!

The Avadhut heaved a deep sigh and stirred himself from his several-hour contemplation. Midafternoon had come and was fast receding, soon to transform into late afternoon and dusk. He must move through the forest and reach the other side before dark, for he did not favor sleeping among the trees at night, preferring the grassy hillocks or the low-lying mountains. Therefore, he packed his few belongings and plunged into the forest at a faster pace than usual.

After a few hours of swift hiking, Ekanta penetrated the woods and emerged from the other side. He was standing in a clearing facing a large pasture, at the other side of which sat a cottage bordered by a stream. A wisp of smoke rose from the chimney and a pastoral atmosphere pervaded the entire scene. In a flash Ekanta realized that this was the distant cottage he had seen early in the morning from his high vantage point miles away. As it was getting dark and Ekanta had procured no food along his swift hike, he decided to approach the house and beg for his supper. With this plan in mind, he brushed himself clean of leaves, cobwebs and bits of branches and started out across the pasture towards the quaint cottage near the stream, the forbearing earth supporting his every step.

# — Chapter 2 —

# Teachings On God Dwelling in Mankind

THE SECOND GURU —The Arrowmaker

THE LESSON —Concentration

*Upon beholding the arrowmaker at work on his craft, I learned about intense concentration leading to success in all endeavors, whether worldly or spiritual. Noticing with interest and appreciation that the arrowmaker did not look up from his work even when the king and his processional passed by his shop, and applying this unique example of focus to spiritual life and practice, I concluded that life, spent in whole-hearted concentration on Brahman, Atman and Ishvara, devoid of all distractions, lapses and deviations from the goal, leads to full realization. Thus, should one spend his or her time on this earth.*

As the Avadhut approached the cozy looking cabin, nestled comfortably amidst stands of trees and bordered by a murmuring brook, he noticed signs of life within. The warm and natural ambiance of the wooded surroundings added a homey atmosphere to the cabin, which itself was rustic by design but extremely well built. A master craftsman had undoubtedly been at work here, for closer inspection revealed that foresight had been utilized in every detail. Appearance had obviously been of secondary importance to the builder, while of prime concern had been sturdiness of design and longevity. The outlying lands were also well-tended, providing a garden for vegetables and small groves of fruit and nut trees. A few animals grazed near a small but well-constructed shed which probably acted as shelter for them in cold and rainy weather. There was no excess of money here, thought Ekanta, but the owners secured a decent living and lived a life which many would envy.

Ekanta reached the footpath just before dark and made his way up to the front door. Not knowing what to expect, having received many different receptions in the past, he reverently saluted the house with folded hands, for Narayana — God in human form — dwelt inside. There were various sounds of moving about inside, but the sound of his knock stilled them all for a few brief seconds. There followed a hushed exchange of words between two people, uttered in low voices so that the words were indistinct. Then, the door swung open and Ekanta found himself face-to-face with a rather tall figure. He noticed a woman standing near the back of the cabin looking on with curiosity. A few moments of tense silence passed as the tall figure searched Ekanta's face.

The owner of the house was evidently satisfied with what he saw for the welcome words "Om Namo Narayanaya," rang forth from his lips and Ekanta knew he had come upon the right place. No words could have sounded so sweet to his ears and no greeting could have conveyed deeper sentiments. Even the traditional "namaste or namaskar," though it would have been welcome, could not have surpassed this, for upon hearing it Ekanta knew that he was in the company of another man of God.

The smile that lit up Ekanta's face must have been appreciated for what was behind it, for no sooner had this brief but poignant moment of mutual greeting passed than he was whisked indoors without further delay. Without wasting words, the stranger indicated a seat for Ekanta to occupy and a place to lay his belongings. The woman, no longer holding back, was in front of him offering him drinking water from a clay mug. Accepting their hospitality, Ekanta took a few swallows of water and sat himself down cross-legged on the floor. Glancing around the cabin, he found it neat and orderly with not a bit of wasted space. Two oil lamps,

burning brightly, cast adequate light about the dwelling and indicated a freedom from impoverished conditions combined with an
eye for curbing any wasteful tendencies.  All in all, the whole
scene was harmonious and Ekanta felt immediately at home and
free from any awkwardness or uneasiness.

Turning his attention on the couple, he found the man and
woman young-looking, healthy and with calm dispositions.  He had
received warm receptions before, but many had been accompanied by a thousand questions before he even had time to catch his
breath or take water.  The easy and straightforward way in which
this couple received him spoke of wisdom and peace of mind, a
combination that was rarely seen, even for the Avadhut who had
met many beings in his travels.

He was not the only one analyzing everything with a keen eye,
he discovered.  It was evident that he was under study as well.
The two were sizing him up in a calm and deliberate fashion, without seeming to be rude or forward.  That they liked what they saw
was also evident, for the light dancing in their eyes communicated
a subtle delight in having such a special guest at their humble
dwelling.  Before any embarrassment could develop due this quiet
demonstration of mutual regard, the man spoke with a voice that
was both compelling and soothing.

"You have come through the east woods, friend."  The direct-
ness of the statement, coming in place of the anticipated question,
caught Ekanta off guard for a moment.  He was also curious how
the man could know of his whereabouts at a mere glance.  His
response, however, was equally disarming and immediately
earned him two smiles.

"My body indeed has penetrated the east woods, good sir, but
the real I moves not, pervades everything and exists everywhere."
There was not the slightest trace of affectation in any of these
powerful statements, nor was there force or constraint.  The naturalness of easy communication prevailed at all times.

"Revered sir," ventured the woman, "I see that we are blessed
by the company of a knower of Brahman and are in store for an
evening of divine discourse."

"On the contrary," Ekanta returned, "it is I who have come to
listen and learn from you.  The river flows to the ocean, not the
other way around."

Stirring from his seat, the tall man laughed at this exchange and said, "Sir, you afford us too much honor with such words. We are merely simple country folk and you are obviously a world traveler. Therefore, do not deprive us this evening of your broad experience and your wisdom. But come, let us take our evening meal. We were just about to partake of the Earth Mother's bounty. Will you kindly join us?"

Nodding his consent and voicing his gratitude, Ekanta moved with the couple to a large table near a clay oven where the smell of freshly baked Indian bread was filling the air with its inviting aroma.

The evening meal was a rare event. Profound silence and animated talking vied for the upper hand during the entire repast, but whenever speech was utilized, the subject matter was always the Supreme Being and Its many modes of expression. Gradually, by both outward and subtle exchange, Ekanta found that he was in the company of a rare combination of man and woman, the like of which had been manifest on earth in the times of the great Rishis. Those enlightened beings, many of whom were householders with families, had acted as open channels for the reception of powerful spiritual insights that were duly passed on to their children by means of concentrated study and exact memorization. These insights were collected, recorded and eventually compiled by great beings such as the venerable Vedavyasa, revealing themselves over time as the perennial Wisdom of the Ages, the written word of God. As the Avadhut began to ruminate about the Rishis, he could not help but notice the striking similarities between this humble couple, the revered vanaprastin teachers of his youth and the ancient ones who were vessels for the sacred Upanishads. This made the evening all the more special.

Observing the subtle interchanges between his hosts, the Avadhut was occasionally launched into spiritual reverie about stories and teachings he had heard from other beings regarding the Divine Couple. Though he was a solitary person and had taken the great vow according to his calling, he also cherished the ideal of the Divine Couple, Shiva and Shakti, and saw Their presence and Their workings in everything.

*"Everything one sees in the universe has come about due to the union of Shiva and Shakti,"* his teachers had once told him.

Ekanta had seen the Divine Couple in the meeting of the mountains with the sky, in flocks of birds penetrating the inner recesses of a spreading tree and even in the simplest acts such as bringing food to the mouth or lying down to sleep. In human couples, though, especially those whose union was consecrated with commitment, bound in selfless love and based upon the truths of the scriptures and mutual seeking after the highest attainments of spiritual life, he had witnessed Shiva and Shakti sporting in the world fully manifested.

Ekanta's mind was free from fault-finding. His powers of discrimination, however, were honed to a fine degree. He knew the difference between these two.

*"To judge spiritual progress is nothing but vanity based upon speculation,"* his guru had told him at one point. *"It is hard enough to ascertain one's own progress and spiritual stature let alone another's. This is because spiritual growth is subtle and involved with the internal workings of the mind. Only one gifted with the ability to clearly see the various attributes contained in people of differing temperaments is qualified to instruct others. This is the guru, and the power inherent in such a one is granted and overseen by the Mother of the Universe Herself."*

Therefore, Ekanta was aware of how fortunate he had been to have the company of several such gurus. They had taught him how to be reliant upon himself in spiritual matters. After leaving home and entering into the renunciate phase of his life, he had met many beings along the path who shunned all modes of expression besides their own. Among those who renounced and wandered, he had spoken with many who judged and criticized the sacred union of man and woman as something below the highest ideal. Even among the so-called leaders of religious institutions that he had visited, many of them famous throughout the world for their erudition and high learning, he had found this condescending attitude towards the householder existence. It made no sense to him, for worldliness and ignorance were as common among monks and renunciates as they were among householders. Both paths had their share of hypocrites and of adepts. Ekanta had noticed, however, with what humility many of the householders approached the renunciates and how they learned from the respective austerities and insights of these beings. Often, while this benefited the householders in many ways, it only served to foster pride among the monastics who somehow equated this process with their own superiority. This often resulted in spiritual egotism and a falsely inflated sense of their own self-worth.

Watching his humble, sattvic hosts, Ekanta thought of the many examples of divine couples who had appeared over time, all in differing relationships to each other and to the world. Sita and Ramchandra, Jesus and Mary, the Buddha and Yashodhara , Radha and Sri Krishna, Shiva and Parvati, Yagnavalkya and Maitreyi, Agastya and Lopamudra — the list was endless. He thought of the great Rishis, many of them married yet capable of receiving and transmitting the highest teachings. Powerful transmissions of spirituality came through illumined couples and always had. The monastic stream was one way of receiving teachings and it had its strong points, but a unique warmth and dynamism came through in those teachers who were living in the world and working with its peoples.

As these thoughts crossed Ekanta's mind, an interesting teaching contained in the Avadhuta Gita, a revered scripture of his order, came to mind. His teacher had repeated it several times to him, as if to free him of formulating any limited conceptions about Truth and its transmission:

> Whether a teacher be advanced in years
> or younger than the student, this is nonessential.
> Whether such a one is a scholar or an illiterate,
> a monk or a householder, a servant or a master,
> male or female, none of this need be considered.
> Even if such a one is apparently addicted
> to the pleasures of the senses, this too may be overlooked.
> A worthy student should seek only for the essence.
> A diamond fallen into excrement still retains its value.
> A ferryboat, undecorated, still allows beings to ford impassable rivers.

Ekanta had learned from many beings, and he still continued to do so. His initiatory gurus, the vanaprastin couple, had supplied him with most of his training, but they had also made sure that he was oriented towards continual experience and not stymied by any preconceived and premature notions.

*"Perfection,"* they had told him, *"is your very nature. Come to comprehend that fully, but do not take it to mean that you should stop living life or gaining experiences, both in this world and beyond it. The experiences you get from spiritual realization are best digested by testing them in the world. It is here where they are fired in the kiln of practical application."*

"Revered teachers," he had asked sincerely, "if my Atman is ever-perfect, and if I realize It in this life through total identification with It, what else is there to attain?"

*"The Atman is indeed beyond growth and decay,"* came the answer, *"transcendent of both knowledge and ignorance and alien to the idea of bondage and liberation. But, Ekanta, It is busy sporting in the world, as it were. Its radiance is lighting the universe. With this advance wisdom of your perfect nature a given and direct knowledge of your ever-unified condition of awareness with the Supreme Being an accepted fact, you will be free to explore God's universe without fear of separation and completely appreciative of this amazing creative process."*

"Is there an end to growth?" Ekanta had questioned. "There seems to be some who think so and these declare themselves to be fully illumined."

*"There is an end to ignorance,"* answered the guru, *"then substantial growth proceeds. Next, there is an end to the idea of growth and that is where pure expression takes over. But do not, dear one, fall prey to pride or misconception. Let others declare themselves to be masters, or settle into the belief that the goal has been attained. Let them imagine, even, that the universe itself comes to an end with the acquisition of some supremely illumined and exceedingly rare state possessed only by them. Let them think this according to their own understanding. But you, my boy, follow the way of beings like the Buddha, the Tathagata, who taught both a way out of suffering and an eternal state of completeness."*

"What were His teachings like, revered sir?" Ekanta had asked.

Pausing, his preceptor stared off into space for a moment. *"He said, for instance, 'Never satisfied with their present condition, true aspirants, as well as illumined beings alike, are ever seeking higher spiritual atmospheres, like wild geese that leave their mountain lake for more pristine waters at higher altitudes.'"*

"That is beautiful," replied Ekanta with awe. "That will definitely be my credo."

"*Good,*" said the guru. "*And remember the words of another avatar in this respect: 'No matter how high a bird may fly, there are always more lofty regions to explore.'*

"*God is infinite, Ekanta, and ever-perfect,*" the guru continued, after a few moments of silence. "*Even where imperfection exists or seems to persist, it is God alone in the aspect of guide and protector that maintains it. In this way, the Mother keeps beings in their present condition in order to affect total consummation of all limited goals and the fulfillment of all desires at the right and proper time according to the Supreme Will. As the mixed and negative energy from their various thoughts and actions becomes depleted and a certain karmic neutrality is attained, then they are fit for higher understanding. At this juncture, old habits and concepts can be dissolved without danger to the delicate human psyche and fresh insights can visit the mind. It is a meticulous and very exacting process, masterminded and directed by the Master of karma.*"

"If it is God who keeps us in ignorance," asked Ekanta, "why should we strive at all to awaken to Truth, since all will happen in time anyway?"

"*In Truth,*" responded the teacher, "*we are nothing other than the Divine, but our divinity is sleeping as it were, unaware, as yet, of Its infinite power. Take, for instance, the case of a chick still inside the shell. It stirs but is imprisoned, so it reverts back to an unconscious state. As it wearies of its limited condition, upon awakening it struggles harder and perhaps cracks the shell a bit. Meanwhile, on the outside of its little world, the mother hen is busy watching the progress of her chick and encourages it in various ways to struggle. At the appropriate time, when the chick is ready, she helps it crack the shell and it emerges into the light. Then it gains strength and opens its eyes to a greater reality. In like fashion then, Ekanta, you must struggle and open your eyes to this infinite Reality.*"

After a time, the preceptor continued. "*Who knows why this process should be as it is, Ekanta? But since it is this way we should not complain but rather find a way out of the maze. There is a certain wisdom in working with our limitations*

*until an auspicious time arrives and there is a difference
between the moderate way and the way of outright stubbornness
or complacency."*

"What are the signs that allow us to comprehend the distinction, revered teacher?" Ekanta had asked.

*"There is a word in Sanskrit for this stunted condition,
Ekanta. The Vedanta calls it Anavasthi-Tattva, a stagnant state
where the aspirant falsely assumes that he or she has reached
the highest realization and need not proceed any farther. You
will notice quite a few beings laboring under this delusion.
There are obvious signs and indications of ignorance and pretension which surface while in the proximity of these misguided
souls. Some become self-declared luminaries and teachers,
advertising themselves in all sorts of sensational ways. They
declare themselves to be supremely enlightened or begin to call
themselves Avatars. Sitting on thrones, gathering gullible and
wealthy disciples around them, dressing themselves up like gods
or goddesses complete with various ornaments which act as
mere stage props for their vain antics, these beings make a mockery of authentic spiritual life based upon hard self-effort. They
also make a sham of the precious guru/disciple relationship. The
difference between these charlatans and true teachers is vast
indeed."*

"I have seen such figures here and there, revered sir," mentioned
Ekanta. "There is much fanfare going on and they are always
accompanied by crowds of restless, glamour-seeking people. It is
all for show and very little beneficial teaching occurs, if any."

*"That is true, Ekanta, and very perceptive of you. The
emphasis at these gatherings is placed upon an ego-centered
spectacle. It is all pseudo-religious theater where thrills connected with name and fame form the basis for all seeking. Both
the guru and the disciple of this orientation hold a distorted
view of darshan. It is all, 'see me, appreciate me, worship me.'
Nothing is done to benefit the needy, to remove the suffering of
others or to perpetuate the spiritual evolution of the devotees."*

"What characterizes normal behavior where authentic spiritual
circles are formed, dear guru?" Ekanta had asked at this point.

*"In authentic spiritual circles, Ekanta, teachings of the
highest import are given, designed to transform the sincere*

*seeker into a Self-realized being. No concern for selfish motive can exist where a dedicated guru and his or her sincere disciples are meeting. Only the drive to awaken the aspirant to the internal perfection of the Atman exists in the heart and mind of the true guru and such a one uses powerful methods to accomplish this. Those seeking niceties, who are searching after the 'all love and light path' in a superficial sense — these will not be found where the hard work of perfecting human nature is being accomplished. As Sri Krishna has said, the path of yoga is not for the weak or the insincere."*

"Revered sir," asked Ekanta, "can you outline briefly the differences between the authentic guru and the charlatan?  I have noticed that the impostor can be very charismatic, attracting many followers."

*"This is true, Ekanta,"* replied the guru, *"and perhaps some desires of the spectacle seekers get satisfied around such as these, but it is a far cry from the transforming power of yoga.  The pretender loves to be admired and served while the true guru bends all energies to the service of others.  One dotes on ostentatiousness and sensationalism, the other works silently behind the scenes.  One covets wealth and material goods, the other owns nothing and seeks the removal of ignorance from the minds of sentient beings and the instilling of divine qualities into the devotees.  My boy, there is a wide chasm between the two.  Seekers who arm themselves with discrimination can immediately separate the two and act accordingly.  Spiritual perfection is accomplished swiftly and completely in the presence of God and guru which, in the case of the illumined ones, are one and the same thing."*

At one time the Avadhut had come under verbal fire from a group of wandering itinerant monks.  He had stayed at one pilgrimage place longer than usual and had subsequently earned the respect of the sadhus who had gathered there.  The newcomers had disagreed with him on a certain issue and had verbally attacked him with a mind towards demeaning his level of spirituality.

"Have you had Nirvikalpa Samadhi?" they asked, in an accusational tone.

"Oh that," Ekanta had replied lightly yet decisively, "that is my true nature.  My Lord and Master will manifest that through me when the time is right. He decides such matters so I leave them to Him. My duty is to love Him, chant His names and glories, be devoted to the guru and the teachings and share what knowledge I possess with my brothers and sisters." This answer had endeared him all the more to his companions who were looking on.

Not satisfied to leave it at that, though, his examiners had asked, "Yes, but have you seen God?"

"I have seen only God ever since I opened my eyes on this earth, as have you!" The practical and evident tone of this statement combined with the force of realization coming from Ekanta's words served to silence his would-be antagonizers. Muttering among themselves, they had withdrawn to contemplate the evening's exchanges.

Ekanta turned his attention once again on the wonderful couple before him. Their regard for one another was more than mere respect, it was actual reverence. He remembered some of the questions he had asked the vanaprastin couple regarding married life as opposed to monastic life.

*"It is your choice,"* they had told him, *"but seek your swadharma first and let such matters be worked out in accordance with the realization of that. Ultimately, it matters little what the outer circumstances of one's life are if one is fully focused on the Atman in the proper way."*

This teaching had echoed the Christ's own words when he had advised seekers to first seek the kingdom of heaven and all else would be added in due time. Thinking about the differences between the monastic way of life, the householder path and the way of his own gurus who were vanaprastins, brought back more teachings from the past:

*"There are many ways of living and a vast array of differing modes of expression, Ekanta,"* the Mataji had said one day. *"Regardless, it is all very complete somehow. Actually, the teachings regarding the householder path differ very little from monastic living. The lifestyles of the monks we have known, when examined, are very similar to the way in which illumined householders exist. If the teachings are followed carefully, my dear, by all and in accordance with their capacity, enlightenment will surely dawn and life will radiate divinity. So many of the Avatars and great prophets have remained in the world,*

*Ekanta, accepting wives and husbands while still exemplifying the highest ideals. It is wonderful! So do not get attached to the path but simply go forward with your mind on the goal, knowing it to be your true home and your very essence."*

Now, resting in this sacred home of the Lord's children and watching the interchange between this blessed couple, Ekanta was inspired and realized the full scope of the Mataji's words. In many of the houses he had visited, he had noticed that the presence of spiritual communion and reverent regard for others was sorely missing. Even when graced with all manner of boons, many families still fell into the traps of mundane habit and complacency. Such a state was not only unfortunate but wasteful. It created a condition akin to spiritual suicide. Ekanta shuddered at the thought and he placed his mind back on the positive aspects of existence in the world. A description of the exemplary householder couple came to mind.

One day, the Avadhut had asked the Bengali ecstatic, Ramakrishnadas Baul, "Are divine couples still to be found on this earth?"

*"Yes,"* answered the baul, *"I have seen them. Some do exist, though they may be rare. Such beings succeed only if they both lead a spiritual life and practice disciplines. God's special Grace is upon them and they both taste the bliss of the Atman. Otherwise, disagreements will occur, life will become miserable and one will have to leave the other."*

"What are the characteristics of such a couple?" the Avadhut had asked.

*"Their love is indescribable,"* came the sure answer, *"and they feel about each other that there is no one so near and dear, in life and in death. Both of them are servants of God — His servant and His handmaid. After the birth of one or two children, if that is destined, they live as brother and sister. The family is spiritually oriented and the children are taught the scriptures from a young age. The community looks upon them as great inspirations and learn from their example. Ultimately, they know that God is their very own. Despite all troubles, they remain firm in their faith and commitment. They are like the Pandava brothers and their wife: they do not forget God in happiness or in sorrow."*

Dharman and Gramani, the householder couple who fed and sheltered the Avadhut that evening, were hardworking members of the merchant class whose families had both met with disaster. This painful experience had brought them together in mutual understanding and they had gradually formed a powerful bond of friendship that had matured into love, resulting in the consecrated union of marriage. They had inherited the land they were farming due to the death of Gramani's parents and had moved away from the city where their respective families had lived. They had one child, a daughter named Puspi, who had just gone away for a week to visit relatives. Partially for this reason, the couple was very happy to have some company in place of their beloved child.

Of the many subjects that bore inspection that evening, the favorite, not surprisingly, was Truth. While describing the state of affairs of society and the world, observed during his recent travels, Ekanta had at one point stopped and apologized for seeming to be so critical of the human condition, of the insensitivity of living beings towards the presence of God in all things and of their dishonesty and deception.

Dharman excused him expediently, stating simply, *"The tusks of an elephant go out, but should never circle and grow back in."*

Ekanta had recognized this teaching from his own upbringing and knew that it referred to the spoken words of a human being. Using the example of a rogue elephant, who suddenly goes mad due to the curving tusk that grows back into its jaw bone or skull, the saying explained nicely the unfortunate but timely repercussions experienced by a person whose words were bereft of honesty and sincerity. These dishonest words, like the tusk, would only return and cause pain to the one who thoughtlessly uttered them. Such was the condition of many of the people of this time that they would callously deceive and manipulate others without thought or consideration, placing their own selfish and often petty concerns above the well-being of others. This apt example of karmic retribution had inspired Ekanta's mind and brought forth all manner of applicable teachings, many of which had delighted the couple immensely.

"Have you noticed that the mother cat treats her kitten in one way and a mouse in a completely different manner?" Ekanta asked them. "The Mother of the Universe is no stranger to delusion, being Mahamaya Herself, the very power of the Lord and the infinite repository of illusory appearances. Those who take refuge in Her have nothing to fear, for She bears their burden within Herself and protects them from that moment onward. The ignorant, however, like the mouse in the claws and jaws of death, suffer horribly due to their negative actions, their stubborn pride and their failure to return to the protective sanctuary of the Feet of the Lord."

As the meal drew to a close and the three retired to the sitting area, Ekanta noticed an interesting display on the wall. Several arrows, obviously of authentic-quality workmanship, had been cleverly arranged in artistic fashion. Asking about the display earned Ekanta his first insight into the profession of his male host. Dharman was an arrowmaker and made his living at this craft. The king of the province in which he lived often employed him when he needed to outfit his militia with proper weaponry. This notable distinction was sufficient to earn Dharman a more than adequate living which he in turn used in the service of the holy and the maintenance of his property. The discussion of this lifestyle and its benefits gradually turned the topic of the conversation towards Ekanta's plans.

"Where are you headed next, revered sir?" asked Dharman.

"I have no fixed plans," Ekanta admitted, "but desire to visit the city for a change and soon. A great manifestation of God is present where many gather."

"There is no doubt of that," said Dharman. "As it turns out, I must go to the city tomorrow to finish an order of arrows placed by the captain of the king's army. Perhaps we can travel that distance together, if you would care to keep my company."

"I would like nothing better," stated Ekanta, for though he usually traveled alone, he had taken a great liking to this noble person and his pure and gracious wife and wanted to know them better.

"It is settled then," said Dharman. "We should leave at first light after morning worship and breakfast. It will take several hours to reach the city and I must accomplish a major part of my work before dusk tomorrow."

Having settled all plans for the morrow, the couple showed Ekanta a small adjoining room where he could relax at ease and in partial privacy. Where there had once been a door a large sheepskin hung instead. There was another thicker skin laying on the floor which provided padding for a comfortable bed. The Avadhut sat for awhile, enjoying the deep silence and wholesome atmosphere of the place. The fire in the hearth burned low, casting darting shadows about the outer room. Ekanta's mind gradually began to soar, as was its natural tendency when the late night hours of Brahma Muhurta began to arrive. It was his teacher who had pointed out the powerful effects of this midnight period to him, indicating the heightening of intensity of one's consciousness during reflection and meditation accomplished at this time. Ever since then, Ekanta had made it a habit to either remain awake until others were asleep and the early hours of the morning had arrived, or, according to schedule, simply wake up during this auspicious time and sit to contemplate the glory of God's subtle presence within him. Many of his most sublime spiritual experiences had taken place at this rarefied late night hour when the Mahavayu, the subtle spiritual wind, was blowing free and unimpeded.

Such had been the case the past evening on the hillock, Ekanta remembered. Thinking back on that wonderful experience, Ekanta's mind immediately fell into a deep reverie. That especial vision — the perception of experiencing the Divine Being simultaneously without and within — was again coming upon him. He wondered if this condition was recorded anywhere in the scriptures, for he had seldom heard it spoken of and had never read about it. What type of samadhi it was seemed beyond classification, but Ekanta was certainly not about to mar it or detract from its blissful intensity by attempting to categorize it.

This evening, though, the teachings which came from the living, conscious Presence were of a different type. Instead of being nature-oriented they were more internal and Ekanta felt a shift which caused him to perceive his surroundings from an omniscient standpoint. His senses were not as heightened but instead were transcended without seeming to be shut off. At first he was aware of other living beings. In a distant room, Dharman and Gramani were breathing rhythmically in deep sleep. Suddenly, the teaching of Soham — That am I, and Hamsa — I am That, entered Ekanta's mind with surprising force. He had learned of these perpetual breathing mantras, called Ajapa-Mantra, from a yogi who had passed through his village when he was a young boy, and had confirmed the teaching with his own guru. Now he was experiencing the profundity of this ancient principle in a new way. Thinking back, he heard his guru's voice once again, echoing in his inner memory:

*"The indrawn breath, the yogis say, is naturally accompanied by the inward prayer, Soham, affirming the eternal presence of the Supreme Being. Breathing out, the prayer Hamsa naturally occurs, which reveals the constant unity of the apparently individual soul, jivatman, with the eternally perfect and all-pervasive existence called Paramatman. Along the Mother path, by becoming aware of this natural breathing and by using Her mantra and utilizing the knowledge of Her Word, the spiritual energy called udghata gets stirred up. It is the precursor of the appearance of Kundalini Shakti, which rises and penetrates the spiritual centers of human awareness, bringing with it substantial illumination. Different from this natural combination of breathing and mantra, are certain breathing exercises called basic pranayama in yoga and anapanasati in Buddhist practice. They are designed to calm the mind and make it fit for enlightened states. These, being rudimentary and potentially dangerous, however, should be practiced only under the guidance of an adept."*

Ekanta was no stranger to this process of awakening, having both studied it intellectually and experienced it for himself. He had occasionally been transported into an omniscient state of mind by its direct presence in manifestation. At this moment, sitting in the warm, dark house, he felt simultaneously observant as a witness and inherently involved as the experiencer. The breathing of his two hosts, sleeping in the nearby room, was fraught with significance and meaning, for it somehow confirmed, in an unexplainable way, that Reality was a living, breathing presence, as inclusive of life and mind in a relative sphere of existence as it was of transcendent and absolute states of pure conscious Awareness. Immediately, Ekanta's memories of his studies of the great Mandukyopanishad came to the forefront of his mind. Silently, barely audible, he chanted the appropriate Sanskrit verse which moved him the most:

*Sarvam hi etat brahma ayam atma brahma,*
*so'yam atma chatuspat.*

The ultimate Truth is that Brahman contains everything.
The Self within, that too is Brahman.
That which is within all beings, called Atman,
appears with four apparent divisions.

At this point, Ekanta's mind searched through an entire host of teachings, placed in his mental faculty as consecrated memories associated with vibrant transmissions from his teachers. His inherent ability to retain this vast field of wisdom was due in part to the practice of pratyahara, a yogic discipline that required the withdrawal and storing up of all the energies associated with the five senses and placing them as a concentrated force within the lotus of the heart. This practice, together with others, penultimate to the attainment of true, one-pointed focus, created in Ekanta the intellectual foundation upon which retentive memory in a vastly expanded condition was formulated and achieved. The mind, illumined by this subtle secret of inward practice, was then capable of drawing in upon itself infinitely. *"All knowledge lies within,"* came the teaching from his memory.

The Avadhut had realized many things by this age-old method, not the least of which was that the Supreme Being, Brahman, was a timeless and spaceless Reality. The implosion of the original and primal intelligent force, called the Adishakti in Tantric tradition, willfully manifesting Itself as the universe of name and form for the playful sport of indivisible Consciousness could, at any time, turn back in upon Itself and experience Its primal Essence with complete fulfillment and natural ease. All that was needed, from the standpoint of relativity, was an initial practice pursued under the guidance of an adept teacher which, when activated, was capable of breaking the bonds of habitual thought and limited conception. Once, just before leaving family, home and gurus, a matured Ekanta had asked his revered teacher for information about Kundalini Shakti, having begun to experience its flood tide of renovating power.

"Revered Guruji," the young man had inquired, "my whole outlook and many of the truths I once held sacred are now being transfigured into something higher and less cumbersome. This is strange and I am not sure what is happening to me half of the time."

Laughing softly, the guru said, *"Blessed disciple, what we have taught you through these past twelve years has been powerful by way of teachings and certainly of a much more potent transmission than most students receive. Now, you are beginning to have anubhava — direct spiritual experience of what has been conveyed — for you have striven hard to put these principles into practice rather than merely listening and intellectually comprehending them as most do."*

"Respected teacher," replied Ekanta, "I feel now as if I have met the Mother face-to-face, at least in brief encounters. She is..." at this point the young man faltered, searching for words..."terrific, but how do I cope with what She is doing to me, inside of me? My mind is sometimes in a whirl, though I feel no danger or discomfort. I feel as if nothing is real....except Her."

*"Ah, my dear student,"* returned the loving preceptor, *"in these many hard-working years that you have been with us you have accomplished what the teachers of the highest aspects of spiritual life call, Tattvashuddha, the purification of all external principles."*

"Revered Guruji," Ekanta had objected mildly, "I have done nothing but control and purify the mind."

*"Precisely, dear student,* replied the teacher, *"and since the mind is everything, and everything in this phenomenal universe has proceeded from it, its purification and control amount to nothing short of illumination. As the Avatar has stated, pure mind is God. That you have placed the mind's contents in order and learned the art of detachment from the world is no small accomplishment. This is what is needed for success in spiritual life. Essentially, successful Tattvashuddha culmination is called Sattva-Purusha-Nytakyati, the realization that the Atman is different from all created things, in other terms, that It is the only stationary and immutable Principle.*

*"You see,"* continued the guru after due consideration, *"it is involution that we are speaking of here, not evolution. At one point, inside of the scope of intense, transformative sadhana, the aspirant stops the process of incessant change by refusing to indulge in pain-and pleasure-bearing activities. Remaining*

*firm in sadhana for years, a neutralization of karma is finally achieved and an end to the regime of universal compulsion is effected. As involution takes place, that being a turn inwards towards the Source and away from the mirage-like appearance of the universe, each of the elements and aspects of creation are examined and found to be lacking in permanence. One by one, from the five elements on up to the highest and subtlest expression of Brahman called Mahat, the Cosmic Mind — all are seen through, are seen as they are, and renounced due to their mutability and their involvement with the process of unfolding.*

*"The unfolding process, called evolution, is put into perspective as a relative truth by the practice of proper observation. After this is achieved, the whole facade comes tumbling down like a house of cards due to the death of all processes. As soon as the twenty-four cosmic principles are rejected on the grounds of mutability and creativity, the purification is accomplished. It is then that one knows the Atman to be completely separate from all created things, 'entirely other' as the Upanishads state.*

*"Successful involution, then, is to become stationary," con-tinued the guru, "like Reality. It is abiding in the Atman. When Mother Kundalini awakens and rises, everything is destroyed, that is, all that is not ultimately Real is revealed as such. Attachment to noneternal things, fanciful and imaginative thoughts as well as solid objects, then dies. What is left over is, indeed, Essential Reality, Satchitananda. Praises be to those who accomplish Tattvashuddha. Knowing themselves to be eter-nal, they enjoy the universe in a way unlike any other."*

Ekanta had seen the various rides offered to the public at festival gatherings in big cities. One particular ride had many individual cars, all connected to a main circulating overhead beam that took the occupants round and round in a rapid circle. The screams of the riders bore testament to the great fun they were having. Though each car was independent from all the others, they were controlled by the same mechanism, and though all the riders were also separate from one another, they were still enjoy-ing the same sensations. This spectacle, demonstrating, among other things, the interconnectedness of all beings, had brought obvious spiritual teachings and correlations to Ekanta's mind. If all beings could accomplish Tattvashuddha, he reflected, taking the time and the steps necessary for personal spiritual advancement, they would discover the intrinsic Oneness at the root of their being and would learn the secrets of merging with It. This would be a source of great bliss for them, a way into divine life.

With his mind floating in a high and refined state of awareness, focused upon the subtle repetitive prayers of the sleeping Dharman and Gramani, Ekanta recalled the teachings about the four quarters of Aum, the word symbol for transcendent Reality:

Vaishvanara, the normal condition of all embodied beings,
know that to be the first apparent division of Reality.
This, the waking state, where consciousness is attached to
external manifestation through which it enjoys objects by the
means of seven limbs and nineteen mouths,
is the playground of the Universal Soul called Vishva.

Ekanta's gurus had schooled him well about the seven limbs — the heavens as Vishva's head, the sun and moon as His eyes, the air as His breath, the sky as His body, the water as his lower organ and the earth as His feet. In addition, His nineteen mouths — the five sense organs, the five motor organs, the five vital breaths and the four aspects of mind — were known as the ways in which this all-pervasive being, seemingly split into many parts, enjoyed the waking state. Still, with all of this before them, human beings seldom contemplated these modes of existence. Recalling the scriptures once again, Ekanta muttered the following verse:

Playing in a subtler field, the realm of dreams,
the shining one, Taijasa, remains inwardly aware
and experiences the refined enjoyment of the dream worlds
with seven limbs and nineteen mouths.

Thus, the scriptures stated, the dream state afforded the experiencer of this realm, Taijasa, the opportunity to enjoy subtle objects instead of the gross physical ones, which were, it was admitted, only stored up impressions formulated in the waking state. Ekanta had always thought that this experience pointed directly to the transcendence of death, which was a power that exerted influence over material objects only. Even a dream death was revisited by another dream life, showing the nature of Reality to be witness of both dreams and therefore beyond both. This was brought into further clarification by the third state of consciousness.

The third state, his guru had told him, was full of transcendent joy — ananda-mayah — and was characterized by ghanananda — an indefinite mass of bliss. This was called Prajna, the all-knowing intellectual condition having direct access to the portal of Absolute Reality:

In deep sleep,
in indivisible union with the source of ultimate cognition,
Prajna sports in a field of ecstatic knowing,
enjoying unfathomable joy and permeated by it
in perpetual and blissful awareness.

Ekanta knew, though, that the bliss experienced in deep sleep was of the negative variety. It had different characteristics than the bliss of the Atman. The literal definition of Prajna as pointed out by his gurus, which meant "one who knows properly," pointed to this fact. The Sanskrit word, chetomukhah, defined as "mouth of knowledge," indicated the third state as a gateway through which the conditions of waking and dreaming were experienced. As beings did not really remember their experience of deep sleep, it was fitting that it not be assigned the position of ultimacy and be looked upon as a portal through which Consciousness enters the external realms of existence and, conversely, through which It returns to Its point of origin.

Still, the Mandukyopanishad named the third state of Prajna as Sarveshvarah, the Lord of all. This, thought the Avadhut, equated it with Ishvara, the Lord and Master of the Universe, for as all things came out of Ishvara — God residing inside the universe of name and form — so too did all manifestation and phenomena spring from consciousness in the deep sleep state, resulting in the experiences of waking and dreaming. This, in turn, brought up the natural inquiry into the Source of these three states. If Aum was the primal vibration holding these three realms of experience, there must be something beyond it and of the nature of absolute unity or totality. The Rishis had named this Source simply as

Turiya, the fourth, a state of Consciousness which was not a state at all but something simultaneously all-pervasive and transcendent:

> It is the essential, indivisible self-awareness
> common to all states of consciousness.
> Peace, bliss and nonduality
> of the ultimate nature are there in It,
> and It must be realized.

Despite the cerebral nature of these teachings, Ekanta had always appreciated the way that the Rishis, the wise ones of old, had mixed philosophy and direct perception with practical sense and good humor.  The description of these four states as the Four Feet of God was an example of this.  The thought of these great realms of existence being the feet upon which God, as Consciousness, got around, always brought a smile to Ekanta's face.  The metaphor of four "divisions" was too misleading anyway, especially for an eternal and infinite Being that was supposed to be indivisible and homogenous.  Thinking of God with four feet, Ekanta could immediately relate to all phases of the Supreme Being's manifestation, and this was acceptable without detracting in the least from the transcendent and absolute nature of Divine Reality.

Ekanta knew himself to be both a jnani and a bhakta — a wisdom knower and a devotee of the Lord.  It was this combination which had caused his teachers to proclaim him to be an adhikari, a qualified student at a very early age.

*"You have two wings,"* said his guru one day, *"now open them, exercise them and learn to soar."*

His devotional side now began to emerge as he thought of the Four Feet of Brahman.  It reminded him of a certain holy man he had met, a mysterious figure who had appeared in his village one day and had disappeared just as suddenly two weeks later.  Ekanta, though he had never known his name, had been attracted to him intensely and this had given him ample opportunity to exercise his detachment when the holy one departed.  Thus had the holy man taught him profound lessons, in deeply contrasting ways, during a very short time.  One night, as they sat around the dhuni fire together, the enigmatic figure had suddenly asked him a question:

*"What is the greatest thing in the universe, my boy?"*

Ekanta, taken off guard by the suddenness of the question, had stammered in a questioning voice, "God, sir?"

*"The heart of a holy being is the greatest thing in the universe,"* came the reply.

After a short silence, Ekanta had questioned him by saying, "Is this because God is not in or of this universe, revered sir, being entirely transcendent?"

*"Don't speak in half truths, son; of course God is here. Otherwise, where is the support for all this phenomena? Even a reflection has to have a medium like glass, water or a mirror on which to appear. A mirage, for instance, needs air, heat and sand as a backdrop to effect its illusory presence. What you are saying is a subject for vain philosophical speculation. Seek higher, go deeper. Don't end up as a dry jnani. There is much more beyond the mere surface of religion. Remember, the six darshanas — the six orthodox systems of philosophy — are the Divine Mother's perpetual streams of Wisdom. She reveals them, but they can never fully reveal Her."*

After another pregnant silence, Ekanta had summoned the courage to ask, "Why is the heart of a holy man the greatest thing in the universe, revered sir?"

*"I did not say a holy man, my boy, I said a holy being. My greatest teacher was a woman, and remember, the Atman has no gender. One should never limit the Supreme Being, nor is it even possible."*

Another period of silence ensued, when finally the holy man emitted a laugh. After his mirth had subsided, he stated grandly:

*"When we look out upon the world, it is the earth that impresses us as the greatest thing. By learning about our world, though, we find that the ocean is of greater volume than the earth. Upon further inspection, we perceive that space is more vast than either earth or the waters and we then think this to be the greatest thing. Finally we learn from our guru that Vishnu, the Lord of the Worlds, covers all three — air, earth and water — with one of His Blessed Feet. The holy ones, however, have both of Vishnu's Feet enshrined in their hearts. Therefore, the heart of the illumined being is the greatest thing in the universe."*

There was no need for any more conversation for the rest of the night. Together, in one of the most profoundly moving meditations Ekanta had ever experienced, this unique and strangely familiar being and the exceptional young boy had spent the night absorbed in communion with the Supreme Being abiding eternally within their hearts.

With the prayers Soham and Hamsa repeating in the background, over and over again in constant testament to the existence of a benign Creator, the Avadhut searched deeply in his consciousness for more of the Divine Mother's teachings. He was not yet sleepy.

In the distant past, late one night, his teacher had told him, _"Dear child, you have acquired the yoga of insomnia at a very early age. You will make the most of this life, to be sure. I have no doubt."_

One of the songs of his boyhood suddenly danced into his mind:

I have lulled sleep to sleep forever
and have placed death in its own grave.
Even my fear has now become frightened of itself.
What additional concerns can possibly plague me now,
in a universe where my Divine Mother is the sole sovereign?

Dawn came early as Ekanta awakened. He had not even been aware of his slipping off into deep sleep but he was aware that he had experienced some profound dreams in the early morning hours. His hosts were already up and around and gradually the aroma of incense began to make its presence felt. Ekanta took this as a sign that morning worship was beginning and he rose up and dressed himself appropriately. Coming out of his room, he found that Dharman and Gramani were already seated at the altar in a distant corner of the cabin. Smiling, yet remaining silent, Gramani turned and indicated a place to wash just outside the door of the cabin.

Ekanta went through the door and moved towards the trough of water by the porch steps. He pumped some water for his use, washed himself and dried his face and hands. It was still a bit dark but twilight was beginning to spread over the countryside. The earth was waking up and signs of that awakening were evident.  It reminded Ekanta of spiritual awakening and the systematic opening of sublime awareness from center to center from the base of the spine all the way to sublime heights at the crown of the head.  His own consciousness was so heightened at this moment that he saw the entire physical universe as a mass of indefinite sparks of light, dancing behind the appearance of objects and elements.  The eyes, though, were just not capable of such vision, he thought.  Better to shut them and perceive the inner Reality without any outer impediments or obstructions.  Thinking so, he turned to go inside.

Once in the house again, he moved to his place instinctively and was seated and plunged into meditation before his mind even realized what was happening.  All that he was aware of was light, dancing and leaping about, illumining, as it were, the four quarters.  A powerful yet subtle energy within him, seemingly centered in his spinal column, was leaping as well, *"like a monkey swinging from branch to branch"* his memory seemed to say.  Whenever he became aware of the body and the world at all, it felt as if he had levitated and was floating far above the normal habitat of the body.

This inner sensation, whenever it occurred, always reminded him of a funny incident that had happened during his travels.  He had been journeying in a part of the country that was particularly devoid of inhabitants and towns.  Darkness had caught him in the middle of nowhere and as he was about to lie down and sleep where he was, he saw a light in the distance.  As he approached the encampment, his joy at finding human beings was matched only by his surprise at the spectacle before him.  Gathered around a fire was a group of beings who were seated in lotus position.  They were attempting to launch themselves into the air and Ekanta could only surmise that they were trying to defy gravity.  Unfortunately, their attempts resulted again and again only in an unceremonious and probably painful landing on their haunches.  Still, they did not give up and continued to bounce around the circle.  Others watched and occasionally encouraged them in their folly.  Ekanta had to exercise some very strong self-control to keep from laughing out loud.

The man who welcomed him had barely given his name before he had embarked on an explanation of what was occurring.

Evidently, from what Ekanta could gather, the group consisted of hatha yogis dedicated to practicing physical exercises and forced breathing in order to attain supernatural powers. They were convinced, as well, that the feeling of levitation experienced at times of meditation was a physical reality that happened to the practitioner at a certain stage of spiritual growth. The description of an elevated feeling stated in traditional yoga sutras was intended, the guide declared, to encourage aspirants to attain the power of levitation. Therefore, drawing away from society in secret, this group had embarked upon a strict sadhana in private with the intention of achieving this end.

"Have any yet succeeded?" asked Ekanta of the man.

"No," he answered, "but one yogi has managed to stay in the air for several seconds longer than any other. Our group has great hopes that this man will soon levitate and float in the air to any location he chooses.

"Do you want to join the group in its attempts?" asked the man hopefully.

"No thank you, dear sir," answered the Avadhut politely. I much prefer to walk to my next destination rather than fly."

Judging by the painful expressions on the faces of the "yogic hoppers" and the considerable bruises on their backsides and thighs, Ekanta wanted no part of this particular delusion. He had withdrawn to the edge of the camp, secured a little food, eaten, contemplated the Lord and had finally drifted off to sleep. Early morning found him miles from the encampment, happily moving forward under the animating force of his own legs and free of sore haunches.

Later, in his own sadhana, he had experienced true levitation — the rising of Consciousness, called Kundalini Shakti, from the base of the spine through all the subtle centers. This morning, sitting in meditation with Dharman and Gramani, he was again experiencing this profound inner feeling. It was not accompanied by perspiration and painful bruises, though, but rather by blissful light and the sound of the primal Aum.

The Avadhut knew that such descriptions recorded in the sutras referred to the rising of awakened Consciousness and its arrival at the Sahashrara chakra in the crown of pure mind. The Avadhut knew as well that all powers such as omniscience, diminution of form to the size of an atom, floating on air, walking on water and other phenomena were accomplished by illumined Consciousness, not by limited willpower attached to physical matter. Those who desired to go beyond the laws of the universe could definitely do so, not by accomplishing the physically impossible but by realizing themselves to be eternal Spirit, the Atman, and transcending mental and physical realms entirely. This way also saved the aspirant from the dangers of the acquisition of the eight occult powers.

Ekanta had learned early on from various teachings and by the examples of liberated beings that occult powers were an obstacle to the attainment of Self-knowledge. It was therefore unbelievable that beings would ignore the advice of the wise ones and seek out such powers. As Ekanta considered this, the words of Sri Krishna came into his mind.

"My friend," Sri Krishna had said to a beloved disciple, "if you have attachment to even one of the occult powers you will not be able to realize God."

The Mataji, his revered female preceptor, had put in another way: "Those who succeed in this grandest of all achievements, the realization of the Atman, have powers come to them unasked for yet seldom, if ever, utilize them for any purpose. What a stark contrast there is, Ekanta, between those rare few who naturally proceed along the path towards enlightenment, free from goal-oriented, process-oriented sadhana, and the deluded masses who grasp after the glitter of occult powers and the transitory and limited experiences that they bring."

"What are the eight occult powers, Mataji?" Ekanta, at that time a young man of sixteen, asked her one day.

"Anima, laghima, vyapti, prakamya, mahima, ishitva, vashitva and kama-vasayita," the wise preceptor answered directly. "If ever they manifest in you, or if ever you see them manifest in others, simply disregard them or merely witness them and focus on the Atman within. This will automatically regulate these forces and will guide you in dealing with them."

"How will I know them if I see them, revered Mataji?" the young man asked. "Can you tell me something about them?"

"The Eightfold Supernatural Powers, the Asta Siddhis," began the vanaprastin guru, "were, originally, and according to the

_Shaivite Tantric path, blessings bestowed by Lord Shiva on special devotees. Since beings did not become perverted in those days by using them for show, out of pride, to control others, to amass wealth or to effect some selfish attainment contrary to spiritual growth, they were enjoyed in secret among the few and used wisely only by certain great and perfected masters."_

"What do these eight accomplish, revered teacher?" asked Ekanta curiously. "What powers do they confer?"

_"Anima allows one to reduce the body to an infinitesimally tiny unit of matter, so small that others cannot possibly notice or perceive."_

"But Mataji," stated the young man, "if a yogi can project his consciousness through the flow of prana, by using the subtle body, and more importantly, by simply being aware of the all-pervasive nature of the Atman, of what use is this power?"

_"Indeed,"_ came a voice from the door of the ashram. Looking up, Ekanta beheld his male preceptor, the Mataji's husband, standing there, and the two saluted him reverently. The preceptor, beaming profusely upon his young charge, gave him a sign of blessing and proceeded to sit down in yogic fashion beside them.

_"I am so gratified that you use your mental faculties so well, Ekanta,"_ the guru praised him. _"Instead of losing yourself in awe or admiration of paltry attainments, your powerful reasoning and discrimination saves you. Lord, I wish that the Divine Mother would send me a dozen like you. I could then change the world!"_

"Guruji," came the young man's response, "you have always told me that the world is fine as it is, that it does not need changing. Have I misunderstood?"

Breaking into laughter along with his wife, the teacher smiled even more broadly and said, _"No, Ekanta, you have not misunderstood me. Rather, you have caught me! What I meant to convey is that I could then help to change human nature, not material nature. The five elements and this universe are doing fine without the intervention of humankind. However, let us proceed with the subject of anima. It sounds as if you were discussing the Asta Siddhis before I arrived."_

_"That is correct,"_ replied the Mataji, _"and your interruption_ *is welcome, for you can help me explain this difficult subject. Please, tell him what you know."*

The guru was quiet for a few moments. Then he said, *"You are perfectly right in seeing through the comparatively unimportant function of anima, Ekanta. It is those of small attainment, who do not have the greater abilities that you mentioned, that use the power of diminution. This power is used for a whole host of inferior reasons, such as escaping impending danger, to effect unwanted contact with others, to see things that are either difficult to witness or are not meant to be seen or in order to escape detection and so forth. In truth, nothing very beneficial, spiritually speaking, comes of any of these eight powers. Their acquisition by way of sadhana is a waste of time and therefore an impediment to more helpful and crucial pursuits."*

*"We shall finish the description of the other seven though, my dear,"* said the Mataji, *"for it may be of use to you in the future. Laghima confers the power of weightlessness on the practitioner. Though floating around in the atmosphere has no actual benefit with regards to spiritual life and can be physically dangerous as well, beings are nonetheless attracted by the thought of transgressing natural laws. Therefore, you may come across some who seek after this power. It is called levitation. It is best to steer clear of it and of those who seek it. They are in a deluded frame of mind at that time and one can only hope that they will give it up and go forward towards more essential practices."*

*"You may have heard of the famous story about the two brothers,"* interjected Ekanta's guru. *"They parted and each went away for five years to study. When they returned, the first said to the other, 'Brother, look what I have learned.' Saying so, he proceeded to walk across the river. The second brother, procuring a small coin from his pocket, paid the boatman the fee and was ferried across the river. Approaching his brother, he said, 'Is that what you have spent five years learning? For a few cents I was able to accomplish the same feat!'"*

*"So you see,"* the Mataji said, returning to the subject at hand, *"occult powers are not only detrimental to spiritual growth, they are time-consuming and practically useless besides. They are sometimes used by the great ones for particular purposes, but this is seldom and for specific reasons. Importantly, it is only*

*these special manifestations of Mother's power that can remain untainted by them.*

*"As for vyapti, if one can shrink to nothing, as it were, one should also be able to increase in size. Of what good this is, well anyone might venture a guess. One could possibly win the fattest-man-in-the-world contest, I suppose, or be able to literally crush one's enemies, but here again you may see my point. It has no spiritual value that we can see, though in ancient times the siddhas must have had some good purpose for it."*

*"Yes,"* continued Ekanta's male guru, laughing at his wife's description, *"but in those times people were not nearly as gullible, nor were they ignorant of their Atman, nor were they given to all manner of delusion such as selfishness, greed and the misuse of power. As an example of the dangers of the possession of these powers by unqualified beings, take prakamya, the fourth occult power, for instance. It aids one in fulfilling any desire that comes to mind. Can you imagine what havoc would ensue if beings living in this day and age would get a hold of that? I shudder to think of it. If power-hungry people were able to have anything they wanted — name, fame, power, wealth, etc. — these desires would be satisfied at the expense of others. Such dictates go against dharma and upset the world order. During these present times we are seeing the effects of such behavior, even without the eight occult powers brought to bear."*

A few moments of silence followed as the three pondered what had been said.

*"The fifth power, Ekanta, called mahima, makes the body radiant, glorious to behold, full and robust."*

"Does not a good diet, exercise, proper posture, meditation and chanting the names of the Lord accomplish this ever better?" asked Ekanta innocently.

The two vanaprastins turned and looked at each other as if on cue. *"What more need be said?"* uttered the Mataji with a smile.

*"Though this seems a bit wasted on you, my dear,"* she continued, *"I shall explain the final three siddhis. Ishitva enables one to dominate over others, causing them to do one's exact bidding, and vashitva is a power of attraction that draws others inexorably and helplessly near."*

"What about Yogamaya, which you have taught me about?"

asked Ekanta. "That, too, is a power of attraction."

*"Yes,"* responded the Guruji, *"but that is a power so far beyond these which we are discussing that they literally pale to insignificance. The Divine Mother's own power of attraction is pervasive at all levels of creation and at every level of manifest being. It is extremely positive as well, and all-auspicious, unlike the siddhis which are oriented towards and relegated to the individual and his or her small concerns. Again, young man, you have pointed to the essence, easily and effectively placing inconsequential concerns where they belong."*

*"Finally, Ekanta,"* the Mataji continued, *"there is kama-vasayita — the power to enjoy all desires."*

"How is that different from prakamya, Mataji?" Ekanta asked.

*"One can attain the power to fulfill all desires, my dear, but this is the power to thoroughly enjoy desires. There is a distinction. Imagine the feeling of enjoying each desire as it actually gets fulfilled, rather than just acquiring them and being done with them. Many beings get trapped here, pursuing the various joys that this power brings and thereby stifling their growth and spiritual potential. So you can see how dangerous these siddhis can be. Many spiritual aspirants, lacking sincerity and tenacity, seek these out, Ekanta. In so doing, they make their way, slowly, along a well-worn road that is beset by attendant dangers. The wise ones caution against going down this pathway, dear one, but you will escape such trivial pursuits, have no fear."*

Concluding thus, his revered female preceptor held up the abhaya mudra, conferring a blessing upon her beloved student, and the matter was never mentioned again.

As the Mataji predicted, the path less traveled became Ekanta's selection. He had never regretted that decision. As he considered the difference between these two distinct approaches, wisdom teachings from Yogindra Yogi came to mind. The yogi, who lived in a cave in the mountains behind his boyhood village, exercised a profound influence on Ekanta as he was growing up. Often, in the late afternoon, Ekanta would undertake the arduous uphill hike in order to arrive at the cave just after dusk so as to take darshan with this powerful being. Between the monastic presence of the yogi, the vanaprastin couple at the forest ashram and his parents who upheld the noble way of pious householders, Ekanta's entire being had been fortuitously shaped.

*"The Advaita Vedantist has no practice as such, my boy,"* the yogi stated gruffly one evening while the two sat around the sacred fire. *"However, if the term 'practice' can be used in this regard, the Advaitist proceeds upon the premise that the inner Self, called the Atman, is always pure and stainless and ever accessible: 'as tangible as a fruit placed in the palm of the hand,' as the saying goes. Thus, the Advaitist views the ascent into the spiritual realm as an exploration rather than a search. Perfection, the Atman, is already the essence of his nature. All else is superimposition."*

"Revered sir," Ekanta half objected, "why then the push to achieve perfection through spiritual disciplines?"

*"Sadhana, spiritual discipline,"* came the swift retort, *"is necessary for those who still labor under the presence of ignorance in the mind. As long as the Advaitist is aware of this imposition, so long will he or she exert spiritual effort. For such as these, though, sadhana is an art form, guided by an expert, to be performed with grace simply to express what is subtle or unseen. Other approaches, Ekanta, mainly dualistic, prescribe rigorous exercises that tax the body, wear out the life-force, and confuse and deceive the mind by embroiling it in thoughts of power and gain. You choose!"*

"Outline for me the real differences in these two approaches, revered sir, and I will tell you my choice," said Ekanta with a wry smile.

*"You have already made that choice,"* growled the yogi half-humorously. *"It is in your very makeup. You just want to hear me talk. I came to this mountain to be free of flapping my gums and hearing others do the same. Now you have found me."*

Yes," laughed Ekanta, "to my good fortune and to your botheration."

The yogi, half smiling and half frowning, continued on with his powerful discourse.

*"Two things distinguish the 'practice' of an Advaitist from others. First, as I have said, the Advaitist goes forward with the resolve that perfection is already within and that all that clouds its vision, which is actually illusory and nonexistent,*

*will fall away naturally as he comes near to the Source. Next, as long as sadhana is necessary, the Advaitist indulges in it with full commitment and with an attitude of acceptance and positivity. A lukewarm or an on-again/off-again practice is unacceptable. Armed with the resolve that his true nature is Divine, he swiftly approaches the gates of nondual realization and eliminates the vain wanderings characteristic of other less-direct paths."*

After a short pause, during which the crickets added their advice, the yogi continued.

*"There is one more thing that comes to mind about the Advaitic approach, my boy. Once ignorance is utterly gone, the illumined ones continue to perform sadhana in order to keep the internal and external organs clear and clean. This show of self-effort also acts as an example to others who are attempting to free themselves from self-imposed bondage to relative existence."*

"What else can you tell me about Advaita Vedanta sadhana, revered sir? It is fascinating and I have always wanted to hear such things articulated."

*"Yes,"* agreed the yogi, *"it is fascinating. It comprises the Supreme Way and is not limited to Hindu dharma alone, but is the essential element in every religious tradition. What it seeks to accomplish is unique. Whereas many practitioners view their sadhanas as a way of being grounded in daily life, the Advaitist simply remains grounded in the Spirit. This act, subtly effective and deceivingly simple, transforms daily life and allows it to conform to the dictates of the highest power operating in the universe. This, in turn, leaves life free of mis-guided interference of the individual ego. Other approaches leave the aspirant open to variables based upon hopes and desires, an indeterminable condition that has them looking to the past or the future for fulfillment instead of realizing the Truth here and now.*

*"To conclude, I can say from experience that many practi-tioners undertake their sadhana with the idea that the Self undergoes evolution. The Advaitist never labors under this mis-conception. Such a one is aware that the Atman never learns, never grows or expands. So, my son, you can now think about what I have said and compare approaches. Dualism has its*

*strong points, but these points must have a basis. Advaita pro-*
*vides this basis and more."*

Stirring themselves from their own deep meditation, Ekanta's hosts bowed low before the altar. A bell tolled. Its note was sweet and inspiring, floating on the morning air which was still spiced with aromatic incense.

"Meditation is feeling the presence of God," Dharman said, breaking the silence.

"Yes," Ekanta joined in, "an auspicious time in which to enjoy communion with the Lord and the bliss of His very own Self dwelling within us."

"It is so wonderful to have you with us," Gramani ventured. "Our meditations were lifted considerably by your presence."

Before Ekanta could speak, she was up and moving towards the kitchen. Soon, the aroma of delicious food was also floating on the air. The rising of the scents of delicious food, Ekanta thought to himself with a wry smile, this is my favorite type of levitation. In due time, all three gathered at the table. A food blessing rose spontaneously to Ekanta's lips:

*Harirdata harirbhokta harirannam prajapatih*
*harih sarva sharirastho bhunkte bhojayate hirih*

The Supreme Being is the giver and the enjoyer.
The Supreme Being is also the food and the act of offering.
Being everywhere, as well as in the body,
the Supreme Being is the one who partakes and sustains.

As the morning sun began to spread its healing, warming rays through the windows of the house, the three devotees of the Lord quietly and reverently enjoyed their meal among good company. The only topic which arose during breakfast concerned the act of formal worship.

"I notice that you both bow before the holy images on your sacred altar," mentioned Ekanta.

"Yes, we do," said Dharman, "for God exists in all things, but manifests a special holy presence through the object or image that receives the loving attentions of the worshipper."

With wide eyes, Gramani added, "Kind and revered sir, is there any harm in ritual if the one nondual Consciousness is perceived and honored there in the image?"

"Dear friends," Ekanta lovingly said, "I found your worship exceedingly inspiring. Personally, I find that external worship completes the picture. That is, if one is without such observances, the mind tends to lose track of the hidden sacred presence which underlies all of existence. One begins to take the creation for granted and a sort of complacency visits the mind, which then becomes indifferent to the living Awareness that animates all things. There are, of course, exceptions to this rule."

"Explain that to us, sir," asked Gramani.

"How long do girls play with dolls?" explained Ekanta. "Only so long as they do not have children of their own. In other words, there are a few beings who, having realized fully the presence of God existing in all things, are filled with the Spirit and see only That at all times. My teachers used the example of a man who looks at fire for a long time and then, as he looks around, sees flames dancing everywhere.

"On the other hand, there are those of immature outlook as well. Traveling far and wide, I have come across beings who are averse to image worship and ritual and who shun it. One audacious person who, seeing several of us bow before the sacred image of Shiva at Benares, actually said to us, 'I spit on bowing before images.' How can anyone think of spitting with distaste on anything, sentient or insentient, not to mention a venerable image or those divinities who offer their salutations there? It is unthinkable. Such beings are deluded and without reverence for God's presence, thinking themselves to be higher and mightier than others. They have a definite problem in the mind/ego complex which usually stems from a hidden desire to be worshipped themselves. When they see others bow before the sacred image, they become jealous."

A profound and thoughtful silence followed these words. Before the meal was over, Ekanta offered some more of his insights.

"It is the one immaculate and eternal Self that has become all of this — trees, beings, bodies of water, the graven image and so forth. All objects of perception are externalized bits of Its Consciousness, are formulated, sustained and dissolved in That. Seemingly fragmenting into many parts while simultaneously free of divisions, the Supreme Being accomplishes the birth, preservation and destruction of the Universe without ever acting or changing Its sublime and immutable nature in the least. Those who truly know this are absolutely reverent of all things at all times and are both thrilled and humbled by the vision. They think to themselves, 'Seeing God everywhere, in everything and at all times, what should I bow to first, to whom, and at which particular time?'"

Later on in the morning, before Dharman and Ekanta set forth towards the distant city, Gramani found the Avadhut outside near the stream, gazing off towards the distant mountains.

"Am I still playing with dolls then?" she queried.

Ekanta laughed and said, "Mother, please forgive me for even suggesting such a thing. Please do not take it out of context and kindly be at peace. Of the many holy cites I have visited, there are some which are much more intensely spiritual than others. One can feel a palpable presence exuding from the sacred images there. What can account for that? I feel it is a combination of God's actual presence, the quality of devotion of the pilgrims, the austerities practiced there by the holy ones and a mindfulness and attention to the worship."

A short silence ensued while the two gazed upon the beautiful creation all around them.

"This mindfulness is extremely important," the Avadhut continued. "Perhaps you have been to certain worship ceremonies during the holy days and have seen people sitting about in the shrine room in the vicinity of the altar, talking glibly about this and that worldly matter. There before them is the sacred image, the auspicious time of worship is upon them, yet they treat the image and the altar area as if it were any common place such as a parlor or a tavern. It was just this sort of thing that angered even the great Avatar, Jesus, when he chased the merchants away from the temple precincts.

"Imagine, the entire earth and its vast resources are used for commerce, and people spend a greater portion of their time pursuing wealth and gain, often in illicit fashion. Then, with characteristic callousness and mindless brazenness, worldly people bring business affairs, superficial chatter and their countless petty concerns right into the holy residence of the Divine Being. They will not humble themselves even for a moment and make no attempt to invoke what is holy. Is there no place, then, that can be considered sacred? If this be the attitude of worldly people, why have a temple, a sacred image or an altar at all? Why even practice spiritual disciplines? It is only a pretense in this case, so why maintain appearances? By their actions these fools are actually saying that God is a nonentity. If God matters that little to them, if they have so little faith and believe God to be so insignificant, they may as well continue on in their worldly folly and let name, fame and wealth rule their existence. In actuality, this is often what occurs."

Pausing briefly, the Avadhut went on.

"If you were the Supreme Being residing in the shrine room, in the sacred image, or in the illumined being, what would you think upon being ignored in such a deplorable way? How does any person feel when treated in that fashion? But alas, beings ever fail to understand that God is a living, breathing presence — the very Soul of their soul. Yes, this Supreme Being exists beyond time and space and outside of the universe, but It has also created this mode of existence called relativity and has entered into it as conscious Awareness. To deify the universe as God in external form, then, must be the first step towards sensitizing dull and lifeless mental consciousness to this all-pervasive verity. Again, seeing God in everything is the final step in spiritual life in the world as well. There must be one place where worldly beings seeking release from ignorance and its resultant suffering can forget these worldly tendencies, purge themselves of mundane human convention and ease their minds of suffering. Is it even possible that they might be able to transcend, at least for a moment in time, the transitory body and mind and experience an instant of peace? After all, if all remembered their divine origin from the outset, there would be no need of spiritual disciplines."

Gramani was struck dumb by these words, which not only affirmed her own beliefs and practice but brought them to a more clarified expression.

"God will not come into a place that is not pure and sanctified," proceeded the Avadhut after a short pause. "Just look, beings have all sorts of impurities which they allow access into their minds. Abiding there with permission from the owner, as it were, this contamination obstructs the advent of God's presence. He wants to enter there and fill his children with all manner of joy and knowledge but how can this be accomplished?  These same beings then complain that God will not help them with their problems.  If ever God was helpless, it is here in this unfortunate situation.  But what can He do?  He is ever free and never bound, the very essence of pristine Awareness.  It would be more likely that the earth's waters all suddenly rise into the skies of their own accord and put out the sun's fires than it would be for God to dwell in an unholy place!"

After another pause and some reflection, the Avadhut added:

"Thank the powers that be that perfection and sanctity constitute the nature of Brahman.  That there is one unblemished and immaculately pure thing in this universe is cause for great celebration among His devotees.  This is why we claim victory in typical Sanatana Dharma fashion, crying 'Jai, Jai,' to the heavens. If the truth be known, the jiva is Shiva.  Human beings are expressions of the Divine Being, exact replicas cut in His image.  They are therefore inseparable from God.  But they must know themselves as pure Spirit and be free from attachment to relative existence and never bound by the insidious egotistic notions that they are owners, agents and individuals.  A song my guru taught me expresses this well.  One line states:"

With an abundance of God-given gifts,
and His own pure diamond essence abiding in you
as your very Soul,
what a fool your mind makes of you, my friend,
that you would trade the pure vein of gold
at the center of your being
for a glittery world of cheap tinsel and mere colored glass.

"I am well aware of the impediments that the mind places in the way along the path towards enlightenment," said Gramani.  "I have experienced them myself and have suffered long at the hands of others, trapped in the desert of the world.  It is by the Divine Mother's Grace alone that I have met my husband and have been saved from further trials.  Therefore, I am ever on the search for clues to the mystery of the union of Shiva and Shakti.  Please tell me more of the absolute identity between mankind and the Blessed Lord."

"You are a true devotee, my sister," stated the Avadhut, "this is clear. The powers of the Lord, called Maya, are indeed difficult to see through and overcome. In sacred scripture, Lord Vishnu tells us that anyone and everyone who has taken birth in these three worlds of name and form is subject to and comes under the control of Mahamaya, the Great Enchantress. The best thing we can do after completely surrendering ourselves to Her with utmost sincerity is to cling to the Lord with all our strength. It reminds me of a story.

"Once, while traveling through the farmlands of the grain merchants further south, I was befriended by one of them and taken into his household. On one particular day, he took me to the mill where he ground his grains into flour for selling at the market. As I watched the grinding process, I noticed that two very large and heavy stone wheels, placed one on top of the other, were responsible for powdering the grains that were fed into the mouth of the mechanism. This, I thought, represents well the dual forces of the universe that forcefully press worldly-minded beings with weights such as poverty, misery, ignorance and suffering until death is the only recourse. As I drew nearer, and on closer inspection, I noticed that a huge wooden pole extended completely through the two stone wheels in the middle and by turning, caused one of these heavy weights to turn as well. There was, however, a tiny space all around this center pole and I noticed that a few grains of rice had slipped into that indention and were free from destruction. The thought immediately flashed in my mind that these few grains represented the clever and dedicated devotees who cling to God and stay ever close at His side. By remaining at the center of their being, they escape destruction. I have never forgotten that teaching.

"About the identity between jivatman and Atman, between Atman and Brahman, much can be said. The great Devarshi, Narada, has written in his famous Bhakti Sutras, '*God and His devotees are one and the same.* This explains the matter very well, but beyond the outlook of an illumined human being, the Avatar, a greater manifestation of divinity, has described it even more succinctly. Uddhava, Sri Krishna's precious devotee, once asked Him:

*"Lord, now that I have found out Your true identity, I never want to lose You again. This is my fear, that when due to the nature of life in the world, we become parted, that I may never be able to find You again.'*

*"'Uddhava, my beloved one,' said the Lord, 'if ever we are separated in this life or in any other, seek the company of holy beings who are dedicated to chanting My names, singing My glories and discussing My teachings. I dwell within the hearts of all such beings and knowing this, you will never be without Me.'"*

Gramani gave a deep sigh and wiped away a tear. "How can I achieve that kind of devotion, revered sir? How can I make God love me with that type of intensity?"

The Avadhut remained silent for a few moments, then spoke again.

"After the destruction of root ignorance has been achieved, the entire matter rests upon the fact that the presence of God exists more intensely through mankind than through other things in the universe. The 'two-legged city,' as Sri Bhagavan has stated, is His most favorite metropolis. Have you ever heard the story of the merchant and Vibhishana?"

Without waiting for an answer, the Avadhut plunged onward with his divine discourse.

"A merchant became shipwrecked at sea near Ceylon and was washed up on its shores. Ceylon was at that period of time inhabited by the asuras and men were seldom ever seen there. The asura Vibhishana, the brother of Ravana, was a great devotee of Sri Ram and had this man brought before him. Seldom having seen a human being before, Vibheeshana looked upon the merchant and exclaimed, 'Wonder of wonders, he resembles the image and description of my Ram!' Therefore, he clothed the merchant in fine silks and fed him sumptuously and the merchant's troubles and dangers were over.

"Realize your true nature and then you will see that no separation between your true Self and God is possible. All is verily oneness, a comprehensive and homogenous unification of Consciousness. Even to speak about it in terms of unity is to limit It, for the idea of unity is predicated on the lack of unity and such a thing never occurs in Brahman. After realizing this pristine condition to be your only real mode of existence, live in the world like a female turtle which swims the vast ocean. It is active, no doubt, but its mind is always fixed on its eggs lying buried in the sand. Keeping your mind on God in this fashion after the realization of the Atman, no want or calamity can ever really touch you."

Gramani was about to touch the feet of the Avadhut in the traditional respectful salutation when she heard Dharman's voice calling her from the cabin. When she looked back towards the Avadhut, she found Ekanta bowing to her. Before she could voice her objections he was on his feet and moving swiftly towards the house.

"I must gather my belongings so as not to detain your revered husband on his journey," came his voice, drifting back to her. Gramani, not to be cheated of her chance to pay her obeisances, saluted him from a distance and began moving towards the cabin while thinking back over what she had just heard.

Departure from the little cabin and one of its precious occupants was not easy. The nature of Ekanta's lifestyle made it impossible to determine whether or not he would ever return. Knowing this, both he and Gramani remained silent on the subject, contenting themselves with the inner wisdom which adamantly declared the inseparability of all things, of all beings. When Dharman and Ekanta had reached the edge of the meadow, and before plunging into the west woods in the direction of the distant city, they had both turned to find Gramani waving from the porch of the little cabin. With hands folded in reverence, Ekanta saluted her. As they walked on in silence, Ekanta could not help thinking about the precariousness of human existence. Whether or not Gramani's husband would ever return to her again was as indeterminable as the fates that brought them together after so much suffering in this lifetime. Ekanta found a prayer spontaneously bubbling up in his mind for the well-being of this divine couple and their child whom he had never met.

After about an hour's hike, Dharman broke the silence. "Did you see the tiger's tracks behind us earlier?"

"Yes," Ekanta returned, "but I did not care to follow in his path. I always salute the tiger God from a distance."

Dharman laughed heartily at this response and voiced his own verbal consent. "Yes," he laughed, "but what of the one who has mastered the Yama of Ahimsa — total nonviolence in thought, word and deed?  The successful outcome of such a practice is said to result in the complete cessation of all animosity in the yogi's presence."

"Such masters are indeed rare on this plane of existence," retorted Ekanta.  "I see that you have knowledge of the Patanjala system of Yoga.  You did not mention, though, that you have studied philosophy."

"My knowledge is very rudimentary in some ways," said Dharman, "but I am generally well-studied due to my father's insistence on my knowing the Jnana Yoga at an early age."

"This is a key of great importance," stated Ekanta.  "If more parents would teach or transmit to their children the perennial wisdom of the ages, they would then become free from life's usual problems and be a boon to society as well."

The two men walked on, following a well-marked trail that occasionally took them by other travelers.  Gradually, the occurrence of these meetings became more and more pronounced until eventually they knew that they were nearing a large concentration of humanity.  Ekanta picked up the tail end of the previous conversation as if no time had elapsed at all.

"Of course, in order that parents be able to transmit spiritual knowledge to their children, they themselves must know it.  How few people among the householders have any working knowledge of the scriptures nowadays, and if they do, they are not encouraged to share or spread it broadcast.  Such fear and narrow-mindedness now occupies the minds of men and women who hold prominent positions in religious organizations and schools of higher learning that if the slightest glimmering of awakening graces the minds of aspiring people with teaching potential, it is immediately stifled.  This mean-minded and petty tendency has been a major cause of the downfall of religious fervor in the country.  Due to the greed for power and the leaning towards complacency, it has not been remedied."

"I too have noticed that negative influence more and more over time," mentioned Dharman.  "The ashram I attended earlier is now run by hypocrites who exercise their power over others in despicable ways.  There is not the slightest atmosphere of holiness around them, yet they presume to be able to teach others based upon their titles and assumed station in life alone.  It is most

unfortunate. Yet I see another more favorable manifestation arising. Since spiritual aspirants cannot depend on quality guidance
anymore from traditional sources, they are forced to depend more
readily upon themselves. Direct experience, even with all the mistakes that occur early on in the path leading towards perfection,
is now acting as the teacher, and this is producing some illumined
beings in the private sector and among the ranks of the householders."

"Yes," agreed Ekanta, "and this reminds us of the olden days
when great Rishis walked the earth, teaching their children the
eternal message of Sanatana Dharma. We must always remember
the great ideal of the Divine Couple who blend perfectly the
monastic and householder ways. Neither the mundane habits or
superficial preoccupations peculiar to the householder path or
aversion to the world and the life-negating sterility found in the
monastic path can be allowed to ruin or obscure the way of the
ancients."

"Well put, my brother," said Dharman. "Take Sita and Ram for
example. When we look at such exemplary lives we find a wealth
of comprehensive teachings on all levels of existence. Sri Ram,
in His Nine Limbs of Bhakti, tells us that spreading the teachings
is of the utmost importance. This practice proceeds only after
holy company is discovered and enjoyed. Before, in earlier times,
there were many solitary yogis and yoginis wandering the earth,
and many vanaprastin couples and other venerable teachers
available and accessible to mankind. Now, where is this rare thing
called holy company to be found?"

"If the well dries up, one either digs deeper or moves to
another location," said Ekanta. "As you said, one learns to rely
upon the primal teacher within, called in Vedanta philosophy, the
Atman. In my own case, I was blessed with a few of the thoroughly illumined monks of the old style as teachers as well as a
vanaprastin couple who completed my training. I cannot now
imagine being bereft of either of these expressions of divinity.
Through this powerful combination of gurus, the Atman within me
could not help but shine before my inner gaze. If It had remained
obscured amongst such company then I would have known
myself to be a sea of darkness, ignorant to the bone."

Dharman broke out laughing at this expression, almost tripping on the uneven trail.  That they were nearing a city was evidenced by the increased activity along the path and the thick atmosphere of smoke closing in around them.  It was not long before a road made itself visible and their feet left the dusty trail.  This made the going a bit faster and soon they were skirting large groups of people on their way to and from the city.  It was not possible to remain free from the rushing hordes for long.  Swept along in spite of themselves while striving to remain together among the swirling masses of humanity, they eventually caught sight of the city.

In the distance, a large gate seemed to spring up from the plains, seen through the rising clouds of dust raised by the footfalls of cattle, people and other living things.  Merchants with wares, families searching for employment, troupes of entertainers, wandering ascetics, impoverished beggars, caravans carrying dignitaries and notables — all these and more were pouring into the city.  The spectacle reminded the Avadhut of Vishvarupa Darshanam, the vision of the Universal Form in the eleventh chapter of the Bhagavad Gita.  In this passage, Sri Krishna, the Blessed Lord in human form, grants to His disciple Arjuna a fantastic gaze at the Cosmic Body of Ishvara.  Amidst the increasingly thunderous noise of madly marching humanity, Ekanta found himself repeating from memory a most significant part of the chapter:

An infinite array of shining weapons rose and fell, causing death on all sides, yet nothing died! With every shocking and awe-inspiring movement, another of hundreds of sparkling and shimmering divine ornaments vibrated, causing a cacophony of rapturous, spine-tingling sound to spread like some celestial symphony over the vaunted battlefield. An immeasurable number of ears were strangely arrayed across that boundless Form, listening intently, and countless rolling eyes filled with unique and peculiar beauty gazed into space.

Arms of power, arms of beauty, too many to count, graced that stupendous living configuration, and upon which leg, of millions present, that It moved could not be discerned. Gazing higher, with bated breath and mind in awe, the Pandava saw faces so celestial and terrible as to entirely

escape earthly description. Suns and moons and flashing
stars were there absorbed in numerous eyes, and perched in
sweet, pungent stacks about a forest of towering necks were
flower garlands of such unimaginable beauty as to shame
the gardens of heaven.

All about, pervading and penetrating, an unintelligible Light
flowed outward and upward, in all directions, infusing every
modicum of existing substance with palpitating, scintillating
life. The universe with planets, stars, suns and moons,
whole solar systems and their inhabitants, were resting in
impeccable fashion within the fathomless receptacle of that
great Atman.

The consummate warrior then cried out in mingled awe and
deep consternation: "O God, I see my essence in Thee.
Hosts of luminaries also dwell in Thy immutable Being. Is
that the four-faced Brahma, chanting Soma hymns, and that,
a forest ashram full of illumined Rishis, mentally drinking
Thy teachings? There, that is my own blessed guru, dearer
to me than life itself, and all around are multitudes of divine
serpents. Above and below, on all sides, are spread an
overabundance of gradated realms with countless living
beings, all occupied in Thy service, knowingly or unknowingly.

"Where is Thy end, O Father? I now deem that You have
none. If this be the case, then no beginning is possible
whatsoever. Thy middle is too vast for my limited human
comprehension, O Lord, for indeed, though there are infinite
forms filling my wonder-struck gaze, You are ever One, I see
that now. Arms, legs, stomachs, eyes, ears, mouths—O those
wonderful and horrible mouths—I cannot imagine such
plenitude and remain trembling with amazement.

"O Thou of Absolute power, worthy of deepest veneration,
it is You who are the ageless and imperishable guardian of
the eternal Truth, who protects the universe throughout
interminable periods of time. Your Divine weapons
surround existence itself, and Your protective power is

resilient with the combined lights of all-consuming suns and blazing wildfires.

"I cannot perceive You, O ancient and primordial One, though I stare with wide eyes into Thy Being. How to realize that which is beyond thought and which created all minds out of pure paradox! The warmth of life and the dread cold of death are both Thy gifts through which the miracle of immortal existence continues on inexorably.

"All-devouring Time is robbed of its powers by Thee, O Omniscient One, for infinity is Thy nature. Thy mouth of fiery nondual knowledge sets the insentient universe into motion and also reduces it to ashes, while in between, innumerable arms are occupied facilitating Thy Supreme Will.

"Where is the place that You are not present! Heavens, earths and hells and even the interspace is filled with You alone. Now that I see Thee, along with gods, goddesses, saints, sages, demigods, demons, celestial musicians, perfected luminaries and an entire host of beings, I tremble with combined joy and fear. We all gaze at You, transfixed!

"Many of these great ones merge in Thy essence, while others remain apart, extolling Thy virtues. Some are lying prone before Thee, weeping copious tears of heartfelt devotion, and others chant especially beautiful hymns in Thy honor. All are asking for Thy most excellent Grace, O Beloved. May Thy incomparable presence guide and protect us eternally.

"This is overwhelming, O Divine One! Courage and peace have fled my mind. Gaping mouths with teeth and tusks, endless voids filled with blazing eyes, visions of enthralling world-transcending forms, this and more perplexes my reason.

"Behold the sons and daughters of earth, warrior chiefs, elephants, chariots, and kings, armies of good and evil alike, rushing towards Thy infinite mouths. Caught in Thy many tusks and fangs, screaming and kicking in throes of life and death, and all the time, from those yawning cavities poised like voids over the battlefield, flow rivers of blood filled with severed heads, trunks, arms and legs.

"These beings are like torrential raindrops which fill a million rivers of humanity, all flowing ceaselessly towards the Brahman sea. Like a million moths rushing headlong towards a forest on fire, this do I behold, O Lord, with heart-palpitating fear.

"Are they all mad, then, these myriad creatures, throwing themselves into Thy boundless expanse like hailstones into an ocean! They are the fuel and You the fire, and the radiance from that blaze lights up the entire phenomenal universe.

"What is the purpose of this fearsome display! Reveal to me Thy nature, as I bow down to the ground. Who are You, primordial flame, so fierce and mighty! Bestow upon me Thy mercy and make me calm."

The Avadhut returned slowly to normal consciousness. At first, he could just dimly make out a few figures. Then one of them, strangely familiar, was bending over him speaking words he could barely understand. Finally, he recognized Dharman and suddenly he could see and hear once again. He was seated in lotus position by the side of the road which they had been walking on. A number of interesting-looking beings had gathered around him, forming a circle. Outside that closed circle, he sensed that others were trying to get closer. He looked in wonder upon the scene, trying to gain a perspective.

"Are you again amongst us, dear friend?" asked Dharman. "Do you understand what I am saying?"

Heaving a long sigh, as if his lungs were just beginning to function again, Ekanta was barely able to stammer, "I am here." Then, searching for words, he uttered, "In fact, I see nothing but the 'I' here. What is this state? Oh, I have done it again!"

"What are you talking about?" asked an elderly man squatting nearby.

After a brief pause, Ekanta went on. "No, it is not I that have done this; it is Thou, Oh Lord! Oh bother! This is all too complex. None of it makes any sense whatsoever. Take me back, Mother!"

Next, Ekanta became aware that Dharman was offering him water, which he drank of sparingly. His mind, which seemed numb before, like an arm or a leg that has not been used for some time, responded to the liquid element as if it were some magical grounding force and began to function somewhat normally.

"Thank you, Mother," he said to Dharman, still a bit intoxicated.

A surprised look spread over Dharman's face upon being addressed in this way. Seeing that quizzical look, at once perplexed, concerned, gratified and dumbfounded, Ekanta burst out laughing. This laughter, becoming more and more uncontrollable as moments progressed, had a transforming effect upon the gathered crowd. They too started to join in, at first with giggles, guffaws and short spurts of merriment, but soon with thundering peals of nonstop laughter as the entire assembly gave way to spasmodic, side-splitting mirth. It was as if an avalanche of good humor had poured down on the little group. At last, even Dharman was caught up in this happy tirade and was soon rolling on the ground.

For the participants, there was no telling how long this went on, but the sounds of laughter certainly attracted more people. Even those who did not know the reason for the merriment were nevertheless caught up in the gay mood and laughed in spite of themselves. When it ended, trickling off with plenty of leftover sporatic eruptions, all were grateful, for lungs, sides, throats and heads had borne a terrific impact.

"Such an intense and contrasting variety of moods I have never experienced in such a short time span in my entire existence," spoke Dharman, as soon as he could gather his breath to speak. "One moment you are sitting at the side of the road, body ramrod straight, vibrating with an unearthly electricity, chanting out our Lord's awesome verses from the Bhagavad Gita in a voice charged with divine emotion and the next moment you are practically incoherent. Then, without warning, you force us into unbridled hilarity, almost at the expense of our very lives. Literally, I declare, for some moments there I could not even breathe!"

Various forms of assent came from the bystanders, who by now had drawn back a bit to behold this strange man. There was little light left from the sun, which had already set, and there was no fire either, so no one could get a good look at this intriguing figure. This was just as well, thought the Avadhut, who was beginning to feel a little uncomfortable in this particular setting. Still, the energy left over from the laugh festival was helping to maintain a somewhat balanced atmosphere among the group. People were still catching their breath and had seated themselves or were picking themselves up off of the ground.

At this moment, an interesting being stepped forward from the periphery of the circle. He was dressed in the garb of a sannyasin and had an orange turban wrapped in Muslim style around his broad forehead. His dress gave him away as a swami of a Hindu order, however, and his manner was immediately endearing. He exuded great confidence and was evidently used to being in the forefront of the action and comfortable with people's attentions.

"I witnessed the entire spectacle over this past two hours," said the swami. I have seen the like of it only rarely as I traveled the spiritual path. How are you feeling, revered sir?"

"At the moment I am feeling okay, though a little disoriented," answered Ekanta. "I know not of what spectacle you speak of though. It seems only moments since I was walking this road with my friend here."

The swami remained silent for a few moments. Then he spoke again.

"I was here, helping an elderly woman secure a drink of water by the side of the road, when I saw you approach. You seemed to be indrawn, muttering something to yourself. All of a sudden your arms went up in the air and you began to chant in a loud voice. I recognized the verses to be Sri Krishna's words from the sacred Bhagavad Gita. At one point you stumbled and your friend here helped you to sit by the side of the road."

"This did not stop you from broadcasting the message, though," stated Dharman. "Sanskrit slokas were flowing from you like bees from a broken hive! Hearing it, my hair stood on end and my skin began to crawl. I had heard you speak previously, but what I heard just recently was not your normal voice."

"This is a type of divine descent," said the swami. "I have seen it only a few times in my life. It manifests differently in various vehicles at different times. Such a discourse should not be missed. We were most fortunate to be here to hear it. It must be somewhat like the way Arjuna heard it in the original! I, too, was thrilled to the very marrow of my bones."

Ekanta struggled to his feet. Feeling a little dizzy, he began to reel slightly. Both Dharman and the swami were there by his side instantly, steadying him on his feet.

"I have experienced this particular type of service more often," said the swami, as he supported Ekanta. "My guru, an illumined rajarshi in central India, used to have ecstatic moods come upon him quite frequently. I was always wary that he might fall and injure himself, so, as a young boy, I served him day and night."

"How fortunate for you," stated Ekanta. "I have seen many beings under the intoxicating effects of blissful experiences before but I have never had the privilege of serving them so intimately. As for ecstasies, they are overrated. The truly illumined are more concerned with alleviating the suffering of humanity than with enjoying personal bliss. What is more, the greatest beings are a seething mass of subtle bliss on inside but it never shows the least on the exterior unless it would suit the Lord's divine purpose. The waters of a small village pool rocks with waves when an elephant enters, but the same elephant entering an ocean causes no stir whatsoever. I am still a small pool, it seems, manifesting sensational experiences outwardly in an uncontrollable fashion."

"Oh no, sir," ventured the swami. "As you said, the Lord has a certain use for your demonstrations. Otherwise, why should such an interested group gather about you? Please, tell us of your life and experiences."

"I beg to be released from that chore," pleaded Ekanta, "for I have already detained my companion past dark and he has important business in the city for the king. Therefore, we must take our leave immediately."

"Indeed," said the swami, "that sounds pressing. We will honor your request, no doubt. Please consider this though, dear sir. I am on business in the city as well.   There is a gathering of luminaries from different parts of the country all meeting for a religious discussion.   It is more of a chance for sharing the wisdom of different traditions than an opportunity for debate.   My name is Swami Advaitananda and I have been invited to attend and present some knowledge from my tradition at this meeting.   Please come as my honored guest and I will forthwith release you from our company here at present."

"Since you put it in such a manner," laughed Ekanta, "I should be delighted to attend, but only as an observer."

Swami Advaitananda and the Avadhut exchanged information about addresses and the location of the sacred meeting and went their separate ways.   Soon, Dharman and Ekanta were on the road and approached the gates of the city.   A small group of people had followed them, being impressed with what they had witnessed, but increased speed and a little weaving in and out among the masses soon took care of that.

"You almost had a following of disciples there," said Dharman.

"Just what I need," returned Ekanta.   "Remind me to chant the sacred Gita only in solitude from now on."

Dharman laughed again, grabbed his side and quickly shut up. "O gods of laughter," he mumbled, "all respects to thee but kindly do not visit me again too soon in the future."

The two remained silent as they entered the city.   This was not by choice but by necessity.   It would have been impossible to hear anything but shouted conversation under those circumstances anyway and besides, there was so much to look at.   With Dharman in the lead, threading them neatly and swiftly through the streets and byways of the grand eastern metropolis, the two made excellent headway and were soon in quieter surroundings.

It had been months since Ekanta had been in a large metropolis.   Though it was just past dusk, it was a favorable time to be there, for worship was still going on in all the temples and private homes around the city.   Eastern peoples were fond of their rituals and observed them several times every day in order to worship the Blessed Lord of the Universe manifesting in so many forms, in so many ways.   The aroma of incense wafted by on the air, as did the sounds of temple bells and conch shells.   Shopkeepers took time off from business to salute the Giver of all Success and even the beggars seemed less inclined to extract their due from passers by. Ekanta felt moved by a higher power and was barely conscious of his individual self. A flavor of intoxication still lingered in him from the roadside experience and this was kept alive to a certain degree by seeing God in so many forms, gathered so densely in one place. He moved on as if he were floating on the earth and the way people looked at him he wondered if, indeed, he was actually levitating.

Turning a corner and stopping before two large ornately carved wooden doors, Dharman produced a key from somewhere on his person. Fitting it in the massive lock, he opened it and pushed his way through the entrance. Ekanta followed quickly so as to leave behind any curious onlookers. The smell of wood smoke and other earthy aromas entered his nostrils and he felt an immediate warmth inside of him, associated with other pure places he had visited. Dharman shut the two doors promptly and put the open lock through an inner hook to keep unwanted outsiders from entering. Safely inside, the two groped their way in the dark until Dharman found a lamp. Leaving through the two doors, and asking Ekanta to admit him again when he knocked, he returned shortly with red-hot charcoal and eventually had the lamp lit and trimmed. A few candles were also lighted which lent the place a comfortable atmosphere.

Laying blankets on the floor in two places, Dharman asked Ekanta to recline and rest. He was gone again before long and returned after some time with lentils, a few spices and some legumes. As Ekanta drowsed, a fine soup was made and before long the aroma was drifting on the air, causing feelings of hunger in the tired travelers. From a bag Dharman took a loaf of bread, unwrapped it and placed it on the rough round board that acted as a table. Soon, the soup was ladled out into bowls and, tearing the bread into two halves, the friends sat for the evening blessing.

This time, Dharman offered the prayer, stating beforehand, "Food not offered first to God is impure. One eats sin who verily forgets to acknowledge the Lord for nourishment and sustenance." A wonderful prayer then sprang from Dharman's lips as the Avadhut listened with rapt attention, head bowed in reverent salutations:

*Aum annapurne sadapurne shankaraprana vallabhe*
*jnanavairagya siddyartham bhiksham dehi cha parvati*

O beloved Shakti of Lord Shiva,
Thou who art all-pervading, complete,
and fully manifesting as the nourishing power in this food.
Sustain us with this prasadam
so that we may attain knowledge,
mature detachment and spiritual perfection.

After a satisfactory meal and a little water drawn from Dharman's tank, the two men laid down on their beds to sleep without another word. As the sounds of the city gradually diminished outside, Ekanta gave thanks to his chosen ideal for safely bringing them to their destination and for all the unique experiences that spiritual life in the world was prone to bring. Meditating in a prostrate position for a half an hour, he then saluted the Lord and with his thoughts contemplating the Mother of the Universe, slipped off into a deep and refreshing sleep.

Dharman's stirrings awakened him in the early morning. A little light was filtering through the shutters on the street side of the building and by and by Dharman had the upper window opened after climbing to the second story via a ladder near the back of the room. This provided light from the loft above and illumined the room, giving Ekanta his first good look at his surroundings. The room was basically clean, but signs of soot on the walls gave away the profession of the occupant. In one part of the room near the door, Ekanta saw the tools of Dharman's trade, similar to a blacksmith's setup though with less equipage. Perfect arrows were formed here which then graced the scabbards of the king's foot soldiers and horsemen.

Dharman was already at work, preparing the preliminary setup for starting the fires. Large, well-shaped pieces of wood were neatly stacked against the wall nearby. These would provide the shafts for the arrows, Ekanta surmised. Dharman's voice brought him out of his study of the place.

"I have lost time due to yesterday's delays," he said. "Therefore, I am starting early. Please excuse me for not being able to serve you in the desired way. Also, I do not know your morning habits. I meditated earlier and usually do not eat until noon. What is your schedule, or do you keep one?"

"I am free and without agenda most of the time," said Ekanta. "Actually, I am wanting to make my way through the city. There are several things I can accomplish by this, not the least of which is to return with food for our lunch. I will see you some time around midnoon then."

Sounds of an awakening city greeted Ekanta as he washed and dressed in clean but basic garments. The Avadhut was not a gourd and loincloth type of renunciate nor a naked sadhu, but preferred the standard dress of his village and vicinity. He carried a sacred cloth given to him by his teachers and this he used for meditation. He also often carried a staff but precious few belongings inhibited his movement and he preferred it that way. Within a few minutes he was ready to embark into the city.

Stepping out of the doorway, Ekanta almost stumbled over an elderly man laying on the ground. With hand extended upwards for alms, the beggar pleaded for a handout. A smile was all that he got from the penniless Avadhut as Ekanta walked around him and made his way into the city, thinking that he would give him alms later. Even as spiritually intoxicated as he had been the night before, Ekanta had remained aware of the general direction that they had come the previous night and had also mentally noted a few important landmarks. It was not long before he was walking the most busy sector of the city, already teeming with humanity at this early hour.

The Avadhut soon saw his destination, a less busy side street off of one of the main thoroughfares. Here he sat himself down near a water outlet, silently assumed a pose of contemplation and was soon lost in concentration on the Feet of Vishnu, a favorite mode of meditation for him. In the interim, several people approached him and placed annas, half rupees and an occasional rupee on his carrying bag. This they did with a profound salute. They obviously felt that it was their good fortune to be able to give to a holy man. No thought of doing good to others polluted their minds in this regard, unlike the egoistic tendencies that usually accompanied the charities of the rich, the arrogant and the deluded.

After awhile, Ekanta took his mind off of the Feet of Vishnu and opened his eyes. It was at that very moment that a street urchin had been stretching out her hand to take some of his alms. Seeing him suddenly open his eyes, the child quickly withdrew her hand, drew back flinching and braced her body for an inevitable blow. Instead of a hand raised to deal punishment, however, the child was surprised to find a hand extended in charity. There, resting on the Avadhut's palm was a full rupee, a small fortune to this unfortunate waif.

"Asking is always better than taking, child, and better than taking is giving. Think about that before you act next time."

A smile of mixed gratitude and disbelief crossed the little girl's face as she took the rupee and disappeared into the crowd.

Several other people left alms in the form of money and foodstuffs. The Avadhut smiled graciously but said nothing, nor did he look at his benefactors. Sitting still, wrapped in subtle bliss and abiding in his Atman, he had long since gotten used to this chosen way of life. Nothing bothered him anymore, for he knew himself completely and was the master of his mind and senses. He who owned and coveted nothing had nothing to lose. It was a simple rule but effective. It also kept him free from the extremes of poverty which was, he had discovered, a negative state of mind based on assumptions of lack or want, and free as well from the bizarre diversion of attachment to heightened pleasures, which was nothing short of an ignorant stifling of spirituality. Much better, he thought, is the perfect balance of equanimity and absolute trust in God for all things.

As Ekanta gazed peacefully at the multitudes moving past him, he suddenly caught a glimpse of someone familiar amidst the crowds that lined the streets. It was Swami Advaitananda, moving at a fast gait and skirting the crowds like an experienced city dweller. He was already out of range of hearing but Ekanta quickly gathered his coins together and moved off after him. He wanted to find out the location of the coming spiritual gathering beforehand. The swami turned up several different streets and finally came to a large building that obviously contained a hall for gatherings. The swami disappeared inside. Ekanta approached the doors of the building and, telling the guard of his intention, also passed inside. The hall was very basic but had accommodations for a large number of people. The swami was nowhere to be seen but Ekanta did not cherish a meeting at this moment anyway.

Taking note of the lay of the building from inside and out, Ekanta again plunged into the crowds on the streets outside.

After a half an hour's walk back towards Dharman's shop, the Avadhut stopped at a nearby store and made a few purchases for lunch. Special Indian bread called luchis and pakoras, deep-fried vegetables dipped in batter, took most of his morning's alms. Ekanta mentally saluted the generous people who gave him the alms, the shopkeeper for supplying the foods and, of course, the Blessed Lord for watching over him and providing him sustenance. Departing the marketplace, Ekanta walked the few blocks to Dharman's shop. Looking in, he found Dharman hard at work in the afternoon heat, laboring over the fire. A small pile of fine-looking arrowheads lay nearby, testament to the fact that hours of labor had been successful. The harder task of fastening them firmly to wooden shafts was presently underway. As the Avadhut watched, he noticed that Dharman was using some arrowheads from a bag that he must have made days earlier. This allowed the fresh ones to cool properly.

"Om Namo Narayanaya," came Ekanta's greeting. Looking up from his work, Dharman returned the greeting.

"You have arrived at a perfect moment. I can now take a break for lunch. If I work hard this afternoon, I can retain the original integrity of my intended schedule."

"This is indeed good news," said Ekanta. "I was beginning to think that my presence on this journey was an imposition."

"Banish the thought," declared Dharman. "What I have learned from you and what I have witnessed in these past few hours is a true Godsend. Divine visitations and spiritual teachings, as rare as they are, are much more important than even the most critical worldly duty."

"Would that all people thought as you do," replied the Avadhut wistfully.

Ekanta was already at the table, arranging the purchased foods for lunch. Dharman brought water from his small tank and the two sat for supper. After the meal was finished, Dharman immediately began his work again.

"The city has worn me out in a few short hours," said Ekanta. "I am going to nap."

"Good," said Dharman. "Please rest easy and awake refreshed.

If all goes well we can take our meal out at a friend's house tonight. He came by earlier and when I told him about your visit he invited us to a fine repast."

Shutting his eyes, Ekanta fell into a light sleep. When he awoke, he noticed that Dharman was still hard at work. Ekanta got up and wandered outside without bothering his friend. Their eyes met briefly in a mutual silent greeting.

Next door and at several locations down the road, blacksmiths and goldsmiths were plying their trade. This neighborhood had several such craftsmen. Ekanta looked inside one shop and saw a goldsmith hard at work. His foot was working a kind of ventilation system that brought air from below the mechanism onto the coals. A lump of gold sat upon a small thin metal dish directly over the hot fire. With the left hand the goldsmith was working a fan to give added wind power to his chore. His right hand was operating a bellows that fanned the flames from the opposite side, to achieve as much heat as possible.

Ekanta watched closely. He had not realized how much effort was involved with this undertaking, nor had he known how much heat was needed to melt gold. Besides, the gold was precious; no mistake could be made. Firewood and coal were expensive as well, especially in the city, and the present load was burning down swiftly. Ekanta wondered if the goldsmith would achieve his goal.

The man, obviously under considerable stress, sweated profusely, but he did not waver in either his efforts or his attention. At a certain moment, due to a change of conditions known only to the goldsmith, he brought his mouth to a tube hanging in front of his face which extended down into the fire and began to blow furiously into it. The fire swelled even hotter and all of a sudden the lump of gold began to disappear. At this critical moment it seemed that there was no rest either, for the entire piece of gold had to be melted completely. The pumping, fanning and blowing seemed to Ekanta to go on forever, until simply by watching the process, he felt hot, dizzy and tired.

All of a sudden the activity ceased abruptly and the goldsmith quickly took the hot dish off of the fire with a metal tong. Moving to the table nearby, he poured the precious liquid gold carefully into a mold and placed the mold aside to cool. Then, wiping his brow with a piece of cloth, he sank down onto a stool, breathing hard.

So much work and activity, thought Ekanta, and now all is still and peaceful. To the Avadhut, who was always looking for inner meaning in life's situations, the direct parallel to spiritual life here was obvious. Initial effort resulting in the accomplishment of one's goal leading to ultimate peace, this was the way of both worldly and spiritual life in the world. In the same fashion as I have seen here today, thought Ekanta, just so must a spiritual aspirant be up and doing in the early stages of sadhana. Additionally, the sadhaka must remain watchful for the approach of potential dangers that might crop up and must persevere through all difficulties until the goal is reached. In a flash, a famous declaration from the Upanishads came into Ekanta's mind:

*"Utithasta, Jagrata! Arise and awake and stop not until the goal is reached!"*

Then, and only then, can the aspirant truly rest and enjoy peace, peace, peace. It is so true, thought the Avadhut.

Walking back to his friend's shop, Ekanta remembered the wife of a rich merchant who was landlord in his village. She was a hard worker, served her husband, his brothers and in-laws, the many children of the household and even the servants as well. From early morning to late night she would toil on the behalf of all concerned. One night, Ekanta had come to the merchant's house to perform some small chore. It was getting late and the merchant's wife was not to be seen. Wondering at this strange occurrence. Ekanta had asked the merchant where his wife was.

"She has gone for her bath, my boy. Nothing can now bring her back."

"How is that possible, sir?" queried Ekanta. "She is always working."

"Nevertheless, it is true," replied the merchant. "One night, in a jocular mood, I yelled to her through the bathroom door that the house was on fire. Her response was, 'You put it out, I am taking my bath.' Therefore I say, that when the lady of the house goes for her bath after working all day, she will never come back, even though you may yell yourself hoarse!"

Ekanta had detected a similar meaning in that experience comparable to the one he had just seen at the goldsmith's shop. Now, thinking back, he remembered the Mataji's comments about work and liberation.

*"Having experienced the activities of the world after working hard, a person should attain spiritual realization, Ekanta. Once tasting that especial kind of peace which comes from illumination, one will never return to the mundane world of stress and toil in the same way again. What is more, my dear, if spiritual enlightenment dawns upon any struggling aspirant at the outset of spiritual life or along the way, all duties will naturally and gradually fall away, leaving time to contemplate Reality. This is the law of spiritual life. Alas, how few attempt to gain the highest goal of life and thereby prove this eternal law to be true."*

Dharman was more intensely concentrated than ever. Ekanta sat just inside the door of the shop and watched humanity sweep by in torrents. He had a good view of the street through the two huge open doors and he was also positioned perfectly in order to see his friend perform his craft. Waves of sound literally pulsated through the double doors but both Ekanta and Dharman were in other worlds. The noise from the city was not penetrating their consciousness whatsoever. As for Dharman, his mind was fully focused on the task at hand. For Ekanta, all sounds had become mantras, uttered by the holy lips of his dearly Beloved who was the underlying foundation of all activity. Whether receding or crescendoing, these sounds never spoiled his calm, detached mood.

An old women with a staff suddenly stood before him. "Get busy and accomplish some work you lazy good-for-nothing," said the cranky old woman.

Ekanta only smiled amiably and the woman, nonplussed, went away muttering something inaudible under her breath. Minutes later, he found himself thanking this woman and her rude intervention into his reveries, for she had reminded him of a holy man who had frequented his village when he was a young boy. That man, too, had been relatively young for a renunciate. He spent most of his daytime hours lying down flat on the ground with his cloth pulled over his body and head. People had wagged their tongues furiously about his worthless and lazy nature. Ekanta, too, had believed him to be practically useless.

One day, Yogindra Yogi, a respected holy man of the vicinity, had entered the village for alms. Receiving a few items from the local store owner, he spied the young renunciate lying nearby in the grass. The wife of the store owner was present, as were a few of the neighbors. Ekanta had witnessed the entire incident as well.

Noticing Yogindra Yogi's gaze fall upon the young man, the shopkeeper's wife exclaimed rashly, "Please do not bother yourself with that one, revered sir. He is a no-account, completely worthless and of no benefit to anyone."

"Yes," joined in a neighbor, "he just lies about all day and by night he disappears to no one knows where."

*"I will tell you where he goes at night,"* said the holy man. *"He visits me in my cave and we talk about the Divine Mystery into the wee small hours of the night. Sometimes he frequents the graveyards to meditate on the stainless, eternal Reality beyond birth and death. He is one of the finest men I know and of unsurpassed intellectual prowess. He also has a compassionate heart. His actions and duties, however, in this, his last incarnation, are over with for good. I pay him my highest salutations."*

Stating this, and saluting the younger man who was oblivious to all that was going on, Yogindra Yogi turned and left the shop. The silence that ensued was palpable. Yogindra Yogi was the most highly respected holy man in the area. His word was taken at face value, even among the enlightened ones who passed through from distant provinces. Ekanta had been much impressed by this event, but extremely perplexed. The next evening, he had gone to Yogindra's cave to inquire further about the enigmatic young holy man. Arriving at the cave which was at a much higher elevation, Ekanta announced himself.

*"Namaste Ekanta,"* came the greeting, *"please enter. Why have you come? Here, take some of these berries and rest. The steep climb must have winded you considerably."*

When Ekanta had settled himself comfortably, he proceeded to question the mountain yogi. "Revered sir, you stunned all of us the other day with your evaluation of that young man who seems to sleep all day. I am perplexed by this and seek clarification. What does he accomplish and how is it that you praise him so highly when he shows no signs of holiness. In fact, if one judges according to the scriptures, he appears to be very tamasic."

*"Yes,"* came the retort, *"and this is why they say that appearances can be deceiving. Just as the senses fail to perceive the essence of an object due to their singular external orientation only, so too is the mind unable to evaluate a situation perfectly for the same reason. Having little or no internal discrimination and devoid of any power of proper analysis and insight, people nevertheless deem themselves to be so knowledgeable. They know nothing of God's majesty or glories and therefore have no understanding of what goes on in the mind of a holy person, God's abode on this earth.*

*"With regards to the scriptures, Ekanta, they are like precision instruments. Be sure that you know how to use them effectively. They must be interpreted carefully, for they contain a mixture of sand and sugar. One must become an ant and take only what is essential, leaving the rest aside. Let me explain using our young friend as an example. In fact, I will tell you a story which actually happened and which I was a part of.*

*"There was a well-known holy man, Jagachakshu Muni by name, who lived in the south of India near Madras. He had set up an ashram and had many disciples and students who frequented the place. I was then traveling over the whole of India during my pilgrimage days and happened to stop there for a few days for accommodations and prasad. Many holy men stopped there for alms as they were plentiful and the muni was extremely generous. While I was there, a certain student of Jagachakshu Muni was scolded by him for being lazy. I can still remember his scalding words, for he had a volatile nature where laziness and complacency were concerned.*

*"'This tamasic condition in you will never do,' roared the muni at the surprised student. 'No progress can be made in spiritual life until slothfulness is conquered in the mind.'*

*"The student objected to this scolding and indicated a certain visiting holy man named Adbhutananda lying down nearby.*

*"'He is always lying around and does nothing all day,' complained the disciple. 'He simply spends his time sleeping with his cloth covering his face and entire body so that none can see him. Yet all respect him and call him very sattvic. What is the difference between us, Master, I do not understand.'"*

*"The muni laughed out loud and said, 'Listen to what he is saying. He thinks Adbhutananda sleeps all day!' Turning to the holy man he said, 'Well Maharaj, what do you say? Did you get good rest today, lying there in such a tamasic condition? It is strange, but I have never heard you snoring!'*

*"With all eyes directed towards him, Adbhutananda sat up, removing the cloth from his body and face. No signs of sleepiness were present on his features and instead, his focused gaze burned with deep intelligence. Rather than giving a defensive retort or even adding to the muni's jocular statements, the silent holy man surprised everyone with an immediate quote from the scriptures:"*

That mind which can properly distinguish
between work and renunciation
as well as right and wrong action, which is fearless,
having transcended ideas such as bondage and liberation,
that is the truly sattvic mind.

The opposite condition called tamas,
shuns righteous work accomplished selflessly
and instead attaches to unrighteousness as if it were good.
Perversion, darkness and indolence are its characteristics.

*"'Please explain further, revered sir,' said the muni, 'for the elucidation of all present.'*

*"'When a tamasic state befalls the mind of a normal man,' stated Adbhutananda, 'he gets plunged in sleep, fear, grief, despair, conceit and other impurities. Such a person even gets attached to these conditions as if they were perfectly acceptable. Thus has delusion become the norm all over society in this present age of darkness. The mind of a holy man, however, has developed the power of detachment from all such impediments, having mastered the mind and senses. Slothfulness, trepidation, insecurity and other obstructions to spiritual life are alien to him, for he knows himself to be pure Spirit rather than the mind and its contents.*

*"'Do you think that I lie here and sleep all day, my boy?' said the swami, turning his attention on the muni's student. 'Most*

*of my time these days is spent in contemplation of the radiant mind, though once I had charge of three ashrams and many students. The contents of the illumined mind-stuff is not only free of impurities, it is full of spiritually significant knowledge which brings an abundance of sublime experiences. You must have heard the famous song by Milarepa in this regard.' Saying so, the swami sang in a voice that inspired all present:*

Lost in snow-capped splendor at the foot of the Himalayas,
the yogi, Milarepa sings,
nondual wisdom is the eternal principle
which permeates the pure mind with strength.
Purity itself is strength without end.
Freedom from discrimination and nondiscrimination
is the meditation of strength,
and the Great Light Itself is boundless strength.

Relax, abide in peace and observe mindfully.
This act alone, in itself, confers great strength.
The primordial source of Absolute Reality is strength.
It abides within all forms as undiluted strength.

Make of all life a meditation
and strength will enter you fully.
Apply this practice moment to moment, with great care.
When all the universe is perceived as your own being,
your own mind,
great strength will emerge and sustain you eternally.

*"'The lovers of God never tire of contemplating this light-filled expanse of pure Awareness, my boy,' stated the swami after the song was over. 'You should know this too, however. The mind of an enlightened being is also subject to the movement of the three gunas. The tamasic state comes to the mind of every being. The difference is that the illumined have the power and ability to withdraw from the mind, its cycles and its limitations whereas the worldly and deluded do not. These fortunate ones have access into the Atman and, once experiencing That, desire only to abide there forevermore.' Saying this, the knower of Brahman rose*

*from his position and swiftly departed from the company of the group."*

Ekanta had marveled at the yogi's stories all night. In fact, that evening he took a personal resolve never to judge things on face value alone, but to always search for inner significance and meaning. This resolve, now fully developed and realized, was one of the salient characteristics of the order of Avadhuts. They were not critical of the world process, for they knew God to be its author, but were nevertheless committed to the removal of ignorance from the minds of living beings. Even this was seen as God's will.

*"An instrument never moves except by the power of its wielder,"* they often affirmed.

Ekanta's mind was abruptly drawn back to the external world. A different kind of noise had roused him from his fond recollections. At first, it seemed to be a strange combination of city noises, but soon it became apparent that something else was contributing. This became all the more evident when Ekanta noticed that people in the streets were beginning to gather and run to and fro. As the noise became more audible, coming closer with every minute, a distinct atmosphere of excitement began to charge the air. A parade is approaching, thought Ekanta. He had experienced this before.

Ekanta did not leave the building, for he was averse to being pushed and shoved in the crowd outside. As it turned out, he did not even have to get out of his seat, for at that moment, up the street on which all the blacksmith and goldsmith shops were located, a huge elephant carrying a brightly adorned carriage filled with people turned the corner. Behind it came a processional fit for a king's eyes. As a matter of fact, from what Ekanta was able to make out from the excited talking nearby, it was the king's processional. Soon, streaming past the double doors of Dharman's little shop, came elephants in lines, holding onto each other's tails, groomed and decorated horses carrying handsome riders in full uniform, lines of musicians playing all manner of instruments and carriages of beautiful women belonging to the king's harem. Interspersed and interwoven with all of this phenomenal show were the many jugglers and clowns who caused riotous laughter amongst the gathered crowds and who passed out sweets to the children.

Soon, the king's courtiers and the inner chamber officials could be seen approaching with all pomp and ceremony, attended by a bevy of lesser officials bent on keeping the crowds at bay and under control. The king's own military band and personal guard followed this spectacle and all became certain that, not far behind, the king and queen would soon make an appearance. At this point, despite the increased excitement, Ekanta remembered the words of his guru once again, spoken after the two had witnessed a parade in his village when he was a boy.

*"The realization of God is somewhat like the mounting grandeur of a parade,"* said the guru as they left the festivities behind and made their way towards the ashram. *"It all occurs on subtle inner levels, however. One first perceives certain inward signs such as an upward current of spiritual feeling accompanied by wonderful inner visions. Then there are outer manifestations like the horripilation of the flesh which results in goosebumps and profuse coloration of the skin. Copious tears of joy also flow from the corners of the eyes. When these things occur in succession, one by one, it is certain that the finale is not far behind. One knows that a direct experience of God is about to happen!"*

No sooner had Ekanta finished reliving his memory, than with an increased blast of fanfare from the musicians accompanied by a blatant roar of enthusiasm from the crowds, the ornately decorated elephants bearing the king and queen rounded the nearby corner and came into view. People were beside themselves with joy and excitement. Ekanta could feel the eagerness and ardor of the people as a palpable force pervading everything. The ground shook with the footfalls of elephants, horses and the many people who had gathered. It was an unprecedented event that had all present in a firm grasp of absolute enchantment.

It was at this moment that Ekanta glanced over at Dharman. What he beheld there was enough to take his attention immediately off of the parade. Dharman was in the middle of his arrow-making task and for all intents and purpose had not stirred for hours. Neither was his concentration broken in the slightest degree by the appearance and passing of the marvelous cavalcade outside his doors, for he was absolutely riveted on the important task of fashioning perfect weapons for the king's army. Indeed, these very legions and the mighty king himself were now outside his own dwelling place, yet Dharman, completely oblivious to what was going on all around him, remained concentrated on his task. It was an unbelievable demonstration of one-pointed focus. Such was the intensity of his friend's attention, Ekanta believed, that if the king himself would have stopped in front of Dharman's shop, dismounted from the elephant and entered the premises, it would not have been sufficient to cause the arrowmaker's attention to deviate one iota from his present project.

This simple representation, superimposed amidst all the pomp and splendor of the moment and heightened and emphasized by the stark contrasts present in the situation, caused Ekanta to stand and salute the arrowmaker with heartfelt reverence.

"As the Mother Earth has become my exemplary teacher of forbearance," said the Avadhut aloud into the din, "so too is this arrowmaker fully worthy of being my teacher of concentration, revealing to me the very essence of one-pointedness."

The procession gradually went by and both the noise and the excitement began to wane. Ekanta's attention, however, continued to remain on his friend the arrowmaker who, for several hours afterwards, did not look up even once. All his motions, too, were made in a concentrated way. There was no waste of energy and no deviation from the task at hand. It was an inspiring sight. At last, as dusk began to fall, the Avadhut watched as the arrowmaker breathed a long sigh, straightened his back, stretched his arms and stood up from the table, his important task finished in perfect fashion. Taking note of Ekanta staring at him with obvious interest, and suddenly becoming aware of his surroundings once more, these simple and astonished words fell from his lips:

"My friend, revered sir! What time is it? Oh, forgive me! I have lost track of the time and have forgotten to serve you. What a wretch I am!"

# Chapter 3

# Teachings on the Way of Tranquillity

THE THIRD GURU —The Maiden

THE LESSON —Peace

*In the city, as I gazed upon the maiden who was busy husking rice, I learned the importance of peace of mind. When her suitor came calling, she, with her parents temporarily away from the house, had to admit him herself, there being no other recourse. As she returned to her chore and while the suitor waited for her parent's return, she became ashamed due to the noise that her cheap conch shell bracelets made while she husked the rice. Perhaps she thought that this would give away the family's impoverished condition and, coming to know this, the young man would go to search for a more suitable wife. Finally, breaking a few of the bracelets off of each arm, she continued her task, but still the noise persisted. In the end, she broke all the bracelets except for one on each arm. Peace then reigned supreme, both in her house and in her mind. Thus*

*the lesson came to me that where there are many or*
*even two, there is cause for worry and dissension,*
*but where only one resides there is eternal*
*peace, peace, peace.*

The Avadhut looked around himself, taking note of the entire assembly. The people gathered there were buzzing with quiet intensity, for many luminaries were appearing through the front door and the vacant seats reserved for the spiritually elite were swiftly becoming occupied. Organizers were running to and fro in order to accommodate all involved so that the morning's program could begin relatively on time. The hall was almost full and standing room was beginning to be taken up as well.

Ekanta had arrived early and proceeded to secure a good front-row seat. He had said good-bye to Dharman earlier that day but had promised him that he would come to dinner again in the evening at another friend's house. Therefore, Ekanta's schedule was to attend this gathering to hear some of the speakers in order to make good his promise to Swami Advaitananda and then go to the dinner gathering. After that he would leave the city, for he was looking forward to being alone again, lost in the wilds, contemplating both the inner and outer beauty of Brahman.

The sound of a conch shell brought most of the talking to an abrupt end. The master of ceremonies was standing on the platform already and waiting for silence. Ekanta could see the entire group of luminaries — about a dozen or more — seated in cross-legged fashion, awaiting their turn to give discourse. The familiar face of Swami Advaitananda stood out in their midst, and Ekanta hoped that he would speak early on in the program so that he could depart at an appropriate time and in diplomatic fashion.

"Welcome to this auspicious gathering of the devotees," came the voice of the speaker, "and salutations to all present. I would like to ask Swami Advaitananda to give the opening chant and invocation."

Dressed in the gerua cloth of his order and with turban wrapped around his head, the swami cut a fine figure as he walked to the front of the platform. Soon, after an appropriate silence, his sonorous voice was ringing out, carrying the timeless words of the ancient Rishis to the assembly of people gathered there for inspiration and edification:

*Om! Asato ma sadgamaya*
*tamaso ma jyotir gamaya*
*mrityor ma amritam gamaya*
*abhir abhira mai edhi*
*rudra yate dakshinam mukham*
*tena mam pahi nityam*
*Om shantih, shantih, shantih*

May the Divine Being lead us from ignorance
to ultimate knowledge.
May that One dispel darkness
and fill our minds with radiance.
May the unreality of death be revealed unto us
and may we ever identify with our eternal Self.
May the transforming touch of the Absolute
saturate us with everlasting peace, peace, peace.
May peace reign supreme in all hearts and minds.

The swami's rich and melodious voice combined with his devotional feeling placed the entire group in a deep mood. This was exactly what the master of ceremonies had counted on, for no sooner had the swami returned to his seat than the first speaker was announced. This speaker, given such an important position, was the leader of a monastic order in North India. Being a worshipper of Shiva, his discourse was on certain salient aspects of Kashmira Shaivism as compared to other ideals and doctrines. Though his speech was eloquent, thought Ekanta, it lacked life and was decidedly oriented in favor of the Shaivite tradition.

The second speaker was an Advaitist of the Shankara order of monks and he was followed by a well-known yogi who enumerated the virtues of the Patanjala system of Yoga. Others followed, including a Jain speaker in favor of extreme nonviolence and a Buddhist monk from Tibet. Ekanta sat straight and still through all of them, remaining open-minded and attentive. The Truth, he knew, was reflecting through each speaker present, though in different ways. It reminded him of a teaching from his Mataji:

*"Truth visiting the receptive mind is like water falling from the heavens, Ekanta. It is like rain that deluges the rooftop which then rushes down into the mouths of various animal-shaped spouts situated on the four corners of a house. All Truth comes from Brahman, the limitless ocean of nondual Awareness, and enters into the minds of holy beings according to their capacity and orientation. Like rain flowing out of these water spouts, then, some teachers transmit Truth in steady streams like that which comes through the trunk of an elephant. A few bestow It in huge gushes as through the teeth of a lion. Others are capable of giving only in an arching spurt like that which comes through a fish's mouth while others are only able to give in a thin sprinkle like that which emits from the mouth of a monkey. It is the way of the world, my dear, that most beings listen only to that teacher who matches their particular level of understanding. This is natural spiritual evolution, Ekanta, and as long as stagnancy, complacency, narrowness and deception are avoided, all will make their way, swiftly or gradually, to the goal."*

The intermission was announced, but just before the break, Swami Advaitananda was to speak. This was perfect, thought Ekanta, for he wanted to depart and he longed for direct experience with the Lord in deep communion rather than secondhand dissemination from a platform. He knew, however, that the swami had some inner realization and would probably speak in an entirely different manner than the previous speakers. His intuition was not wrong nor were his expectations disappointed in the least. The swami gave a brilliant talk on Sanatana Dharma, citing its universal scope and its profound depths. His talk was accented with quotes from the Vedas, the Upanishads and the Bhagavad Gita and he drew many parallels with other religious traditions.

Warming up to his topic, the swami said, *"We need not be too concerned with the name we call this wonderful living verity, nor should we be ashamed in the least in standing behind it. Truth will suffice as a name, but if we need a particular title then Sanatana Dharma will do nicely, for this is inclusive of all lineages of the Indian tradition as well as all scriptures of the world at large. Vedanta describes what we believe, no doubt, but we cannot all fit into that expression for there are many approaches to*

*Reality, considered unorthodox by Vedantic definition, that will not agree in total with the Vedas. Besides, the scriptures of Islam, Christianity and Buddhism have all proceeded from the Cosmic Mind of Brahman and they all possess validity and authority. I have studied them and find them to be not only enlightening but complementary and revealing.*

*"Sanatana Dharma," continued the swami, "describes the everlasting and the conditional truths of religious life. It states that Truth is indivisible and eternal by nature but allows for all systematic approaches as well, even of dualism with its many wonderful expressions. But we cannot make the same mistakes that the Brahmin priests have made in the past — of either hiding the teachings inherent in the Vedas from the masses or of insisting that they possess the only way to enlightenment. We must understand the Rishis as complete nondualists who were never pressed by the imposing weights of sectarianism.*

*"Speaking from the relative standpoint, as there was no such thing as Buddhism when the Buddha lived and nothing called Christianity when the blessed Christ walked the earth, so too the term Vedanta did not exist in the times of the great Rishis. Yet all of these streams of spiritual knowledge are present in the ultimate sense at all times, being facets in the diamond mind of Brahman, of God, of Allah. Therefore, I say that Eternal Truth should be our emphasis, complemented by an open-minded acceptance of all religious systems based upon Advaita — nondual realization. The many zeros placed end on end add up to nothing without a one placed before them. This one, in regards to spirituality, is the perfect enlightenment that, as Gaudapada, the great Advaitan says, perceives no distinction between creature and Creator, between nature and Spirit, between God and mankind. I feel so strongly about this that, as a monk, I have taken the name, Advaitananda."*

One of the many fine points of the swami's talk was his elucidation of the six systems of Indian philosophy. He captured the audience completely and never allowed a dull moment to exist. Whenever such a feeling entered the atmosphere of the hall, the swami would break the inevitable monotony of words with thrilling excerpts of songs from India's massive storehouse of devotional music. The master of ceremonies had planned well.

With this talk on their minds — a divine discourse reminiscent of the days of the ancient Rishis — people would be certain to return for the second half of this auspicious gathering.

At the break, Ekanta wanted to bid farewell to the swami but too many people had gathered around him. He decided instead to forget this plan and started to make his way towards the door. A voice from behind stopped him in his tracks. It was Swami Advaitananda, who had noticed him early on and had been keeping an eye upon him.

"No farewell, revered sir?" he asked.

Ekanta swung around and with a sheepish smile said, "Where would I go, swami? According to your wonderful talk, my true Self knows no location, no span of time and certainly perceives no difference between you and I."

"Well spoken," said the swami. However, I am evidently not able to realize the import of my own words since I feel the need to offer you my good-byes in person. Please go in peace, as I know you will, and if you are ever in central India you must stop and receive your share of alms at our ashrama."

"That shall be my extreme good fortune," returned Ekanta.

"Where is your next destination?" said the swami, who was obviously reluctant to part company with the Avadhut so quickly.

"Nowhere and everywhere," admitted Ekanta, "for there is no place where I do not exist nor is there a locale that is devoid of the all-pervasive presence of my Beloved."

"In that case," said the swami, "I should not miss you, for our inseparable oneness is a matter of fact rather than of speculation."

"How true this is," responded Ekanta. "Like the many stars in the night sky, held and supported by the infinite expanse of darkness surrounding them on all sides, so do living beings, though they appear to have independent lives, truly rest and have their existence in the immeasurable firmament of Brahman alone."

"What of the earlier speakers," stated the swami, "many of whom expounded the Absolute Reality in terms of an ultimate form such as Shiva, Krishna or Kali?"

As a conversation sprang up between Swami Advaitananda and the Avadhut, many of the nearby attendees of the gathering began to congregate around the two figures. As they listened to the enthralling exchange, they became riveted on what was being said.

This verbal interchange between two truly illumined beings was intriguing and compelling and no one wanted to miss it.  Word began to spread around the crowd that two spiritual beings were communing in the presence of all, for all to see and hear.  It was not long before most of the assembly had formed a circle around Swami Advaitananda and the Avadhut and were hanging on every phrase that sprang from their divinely inspired lips.  This proved a problem for the officials who were attached to a formal and sequential order of events.  Wriggling his way through the crowd, the master of ceremonies finally reached the inner periphery of the circle and beheld the two holy men entirely engrossed in their exchange and practically impervious to all those who had gathered around them.  Due to the intensity of the conversation, the official did not dare interfere and merely stood there with mouth agape, helplessly resigned to his predicament.

Ekanta was still considering the swami's previous question.  "As to your statement about God with form, there is no denying that the Absolute has achieved a purchase hold here in this world of relativity.  The blessed forms of Brahman called Shiva, Krishna, and Kali by three complementary religious traditions, are white, blue and black respectively, signifying transcendence, infinity and all-pervasive inclusiveness.  Even the attributes of these three great Ones, then, for all intents and purposes, are attributeless."

"Yes," broke in the swami, "and what does this tell us about Ultimate Reality?  That it is simultaneously present and transcendent, even in its apparent workings in the phenomenal universe.  As the Samkhya Yoga philosophy tells us, when the Divine Being becomes the universe and all living beings and appears as nature with its five elements, It still remains infinite."

Before the swami could elucidate on this point, an old man lost in the inner recesses of the circle yelled out, "Revered sirs, kindly speak up.  We cannot hear in the back.  What was that you said about five elephants?"  Some laughter broke out in the crowd due to this misunderstanding and this gave the master of ceremonies a chance to intercede.

"Please sirs, so rare an exchange must be properly staged.  Kindly move to the platform where all can share in this wisdom."

Ignoring this outbreak due to his intense inner involvement with the conversation, the Avadhut went on, oblivious of the interruption.

"So what if the six schools of orthodox philosophy define the Supreme Being in various ways. Let them assign Him different heavens, decorate Him with diverse attributes and render him complete with a multitude of forms or with none. Of what import is that to the lover of Reality? Blocks of ice solidify in the ocean and then melt with the approach of the sun's heat. It is all water nevertheless. God remains indivisible and full of bliss whether He takes form or remains homogenous. There is only one substance here, all about us, within us and everywhere and that substance is pure Consciousness called Brahman. Love, Bliss, Truth, Knowledge — these are all sublime expressions of Brahman. Without them, the people of earth would not know of the existence of anything higher."

"It seems then," said Advaitananda, "that what we are proposing is unique and unprecedented, a comprehensive understanding that is vast and universal. It is an idea whose time has come. That God is both in the world and beyond it was no secret to our ancient forefathers but this subtle secret has been forgotten in these troubled times. What is more, that Brahman remains untouched and unaffected by all that goes on in the universe, despite the cries of weak, feeble-minded people who think Him callous, unjust and uncaring, is a great insight into what is true. It is a direct pointer to the need for strength and forbearance along the spiritual path. Only those who are fit can undertake a pilgrimage to Kedarnath or Badranath, for the elevation is thin and the atmosphere, both internal and external, is rarefied indeed."

"I know the truth of your statement from direct experience," said Ekanta, "for I wandered the highlands in fierce winter conditions. Indeed, strength and fearlessness are necessary in order to gain direct experience. It follows, as well, that direct experience is needed in order to realize Brahman and His Shakti. Some wise men talk glibly about Brahman and Shakti, assigning the position of creator, preserver and destroyer to Mother Shakti. If Brahman has Its power, called the Mahashakti, then so does Mahashakti have Its power. In part, it is called Prakriti. The Mahashakti, being one with Brahman, does not get involved in the movements of the empirical process either. She is as untouchable and as pure as the formless Brahman. She lets the forces of nature accomplish all acts while She simply oversees from a detached witness position. She sets up the universal laws and sets them in motion too. The Blessed Lord, Sri Krishna, explains this lucidly in the Bhagavad Gita. Therefore, one must be careful how one defines shakti. She is not creative power. She is the unattached wielder of creative power."

These remarkable words caused a profound silence for a few moments. The speakers for the gathering and many notable wise men had also drawn near, interested in the new direction of the discussion. Several exponents of Samkhya Philosophy as well as a few Tantric adepts stood with mouths gaping to hear this unique exposition which merged the Prakriti of Samkhya Yoga and the Shakti of Tantric Philosophy. Taking advantage of the silence, Swami Advaitananda, who knew about the true stature of the Avadhut — despite being uncelebrated, with an unkempt appearance and standing there with ragged clothes and unpretentious demeanor — directed a question at him.

"Given that beings are of differing temperaments, that some hold to the ideal of the formless God while others desire to see God with form, is there any ultimate answer or absolute standpoint?"

Without skipping a breath, the Avadhut launched into further elucidation on the topic, a divine light beginning to radiate from his being.

"Liberation is coveted highly by the knowers of the formless Brahman, whereas devotion is preferred by those who perceive the highest Reality as being possessed of form. There is no real contradiction here, nor should there be any dispute. The scriptures of Divine Mother Reality declare that mukti is without service and that bhakti is with service. Therefore, the lovers of Krishna, Ram, Shiva and other Ishvara forms covet the Supreme Personality as their ideal, for not only do they long to see the Lord with these very eyes, they also love to serve Him and His creation. Yet, one cannot serve in the proper spirit, free from egotism and as a true benefactor to all beings unless the sense of individuality has been effaced. The best instrument to achieve this end is liberation, for the rascal ego is dissolved in that state and ultimately this is accomplished not by self-effort, but by God's Grace.

"Therefore, it is God's will that beings become liberated and this is so that they can become better karma yogis and yoginis — serving the Lord's creatures; better bhakti yogis and yoginis —

perceiving and loving all beings as representations of Divinity; better jnana yogis and yoginis — becoming adept at understanding the nature of Reality while teaching the lessons of the impermanence of temporal existence to others; and better raja yogis and yoginis — attaining the ability to meditate on and dissolve into Ultimate Reality with the full capacity of their being. The gist of this is that true love is not possible or attainable without the acquisition of nondual Wisdom and authentic nondual Wisdom is not comprehensible without pure, selfless Love. The two are the reverse and obverse sides of the same coin.

"Imagine that there is an ocean called formless Reality," the Avadhut continued, his voice now filled with deep resonance. "Around its shores are countless illumined beings. Occasionally, these beings plunge into this nectar sea of immortality and lose all sense of individuality. Then again, they sometimes emerge from that immortal bath to converse with those dwelling on its shores. Yet, outside and all around there is nothing but infinite splendor, albeit in a solidified or manifested mode. Within the ocean, too, there is a boundless expanse of Light, but that conscious Light illumines another infinite expanse of experience, in this case, of an extremely subtle and indescribable nature. Wherein lies the problem here? Am I to prefer one infinite and blissful mode of Brahman experience to another infinite and blissful mode of Brahman experience? The true lovers of God are never caught in such divergent philosophical predicaments."

At this point, the crowd of devotees remained still, waiting for more words of wisdom from the Avadhut. Even the officials had forgotten their individual duties, intrigued by this man's lucid and personable explanations.

"God my Father, the formless Brahman, and God my Mother, the playful and blissful Shakti — these are both sacred and equally loved by me. Can I give up one for the other? Is it even necessary? A child loves the father and mother for different reasons, perhaps, but they are both dear to it."

Another profound silence followed these words. Finally, the Avadhut spoke again. "There is such a thing as the eternal form of God, as well."

"Please tell us of that," revered sir, said a Vaishnava teacher who had come to speak at the gathering.

"The water of formless Consciousness becomes congealed into the ice of Ishvara or Avatar through God's Grace due to the desire of the creatures to behold the Divine Essence with form. Then, with the rising of the sun of nondual Wisdom, these forms melt back into their original unmodified state again. However, there is the case of a particularly powerful iceberg that, instead of melting, crystallizes and turns, as it were, into quartz. In the case of the Eternal Form, this undying, insoluble mass of congealed Consciousness is present throughout all cycles of creation and over an entire Mahayuga. Even during Pralaya, the dissolution of the very idea of name and form, this Being remains fully present, whether as a subtle seed or as an ever-present Reality, no one knows. Still, what can account for the existence of all things sacred and secular, that continue to exist and re-emerge from that condition of total annihilation?"

After these words had been delivered, a huge sigh seemed to emit from the entire assembly simultaneously. They were listening to the most precious secret — that which they had always known in the depths of their being, but which was being articulated so clearly by this wise man.

Seizing the moment once again, Swami Advaitananda said, "This is why we call the Vedas, our eternal scriptures, Nitya, eternal, Anadhi, without beginning, and Apaurasheya, not ascribable to human authorship. From out of the Divine Being Itself comes the Truth of immutable, ever-perfect existence. Those who comprehend this can do nothing other than try to live a divine life in accordance with what is written by the Divine Mother's own precious hand."

"Certainly what the swami says is true," stated the Avadhut, "and besides, what is the alternative — a return to phenomenal existence where the highest bliss is in the senses and this bliss being always accompanied by the six transformations of birth, growth, disease, decay, old age and death and attended by the pain-bearing obstructions of ignorance, egotism, attachment, aversion and clinging to life? Is this why we have been born on earth? The passions such as lust, anger, jealousy, avarice and the like, as well as their sons and daughters like disappointment, hatred, remorse, depression, stress and others also plague the poor soul trapped in Maya. Knowing this, as the swami says, what other direction is possible for us, or even desirable?"

"These are precious words," said one of the invited speakers, "the likes of which I have never heard before. I feel the definite presence of the Divine Being here amongst us now."

"There should be no great surprise in that," responded Swami Advaitananda. "Did not Sage Narada tell us that God and His devotees are one and the same? What is more, Sri Krishna affirms that where loving beings gather to speak of the Divine Being and other spiritual subjects, God is definitely present."

"This may be true," joined in another, "but can it ever be possible for mere humans to contain the uncontainable? I, for one, cannot see the validity of the Advaita. It is impractical as well."

This statement brought out the ire of several of the speakers standing nearby and an argument sprang up immediately.

"Gentlemen, gentlemen," said Swami Advaitananda trying to mediate. "Let us hear the Avadhut's response to this assertion."

The people all gave their assent to this proposal, but when the assembly turned their eyes towards that engaging figure, he had disappeared.

Before there could arise any complaint at this strange event, the master of ceremonies began directing people's attentions back towards the platform where speakers were already gathering. The crowd slowly dispersed, though they were loath to lose the presence and wisdom of the graceful figure that had so recently inspired their minds. As the group moved away, the last left standing there was the swami who gazed around wistfully, hoping to catch a final glimpse of the Avadhut, his new friend. When no sign of him was evident, the swami gave a mental salute and swiftly turned to take up the duties at hand.

Ekanta's withdrawal from the crowd and his unnoticed exit was aided by his study of the hall on the day before. An obscure and seldom-used door in the supporting wall near the east end of the hall had provided him with a fast departure. He had, as well, felt the oncoming dissent of certain of the more conservative and bigoted factions present at the gathering and he had not wanted to be around when the acidic effect of the radical Truth he had injected into them began to percolate down into their narrow analytical minds. Let those who will hear such natural truths with open-minded and childlike acceptance, benefit, he thought. The rest will never be able to imbibe them and must follow a more pedantic pathway towards universalism. They call themselves followers of the Vedas, thought the Avadhut, yet they are unable to comprehend the boundless and universal scope of Vedanta and the unique, broad and expanded awareness of the ancient Rishis. Such are the effects of Maya in this age, he thought, and he proceeded to join the thick crowds flowing through the streets of the city in vast numbers.

It was still midafternoon as Ekanta made his way towards the home of Dharman's friend, following the instructions he had been given. He arrived at his destination early, nearly two hours before the scheduled appearance of the other guests and proceeded to sit himself down near the door to wait. The house was a smallish old dwelling, not very well kept up and evidently accommodated people of a poor caste or those fallen on hard times. All habitations in the cities of India have that well-worn look, thought Ekanta as he settled himself to wait, even the mansions of the rich. This was due to both the smoky atmosphere and the considerable age of most of the dwellings.

As the Avadhut sat still, occasionally receiving the salutes and sacred offerings of passersby, he suddenly noticed the approach of a handsome young man. The man turned up the walkway leading to the house, passed by the Avadhut and knocked at the door. Soon, a maiden came to the door, peaking from behind it due to her modesty. This is strange, thought Ekanta. No young girl will ever receive a man when her parents are not home. The parents must be out, he surmised. A few fragments of the conversation came floating to Ekanta's ears.

"I have come, as prearranged, to discuss plans with your parents," said the young man. "Are your parents here to receive me?"

"I regret to inform you," said the girl in an abashed voice, "that due to the attendance of guests tonight for supper, my father and mother had to go out to procure certain supplies. It is very regrettable and cannot be helped, but they have informed me to tell you that you are welcome to sit and wait in the outer chamber until their return, if you do not mind."

"That will be well," said the man, and he was admitted.

Ekanta was seated almost directly facing the house. Therefore, though happening by chance only, he was perfectly situated to be able to see what went on in the lower floor of that dwelling. At first, he noticed that the man had taken a seat in the outer chamber as discussed and only his head was visible to Ekanta's gaze. Next, he saw the young girl enter another room and take up the task which she had been in the midst of doing when the knock on the door had interrupted her. This was the chore of husking paddy, which no doubt, thought Ekanta, would be used to feed the guests tonight at the dinner gathering. The sound of paddy being prepared proceeded to emanate from the room next to the chamber where the man sat patiently. He turned his head at the sound and Ekanta heard him say, "I hope that I did not interrupt you in your task. If I did then please forgive me."

"There is no need for apologies," called back the girl, though she looked a bit embarrassed since she knew that he could hear everything that she was doing.

As the husking chore proceeded, another sound could be distinguished, making itself heard gradually to the ear as it adjusted to the initial all-too-familiar sound. Ekanta suddenly realized what the sound was. The girl was wearing many imitation conch shell bracelets around her wrists, the kind that were easily affordable and favored by girls and women of poor families. They were very common and everyone naturally identified them with the lower class. The young girl, too, was now aware that her bracelets were making too much noise and stopped her chore to consider. Ekanta could easily guess what was going through her mind. She was now even more embarrassed due to the sound of the bracelets accompanying her work, not because of the presence of noise which always permeated the atmosphere of the city anyway, but because they were giving away her impecunious condition and calling attention to her station in life. Perhaps, thought Ekanta, she was thinking how the nice man in the next room might begin to ruminate on the poor condition of the house, the lack of servants and the impoverished state of the family. This, in turn, might cause him to think that he might do better for himself if he looked for a wife that could provide him with a suitable dowry which would give him a much better start in his householder existence.

As the girl pondered her dilemma, the Avadhut watched curiously. All of a sudden, the girl came to a decision. She began to remove the bracelets from her wrists, but as was often the case, hard work and time had caused her hands to swell slightly and the bracelets would not come off. As he watched, she took a small rock used for other chores in the house and began to break them one by one. As she obviously desired to keep them, since they represented the only jewelry that she owned, she left three of them on each wrist and again took up her task.

The sound of conch shell bangles rattling together persisted, however, and she had to stop again and break one more on both arms, leaving only two on each wrist. As she continued her work again, she found that these two bracelets also proved to be too many as they continued to clatter together, causing that embarrassing sound. Finally, in exasperation, the girl broke one more bracelet off of each wrist, leaving only one conch shell bracelet hanging on each side. This proved to be the solution, for as she continued husking paddy for the meal, the one remaining bracelet made no sound whatsoever and peace reigned supreme, both in the house and in the maiden's mind.

The Avadhut stood up, reeling a bit from his newly inspired state, and faced the girl. Since she could not see him and did not know of his attentions, she would also never know that he saluted her profoundly and took his seat again. As he pondered the situation, his mind began receiving the influx of spiritual insight, for what he had just witnessed had brought back to his consciousness countless teachings.

"I salute you, maiden," whispered the Avadhut reverently, "for you teach me the meaning and efficacy of true Peace."

The Avadhut's own lifestyle, his personal preference, was to keep aloof from the society of human beings, only frequenting the company of the holy. His natural ability to remain fully satisfied in his isolation was a source of amazement to people engrossed in worldliness. Most misunderstood his penchant for seclusion while a few wanted to engender it in themselves. To the Avadhut, however, it was a matter of practicality blended with wisdom. The scriptures, he knew, gave ample support for his mode of living. If one wanted higher attainments, there were certain rules and exercises to follow:

Controlling the tendency of too much talking
is the first portal leading towards yoga.

The second is the complete domination of the mind.
Attempt to perfect this by practicing renunciation.
Expectations, desires and attachments must be overcome
and this is effected by solitude.
Retreat, be alone and subject the senses to higher thought.
You will then attain peace of mind.
Accomplishing that, the insubstantial ego vanishes.
Then only will the bliss of Brahman visit you.

From the recesses of his wonderful memory drifted the sacred words of many other ancient scriptures as well, replete with all manner of precious teachings. He could still hear the voice of his guru reading to him from years gone by as he listened with rapt attention:

Where there are many, there is fear,
and where there is fear there can be no peace.
Where there is only one, however, no fear can enter,
for there is no second thing to be afraid of.
Peace reigns supreme in such a condition at all times.

Teachings about authentic Peace had come often from his respected vanaprastin teachers. One day, as Ekanta enjoyed the presence of these two unique beings in a relaxed atmosphere, the topic of Peace and that which stymied it came up for discussion:

*"True Peace is based upon Oneness, upon Unity, Ekanta. There is hardly any other quality valued so highly by the ancient Rishis. Consider the many gems from the various Upanishads which have come to be known to the devotees as the 'Peace Chants.' They are descriptive of that sublime condition that was enjoyed by the ancients who kept Brahman at the forefront of mind and existence."*

"Where has that peace gone?" asked the boy innocently. "I have little to compare it to but in my short experience with this world it seems as if most beings are unhappy, restless and fearful."

*"Your experience is not misleading you, my son,"* answered the guru. *"As the scriptures declare, though there are many impediments to the attainment of peace of mind, certainly fear could be said to be the greatest. Anxiety comes to the mind due to fear*

*of negative repercussions. The problem of greed and selfishness
is most often due to the fear of lack or the want of something.
Jealousy, too, occurs through the fear of losing something or the
projected fear of not possessing it in the first place. It is an
insidious process and it destroys that upon which the very foundation of contemplative life is based."*

"Revered teachers," he had asked, "two of my relatives have
recently begun fighting over what I see as a minor disagreement.
Great unrest has visited us as a result. How is it possible for such
small matters to ruin the peace of the household?"

After a silent moment, a response came in the form of a quote
from the scriptures. With compassion blended with detachment,
his guru recited:

> The rich fear thieves and the proud fear humiliation.
> The politicians fear slander while
> the beautiful fear disfigurement.
> The businessman fears competition and
> the pundits fear the more learned.
> All fear is predicated upon multiplicity and diversity,
> all peace upon harmony and unity.
> Still, the world clings to duality and will not give it up.

The validity of this teaching struck home in a deep way. How
could one expect contentment to visit the mind, not to mention
higher spiritual experiences, when the mental state was so frenetic? Ekanta had met many aspirants who had complained of
the restless mind, but even though they could not meditate with
any positive results, they would not practice the necessary prerequisites needed to calm the agitated mind. What a paradox this
created, resulting in abandonment of spiritual life, the compromise
of the highest ideals and even pretense and charlatanism.

The Avadhut was very well informed about the eight-limbed yoga
system of Patanjali called Raja Yoga, and he favored it highly. His
own observation, however, was that too many people, both teachers and students, misused it. The lack of proper understanding
as well as the failure to comprehend the full ramifications of the
Yogic tradition was responsible for its misapplication. In the first
place and to the great regret of pure-minded, authentic teachers,

aspirants who were physically-oriented used the third limb, called asana, almost in place of the entire Raja Yoga system. This relegated this sublime method to a system that catered to those who were obsessed with the body and senses. This, in turn, justified the sentiments of all who were comfortable dwelling in the three lower centers of human consciousness.

*"Yoga is meant to lead the aspirant out of suffering and bondage and to the liberated condition of freedom,"* his Mataji had often told him. *"The embodied condition is fraught with potential dangers and these must be overcome. Transcendence of the world of name and form with its many limitations is not escapism, my dear, but practicality based upon knowing one's Self to be beyond the body and the senses. Be in the world but not of it. Coming to realize your true nature as Spirit, detach from the world of becoming and abide in pure Being. Yoga will help you to accomplish this, providing that you use it properly and according to Patanjali's original inspiration and intention."*

*"Freedom from the senses, not freedom to the senses,"* came the uncompromising words of his teacher as she continued the transmission. *"This is what we want in spiritual life. Anything else is a mere caricature of true spirituality. Is it ever possible that the illumination of the mind, let alone its peaceful condition, can be attained by assuming various body postures or by practicing breathing exercises. Have you not read Patanjali's own words on the subject? He de-emphasizes the physical yoga and points to mastery of the mind and the transcendence of the phenomenal universe in samadhi. Yet materially-oriented people always lean towards the sensational rather than the subtle, towards the physical and away from the spiritual. Flexing the muscles is flexing the ego and the more versatile the body can become, the more impressive it is to onlookers which, in turn, is another pleasurable stroke for the ego. This sort of thing gives rise to worship of the ego, the desire for power and attachment to earthly existence. This is clinging to life, the very thing Patanjali warned against. Few want to transcend such vanity and foolishness. Truly, it is all a vexation of Spirit."*

"How can one rise above such heavy tendencies?" Ekanta had asked his Mataji one day. "Postures and breathing are obviously not enough for the attainment of enlightenment. If they were, most of the spiritual community would be illumined by now, since that is all they ever do."

The Mataji laughed aloud to hear of Ekanta's astute observation. When her laughter had subsided a bit, she said, *"The best way to peace of mind is to see the Self as being perfect at all times. Raja Yoga is a fine system, but Eternal Truth — Advaita or perpetual Oneness — gives it its efficacy, as It does for all of the philosophical systems, and, indeed, all religions. Knowing one's intrinsic perfection to be covered up or sublated by Maya and taking definite steps to uncover It is very different than blindly groping along under the mistaken assumption that perfection is far away or nonexistent."*

Pausing for a second, the Mataji said, *"Listen to a story that illustrates this point, my dear.*

*"Two men, searching for a hidden cave, stumbled upon its hidden entrance independently of each other and, although without flame or torch, they were nonetheless determined to go through it. One of the men had consulted the discoverer of this cave and had been told that the cave took one hour to move through, that there was an exit at the other end and, importantly, that there was a key to a successful outcome.*

*"'Three quarters of the way through the cave,' the old man said, 'there is a welcome shaft of light that descends from the ceiling of the cavern, lighting your way. So, although you will be in pitch darkness for most of an hour, you will be gratified to know that there is light up ahead and that it signals an end to your quest.'*

*"The man entered the cave and, though trembling with fear while feeling his way along the dark interior, nevertheless prevailed due to his mentor's prior instructions. Emerging from the other end of the cave, he felt exalted and enjoyed his victory. The second man, not equipped with the fear-dispelling knowledge of the more experienced, gave up after only a few minutes in the fearful darkness and swiftly retraced his steps, plunging out of the mouth of the cave with a relieved gasp but never fulfilling his initial intention. Do you get the gist of this story pertaining to what we were just discussing?"* asked the Mataji.

"Yes," returned the boy, "I see that those who are in the know about their true nature, their oneness with Brahman, will complete their life's mission with minimal difficulty, while those who are without such essential knowledge will falter and maybe even fail."

*"Well put, my dear. If you maintain your studies here at the ashram with us, there is no doubt that you will emerge from the student phase of your life in full awareness of your true nature. Remember, too, the hidden facet of this story — the discoverer who gave the explorer this crucial information. It is the guru who gives the key of nonduality to the disciple early on in the path and guides him or her accordingly thereafter. Armed with that crucial knowledge, all dangers are easily dispelled and anything is possible."*

After a short pause, and in order that these profound words would sink in to the boy's intelligence, the Mataji continued:

*"Only after falling into the delusion that the Atman is tainted in some way — either by division, by limitation, by transgression or other self-imposed and imagined deceptions of the mind/ego complex — does one begin a descent into depression and depravity. Then it takes spiritual effort, sadhana, to reverse and overcome the adverse effects of this downward trend. There would be no need for sadhana if all knew themselves to be exactly what they truly are — the eternal Spirit. This was the blessed Christ's favorite attitude as well and He described it by stating, 'Be thee perfect, even as thy Father in heaven is perfect!'*

*"If beings fail to know themselves as inherently perfect, then a secondary way is open to them. They can strive hard to know the Truth, using the many devotional and philosophical systems that the Divine Mother of the Universe, in Her boundless Grace, has placed in this terrestrial realm for our salvation. These wonderful spiritual pathways represent Her Lotus Feet, planted like the roots and stalk of that lovely flower in the very fabric of relative existence. Taking recourse to these and in accordance with the guidance of Her illumined children, beings can transcend the effects of both personal delusion and the appearance of the false superimposition of the world of name and form over Brahman. Then they will remember what is real and what is illusory, what is true and what is erroneous, what is essential and what is superfluous, what is important and what is not.*

*Sri Krishna, in His Song Celestial, has aptly called this process Abhyasa Yoga, the way of constant practice."*

"These two ways," asked Ekanta, "the way of the ever-perfect and the way of aspiration, do they not correspond with Advaita and Dvaita, nondualism and dualism?"

*"Yes,"* declared his teacher, *"an important parallel can be drawn there.  Take for instance the attitude of a dualist who believes in God but still retains a strong sense of agency.  Such a one thinks that by his or her own self-effort, enlightenment can be attained.  This is half correct, but the crucial half is missing — that being God's Grace.  The self-surrender of such an individually-oriented being is incomplete, is it not?  The ego still poses a great problem by constructing the formidable barrier of 'I am doing, I am accomplishing.'  This is sheer lunacy.  Who is doing and what is being done?  One should ask oneself these important questions.  After the sense of ownership is effaced — that being one of the ego's favorite pastimes — the sense of agency is the next hurdle.  First, one must take the attitude of overseer or custodian of all belongings to destroy the sense of ownership and the covetousness that accompanies it.  Then perceive clearly that it is God alone that operates the universe from His detached witness position and affirm, 'I am not the doer,' or, 'Not I, but Thou, Oh Lord.'  Ultimate Peace comes from such assertions."*

His wonderful teacher had paused for a while.  Then she continued.  The boy hung on every word, on every fragment of precious knowledge that flowed from her illumined mind.

*"Can impurities stick to the wind?"* she stated emphatically. *"Can the sense of sin taint a young child's mind?  Slough off this insidious ego and be free in a moment!  This is the way of the Ever Free, the Nityasiddhas.  The scriptures declare this immaculate way as well.  Have you not heard, my boy?"*

Saying this she chanted:

*Sadanga yogan na tu naiva shuddham*
*mano–vinashan na tu naiva shuddham*
*gurupadeshan na tu naiva shuddham*
*svayam cha tattvam, svayam eva buddham*

The Self is not made pure by spiritual disciplines.
Neither is it purified by bowing at the guru's hallowed feet.
It is never purified by the destruction of the mind's thoughts.
It is of the very nature of purity itself, it is Truth unchanging!

"So, dear boy, if you were given something absolutely pure, would you subject it to all sorts of impositions? Must we then twist ourselves into ungodly shapes and subject our bodies and lungs to painful contortions in order to realize that which is beyond body and breath? Even if you were not quite convinced of this eternal verity or of your own identity with It, would it not make more sense to find an illumined preceptor and consult the scriptures concerning It? With this done, you could then learn what it takes to realize the Atman: to sit peacefully in one posture long enough to catch a glimpse of It; to regulate your breathing long enough to attain the breathless state necessary for the experience of higher states of mind and to control the outgoing tendencies of your senses and master the mind's penchant for desires and attachments. These practical steps make up the noble yogic path, not posing, posturing, pleasure-seeking, pain, pretension or powers."

"From what you say, Mataji, I assume that there must be other steps penultimate to the practice of basic posture and natural breathing. What are these and why do people ignore them?"

"That is a profound and practical question, my dear," said the Mataji. "Raja Yoga and the great founder of the system, Patanjali, recommends recourse to ten steps or practices before one begins to sit formally. These must be done in the company of and in consultation with the guru and the scriptures. Anyone who imagines that they can make their way through the morass of internal and external obstructions of mind and matter without a guide is extremely deluded. These unfortunates eventually either give up completely, having no one to correct or support them in their strivings, or end up pretending that all is fine and proceed to make a fool out of themselves and a mockery out of spiritual life. Besides, by sliding back into the ways of the world they open themselves up all the more to the adverse effects of their own inherent karma. This brings an important teaching to my mind."

The revered Mataji collected her thoughts for a moment, then went on. *"The guru, the teachings and the sincerity of the student act as interdependent defense mechanisms against dangers from within and from without. Certain karmas, both internal and external are, as it were, heading for a point of convergence in life and are destined to fructify and emerge. If they surface during a period when the mind is in a tamasic state, or when it is not protected by holy company in the form of guru, dharma and sangha, then great disaster may ensue. It will be extremely difficult to reverse those effects as well, and one will have to live through them in due fashion.*

*"Have you not seen the turtle surfacing unawares for a breath of air and being caught by the fishermen of a nearby boat? It inevitably ends up as turtle soup or turtle steaks in someone's kitchen back on land. The turtle that rises to the surface conscious of apparent dangers, however, can take a swift breath and disappear below the surface before the fisherman can throw the net. It then remains free from impending doom. The devotee that has faith in God, in His sacred Word called the scriptures and in the guru who is simply God in human form, is like the clever turtle and seldom, if ever, has to worry about karmic dangers. If karmic propensities are to occur, they are at least greatly diminished due to the proximity of the triple gem of guru, path and teaching."*

"Mataji," Ekanta had asked, "you mentioned the ten practices to be utilized and mastered first before embarking on the Sadanga Yoga path of Raja Yoga. Sadanga means six-limbed, and the Patanjala Yoga system speaks of eight only. If there are ten prerequisite steps then is not the Raja Yoga system a sixteen-step process?"

*"That is very astute, my dear,"* commended his teacher, *"and in truth, the way I think of it is just so. It is because the first ten steps have been so lightly treated by those who blindly and carelessly rush into the practice of asana or yogic postures, that certain problems and distortions of spiritual life have arisen in them. If you study the Raja Yoga traditionally and comprehensively, which is recommended by the wise, you will find the first two limbs to consist of ten prerequisites — the yamas and niyamas. The yamas, moral and ethical observances that*

*purify the mind, are five in number and include noninjury, truthfulness, noncovetousness, chastity and non-receiving of gifts.  The niyamas, regular habits and practices, also amount to five and consist of austerity, study, contentment, purity and devotion to God.   These should be understood and practiced before going on to the six consecutive steps."*

Ekanta was amazed by this statement from his teacher and asked incredulously, "Do you mean to say, Mataji, that there are beginning students who would presume to practice the intermediate levels of yoga without first taking recourse to these basics?"

*"Yes, my dear, that is a sad fact,"* replied the guru.  *"And many of the calamities in religious growth occur due to this oversight. It is the fault of aspirants who, full of pride, embark upon the early practices of inner contemplative life such as asana, pranayama, etc., thinking that they do not need a teacher.  Then again, it is sometimes the fault of poor teachers who do not follow the progress of the student and provide proper guidance while insisting on adherence to the practice of essential basics such as the study of the scriptures, devotion to God and others."*

"What are some examples of these disasters, Mataji," the young boy had asked.

At this, the preceptor thought a while.  Then she stated:

*"To illustrate that in part, let us take two of my favorites that are deemed by superior teachers to be essential to the successful mastery of the critical six limbs.  These are Ishvara-pranidhana and Svadhyaya — devotion to God and the study of the scriptures.  What can be said that is not obvious here?  Only the stupid, the belligerent or the lazy could be so blind as to ignore these prerequisites.  I like Svadhyaya, the study of scriptures, for several reasons.  Firstly, it is obvious that when one first reads the scriptures, written by the illumined ones, that a guru is necessary in order to interpret and elucidate the teachings properly.  In addition, one then finds out how difficult the spiritual path is, what subtleties attend it and what care must be exercised in following it.  Next, a true aspirant uncovers the essential keys to a peaceful existence in the world as well as success in spiritual life by rightly understanding the scriptures. Finally, the existence of God becomes apparent through this deep study and initial belief is transformed into absolute Faith.*

*"This brings to mind my other favorite, Ishvara-pranidhana, devotion to God. How people imagine that they can make sense out of this creation, their individual awareness and life in the world if they do not have a relationship with the Creator of the universe, the Master of Consciousness and Source of all existence, is beyond me. It simply does not follow! Devotion to God is the basis for everything. The only reason that the revered father Patanjali placed moral and ethical procedures in order before the worship of God is because beings, in this day and age, caught in this universal drama, are bereft of their subtle senses and rely on their physical ones instead. These, being connected to the mind made impure by ignorance, egotism, attachment, aversion and clinging to life — what Patajali calls the five kleshas or impediments to spiritual progress — can never give an actual reading of Reality and therefore delude the intellect further. Basic practices are then necessary at first in order to catch a glimpse of this wondrous Being. The mind's ignorance must be effaced to a certain extent before insight and vision occur."*

"Revered Mother," Ekanta had asked, "you mentioned the adverse effects that ensue later in spiritual life if one fails to observe these ten practices. What would happen to the aspirant if these two niyamas, for instance, were not followed?"

*"If aspirants fail to worship God,"* responded the guru, *"even if they be possessed of the most astute intellect, their attempts at knowing God will fail or reach only partial maturation. Becoming enamored with their own intellect as the ultimate guide and falling under the delusion that they know everything, they become puffed up with pride and develop a subtle spiritual ego which colors everything they say, do or think. Too late will they find out how incomplete is the limited human mind and intellect and how deceptive is this nefarious ego.*

*"With regards to study of the scriptures, so many mistakes will visit the student that it will be impossible to see his or her way clear without a spiritual guide's intervention. Spiritual study, according to Patanjali, is supposed to fructify in the realization of one's intended deity — one's Ishta, or chosen ideal. Without knowing the scriptures, one never finds out that a chosen ideal need be selected in the first place or that one even exists. How are we to know the proper thing to strive for if there*

*is no concrete ideal? Do you know what happens to the greater percentage of students in this case? They end up worshipping their own small self and the ego strikes another blow of victory — a blow in favor of spiritual suicide. This is like the story of a sculptor who, with the best of intentions but no teacher or model, sets out to create an image of God from a huge block of stone but ends up forming nothing more than the image of a monkey."*

"Is it possible for you to give a synopsis of what occurs when the other yamas and niyamas are ignored?" asked Ekanta.

*"I can certainly try,"* replied the guru. After a pause, she said, *"If one does not practice Ahimsa — non-injury in thought, word and deed — until mastery is attained, enmity from others and the dangers of karmic retribution will certainly ensue. All must die, but the time for that is determined by God, not by one's actions. Suffering, however, is another matter and very definitely follows our actions.*

*"If one fails in Satya — truthfulness in thought, word and deed — then all beneficial and righteous desires will be stymied and will never come to fruition. Besides this, what emerges out of one's mouth and what occupies one's daily thoughts shapes character. An honest person literally remains honest without the slightest bit of effort while the devious or untruthful wretch wallows in all manner of deceit. Even if higher tendencies emerge due to past good karmas, their beneficial effects are greatly minimized. Bad habits are extremely hard to break.*

*"If a person does not observe Asteya — noncovetousness — and remains desirous of another's goods or attainments, a condition of intense want develops. This is interminable and affects one's entire life, plaguing it with unfulfilled desires and destitution. Such a virtue is not to be trifled with or held in low regard. I have seen the impoverished condition of many unfortunates and found most of them to be very selfish and jealous of others' wealth, belongings and status. This is no way to live, but if one persists like this, the effects are nonetheless deserved.*

*"A lifeless and pallid existence is the result of the nonobservance of Brahmacharya — continence. Chastity is to be taken seriously, and by chastity we mean absolute abstinence during periods of important practice and moderation at all times.*

*These rules differ for the enlightened, the monastics and the householders according to stages of growth, but those two directives apply overall. Sublimated energy is desperately needed for spiritual life and those who disregard this basic virtue deplete this primal source of power and spoil the greater potential of their lives. Later on, when the concentration of the mind is essential, they often fall from the ideal due to ignoring this prerequisite and find ample reason to regret it.*

*"If one receives a gift from another — Aparigraha — a stipulation or expectation is nearly always attached. This puts a damper on one's progress, for the mind is made captive by such an imposition. Again, there are countries around the world that orient most of their holy days around the giving of gifts. The result is nearly always a dependence upon external objects and the good graces of others for personal happiness and a regression into the unwholesome mode of materialism. A mass collective delusion is formed by these practices and the fall of society into a depraved or superficial condition ensues. On the individual level, by depending upon or being fond of gifts, one forgets what is important and becomes seduced by outer stimuli. It is like the cows who, when they are offered oil cakes mixed with fodder, gobble it greedily and forget everything else — even the nursing of their offspring. Such is the danger of accepting gifts without performing an exacting discrimination within one's own mind while simultaneously observing a close inspection of the intentions of others."*

"Mataji," said Ekanta eagerly, "you have nicely answered my question regarding the yamas. What about the niyamas?"

*"Patience, my child,"* said the elderly woman humorously. *"You would literally suck me dry of teachings, I am sure. Allow an old woman a chance to get a breath!"*

Ekanta, ever on the alert for any tendency of disrespect in himself, bowed down at her feet in humble salutation. "Excuse me, revered teacher," he said humbly.

*"Rise up, my dear,"* said the guru. *"I would have you no other way than this. Besides, what have I left to do except to lavishly give out what I know right up until the time of my departure?"*

"Mataji," said Ekanta, assuming his former position, "you have always told me that an illumined person merges with everything, never departs anywhere."

*"Sometimes you amaze me, my boy,"* breathed the woman appreciatively.

After a moment of thought, she continued on with the teaching of her beloved student.

*"A person who practices no austerity, that called Tapas, acquires very little power in the body or the mind. By this, I do not mean just strength as we normally understand it, but the ability to bear with physical, mental and spiritual trials. Real resolve and authentic forbearance are rare things. A strong body, pumped up by exercises, and a strong mind, made so by individual will, is seldom able to bear with the subtle difficulties of spiritual life. Like the poet-saint sings, the white beetles of a perplexing nature come out from the eaves and the woodwork in swarms and cause great agony and frustration. Muscles and will power cannot cope with them. What is needed is insight, inner perception and peace of mind. I have seen big, strong men act like babies before the onslaught of simple spiritual problems. Austerity is equal to purification, and it is the mind that harbors impurities. The rest of the creation is fine as it is. Those devoid of austerity find it hard to achieve purity as life advances. No one would want to be in this deplorable condition in later life, especially as death nears and the mind gets fearful and unruly. What will they fall back on at this critical time?"*

The guru took a sip of water from an earthen mug, then she continued.

*"About contentment, Santosha,"* the teacher said in a reverential tone, *"one could talk or write volumes on its efficacy. Suffice to say, though, that those who do not cultivate it achieve no lasting happiness and are ever at odds with the world, its ways and its creatures. These beings are impervious to the eternal blessings which come naturally to all beings and always have their sights set on extra benefits, usually of a distorted variety. Contentment, penultimate to peace of mind, never visits the likes of these and their lives are unbalanced and negatively influenced by this lack of equanimity.*

*"If the attribute of purity, Saucha, is overlooked or ignored in one's practice, attachment to the senses, gloominess and an*

*unhealthy preoccupation with both mind and body ensues. In addition, an inability to concentrate is experienced, for the mind will be inexorably called back to its impure condition. Physical disease can be a horrible impediment to spiritual practice and even if one is lucky enough to avoid that to a certain degree, the mind's disease is equally as formidable. Hindrances of all types attend this life. We have enough of them inherent in the world process, what with the body and nature to deal with. The mind and one's personal delusions and ignorance brings another set of them to bear on consciousness. Throughout it all, beings disregard or repudiate the teachings which the Universal Mother places at their disposal. Instead, they hold to base delusion as if it were Truth itself. This is why delusion is often placed on the list of the six passions. Perhaps you have seen jackals feasting on a long dead animal, even though its carcass is putrid and rotting? Later, they vomit horribly, yet they still return and gorge themselves further."*

Intrigued by the tenor of the conversation, Ekanta then asked his teacher, "Revered guru, why are beings fooled so completely? What makes them cling to infantile ideas?"

*"Some beings,"* came the answer, *"are like animals experiencing their first human birth. Don't you notice them sniffing around what is unclean, like a dog around heaps of garbage? The scents that attract them in early human evolution, however, are such things as the pungent and unhealthy smoke from dried plants, the taste of bitter and fermented liquids, an attraction to the scent of cheap perfumes and those who wear them and the desire to consume dead flesh.*

*"Other beings, having tried and failed in their early efforts to rise above gross human nature, give up and simply revert to old habits and tendencies. They make a dubious art of pleasurable living, seeking after things that attract them while shunning things that repulse them. Yet, negative experiences often bring the most valuable lessons while pleasurable experiences usually bind the experiencer to superficiality and mediocrity. These latter are worldly to the bone, petty and jaded. They, as the scriptures relate, do not think of God even by accident."*

"What happens on a higher level of comprehension?" Ekanta had asked.

*"Those moral fundamentalists come next,"* came the reply. *"Unable, as of yet, to reach the heights of spiritual attainment, they cling to a reliance on dualistic religion based on narrow beliefs and rigid rules of conduct. Highly critical of others and mentally condemning them to unspeakable hells, these kind have no real contentment in life, nor does compassion get born in their hearts. They go from birth to death and death to rebirth reaping the bitter experiences of such a condition until a greater awakening finally dawns on them.*

*"When this occurs, we find human evolution at the beginning of true spiritual life. The next group of evolving beings are people of good moral fabric who understand, to some extent, the rules of Karma Yoga. They have had enough experience in this school of hard blows called the universe to know that what they sow they will also reap. These experiences have made them more broad-minded. The long-winded death of the rascal ego is taking place for such as these, and if conditions are auspicious they gravitate towards holy company. Then, they secure spiritual teachers, an absolute necessity in this illusory world, and thereby acquire a taste for the teachings of the scriptures. If this fructifies due to commitment and perseverance, then knowledge of the Atman and a desire to realize Its eternally pristine condition grows in the heart and mind.*

*"This latter group is comprised of a few rare individuals and as spiritual evolution becomes more subtle and refined, they seem fewer and fewer. This is because the heights of nondual realization cannot be perceived from the normal human station and with the ego gone, melted in the bliss of absorption into Absolute Reality, there is nothing left to declare a separate existence. All that reigns, as the Upanishads declare, is peace, peace, peace! This peace is not a period of quiet or a sterile silence. It is not mere rest or repose, nor is it just freedom from stress and travail."*

Here, his guru had paused again as if battling with some inner emotion. Finally, after Ekanta had seen a few tears form in her eyes, she said, *"What it is cannot be described but must be experienced."*

"How does one acquire such a wonderful state," Ekanta had asked with wide eyes.

*"With the kind of sincerity that I just heard in your voice,*

*young one," said the guru, "combined with the wonder present in your eyes right now. Peace will certainly attend those who love the Lord with their whole heart and mind, who think of no other and who see that beloved One permeating all things. You know the famous Peace chant from the scriptures, dear child. No true God-lover who, ever having heard it, could ever forget it."*

Saying this, the elderly woman, eyes glowing with love for God, chanted melodiously:

*Om dyauh shantih, antariksham shantih*
*prithivi shantih, apah shantih*
*oshadayah shantih, vanashpataya shantih*
*vishvedeva shantih, brahma shantih, sarvam shantih*
*shantir eva shantih sa ma shantir edhi*
*Om shantih, shantih, shantih*

There is peace in the sky, there is peace on earth.
There is peace in the heavens, there is peace in the world.
There is peace in the waters, there is peace on land.
There is peace with the plants,
animals, flowers, insects and herbs.
There is peace with men
and peace with women and children.
There is peace with the gods and peace with the goddesses.
Brahman is this ineffable peace.
May this all-pervading peace enter into us
and permeate us to the very core of our being.
Om peace, peace, peace.
May peace be unto us, may peace be unto all.

Ekanta brought his attention outward again and found himself looking up into the sky. He turned to look at the house where lessons of eternal peace had been transmitted to him in a most unique way. There sat the maiden, finishing up her chore of husking paddy, the single conch-shell bracelets moving up and down on her wrists in absolute silence. Perfect peace abides where there is only one, thought Ekanta, but there is potential cause for all sorts of unrest where two or many reside. Almost immediately the question, "What about loneliness?" sprang into his mind, not due to consideration for himself, but because of the many times that this question had been posed to him by others who were seeking fulfillment.

Ekanta knew that having the Atman first and foremost, as guide, companion and beloved, destroyed all intruders such as loneliness, boredom, unhappiness and the like.  It was, however, almost an impossibility to explain this to others or to convince them of the truth of this.  He only knew that the love of solitary existence was a part of him and that dependence on others, except for Holy company, was not only alien to him, it was wholly undesirable.  It was not that he had an aversion to the company of people or society, for he saw God at work therein.  It had to do, at least in his case, with a love for unity that recognized the experience of true peace and contentment to be contingent on a totally free and independent state of being.  Accepting anything less was a betrayal of that lofty principle which inevitably led to the gradual degradation and loss of the freedom natural to the Soul.

This unfortunate and lamentable bereavement was the cause of all manner of attachment and misery everywhere he wandered.  In some beings, this tendency towards reliance on others and upon external circumstances proved to be downright demeaning.  Teachings from his gurus had substantiated this for him.

*"Freedom and peace are nearly synonymous terms,"* came the words of Yogindra Yogi one day as the two strolled outside the village precincts. *"If you lose one, the other is sorely affected.  The same could be said for truth, devotion, grace and all other eternal divine qualities, my boy.  They are all so interconnected that losing any one of them is like cutting off a limb or allowing one leak to remain in the hull of a ship before a long journey at sea.  Sooner or later this loss is bound to show in regrettable ways.  It all amounts to loss of freedom in the end, no matter which way you look at it.  The result is dependence in its many deceptive forms.  What beings call freedom, when examined, is seen to be attended by all manner of subordination to external things which bind.  This is not freedom.  True freedom has been forgotten in this day and age.  If it were not, we would see everyone at peace — calm and contented."*

The late afternoon's peaceful and reflective activities were very satisfying to Ekanta.  Soon, the parents of the girl returned home and there was a brief meeting between them and the suitor.  Not long after the young man had gone away, Ekanta saw Dharman coming his way along the crowded streets. The waning light of dusk told him that the time for the evening meal was nearing, so he stood up to greet his new friend. Dharman was in a good mood and this was somehow reflecting in him in an imposing manner. Taller than most Indians, the crowd seemed to part for him as he wended his way along the streets while beggars and street urchins thought better than to impede his progress.

"Salutations," cried out Dharman to the Avadhut, as he made the traditional gesture of respect with hands placed together in reverential greeting. "I am so happy to see you again. Knowing of your penchant for wandering in a solitary fashion, I wondered if I should ever see you so soon again."

"Stronger than my love of moving about freely on my own is my insistence on keeping my word," said Ekanta. "It was you who reminded me of the story about the tusks of an elephant. A man is only as good as his word, is he not?"

"Yes that is true," replied Dharman, "and in that case we are extremely lucky that the word of the holy ones binds them to righteous action, for where would the rest of us be without such fine company and such sterling examples?"

"Funny you should mention that," returned Ekanta, "for I was just noticing again the pitiable circumstances of those who have lost their love of freedom and their reliance on Truth. Peace of mind cannot survive without the likes of these qualities. They are, besides being natural attributes of the gods, formidable weapons and shields in the ongoing battle taking place all over the field of terrestrial existence daily. It is unthinkable that one might go through life without them. Yet, there you have it. All around and in every quarter, people have given up their love for higher values and have accepted the most mean intentions instead. What can be the lot of those who work the land yet disregard the harvest? It is most difficult to understand."

Dharman straightened up and a serious expression came over his face. He was noticeably affected by the words of his friend, spoken not out of criticism but out of compassion for the sufferings of humanity.

"This is an untenable and unacceptable situation," he replied emphatically. "A worm dies if you take it out of filth and place it in white rice.  A great amount of growth must take place in order to prepare the mind for the comprehension and implementation of higher values.  I prefer to believe that all beings have knowledge of these superlative qualities and have only forgotten or covered them up.  It is a matter of recalling or recapturing a once noble condition, not of attempting to create something out of nothing."

"Yes, I agree" said Ekanta.  "Forgetting the true nature of the Self due to the mind's preoccupation with Maya, beings allow themselves to be seduced and barter away their precious store of divine attributes for a handful of cheap trinkets."

"And these are short-lived," returned Dharman, "yet people cling to them as if they possessed the power of satisfaction itself.  The world, in this respect, is like the hog-plum fruit.  It is all skin and stone with very little flesh and eating it gives one a case of indigestion."

"That is an apt analogy," said Ekanta with a laugh.  "I will have to remember that."

Dharman smiled and said, "I can see that we are both in a fine mood for reforming the world.  However, before we instigate all our favorite changes, I suggest that we eat first."

Saying so, he directed the Avadhut up the front walkway and into the house of his friend.

The evening was enjoyable enough, for the family was spiritually oriented and talk tended to remain on higher things rather than on the mundane or superficial.  Ekanta was greatly relieved.  In earlier days he had occasionally been subjected to the kinds of gatherings where all people did was to talk about insipid worldly matters, drink intoxicating beverages, laugh at off-color jokes and consume vast amounts of food without the slightest regard for anything sacred whatsoever.  Then, feeling very happy with themselves, they would stagger home to their beds and fall into a tamasic sleep after indulging their insatiable sensual appetites.

*"What one eats, one becomes,"* came the words of his teachers.  *"If one eats radish, one belches radish."*

These sayings described perfectly the pitiable condition of worldly people, who literally consume impurity with body, mind and senses.  Ekanta often did not know which way to feel about this: distress for their unfortunate condition of self-imposed bondage or happiness in his own freedom.

With the meal over and the evening drawing to a close, Ekanta and Dharman bid farewell to the lovely family and departed. The Avadhut would never forget the young woman of this family, the maiden who had reminded him in such an endearing way about how to fulfill the conditions penultimate to the attainment of real peace. Saluting the entire family, Dharman and Ekanta took their leave and returned to the city streets, now practically deserted due to the late night hour.

"You must come and sleep at the shop," said Dharman. "Then you can make your way in the morning."

"As much as I would like your company another night," said Ekanta, "I think that I would like to leave the city before the rush of the early morning crowds."

"Ah," said Dharman, "I understand this well. Besides, you can spend some nocturnal hours on the hills outside the city, gazing at the stars and meditating on the Eternal One, is it not so?"

"You understand me well, my friend," returned the Avadhut, "and through the grace of the Divine Mother I have received enough alms this afternoon to provide for my immediate travel needs. Therefore it is time to part company, if only for a time."

"Yes," said Dharman, "but when you find yourself in these parts again I want you to visit us at our country home for a few days and meet my daughter. I feel that a strong connection will be forthcoming there."

Ekanta assured him of this eventuality and the two embraced and saluted each other.

There were no long good-byes that night, for neither wanted to dwell on the thought of separation. Nor did either believe in such a condition. As Dharman headed for his shop, however, he turned once to catch a glimpse of this amazing being he had met. The Avadhut, sensing powerful eyes upon him, turned at the end of the street and gave a sign of respect and benediction upon his new friend. Then, throwing his wearing cloth around his shoulder against the cool of the evening, he turned and disappeared into the darkness of the great metropolis and made his way through the silent streets towards the distant gates of the sleeping city.

# ~ Chapter 4 ~

# Teachings on Sensitivity

THE FOURTH GURU — The Moth
THE LESSON — heedfulness

*The moth was an apt teacher, O Prince, for from
its actions I learned the nature of attraction,
both in a positive and in a negative sense. As the
moth hovers about the fire or flame, trying to merge
into it due to the powerful force of its attracting light,
so too should the devotee of the Lord rush unto the
Lord.*

*In another sense, though, one should not emulate
the moth's irresistible attraction for the flames. These
flames are like the worldly man's longing for
pleasures of the senses that would sap his energy
meant for the realization of the Atman and thus
bring about his ruin.*

As his friend Dharman had predicted and in keeping with his
own plans, Ekanta found himself moving across the rolling hills
which surrounded the city by late evening. In the distance he
could still see the looming gates he had left behind, now almost
imperceptible to the eye and he could barely detect the many
lights burning there in the houses and shops of the denizens of
that gathering place. He knew that Dharman and Swami Advaita-

nanda were also still there and he saluted them profoundly before turning his back and walking on.

He had made a swift passage through the city, his only detainment being the appearance of a courtesan who, until she could make out his features, had approached him to solicit his attentions. When she saw who it was she quickly and apologetically saluted him and withdrew. He wondered at the condition of such a life but, as usual, his thoughts were entirely devoid of judgment and full of concern.

At the gates of the great city he had stopped to have a few words with the night watchmen. They had offered him a smoke, thinking him to be one of the ordinary sadhus who passed by at night, but he good-naturedly refused and spent some minutes conversing with them instead. They had found him very amiable and even offered him a meal and a place to sleep. Soon, he excused himself and slipped off into the night, a single solitary figure with apparently nowhere to go and nothing to do. After he had gone, the two night watchmen lamented that such a nice man could be so forlorn and lonely, without home and family and bereft of purpose.

Unlike some other sadhus, though, who gave up the world due to laziness, aversion and a whole host of other reasons, the Avadhut's renunciation was mature. His was an identification with and a deep love for Reality that simply accepted nothing less than the Absolute. He had made his choice to know and dwell in this ultimate condition early on and had never regretted that decision. After wandering away from home, family, friends and even his revered gurus, Ekanta had headed straight for the Himalayas, intent on getting the darshan of Lord Shiva there.

What he received during this period of travel was much more than just a temporary darshan of the Lord. After two years of wandering as a reclusive sadhu and somewhere around his twenty-fourth birthday, he came across a group of renunciates known as Avadhuts who had amidst their numbers an old and venerable teacher. Having heard wonderful things about them from his vanaprastin teachers, Ekanta decided that this was his destiny in the making and kept company with them for a time, eventually taking initiation into their order.

The entire series of events leading up to his meeting with this ascetic order had been fortuitous. After leaving the sacred mountains, he reached the plains of central India.  There, while filling his water skin at a lonely desert pool, a naked sadhu approached him.  After conversing for a time, the sadhu asked him to come to his campsite where others of his order were observing austerities for an extended period.  Ekanta, young, unkempt and wild looking, fit in well with the group, having just come down from the mountains where he had stoically endured extremely cold temperatures.  Applying some healing balm to his frostbite wounds, the leader engaged Ekanta in conversation and the two became fast friends.

Realizing the unique character of this young luminary, far beyond the level of awareness of even his brightest followers, the leader of the Avadhut order asked Ekanta to join them in three weeks of austerity.  Feeling the Divine call in this, Ekanta plunged into an intense sadhana period with the group of sadhus and experienced several days of deep samadhi as a result.  Perceiving definite signs of profound insight mixed with ecstasy in the young aspirant, the Avadhut leader arranged an initiation ceremony one midnight and conferred authentic and formal sannyas upon Ekanta while he was still in partial samadhi.  Both guru and disciple experienced powerful awakenings due to the intensity of the ritual and all felt the palpable presence of God during the ceremony.

Emerging from the effects of the samadhi after the initiation, Ekanta looked at the leader and said haltingly, "How am I changed?"

*"All change has come to an end,"* replied the old Avadhut.  *"You have given it back to Mother.  It is now only an external show, a mirage performing its many colorful tricks in front of you.  Never again will you suffer from it, act upon it or truly believe in it.  It will dance around you — the center, the living Shivalingam.  You will not dance in it or due to it anymore.  All is fullness now."*

After saying this, the old Avadhut chanted:

> *Kevala–tattva–niranajana–sarvam*
> *Gaganakara–nirantara–shuddham*
> *Evam katham iha sanga–visangam*
> *Satyam katham iha ranga–virangam*

Behold the Truth, resplendent and ever immaculate,
impervious to even the idea of impurity,
of the form of formlessness, like the boundless skies.
Where is involvement, where uninvolvement?
Indeed, how can there be sport or its absence?

"I declare thee the Avadhut, young man, ever-pure and ever-free," stated the elder after his chant was concluded. "This is the ultimate station in life for you and from here, due to your consummate training and your strong endeavor, you will be a blessing on the world. Indeed, life and death in the ordinary sense are dead to you. The myth of evolution has been exposed. It is now naked, like all of us. There is only perpetual existence now, inherently complete and of the nature of blessedness. Repeat after me:"

Asha–pasha vinirmuktah adi–madhyanta–nirmalah
Anande vartate nityam akaram tasya lakshanam
Vashana varjita yena vaktavyam cha niramayam
Vartamaneshu varteta vakaram tasya lakshanam
Dhuli–dushara–gatrani dhuta–chitto niramayah
Dharana–dhyana–nirmukto dhukaras tasya lakshanam
Tattva–chinta dhrta yena chinta–chesta–vivartijah
Tamo'hankara–nirmuktah takaras tasya lakshanam

Ekanta repeated the preceptor's words. Then, the elder Avadhut came close to Ekanta and whispered the meaning into the young Avadhut's right ear:

"The letter 'A' in Avadhut, came the teaching, "signifies your freedom from all bondage and further indicates that you are completely pure in the beginning, the middle and the end, as all these three are one.

"The syllable 'va' in Avadhut is meant to convey that all desires have been fully renounced. Also, that thought, word and deed are all perfect and unified and manifest only in the eternal present.

"The syllable 'dhu' in Avadhut represents dust, which is the only clothing of the Avadhut. It further symbolizes one of perfect health, who is not dependent on anything external and who *has no further need for practices such as concentration and meditation.*

*"The syllable 'ta' in Avadhut affirms that such a one is reliant only upon Truth, whose only thought is of Truth and is therefore free of ignorance and egotism forever. I now pronounce you of our order — an Avadhut."*

As these memories flooded through his consciousness, the Avadhut hiked until he could no longer see or hear any trace of humanity. Then he looked for a good place to spend the night. A high, grassy knoll provided that space and he gratefully took his seat and gazed up at the stars. Here was a teaching, he thought. Always manifest, but apparently disappearing at the approach of daylight, they all seemed to cry out to humanity that God was ever-present, even though the puzzling presence of Maya shrouded that august Being. If beings would only sit, wait and contemplate the existence of the Supreme Being, the distorting and obscuring powers of Maya would gradually fall away to reveal this Eternal Verity. Was not such a vision worth waiting and striving for?

Ekanta shivered in the cold of the evening. He stood up to search for firewood and was soon rewarded with a scattered supply of it in a nearby wooded area. Striking a spark was a considerably harder task, but by repeated efforts he ignited the paper he had carried with him from the city and was soon basking in the warmth of a small fire. Constancy, he thought. All comes to the one who perseveres. Thinking about that wonderful quality, he recalled the teachings of his Mataji regarding what she often referred to as "the three p's." Sitting up straight and drawing close to the soothing fire, he gazed into the night heavens and listened to her inspiring voice once again:

*"Purity, perseverance, and patience, what could ever thwart the sincere aspirant who has possession of these three attributes, Ekanta? Purity and innocence come hand-in-hand, and provide the seeker with a natural protection against all manner of ills. Like an undisturbed field of pristine, white snow in a high and inaccessible Himalayan meadow, the devotee invested with purity naturally radiates the spontaneous presence of the Lord. Such a one will easily bypass the troublesome impediments encountered in sadhana when they arise. Problems will either simply fail to materialize or will disintegrate in*

*that guiltless and worry-free atmosphere. In addition, various virtues, like healthy plants, will sprout and grow swiftly in the soil of purity, turning a potential wasteland into an aromatic garden. Once virtues are developed, there will be no failing or falling off."*

Ekanta waited for a few moments while the Mataji contemplated her next subject. It was not long before she continued on:

*"Though spiritual life is full of wonders after the early struggles and triumphs have occurred, it is still a long ascent to reach the mountaintop of nondual realization. After impediments have been destroyed, the devotee comes to know that there is an endless expanse of experience to be gleaned that will add to the individual storehouse of subtle power needed to realize the Atman. At this stage, a certain tenacity combined with watchfulness becomes necessary to ward off the complacency of merely resting on one's past attainments. This is called perseverance and it means not only bearing with circumstances, although that is helpful at times, but is also intrinsically intertwined with inner strength and deep insight so that as one maintains ground in spiritual life, additional growth in subtle areas will continue.*

*"What is more, the quality of perseverance insures that no pessimistic or fatalistic tendencies, should they arise, will be allowed to spoil the progress already made along the path. Giving up before the goal is reached, or even slackening one's pace in the interim, are both attendant dangers in ongoing sadhana and should be guarded against. Whatever the degree of attainment, though, and whatever the speed of attainment, perseverance will guarantee an eventual arrival at that which all sincere spiritual aspirants seek, either knowingly or unknowingly.*

*"As a necessary prerequisite to both purity and perseverance, dear boy,"* the Mataji continued, *"patience is invaluable. I have seen many well-formulated and successful assaults on higher realization stymied and waylaid by anger, depression and other forms of weakness. Patience is actually strength, though of an inner variety, and will stand one in good stead throughout all the variations and ups and downs of self-effort. On a more nondual note, patience is truly the Mother's Grace shining upon us and She fortifies us with it so that our strivings will bear fruit*

*and result in culminative successes and ultimate victory.  So have patience with yourself, Ekanta, but do not compromise your spiritual efforts by mistaking complacency for patience. The two are vastly different, one being a friend of weakness and the other being a form of strength itself."*

"Mataji," the young man had asked at this point, "you began this talk with the quality of purity.  That quality and its benefits has always seemed obvious to me.  Is it just simple or am I missing something or overlooking something about it?"

*"Its simplicity makes it subtle and easy to overlook,"* replied the Mataji. *"In your case, purity is an attribute that has been developed in you over past lifetimes and now has become a part of your inner nature.  However, there is more to tell about it according to the scriptures.  Listen well.*

*"There are basically three purities that we need to be aware of: purity of place or object, purity of action, and purity of thought — called Dravya, Kriya and Chitta Shuddha respectively.  The first, Dravya, corresponding to purity of place and object, concerns external things and locations.  Where we go and the objects we come in contact with in those vicinities must be pure, must be clean.  Place and object tend to reflect the way in which they are perceived and treated, just like a living thing. Disregard and indiscriminate behavior and attitude towards the earth and its objects darkens the vibrations associated with them.  Physical bodies, for example, are objects.  Are we to treat them disrespectfully?  Divinity dwells within them, as it were, and will be brought to the surface for all to appreciate through loving kindness.  Thus you see my point.*

*"It will become increasingly obvious as I speak, Ekanta, that all three purities are interconnected.  Kriya Shuddha, indicating one's actions in the world, concern what I just said about places and objects.  Each motion, every movement inside of this relative world must be considered from an intelligent and sensitive perspective.  How difficult this is in this day and age as people rush about performing any and all kinds of activities — most for the sake of selfish reasons.  On the other hand, how wonderful is the well-considered and perfectly worked out plan of action.  The art of contemplation has been lost to the peoples of this age, Ekanta.  There was a time when beings would not*

*venture out of their habitations until they had considered the consequences of their actions carefully. Now, it is all thrown to the winds of chance and the powers that be, those powers being intermingled and often conflicting karmas.*

*"These first two shuddhas are relatively easy to attain, my dear," said the Mataji, "but the third, Chitta Shuddha, is difficult of access. That is why it is so treasured among the wise. A pure mind, according to some, is tantamount to a God-aware state. If one's consciousness be pure, free of passions, desires and crookedness, it is just like living with God, in God. Obversely speaking, the Lord loves to come to rest in such a vehicle. But as I said, it is hard to free the mind of all impurities, which seem to surface even after one undergoes the most exacting cleansing process. Still, the benefits of even a little of this kind of internal work are far-reaching and satisfying, giving rise to periods of peace and contentment. In fact, peace, a fourth 'p,' is the welcome result of Chitta Shuddha. Strive hard to attain it, Ekanta. There is hardly any more wonderful possession on the face of this earth."*

Becoming aware of the outer world again, it was not long before Ekanta sensed a few curious eyes fixed upon him. These night visitors were not uncommon and he had gotten used to their appearances. A deer glided by outside of the periphery of the firelight and it was soon followed by a few others. One even drew up closer to the fire and looked at him, as if it wanted to be near a human being, or perhaps it was mesmerized by the fire. It was just this sort of curiosity that got deer into trouble, Ekanta remembered. In the nearby trees, where he had gathered wood in the dark, an owl occasionally sounded off, sending its eerie call into the evening stillness. Around his scanty belongings, two mice played and looked for food, scurrying about and remaining stationary in turns, as if frozen in fear at the advance of a predator. Ekanta fed them a few crumbs of the bread he had received as alms in the city and they took it straight from his hand, knowing no fear whatsoever in his presence.

After partaking of the prasad, sanctified food offered to the Goddess, the Avadhut sat for meditation and was soon soaring high in his own pristine awareness. After an indeterminable time had elapsed, a sound called him out of his meditation. As he opened his eyes, he noticed that a large luna moth was darting and diving around him, attracted by the light of his fire. At first he thought that it was a bat, one of the small variety of fruit bats that frequented the area feeding on various fruits. But on closer inspection he noticed the exquisite markings on the moth's wings which formed a beautiful design. It seemed to have a phosphorescent glow to it as well and its small eyes glowed a luminous green when the firelight caught them just right.

The moth was of the type that were somewhat rare, for its size put it apart from other moths. Its wingspan reached at least ten inches and it was easily bigger than a man's hand. Ekanta remembered seeing one in a distant village one night long ago that was a foot-and-a-half wide. Its size had caused a stir and the children had all come out of their huts and chased it around the bonfire which had attracted it. At that size and at first sight, it resembled a large bird rather than an insect.

As the Avadhut watched, he felt that blissful feeling return to him that he had experienced several nights previous. A powerful teaching was coming upon him and he felt that the Divine Mother was preparing him for it. Suddenly, the moth made a particularly radical dive and actually entered the fire for a few moments, singeing its wings and scattering sparks everywhere. Ekanta felt a thrill of bliss mingled with alarm and remorse as he watched to see how the moth would recover. The huge moth arced into the air again and continued its aerial dynamics about the fire. It was as if its body was of no consequence compared to the thrill it received from merging into the flames. Seeing it sport about the fire like that, attracted by the light, Ekanta was immediately drawn inward towards profound teachings given to him in the past:

*"Always contemplate the pure mind and its immersion into Brahman, Ekanta,"* said the Mataji one evening. *"Like the moth around a fire, the jiva, or embodied being, longs to merge into the light of pure Consciousness, but its embodied condition as well as its mental limitations keep that from occurring. The mind, attracted towards the objects of the senses, places many barriers in the way of this absorption. It is like the paper kites that you have seen and played with as a boy, Ekanta. They become airborne so swiftly and float aloft in the sky high above*

*the earth, but occasionally a heavy downward draft of wind drives them from their position and smashes them into the earth. Such is the condition of the awakening human being, too, who in a natural state, remains poised in spiritual bliss but, who, on account of encountering the vicissitudes of this world and the latent karmas of the subconscious mind, falls from that elevated plateau and suffers."*

To enter the world of relativity is at once a great danger and a mystical journey, thought Ekanta. A few lines from the song of a Bengali poet-saint came to mind:

> Smiling your transcendent smile, O Mother,
> you bade me descend into the worlds below,
> but not before giving me a profound wink.

This "wink," Ekanta knew, was meant to convey that wayfarers on this earthly plane of existence should never, under any circumstances, forget their point of origin and fall under the delusion that they are mere physical beings. They must always remember that the earth is not their true or permanent abode. The words of Yogindra Yogi came to mind in this regard:

*"One should bear with the trials and tribulations of this earth, knowing them to be part of the divine plan, and remain firmly fixed in the inner Self, the Atman. Remember the ancient scriptures, Ekanta: 'Abiding ever in the light of pure Consciousness, the Atman dwells in its own pristine nature, free from the impositions of name, form and false identity and liberated from the mind's conceptualization of time, space and causation.'"*

As if in response to this Sanskrit sloka, the huge moth abruptly executed a spiral dive and entered the flames again, hitting the coals so hard that several pieces of wood sprang from the fireplace and landed several feet away. Before Ekanta could move and try to save the moth from a fiery death, it lifted itself out of the flames and, streaming sparks like some wounded air-born craft on fire, flew off into the darkness of the evening.

This new sequence of events threw Ekanta's mind into a different vein and teachings concerning Maya and its illusory effects began to surface. Seeing the powerful attraction of the moth for the hazardous flames and the detrimental effects and outcome of its careless actions brought a whole host of memories to the forefront of his mind.  Yogindra Yogi, the mountain holy man, had taught him, at Ekanta's request, many lessons from the ancient scriptures of the Universal Mother.

"What is the nature of Maya," he had asked guilelessly one night, "and how does it exercise so much power over human beings?"

*"Why, Maya is of its own nature,"* retorted the yogi, *"and no one can truly explain what that is. Even the scriptures are helpless to explain fully."*

"What do the scriptures tell us about this illusive power?" Ekanta asked.

The yogi entered a deep silence for a time, then he began to chant aloud, his voice echoing through the cold air of the dark mountain cave:

> Listen, O lover of Truth, thou who will drink no other elixir
> than the powerful, relativity-destroying liquid of immortality.
> The great Vedavyasa proclaims,
> that the entire cosmos of sentient and insentient beings,
> resting on the support of the three worlds,
> is comprised entirely of Maya.
> The master of this power,
> Who is also the pure Consciousness of Brahman,
> is Bhuvaneshvari, the Supreme Lady of all the worlds
> known as Mahavidya Mahamaya Bhagavati Durga Devi
> and by other profound and exceedingly beautiful names.
> As a master puppeteer magically makes wooden dolls move
> according to his own sweet will by use of invisible strings,
> so too does the Divine Mother's Maya,
> consisting of the triple gunas of tamas, rajas, and sattvas —
> stupidity, avariciousness and peacefulness —
> cause the entire world and its living beings
> to dance according to Her design.
> As a cloth cannot exist without thread,
> as a pot cannot exist without clay,
> living things cannot live without the three gunas.
> This is Her will, Her play, and none can doubt or change it.

This had been Ekanta's first real encounter with the scriptures of the Goddess, since few beings, even among the holy and illumined, were well-versed in them. This was due, he later found out, to the enigmatic nature of the Goddess and Her esoteric wisdom. Her teachings and presence, both, were held in such high regard, such reverent esteem, that none would venture to describe or converse about them. This had impressed him completely and being the unique character who he was by nature, he had secretly vowed within himself to spend his entire life and any lifetimes after that in the pursuit of Her teachings and Her Grace.

After the chant had died away, while the holy man remained poised in some deep reverie, Ekanta had asked, "What about the gods, the goddesses and the illumined and liberated souls? What happens to them under the influence of Maya?"

*"In the Srimad Devi Bhagavatam,"* came the reply, *"Vedavyasa has stated:"*

> All embodied beings, whether they be of earth,
> heaven or the higher worlds, labor under this Maya.
> No one works independently of It.
> Shiva is pleasant when He is blessed by Her sattvas,
> but when She moves Him to tamas He becomes Rudra,
> the power of awful destruction itself.
> Brahma creates under a sattvic influence with joy
> and creative spontaneity,
> but when She shoots Him with dark tamas
> he mourns and forgets his mighty powers.

Ekanta had sat stock still, stunned to hear this message. What simple and natural sense it contained. Later, when he meditated on the day's discourses and teachings which was his evening habit, he clearly saw that there had to be some reason for what is unreasonable in this universe. So many perplexing things were occurring constantly and all seemed helpless to prevent them. Even the wise seldom knew what was going to happen next. Thoughts such as these prompted him to formulate certain questions for the yogi the very next day.

"Revered sir," he began, after saluting his monastic guru with a full prostration, "how does one escape this enchanting power of delusion? There must be a way. Otherwise, where is the point to all this suffering and confusion?"

*"Right you are, my boy,"* said the yogi. *"You are an extremely bright and worthy student. To answer you, Vedavyasa prescribes intense concentration on the Devi Herself. In the Srimad Devi Bhagavatam, he says:*

*'Know, all thee lovers of the Supreme Truth, that if anyone can effectively fix their hearts and minds on the highest Devi — the Samvit — Her Maya, born of a perplexing mixture of what is Real and unreal, will recede as a matter of course and revelation of a transcendent nature will come upon them. No harm or delusion will then ever befall them. This darkness of the gunas, none can destroy besides Her. The light of the sun, the moon, of fire or even of astute individual intelligence — all are powerless to dispense with it. Therefore, with a cheerful heart and a mind completely surrendered at Her Feet, worship the Devi Bhagavati with all your being. She Herself will then remove the debilitating effects of the triple gunas and free you from the darkness of ignorance.'"*

In the light of these teachings and while recalling them from his past, the Avadhut again thought of the moth. Another lesson the moth had taught him came to mind. He had been attending an agni-hotra celebration in his village one evening and was sitting by the large bonfire afterwards. Most of the townspeople had retired to bed. The fire was situated near the great wall of the town's most prominent shop. As Ekanta watched the fire, he began to notice the shadows it was causing on the nearby wall. These in turn, led him to notice the many lizards that had climbed up the wall in search of moths that were attracted by the reflected light. The lizards were having a feast and Ekanta could not help but compare these moths to the many deluded souls who were inexorably attracted to mundane attractions such as found in nature and conventional human existence. Like these moths on the wall, such beings exposed themselves to many dangers at every moment of their precarious existence, being without the protection that spiritual practice afforded.

As Ekanta watched this small drama, a large moth, too big for a lizard to swallow, landed on the wall. The lizards, attracted by the flapping of its huge wings, immediately rushed towards it.

Upon drawing near, however, they drew back as if in awe or fear and left the newcomer alone, returning to their search for smaller and more easily manageable fare. It was then that Ekanta thought of another way to defeat Maya. Whereas most aspirants followed the path of becoming minute so that Maya could not find them, some grew so tremendously large that Maya simply could not handle them. Slipping through the tiny holes in Maya's net or outgrowing the net entirely, these were two solutions to the problem. Primarily though, he surmised, one had to become aware of the presence of Maya to begin with.

After Yogindra Yogi had transmitted the Mother Wisdom to Ekanta on that occasion, both he and the boy shed profuse tears from the corners of their eyes. The holy man simply could not speak any more and after a half an hour had passed, Ekanta took his leave after bowing low in reverence. From that day forth, Ekanta was in possession of a new ideal and he often thought back on that evening, knowing it to be a major turning point in his own spiritual evolution. He had also gone back to the cave of the yogi several times to inquire further into the mysteries of the Goddess. He had then found out who She was and had begun to think of Her as the Divine Mother of the Universe, for this was what the yogi often called Her. What he learned of Her changed his life forever.

One evening, as the two emerged from the cave to behold the stars sparkling overhead, the yogi bestowed another rich experience on him. Ekanta, after some reflection, had inquired reverently for some more information about the Devi, knowing that the yogi might not give it due to his need for a certain special mood in order to speak of Her.

Considering Ekanta's request, the yogi said, *"Last week, my boy, due to your pressing questions, I nearly left my body for good. What you prompted in me by thinking so profoundly on the supreme Goddess kept me in a high state for the entire night. I had the utmost difficulty in retaining body consciousness, even by the morning light. Therefore, you are a wonderful rascal, I deem, sent by Her to elevate me beyond my present spiritual position."*

Laughing mischievously and knowing that the yogi had evidently enjoyed his high state, even if it had been precariously elevated, Ekanta teased, "Revered sir, previously I understood that you had no fear of leaving the body."

Raising his eyebrows and fixing the boy with a serious gaze, the enlightened man feigned a mood of aggravation and said, *"May I be around when you experience such moods so that I can drive your mind into unimagined heights. Then we shall see how you fare."*

The two exploded into side-splitting laughter and the outlying wooded areas reverberated with these sounds, much to the amazement of the creatures living there. Later, when the mood had again become deep and indrawn, the yogi began to answer Ekanta's earlier question.

*"What do you want to know then, my son?"* he asked.

There was a pregnant silence. Finally, Ekanta was able to formulate his question.

"Who is She?" came the boy's tearful reply. "How can I know Her?"

*"The first question is impossible to answer,"* said the yogi directly, *"though you can consult what the scriptures say and strive for direct perception of Her in meditation. As to the second question, you know that already. Follow implicitly the instructions of your guru without flagging for as long as it takes you to develop a relationship with Her. Keep holy company, renounce the company of the worldly-minded and shun evil company. Offer all of your actions, thoughts and aspirations to Her in a spirit of complete detachment and absolute self-surrender and above all, love Her with all your heart. She is irresistibly drawn to pure love and adamantine devotion."*

"Are there any references to Her with regards to Her direct intervention in the affairs of humanity?" asked the boy. "Has She ever spoken to us and, if so, what is the nature of Her transmission?"

The yogi continued to adeptly field Ekanta's perspicacious questions in a masterful way.

*"She intervenes in the lives of humans but rarely and even then only in times of great need or during a profound sacrifice. She seems to love the atmosphere of striving and struggle, even chaos and the like, and dotes on challenges. It is said that She makes the impossible possible, like harmonizing contrasting pairs of opposite forces. In short, She is a complete enigma. But let us see what the scriptures have to say about Her mode*

*of communication."*

Saying so, the holy man went to fetch a large book, one of the very few he kept near him, and began to flip through its pages.

*"Of course, when She talks to the illumined beings it may be in the form of a type of communication that is transcendent of words — an intimate subtle message, as it were, received by the intuition. In the scriptures, however, when She talks to the gods, we get an interpretation of that transmission in understandable language."*

The yogi then quoted a passage from the Srimad Devi Bhagavatam for Ekanta, who sat totally engaged and fully focused.

> I am the indeterminable One, known only in part
> to the precious spiritual children who take refuge in Me
> and who surrender all individual considerations.
> I am birthless and deathless and so being,
> I am eternal and all-pervasive.
> Though I am formless in essence,
> I take forms for the purpose of sportive existence
> and it is My power alone that creates, preserves
> and destroys the worlds.
> I dispense justice in my creation
> and mete out retribution for injustice as well,
> for to preserve virtue and religion is my intention.
> I desire nothing, need nothing
> and have no enmity for any living being.
> The many avataras, all of one Essence,
> take births by my bidding
> and perform all actions under my supervision.

"Those are profound words," said Ekanta. "Is there anything relating to Her Wisdom that is written?"

*"All that is written is Her Wisdom, either higher or lower as the subdivision falls,"* responded the yogi. *"However, here are some of my favorite excerpts which go deeper and will no doubt satisfy you more fully:"*

> Hear Ye Immortals, declared the Supreme Devi.
> Before the creation, I alone existed in My formless Essence

called Chit, Samvit, Parabrahman and others.
The Atman is My essence, too, beyond mind or mentation,
transcendent of name, form and all transformations.
I am Nirguna, but when I am united with My shakti power
I become Saguna and cause the worlds to appear.
This Maya is also My power, divided into two,
called vidya and avidya.
Vidya liberates whereas avidya creates.
When My Maya mingles with intelligence,
it forms the efficient cause of the Universe,
whereas when My Maya gets united with the five elements
it becomes the material cause for the Universe.

Stopping his reading, the yogi said, *"You will have to read this, my boy. It makes an excellent study, besides being extremely informative and revealing of our Divine Mother."*

"Yes," Ekanta agreed, "there is much I have to do in the way of study. I will speak to my father tonight in order that I may acquire some of the holy texts and begin this part of my training."

*"Well done,"* said the holy man. *"Such a journey, mixed with your excellent resolve, will result in all manner of blessings upon you. There can be no doubt of this, for myself and many others that I know have had our minds enlightened by similar exercises. God speed to you, dear boy, in this undertaking."*

Ekanta had made good on his vow. From that day forth his mind had remained immersed in various holy books and he had never regretted it. Along the way, he had met beings who looked down on book learning and who considered knowledge to be unimportant as a spiritual pathway. His guru had mentioned this stunted approach to him before:

*"There are beings who hold a rather foggy notion that love and devotional exercises are all that are needed for spiritual life, Ekanta. This depends on the quality of the devotee, for most of those who are critical of the wisdom path are very shallow and unable to exercise the deeper powers of their intellects. They probably have never attempted to engender higher knowledge in themselves. Their so-called love for the Divine Being proves time and time again to be extremely conditional, for they did not possess the realization that comes from a strong and well-rounded*

*sadhana based in Jnana Yoga. Therefore, when trials and chal-
lenges come their way, and this is unavoidable in terrestrial
existence as well as in spiritual life, they are about as strong
as leaves blown before the onrush of a hurricane. In most cases
they resort to pitiable pleading and the offering of ineffectual
prayers, whimpering and wallowing in their weakness and their
misery."*

To Ekanta, what was required for success in spiritual life was
obvious. Even with his natural ability in this area, however, he
had needed to have things clarified on many occasions and inten-
sification of spiritual life was always an ongoing consideration of
utmost importance to him. *"The two wings of a bird —"* that
phrase occurred to his mind over and over again. Thinking of it
again prompted more memories of his teachers:

*"Bhakti and jnana, devotion and wisdom, Ekanta, these are
an unbeatable combination. No obstacle in existence is able to
resist them when they are united and utilized properly. Yet,
even knowing this and being told time and time again by the
guru, beings either overlook, ignore or refuse to acknowledge this
supreme way, opting instead to take all sorts of time-consuming
detours fraught with innumerable dangers. These avenues only
appear to be short-cuts, that strange phenomenon which is so
attractive to the peoples of this day and age, when in actuality
they are often dead-ends, requiring extra time and energy to
backtrack. Such are the dictates of bad habit, however. Few ever
listen or take heed."*

This teaching reminded Ekanta of a story that an Islamic trader
had once told him as he had passed through the village on the way
to Central India. The man possessed a few camels, which were
rare in Ekanta's part of the country, and when the boy asked about
them the trader laughed and described them as being stupid and
stubborn.

"Once," said the trader, "I was crossing a desert that was hedged
around by several mountain ranges. My camel train had been
across these flats many times in the past and the animals knew
the way by heart. Even in a sandstorm, I could rely upon their
instincts to guide me in this matter completely. On this particular occasion, I met another trader, unknown to me, who informed
me that I could reduce my travel time by several days by taking

a particular mountain pass, also unknown to me, that skirted a significant part of the desert tract.

"Needless to say, I was eager to give it a try and as I drew near the turning point described to me by the trader and marked on a map that he had fashioned for me, I attempted to turn in that direction. The camels, however, having developed a habit of going the old way, remained fixed on the old path and nothing I could do would dissuade them from following it. In the end, I was relegated to the old path and was therefore unable to discover for myself this new and better route."

To Ekanta, this humorous yet frustrating story epitomized people's attachment and their penchant for outmoded ways of doing things, both in worldly and in spiritual life. What a shame, he thought, that heedlessness and lack of sensitivity and lack of open-mindedness resulted in such narrowness.

So many times and at so many locations, Ekanta had been witness to the reckless deeds of human beings. What seemed astounding was that, despite powerful negative repercussions, people continued to perform similar acts and inevitably suffered the consequences, never attempting to correct or neutralize the root of their problems. Such behavior was mind-boggling to Ekanta, but he had finally given up and accepted that this was the way of the worldly-minded. They grieved and suffered in exact proportion to the extent that they rejoiced and enjoyed. As long as they were content with that exchange then who was he to try to change them?

The Avadhut, however, was not into compromise. Nor was he one to torture the indwelling Spirit within him, for he knew that the presence of God dwelled inside of all human beings. That sacred presence was, no doubt, greatly hampered in its natural flow by the congestion of limitations, bad habits and misconceptions that living beings placed in the way, but nevertheless, the all-pervasive Atman resided within them. He remembered Yogindra Yogi's oft-repeated words in this regard:

*"To become conscious of God is to have God become conscious of you."*

This law of divine attraction was, at least in the terrestrial world, the only way of securing a relationship with the Lord, for He would not make Himself known without the sacrifice of the lower self and the giving up of petty things that it was attached to.

This was the meaning behind the sacred symbology of Mother Kali and the severed heads She carried, his teachers had told him. An offering to the Goddess of all lesser considerations and a willingness to rise out of the depraved and constricted condition of worldly life constituted the classic way of transcendence in spiritual life. Then, and only then would the true purpose of life be revealed and the divine status of humanity be remembered. As the Upanishads declared:

> To the spiritually illumined comes Peace sublime.
> None else have access.

The Avadhut moved a little closer to the fire in order to stoke the coals. Piling a few more small pieces of wood on it, he recollected his travels through Tibet where he had met and communed with many of the holy beings that frequented that country. The Buddhists were particularly oriented to the teaching of heedfulness or mindfulness. Their sensitivity in this regard was refreshing and Ekanta had enjoyed the care with which they treated each other and the reverence they had for spiritual teachings. Such subtlety could well be wished upon the minds of men and women of the world so that the earth could be a place of joy and happiness. If the moth, for instance, was more mindful of the dangers of his predicament, he could enjoy the fire's glimmer and radiance without experiencing such negative results. The words of his teacher regarding heedfulness came into his mind at that moment and he let himself dwell on their profound meaning.

*"The worldly mind finds all manner of reason to brood. This tendency has to be destroyed or transcended. The brooding mind must be turned into thinking mind and the thinking mind transformed into illumined mind. The entire process proceeds through sensitivity and self-effort. What is callous, crass, base and banal must be remade into more subtle material. Uncaring thoughts and feelings must be identified as being born from selfishness. Removing selfishness from the mind, however difficult it may be, is not enough. One must replace it with generosity and compassion. Likewise, after removing other negativities from the heart and mind, one must proceed to install divine*

*virtues in their place, one by one. Writing a book begins with the formulation of the first sentence. One must begin, a start must be made. Be up and doing, for the world will not tolerate slackers and weaklings."*

This small but intense set of teachings had come to Ekanta as a young student in the form of a scolding. His teachers and his parents had not been easy on him, though he seldom gave them reason to complain or scold. In the case of the people of the world, however, much hard work and attention to detail was necessary before higher spiritual truths could dawn upon their minds.

*"If the teachings and the guru are not consulted, Ekanta,"* came the advice one day, *"and this with an attitude of reverence, then the many obstacles to spiritual attainment will prove too difficult for most seekers and the pursuit of Truth will be abandoned. In addition, the aspirant must not merely consult the teacher, must not merely hear of the existence of God, must not just speculate on one's inner perfection. The seeker must also take sometimes drastic steps to realize what the guru and the scriptures reveal and epitomize."*

The huge luna moth, then, taught the Avadhut a fine lesson. The need for heedfulness or mindfulness was crucial to the process of spiritual awakening. As he ran through the teachings in his mind, Ekanta remembered the list his guru had given him for future reference:

*"First, dearest disciple, one must be sensitive to one's own inner voice, which is the Blessed Lord's own presence attempting to manifest in the human mind. Secondly, an openness to the words of the teacher and a healthy reliance on the timeless message of the scriptures are essential, for one must listen to the wisdom of those who have gone before and are enlightened about the path. Third, a type of sensitivity that acts as a safeguard against the impositions and intrusions of Maya is indispensable. Like a sleepless sentinel always on guard, Ekanta, this powerful discrimination is the quality of mindfulness operating in a practical mode. Finally, a sensitivity to the suffering and needs of others completes the list, for maturity along the spiritual path is demonstrated by the manifestation of realization in action. This is a sorely missed element in the contemporary spiritual life of the world."*

Thinking about this formula, the Avadhut began to consider the different kinds of people he had met. There were the worldly-minded beings he had known. For the most part, they were selfish and devoid of higher attainments. The scriptures called them "nonentities" and from the ultimate standpoint, Ekanta believed this to be an adequate summation.

*"They have no belief in a higher existence and prefer sense life instead,"* stated his guru, *"despite the many obvious proofs all around them and an entire expanse of wisdom teachings to rely on for elucidation. They are generally hapless beings who give their life energy to physical existence and marry their minds to work and to nature. The spiritual law, Ekanta, which the illumined declare, is that the mind's precious consciousness becomes what it concentrates upon. Affirming one's identity with physical matter such as body, senses and nature is equal to spiritual suicide. The whole gamut of higher Truth simply remains out of reach in this case. Rebirth in the basic mode of relativity, characterized by cyclic rounds of mundane habit and convention and attended by alternating cycles of superficial happiness and continual suffering is the agonizing result."*

His gurus had informed him of the distinctions between various levels of seekers as well.

*"Among striving and illumined beings, Ekanta, there are some interesting categories. The first group are those who have only an intellectual grasp of the teachings but who have not yet put them into practice. Among this group, there are some who are satisfied with this particular level of experience and have no desire to go forward. Possibly, they consider themselves to be enlightened.*

*"There is a higher class than this, though, my son,"* said the guru, considering the subject further. *"There are beings in existence who have already reached the goal of human existence and are free from the detrimental effects of worldliness and absolved of all karmas. Their comprehension of the laws of the universe as well as their knowledge and conformity with the spiritual laws wielded by the Creator make them ideally fit for the experience of enlightenment. The trouble here is that many of these are possessed of a kind of spiritual selfishness or elitism that robs them of their opportunity to be of service to God's needy*

*creatures.*

"*Therefore,*" continued the guru, "*we cherish an ideal of realization combined with compassion and service. The old style of renunciation has become practically outmoded in the present day and age, except in rare cases, and a crying need for the manifestation of divine virtues in the world has become of paramount importance. What is needed, Ekanta, is more of that type of being who, whether they be fully perfected or not, can adopt strict measures in order to carry out a policy of education that is based upon spiritual values and which proceed upon practical guidelines. By feeding the hungry, for instance, providing for the weak and impoverished, supplying healing for the infirm and generally uplifting the masses while simultaneously and in proper course giving them the fundamental spiritual teachings which will transform them, a balance can once again be struck in the world.*

"*This policy, Ekanta, will not be possible until a change in human nature and in human outlook can be effected. Society must lose its selfish attachment to pleasures and possessions and begin to look around and notice the unfortunate condition of their brothers and sisters. Giving freely and without consideration for the base human tendencies of hoarding, storing up for the future and placing personal needs and desires above those of others is what is needed now. This can only be made clear to sleeping humanity if they become convinced that the Divine Being provides everything, unstintingly, to the peoples of the world and that since God is infinite, so too is His supply infinite, as is His love and His mercy. This process is based upon a type of sensitivity and heedfulness that transcends other approaches, for it perceives the abiding presence of the Blessed Lord in all beings and places all materials and benefits at the service of that all-pervasive Presence without regard for individual considerations.*"

The Avadhut sighed loud and long. His heart was pining for the Absolute while at the same time full of concern for the beings of the world. There was no fully satisfactory answer for the problems and the purpose of relative existence, nor was it his business, he had come to know, to try and invent one. The Divine Mother knew what She was doing and would take care of all matters pertinent to the universe of name and form. After all, even a human mother conceives of a newborn child in full knowledge of the conditions that it will be born into, including all the difficulties and imperfections of life. Still, this does not stop her from giving birth and watching over her children.

The Avadhut stretched and yawned. The evening's mental activities had taken him on a fine journey through some choice wisdom teachings. He knew that there was a boundless expanse of spiritual wisdom available to the aspiring mind and that it would take many lifetimes to fathom even a portion of it. As he lay down to rest his body, a timeless and profoundly significant chant crept softly into his memory:

*Purnamadah, purnamidam, purnat purna mudachyate*
*Purnasya, purnamidaya, purnameva vashishyate*

Laden with divine perfection is this phenomenal universe.
Saturated with incomparable excellence,
the infinite presence pervades it.
Both the comprehensible and incomprehensible
are exquisite and immaculate.
While one reveals the other, both retain
their inherent perfection.

With this wisdom chant coursing through his very being, the Avadhut pulled his wearing cloth high over his shoulders and slipped into the deep sleep of superconscious Awareness.

# — Chapter 5 —

# Teachings on Sensuality

THE FIFTH GURU —The Elephant
THE LESSON —Detachment from
Sense Objects

*From the elephant, I have learned that to be enamored with sense life alone is to court disaster. I also learned of the efficacy of holy company and the need for withdrawing from the atmosphere of the worldly-minded. I found that men and women of a discriminating character who are desirous of acquiring divine virtues and realizing their true nature, should avoid the locales and doings of beings whose concerns center upon earthly matters alone as well as who delude themselves with passionate and mundane preoccupations.*

The next morning, the Avadhut left the low-lying hills and headed in the direction of the road once again. His intent was to follow it as far as the mountains to the west and then skirt the mountains before entering Madhya Pradesh to visit a few holy sights. Then, he planned to turn south towards Kerala where he would pass the rainy season. The monsoons would soon be upon this region and he did not want to be present for that deluge.

Ekanta found the road a few miles outside of the city.   He headed west, away from the city, enjoying the countryside immensely.  Before going even a mile, however, he saw ahead of him a strange sight.  As he drew closer, he realized that a group of mahuts, elephants drivers, had stopped alongside the road at a bathing ghat located at a rather large lake.  Here, they were beginning the considerable chore of bathing their elephants.  Ekanta stopped to have a look at the huge beasts and to observe the process.

The elephants were covered with all manner of designs.  There were sacred symbols, symbols with worldly overtones and even some with political overtones, existing side by side without any special consideration.  The artists had taken much care in execution, though, using bright colors of every conceivable hue.  In a flash, Ekanta knew that these were the elephants that had carried the nobles and participants in the festive parade he witnessed from the door of Dharman's shop the day before.  Perhaps the very elephant that had borne the king and queen was present.  The mahuts probably brought them to this ideal lake outside the city in order to wash, feed and exercise them.

As the Avadhut watched this difficult task being undertaken, his mind drifted back to a time in the past when he had been on pilgrimage in the Himalayas.  Coming out of the mountains and entering the foothills of those most sacred of mountains, he  crossed the border over into northern Uttar Pradesh and unknowingly entered a wildlife sanctuary.  There, he suddenly came upon a group of wild elephants.  Due to his close proximity to the herd, the male elephant became anxious and thundered forth to protect the females.  The Avadhut stood stock-still and the male elephant, seeing no threat, withdrew.  The Avadhut, too, quickly drew back away from the herd and sat down at a distance to watch them.

The majestic creatures were associated with India in so many ways, mused Ekanta, and with its philosophy as well.  Ganapati, or Ganesha as He was more popularly known, was an elephant-headed god responsible for removing obstacles in one's spiritual path.  Good fortune and beneficial wisdom were his boons.  Unfortunately, the elephant was not always so wise, as Ekanta was about to find out.

Being in no particular hurry, Ekanta had followed the herd at a

distance throughout the day, observing their habits and mannerisms. Gradually, he skirted the behemoths and headed out in front
of their meandering pathway. After going about a mile, he noticed
what appeared to be a campsite ahead. Not wanting to encounter
anyone in this wild country where all sorts of temperamental types
were apt to gather, the Avadhut detoured to a small rise outside
the camp and climbed to the top, seating himself to observe the
countryside.

Soon, he became aware that there was no one at the campsite.
As he looked around, he noticed instead that there was movement
in the bushes nearby. As he looked more closely, he detected a
group of hunters crouched there, evidently waiting for the distant
herd of elephants to approach. It was not long before the lumbering giants came near the camp. Sensing the men, however, the
male elephant raised his ears and trumpeted loudly. Then, he led
the herd off in another direction.

The Avadhut was glad that the elephants were safe and watched
their hasty retreat with satisfaction. As he looked with gratifica-
tion upon the retreating herd, teachings from his Mataji came to
mind:

*"By sensing danger in advance, Ekanta, the aspirant treading
the spiritual path saves much wasted time and saves considerable suffering and grief as well. When beings act in day-to-day
life, they become habituated to a routine. This robs them of spontaneity and encourages the descent of complacency into their
lives. There are even those who have their daily routine perfected
and go on as if everything is under control. Such beings turn
the guna of rajas into a profession. What is missing in such a
condition is the art of nonaction, the ability to do nothing. The
Universal Mother wants us to cease and desist at times, to leave
off with all ego-centered preoccupation with schedules and personal concerns. She has important things to show us, to tell us,
but we thwart Her attempts to communicate by sticking inexorably to our own selfish ways. Therefore, my precious student,
learn to listen internally and pay heed to a higher prompting.
Dare to set your schedule by Her timepiece. The wise aspirant
must be flexible enough to deviate from the usual and conventional mode of progression at times in order to achieve his or
her own best good. Her guidance aside, this act alone, even*

*without Her instructions, often saves one from danger."*

Ekanta's happiness at the elephants' safe departure was short lived. The hunters had anticipated their actions. As he stood up to watch, he saw another group of hunters off to the west in the distance. This group had an elephant in tow with them and they had tied it to a stake in the ground and were waiting for the herd to advance.

With increasing clarity, the plan became apparent to Ekanta. He knew from his travels that elephant hunters, especially those who hunt for capture rather than for prize or sport, used female elephants whenever they desired to attract and trap a wild male. This was what was evidently going on now, for all contingencies seemed to be provided for and all the elements were in place.

Despite a growing sense of foreboding in the pit of his stomach, somewhere inside of Ekanta was a hope that the male elephant would be smart enough to avoid this trap as well. As he watched, the herd came closer to the domestic female staked directly in their path. When the male elephant saw the new female, he charged straight in its direction, stopping at a short distance to survey the situation. After a few moments, in which the big male saw no other male elephant around to return his challenge, it proceeded to draw closer to the bait.

The hunters waited no longer than necessary. What Ekanta saw next was out of sequence due to his distance from the scene. The male elephant suddenly toppled to the ground while a split second later the sound of a gun being fired could be heard. After that, some gun smoke rose in the air from the bush off to the west. The hunters had claimed their prize.

At first Ekanta mourned the death of this fine specimen, evidently taken for its ivory, but soon, as he observed the men gather around its body, he noticed that the elephant raised its head every now and again. With a feeling of conditional relief, the Avadhut realized that the mammal was only sedated and that the gun had contained a drugged dart. He remembered hearing about this from some sadhaks who had shared a dhuni fire with him one night. In the olden days, pits were dug or nets were cast from trees to entrap the elephants. Nowadays this new method — safer, less cumbersome and more effective — was being used.

As the day wore on, Ekanta watched the enslavement of the

wild male elephant take place. Short chains were fastened on its legs and stout ropes tied around its neck. The herd, now without a mature male to guide it, wandered off in haphazard fashion, available to any other regal male that happened along and survived the challenge of battle. The Avadhut had witnessed such a battle of the titans before. Fighting for supremacy over the herd, males would do battle and inflict great injury on one another for the sake of domination and satisfaction. This made Ekanta think of the great lessons taught to him by his gurus.

*"With a disoriented mind, the ego out of control and the body's desires as the foremost consideration, living beings impetuously rush to enjoy that which their senses deem to be fair taking. Without consideration for the consequences and failing to take heed of the needs of others or what is in keeping with dharma, this course of action brings untold agony, suffering and even danger to bear on human existence. What is more, Ekanta, such ill-considered actions meddle with the divinely intended order of things in a person's life, waylaying or deflecting the positive and auspicious events that are to come as a result of natural dharmic living. After enjoying the forbidden fruits of such way-ward deeds, people then experience the usual negative reper-cussions and complain bitterly, crying, 'Oh, where has this curse come from,' or 'What have I done to deserve this?'*

*"The end result of all such doings is bondage, Ekanta. Like the sense-driven elephant, surrounded by the net of captivity, plunged into the pit of despair and pierced with the arrows of remorse and suffering, human beings fall victim to the uncon-trollable desires of sensual appetites and seldom take recourse to spiritual disciplines. Sadhana, accomplished under the guid-ance of a guru who knows the essence of the scriptures, renders the mind and senses subject to a higher power which bestows peace, bliss, mastery and freedom."*

After a pause, as if to consider some hidden voice, Ekanta's female vanaprastin teacher had continued.

*"Though it is unfathomable, the Divine Mother's hand guides everything. She places all that we need within our grasp. The same rope that binds us can be wriggled out of and used to climb out of our prison hole. We can free ourselves or remain bound, and it is difficult to watch the folly of people if they remain*

*imprisoned. The individual can remedy this imbalanced situation. When beings finally tire of the world and its insubstantial enticements and cry out with a sincere plea for something higher, the Mother will take them in Her arms and reveal to them their destiny — their dharma or swadharma. This auspicious moment is a marvelous thing to experience and to behold."*

Returning to the present, the Avadhut gazed down upon the interesting scene below. One by one, the elephants were being led to the water where, with brushes attached to long bamboo poles, they were scrubbed from trunk to tail. It was quite a sight, for one elephant required the combined attention of five or six little brown men, who climbed like ants over the entire expanse of the huge animal. All the while, the elephant stood still and majestic, bearing this human swarm patiently and seeming to enjoy the experience as well. When all of the paint and dirt was washed from the animal's body, it was led out of the lake and chained to a stake near some food. Thus was it cleansed and pacified, completing the job.

At one point, a certain elephant decided to roll in the dirt immediately after leaving its bath. The servants swiftly scattered as the two-ton beast laid its massive bulk on the ground in the mud near the lake. Immediately the chief mahut was on the scene, shouting commands and using a metal-tipped wooden goad to strike the elephant in sensitive places in order to get it on its feet. The leviathan responded as ordered and the entire job had to be done again. This time, only a rinse was necessary and the mud came off quickly and easily. The incident reminded Ekanta of a teaching that he had heard from his teachers which came from the inspiring treasury of stories from the Avatar's life. The conversation had proceeded from Ekanta's questions regarding death, rebirth and karma.

"What happens to those who deviate from the spiritual path or are unable to reach the goal before death, revered guru?" he had asked his teacher one day.

*"These are two different cases, my dear boy,"* came the answer. *"For those who turn away from the path, becoming rebellious, complacent, lazy or simply forgetful, the stored up impetus of their past spiritual effort will at some point cause them to return and finish what they have started. A tiny banyan seed*

*eventually grows into a huge, spreading tree. Only the right conditions and the proper time are needed. A certain story illustrates this well.*

*"Once, a seed fell onto the cornice of a house and laid there dormant for many years. In time, the house was deserted and gradually fell into a dilapidated condition. Finally, the walls gave way and the house crashed to the ground and the little seed was thrown onto fertile soil. The rains came that evening and thus, at the right time, it received all that it needed to sprout and reach fruition. This indicates that everything happens by the will of the Supreme Being at the proper and predestined time.*

*"As for those who strive, yet fail to reach the goal in this present life, they too return and take up the thread of their past good karma, following it to consummation. Sri Krishna mentions this in the Bhagavad Gita, His Celestial Song, wherein He states: 'Beloved one, annihilation never occurs to those who practice yoga with any sincerity. The higher worlds open to receive such pure-hearted beings. When the proper time presents itself, such a one comes again into the world of mortals, attended by a noble family and resources plentiful enough to complete their spiritual evolution. Even a higher condition, such as taking birth in the household of illumined yogis, is possible for these fortunate beings. A birth of this caliber is rare indeed in the realm of becoming.'"*

"Revered Mother," said Ekanta, "I have noticed that there are beings who do no practice yet live a life of perfect harmony attended by the grace of the Lord. How do they deserve this?"

*"My boy,"* said the guru, *"it is of no use to give the elephant its bath early in the morning. It will only roll in the mud and dirt, raising a cloud of dust as well. If, however, one places the animal in the stable at evening time, immediately after its bath, then all is well. Likewise, there are beings who have realized the goal in past lives who now appear before us filled with balance and Grace. They are examples of successful spiritual practice, placed here on earth by the Divine Mother to demonstrate to us what is possible. Their 'bath' was accomplished previously, and they were admitted to the 'stables' of the Lord immediately after their enlightenment, emerging fresh and pure in this present life. Perhaps they have a few small desires left*

*to experience or have come to help others."*

A tremendous noise roused the Avadhut from his reverie. A large male elephant, which the servants had obviously saved until the end, was refusing to enter the water. Raising its trunk to the sky, it trumpeted loudly, stamping its powerful legs and rocking to and fro. The servants all gave way from the sides of the elephant and quickly gathered at its head to man the chain hanging around its neck. Together they pulled heartily, but to no avail. The elephant stood firm, remaining impervious to all lesser wills. Even bananas and other delectable fruits could not tempt it into the water. An impasse was reached and none could figure out a solution.

Again, it was the chief mahut who came to the rescue. Returning from a much needed break, the man shouted orders and used the metal tipped goad once again. This huge male elephant was strong willed, however, and would not budge. As any additional force might prove disastrous, the chief mahut retired and began to think. Soon, he stood up and gave a nearby servant an order. A group of men then headed west to the right side of the lake where another elephant, heretofore unnoticed by Ekanta, was staked to a chain far away from the others. Bringing this smaller elephant with them, the mahuts took it into the lake near the belligerent male elephant. This simple act produced profound results, for no sooner did the smaller elephant enter the water than the large male plunged in too, duly accompanied by a group of servants who swiftly began to wash its body. Puzzled by this, Ekanta approached the chief mahut for clarification.

"Sir," he shouted from a short distance, "what has induced this beast to enter the waters even after all else has failed?"

Turning to face the Avadhut, the elephant trainer saluted him and said, "Revered sadhu, a female elephant in its mating cycle has done the trick!"

The Avadhut drew away, amazed at the ingenuity of the man but absorbed by other thoughts as well. Out of the past came the words of his teachers once again:

*"Impossible tasks and tenacious impediments can pose considerable challenges to the aspirant seeking perfection, my dear. But remember, a tiny microorganism such as a germ can kill an enormous elephant."*

Intrigued by his guru's metaphor, Ekanta asked, "Can you

explain exactly what you mean by that, Mataji?"

*"The efficacy of japa, my dear,"* she returned with a smile, *"that is what I am referring to. Do you know the meaning of the word 'japa,' Ekanta?"*

"Why no, Mataji, and I have never thought about it."

*"It means 'whisper,'"* came her answer. *"That powerful utterance, that small seed syllable and holy phrase called the mantra, repeated over and over again out loud, quietly or silently, destroys the considerable imperfections lying in the subconscious mind. Aspirants imagine that nothing is happening when they use the mantra. They do not realize that after they begin to use the mantra, everything in their life is affected. The very problem that they complain of which rears up to challenge them in life is actually brought to the surface by the mantra, and they complain that it does nothing. All wonders that visit their existence after mantra diksha are directly connected to the use of the mantra bestowed upon them by their guru through the Divine Mother's grace, and they complain that it does nothing. It is the power inherent in the activated mantra that causes them to destroy the roots of all future problems and increase the appearance and growth of wonders in their life, yet they complain it does nothing. If the truth could be seen and known by them, they would see that it accomplishes everything. It is the simplest solutions, Ekanta, subtle and unseen, that effect the greatest miracles."*

The Avadhut's mind worked conversely and inversely with regards to spiritual teachings. Contemplating the entire morning's series of incidents, he seated himself on a nearby hill overlooking the men and elephants and pondered the different ramifications of the situation. What affected him most strongly, being a lover of freedom, was the ease in which the male elephant's mind was brought under submission and the almost effortless conquest of its will, all effected by appealing to the body, the senses and their desires. It struck the Avadhut profoundly and the lessons he had imbibed from his teachers about bondage and attachment came bubbling to the surface.

Since freedom was so highly prized among the true devotees of God, there were endless teachings surrounding the subject, pertaining both to its loss and its attainment. Many of these

powerful instructions now came flooding into Ekanta's consciousness, replete with the many beings and situations which had
accompanied them. Through these teachings, he had learned
about the constituents and the process of bondage. Distraction,
forgetfulness, delusion, covetousness, desire, attachment — they
were all interconnected. The great Shankaracharya had written:

> Never neglect the contemplation of Brahman,
> for the mind will then encounter and become enamored
> with the objects of the senses.
> Like a ball that falls down the stairs of a house,
> bouncing inexorably down each succeeding step
> and finally reaching the lowest level,
> so too will the mind, devoid of thoughts of God,
> descend from the heights of nondual awareness
> and become bound to matter.

As Ekanta was contemplating this teaching, he noticed a movement on the road below. A farmer was drawing near and he was
driving a pair of oxen that were roped to a wagon containing a
huge load of sugarcane. Whenever the two oxen slowed their
pace, the farmer would dangle a carrot or sweet beet in front of
the pair to make them hurry forward. After the wagon had passed
by, the Avadhut remembered one of the teachings from his boyhood:

*"The bullock carries a huge bag of sweets on its back, but can-
not taste them."*

Intrigued by this example of bondage, Ekanta had asked his
Guruji for more sayings of this kind, illustrative of this danger.

*"Here is another, then,"* the teacher complied. *"The snake,
according to ancient mythology, has a jewel lodged in its brain,
yet it is content to eat a mere frog. You see, my boy, beings are
given all that they require at birth in order to make their way
home to the Divine Mother of the Universe. Driven by the sweet
carrot of desire, however, worldly people get waylaid and engage
in all manner of selfish work in order to acquire short-lived
pleasures, remaining unconscious of the rich store of boundless
bliss that is within them in the form of the Atman. With this
priceless treasure lying there, waiting to be discovered, they*

*instead settle for shiny trinkets that have no value."*

With these teachings circulating in his mind, the Avadhut recalled an incident he had witnessed when accompanying his teacher to town on business one day. The two had been walking past a storehouse when, all of a sudden, they heard a commotion. Looking through the doors of the storehouse from a distance, they had seen two men grasping a long wooden box at its two ends and pulling hard in opposite directions. Neither would let go of the box and each in turn was yelling at the other.

"I claim this; it is mine," screamed one man, a jealous rage over-coming him.

"That is a lie and you know it," insisted the other. "It is I who found it just now; therefore it belongs to me."

As Ekanta and his teacher watched, the two went on tugging and pulling, but neither could force the box from the other's grasp. Suddenly, one of the men lost his footing and this finally brought the tense situation to an end. As a result, the box slipped from the hold of both men and fell to the ground, splitting open and spilling its contents — dirt and rusty pieces of iron — on the ground. Both men were struck dumb with disappointment and were left looking at each other in shame.

"Attachment is a horrible thing," said Ekanta's guru, and walked on.

Such is the nature of the human mind, thought the Avadhut, that even spiritual people get caught up in attachment. Once, as a young boy, when he had been spending the late night hours with a few holy men along the roadside near his village, an interesting incident had occurred. Two dacoits, passing by in the darkness, had come to blows near the encampment and the holy group had seen and heard the entire exchange.

One of the robbers was overheard to say, "Give me my share now."

The other responded, saying, "There are only a couple of rupees and a few annas. It is hardly worth splitting. I will keep it and you can have the next take."

The fight that ensued was horrible and both of the men were injured during its duration.

After the commotion had died down and the two thieves had left, one of the sadhus broke the silence, muttering, "All for the sake of a loincloth."

Instantly, there were laughs and guffaws on all sides. Ekanta was in the dark as to the nature of the joke and had asked for an explanation.

*"Once there was a sadhu,"* came the response, *"whose only possession was a loincloth. One morning, after returning to his asana after taking a bath in the sacred river, he found that a mouse was busy chewing on his loincloth. Since this was unacceptable, he immediately acquired a cat to keep the mouse away. The cat, however, would not remain nearby due to hunger so the holy man purchased a cow to supply milk for the cat. When the cow would not give enough milk, he had to beg for feed and eventually acquired a field where the cow could graze. Due to this, servants were hired to work the field.*

*"Soon, in order to oversee all of the activities on the land and mind the servants, a wife was needed, who then requested that a house be built where she could be sheltered. What followed was a host of children who could manage the estate after the demise of the parents. In a short time, then, a huge family and estate grew up around the holy man. One day, an old friend of the sadhu happened by and seeing the amazing buildings and farmlands where only open land had been before, inquired therein for alms. When he saw his friend ensconced in the activities of the world and in possession of vast resources, he asked in amazement, 'What has happened to you?' 'Oh,' said the sadhu, 'it is all for the sake of a loincloth.'"*

The insidious nature of attachment thus dawned on Ekanta's mind at a very young age and this was later observed firsthand during his travels across the continent. Once, during his journeys, he had seen a female monkey that was sitting by the side of the road. It seemed to be brooding and as Ekanta drew near he saw that she was clinging to the carcass of a baby monkey that was long since dead. The female monkey had bared her teeth at Ekanta in warning and then moved away slowly, still clinging to the dead form of her baby. This was an apt illustration of unreasoning attachment and the misery that it brought in its train. His teachers had warned him that attachment was a bane on existence, even while admitting its place in the cosmic scheme of things.

*"This pervasive clinging, Ekanta, is operative at all levels of existence and normal life can scarcely go on without it. Sadhus, worldly-minded beings, animals and even the gods illustrate this tendency towards attachment. In the early times, my son, as the secondary scriptures relate, the gods and demigods all got together to churn the ocean of existence in order to receive the nectar of immortality. While the churning was taking place, all manner of wonderful things came forth from the ocean. The gods and asuras fought over these things as each wanted to personally possess them. In the interim, the nectar was forgotten, and a horrible poison came forth as well. At both ends of the evolutionary chain, then, and everywhere in between, attachment holds all firm in its viselike grip."*

"If all are caught in the web of Maya, Guruji," asked Ekanta, "how will we ever reach the goal of freedom and transcendence?"

*"Do not get perplexed by the tendency towards attachment in human beings, my boy,"* answered the guru. *"Eventually, human beings will take the natural steps to evolve beyond this stunted condition. A certain amount of ignorance is necessary at the early stages of growth. It acts as a protection until the powers lying latent and potential within can come to fruition."*

A silence ensued as the two beings, guru and disciple, sat thinking, each contemplating the mysteries of life. After a time, the guru had asked Ekanta a question.

*"Have you ever tried to eat the skin of a mango?"*

"Yes," answered Ekanta, "but it is bitter and inedible."

*"True,"* said the teacher, *"but it is necessary for the fruit's growth and protects the inner flesh as well. The sweet cannot be enjoyed without the sour."*

"Is the teaching, then, that good and bad exist simultaneously in this world?" asked Ekanta.

*"In part,"* returned the guru. *"Additionally though, the teaching may be given that ignorance acts as a protective coating over the developing human faculty until one is ready for the direct and powerful experiences of enlightenment. It is a case of lower truth to higher Truth. Thus does the Mahashakti protect us by keeping avidya present in us until the time for awakening is near. Then, at the right time, the bitter skin of ignorance is peeled off of the mature fruit and the sweetness of spiritual existence,*

*called enlightenment, is enjoyed to its fullest."*

Memories of this discussion brought the Raja Yoga system into the Avadhut's mind. Patanjali, the founder of this eight-limbed path, had listed attachment as one of the kleshas, or pain-bearing obstacles, that must be overcome before illumination could dawn on the human mind. He remembered Yogindra Yogi's words on the subject.

*"So many detrimental tendencies and results come forth from attachment, Ekanta,"* the yogi said one evening as he carefully placed a piece of wood on the fire. *"According to the differing types of attachment, such diverse problems as greed, jealousy, covetousness, grief, disappointment, remorse and anger make their torturous appearances. Yet, there is also ample justification for this negative quality, my boy. A mother's attachment for her child, for instance, allows the young one all manner of ensuing benefit throughout its young life. A husband's attachment to his chaste wife who possesses a spiritual nature also effects positive outcome. What is more, my son, if sadhus did not possess attachment for the Truth, where would we be? Some types of clinging, then, do not bear only useless painful repercussions. Of course, these can not be classed as attachments in the usual sense of the word."*

"Yogiji," the young man had asked at this point, "I have read that Patanjali classifies attachment as one of the five kleshas, along with egotism, ignorance, aversion and clinging to life. These are noted by him to be impediments to yoga. Elsewhere, I have read that there are many more kleshas besides. Do you know anything about these?"

Considering this question, the yogi answered, *"I, too, in my earlier life, heard such assertions made and wondered if they were true. Then, while wandering for a time with some Buddhist monks of the Theravadan school, I found out that Lord Buddha's teachings make mention of the kleshas. They make an interesting study, and though the list is different from Patanjali's, the idea is much the same. After all, Lord Buddha was born a Hindu and spent most of His life in India. He was acutely aware of all the scriptures of Sanatana Dharma, only He formulated His philosophy and way of life around fresh tenets due to the deteriorated condition of Vedic dharma at the time of His incarnation. One could even say that it was because of the deplorable conditions of religion at that time that He visited us with His great light of compassion and understanding."*

"Revered sir," came the inevitable request from the student, "do you remember the list of kleshas as outlined by the Lord Buddha and can you tell me of them?"

*"That venerable and auspicious one uncovered and contributed a wealth of teachings to the perennial wisdom of the ages, my boy. The orthodox and the unorthodox alike with respects to Indian philosophy both revere Him. He was, like other Avatars, the epitome of true religion and the adept purveyor of high-minded philosophy. His power for good reached far beyond the shores of India, influencing thousands of minds in oriental countries and beyond."*

The yogi paused and, not hearing the usual response from his young charge, eyed him momentarily. Then, noticing Ekanta's expectation, he laughed out loud.

*"The kleshas, of course! I should not keep the student who is thirsty for knowledge waiting."*

Fidgeting a bit due to both impatience and embarrassment at being so adeptly found out, Ekanta remained silent, looking at the ground.

Smiling a knowing smile, the Yogi began, obviously enjoying this rare advantage over his precocious student.

*"The kleshas in Buddhism, from what I was told, relate to the Sanskrit term 'akushala,' which Buddhism defines adequately as 'unwholesomeness.' All such tendencies tie one up into repeated births in samsara. There are also subdivisions, Ekanta, called the mulakleshas and the upakleshas. So, the subject is much more involved than Patanjali's version, which, on the other hand, was nicely compacted down into five elements that cover the essentials perfectly.*

*"The kleshas according to Buddhism, what practitioners would call kilesa, are harder to enumerate due to the many treatments that they received from various Buddhist scholars and the different Buddhistic schools. I remember that there are those such as dristhi, trishna and vichikitsa — holding false views, craving for sense life and the entertaining of detrimental doubts. The first is of particular interest and, though hard to spot, is*

*relatively easy to get rid of. The others, which are easier to spot, are somewhat more difficult to destroy. They correlate closely to what we would call the six passions and the five fetters. They are such negative tendencies as pride, delusion, hatred and shame. To complete a list of ten that is more defined, one would add inflexibility, impetuousness and lack of conscience."*

"Yogiji," the young man asked, "you said that the problem of holding false views was of particular interest to you. Can you expand on that?"

*"Why yes, dear boy, I can,"* the yogi responded, *"and it relates to what we were speaking of a bit earlier regarding attachment. There are many types of attachment other than the typical varieties which we see around us, but a healthy spiritual life begins by doing away with various surface attachments. Clinging to the unreal: that is the problem. Beings must first be ready and willing to give up grasping after such obvious illusions as money, fame, power and possessions. After that, a definite start has been made, one that will gradually or swiftly, according to resolve and sincerity, return one to the Source of all happiness. Actually, one could make a strong point that all attachments we perceive daily come from the mind. If that be known as a fact, the seeker after Truth can modify his or her views accordingly and relieve life and mind of some heavy burdens. This is what Lord Buddha wanted, in part: a cessation of suffering."*

"Pardon me, revered sir," Ekanta interjected. "Can you be specific about these subtler attachments of the mind?"

*"Getting to the essence as usual are we?"* said the yogi, turning his searching and often discomforting gaze upon Ekanta. *"That is good. This is where it gets interesting, for we hear the same old teachings which are continually given to novices quite often, but we seldom plumb the depths of the conditioned mind and its complexities with regards to advanced perception and the subtle barriers that are encountered there. Let me think a moment."*

After a time, the yogi spoke, his deep voice echoing slightly in the recesses of the dark cave behind them. Ekanta moved a bit closer to the fire and listened with rapt attention, not to fairy tales and fantasies, but to the many facets of perennial wisdom that always flowed where lovers of God were prone to meet.

*"Attachment in its many obvious forms plagues existence, causing sorrow in many ways. The solution lies, as I have said, in modifying one's view, one's perspective. This has to be accomplished in the company of the holy if one desires Truth, for there in that sanctified atmosphere, concepts are broken down and the true nature of existence is revealed. That is the particular specialty of the illumined ones. Just as a doctor who specializes can locate hidden diseases and their causes due to certain symptoms known to him only through his own experience, so too can the guru pinpoint problems in the mind and dissolve them in the light of higher perception.*

*"This gets down to the fine points, as I have mentioned. For instance, most beings, even if they are able to diminish their attachments to the world and check the desires of the restless mind, cannot understand the subtle and disconcerting need for the destruction of that bothersome facet of individuality called the ego. It persists, Ekanta, well into the advanced stages of spiritual growth and this is so because people believe in it. Even after they hear that it must go and begin to take steps for that end, they continue to foster it in various ways. Is this not passing strange? In truth, belief in the ego, in that complex knot of limited consciousness called the separate individual, is a false view. This is one of the mulakleshas. It is, as I have said, hard to locate and encounter in oneself but, once perceived in the right perspective, easy to do away with. Holy company, called darshan, is the solution here. And by holy company I mean interaction with the guru, the sangha and the holy scriptures as well as the very best holy company in the ultimate sense — communion with one's Buddha nature, what we would call the Atman."*

"What else, dear teacher?" Ekanta broke in, a huge smile taking over his entire face. "Are there other mulakleshas?"

*"How about this one, thirsty student?"* replied the yogi obligingly. *"Laboring under the misconception that false views can lead one to liberation. There are a whole host of confused aspirants that dally in that stage of stunted spiritual growth. This is where attachment is known as pervasive clinging, tenacious and insidious."*

A silence followed these words as the two wonderful beings pondered the teachings coming forth. Finally the yogi spoke again:

*"Denial of the law of karma, there is a knotty problem for you, my boy. One of the Buddhist monks that I wandered with for a time sat up with me late one night speaking for hours on that issue alone. Cause and effect is all around us, is in the nature of the universal manifestation. People can accept this if it is proposed by science and applied to the physical universe but they have the most terrible time understanding its place in spiritual life. Again, it is hard to spot, this denial of what is obvious, but once one notices and accepts, modifying the view and doing away with old concepts, life changes accordingly and is never the same again. Spiritual teachers welcome the advent of such comprehension in their students, for it marks the beginnings of real living which, after all, is supremely natural and spontaneous.*

*"Finally, Ekanta, there are some very perplexing beliefs that press on our consciousness. In classical fashion, similar to our Advaitic wisdom, Lord Buddha pointed out that the belief in eternity as well as attachment to the idea of nihilism are both impediments, mulakleshas. This strikes deep into the heart of the conditioned mind, tearing at the very interior fiber of our samskaras from past lives. So much psychic sludge and muck lies there, my boy, but darshan will do away with it. Is it any wonder why every religious approach values holy company so much?"*

"No, indeed not," breathed Ekanta, looking at the holy man with fond admiration.

A few minutes passed as the yogi and the exceptional young aspirant listened to the fire speaking its own soothing language. Both were obviously enjoying the fullness of an elevated consciousness. Finally, Ekanta broke the silence.

"Sir, I am very satisfied. However, you stated that some of the kleshas are harder to get rid of. If darshan can dispel the impediments associated with false views, how can the others be destroyed?"

*"Desire, hatred, pride and so forth — those can only be done away with completely by dhyan, meditation, combined with dharana, concentration. Actually, a small trace of these must persist so long as the body and mind exist, but they must be reduced to a minimum. People try a thousand ways and methods to be*

*rid of these troublesome passions. They listen to any and every charlatan who comes along and even to well-intentioned but poorly informed advocates in professional and intellectual circles, but to little avail. One must free the self, by the self, after listening well to one who knows the Self. Thus do grace and self-effort, that harmonious couple, marry happily again. There is no other way."*

The Avadhut spent the next few hours contemplating the precious benefits of holy company. This was surely the way to transform the tendency to cling to the things of the world, to falsehood and deceit, to what is insubstantial and ultimately unreal.

Eventually, Ekanta was called forth from his radiant internal state by noises near the lake below. Looking up, he saw the mahut mount one of the elephants. The feeding was over and it was time to return home. The elephant had other intentions, however; and seeing a bunch of unripe bananas hanging from a nearby tree, it stretched out its trunk to take them. The mahut immediately brought the steel-tipped goad down on its trunk, letting it know that this was an unacceptable action. The fruit was unripe, the elephant had already been fed and these bananas belonged to others, besides. Bringing the elephant around, the mahut called out to the others to line up the animals for the trip back to the city.

Witnessing this final scene, the Avadhut could not help but compare the actions of the elephant with the acts of novices and worldly people in the presence of holy company. Some harsh lessons are meted out, no doubt, he thought to himself, but in that atmosphere one swiftly finds out what is acceptable and what is not, what is beneficial and what is detrimental, what is encouraged and what is forbidden. He, the Avadhut, was living proof of this, for throughout his life he had received teachings from the illumined that had inexorably shaped him and brought him ever closer to the goal of human existence. As the line of elephants filed out onto the road leading back to the city, the words of Ekanta's venerable vanaprastin teacher, the Mataji, came to mind.

*"One's mistakes, Ekanta, are much more important than one's successes, especially at the outset. Through these seemingly negative occurrences, which surface and get corrected in the presence of holy company, attachment is converted into detachment*

*which in turn is transformed into mature renunciation. This,*
*dear one, is the way of spiritual growth in the world."*

The elephants were now lined up on the road and, with a
signal and an order from the chief mahut, they began lumbering
in the direction of the distant city. The Avadhut stood up and
reverently saluted the majestic animal which, in this case, had
taught him many valuable lessons in nonattachment. As the line
of behemoths gradually disappeared in the distance, another
smaller figure, unseen by any, reached the road and turned in the
opposite direction. The Avadhut, satisfied within the Self,
detached, free from worldly impediments and contented under all
conditions, wended his way towards the south where warmer,
dryer weather awaited him.

# Chapter 6

# Teachings on Clear Perception

THE SIXTH GURU — The Moon

THE LESSON — Discrimination

*O great Prince, by observing the moon and its apparent cycles, I have learned that things are not always as they appear to be — that illusions of all kinds delude the perception of the limited mind connected to the five senses. Also, Sister Moon taught me the ultimate lesson of transcendence — that one must be able to rise above and see beyond the mirage-like stream of time and its flow of events.*

Ekanta had walked all day, eventually leaving the road and plunging through the undergrowth that separated him from the distant mountains. By dusk he reached the foothills and soon had secured a perfect location to spend the night, free from insects and stiff breezes and offering a perfect vantage point of the lands below. After eating the remainder of his scanty foodstuffs which were gathered in the city and along the way, he quenched his thirst in a small stream nearby and settled himself down in a prone position. His legs had taken a stiff workout and it felt very good to stretch and relax them.

As darkness fell, the stars came out. Properly expressed,

thought the Avadhut, they are not "coming out" at all, but are simply revealing their constant presence. As he watched the scintillating spectacle, he began to notice that the stars were becoming less brilliant with each advancing moment. This is unusual, he thought, for they should be increasing in brilliance. As he was puzzling over this phenomena, he suddenly noticed that the horizon to the east was becoming radiant and it was not long before the cause of the stars' receding light became evident. The moon, at first almost yellowish-red, was making its appearance on the nocturnal scene. It looked bigger than Ekanta had ever seen it due to its proximity with the horizon relative to his position in the foothills. It was now nearly full and the sight of it, waxing brilliantly towards the consummation of its monthly cycle, filled Ekanta's mind with all manner of teachings and divine associations.

As the light of the rising moon flooded the landscape with a soft luminosity, the Avadhut's thoughts lit up in similar fashion. The burgeoning moon reminded him of one of his favorite dialogues in the Ramayana. In this epic spiritual saga, Ravana had stolen Sita away from Her precious Ram and was keeping Her prisoner in Sri Lanka. One night, as Sita spurned Ravana's advances in Her usual chaste fashion, being ever faithful to Her beloved ideal and husband, Sri Ramachandra, Ravana asked Her: *"Dear woman, why do you avoid my advances, even after so much time has elapsed? I am handsome and powerful, even more so than Ram. Why do you prefer him to me?"*

Smiling to herself, the ever-pure Sita replied diplomatically:

*"Oh Ravana, you are like a full moon which has reached the limit of its cycle and is now beginning to wane, but my Rama is like the crescent moon on the second day of the bright fortnight. He is just beginning to manifest and demonstrate his infinite power."*

Once, when Ekanta was a young boy, he had been sitting in meditation under the full moon with one of his vanaprastin teachers. Eventually, he said, "Revered Mataji, I hope that my mind will become as pure and radiant as the full moon someday."

After reflecting on these words of her young student, the guru said, *"Dear boy, my prayer for you is that your mind may become even more clear and bright than the full moon. Even*

*the moon has imperfections.  There, do you not see them, cov-*
*ering the face of that splendid orb?  Therefore, may the light of*
*Pure Consciousness that is ever abiding within you shine forth*
*from a mind that is completely stainless and eternally free from*
*blemishes."*

With thoughts such as these floating through his mind, it was
not long before he could detect the up-draft of the subtle spiritual
wind called Mahavayu rising within him again.  This was often
accompanied by an intoxicating aroma which seemed to emanate
from the crown of his head.  It was wonderful the way that everything transformed under the influence of this intense feeling.  All
of his faculties seemed to become infinitely more sensitized and
this in turn allowed him to behold the creation in entirely new and
refreshing ways.  This is how God must see the world, he often
thought to himself, and as much as he marveled at the experience,
he also lamented when this intense devotional feeling withdrew.
At least, he comforted himself by thinking, I know what Grace is.
Someday, he thought, the Divine Mother will plunge me irretriev-
ably into the ocean of Her boundless Grace and dissolve me into
Her completely.

Contemplating the extreme differences between mundane
awareness and heightened consciousness, the Avadhut began to
ponder over the dilemma of habitual preoccupation and its resultant attachment.  The elephant teacher and the lessons the animal
had transmitted were still strong in his mind from the past day's
experience.  The moon, however, seemed to express a different
teaching.  Like the stars whose presence was always constant
though often unseen, speaking silently of the illusion of false
appearances, the moon, too, communicated similar lessons.

The Avadhut thought back on the past month of travels.  Almost
every night he had seen the moon in different phases of its cycle.
Essentially, it was as if a different moon was appearing each
evening.  All of a sudden, a unique thought struck him, one that
was deceptively simple and which he had never perceived in quite
this way.

"The moon has no cycles," he said abruptly and out loud.  "It is
all an appearance."

Ekanta laughed heartily.  An echo of that laughter came back
to him a few seconds later, bouncing off of the hills and canyon

walls nearby. Every evening, he thought, people look up at the moon and say, "Look, the moon is almost full," or "See what a beautiful crescent moon is out tonight." However, the moon itself never changes. If seen from a different vantage point, off in space and away from the earth, it would be always full, always shining, its luminosity unimpeded as the sun's rays shone upon it.

This was not new knowledge or even anything very profound, yet the Avadhut could not help but view it in accordance with the tendency of the human mind to fabricate illusory appearances that obscure the essential Truth. As he thought about this, he remembered a conversation he had held with the Mataji just before he parted from her to wander the world.

*"My dear,"* said the Mataji one evening, after a discussion had sprung up regarding discrimination, *"human beings are forever constructing false notions, erroneous concepts which they then live by for years, in some cases even for lifetimes. They habitually misconstrue information pertinent to both spiritual and secular life. These misconceptions, many of them simple and harmless at first, eventually gain a foothold in human awareness and turn into recurrent ways of thinking. The mind gradually fosters them through the lack of proper discrimination and then substantial delusions form. Before one knows it, what is fallacious has become true and what is true has become a fabrication or superimposition. I have seen this occur on many occasions in my interaction with the people of the world. In fact, many of the beliefs that contemporary society holds are simply the product of collective delusion."*

"Can you cite some examples, Mataji?" Ekanta had asked.

*"On matters of a simple nature, consider our habits of sleeping and eating. The illumined tell us that four to five hours of sleep per night is plenty yet, because society places their faith in conventional wisdom and those who make their living peddling it, most people oversleep and still they wonder why they are always drowsy or tired. If you overwork an ox it gets worn out and if you do not work it at all it gets lazy. A balance must be reached. With regards to spiritual life, however, there is a potential dynamo in each person that, when accessed, will awaken, invigorate and increase one's abilities manyfold. To find this power, one must be willing to break out of conventional*

*modes and experiment, under the guidance of an adept, with different methods and schedules. The illumined preceptor will help you uncover and develop your discriminatory powers. This is the beginning of learning how to live a divine life in the world. The alternative is to remain asleep to higher potential, as I said, possibly for one's entire life."*

Intrigued by the subject and desiring more information, Ekanta then asked, "After beings break through these barriers, Mataji, what kind of misconceptions do they encounter then? Surely, a little discrimination does not enlighten them thoroughly right away."

*"That is true,"* answered the guru, *"at least in most all cases. Though occasionally a unique being will get transported instantly by initial contact with radical teachings, most ease in a bit at a time. It is like entering the ghat for one's bath or for a swim. You can enter slowly, getting your body used to the cold water a little at a time, or you can jump into waist-deep water and get the other half of the body wet later. Again, someone might come along and shove you from behind, getting the entire matter over and done with in an instant. In all these cases, though, the end result is that you get wet.*

*"In the interim, however, there are many subtle barriers that come crashing down as well. Belief that the world of external manifestation is the only reality, assuming that wealth and possessions belong to you, thinking erroneously that wife, family and relatives will always be there for you or that you will be there for them, imagining that your health, well-being and peace of mind will remain constant — these and other misconceptions will get substantially adjusted or completely done away with as spiritual growth takes place. The Mother of the Universe simply will not allow the devotees to forget their true nature, their spiritual origin. She is ferocious in the face of our fear and tenacious with regards to our complacency."*

The Mataji stopped for a time to consider. Returning to her subject, she continued to discuss the nature of impediments with regards to true living and the discrimination needed to attain success.

*"One of the most daunting barriers in life, around which people construct innumerable fantastic notions, is death. Of course,*

*I mean the death of the body. Illumined beings, even sincere spiritual aspirants, take it for granted that Consciousness is eternal while the body is not. However, you would be surprised how many remain in the dark, completely uninformed as to the nature of Reality. Short of the contemplation of eternity with regards to Absolute Reality, to know death is a wonderful thing. It is an energy under the control of Ishvara that provides so many important functions. It liberates us from the old and diseased body, it shows us realms we only dreamed about or imagined. For all those who are still desiring to embody in the various realms of name and form, death is an essential process and an important personality."*

"Mataji," responded Ekanta, "how can death have a personality?"

*"On the ultimate level,"* she said, *"there is only Consciousness. Matter is not really living. In that sense, Ekanta, you and I are not living since we are not matter. Chaitanya Shuddhaham — We are pure Consciousness. It follows, then, that we cannot die since that which is eternal can experience no death. Consciousness does not labor under the constrictions of ego and personality, you see."*

"But Mataji," Ekanta replied, "what are all of these beings around us then? Are they not living?"

*"'Who are all of these beings' might be a better question, my dear,"* came the response, *"and no, they are not truly living so long as they are identified with the body, as long as they believe themselves to be material in nature, if they indeed assume themselves to be the individual ego, the limited personality. That is why I called death a personality. He is not truly real, though for those who have lost their spiritual orientation, he acts as an avenue of return to the radiant Reality."*

Ekanta stared at his teacher in disbelief. He felt as if his mind were undergoing surgery. A feeling of heightened awareness was coming over him associated with something important, something essential that he had known before or that he had always known down deep. The Mataji merely stared back into his eyes, head nodding, her whole demeanor permeated with a look that told him she understood what he was experiencing. Finally, he managed to speak.

"I see," he stated briefly. "We were speaking earlier of misconceptions. You have led me in a most clever way to the most deceiving fallacy of all. Previously, you and Guruji have mentioned the illusion of death to me many times in various teachings. Now, I see all of this in a very special way. But Mataji, you were speaking of the personality of death. He must be the supreme personality in a sense, since he comes to us and dissolves the mistaken notion of our own personality."

"_Yes, young man,_" she affirmed. "_It is a matter of the dead coming unto the dead and revealing to them eternal life._"

The two laughed uproariously at this statement.

Catching his breath, Ekanta added, "Yes, or if seen in another way, what is truly alive must enter the world of the walking dead and convince them that they, too, are immortal."

"_Yes,_" the Mataji continued, "_it is quite a conundrum.  The world of insentient matter borrows Spirit and all becomes suddenly animate.  What is dust, as Lord Jesus has implied, receives the breath of the Almighty and rises to walk and talk among a trillion stars._"

After a short silence, the Mataji spoke again.

"_Even Ishvara is ultimately unreal, Ekanta,_" she continued, wiping away a few happy tears. "_From the Advaitic standpoint, there is nothing but Consciousness.  All existence is Brahman, as the Upanishads state.  But only true existence is Brahman, my dear, not false existence.  We cannot accept what is not real in place of Reality.  If we do, we fall asleep to our higher nature.  Careful!  Exercise caution!  Time, space, and causality are all false notions and so is the individual ego complex that believes them.  Consciousness may sport with them, in them, around them, but that is as far as it goes.  If Consciousness seems to solidify around them, giving each a sense of Reality, this congealing marks the acceptance of limitation and a bittersweet dream of cyclic happiness and suffering ensues._

"_This brings me back to death, which is called Yama in our tradition.  We have instructed you in the Kathopanishad so you are well aware of the predicament of Nachiketas and his revealing and enlightening visit with Yama.  I have not told you about the Yamastakam, however, and this might be a good time to recite and explain it._

"_Yama is a power of Ishvara, or Ishvari,_" the Mataji explained, "_and Ishvari is one with Brahman.  Again, and to_ *avoid confusion, it is the true nature of Yama and of Ishvari that is ultimately Real, not the form appearing in the realm of time, space and causality. The essence of Consciousness is never subject to time, space and causality, though it may appear there. It is like trying to saturate a lotus leaf with water. The water simply will not be absorbed. The leaf resists the liquid as a matter of course. In like manner, this Consciousness, called the Atman, cannot be forced to take on characteristics. You have read as much in the scriptures, which state that fire cannot burn It, water cannot wet It, wind cannot dry It, and so on. Well, matter cannot prevail on It either; time cannot seduce It into cosmic cycles and space cannot contain It. Further, cause and effect have no existence in It.*

*"Let us look at this in accordance with death, then, my dear. For those congealed bits of limited awareness that mistakenly imagine themselves to be the body, who associate with the vehicles of body, mind and intellect instead of identifying with Consciousness, death is the liberator. As a power of Ishvari, Herself a compassionate appearance in the universe acting as a reminder of all that is true and real, death is a cosmic force that moves us. Out and away, my son, in eddies and swirls, life-energy breaking free and pulsating with renewed inspiration and joy! She sends death into this constricted world like a brisk wind amidst dead leaves and literally sends us flying out of our grief, our despondency, our petty concerns and minuscule plans.*

*"It is impossible, under death's powerful force, to grasp onto anything, any concept or limited belief. The only anchor there is the Atman and that is why those who have realized It go nowhere — for there is no space, and do nothing — for there is no cause and effect. To fashion another home in the terrestrial world — these great ones do not desire that. That would be to relegate their awareness to cycles of time, the master of cosmic sleep, the devourer of insightful memory.*

*"About the true function of death, what is already essentially lifeless cannot be killed. Therefore, death is not really a destroyer but is a prime mover of all consciousness that is associated with name and form, even obsessed with the same. He unties knots, assists in flowing what is stagnant and frees those*

*bound in fear by releasing their vice-like grip on matter and temporality. That is why the illumined revere him, why he is worthy of worship. They see him as he really is. Listen as I sing his praises."*

Saying so, the Mataji entered a meditative state and began to sing the Yamastakam, eight verses of death personified:

All praises be to Dharmarajan,
the lord of all pathways leading away from limitation.
Victory to Samana, the witness of multitudinous
embodied states who sees all equally.
My salutations to Kritanta, who steals away
my earthly life and puts an end to action.
Obeisance to Dardadhana, who holds the rod of justice
and destroys the sins of mortals.

Free me, O Kala, O primordial one,
who dissolves the universe of space and time.
Reveal to me my Essence, O Yama,
who finally restrains the wayward, outgoing senses.
I worship thee, Punyamitra,
who graciously purges the sinner and uplifts the virtuous.
Burn away my attachments, Brahmagni,
O great purifier, O fire of Brahman.

After the hymn was complete, the Mataji remained still for a time. When she spoke again, her voice was soft and tender with concern:

*"These eight names of death, my dear, I give to you in sacred transmission so that you will always be protected from danger. True death is not death of the body, but ignorance of the Atman. With these eight guards to remind you of the nature of what is real and what is not, go into the world and spread the wisdom we have shared with you due to the Grace of the Blessed Lord and Divine Mother of the Universe."*

The Avadhut rose to his feet. Turning his face towards the glorious moon, he saluted it profoundly.

"You are my teacher of discrimination, Oh radiant moon," he said aloud. "Whenever I see you, from this day forth, I will always remember the importance of perceiving things correctly, of never falling under the delusion of the false appearances of duality which accompanies the world of name and form."

Taking his seat in a meditative posture, the Avadhut continued to contemplate the moon. There, in the nocturnal skies, the moon rested interminably, encouraging all to discriminate, revealing that things are not always as they seem. His mind began to ruminate on the possibilities that this radiant teacher brought forth. As he thought about the golden orb appearing there before him, he remembered that the Blessed Lord, Sri Krishna, had indicated the moon to be one of His foremost powers in the Bhagavad Gita. It was not long before the appropriate sloka emerged from his retentive memory:

> Of luminaries by day, I am the brilliant sun,
> and by night, the incandescent moon.

Inspired immensely by this thought, the Avadhut was seized by an inner desire to pay obeisance to the moon. Standing, he began to do multiple prostrations before it, laying himself on the earth face down and rising to standing position over and over again, all the while repeating sacred mantras.

In due time, the uprush of divine energy, now formally propitiated, began to submerge within him and he found himself once again seated in yogic posture. The quality of discrimination had been the mainstay of his early Vedantic training. That he had found an ever-present teacher for it in the phenomenal universe caused him exceeding joy which he could barely contain. At once, teachings from his guru touched his mind, lessons which had never been forgotten and that had stood him in good stead throughout his life.

"*Before discrimination visits the mind, Ekanta, life is like a storm sporting high winds. All objects in a storm take on a similar appearance and cannot be discerned easily from one another. When the need to discriminate surfaces in the confused and oppressed mind, however, clarity is at once experienced. This is like perceiving various objects through the clean, clear and peaceful air after the storm has subsided. Everything can then be seen for what it truly is.*"

The Avadhut thought back on his own spiritual awakening in all its various phases.  There had been times when the truths of the scriptures, transmitted to him through the wonderful abilities of his spiritual teachers, had seemed obscure and hard to grasp. A little effort was, in the end, all that was needed to break through such barriers and emerge into the clear light of understanding once again.

*"Grace and self-effort always go hand in hand, Ekanta,"* came the voice of his guru.

Exercising discrimination had always been emphasized by all of his teachers.  They had given him the unique perspective that all such qualities like detachment, faith, devotion and the like were actual manifestations on the earth plane of the Divine Mother of the Universe, coming through the human vehicle.  Through these sacred attributes, one could actually infer Her existence and then begin to commune with Her benign presence.  While others of dualistic leanings were busy trying to acquire a vision of the Goddess with four, eight, ten or sixteen arms, Ekanta had been directed to behold the Goddess at every moment of his existence as She appeared to him through these various energies.  Thinking thus, he began to recite a favorite verse from the Divine Mother scriptures:

We praise endlessly and with every breath of life,
the Bhagavati Durga Devi, the Parashakti.
"Sha," the primal root, denotes prosperity and divine powers,
whereas "Kti" means fortitude and insurmountable strength.
She possesses and bestows these qualities
and appears through them as well.
Thus, She makes Herself known through such energies as
intelligence, without which all beings would be ignorant
sleep, without which all would become devoid of energy
hunger, without which all would become weak
thirst, without which none would seek fulfillment;
fatigue, without which none would seek rest and repose
memory, lacking which no one would know themselves
forbearance, without which all would give up all pursuits
peace, without which all would become slaves to work
beauty, devoid of which the entire creation would be drab

consciousness, without which nothing could be perceived
at any level of existence, and a whole host of other qualities.
Eternal victory unto Her!

After meditating on this wisdom for awhile, the Avadhut detected another wisp of memory floating through his mind. Thinking back, he remembered a certain situation where he had witnessed a conversation between a poor householder and a wandering sannyasin. It had taken place just outside his village.

Ekanta had been running an errand for his mother and was briskly walking down the road that led out of his village to the rice fields beyond. Turning a corner, he had come upon a couple with several children traveling towards the village. The woman, carrying a heavy load, had just slipped, lost her footing and fallen, scattering the family's entire belongings all over the road. The husband, a large and arrogant fellow, was irate and instead of assisting the poor woman, was busy berating her, occasionally adding a blow or two to her person to emphasize his point.

Ekanta was almost ready to intercede on behalf of the unfortunate woman when, all of a sudden, from the trees bordering the road emerged a tall holy man carrying a thick wooden staff. It was this intimidating figure that came to the rescue of the lady, staff raised as if to strike and face flushed with outrage. Seeing this imposing person, replete with auspicious holy markings which demanded respect, the incensed husband fell back and refrained from the physical beating and his verbal abuse.

Helping the woman to her feet, the holy man turned to the man and said sternly, *"Never strike a woman! Such behavior is degenerate. The Divine Mother of the Universe resides in them. If not out of respect for this fact alone, then at least refrain due to practical sense and a regard for your own safety."*

Nonplussed, but still offended by this untimely intrusion, the husband lashed out with words belying his own ignorant state.

"Women are worthless, especially ones such as this, so you be off and take care of your own business and leave me to mine. The Goddess, all respects to Her, is far beyond the likes of this poor specimen, so your apparent concern and good intentions are wasted here."

The demeanor of the holy man suddenly changed. He then began to speak words of a calm and reassuring nature.

*"Dear sir, forgive my intrusion, but your actions are unbe-coming of your station in life. You are a family man, and that is a holy occupation. You are Shiva, the transcendent, the Absolute Brahman Itself. Your wife is Shakti, the one who pre-sides over the world of name and form. You are the Father, the Karya-vibhavaka that wills what She does and She is the Mother, the Karya-vibhavini Herself! Knowing this, there should always be harmony between the two of you, if for no other reason than the maintenance and instruction of the children around you. When she has blessed you with these, how can you treat her in any other fashion than profound respect, not to mention extreme reverence."*

These words had a transforming effect on the man who now showed the holy man a completely different manner. With a voice noticeably affected and occasionally choked with stifled remorse, the husband asked, "Revered sir, how can I, how can we, live up to these lofty ideals? We are simple, poor and impoverished beings barely able to cope with the world's repeated blows."

Saying this, the man placed his head in his hands and wept silently.

*"What the world deals out to you must be borne with equa-nimity,"* said the holy man. *"One must not trade blows for blows. Even the Avatar, the Divine Couple, accepts straitened circum-stances in every incarnation and bears them patiently in order to instruct us accordingly. Your own change of nature as well as the restructuring of society will proceed upon instigating a new standard with regards to the worship of shakti. As long as our women are treated poorly, left uneducated and relegated to an inferior status, their infinite potential left lying dormant and undeveloped, so long will the world suffer the agonies of the Divine Mother's wrath in this regard. Like any other karma that is left untended and unneutralized, this blatant oversight will return to haunt the world's peoples until a solution is effected."*

A silence reigned among the small group for a few seconds. The husband was tongue-tied, the wife and children stood with mouth agape and even Ekanta waited with bated breath to hear more teachings from the wise one.

*"The Goddess resides within all,"* continued the enigmatic figure, *"not just in women. She is beyond gender and ultimately*

*transcendent of all form as well. In woman, though, as in man, She manifests certain blessed qualities. The wretch who does not behold them is indeed unfortunate and wastes his precious time on this earth, which is Her domain."*

The attention of the group was still focused upon the holy man. Each sentence was somehow charged with a power that caused all present to hang on every word. It was if the Divine Mother Herself was present, using this situation to confer instruction and blessings upon all present.

*"From the union of Shiva and Shakti,"* the wise one continued, *"this whole vast creation has proceeded, yet it is She who oversees the functions and cosmic laws that operate here. Knowing this, can we afford to neglect or disregard Her? Shakti is not merely a diminutive figure who is seen on the lap of the images of Indian gods, to whom is assigned the subordinate position which some deluded ones consider that a Hindu wife should occupy. She is not just a handmaid of the Lord either but the Lord Himself in His aspect as the Mother of the Worlds. Therefore, this Shakti is both Nirguna and Saguna, that is, both Chit Shakti and Maya Shakti. If one knows this, as spoken by the true knowers of Brahman, life becomes blessed and a new awareness visits the mind."*

The husband, now streaming tears of remorse, abruptly turned to his wife and saluted her, much to the surprise of all present.

"Forgive me, Mother," he managed to say through his sobs. Then, with new energy he immediately set about gathering the family's scattered goods which still lay upon the road, placing them on his own shoulders. As soon as this was achieved, the man turned to thank the holy one, but he was already gone. Not even Ekanta had seen his departure, so caught up was he with the miraculous unfolding of this unusual scene. He then continued on his merry way, thinking back on the words that he had heard with immense appreciation.

The moon had now climbed higher into the evening sky. There it was, lighting the world with its loveliness, saying, as it were, *"existence will become permeated with peace and bliss if the light of proper understanding is utilized."* Discrimination, thought the Avadhut; it is the essential foundation of peace in the relative world and the pathway to right knowledge and higher wisdom.

About it, he remembered, his guru had told him:

*"In the nondual texts, Sri Ramachandra relates the necessity of discrimination to us clearly and succinctly:"*

Ignorance and delusion persist
in the mind that is devoid of discrimination.

*"Therefore, Ekanta, never fail to implement this practice into your sadhana, for spiritual discipline will not bear fruit without it."*

*"Pick your favorite divine qualities, Ekanta,"* his guru had said to him one day.

"Love," came forth the boy's reply.

*"Human love without discrimination results in promiscuity and surface emotionalism,"* replied the preceptor.

"How about truth?" said the boy.

*"The two, truth and discrimination, are part of the same package,"* said the guru. *"It is impossible to separate them. Pick another."*

"Grace," came Ekanta's reply.

*"It will not be possible to recognize grace when it descends upon you until you possess the jewel of discrimination,"* returned the guru.

"You are calling discrimination a jewel, Master?" asked the boy. "How lovely. Where does that expression come from?"

*"The great Adishankaracharya has named one of his most profound spiritual texts by the title of Vivekachudamani — the Crest Jewel of Discrimination,"* replied the teacher. *"It is a great testament to the power inherent in this precious quality."*

"Can you recite for me your favorite sloka from that text, revered sir?" asked the boy.

*"Regarding favorites,"* said the guru, *"you pose me an impossible task, but I will recite one having to do with discrimination."*

After a moment's silence, his teacher's rich voice came forth:

The brisk and deceiving wind of Maya
that creates waves of ignorance in the mind,
is stilled forever
through the power inherent in discrimination.

Such waves dissolve completely
under that profound influence.
What remains is the Self, the true I,
which is always one indivisible ocean
of homogenous Consciousness.

"That is wonderful," said Ekanta, truly moved. "I have received the gift of goose bumps from your sloka. Have you any other? Is there one that states the essence?"

The teacher did not have to think long. Soon, in tones of contained rapture came the words that were to fill Ekanta with wonder for the rest of his life:

Though discrimination has many faces,
a multitude of uses, the essence of it is this:
Maya creates everything,
including places, names, forms, mind, prana, etc.
All these are objects and concepts projected over Reality,
like mirages in a desert or the passing fragments of a dream.
All this, then, is ultimately unreal and only thou art true.
Know yourself, then, and affirm 'Thou art That,'
in deep silence.
Truly, you are ever one with the Supreme Being.

When he was older, Ekanta secured a copy of the Viveka-chudamani and read it silently in the forest by himself. Those days were never to be forgotten. While other children played about the house or in the vast fields outside, Ekanta had withdrawn from such sport for the most part and had studied the wisdom of the ages. Though Ekanta never minded spending his time and energies in this manner, the sacrifice of his young years in the service of acquired wisdom was not without regrets. He was unable to relate with anyone his own age as a result, and had even left the company and conversations of his elders far behind since most of them were inevitably oriented towards mundane affairs and superficial preoccupations. In the end, he had decided that it was his destiny to travel the lonely road that led to Self-Realization — "the flight of the Alone to the Alone," his teacher had called it.

It was this "love of lonely study," as Sri Krishna had called it, that had shaped him into the Avadhut. He could neither deny its efficacy or regret its implementation into his being. In fact, a time had come when he realized that he, the Avadhut, was doing nothing, accomplishing nothing. All knowledge was in him and after the different karmas had run their course, eventually drying up like river beds in the desert, this internal wisdom, inherent in the Soul, simply exuded out of his very being, filling the mind with infinite teachings and transforming the world into a paradise.

These teachings were always perceived from a witness standpoint, in effortless fashion, as if a great scientist was searching the entire creation with a huge microscope that left nothing to chance and caught every detail. His illumined mind was that instrument and the Great One gazed through it in omniscient fashion, beholding with joy the very universe It projected. Therefore, the Avadhut was no one, was nothing, and being so he was everything. This was his secret, scarcely even apprehended by himself, and the singular secret of all illumined beings. He was grateful for this unique state of mind, or of 'no mind' as he had heard it expressed, and he owed much to his teachers as a result. With reverence, he recalled what his Guruji had told him early on:

*"This egoless condition, Ekanta, it is the 'Nothingness' spoken of by Buddhist adepts, the 'Oneness' emphasized by the Advaitans, the 'Union' coveted by the yogins and the Primordial Presence into which all beings seek to immerse themselves. The only necessary prerequisite — the price of admission into Its indescribable realm — is the sacrifice of the ego, that persistent and troublesome sense of individuality that encourages such qualities as selfishness, desire and attachment. Transcending it, disidentifying with it, discriminating it away, effacing it or offering it up with sincerity — in whatever way one is able to reduce its influence, that is of crucial importance. Remember what the great Advaitan, Shankara, has said in this regard:"*

May you, who have been bitten
by the great black serpent of egotism,
take recourse to discrimination
and free yourself from this vexing imposition.

After quoting this sloka from the Vivekachudamani, The Crest Jewel of Discrimination, the preceptor put the scripture away and looked at his young student.  Ekanta steadied himself and made ready for personal instruction.

*"To get rid of the tenacious encumbrance called the ego is no easy matter, my son, but discrimination is one of the most important keys.  In fact, it is indispensable.  After one has come to grips with the ephemeral nature of the universe, seeing through its illusory appearance, there is still the mind to deal with.  It is the mind that created the universe and it is also the mind that sustains the phenomenon of its existence.  Therefore, learn how to dissolve this mind into the subtlest substance possible.  Our Rishis knew this secret well."*

Saying this, Ekanta's vanaprastin guru reached for another scripture, one that he seldom read aloud from but one that Ekanta thrilled to every time he listened to the wisdom it contained.

*"Our revered rishi, Ashtavakra, has described the process in brief in a very nice fashion.  Listen well."*

Next, came forth a beautiful sloka from the Ashtavakra Samhita:

> The vision of the cosmos rises from the mind
> as bubbles rise from an ocean.
> Merge the mind into the Self
> and be free from attachment to external appearances
> forevermore.

With wise counsel such as this, the Avadhut thought, it was nothing less than spiritual suicide to live in the world without the shining armor of discrimination.  One day, under the bright sun, sitting in a clearing in the forest, the revered Mataji had explained to him the connection between the mental sheath and the universe.

*"The wise ones tell us that just as an inventor thinks of the invention by drawing it from his subtle inner awareness, so too does the Universal Mother, when She wants to indulge in creation, manifest the universe by materializing objects from subtle seeds lying fallow in the Cosmic Mind, what the Vedanta and the Samkhya call the Mahat or Hiranyagarbha.  Therefore, the Cosmic Mind produces the universe and all individual*

*minds, which are merely expressions of the Mahat in a micro-cosmic sense. These little minds act in similar fashion in the terrestrial world: creating, preserving and destroying on a very limited level."*

Gazing around at the beautiful scenery, the guru continued. *"Do you see all of these wonderful objects,"* she said, *"different species of trees, plants, and animals, the birds and insects, the waters flowing by and the various elements? The universe is God's creation and reflects His infinite nature. If you were to come with me and go into the cottage hermitage nearby, we would see the various objects fashioned by mankind out of wood, metal and other materials of the earth. All created things, including the bodies of living beings and the diverse energies flowing through them are concepts that have their origin in the Cosmic Mind. They exist in subtle form first and later manifest as solid objects due to the will of the Creator."*

"Everything seems to come out of nothing, then," rejoined Ekanta. "Is that why the Mayavadins call this universe an illusion?"

*"You cannot create something out of nothing,"* returned the guru. *"Do not fall into the trap shared by the nihilists and certain Buddhist and Indian philosophers. One can deny everything in classic discriminatory fashion, step by step, phase by phase, right down to the last subtle manifestation, but one can never deny the existence of the denier. There certainly is something, an indescribable Essence, beyond the Cosmic Mind. We often refer to It by saying Devadevi Svarupaya — the sum total of all powers inside and beyond the universe. Its formless mode is admitted simply because it cannot be adequately expressed or grasped by the mind and senses. What some call the void, or shunya, is simply one of Its aspects. The Essence, on the other hand is, the wise tell us, the substratum of all that is created and the foundation upon which all rests. The mind cannot comprehend That, for It is an instrument used to both manifest and perceive the creation. Its wielder, the Parabrahma and Parashakti, whom we call the Divine Couple when They manifest in the worlds of name and form, is that Essence and cannot be adequately described or conceptualized."*

"But It can be experienced, is this not true, Mataji?" asked Ekanta in a pleading voice.

*"Yes,"* she laughed, noting his anxious tone, *"It can and It has. There are many who have testified to this and they are all of sterling character. Knowing them, even a little, it is impossible not to believe. So have no fear and hold no doubts within you, my son. Belief gradually culminates in Faith. Even if doubts persist, you must always go forward with your practice, utilizing discrimination, detachment and devotion until that glorious day will dawn when you, yourself, will behold that radiant Reality and rest forever in the ultimate Truth. As the Upanishads say about those who have truly seen, 'To them belongs Peace and to none else.'"*

Ekanta looked up at the moon once again. There was yet another teaching that it illustrated. To discriminate about appearances was to arrive at the truth of any given matter and then transcend the illusion associated with it. Therefore, the moon was communicating messages about transcendence as well. Gazing at it, floating there in the sky above all other things, the Avadhut communed with it deep within his intelligence. Lightning swift, new insights began to pour into his mind until finally he comprehended its additional message. The moon, he thought, is telling us to transcend time. Its cycles apparently come and go, it seems to change, but in actuality it never does. Its cycles and changes are mere facades.

*"Be the immutable Self,"* his gurus had taught him, *"poised and enduring amidst all apparent changes and seeming alterations. Timeless therefore changeless, deathless therefore birthless, without beginning and end and therefore eternal. In whatever way the external circumstances of universal manifestation proceed, one is to know without a doubt that the Self is real and all else is illusory."*

These words brought forth a memory of another conversation which he had instigated with his guru.

"Then, dear guru," the young man had stated one evening, "the Atman is the only unchanging and eternal verity."

*"This is what I have been harping on for years, dear disciple,"* came the words of the guru in mock exasperation, *"and you have only now just understood?"*

An abashed Ekanta had only smiled sheepishly at this sweet admonishment, waiting for further elucidation.

*"We see it in these terms, Ekanta, clear and concise. There*

*is always one, though It appears as two or many.  This applies, as well, to Brahman and the creation.  This is known among the lovers of Reality as Being and becoming.  This twofold designation places Reality as unchanging and all else as that which changes or evolves.  Brahman is pure Being; His universe is becoming.  Purusha is pure Being; Prakriti is becoming.  The Atman is pure Being and the twenty-four cosmic principles are becoming.  In short, dear one, what is Real does not evolve while all else is involved in ongoing evolutionary states.  One is constant; one is constantly inconstant."*

One evening, while contemplating Reality, Ekanta had complained to his teacher.

"Revered sir, I will never be able to realize the nondual mode of meditation, I fear.  What would you advise in this case?"

After due consideration, the guru replied:

*"Many feel and have felt the way that you do now about this issue, my son.  Is nondual realization such an easy thing to come by?  Even the basic powers granted by the Lord of the Universe such as Sri, wealth, and Bala, omniscience, are difficult for mortals to come by, and they often bring more difficulties in their train as well.  When such powers as these are hard of attainment, how much more precious and rare is the Advaita experience, that which the seers call the 'pearl of great price?'  It is as uncommon as the appearance of Prema Bhakti, Pure Love."*

After a short pause, the guru went on.

*"We feel that this experience, being synonymous with Nirvikalpa Samadhi, is only granted at the perfect moment to the sincere and aspiring seeker through the will of the Divine Being.  The Rishis noted this down in the Upanishads, saying:*

The Atman, the immortal Self of all Beings,
selects only whom it chooses for Its revelation.

*"Therefore, Ekanta, if you want a formula, you will require auspicious timing, your own dedication, self-effort and the Grace of the Divine Mother who will release you from attachment to the world, clinging to the ego and from misconception concerning what is real and what is unreal.  Beyond this, the Atman must accept you, so I would advise loving the Self with*

*your entire being and concentrating upon It as what It is —*
*your essential nature.  In addition and in the meantime, we*
*have the testament of the scriptures to drive us onward.*
*Ashtavakra, for instance, told his disciple, Janaka:"*

> Have faith, dear student, and eliminate all confusion
> that arises in the mental sheath regarding your true nature.
> The Supreme Knowledge abides within you
> and you are its sovereign.
> Know yourself to be the Atman,
> eternally perfect and beyond nature.

With these precious teachings occupying his calm and satisfied
mind, and feeling full and complete as if having taken a nutritious
meal, the Avadhut placed his mind in a restful mode and was soon
plunged into deep sleep.

He awakened early in the morning, refreshed and still fixated
on the evening's communion with Reality.  Standing up and climbing to the top of a nearby pile of rocks, Ekanta gazed westward
and was rewarded by a long look at the morning moon, receding
off into the distant horizon.  Seating himself atop this grand perch,
like an eagle surveying the land, the Avadhut once again pondered
the moon's hidden teachings.  Forgotten was the body condition.
Thoughts of food did not even enter his consciousness.  His was
the realm of the illumined mind given to the Atman and he was
eternally happy abiding there within it.

As he gazed at the distant moon, he again pondered its teachings.  The moon is setting, he thought, and will soon disappear.
Then, laughing at his naiveté, he corrected himself.  The moon is
not setting; the horizon is, as it were, moving up as the world
turns, following its orbit.  Also, he reminded himself, the moon
does not disappear nor does it wax or wane.  It is all an appearance, just like every other created thing in the universe.

Gazing lovingly at the sight, the Avadhut gradually picked up
on another teaching that the moon was communicating.  The stars
had long since disappeared, apparently, their light unable to penetrate through the more imminent light of the earth's sun.  Yet, the
moon was still present and though its light was faded compared
to the previous evening's display, it still shone distinctly in the

morning firmament. "The true nature of everything is subtle," it appeared to be saying, "and all appearances are fleeting and illusory," for Ekanta knew that with the increasing brilliance of the sun's light, the moon, too, would seemingly vanish as the stars had done. It reminded him of the teachings in the Vedanta scriptures, quoted to him by his blessed teachers:

> The light of the intellect is like the light of the moon,
> which shines by borrowed light.
> The light of the sun, however,
> is more akin to the Atman's radiance,
> for it is svayamjyoti — it shines by its own light.
> Realize your own essence to be svayamjyoti — Self-luminous.

Half an hour later the moon had disappeared below the far horizon. The Avadhut, too, had left his seat and departed. From the vantage point that he had recently occupied high atop the rocky hill, he could be seen wending his way through the various rock outcroppings below on the valley floor. Then, he too gradually vanished, blending with the changing landscape and fading into the distance in the general direction of the Indian Ocean.

# Chapter 7

# Teachings on Acceptance and Rejection

THE SEVENTH GURU — The Osprey

THE LESSON — Renunciation

*O*bserving the osprey, a small hawk that eats fish
and rodents, I gained valuable insight into the
crucial lesson of renunciation. Carrying a nice fish
and, as a result, pestered to the limit of its endurance
by crafty crows desirous of a feast, the osprey finally
gave up its piece of meat and flew away unhampered
and free from harassment. I concluded from this that
if, like the osprey, beings would let go of attachments
to name, fame, power and possessions, they could be
free and would then dwell easily and naturally in the
Atman.

It was the dark fortnight of the new moon. The Avadhut had
traveled across the holy land of Bharat in a westerly direction as
far as Madhya Pradesh and, penetrating that state, had then turned
south towards the tip of the sub-continent. Many experiences had
marked his passing, not the least of which were his visits to various pilgrimage places along the way, both notable and obscure.
Ancient caves where Buddhist monks and venerable Rishis had

208

once dwelt detained him for a few days and deep within their confines he had plunged into profound meditation, surrounded by nothing but rock walls, darkness and silence.

In this atmosphere of extreme sense deprivation, where most human beings would have been deluged with a host of their most horrific fears emerging from the recesses of their subconscious mind, the Avadhut had, instead, beheld the luminous radiance of his inner being.  This inner Light was all the more sublime in contrast with the dark depths of the mountain caves and the sound of the primal Aum was heightened as well due to the pervading stillness there.  In that sublime state of awareness he had discovered, first hand, the truth which the yogis adamantly proclaim.  This, he spontaneously expressed in a song which he composed in an ecstatic state after emerging from the caves:

> There, set against impenetrable darkness,
> in sharp contrast to the jet-black expanse of inconceivability,
> the essence of pure, conscious Effulgence appears,
> wrapped in formless splendor, infinite and sublime.
> Against the backdrop of cold stone walls,
> undetected by helpless, staring eyes,
> whose blackness enhances the sparkling magnificence
> of Thy splendor, seldom seen,
> shafts of love's lightning illumine the awestruck mind,
> while fear, terror and confusion bow low to Peace,
> tranquil, serene.
> Your thrilling Aum-laughter, O Mother,
> how it resounds here,
> spreading through the silent recesses of my mountain cave
> like seething waves of living Bliss.
> Here, the dark becomes You more, O Goddess of my soul.
> Come, reveal to me the mysteries of sweet absorption,
> and immerse me irretrievably in Thy ecstatic expanse.

After his profound experience in the caves and at this time barely aware of the body, he had wandered around in circles for an entire day.  Finally, amazed at his own inability to navigate the physical body according to his will, he finally stopped to consult the Divine Mother directly about this dilemma.  After contemplating Her for some time, he had received an answer. Standing up, he took note of where he was and where he had come from. Retracing his steps, he quickly determined that his seemingly random course revealed profound meaning. In the day's wanderings, he had circumambulated the entire mountain, caves and all, making a complete circuit of the holy place! It was then clear to him that the Divine Mother had willed him to accomplish this auspicious task and as soon as it was finished, his mind became lucid and clear and he was able to guide himself easily towards the next destination.

Many weeks later, after walking nearly half the country and as he drew near to the proximity of the border state of Kerala, he came across a charming location. Surmounting the incline of a particularly steep grassy hill, he came over the rise to face a magnificent scene. The green and lush valley that lay below could not be adequately praised with words. His eyes had to linger long in order to drink in the vast beauty of this paradise. As he looked out over the place, descriptions of heavenly lokas from the various sacred stories of the secondary scriptures of India came into his mind:

> High on the holy mount, Garuda, Narada and Sri Hari swept passed an abundance of heavenly realms. All manner of dwellings dotted the land including the farmhouses of cultivators spread over vast tracks of seeded fields and the huts of cow-keepers surrounded by lowing herds of healthy cattle. There were mountain dwellings set amidst the highlands, streaked with winter snows, and forest hermitages blessed with verdant woods full of an array of woodland creatures and peopled by illumined beings enlightened by the wisdom of the ages. Tanks and lakes filled with lovely lotuses and banks of aromatic water lilies of various hues graced the land below like a series of shining jewels. The waterfowl, geese, swans and a variety of songbirds with multicolored feathers were all singing and making cackling sounds which blended with the humming of bees and insects, all intoxicated with the lush and pristine atmosphere.

With these memorable descriptions impressed upon his mind, the Avadhut felt that he had suddenly entered one of these blissful realms.  Below him and off to the right was a deep blue lake and the low-lying sun was causing mirror-image reflections to grace its still and glassy surface.  It seemed to call to him, not just with the alluring charm of nature, but also for deeper unexplainable reasons.  Though the lake was out of his way, he could not resist a visit to its vicinity and, starting off downhill, soon found himself on a grassy area just overlooking its pristine waters.

Seating himself for a rest and some sustenance, Ekanta gazed at the scenery while he ate from his store of fruit, gathered along his journey across the more fertile southern lands.  Banana and papaya trees had become frequent as he entered the warmer climates and the householders, too, seemed more friendly and willing to share the bounty of Mother Earth's abundant stores.  During his earlier trek across less accommodating terrain, Ekanta had been forced to pick up a gourd at a small mountain village so that he could carry enough water to last him through dry mountain passes.  Thirst was a considerable problem, and though the Avadhut could do without food for days, even for a couple of weeks if necessary, water to freshen and lubricate a hard-working, well-traveled physical body was more of a necessity.  As Ekanta pulled from his water gourd, he noticed that the liquid had taken on a pungent taste.  Thinking this to be a good time to clean his gourd and take on a new supply of water, he rose from his seat and walked to the edge of the lake.

The peacefulness of the lake was indescribable.  Waterfowl abounded on the shores and many fish were seen in the shallows near the banks.  If Ekanta had not been a vegetarian, he could have had a veritable feast here, for the fish were tame and came right up to nibble on his toes when he entered the water to wade.  As he looked across the lake and off to the west, he could make out a marshy area full of wild growth and much to his surprise and delight, his roving eyes found a stand of beautiful red lotus flowers in full bloom.  Immediately, his already intoxicated mind entered a sublime state as a host of spiritual stories associating the sacred flowers with the many holy personages of the scriptures flooded his consciousness.

As he was mulling over these stories and the various anecdotes contained therein, Ekanta absent-mindedly shed his clothes and began washing the dust and dirt from his body. The water was sweet to the taste, cool and refreshing. A healing atmosphere permeated the lake and the entire region and Ekanta felt days of fatigue gradually drain from his body.

Eventually, he returned to the banks of the lake and washed his clothing while standing on shore. He then wrung out his clothes and laid them on the nearby grasses to dry. Reclining on a log that lay lengthwise across the bank with one end in the lake, he dipped his feet in the cool liquid and gazed off across the expanse of water, letting his mind enter an easy and natural flow of contemplation.

As his fertile spiritually-oriented mind opened in upon itself, the powerful humming of the primal sound, Aum, began to permeate his inner awareness. It did not block out the various sounds of nature that surrounded him, such as the lapping of the water, the buzzing of bees and the calling of songbirds that echoed across the water, but instead pervaded them all. In fact, Ekanta had realized that all other sounds were emanations of the Aum and all objects were expressions of its essential and singular vibration.

Everything, the Avadhut knew, had a sound vibration associated with it. The silent sound, Aum, was the sound of Reality, the voice of Consciousness, the primordial vibration that was ever one with the almighty Creator. His guru, blessed be her memory, had called it the "Song of Peace." Never apprehended by the ordinary senses, it only became perceptible in states of concentrated awareness or deep absorption. Detecting it in quiet contemplation, the yogis knew that they had located the sublime trail that led inward to the Source of existence itself. All duality was transcended when the Aum manifested in consciousness, for all lesser vibrations of the mind were either taken up and merged into its powerful sweep or shut down completely. This is why his other guru, blessed be his memory, had called it the "Whirlpool of Unification." The Avadhut allowed his mind to revisit his teacher once again.

*"Have you ever seen or heard of a tornado, my boy?"* said his guru one day.

"I have heard that such things exist, revered sir," returned Ekanta, "but have never experienced one myself."

*"Nor would you want to necessarily,"* responded the teacher,

*"at least one created by nature's forces.  There is, however, a tornado of another kind.  Not completely unlike the physical tornado that rips through the countryside, destroying everything in its path, the internal tornado of Aum moves through the landscape of mundane human awareness and annihilates all traces of attachment to name and form.  It, however, is a subtle force, completely transcendent of relativity, yet permeating it entirely. Like the air which, though unseen and undetected, nevertheless supports the flight of birds, the Aum cradles the universe in its all-penetrating grasp, sustaining its every movement and expression."*

Pondering these words for a moment, Ekanta said, "I have heard you speak of this paradoxical thing before, revered sir.  It is wonderful but one finds no basis upon which to accept it.  How can a thing be transcendent and present simultaneously?"

*"Wonderfully put,"* exclaimed the guru, inspired by his student's powers of expression, *"but do not expect me to be able to explain or describe this enigma.  It is a matter for open-mindedness followed by acceptance leading to direct experience.  Have you not heard the teachings of the Blessed Lord in the Bhagavad Gita? There, in that amazing scripture, Sri Krishna, says:"*

Higher understanding lies beyond the comprehension
of those who deny or reject the eternal truths
transmitted by the illumined ones.
Objections and remonstrances only serve
to drive the Truth far away.
Unfortunate, indeed, are those
who would turn a deaf ear to subtle wisdom.

"Who can successfully argue with God?" stated Ekanta.  "I, for one, will listen and take to heart everything I find to be reasonable."

*"That is a fine beginning, Ekanta,"* said the guru.  *"In due time, with such a policy as your credo, all will be revealed to you.  You ask, then, how can a thing be both present and beyond? In the same way that the world perceived by the senses is here and all around you while the world of thought is unseen and invisible, in that way can one begin to comprehend the ability of Aum to be both transcendent and immanent.  The Rishis,*

*pondering the wonderful presence of God that is immanent, transcendent and absolute — all three — knew that It must have a vehicle through which to spread Itself through the three worlds. Aum, the unstruck sound, is this vehicle, symbolized anthropomorphically by Garuda, the huge dragon bird of Sri Vishnu that travels to any location that the Blessed One wants to be taken. The transporting of consciousness and its transmigration through the various created regions, whether physical, astral or causal, is accomplished by this primal vibration."*

"I have understood by your teachings that Consciousness is ever-present and goes nowhere, revered teacher," stated Ekanta.

*"Exactly so,"* returned the guru, *"but that is Consciousness in its unconditioned state called Atman and Brahman. When the Lord creates the worlds, superimposing various coverings over the Atman like wrappings around a gift, Consciousness becomes, as it were, modified by these impositions and takes on properties. One such characteristic is movement which, on a transmigrational level, occurs in the mental sheath. Thus do such occurrences like physical sensations, the movement of prana, the experience of dreams and visions and other expressions of awareness take place. Birth, growth, decay and death also happen only in the body/mind mechanism, for the Spirit is ever free of these."*

"And what of the primal sound, revered sir?" came Ekanta's question.

*"From birth to death and death to birth goes the transmigrating consciousness,"* came the guru's reply, *"taken by the flow of prana and still convinced of its connection with the psycho/physical being. Identifying with nature, one becomes nature, just like a worm that inhabits an apple becomes all apple. Identification with Atman, however, awakens the spiritual force at the base of the spine and riding on the lightning-swift vehicle of Aum, the Mahashakti visits higher spiritual centers and sports there."*

"Do Kundalini and the primal Aum have a correlation, then?" asked the boy.

*"Yes indeed,"* affirmed the guru. *"And many of those who are spiritually attuned will perceive this silent sound upon the awakening of their inherent subtle power."*

"I have heard this sound within," said Ekanta, "but some others I have talked to who I deem to be spiritual have never heard it. How can this be, revered sir?"

*"Not all are so inclined,"* answered the teacher. *"There are some given more to internal visions and others who proceed through the illumined intellect. Still others dance in ecstasy, unaware of anything other than the blessed form of the Lord appearing within them. Just as there are many mental temperaments, Ekanta, so are there many spiritual temperaments too. Just because one does not hear the primal sound does not mean that such a person is unawakened or lacking in spirituality. Such assumptions are the cause of all manner of misunderstanding.*

*"In Truth, Ekanta,"* the guru went on after a pause, *"the Kundalini power does not awaken at all. It is ever-awake. Beings describe It as rising, but It does not move whatsoever, not in the sense that we think of motion. Others describe It as becoming unveiled, but It is never obscured in the first place. An ocean, whipped into a frenzy on the surface, nevertheless remains calm and serene in its depths. Kundalini Shakti is all depths, while what gets manifested as a result of Its pervasive existence are surface waves. What is described as Its dynamism is pure subtlety."*

"What is the correlation of Aum with Kundalini then, revered teacher?" Ekanta asked.

*"As explained in the Vedas and other scriptures, dear boy, they are one and the same. For Kundalini Shakti is the same Divine Mother who appears in the Upanishads as Umavati as well as the very one who is the grand aim of all Tantric sadhana, worshipped as Sri Durga or Mother Kali. If Kundalini is Mother's most sublime body, then Aum is Her voice."*

"If this is the case, revered sir," broke in Ekanta, "how does She speak and what does it sound like?"

The guru laughed out loud in a good-natured manner and replied, *"How nicely put, my dear student, and how typical of your line of questioning. Do you know what comes to mind as I hear your question?"*

"No sir," the boy answered, perking up in expectation.

*"The Four Stages of Ultimate Knowledge,"* the guru asserted.

*"Have I taught them to you before?"*

"No, revered sir," replied Ekanta. "Are they stages of enlightenment?"

*"Not really,"* answered the guru, *"though they are states of meditation on the Nada Brahman. As eternal principles, however, what I am speaking of is on a much higher and more integrated level than mere human understanding. It is the Mahashakti's own way of formulating and expressing some of Her infinite potential."*

After a short silence, Ekanta replied, "That sounds intriguing, revered sir."

*"Indeed it is,"* returned the preceptor, *"and I know you want to hear it. Therefore, give ear."*

For a time, the guru was lost in reflection, eyes closed, head turned upwards. Then, as if accessing some profound secret, he began to transmit one of the Devi's secrets. Whenever this happened, Ekanta always felt himself transported to an ancient time when great Rishis revealed the very highest flights of wisdom to their loving and devoted disciples. Recalling this feeling on every occasion, he became still and silent, imbibing every utterance that fell from his illumined preceptor's lips.

*"Para, Pashyanti, Madhyama and Vaikhari,"* the words came forth like peals of distant thunder; *"this is how it was taught to me long ago, dear disciple. In these four stages, if they can be enumerated so, the Divine Mother brings forth all manner of expression.*

*"At first, on the highest level, where all is in a condition of unfathomable unity, there is no manifestation, no concrete expression, no universe, not even celestial realms or subtler regions. The inconceivable fullness of Brahman is all that exists. This state, to use an inadequate word, is called Para — Supreme. All is homogenous there, everywhere. Space does not exist, either internal or external, so there can be no movement. There is no mind, either cosmic or individual, so there is no time. Being that there is no mind, there is no thought, word and act, so cause and effect — action and reaction — do not take place. If Satchitananda were taken as the essence of Brahman, this level called Para would be Its pure Chit — the highest Awareness. It is Brahmajnana, the very knowledge of*

*Brahman, but beyond the Triputi.  In short, it is the seat of all knowledge Itself, but in an unmanifested state."*

"You have mentioned the Triputi, revered sir," Ekanta interrupted.  "Can that be explained to me?"

*"Certainly,"* the teacher complied.  *"The Triputi is that triad whose relationship contains the knower, what is known and the knowledge that flows between them.  On the heart level, it can be defined as the lover, the beloved and the love that is shared. Any triple aspect similar to these, such as subject, object and the experience corresponding to them can be classified under Triputi.  Many of these exist.*

*"Now listen to what is said about the second stage of Ultimate Knowledge, called Pashyanti.*

*"Somewhere, somehow, though it occurs outside or beyond our tiny human understanding, this ultimate Brahman wishes to enter into the act of Creation.  At this time and on this level, Its boundless and omnipotent knowledge enters a phase where it creates and fills an infinite yet extremely subtle plane or realm with ideas.  Here, then, is Pashyanti — knowledge that, though still amorphous, is yet manifested as pure Intelligence. The correlation to Aum is obvious, of course.  The illumined call it the 'Seeing Word.'  Another term for this is 'Looking Out,' for this wisdom is eventually going to express Itself.  Here, though movement is going on, it is all subtle and still has not become solidified in any way.  Also, the ideas are still very abstract, seeds containing in them a whole host of potentials in greater and lesser degrees of potency and importance.  Here is where the cosmic laws that govern the process are formulated, Ekanta. They had to have had a start somewhere, is it not true?  Well, it is in the stage called Pashyanti that all things have their beginning."*

The guru gave a long sigh and reflected for a time as Ekanta watched, spellbound with anticipation.

*"At the Madhyama level, called 'Intermediary,' pure Intelligence finally gives birth to thought and word, though no external sound is present as of yet.  Positive shape and affiliation between concept and meaning are formed here.  Multiple ideas in many ongoing series are strung together ad infinitum and the connection between what they are in essence and what they*

*represent becomes clarified. One can almost imagine the Vak Devi, the Goddess of the Word, the Wisdom Mother tending a boundless garden of thought forms and linking them up with their appropriate counterparts while infusing them with meaning. This is the birth of the universe of name and form — nama/ rupa.*

*"Then, after the stage is set, all internal work accomplished and the whole macrocosmic conceptualization has been masterminded, all spills forth into manifestation. This is the Vaikhari phase of knowledge, called 'Rudimentary.' It is knowledge coming out of the Divine as speech. It is intelligence expressing itself, albeit on the grossest external level. Here, on the physical plane, many languages comprised of millions of words, all with their corollary sounds and meanings have come into being. And consciousness then communicates with consciousness. What a wonderful play, Ekanta, and as long as those who use the word remain true to the intrinsic meaning and have proper intention, knowledge can penetrate and permeate human awareness, distributing its light there for all to benefit from.*

*"The Four Stages of Ultimate Knowledge, Ekanta,"* the guru concluded, *"reveal, in short form, what has been described in the Samkhya system and other philosophies based in Truth. Advaita represents the highest Principle, Kundalini is the expression and experience of It, the Darshanas describe It to us and Aum is the sacred symbol for It All. Study It, love It, be devoted to It and It alone. All will then be revealed unto you."*

Some intangible and immediate signal abruptly caused Ekanta to bring his awareness out into the external world once again. Bringing his consciousness into his senses, he gazed across the waters of the beautiful lake. As he watched, calm yet alert, a large bird suddenly interrupted its flight pattern, paused in midair and plunged out of the sky above, grazing the surface of the lake. As the Avadhut observed this graceful incident, he saw the huge bird draw its talons from the water and head skyward, a large fish wriggling in its powerful grasp.

That osprey has its dinner, thought the Avadhut, but no sooner had he finished this thought then his eyes detected a group of crows descending upon the large feathered predator from different directions. They seemed to come out of nowhere and since the osprey's two claws were completely occupied in holding onto the large fish, it could not fend off the advances of these tenacious winged thieves. Though it strove hard to shake its attackers and struck out side to side with its sharp beak, the pesky crows easily eluded its offensive maneuvers and continued to hound it by striking with beaks and claws at both fish and carrier.

The Avadhut continued to observe this drama of nature. The osprey, called a kite in some parts of the country, flew in different directions to try and elude the crows, but the group merely followed and harassed the kite all the more. Soon, the kite turned back and flew almost directly over Ekanta's head, offering him a close-up view of the aerial dynamics. He could even hear the intensity of the beating wings and was able to more fully appreciate the struggle that was taking place above. In a last attempt to shake its attackers, the osprey abruptly changed tactics and suddenly headed straight upwards in the sky. The crows, however, unencumbered with any extra burden, merely followed, pestering the tiring hawk beyond normal endurance.

Finally, after flying again over the middle of the lake, the osprey simply let go of the fish. The ensuing result caused the Avadhut to stand up abruptly, for the crows immediately followed the downward trajectory of the forsaken fish and refrained from pestering the kite, who then flew casually on its merry way, bereft of food but free from anxiety.

"What a profound lesson!" the Avadhut called out excitedly. "I salute you, friend, and accept you as my teacher of renunciation, for it is only in giving up that one attains ultimate peace and true freedom."

Ekanta walked up the bank and sat down on the grassy surface. Inspired by the spirit of renunciation, numerous teachings were flashing across his awareness. Conversations with his teachers emerged from his consciousness as if they had occurred only yesterday.

Once, Ekanta had asked, "Revered sir, I see so many different types of spiritual aspirant. Some renounce house and home while others retain these yet remain aloof from them. Some say that the world must be given up entirely and that one should give up the body in the interim. Is the world such a horrible place, then? And if so, should we strive to transcend it?"

*"My boy,"* said the guru, *"these beings whom you encounter are at different stages of their spiritual growth and one simply cannot accurately determine their status. I have met householders, living amidst all manner of material wealth, who are fully illumined and monks, bereft of possessions, that are immersed in worldliness though appearances may say otherwise. Suffice to say that the highest attainment, at least with regards to this plane of existence that we find ourselves in, is the simultaneous attainment of harmony and unity.*

*"Yes, we must transcend the world, if for no other reason than to be able to detach from its pain-bearing transformations such as birth, disease, old age and death. We must also be able to reside in our true nature, free from all impediments and we must have a proper defense against the allurements of Maya, which befuddles even the minds of knowledgeable beings. If we are able to achieve all of this — the most positive results of spiritual life and practice — then the world is shorn of its oppressive impositions and consciousness resides easily and naturally in its original condition."*

The guru was silent for a time. Then he said, *"Renunciation, at its most mature level, is not concerned with having or not having possessions but rather with being free from the sense of ownership and possession that breeds attachment and the desire for more. Those who have, must learn how to be caretakers of God's resources; those who do not must learn patience and satisfaction with what comes naturally."*

"So," rejoined Ekanta, "one need not worry about owning objects or about having to renounce them?"

The guru smiled. *"You still have not heard me. Possessions do not bind the one who has no attachment to them. Yet, keep in mind that attachment for objects is different from caring for them. What is more, giving up attachment willingly is far better than doing so by force or because others tell you it is the thing to do. A man will give up chewing betel nut only when he gets no more enjoyment out of it and not before. His teeth may turn red and even fall out, but he will continue in his habit until he decides to give it up."*

"I understand now," said Ekanta, "but there are so many who seem to think that because they possess lands and wealth and have a husband or a wife, that they are low or unfit and can never become spiritual."

The guru frowned at this statement.

*"The problem here is twofold,"* he said. *"Primarily, feelings of inadequacy and unworthiness are the fault of the bearer and must be gotten rid of. As for those who perpetuate these feelings in others, they are mean-minded, either believing that there is something superior about them because they own nothing, which is a problem with the ego, or consciously trying to manipulate others into such deluded attitudes for their own selfish gains and in order to appear somehow superior. It is all vanity and pretense. In short, renouncing objects and action does not make one more spiritual nor does owning an abundance of things make one less spiritual. Those who hold delusions about this are either immature renunciates or are simply making excuses for themselves."*

"Revered sir," said Ekanta, "you talked about the ideal which you described as a blending of harmony and unity. Kindly explain more of this to me."

*"When renunciation is complete and mature,"* stated the teacher, *"then all that is not Brahman is eliminated and all that is Brahman remains. Since everything, without question, is Brahman, then all that truly is, is Brahman."*

"Dear teacher," laughed Ekanta, "this is perplexing. You are talking in riddles. Have you now become a Zen master as well?"

The guru smiled broadly and responded, *"There is no need for that. It cannot be more simply put, but if you demand an explanation for the sake of the intellect, then listen. That which impedes us is mind-based and deludes our thinking. Some call it Maya, but I call it personal delusion or moha. It has no existence, really, but human beings allow it to live in them. It rushes in and fills in the cracks in our thinking, finding dark crevices in which to dwell and grow. It is like a huge balloon that is all for show. It looks imposing and takes up more and more space as it grows, but a tiny pin thrust reveals that it is nothing but hot air and a loud noise. Discrimination is its hated enemy and its antithesis.*

*"After one has discriminated away moha, a certain desire to detach from the world is experienced. This allows one to perceive*

*nature or the universe as the noneternal Brahman. Discarding this too as the ideal, what is left over after such rejection is the eternal Brahman and with That the devotee identifies. Enjoying this precious find immensely, the devotee still must deal with the world and the body. Coming back to normal consciousness, but retaining knowledge of the transcendental Absolute, the devotee then learns the art of harmonization and is a perpetual blessing upon the universe. Thus does life in the world and life of the Spirit get fused into one thing. This is what I mean by the attainment of both harmony and unity. Some may liken it to Shankara's description of moksha wherein the jivatman, the embodied soul, becomes jivanmukti — liberated while living and under all conditions. I would agree, as long as those who propose this comparison understand what the great acharya meant by moksha."*

"What was Adishankara's original intention in relation to the term moksha, revered teacher?" asked Ekanta.

*"The various commentators who expound on the famous Advaitan's works,"* explained the guru, *"tell us primarily that moksha is not something that can be produced or generated since it is an ever-present verity. Secondly, it is never subject to evolution, development or transformation, for the Atman has no birth, growth, decay or death. Next, it is not the product of self-effort, for the Atman knows no distinction between bondage and liberation, nor does it even cognize such dualities, being ever-free. Therefore, moksha is not a state or condition that allows one into heavenly realms or leads one out of or away from the various earths and hells. It is transcendent of all states or conditions and is of the nature of absolute perfection. An extended period of heightened happiness or excessive joy experienced in an angelic or subtle form, then, is not moksha. Finally, the state of moksha is not attained by purification, for the Atman can never fall or become impure. Such is the partial description of the pristine condition that the jivanmukta experiences."*

After a pause, in which he seemed to consult something or someone within, the guru continued.

*"A great sannyasin once told me, 'Truth rests on Truth alone, never on illusion.' Therefore, what is real persists and what is*

*false is only an appearance.  Maya is simply God's power to enchant or conceal.  Are we to blame created objects, which have only a temporary existence in the world of name and form, for what confounds and ails us?  Objects are not to blame, action is not to blame, nor is any external thing to blame for our predicament.  Objects are only the ideas of God in gross form and action is the way in which God expresses Himself throughout the universe.  Even Maya is not to blame, for how can something which is nothing be the cause of anything?"*

Ekanta laughed at this concluding statement, then said, "I am still a bit confused, yet it is beginning to make sense.  What you are telling me is that my own delusion is responsible for all the problems that I experience and I fabricate these delusions constantly and often unknowingly, all to my own regret."

*"Well put,"* stated the guru, obviously impressed with the boy's powers of assimilation.  *"Search the mind and locate every little adverse tendency that exists there — the judgmental nature, the tendency towards despondency or depression, one's intolerance of others, one's feelings of remorse or shame, feelings of inadequacy and unworthiness and even those nagging fears and misgivings that plague you.  Put your finger on the likes of those, renounce those, and the battle is won!  These thought-phantoms are the very things which one needs to renounce, not the natural mode of spontaneous existence that, when properly understood and executed, is the very basis of spiritual living.  You must make this discipline a daily practice, though, and keep it up for some time until the old habitual mind that allows these negativities to persist is flushed clean of them and a new way of thinking is established."*

"This seems to be a remaking of the mind, respected teacher," said Ekanta.  "It appears simple, but from what I have seen of the internal mind, it is not so."

The guru folded his arms together and suddenly seemed very powerful indeed.

*"Some call this a change of attitude, but surface affirmation without practical application seldom penetrates deep to the root of subconscious problems.  Some locate these devils and, as it were, stare at them, helpless.  Others verbally renounce them and pretend away their existence, but how is it that few ever rid*

*themselves of them completely? Affirmation and negation are
good ways of beginning, but much more is needed."*

Ekanta remained speechless at this point, since he again saw
the guru communing within the Self.

*"No,"* continued the guru, by and by, *"it is not enough to
merely enter the Ganges for a purifying bath. Like sins, the
vultures that were previously perched upon your shoulders and
that had taken flight at the sight of the sacred river, will only
return again when you get out of the waters. One must destroy
them as they revisit, after becoming pure and attaining a position of renewed strength."*

"How is this achieved, revered master?" said Ekanta excitedly.
"You are enumerating the fine points of involved spiritual practice which rarely get explained or utilized."

*"You forget yourself,* the teacher reprimanded. *"Remember not
to address me as master. Truly, there is no such thing in the
entire world, save when the Avatar appears. Any others calling
themselves such are sorely deluded. You should never go near
such a person."*

Ekanta knew how his guru felt about this matter and was about
to excuse himself, but without waiting for an apology, the teacher
plunged onward in his discourse.

*"Once an aspirant perceives these subtle problems with their
gross results, he or she must then destroy them using a type of
detachment that depletes them of energy. One must not give
them renewed energy and this often happens when one grapples
with them under wrong orientation and devoid of proper guidance. This is where the spiritual teacher is invaluable and
advises appropriately. One can use the energy inherent in these
negativities to one's own advantage, coupling this tactic with
what the Vedantists call, Pratipakshabhavanam — the raising
of a positive wave. One cannot give up something, either physical or mental, without replacing it with something else. If you
renounce the world, you must then put God in its place. The
most powerful wave to possess is the knowledge of one's divine
nature, which the guru transmits early on in spiritual life and
supports throughout. After that, there are many beneficial qualities to utilize such as love, dispassion and so forth."*

"So, revered teacher," Ekanta responded, "we cannot give too much attention to imperfections, yet we must somehow find a way of dealing with them.  It sounds precarious."

*"They do not call the spiritual path 'as narrow as a razor's edge' for nothing my boy,"* stated the guru.  *"Suffice to say that the destruction of negative tendencies which leads to peace of mind begets ultimate freedom, and true freedom is always accompanied by responsibility.  Mature renunciation, the illumined being's crowning achievement, is supremely natural and almost transparent.  In the early stages, it is accomplished by determined self-effort combined with perseverance in the company of an illumined preceptor.  What each one experiences along the way is too subtle to be described in detail, but the important thing is to take the steps.  The roof of the house can not be reached without taking the steps."*

Thus was mature renunciation and the various steps leading to it described to Ekanta at an early age and he spent much time in contemplating this important aspect of spiritual life.  This lesson on Maya and moha was greatly beneficial, though it sounded paradoxical.  Later, as he was traveling the mountain passes of northern India, he had come to appreciate it in a new way.

High on the Himalayas one day at sunset, sitting quietly and resting himself, Ekanta gradually become aware of a female mountain lion and her cubs at a slightly lower elevation below him.  The Avadhut had watched, enthralled, as the mother lion played with the small cats, sometimes in a ferocious way.  Putting on airs of extreme anger and occasionally roaring fearfully, the lioness batted the cubs here and there and often took them into her powerful jaws close to those fearsome fangs.  Undaunted, however, the cubs fought on bravely, ignoring the impending danger and set upon their own victory over this imposing foe.  It was all affectation, Ekanta realized, though seemingly real.  As his mind rolled back in time to that discussion with his guru, he then understood, to a greater extent, his teacher's description of the unreality of Maya coupled with its clever assumption of reality.

*"The potentially confusing appearance of Maya must be traced to its subtle source, located, encountered, engaged and seen for what it is.  It is the stuff that creation consists of.  Wherever there is manifestation, you must know that Maya is at work.  As for moha which, unlike Maya, has its temporary existence*

as Brahman's power, it is completely unreal. Destroy moha and see beyond Maya, Ekanta. The Divine Mother, whose marvelous play is all about us, will assist you. Take refuge in Her and invoke Her awesome Presence within you. May She, the primal guide, our refuge be."

Thinking thus, the words of Sri Krishna, the Avatara, entered his mind, adding considerable weight and substance to this realization:

All that is unreal never comes into being.
All that is real never ceases to be.

From high mountain passes and cold winter snows, the Avadhut abruptly returned to warm tropical waters. The osprey had taken him to far away places and to undreamed of heights. It had long since disappeared over the distant hills but its teachings remained present, lodged securely in the open and illumined heart and mind of the Avadhut. Everything is my teacher it seems, thought the Avadhut, and I am the eternal student. What a great boon from the Mother this is. She has brought me to this special place and has introduced me to a true renunciate. The osprey probably flies the evening skies at this very moment, wiser for his experiences, strengthened as a result and unruffled by all trials.

Thinking so, the Avadhut gathered his clothes and ascended the grassy slope above, ready for the approach of evening and the gaze of his ever-present friends, the stars.

# — Chapter 8 —

# Teachings on Perfect Well-Being

THE EIGHTH GURU —The Python

THE LESSON —Contentedness

*After beholding the amazing python, a king*
*among reptiles, I came to understand what inner*
*contentment consists of, for that mighty snake,*
*fearing nothing and always abiding patiently, waits*
*for its food to approach in due time and does not*
*exert unnecessarily. Just so do I now content myself*
*with what is due to me according to my deeds and*
*their outcome, remaining immersed in and subject to*
*the Lord's Will and satisfied with what comes my*
*way naturally. Taxing the mind and body with*
*concerns of abundance and satiation is now foreign*
*to me and I am at peace at all times. This is an*
*indescribably wonderful condition.*

With the rising of the sun, the Avadhut rose as well and by midday had entered the tropical rain forests of Kerala. Fording several small streams along the way, he finally came upon a large river, swollen due to recent heavy rains. Following the course of this river, he encountered a tiny village where he hoped to find a

227

small boat which could take him across the river and a little closer to the ocean, his intended destination.

Searching through the village proved to be no problem, for it consisted of only a few streets, a couple of shops and the simple homes of country dwellers. After trading a few items which he had picked up on his travels in other provinces for a few articles of food and some rupees, Ekanta approached an elderly man who was seated on the riverbank near the small boat dock and asked him if his craft was for hire.

"Yes, I can take you downstream for a reasonable price," said the man.

"How far does this river go?" asked Ekanta.

"It does not reach the ocean, if that's what you're thinking," answered the man, "but turns and heads inland for a time. Eventually it joins with a major waterway and eventually empties into the Indian ocean. It is far faster to go across land or to another river in order to reach the ocean, but one should take this river for a half a day first."

Accepting this information from one who seemed to know the lay of the land, Ekanta agreed upon a fee and entered the boat.

The boatman was a remarkable person. Ekanta found this out during a conversation that took place as the boat lazily floated downstream with the current. At first, there was only silence as the journey got underway, but soon the Avadhut noticed the sidelong looks of the elderly man. He was evidently interested in the Avadhut's appearance and curious about his life, though he was obviously too polite to ask. Ekanta decided to open the conversation.

"May I have your name, sir?" asked the Avadhut.

Grinning a practically toothless smile, the man said, "Surebha, revered sir."

"How long have you lived in this region?" returned Ekanta.

"For as long as I can remember," answered the boatman, "but not too long to forget where I originally came from."

"By the look in your eyes, I take it that you are referring to your essential nature as Spirit, is it not true?" asked Ekanta.

"Precisely so," said the boatman, who continued to pole off of the bottom of the river with a long bamboo staff to avoid rocks and occasional floating objects.

"Can you explain to me what you are describing as this origin?"

asked the Avadhut.

"By the look in your eyes, revered sir," returned the boatman, "I would venture to say that you would be better suited to do that."

"Still," said Ekanta, "I would like to hear your attempt at the impossible."

The elderly man laughed and continued, "Only the illumined know that it is futile to try to describe the indescribable and only teachers of humanity can truly take up the challenge adequately."

"Yes," returned the Avadhut, "my teacher had a story for that. He said that it takes only a small razor-knife to kill oneself, while it takes a sword and shield to kill others."

"What was his meaning in that statement?" asked the boatman.

The Avadhut smiled and sat up straight on the seat of the boat.

"You said that it is only the spiritual teacher who can aptly describe what God is like. It is therefore up to the guru to transfer the proper knowledge to us. This, adequately accomplished, facilitates the death of the ego. So, I say that one needs only a little essential knowledge to effect the death of this rascal ego in oneself, but to deal a death blow to the egos of countless others, one will need possession and mastery of every spiritual teaching and system of philosophy known to humanity. For this reason, at least, the guru is no ordinary person."

"That is a satisfying teaching," breathed the boatman. "I have often wondered whether all this knowledge is necessary for everyone in order to attain realization. Now I understand. But tell me, revered sir, are you such a teacher? For if you are I have a few questions for you."

"I have never thought of myself as such," came the Avadhut's answer, "for I find that there is only one guru — Absolute Reality Itself. I am an eternal student of that One."

"Well answered," came the boatman's response, "but since you are such a devoted student, I deem you to be an adept teacher. Therefore, you will not mind my questions."

"If I can be of any assistance whatsoever, I am entirely at your service," replied the Avadhut.

"To achieve peace of mind and be content under all circumstances, what is needed?" asked Surebha.

"In this world, one will require the knowledge that everything perceived by the mind connected to the senses is finite and therefore only a temporary condition," stated the Avadhut. "Without this key, all that one does or sees or hears or experiences will be attended by some doubt or fear, whether it be subtle or uncomfortably apparent. To know Reality to be entirely transcendent of name and form, beyond earth, hells and heavens, free of conceptualization, and superior to all the alluring appearances of nature, that brings peace of mind. Also, this is not a transcendence that annuls or effaces the universe. Rather, it is a transcendence that is all-pervasive yet independent of all the limitations found in the world and its empirical process."

"What you are saying is true, no doubt, and wise," said Surebha, "but I find that it is not enough. The pundits offer this teaching as well, though in their case it is mostly mere lip service. People hear it and say, 'Oh, that is profound,' but nothing profound happens thereafter!"

"Sadly, this is true," returned the Avadhut, "but this is because no effort is put forth to imbibe and implement the essence of this teaching. My guru used to say, *'Realizing the Self within you and realizing that the Self is in you are two vastly different things.'* To know this Self, the Atman, is to know that It is the only Reality while all else that we see, hear, taste, touch, smell and even think are, at best, transitory."

"Is there a method, then, by which to realize this?" asked Surebha. "I mean something tangible and beneficial that offers direct help rather than loose philosophies that are as insubstantial as the ephemeral things which they seek to get rid of?"

"Yes," answered the Avadhut firmly, "such a method exists. In truth, there are many methods but some are less effective than others. There is one that I know of that, in this regard, 'cuts at the throat,' as we say. That is, if followed and comprehended, it puts a swift end to ignorance of all types, surely and completely."

"Please tell me of it here and now, if you can," asked the boatman, almost pleadingly. Noticing the change of tone in Surebha's voice, the Avadhut readily complied.

The boat coasted on down the river carrying its two precious occupants. Wonderful scenery continued to slip by, changing dramatically from minute to minute. Soon, however, the external view was abandoned for the inner view as the Avadhut and the boatman became engrossed in the subject at hand.

"I have two Sanskrit phrases for you, Surebha, which will both introduce and summarize what I have to tell. One is Tattva-Shuddha and the other is Sattva-Purusha-Nytakyati. The first means purification of principles and the other roughly translates as knowing one's pure nature, called Atman, to be eternal and unchanging."

As the Avadhut proceeded to tell Surebha all that he knew about these two spiritual principles, his own mind echoed the same teachings that were given to him in days long past by his own teachers.

*"You ask me what is the essence of all spiritual practice, young man?"*

These words had come from his guru's lips one evening as the two ended a two-hour meditation together at dusk.

"Yes," Ekanta had answered, "I want to know. I have studied many systems now and I know, by your patient teaching, that each has its sights set on something. What, then, in your opinion, dearest Guruji, is the true attainment?"

*"If you ask this question in reference to the mode of practice, then I should say that Tattva-Shuddha is the consummate goal, done, of course, with the Advaitic orientation. Its result, from the standpoint of attainment alone, is the highest realization and that is called Sattva-Purusha-Nytakyati. These two are to the sacred Tantric path what neti neti and its goal are to Vedanta."*

"Guruji," said Ekanta in sincere astonishment, "you amaze me! All these years I have been studying hard with you and our Mataji, as well as with Yogindra Yogi in the cave on the mountaintop, and I have never heard mention of these two phrases."

Laughing for a moment, the guru cleared his voice and said, *"Do you believe, then, that although there is an infinite amount of knowledge, both spiritual and secular, in the Cosmic Mind of God — so much in fact, that our most illumined saints and sages have only been able to gather a few sweet grains of it from the giant sugar hill of Reality, so much so that even though the Rishis performed intense austerities for hundreds of years to receive what little is contained in the Vedas — that you, a youngster, should now have the entirety of it after a mere ten years of study with three rather insignificant and humble teachers?"*

Abashed at these words, spoken in tones of incredulity from his own guru's mouth, Ekanta had fallen into a dumbstruck silence. Smiling, yet still colored with an aura of power and seriousness, the preceptor finally broke the silence.

"*Your thirst for knowledge is admirable, my brave disciple, but never harbor the idea that the tiny human mind can know everything along the path of Jnana Yoga. Holy Mother, in Her bountiful grace and mercy, has fashioned it so that we will have and enjoy an eternity of fresh, vital pursuit of Her essential Wisdom. You will never find the Mataji or I or any other wisdom knower or seeker complaining about this fact. Unlike the voracious and impatient youngsters, though, those of us with experience have learned this lesson. She, the Mahashakti, is an ocean of pure Intelligence and we are mere fishing boats. The best among us may be ferryboats or huge oceanliners but all are minuscule when set upon such a vast expanse. It would be well to remember this in your pursuit of Wisdom.*"

"Yes Guruji," came the young man's quiet words.

After a short pause, in which the guru sat quietly as if he had forgotten what had prompted this exchange, Ekanta finally asked, "Revered sir, you were speaking of Tattva-Shuddha and one other term. May I know what this entails?"

Gazing upon his spiritual charge with great favor, the guru replied, "*Of course. I thought you would never ask!*"

Saying so, he began to explain the meaning.

"*Tattva-Shuddha is the systematic elimination of all that is moving, changing or evolving, so that the embodied human consciousness can actually perceive, once and for all, that which is stationary, immutable and not subject to evolution. Its process is actually brought to bear by using the same power of mind or mental self-effort utilized in the Vedanta called neti neti. Shuddha means purity, tattva means principle — in this case, the many physical elements and aspects of the creation. Can you list them for me, dear disciple?*"

"There are twenty-four cosmic principles according to Samkhya Philosophy, dear teacher, such things as fire, water, earth and air as well as the constituents of the body, senses and the mind."

"*Yes, that is a beginning, dear student, but Shaivism lists twelve more. Tantra Philosophy refers to them as kanchukas.*"

*They are extremely subtle Divine verities. Using thirty-six in all then, Abhava Yoga asks us to explore them and do away with them. This process, the purification of principles, leads to the realization that the Atman is different than all created things."*

"How does this proceed and how does the realization dawn?" Ekanta asked, breathlessly.

*"First,"* replied the guru, *"you must understand that God's creation is pure and complete from its very inception, Ekanta, so do not think that by negating each of these principles in turn, we are discarding them due to inherent impurities. They are what they are, expressions of Divinity, their only imperfection being their transitory nature. So, purification here means knowing the nature of each to be mutable and involved in the evolutionary process. Water is water, whether pure or mixed with contaminates. Add a purifying agent and the water regains its essential quality once again. In similar fashion, the mind is contaminated by all sorts of deceptions and misconceptions. The process of Tattva-Shuddha rids the mind of these unwanted distortions and coverings by reminding us of what we truly are: the Atman, pure, eternal and indivisible rather than the universe of name and form.*

*"Therefore, dear student, to successfully effect this powerful sadhana you must systematically take each element of your being, which is truly in a state of becoming, as well as every facet of the created universe and reject it outright. Then you will know the truth of Sattva-Purusha-Nytakyati — that all else evolves while the Atman does not. This path of internal practice that the sadhaka embarks upon is actually involution, a point in time when Maya recedes for whatever reason, and the aspirant beholds the veils falling away from his inner perception and sees the necessity of actualizing this process."*

"Revered teacher," breathed Ekanta in awe, "what system does this come from? You mentioned both Vedanta and Samkhya and even referred to Shaivism, but also intimated the Tantric way."

*"Yes,"* responded the guru, *"but the key phrase I used was Mahayoga, the consummate way of the Mahashakti. This is nothing less than that, Ekanta, for such spiritual ascent is facilitated and guided by Kundalini Shakti Herself. You see, then, how important our Divine Mother path is, despite its recessive*

*nature throughout time. All the darshanas, as our poets and saints have sung and told, are so many avenues to Divine Reality. She reveals them, they do not reveal Her!"*

"Dear sir," Ekanta said after some silent reflection, "There must be more to it than this."

*"That is an understatement if I have ever heard one, dear student,"* replied the preceptor.

"What I mean is this," the boy went on, "that the process you described is not so easy as it sounds, for the mind is to be encountered as well and where the mind is, the ego is bound to be lurking."

*"Well put,"* replied the guru, *"and astute as always, but what is it exactly that you want to know?"*

"Why everything, of course, Guruji, but since I cannot have that so long as this limited mind is operative, please tell me what signs there are to measure one's progress while performing the powerful Tattva-Shuddha and reaching for Sattva-Purusha-Nytakyati."

Smiling openly due to the young aspirant's wit and memory both, the preceptor proceeded to answer the question.

*"The Seven Victories, Ekanta: these must be attained in order to realize this greatest of Truths. Accomplish Bhuta Jaya first, which is victory over the elements which support the concept of name and form. Realize that your true nature is not the five elements nor any of their various permutations. Study earth, water, fire, air and ether with the peaceful and introspective mind. You will gradually see them as they are, building blocks, properties of Prakriti. It is Mother Nature, in accordance with individual karma, that adeptly fashioned this body. Mulavidya, root ignorance, springs from the false idea that we are matter, consisting of the constituents of nature. Every other misconception breeds from and upon that. First, know that you are not the body and then use it for a divine purpose. Otherwise it will use you, for attachment to name and form is the ego's playground.*

*"Next attain Indriya Jaya, control of the senses, for nothing can be accomplished without this. In each of the senses there is a subtle power that operates. Get ahold of those, control their outward-going energy and concentrate that force on the heart for a time. A great ability conducive to yoga will then come into your possession. There are various yogas that pertain*

*specifically to this and the other victories I am describing and which all fall under the Divine Mother's comprehensive system of Kundalini Yoga, of Mahayoga. They must be practiced under the tutelage of an illumined preceptor before the ultimate force of Kundalini Shakti will even occur to the mind, let alone rise to the heights."*

Pausing in his explanation for a moment, the guru said, *"Many posture and pretend to know this most wonderful and elusive of sciences, Ekanta, even after only hearing of it secondhand. But few practice and master the Mahayoga. I have saved mention of it until now not only so that you would learn all the prerequisites first and be ready for its message, but also so that you would not get trapped or seduced by any mention of it by charlatans and pretenders. These types reduce the Mahayoga to physical exercises of the body and charts and graphs of the nervous system. They describe the seven centers of consciousness in a way that limits them to the analytical mind and its tiny understanding. In short, they strip it of its direct experience, its natural spontaneity, in the same way that they do to all other approaches."*

After a short silence, in which Ekanta saw his guru calm himself with one long breath, the preceptor continued once again. Evidently, the thought of unqualified beings tampering with the Divine Mother's perfect system affected him deeply.

*"Prakriti Jaya comes next — control and victory over the gunas of nature and the other universal laws. Seeing creation for what it is and knowing its origin aids immensely along the path. Integral to this level of understanding is the knowledge that nature is perfect just as it is, as the Creator fashioned it. This does not mean that nature is the goal to be sought after; for though it contains elements that inspire, it also holds limitations which restrict spiritual evolution. Knowing it as a tool which the Mahashakti uses for divine expression leads the devotee inward to a much fuller state of existence and experience. That is, in fact, the difference between becoming, a shifting facet of nature, and Being, a permanent aspect of Divine Reality.*

*"After these three initial Jayas have been attained, Manojavittvam, the utilization of the mind's subtle powers, is gained. Having this under control, one can move with the speed of*

*thought to any location and it is all accomplished internally. Whereas, in ordinary or unawakened beings, the mind is slave to nature and the senses and riddled with the holes of ego-oriented thought and action, the controlled mind is an infinite stronghold of power for Self-realization. One finds, in this regard, that there are worlds within worlds residing in the subtle internal capacity of the mind, and that all manifest things have been created out of the power and energy of thought. Such realizations and insights unveil, in time and with practice, the secrets of Mahayoga and the presence of the Kundalini Shakti Herself. Such a victory, then, cannot be underestimated.*

*"After achieving Manojavittvam, Vikarana Bhava, the power of perception without the senses, becomes possible. Imagine, Ekanta, what wonder there is in that consciousness that is freed from the habitual and limiting misconception that the senses connected to the mind which perceives the five elements and all created objects — that this constitutes the whole of existence. This is the essence of spiritual discovery and, short of perceiving the Atman, is a marvelous experience. There are many adept practitioners who have attained this power and simply live in a high and refined state at all times. Living within, in sacred communion with the highest principle of unified mind called the illumined intellect, it is not long before both the vision of the Atman and an opportunity to truly merge with It present themselves.*

*"There can only be one more hurdle after Vikarana Bhava, Ekanta, before attaining the Sattva-Purusha-Nytakyati. That is called Pradhana Jaya — victory over the very first creative principle. In Samkhya, the Mahat, or Cosmic Mind, is that hurdle, while in other reckonings there are twelve even subtler levels to transcend. Whatever the case may be, suffice to say that, at this stage, the Atman is perceived as an all-pervasive and ever-present Reality. It is not anything created, nor does it evolve. How glorious! Knowing the Atman to be completely other than all created things and the only permanent Reality, the only true Existence, this is what is meant by Sattva-Purusha-Nytakyati."*

As the Avadhut finished telling Surebha what his guru had transmitted to him regarding Tattva-Shuddha and Sattva-Purusha-Nytakyati, a short silence ensued.

Surebha finally broke this silence to say, "Now do I understand how precious and holy is this sacred land of India and how sacred are its illumined preceptors."

As he tried to take the dust of the Avadhut's feet, even momentarily abandoning the course of the boat along the river, Ekanta took him by the shoulders and embraced him instead.

"That is not necessary," the Avadhut said. "I am only repeating what my guru has told me. You have asked about self-effort and method and I have complied with what I know to be true. It is that simple."

"To conclude, though," the Avadhut continued after Surebha had returned to his chore, "I must say that it is perplexing to me that people expect to possess the rarest jewel in existence when they have nothing with which to purchase it. Neither arguing against or giving up will bring them success. They must begin to explore their infinite potential and persevere until the goal is reached. There is no other way. As the musical sage sings, *'Can a mere scrub bush bear sweet mango fruit?'*"

"Ah," breathed Surebha, "you know about the wisdom songs of the great poet-saints of India! They have been my companions, oh, for so many long years."

"Your name," asked Ekanta, "does it not have something to do with the voice?"

"Yes, dear sir," answered the boatman, smiling proudly. "My father, himself a singer, told me that it translates to mean 'one possessing an excellent voice.'"

"If that is true, my friend, please offer a song to the river gods and goddesses for our safe journey," pleaded the Avadhut.

"Very well," said the boatman, and turned to face forward towards the riverway ahead. Soon, a melodious song came floating back to the Avadhut's ears, sung in sweet Bengali dialect and with all the fine feelings and sentiments common to that people.

O boatman, steer this ship across the ocean of delusion.
Navigate this precious craft in calm and lucid seas.
Avoid three reefs of danger – the heavens, earths and hells.
Steer clear of islands peopled by conventionality.

Anchor firmly in the port of Mother's steady Wisdom.
Make merry in the harbor town of blissful peace of mind.
Explore the inland regions of the Atman's safe abode,
and build a home of Truth
upon the mountains that you find.

Shankari's Feet are steady boats, Her bliss, a mighty river,
which wends its way to Brahman
wherein peace sublime resides.
Meditation is Her thought, Her Name, a skilled companion.
In this, Her stream of boundless love eternal, I abide.

After an appreciative pause, the Avadhut finally spoke.

"Such songs are the stuff that Reality is made of," he said wistfully.

"What was that?" asked the boatman.

"Just an old saying, slightly modified," returned the Avadhut. "Thank you for that delightful song."

"The pleasure is entirely mine," replied the boatman, "but please good sir, kindly continue with your discourse. What else can you tell me?"

The Avadhut reflected a moment, then said, "What one needs next, after realizing the ephemeral nature of the universe, is a way to merge with the Creator of the universe. Since something cannot come from nothing, the wise realize that there is a Source of existence, that the universe is the effect of some cause. By shutting out the senses and concentrating awareness in the shrine of the heart in meditation, that primal Cause, the eternal Subject, reveals itself and is beheld by the sincere seeker. As the poet-saint, Ramprasad has said, 'It is the magician that is real, not his tricks.' Therefore, we must seek and find the Reality beyond appearances."

"Discovering Its existence is one thing," cut in Surebha, "but accomplishing communion and immersion with It is another."

"True," affirmed the Avadhut, "so the wise, at this point, advocate the use of heartfelt love and unstinting perseverance. The Lord cannot resist the intense devotional feelings of the persistent devotee and is bound to appear. Like an iron filing drawn by the magnet, the Lord rushes to the place where sincere devotion is manifesting itself.  Is there any wonder in this?"

The boatman was silent for a time, then he said, "What you advocate, then, is a combination of knowledge, action, meditation and devotion, all accomplished over a long and intensified period of time."

"That is beautifully put," the Avadhut stated with evident admiration.  "The combination of the four Yogas is not unknown to us you know, though it has been lost in recent times due to the diminished understanding of the human mind.  Everything has become isolated, compartmentalized, diluted and obscured in the Kali Yuga.  Is it any wonder, then, that spiritual life has become the same?"

The boat coasted on in a southerly direction, easily and at a good pace.  There was little exertion needed to keep it on its course and this facilitated the moment perfectly.  Finally, the Avadhut spoke again.

"Peace of mind, then, maintained under all conditions, do all of your questions revolve around that, friend?"

"I didn't think so," replied Surebha, "but your eloquent discourse has answered any others that were floating about my brain.  I am indeed fortunate to have you as a companion this day and I thank you."

"It is my gratitude that is extended to you, kind sir," said the Avadhut.  "In your presence, whether in silence or in conversation, I feel the same peace of mind.  If one holds the ideal of peaceful communion with Reality, the shantadasya way, one follows the path of least resistance."

"Yes," agreed the boatman, "it is the way of 'Shantoham, Shantoham,' prescribed by the ancient Rishis — His name and form are Peace Eternal and in silence the devotee realizes this."

As the sun was now high in the sky and past its zenith, Surebha suggested that they stop the boat on the side of the river and take their meal.  Ekanta agreed heartily and it was not long before they spotted a perfect landing sight, complete with a clearing in the jungle nearby.  Anchoring the boat by tying it to a tree overhanging the river, the two worked their way through the thick jungle to the nearby clearing.  Arriving there, Surebha spread a cloth and the two passed around and shared what meager fare they possessed between them.  Along with some pure water brought in

Ekanta's gourd from the now far-off pristine lake, the meal was splendid and satisfying for both.

As soon as supper was concluded, Surebha asked, "Where did you get this sweet tasting water and where has that strange-shaped gourd come from?"

"The gourd," answered Ekanta, "I picked up in central India at a village marketplace in Madhya Pradesh. This wonderful water came from a scenic lake near the border of Kerala. The gourd, I'm afraid, has acquired the tendency of making the water taste bitter at times, but this water is fresh and has not yet soured."

"That reminds me of the story of the dry and austere sadhaka," said Surebha, "who went from pilgrimage place to pilgrimage place, gradually becoming more and more sattvic and sweet as realization dawned upon his mind. His gourd, however, even though it had been to all the same holy sights, remained as bitter as ever. As one's nature is, so does one remain."

"This is true in most every case," responded the Avadhut, "except in spiritual life. In the realm of sadhana, where study of scriptures, austerities and devotional practices hold sway, transformation of base or mundane human nature is not only possible it is guaranteed if the proper orientation and procedures are followed sincerely and with constancy. Such is the grace of our Lord and Divine Mother. They create the universe of living beings, They maintain the illusion of separation in us and They also awaken us at the proper time. Even the desire to exert self-effort in order to realize God is given by Them. Those who know this and surrender themselves accordingly, escape the restrictions of a goal-oriented, process-oriented type of sadhana and become adepts in the Advaita Vedanta sadhana. From this unique orientation do the knowers of Brahman emerge."

Thinking on these and other wonderful teachings, the two men packed up their belongings and headed back for the boat. As they entered the current of the great river once again, the Avadhut likened it to the mind's return to spiritual subjects after being distracted by the world and its activities. Such peace and bliss pervaded the river, his companion and the entire surroundings, that the Avadhut did not care if the journey went on forever. Evidently, Surebha felt the same way, for he showed no impatience whatsoever to be at any particular destination at any given time.

All was, it seemed, left to some indeterminable divine schedule that operated according to an unseen agenda. Both of the occupants in the boat were entirely agreeable to its dictates and rested in peaceful contentment, talking about spiritual life or remaining silent in turns according to their own sweet wills.

As late afternoon fell, the river showed signs of turning in a westerly direction. It was sometime during this change of the river's general course that Surebha moved his craft towards the shoreline. Stopping on a sand spit that jutted out into the river, he jumped out of the boat.

"We have arrived at a parting of the ways, revered friend," he exclaimed. "This is where you should head into the jungle and search for another river to take you towards the sea. I have stopped here because I know of a well-worn trail that will bring you safely to civilization. I will lead you to it since the trail head is less than a mile from here."

Dragging the boat onto the shore and covering it with palm fronds to camouflage it, the two headed inland, Ekanta following the lead of his new friend with complete faith and trust. A complex network of interlacing vines, tropical ferns and shower trees clogged the entire landscape so that there was hardly a minute portion of earth visible. Overhead, monkeys, insects and multicolored songbirds produced a continual din so that it was barely possible to distinguish the call or cry of one species from another. A basic pathway was visible, though it had become mostly overgrown since the last time that visitors had walked upon it. The growth rate in the jungle was so rapid, the Avadhut surmised, that it would take only a brief few days before such a trail was completely obliterated from view.

After a half an hour's walk, signs of a break in the jungle became visible. Rounding a bend in the trail, the two men came upon a small canyon separating the jungle into two halves. Thick greenery grew up the sides of both canyon walls and a few waterfalls could be seen falling from different areas on the slopes below. A prominent trail could be detected up ahead on the same side of the canyon that the two men occupied. It was here that Surebha stopped and turned to face the Avadhut.

"Our all-too-brief time is over already," came his words in a soft voice, "but I want you to know that should you ever visit these parts again, both my boat and my home are open to you without reservation."

The Avadhut gazed upon this wonderful man, seeing only the Lord dwelling there within him.

"I am not certain if our paths will ever cross again," stated Ekanta, "but I know with a certainty that you and I are one. The devotees of the Lord constitute one cohesive whole. They form a caste all their own. No insurmountable differences can exist in that atmosphere, for it is the rarefied boon of holy company."

"It is true," returned Surebha. "The Blessed Lord has arranged it so that those who sojourn in this difficult realm of relativity will never want for sacred communion. Though these episodes may be few and far between in some instances, they are always completely fulfilling when they occur."

"Such has been the case with our meeting," declared Ekanta. "You have been my boatman, ferrying me across the solid earth to my next destination. The journey was exquisite in all aspects."

This compliment brought a huge smile to the face of Surebha, who, after saluting the Avadhut profoundly, turned slowly and began to retrace his steps towards the river. Saluting him as well, the Avadhut stood looking after his friend's departure. As he watched, the melody of a familiar song drifted back to his ears. The boatman was offering a fond musical farewell, the lyrics describing spiritual sentiments appreciated by all lovers of God:

> In boundless seas of sublimity,
> dive deep, Oh mind, dive deep.
> On ocean's floor, too few who know
> the treasures one can reap.
>
> Govinda's clan in Vrindaban,
> from whom we never part.
> Seek shelter there, abiding in
> the shrine within the heart.
>
> The wisdom lamp shines constant there,
> reflecting inner Light.
> And tames the mind and leads it on
> to Atman's dizzy height.

O boatman free, please leadeth me
to spiritual rebirth.
And take this body-boat of mine
across the solid earth.

Who can say how you are called,
Oh guide who knows this game.
Kabir, he knows, and speaks his mind,
'tis Guru, praise his name.

As the final words of the song faded away on the thick tropical air, the Avadhut bade a silent farewell to his boatman and turned to continue on his way. He was surprised at how far he had come in one day, but he was also aware that he would soon need shelter as darkness was approaching rapidly. He did not cherish the idea of spending the night in the open in these jungle areas, for whereas he could bear the intrusion of insects and mosquitoes, there were bound to be predators here as well. Thinking about this situation, he took to the path and was making good headway in no time.

A few hours later, with the considerable impediment of impending darkness encroaching on his forward progress, Ekanta was just about to pick a tree in which to sleep for the night when his eyes caught the rays of a dim light up ahead. Quickening his pace, he soon found himself standing in front of a small hut. Calling out to see who might be inside, he heard no answer. Drawing near the door of the hut, he saw a sign on the door. It indicated that visitors were welcome and should come in. Looking back into the pitch black jungle recesses, Ekanta did not hesitate further and entered the small dwelling.

A lamp, trimmed to burn very low, was lit and standing in the corner of the single room on a small rustic table. Except for a small wooden platform and a few woven articles, this was the only furniture present. Ekanta found a corner and sat down on the floor, taking a small drink from his water gourd. As he sat in this strange place, he noticed how silent it was. Only a few nocturnal insects could be heard, and their sound was distant.

After a short time had passed he heard the sounds of someone approaching. The footsteps lingered outside the hut for a moment, then approached the door.  When the door swung open, Ekanta was surprised to find a woman facing him from the doorway.  She eyed him with a little curiosity, then entered and shut the door.  As he began to introduce himself, she signaled him into silence, indicating that she did not speak.  It was then that the Avadhut realized that he was in the company of a woman muni, someone whom he had never encountered before.

The woman busied herself over the platform, preparing a few jungle eatables into a soup.  The small fire she started was positioned so that the smoke exited through a hole in the wall of the hut which was mostly covered over with a woven screen.  She also prepared some fruits, peeling and cutting with a metal utensil that resembled a knife.  When all was in readiness, she motioned for him to approach the platform and two sat across from each other to eat.

Getting a close up view of the woman, Ekanta noticed that she was dressed in an unusual fashion.  Her attire was not well attended to and her black hair, long and unkempt, fell in tangles over her back and shoulders.  Whenever their eyes met, which was seldom and for very short intervals, he saw in them a strange depth of spirit blended with a wild and untamed look.  It was difficult to guess her age, but Ekanta estimated that she was in her late thirties or early forties.  The two ate in silence, the only sound being the nocturnal noises outside and beyond.

After the meal was consumed, the woman rose from her position and cleared away the articles.  The large fern leafs that had acted as plates were discarded outside.  There was barely any time wasted on cleanup and nothing for him to do, so Ekanta simply returned to his corner and spread a cloth to sleep on.  The woman, too, after attending to the chores, went to a corner and spread a skin out on the floor to sleep on.  Making a motion to attract his attention, the woman pointed to her bed as if to ask him if he wanted to share it with her.  Taken aback, Ekanta shook his head to indicate his rejection of the proposal.  A soft laugh issued from the woman's mouth.  Reaching down, she took a long jungle knife from under the bedding and raised it over her head in mock fashion.  Then, hanging it near her on the wall, she laid down on her back to sleep.  Evidently, he thought, she had been testing him so as to ascertain if he had any untoward hidden intentions towards her.  Smiling to himself, Ekanta released her from any blame, for this unique woman, whoever she was, must have had her share of visitors of all types.

That night, Ekanta had an amazing dream.  The Goddess Kali was before him, accompanied by an entire host of unseen beings occupying the background of his dreamscape.  He had never seen nor felt the like of it before, for the atmosphere in the dream was charged with a palpable blend of emotions and qualities.  For one, the aroma all around was heady.  He could not remember ever having his sense of smell activated so acutely in a dream.  The scent of this vibrant atmosphere almost made him cry and seemed to practically tear his heart from his body.  The sounds in this dream were minimal and all absorbed into one thundering vibration that was incredibly loud yet strangely inaudible.

Everything about this dream was inexpressible.  In truth, it was not a dream at all, but a visionary experience.  He had no doubt that it was the Goddess Kali whose presence he visited, but try as he might, he could not catch Her with his eyes.  Yet, some vision of Her appearance stayed with him throughout, being made up of an entirely different composition than what was usually associated with physical forms.  He felt that his heart was on fire and it beat so loudly that he wondered why it did not wake him up.

Towards the end of this internal experience, the Goddess drew near to him, almost face to face, and he began to be able to comprehend Her form.  As he looked at Her, transfixed, he noticed that Her tongue was a snake and that it was feeling his face as if to memorize every feature.  He felt no aversion to this, nor did he even question that to have a snake as a tongue was something unusual.  As this continued, he began to lose consciousness and this was accompanied by a rush of primal sound so thunderous that he thought he would dissolve.

Opening his eyes abruptly, he immediately saw the female muni, poised over him and staring into his eyes, a wisp of her hair brushing his face.  He started and gave a shout in spite of himself.  Drawing back from him slowly and deliberately, the woman said in a soft but husky voice, "You, too, have seen Her this night."  Saying this, she withdrew, went quickly to the door and disappeared outside.

Ekanta was shaken.  He took some time to look within himself, a strong practice that he had developed over a long period of time and which never failed to calm, reveal or rectify whatever issue or situation he was facing. This proved to be effective and he soon discovered that not only was he all right, he was feeling incredibly charged and vibrant. Sitting up, he reflected on his vision. So much of it was still with him and almost as clear as when it had occurred. This, he concluded, had been a visitation of the primal Goddess, through him and within him. His guru had told him that God was present and accessible in form as well as beyond form. Ekanta's nature, however, was one that had always been drawn to formless heights, so he had not had many concrete visions.

Standing up, Ekanta gathered his things and left the hut. Dawn was visiting the region. As he stood outside, he looked back at the tiny dwelling and experienced a sensation that seemed to associate the small dwelling with the mouth of Mother Kali. Saluting this strange little house, he went to the trail and started walking in the direction he had left off the night before.

After he had gone a few miles, he ran into the woman muni once again. Finding that he had nothing to say, as if he was tongue-tied, he merely saluted her as she approached and moved to the side of the trail to let her pass. She, however, stopped in front of him and to his surprise, began a conversation.

"Where are you coming from and where are you heading, holy man?" came her husky voice.

"Mother," replied the Avadhut, "I am recently from the river and am making my way to the ocean."

After scrutinizing him a moment with her amazing eyes, she said, "I know the boatman."

The Avadhut smiled at this unexpected admission. "You know Surebha? How wonderful! I was much taken with him."

Except for a slight change in the woman's eyes, her expression did not alter in the least, nor did she speak for a short time, but merely stood in front of him. Just as he was beginning to feel a bit uncomfortable, she said, "Few beings are able to experience what you have received last night and this morning. She is extremely particular. She will not accept just anyone. Who are you, then?"

The Avadhut thought for a minute.

"Mother," he finally said, "when I examine myself using that question, I find nothing, no personal identity here within to call my own. As to the visitation, I know nothing about that either. It is all Her Will."

The two stood silent. In her eyes in those brief moments, Ekanta saw a mirror image of what he had seen within the gaze of the Goddess the evening before in his vision. Then, as suddenly as she had appeared, the woman passed and moved a few feet up the trail. Turning, she said to him by way of parting, "I want you to know that I have not spoken with anyone for several years."

Then, she bowed low before him and quickly disappeared into the jungle. The Avadhut was left standing alone, surrounded by miles of jungle and accompanied only by his own inspired thoughts.

For the rest of the morning the Avadhut moved swiftly along the winding trail. Vista upon vista, all restricted to jungle scenery, passed by his roving eyes. There was no lack of food or water, so when he had gathered enough choice fruits he looked for a suitable location to partake of his lunch. Up a side trail, near a small waterfall, he found such a spot and sat down for his meal. After eating, he laid down next to the murmuring waterfall for a nap.

Awakening from a short but deep sleep, a state in which he again felt the exceedingly wonderful presence of Mother Kali, the Avadhut lay quiet, not stirring for a few minutes. He had awakened lying on his side and facing away from the waterfall, so the jungle scenery was open to his gaze. As he looked at all the greenery, stretching out on all sides and for miles on end, he suddenly became aware of a little movement in the trees and vines nearby. Searching the area with a more concentrated gaze, he located the source of that movement and found that he was looking upon a snake. It was no ordinary reptile. This snake, at its middle, was almost as big around as the tree that it presently entwined itself around and though its length could not be ascertained due to the many winds and curves of its body in and throughout the vines, Ekanta surmised that it easily reached the size of ten to twelve feet if not more.

Ekanta watched with amazement this creature that God had created. It barely moved at all, only shifting its long bulk occasionally for a better purchase on tree and vines. Its color had changed to match its environment, for most of it was green except for a unique pattern of brown that extended down its entire form. The head, complete with greenish eyes, was bigger than Ekanta's two fists placed side by side and a huge tongue occasionally came flowing out of its slit-like mouth in slow and menacing fashion.

The Avadhut waited and at last his patience was rewarded. Soon, the snake, a python Ekanta decided, opted to leave the tree and take to the ground. As he watched in fascination, the Avadhut marveled at the snake's constitution and its gracefulness. Gradually sliding itself out of the tree, it made not a sound and hardly caused any stir in the vines as it deposited itself over the earth, revealing its full length. Staying very close to the tree that it had vacated, the snake gradually turned a darker shade in order to blend with the earth beneath it. Laying there, silent and unmoving, the Avadhut wondered what it was going to do next and what its purpose for leaving the tree was all about. He did not have long to wait for an answer.

Eventually, moving along the ground in the general direction of a pool of water downstream from the waterfall near which Ekanta lay, came a small creature. Ekanta did not know what it was. It had short fur and though it resembled a rat, it was too big for one. The animal drank water at the pool and then sauntered towards the web of trees under which the python lay. By this time, the Avadhut was trying to remember what it was that pythons ate. He knew that monkeys were probably acceptable fare, for he had seen them go wild with fear and run screaming whenever a large snake approached them.

The python, however, did not move at all, either when the animal was drinking at the pool and even when it entered the trees close by. For a time, the Avadhut could hear the animal and occasionally catch a glimpse of it as it moved about in the jungle. A half an hour passed and the animal was still lingering around, possibly digging for roots under nearby trees. Coming into view again, closer to both the snake and the Avadhut, it drew nearer and nearer to the python. The Avadhut paid closer attention, feeling that something was going to happen, until finally, when it seemed that the snake was simply not interested in the animal whatsoever, an amazing thing occurred.

With a speed and agility scarcely imaginable for a reptile of such massive size, the snake pounced upon the animal, swiftly wrapping its lengthy coils around the victim and quickly exterminating its life.  It was all over in a few seconds.  The snapping of bones revealed the method in which the snake consumed its prey, for after the animal had been turned into a fleshy pulp by those powerful coils, it was slowly and deliberately swallowed whole.

The Avadhut was mesmerized by the entire afternoon's experience.  It was not so much the life and death struggle that fascinated him, or the day's long build up resulting in this drama of nature.  What intrigued him, in typical fashion, was the snake's behavior and what it communicated to him.  The more he thought about it, the more he appreciated the teaching coming from the python, for it was so in common with how he, the Avadhut, preferred to lived his life.  Therefore, the Avadhut decided that, due to the python's incredible patience and its unassuming manner, it was the perfect teacher in nature for the quality of contentedness.

Standing up and facing the huge reptile from across the clearing, the Avadhut spoke and said, "Brother Snake, I salute you and accept you as my teacher of contentment, as a perfect example of the valuable and much sought-after attribute of well-being."

Sitting back down and watching the python slowly disappear into the jungle, the Avadhut then remembered that the python had been the subject of one of his guru's lessons to him as a young boy.  Thinking back, he tried to remember his teacher's words.

*"Everything in nature reflects the Blessed Lord, Ekanta,"* said his teacher one day, as they sat overlooking the forest.  *"Each thing, each object, each animal created, teaches us if we only have the eyes to see and the proper comprehension.  The python, for instance, teaches us how to be content where we are and with what we have, for it simply waits for its food to come near.  It will neither stir nor exert any energy towards that end but merely lingers until the right time comes."*

Looking up into the sky, his teacher pointed and exclaimed, *"There in the sky is the sparrow hawk.  It is smaller than other hawks, so it limits itself to small game that it can manage.  It teaches us practicality in this manner, for none of us should venture beyond our given capacity until we are ready.  One day I saw a sparrow hawk try to take a small mongoose.  The scuffle that ensued was almost the undoing of the small predator, for the mongoose was beyond its abilities."*

"Revered sir," Ekanta had asked, "you mentioned that even objects in nature teach us lessons. How can an insentient thing accomplish this?"

*"These lessons are built into the creation, my boy,"* came the response, *"and need to be uncovered. Your own intelligence married to an aspiring consciousness will be sufficient to unlock these secrets for you in due time. Listen to a story.*

*"Once, as a boy, I too sought out and learned the hidden secrets in nature. I grew up in parts further to the north, for my father was the preceptor of a forest ashram. All around were trees, huge conifers that shed seeds yearly. At one time, there was a debate among the ashramites. One school held that the organic debris that fell from the trees year round was proper fertilizer for the seeds that the pines gave off seasonally. Others argued that material cast off in this manner only hampered the growth of such seeds and thereby impeded the growth of the forest.*

*"Indeed, it was seen that the latter school of thought was correct for, over time, with the heavy shed of organic material increasing, fewer trees pierced the surface and a fungal disease even began to invade the existing trees. Final proof came after a forest fire caused by lightning swept across the region one year, burning off all the organic cover while fortunately sparing the ashram. Soon after, many of the seeds sprouted again and quickly and easily reforested the entire area. The fires, though earlier seen as a threat, were actually necessary for the regeneration of the land. The entire process was extremely subtle and it took great attention to detail over a substantial period of time to ascertain the truth. This is the way that nature works quite often, Ekanta. Few things are the way they seem. Mindfulness, perseverance and attention to detail are essential."*

"Do all things that we see have only one thing to teach us?" the boy then asked.

*"Not necessarily,"* responded his guru, *"but there is usually one primary teaching that is communicated. Other attendant or complementary lessons also come through."*

"Can you give an example of that, revered teacher?" Ekanta asked.

*"For instance,"* continued the guru, *"I explained that the snake waits for everything to come to it, thereby teaching the lesson*

*of contentment with the Self.    The snake has other valuable lessons to share with us as well.    The teaching that good and bad, though they are present in the world, do not affect God, is another example."*

"How is that teaching detected in the snake, revered sir?" asked Ekanta.  "I do not perceive it."

*"The snake," said the guru, "has poison in its body, contained in certain ducts or sacks, usually in its mouth positioned on the upper jaw.    This poison will prove fatal to others, if injected, but it does not harm the snake.    On the positive side, and ironically, this same poison, when extracted from the snake, can cure diseases.    In similar fashion, though God contains good and evil within Him, as it were, He is never affected by them and is ever beyond such dualities.    They form a part of His Maya, though, and He utilizes them both for a specific purpose."*

"You indicated that the sparrow hawk teaches us to be practical and not overstep our capacities.  What else could it teach us?"

*"The hawk is a bird, Ekanta," replied the preceptor, "and all birds teach us something very valuable.    The bird launches itself into the boundless sky and, without any support, maintains itself there, sporting with delight and abandon.    This teaches us that freedom is in formlessness and that the ability to willfully enter that highest condition is achieved by courageous abandonment of all things material.    The immortal Self is that sky and the bird is the embodied Spirit.    This is mentioned in the Brahmopanishad.*

*"Therefore, my young student, respect and revere everything here in this universe as an expression of Brahman.  Leave nothing out of your love, even the most seemingly vile or vicious.    Valuable lessons are transmitted at every turn, at every second.    Stay open and receptive to them and swiftly reach the goal of human existence."*

The Avadhut sat up and surveyed the surrounding jungle.  Even here, he thought, contentment seems to penetrate everything. Nothing is in a hurry to be somewhere.  People could learn much from nature if they would slow themselves down to the vibration that nature operates at, he mused.  Once, he recalled, he had found a monk sitting before a flowering tree, occasionally bowing down to it in reverential awe.

"Sir," he had asked, "why are you paying obeisance to this tree instead of bowing down in the shrine room or at the altar?"

*"Young friend,"* came the reply, *"in the temple we lay flowers over the image and perform the sacred worship to remind us of divine qualities and personages. But here, I find a puja of unlimited beauty going on naturally, occurring exactly as God intended it. Therefore, everywhere and at all times, there is a holy ceremony transpiring. I cannot help but honor and appreciate it."*

Starting upon his way towards the distant ocean once again, the Avadhut pondered as he walked the trail. Quotes from the sacred scriptures regarding peace of mind and contentment were swiftly entering his mind. He began to recite them as they came forth. Miles rolled by in this fashion as the Avadhut wandered the land, supremely satisfied with the boundless Self within him. Before darkness fell, as he laid his head down to sleep in the warmth and safety of a woodsman's hut on the far side of the jungle, the last words he uttered came from the ancient Rishis, experts on the subject of eternal contentment:

When Absolute Reality is perceived to exist in everything,
whether considered secular or spiritual,
the heart's longings are fulfilled, the mind's doubts subside,
inherent karmas dissolve
and supreme contentment permeates the entire being.

# Chapter 9

# Teachings on Even-Mindedness

THE NINTH GURU —*The Ocean*

THE LESSON —*Equanimity*

*There is hardly a more wonderful and beneficial quality than that of equanimity. This I learned from the ocean. Since all manner of flows, particles and objects enter into it — streams, rivers, rainfall, tributaries, earth, trees, ice, aquatic animals and various species — all without noticeably affecting or disturbing it in the least, I came to know after a time that the ocean was informing me of the fundamental importance of balance and equipoise. This, it seemed to say, should be accomplished both in the face of trials and imperfections as well as during times of happiness, joy and spiritual bliss, for the sea's immense depths are essentially the same in storm or sunshine. May we all learn to be so impervious to extremes.*

The Avadhut was walking slowly, deliberately, reverently towards the source of a distant rumbling vibration that shook the sands upon which he tread. The sound was drawing nearer with each step and as he mounted each succeeding sand dune he expected to catch a sight of that which had drawn him across half the subcontinent of India.

The boundless ocean, besides being the very epitome of magnificence, held precious associations for Ekanta. Several times, in what he had come to think of as some of the most wonderful and potent memories of his youth, he had visited the ocean's vast expanse of endless beaches with his male vanaprastin guru. On those occasions, teachings of great significance had been transmitted to him. He would never forget them, for they were etched upon his memory like ancient runes upon stone. As he drew near the liquid origin of life on earth, he suddenly remembered his preceptor's sublime words:

*"The ocean, my boy, receives the force and volume of hundreds of rivers, streams, brooks and tributaries daily and even accepts the perpetual rains into its broad expanse, yet it never noticeably swells or changes in the least. What correlation could you cite from this with regards to spiritual life?"*

"Revered sir," came the boy's answer, "the illumined sage constantly absorbs intense bliss and prolonged experiences of divine Grace through communion with the Supreme Being, yet never shows the effects of this inner contact on the outside whatsoever. Such a person is steeped in ecstasy but the onlooker would never know it."

*"That is excellently put, dear student,"* replied the guru. *"What you are describing is equanimity, a quality openly coveted by sincere seekers and prized highly by perfected souls. You have learned your lessons well. I am fortunate indeed to have such an apt pupil as you."*

Tears of gratitude had welled up in Ekanta's eyes to hear this rare praise coming from his beloved guru, but try as he might to express this noble emotion, he could not manage words. Seeing his beloved student's predicament, the teacher quickly went on with the discourse.

*"The world is a place of contrasting opposites. Everything here has a price. All must pay for dwelling in this body right down to the last penny. Since this is the case, illumined beings, too, have to experience ignoble whips of pain at times. The true*

*test of equanimity involves this extreme as well. Perfect balance is only attained if one is able to bear stoically with all the trials, vicissitudes, abuse and negativity that the world metes out. What say you, my boy?"*

This fresh inspiration from the enlightened mind of his teacher returned his voice to him. The words came easily, flowing from a clear and insightful mind.

"The ocean also demonstrates this, dear sir," came his response. "These rivers and streams bear with them a rush of impurities carried for miles from swamps, cities and other sources of pollution. Still, the ocean absorbs everything and purifies and transforms as is its nature. One can barely find such a sterling example of evenness on earth or even in the infinite universe. Therefore, the mighty ocean and the radiant mind of the saint have much in common."

This had been one of those rare occasions when the guru did not respond. Seemingly satisfied with the boy's explanation, he simply sat and savored the wisdom of his spiritual protégé's words. Ekanta too, felt a deep contentment within him and together the pair gazed up at the stars in silence. It was not long, however, before Ekanta had felt a question spring into his mind.

Breaking the silence, he asked, "Revered sir, if equanimity is so valuable, why do aspirants ignore it and seek after lesser and more questionable pursuits? It seems that beings are attracted not so much to precious attributes such as even-mindedness, but rather to all manner of extremes. Some desire transitory joy even though it undermines their sadhana. Others covet occult powers, even though the illumined ones warn against them. Who can explain this?"

*"Sensationalism, my boy, nearly always attends the early stages of spiritual life," came the guru's answer. "This is the case, at least, for those who have little substance inside of them to begin with. Perhaps you have noticed the different pastries for sale at the sweet shop? Some are filled with chick peas and pulses, others with condensed milk and some are filled only with mere lentil paste. The former are very expensive while the latter are cheap and easily purchased. Curious and insincere aspirants resemble the inferior grades of sweetmeats, dear boy. Those who are filled with only lentil paste, in other words, those who have no substance in them, these are the ones who chase*

*after fleeting happiness and occult powers.  The rest, though their numbers be fewer, select a path, approach a guru, bend their efforts towards the practice of sadhana and study and contemplate the teachings deeply.  In time, these sincere ones begin to have rare internal mystical experiences such as the different classes of samadhi.  Their commitment and perseverance pays off considerably over time."*

By this time, Ekanta's own curiosity had been perked.

"What happens to those who stray off the path that leads to freedom?" he asked.  "Their fate must be horrible indeed,"

*"If you call the tedium and superficiality which comes from such mundane pursuits and meager attainments horrible,"* responded the guru, *"then that would be as good a description as any.  Sensationalism is a clever and deceitful seducer, Ekanta.  Many fall by the wayside due to its adverse effects.  It produces generations of mystery-mongerers whose interpretation of spirituality is limited to what is distorted or diluted. Some prefer the arcane, others attach to questionable metaphysical pursuits.  Some take to matters that are downright banal."*

"What are the characteristics of this particular level, revered sir?"

The teacher thought for a moment, then said, *"The first group, those who are attracted to arcane or metaphysical pursuits, fixate on astral and mental phenomena, creating a whole realm of superficiality to feed off of.  The attraction for wealth and power over others plays a strong role in this realm.  In the name of omniscience, healing, spiritual guidance and other respectful occupations, beings perpetuate a whole host of facades and ruses.  It is really unhealthy and limited.  What results is a type of psychic circus, complete with every diversion imaginable.  A circus has expensive rides.  In this circus, the expensive rides are offered by the many so-called astral guides and psychics who charge exorbitant rates for advice that only leads the seeker around in circles.  A circus also has side-shows.  In this case, time-consuming nonessential details are dredged from the subconscious mind, flaunted about indiscriminately and labored over endlessly.  Finally, a circus sports the ever-popular house of horrors.  In the realm of the sensational and occult, one's own personal demons and the many that inhabit*

*this pseudo-spiritual marketplace, combine to create a fright-
ening dimension that any sincere aspirant seeking after Truth
would smartly avoid."*

Laughter bubbled up from inside of Ekanta's being. The
teacher, too, laughed in turn at this unexpected description. After
his mirth had subsided, Ekanta continued with this same line of
questioning.

"Can you tell me what the beings experience who frequent the
next level of superficial spirituality, dear sir?" asked Ekanta.

*"The next level is a realm of spiritual menu tasting,"* replied
the guru. *"Running across the planet in search of all sorts of
exciting experiences, taking this guru and then that guru, this
teaching and that teaching, all on a surface level. This accomplishes nothing but a spinning of the wheels. Possibly some
exposure is achieved at this level, but if this exposure does not
culminate in Ishta-nishta — what does that mean, my boy?"* —
came the guru's sudden question in mid sentence.

"One-pointed concentration upon a single ideal until the
essence of that path is realized," came Ekanta's answer.

*"Yes, and if it does not occur then no lasting benefit can come
of it, spiritually speaking,"* concluded the teacher.

Continuing with his description of the rudimentary level of spiritual pursuit, the guru said:

*"It is at this time that beings enter into that curious phase
of contorting the body and playing with the prana. This is no
less than vexation of the mind. Jumping around in a feigned
show of ecstasy, assuming various body postures, making a
spectacle of the protruding tongue, imagining the rise of spiritual power in them, feigning certain self-induced signs of
attainment to impress others and broadcasting to one and all
that they have reached the highest samadhi, this is the ostentatious performance that these beings indulge in."*

"But sir," objected Ekanta, "certainly they do not really believe
that the highest state, that which the illumined call the 'pearl of great
price,' can be attained by mere pretension?" The boy's incredulity
caused a broad smile to spread across the preceptor's face.

*"How are they to know what is authentic and what is not at
the outset of spiritual life, my son?"* replied the guru. *"At that
level they are mere babes playing with teething toys. Do you*

*remember what the Avatar said? 'It takes a jeweler to recognize the value of a diamond.' Until one becomes an advanced spiritual jeweler, one can only wonder what true spiritual experience is like. This process is typical of this level of student, though. The real problem comes when the aspirant gets stuck in these banal expressions and fails to go forward."*

Ekanta marveled at these insights that literally poured from his teacher's mind. He gazed at this enigmatic figure, a simple forest dweller with no wealth and no family except for an illumined wife, and no other recourse than to contemplate Reality. As he inspected his beloved guru, a heightened feeling of thankfulness visited his mind again.

"What else can be said about this surface level of aspirant, revered teacher," he asked, "and when does the appearance of equanimity make itself known?"

*"There is an old saying from the wise that describes the spiritual stature that is accompanied by equanimity,"* replied the teacher. *"They say that grapes that are ripe, must be preserved carefully in a cotton cloth."*

"How does this relate to sensationalism and equanimity, revered sir?" asked Ekanta.

*"Those who jump about and sing and dance wildly, assuming an ecstatic state for show and pretense, are immature bhaktas for the most part,"* rejoined the guru. *"They are unripe grapes, as it were. Those who are mature bhaktas do not need to express in this fashion. If they do, it is under the influence of a power that is incomprehensible and completely devoid of egotism, affectation and other unsightly attendants. The experiences of these rare beings, for the most part, are stored away like ripe grapes ready for eating, out of sight from curious onlookers who would only sour the experience with impure eyes. Truly illumined beings are not given to spectacle and sensationalism. They are like the ocean that contains an ongoing abundance of varied experiences within its internal expanse without ever reflecting them on its surface in the least."*

Ekanta recalled his mind from all of those fond memories and teachings. The sand dunes in front of him were thinning out and now the sound of the ocean was permeating everything. He was about to behold the repository of much of the earth's precious healing liquid.  Looking up at the sky, he estimated that he would reach the sea just about sunset since the light from the sun was beginning to fade.  As he appreciated nature's wonderful qualities, his mind flashed back to what Yogindra Yogi had said about sensationalism.  Ekanta had come to him in his mountain cave one day in a dejected mood.  Noticing this, the yogi asked him the cause of his despondency.

"At the recent holy day celebration in honor of Sri Ramachandra's blessed birth," complained Ekanta, "everyone attended the parade and the feast but no one came to the teachings or to the meditation afterwards.  Being full of prasad and having all their energy expended on the day's frivolities, everyone simply declined to show up for more essential matters.  I was shocked and disappointed."

*"My boy,"* came the yogi's response, *"all do not have your capacity for spiritual matters, nor do they possess your tenacity and thirst for knowledge.  They will naturally be drawn more to aspects of the celebration that provide spectacle and excitement.  Give them time to develop the ability for expansive spirituality and authentic teachings and in the meanwhile act as an example for them.  Let me tell you a story that may help you to understand human nature.*

*"There once lived a boy who was born extremely simpleminded.  Even after he was full-grown, he was more like a child than anything else.  When he came of age, his father gave him sixteen silver rupees which he prized above all else.  The pile of coins, sitting there in all their shining splendor, filled him with delight.  The only problem was, since the man was so childlike, he often lost some of the coins in play and it fell to the father to keep a watch over these precious belongings.*

*"One day, while the young man was away from home, the father decided to turn the sixteen silver coins into one gold mohur, a coin having the same value as the combined silver rupees.  This, he thought, would save his son from the risk of losing some of the coins.  When the son returned, however, he raised such a fuss that the father hurried to return the mohur in order to keep the peace.  While he was away, however, he came upon a diamond merchant who convinced him to turn the gold mohur into a sliver of diamond possessing the same value.  The*

*father took this piece of diamond and returned home. When he showed this small shiny bit of diamond to his son, however, the boy was more dejected than ever.*

*"Finally, the father went out to remedy the situation again, but this time the son insisted on going with him. At the diamond merchant's shop, the father asked for sixteen silver rupees in exchange for the sliver of diamond. The jeweler, however, did not have that many silver rupees and gave instead a whole pile of half rupees and annas. The pile of coins was larger than before. Before the father could object, the son yelled with joy and declared that the pile of coins was even better than sixteen silver rupees. The son then went home happy, though the father had even more coins to supervise."*

"What is the moral and the teaching here?" asked Ekanta. "I think I get it, but please clarify it for me."

*"With regards to sensationalism,"* replied the yogi, *"this story illustrates that most people prefer the spectacular to the subtle, what is gross over what is refined. Though each of the denominations — silver rupees, gold mohur and piece of diamond — were of the same value, the pile of cheap coins were valued most simply due to the spectacle they represented and the sensation that they caused."*

Ekanta breathed loudly. Up ahead, through two small sand dunes, he had caught a brief glimpse of something vast and blue. The ocean, in all its splendor, was near at hand! Coming finally to the top of one last sand dune, the Avadhut beheld a lovely sight. There, stretched out before him as far as his eyes could see, was the immense and mysterious body of water called the Indian Ocean. Not a soul was in sight, for Ekanta had left the beaten path earlier at a location untraveled by many and had struck out across the land in a direct line towards the sea. Now, he was seeing it exactly as he wanted, natural and uncluttered by the rush of humanity or the busy pace of village life.

The Avadhut sat down exactly where he was, on the very spot that he was receiving his first look at the sea. To him, the very idea of water transcended what was conceivable, yet here was a boundless expanse of it, just lying there in all its pristine majesty. It was definitely a living thing.

Liquids had always enthralled Ekanta. It was the property of homogeneity that interested him. To his aspiring and illumined mind, the eternal principle of oneness was aptly illustrated by the liquid property of water, perhaps better than any other existing thing in the universe. Air and ether were, of course, fitting examples of this as well, but they were extremely subtle and represented other attributes more fittingly. Water, to the illumined Avadhut, was nothing short of a religion.

Vishnu, the Supreme Being, rested in supernal cosmic sleep on lucent waters. Lakshmi, Sarasvati and other divine beings emerged from primal waters, seated on huge, wonderful lotus flowers. Sacred waters from the river Ganges flowed like a spring from the matted locks of Lord Shiva, ever plunged in sublime meditation upon Reality. Ganga, Tulsi, Manasa, Vasundhara and other aspects of the primordial Goddess were all closely associated with the liquid of life. Additionally, all creatures owed their existence to water, which was both an essential element and a cosmic principle.

Far out to sea, the Avadhut beheld a large slate-gray rain-cloud. From the mist that was seen to be trailing from it, he could tell that the cloud was shedding its content of rain into the vast ocean. This vision, accompanied by divine associations and enhanced by the solitude of the place, drove the Avadhut's mind into an intense spiritual state. He imagined that thousands of living beings, consisting of pure Spirit, were merging ecstatically into the infinite expanse of Brahman, just like the raindrops were merging in the ocean. As he watched, other rain-clouds started to dump their contents of the precious liquid into the sea as well. This was too much for the Avadhut's spiritually sensitive mind to take.

Standing up abruptly and reeling a little under the effects of natural intoxication, he spoke out loud to the ocean:

"To be sure, you are my teacher of equanimity. You receive it all, but never change in the least. Nothing can affect you, for you have become so vast that all else is insignificant in your presence."

Sitting down again, the Avadhut fell into an indrawn mood. So many rain-clouds, he thought, and all shedding a multitude of tiny drops into the ocean's broad bosom. The vision stuck with him for some time and finally brought about a memory of a teaching he had received from his guru.

_"The Samkhya Philosophy believes in many Purushas, my boy, whereas Vedanta remains firm that there is and can only_ *be one Absolute.   Yet, there is a reconciliation here, if one remains open and flexible.  Like the many clouds occupying one infinite sky, the appearance of many separate Realities is certainly tenable, at least from the standpoint of the clouds.   So long as each individually existing verity is perceived to be an expression of the One, being fully dependent upon It as the substratum of all that exists, just so long can the wonderfully diverse play of the Universal Mother, the Primal Purusha, continue and flourish.   What joy there is, my son, what bliss!"*

From universally-minded teachings such as these, Ekanta had found out that there was no breach in the perfection of Brahman. He had learned, as well, the distinction between vain philosophical speculation, which was usually all for the sake of argumentation and debate, and insightful perception based upon a combination of concentration, meditation and samadhi.

*"There is only one sun in the sky near to us,"* the Mataji had pointed out one day. *"Its light shines on all, regardless.  Different rays or sunbeams flow from its shining surface, and these are likened to the various religious traditions that appear on earth for the salvation and liberation of embodied beings.   They all come from one Source, and return to it as well.   The rays emit from the sun; the sun does not emanate from its rays.  Also, light knows no distinction, no difference, though it reflects on some surfaces better than on others."*

As the Avadhut recalled this teaching, he also remembered some words she spoke about the ocean with regards to universality:

*"The ocean has its waves and they all belong to its surface, forming out of its boundless expanse.  Also, the waves are of different volume, some big and some small, some hollow and some full.  Teachings which the ocean demonstrate are infinite and beyond counting.  As you gaze upon it, Ekanta, apply its abundance of teachings to your human existence, especially around spiritual life and sadhana."*

The Avadhut stood up and began to walk towards the ocean. There were hardly any waves at this time of year and, except for an occasional tiny shore break, all was calm.  Approaching the waters, the Avadhut fell to his knees right at the edge of the sea. Its cool liquid washed around his legs and caused him to shiver with pleasant surprise and subtle delight.  With heartfelt reverence, he took his right hand and dipped it into the ocean, bringing some of the liquid in the cup of his hand to his forehead in symbolic fashion. This worshipful act caused an uprising of devotion in him and tears began to form in his eyes.

As he looked down into the ocean waters, one of the tears fell from his right eye and merged with the sea. "Salt into salt," he murmured softly. Raising his head, he quietly and reverently recited a sloka from the Upanishads, the divinely originated scriptures of the ancient Rishis:

*Yatha dakam shuddha shuddhama siktam tadrgeva bhavati*
*Evam munervijanata atma bhavati gautama*

As pure water falling into pure water becomes the same
so become the Selves of the illumined ones
who realize their identity with Brahman

Sitting there at the very edge of all that water, the Avadhut wondered at its salty condition. Once, a young girl had told him that her father had said that the ocean's salty condition was due to the millions of tears that humanity had cried since the beginning of time. Though a fanciful thought, it was not without intriguing possibilities and certainly provided ample material for poetic expression.

While thinking about the girl's father, Ekanta suddenly remembered something his own father had told him when they visited the seashore.

"The salty content of the ocean is a neutralizing factor, one that aids in the purification of its waters, my boy. Just as an ocean has salt in it for this and other purposes, you should contain the priceless quality of equanimity which is also an ingredient that acts upon impurities. What is more, as the ocean has its purifying elements, so does equanimity."

"What does equanimity consist of, Father?" Ekanta had asked.

"Why, equanimity contains patience and perseverance, for instance. One who possesses this attribute is never without these two mainstays. Knowledge of the existence and efficacy of the Truth is another inherent property of equanimity, Ekanta. If you have the great boon of being in the presence of a holy man or woman, you will notice their balanced state of mind and how it carries over into all actions in life. Such a mind not only enjoys tranquillity itself, it also exudes the same upon all others in its general periphery. Finally, this mind in equipoise literally draws God to it. Therefore, Ekanta, equanimity is conducive of enlightenment, for who could fail to become illumined in the presence of Brahman?"

The two, father and son, remained silent for a few minutes, enjoying communion in an atmosphere of peace and harmony. When his father finally spoke again, it was to further elucidate on the quality of equanimity.

"Equanimity, or evenness of mind, does not just happen to the aspirant, son. One does not suddenly possess it in the way that one might receive a monetary inheritance from a deceased and distant relative. Patience and perseverance forge it into human nature, which in the beginning is restless and slothful in turns. The reactionary mind is always jumping prematurely to conclusions or falling into periods of deep dejection and laziness. Though this is disconcerting for those who desire to control it, the mind gets trained and tempered over time by these contrasting movements and eventually longs for true rest. The attainment of patience and perseverance is necessary in order to be able to maintain authentic equipoise. Until these two qualities are mastered, some unwanted intrusion, whether tiny or considerable, will find its way into the mind's defenses and upset the essential balance. Therefore, strive for this valuable quality, Ekanta, and all the treasures it contains will be yours forever."

As the Avadhut continued to think back on his boyhood, he could still hear his teachers harping on the value of this coveted attribute:

*"In the ocean, as on this solid earth, Ekanta, an infinite life-and-death drama is constantly going on. Just imagine the extent of such a play. Thousands of creatures are born, live and die every day. Millions of waves sport on its surface and merge into it again continually. Storms play across its vast reaches in unending cycles and the winds blow in countless variations and directions. Yet, with all of this occurring daily, the ocean remains aloof and unaffected, transcendent of the entire process. Even when terrible hurricanes rage across it, its depths remain unruffled and silent, peaceful and serene. What does*

*this suggest to you, dear boy? Try to apply its significance to
your spiritual life."*

"My thought is," Ekanta replied, "that though such powerful
happenings are always plaguing the ocean, it bears them all with
equanimity. The storms, winds, waves and hurricanes remind me
of the many intense and chaotic emotions that visit the minds of
human beings throughout their lives. Life and death in the sea's
vast reaches remind me of the attendant transformations such as
living and dying, disease and old age, and other impositions that
you have caused me to consider, dear teacher, for my own good.
If living beings are without the quality of even-mindedness in such
a situation, what havoc and misery they will have to bear."

*"That is very good, Ekanta, and exactly right to a point,"*
returned his guru. *"This aspect of the lesson on equanimity alone
is priceless for aspirants seeking the goal of human existence.
In the sadhana phase of spiritual growth, there is hardly to be
found any quality that benefits the seeker as much as even-mindedness. Making oneself impervious to the world's impositions
and resistant to the intrusions of ignorance from deluded beings
is one of the most practical exercises one can indulge in. It
stands one in good stead throughout life and facilitates success
in both worldly and spiritual matters."*

The guru stopped for a moment to consider, then went on.

*"There is another aspect to this lesson on equanimity that
should be explored as well. Great joy, called Ananda by the
sages, graces those who master the mind and attain perfect balance. The advent of ecstasy is only properly absorbed by those
who hold the quality of equanimity. To those who do not,
excesses of joy only tax the mind, overwhelm the nervous system and wear out the body. A small lake can never bear the
abundance of waters which an ocean receives daily. In like fashion, an aspirant's capacity for spiritual ecstasy must be gradually built up, lest that one be spoiled for life prematurely."*

The Avadhut lifted himself out of the water and gazed into the
heavens. The stars were appearing here and there in the sky,
though it was still light. For the first time in many hours he began
to think about mundane practical matters. Soon, he would have
to find a place to spend the night and secure a few items to eat.
As these things came into his mind, he remembered that he had

stored some food stuffs in his cloth for the evening. Then, he recalled his new location to mind. He was at the seashore, where soft sands were abundant and sleeping was both comfortable and accompanied by the natural lulling sounds of the ocean.

Down the beach in a northerly direction, he found a stretch of sand that was both wide and flat. Setting down his belongings well up the shore to provide for the shifting tides, he laid out his sleeping cloth and sat in half-lotus position for meditation. Dusk was an opportune time to contemplate and worship divine Reality. His teachers had impressed that upon his mind.

*"When light turns to darkness or evening into daytime, those are ideal times for meditation, Ekanta, for it is then that the often proud and stubborn human will realizes that the universe is under the control of a supreme power."*

As darkness fell and the sun's light vanished completely, the Avadhut beheld the evening firmament in all its scintillating glory. After meditating for an hour, he opened his eyes onto this inspiring mystical scene. The nighttime skies never failed to draw him into a deep spiritual mood. "Anantananda," he whispered softly under his breath. There, before his gaze was the bliss of the infinite universe. Why? thought the Avadhut. For God so loved space that he created the endless void, enough room for both the gross and the subtle. Gazing into the night sky and listening to the song of the sea, the Avadhut fell into a deep sleep.

Upon awakening, Ekanta felt something covering his body. As he shifted his position, he immediately felt a rush of tiny legs over his body. Looking down in the dim light of early dawn, he saw dozens of small crabs running helter skelter across the beach away from him. Evidently, they had camped on him overnight, attracted by the warmth of his body. Rising, he shed his clothes and headed for the ocean and his morning bath.

Approaching the huge body of water, Ekanta paused. In the early morning light, with calm conditions prevailing, it seemed to be resting. To see such a vast body of water at peace was intensely inspiring and the Avadhut immediately saluted the ocean with a full prostration in the sand. Then, with cloth in hand, he slowly drew near and, laying his cloth on the sand near the water's edge, entered the liquid expanse.

Compared to the cool morning air, the water of the ocean

seemed considerably warm.  Its aroma wafted up into his nostrils, giving him the feeling of being surrounded by the warm and benign presence of a mother.  As he eased his body down into its waters, at that very moment the sun broke the horizon with a glint of intense light.  Several small fish which had been resting near the shore in the shallows, darted away into deeper waters, reminding him of a famous Bengali song.  He began to sing a few of its lines:

> O lazy surface dweller, you small aquatic being,
> inhabiter of languid waters pleasing and serene.
> Your life is fraught with danger,
> and though you hardly know it,
> a harsh reality will wake you from this liquid dream.

> These shoals which ever bind thee, with daft preoccupation,
> are under death's dominion, under death's perceptive gaze.
> His spreading net will plunder their insubstantial reaches,
> and force you to give up attachment to this shallow maze.

> This playful surface splashing,
> these sparks of mere enjoyment,
> are actions that will only bring his fearful eyes to bear.
> Avoid his cold attentions, his net which misses nothing,
> his hungry curiosity for sparkles, glints and glares.

> Abandon pleasant shallows, dive deep in vast expanses,
> and make the unknown depths your only love,
> your only home.
> Renounce insipid shorelines of limited existence,
> and shed those mortal scales for vast eternity alone.

After Ekanta had taken his morning bath, he left the water and dried himself with his cloth.  Returning to his scanty belongings lying on the beach, he packed them and began his journey once again.  It was his intent to remain on the beach for many miles, begging food from the fishing villages that dotted the ocean shores.  Eventually, he would take to the trails and roads again and wend his way up the coast of the Arabian Ocean towards the huge city of Bombay in Maharastra.

As the Avadhut began his long trek over sandy terrain along-side his beloved teacher of equanimity, he pondered what he had learned and searched for more ways of incorporating it into his understanding.  The ocean was his companion, his inspiration, his sterling example of how to be absolutely unruffled by any and all manner of impositions.  Whether they be of the nature of aggravations, interruptions, disappointments, or grievances, whether they be from subhuman creatures such as animals or insects, individual human beings, societies, governments or semidivine interventions, the Avadhut always had the sea — the personification of perfection in manifest form.

As mile after mile of seashore and blue water rolled past, the Avadhut thought back on several human examples of equanimity he had witnessed.  His own father had been amazingly untouched by external and internal botherations.  On the other hand, though Ekanta had known him to experience spiritual states at times, he neither showed nor talked about them to anyone save his wife, his loving companion on the spiritual path.  As the Avadhut pondered the past, an incident that had impressed him came back into his mind regarding his beloved father.

It was nearing the time of the birth of his parent's second child when this incident occurred.  The blessed couple, Ekanta's father and mother, had been in anxious anticipation of this auspicious day.  When the time arrived, the midwife was present to assist in the delivery, but much to the sorrow of all involved, the baby was received stillborn.  Sorely disturbed by the weight of this disappointment, Ekanta's mother outwardly lamented this tragedy and was unable to control her emotions.  Ekanta had noticed that his father, after observing a short period of silence and fasting, had simply gone on with his life and work as if nothing had occurred at all.  One day, not long after the stillbirth, Ekanta encountered his father in the workshed outside the small family house.

Approaching him, the boy asked, "Revered Father, I am unhappy that we have lost a baby boy or girl.  Mother grieves over this but you seem to show little unhappiness whatsoever.  Please do not misunderstand, Father, but I long to know something."

"What is it, my son?" the father replied.

"Father," the query came, "where does your power of detachment come from?  What is the secret of your even-mindedness?

I long to know this, for I am very depressed."

" My boy," responded his father, "it is not that I do not feel the loss. What is more, I feel even worse for the sake of your mother. There is, however, a safeguard within me, placed there long ago by my father and our family guru. They taught me well the lessons of even-mindedness. The unreality of terrestrial existence is not just a theory concocted by dreamers or philosophers. The truth of the transitory nature of human existence — experiencing events and attaching to objects with the help of the dual mind and the five senses — is not mere speculation.

"Just notice the condition of people who attach to the world as if it were the only reality. Changes occur every second in the creation, yet the ignorant cling to phenomenal existence all the tighter despite this obvious fact. Science now states that the particles of matter which make up our universe have no stability whatsoever, that the universe is in constant flux with no solid foundation upon which to rest. There is nothing fixed here, then, in this precariously balanced realm of matter. Our great philosophers knew this already, but from the standpoint of direct perception rather than from external experimentation. How else could they write:"

The universe of name and form is a projection over Reality,
created by the Lord's Maya.
Consciousness too, is projected there and sports momentarily,
withdrawing Its undying essence to the eternal Source
when all play is over.
That which is anterior to the world of name and form
and which projects the universe is real,
while that which gets projected is not.
With no abiding existence, matter is phantomlike
Those who would attach to phantoms as if they were real
live in vain, beloved student, and follow the way of illusion
until such illusion is withdrawn.

Ekanta stood transfixed, listening to this rare exposition of nondual philosophy by his revered father.

"In the light of what you have said, Father, what has happened to my  brother or sister?" Tears were now beginning to form in Ekanta's eyes.

"Nothing actually happened, my son," said his father. "A dream involving limited existence in relativity simply did not manifest. We have been the recipient of this bitter experience due to our past actions coupled with our fond expectations. The time and energy that we expended to grow this tree of expectation was sweet, but the fruit that grew there turned out bitter on this occasion. Now we must accept this outcome and go forward in the knowledge that the Lord has other things in store for us. To labor over it with remorse and grief will only impede the progression of our future dharma. It will also hinder the soul who was trying to embody here with us. The Lord has an infinite number of potential forms through which He can express Himself. What is more, none of them ever die for they are never truly born. This is the ultimate teaching which has been given to us by this trying experience. Come then, let us presently rejoice in those who are amongst us and become the wiser for this experience."

"I am beginning to understand, Father," said the dejected boy, "but what of us, of you and me and Mother? What is our fate in such a world?"

"That is a profound question, my boy, and one worth pondering. Contemplation of death is a profound meditation and is extremely practical as well. Rightly accomplished, it is never an exercise in futility or morbidity. Equanimity is produced and developed in those who consider the serious questions of impermanence and immutability."

Ekanta's father remained silent a few moments, then went on instructing his son. "A great spiritual luminary once used the ocean for a metaphor regarding death and the fear and depression it causes. I went to him distressed over the demise of a friend. My equanimity of mind was sorely affected and I needed solace in the worst way.

"Drawing close to his sacred presence, which I could feel palpably all around him, I asked, 'Respected sir, what does life amount to when, in the end, we are faced with death?'

"'This world is like an ocean where thousands of bubbles arise constantly,' he told me. "Sometimes, if you look closely, you can see a group of bubbles coming to the surface — a couple of big ones and a few little ones clinging to those. This symbolizes the family unit. People resemble these hollow bubbles, my boy.

_The big bubbles are the parents and the little ones are the chil-
dren, attached and dependent on them. These bubbles make their
upward journey and, encountering the end of their time span,
burst in the ocean that gave them birth._

_"'Make no excuses for it,' the great one went on, 'life in the
world is precarious. It is, as Shankara sings in his hymn, Bhaja
Govindam, "as unstable as a drop of water on a lotus leaf."'_

_"'What is the solution then?' I asked him._ 'Is existence without
purpose?'

_"'No,' he answered. 'Why should it be? Nothing the Lord of
creation does is in vain. Where has your faith gone? One must
analyze life in the world using discrimination and come to a
definite enlightened conclusion. Detachment is the result of
such a process. Faith and forbearance grow strong along the
way. Let me demonstrate the process of discrimination using
this ocean/bubble metaphor._

_"'The ocean, in this case, represents the universe of name and
form where life-forms manifest and consciousness sports
through them. It is the thin, watery covering that sustains the
appearance of the bubble. Without that, the form would be
nonexistent. This sheath or covering, with regards to the living being, is the Upadhi as Vedanta philosophy calls it. It is
the body/mind mechanism made up of the constituents of five
elements: matter, life-force, mentation, intelligence and the sense
of individuality called the ego. Those are the coverings over
Pure Consciousness called the Atman._

_"'Looking at the bubble again, its insides contain nothing but
air. Outside, beyond the ocean, there exists nothing but air as
well. When the bubble rises to the surface of the ocean, that marks
the end of its embodied journey. Upon coming in contact with
the expanse of air at the surface, its thin form disintegrates and
what remains is nothing but air. All the while, then, the bubble
was only an appearance, tracing a path through a relative or
temporary sphere of existence. What was inside of it was its
essence, which is formless and therefore deathless. Therefore,
take away the covering and what is left is Reality, all-encom-
passing and all-pervading. In other words, the embodied being
is nothing but Pure Consciousness, whether in form or not.
With form though, it imagines itself to be other than it really_

*is, experiencing the illusions of birth, growth, decay, disease
and death. Within is Atman, however, and all around is
Brahman. This is the Reality. What happens in the interim is
called life, based upon time, space and causality.*

*"'The Atman, then, that which gives everything life, is a por-
tion of that formless essence within every living being. Beyond
the ocean of this universe, the infinite Brahman exists,
Ultimate Reality Itself, homogenous and entirely free of the
appearance of names and forms. The body/mind mechanism is
formulated either by karmic propensity, out of compassion for
suffering beings, or by the will of Consciousness to sport in relativity. Moving through an ocean of matter and life-force, this
limited structure eventually wears out and gets destroyed. The
Atman within then merges with the formless ocean of Brahman
and all is perfectly unified once again.'"*

"Upon hearing the words of this great enlightened man, Ekanta,
my fears were mostly destroyed. Still, some of my depression persisted, so I pressed him further.

"'What of our human feelings, revered sir, and what of those
who perpetuate death by adharmic actions such as murder and so
forth?'

"'With regards to human feelings and emotions, they surface
naturally in life, due to our various actions. Our attachment
to relative existence and our penchant for enjoying pleasures
must all bear effects. We must remain equanimous through all
such recurring repercussions like the ocean bears with storms
and hurricanes.*

*"'As to those who go against the cosmic laws set up by the
blessed Creator,' the great one told me, 'there is the case of bubbles that burst before they reach the surface of the ocean. The
inner substance of these bubbles does not get the chance to merge
with the formless expanse above and beyond. Applying this to
human existence, the inner essence of deluded living beings
retains the impressions of individual existence and all the coverings return in a superimposed fashion over that essence. In
these cases, and in those where intrinsic perfection has not yet
been realized, a rebirth in the oceanlike substance of matter and
mentation must take place. Repeated identification with name
and form occurs over and over again until full enlightenment*

*about this process matures.'"*

After his father had finished relating this remarkable exchange between himself and the holy one, Ekanta too, had felt much better.

"So," he asked his father, "your own equanimity is due to this knowledge. This is why you cannot lament for the dead or brood over the past?"

"In part, my son," replied the father. "There is another reason as well, maybe several."

"Can you explain them to me?" asked the boy.

"If you ask me, Ekanta, evenness of mind is only possible in an atmosphere of perfect self-surrender. In those who lament and agonize over life's calamities, we see more than just grief and aversion to death. These beings demonstrate an insidious attachment to their minuscule and often paltry little existences. In the interim, they reflect a stubborn and childish rebelliousness that refuses to acknowledge anything outside their own tiny world of insubstantial considerations. Yet, their fathomless and sublime inner essence awaits them, covered over by lifetimes of karmic debris. The Blessed Lord and Divine Mother of the Universe simply must awaken them to this internal verity. The great ones rush to embrace this truth of their being. The others weep and wail and go kicking and screaming, dragging their feet the entire way."

"Self-surrender, then, dear father?" Ekanta reminded him.

"Exactly so, my boy," said his father, smiling. "Only those fully convinced of the Lord's existence and absolutely trusting in His all-powerful will can achieve mature equanimity. Whether He places them in the most exacting situations or showers them with all manner of evident blessings, they waver not in their resolve and devotion to Him."

Ekanta bowed low at his father's feet. Grabbing the boy by his shoulders and raising him up, he embraced his son and said, "Save that for the truly holy ones, Ekanta. You are my very own and I am yours, and that fact is eternal. Thousands of beings have been born in the past and thousands more will be reborn in the future. This is the play of the Lord. We need not be concerned about this in the least. What we are is eternal, Pure Spirit, and nothing can ever truly separate us. Let Maya have its play. We shall worship and propitiate the wielder of Maya Herself and thereby remain ever enlightened as to the nature of relative existence and fully informed about the mystery of Absolute Reality. Victory to the Blessed Lord and Divine Mother of the Universe, my son! Victory to Her!"

While thinking back on his father's amazingly God-centered life, Ekanta had walked miles in the process. Ahead, in the distance, he could see a fishing village nestled on the shore of the massive ocean. Its roof tops of palm leaves shone in the midday sun and a few fishing boats were seen crowding the banks nearby. Mentally saluting the ocean, his parents, his gurus and all the illumined ones who revealed and epitomized the essence of equanimity, he readjusted his belongings on his shoulders and headed in the direction of the village — the first signs of human habitation he had seen in days.

# ~ Chapter 10 ~

# Teachings on Selfishness

THE TENTH GURU —The Fish
THE LESSON —Greed

*The danger of greed is demonstrated by the fish who, not knowing that the hook is hidden inside the bait and not satisfied with the adequate nourishment in its own natural environment, rushes to enjoy this food and is taken painfully and abruptly out of its pleasant existence. Similarly, the hook of karmic repercussion lies hidden in every action and great discrimination must be utilized by aspiring beings to avoid both suffering and untimely death.*

The Avadhut arrived at the little fishing village on the coastline of southern India. He had been hiking along the coast of Kerala for two days and his intention was to work his way up the West Coast of India through Karnataka and visit the city of Bombay. From there he planned to journey further north to pilgrimage points in the Himalayas. He often missed the massive sacred mountains and he was due for a visit to those climes. In the meantime, he was quite content in the warm, balmy weather of South India.

The fishermen and women of the small village as well as the children playing in the streets, turned curious stares upon the newcomer. Since this area was off the beaten path for wanderers

275

enroute to the cardinal pilgrimage points of the south, they did not often see a holy man. This did not mean that they were ignorant about such beings, though, and this was proven when some of the residents began to approach the Avadhut with offerings of food and money as he moved through the streets.

Sitting himself down at a nearby convenient source of water, the Avadhut accepted the humble offerings from the townspeople, returning their greetings of "namaste" and "namaskar" with similar salutations. His broad and smiling face was obviously welcome and encouraging to the children and before long a whole host of the little ones had gathered around him, laughing and testing his patience. Some tried to see how close they could get to the stranger so as to show off for their friends. Making mock lunges and grabs at them, the Avadhut sent them screaming with laughter in the opposite direction. Eventually, the parents of these children, taking pity on the Avadhut and his good nature, came and took the children off to their respective houses.

It was beginning to turn dark and the hour of dusk set in swiftly. The sun had already set behind the hills to the west. The Avadhut was not alarmed at all by this transition. In fact, he was better off than he had been for days. An abundance of foodstuffs lay on his cloth before him, courtesy of the kind villagers, and the endless sands were a more than comfortable bed. Before him, the ocean stretched out forever, providing a suitable altar in front of which the Avadhut could meditate for hours. The stars were also present, peeking out of the dark firmament like so many living eyes of the infinite Goddess. Finally, there was the soft lapping of the waters which was just soothing enough to lull him to sleep. As Ekanta was returning to the beach to find a place for the night, a voice came from behind him.

"Revered sir, please be kind enough to share my humble abode with me this night."

Turning, the Avadhut beheld an elderly man, obviously a fisherman by trade.

Addressing the man politely, Ekanta said, "My gratitude for your kind offer, sir, but I am obliged to keep company with the ocean tonight. I presume that you understand this."

"Oh yes," returned the fisherman, "of the few things that I can comprehend in this life, companionship with Mother Ocean is certainly one of them.  Perhaps I will see you on the morrow then?"

"It is likely," replied the Avadhut, and turned to go his way.

By the time that Ekanta had seated himself in a suitable position for the night, the ocean had changed dynamically.  Taking on various shades of dark orange and misty red mixed with the blackness of encroaching darkness, it made for a truly inspiring spectacle.  Across the surface of the water, a few schools of tiny flying fish occasionally launched themselves in perfectly symmetrical arches out of the sea in a motion almost too quick for the eyes to perceive.  The Avadhut wondered at the sense of freedom that such creatures must possess in this boundless playground.  Thinking thus, he recalled his teacher's words long ago on the subject of liberation.

"*Imagine, Ekanta, that you are a fish that has lived its entire existence in a clear bowl, moving round and round in circles, inexorably.  Suddenly, you are released into a vast ocean with endless expanses of water all around you.  What kind of joy would you experience, then, an ordinary happiness?  No, not likely.  You would feel a rapture of freedom scarcely ever imagined, heightened and intensified all the more by the sense of bondage which you just escaped.  This, then, is akin to what the jivanmukta experiences upon escaping from the condition of imprisonment in the world of name and form.  Nothing of its type can quite compare to it.*"

"Revered sir," returned the boy, "is this what death is like then?  Does the jivanmukta, the liberated soul, have to give up the body in order to experience this sublime state?"

"*Definitely not,*" stated the guru.  "*Liberation of this type amounts to the realization that there is nothing but freedom existing at all times.  One only has to access it by releasing identification with limitations.  Different states of being do not inhibit it in the least.  Therefore, in whatever condition the free soul finds itself, whether in a physical body, an angelic body, a divine body or a disembodied state, that one is always permeated with the ecstatic bliss and pervasive peace that is freedom.*"

Pondering the words of his preceptor for a moment, Ekanta then asked, "How is it that so few beings possess this great bliss if it is so wonderful?  If it is all that you describe, why is it so rare?"

"*It is due to individualization, outgoing mind, uncontrolled senses, desire, sensual pleasure, attachment and greed, in that order, my boy,"* declared the guru. *"In those who are inordinately attached to the world, one finds these tendencies. It is interesting to note that all beings have these seven characteristics within them. Everyone has to grapple with them at one stage or another, often in cycles."*

"My dear and revered guru," said Ekanta, "do even the illumined ones have these impediments?"

*"If they are truly illumined,"* replied the teacher, *"they have either done away with them or completely mastered them. Even in advanced practitioners though, some of these persist. It is the final two, attachment and greed, which must be destroyed at all costs. Individual consciousness is there for all embodied beings, for at least a trace of the ego will remain as long as the body does. The outgoing mind, too, is present in all, for even the enlightened have to apply their mental instrument to some work, for the good of suffering beings for example."*

"What of desire, revered teacher?" pressed Ekanta. "Surely the illumined do not possess that."

*"Not in the ordinary sense, my boy,"* replied the guru, *"but there are desires such as eating, drinking, sleeping and so forth that are a part of the embodied condition. The illumined are subject to these, no doubt, but deal with them in entirely different ways than the worldly-minded. Sensual pleasure, too, is there in the embodied condition, but for the enlightened these pleasures are simple and unostentatious, causing no harm to the spiritual lifestyle."*

Pausing for a moment, as if to consult an internal voice, the guru presently went on.

*"It is the final two, as I said, that are not acceptable under any circumstances. Attachment and greed come into play and life becomes a living hell. The experienced quickly draw away from these and eradicate such tendencies completely before they can become fixed in the mind. One can control sensual appetites and desires if they are present, minimizing them to what is basic and necessary. One cannot, however, successfully control attachment or greed. To allow them room in the mind while trying to minimize them is like trying to force two quarts of milk into a one-quart pot. It is just not possible. Therefore, these*

*two must be destroyed completely, for wherever they are there is bound to be trouble."*

As the Avadhut's memory of these past events and teachings came to an end, he noticed the first few stars gleaming in the night skies. Nature did not exhibit greed, the Avadhut surmised. He had never seen an animal, even a predator, take more than what it needed. Storing up for the future without a needful purpose was also not the way of things in nature. Once, while Ekanta had been hiking through the Sunderlands over a wild game preserve, he had seen a Bengal tiger drag the carcass of a brown-tailed deer away from a host of jackals, storing it in a tree for a meal at a later date. Camping nearby and thinking this strange behavior, he had witnessed the reason for this later the next day when the tiger brought its four cubs to feed on the remains. It was not due to greed, then, but for survival of the species that caused this natural and ultimately unselfish behavior in the tiger.

Ekanta thought back on the teachings of Yogindra Yogi, his precious monastic teacher.

*"Attachment and greed are companions, Ekanta. They are seldom without each other. If you think you notice attachment in someone and greed is not present, then you may know that it is apparent attachment only. Concern and a spirit of taking care of others is not attachment. Neither is the sincere love of a husband and wife for each other or for their children. Love and compassion are present on these occasions, not greed or attachment."*

"What reveals the presence of greed in others, dear sir?" the young Ekanta had asked.

*"Greed has its gross and subtle forms, dear boy,"* answered the yogi. *"The gross manifestations are easily noticeable and we see them amongst the worldly-minded all the time. One could almost say that greed characterizes the worldly-minded, along with lust, anger and jealousy. Dogs rest easily around each other and even lick each others bodies, but throw a scrap of table food amongst them and watch the chaotic result. About food, money, possessions and land, we see just this type of behavior in the worldly-minded ones. They would battle to the death or put each other out in the cold for the sake of a couple of coins, a few morsels, or a few clods of earth. It is unconscionable."*

"And what of the subtle manifestations of greed, revered sir?"

Ekanta asked. "How does one notice them?"

*"In this day and age,"* stated the yogi, *"the most evident subtle example of greed in the world in my opinion is the tendency for all beings to store things up for the future. This insidious habit is based upon selfishness and greed, and it undermines the spontaneous and natural lifestyle which God intended for all human beings to live. Therefore, greed masquerades in this day and age as what beings think of as security.*

*"Once,"* continued the holy man, *"Jagachakshu Muni, whom you have heard me speak of, told a story of the holy man who lost his sacred status due to this type of greed. He had been traveling the road of pilgrimage for a long time. One day, he suddenly heard a voice within say, 'That mountain there in front of you, it is filled with gold ore which none has yet discovered.' The voice then was silent and nothing more was told. This direct statement was beyond doubting and the holy man lost his head and scrambled up on the face of that mountain and began to search for gold ore. After some time had passed, the man came to his senses. He then thought to himself, 'Wait! Hold and desist! I am a holy man who has been trained to renounce since a very young age. What am I doing searching for gold here on this mountain? It is a trap of Maya and I have temporarily succumbed to it.'*

*"Thinking thus, he came off of the mountain and camped below it overnight. During the night and all the next morning, however, the holy man could not bring himself to forget the mountain and its gold. Try as he might, the idea still remained firmly entrenched in his awareness. When it came time for him to head on towards the distant pilgrimage sights, he simply could not bring himself to leave, knowing that the mountain contained a fortune. Caught in a dilemma, he finally waited for a few days and remained encamped there. Days turned into months and finally into years and still the man did not leave the mountain. You see, a strange occurrence had transpired in his mind, that bound him to that location. He thought in his mind that he would not actually lay his hands on the gold but would, instead, simply watch over it and keep it safe for a distant time when he was truly in need. In this way did he hoard the gold in his mind and lay it up for the future. This*

*was his undoing."*

"Revered sir," said Ekanta, "you have talked about vyasti and samasti, individual and collective delusion before. Is this tendency to hoard and store up for the future a result of that? It seems to have become the norm in society everywhere in these times."

*"You have a very retentive memory, little Atman,"* exclaimed the yogi. *"You are a boy after my own heart. Besides that, you have stated perfectly what I am speaking of. This individual and collective delusion is nowhere more noticeable than in the personal and collective financial affairs of people and society.*

*"Once, greed was limited to a few belongings and some small tracts of land. Now, the bizarre diversions that are afforded due to coveting and possessing everything in sight has deteriorated the moral fabric of society. It is no longer fashionable to have just what one requires. It is necessary, instead, to own more than one could possibly ever utilize. People call this planning for the future and say that it gives them security. The wise know that such manipulating of God's resources is selfishness and only brings slavery and fastens the mind on mundane matters, unworthy of the freedom-loving soul. What the worldly-minded call the future is what the illumined speak of as dharma, practical and righteous living, and swadharma, the originally intended and divinely oriented existence. Both dharma and swadharma are greatly distorted by the impositions of greed and attachment. What God has planned for the aspiring soul in the way of wonderful experiences of growth get completely undermined by the ego's penchant for hoarding and storing up for the future.*

*"Once, I came among a group of rich people who were gathered at the house of a devotee friend of mine. They practically winced to see me there. After I had endured a few innuendoes and some ignoble remarks about my station in life, I faced my critics and told them, 'There was once a man who owned nothing. He had no family, no children, possessed no stocks, securities or other financial benefits. He owned no land and did not even know where his next meal was coming from. Do any of you think that such a person could be happy?' All of the rich persons present, to the last one of them, replied that it was not possible for such a man to have happiness. I then told them,*

'The man I have described to you is now sitting in front of you. I am that man and I now declare to you on everything that I hold sacred that I am completely and thoroughly happy. What is more,' I told them, 'my happiness is lasting, is eternal. I am totally free of worries and abide in the bliss of the Atman at all times.' This admission of mine put a hold on their judgmental tongues. I enjoyed the rest of the gathering immensely.

"And so, my dear boy," concluded the yogi, "never fall into the trap of selfishly hoarding things. Storing for the future, whether it be possessions that you can gloat over for years or a large bank account that you think will give you security in your old age, is all delusion. Not only does it take away your right to live freely in an unencumbered way, it also attaches your mind to vain hopes and expectations which may never manifest. Finally, and most lamentable, this store of goods and wealth that you think on day and night takes your mind away from the Lotus Feet of God and His precious spiritual teachings. The Lord and his word are the only things that can bring you true peace of mind. Therefore, nothing can equal this loss."

After a pause, the yogi said, "No, there is no doubt about it. What the worldly-minded call practicality and what the spiritually-minded think of as practical are two entirely different things. This is well-illustrated in a song."

Saying so, the yogi opened his mouth and began to sing a bhajan from the store of India's wonderful wisdom songs:

Tell me, O mind, why have you given up uttering
the Holy Name of Ram?
When you should be renouncing your anger, deceit
and dishonesty, you have given up your integrity
and sacrificed your love of Truth instead.

You flatter the millionaire, yet forget to praise Sri Ram,
though Ram is the owner of the entire universe!
Your mind dwells constantly
on sense objects and mundane habits,
tempted by that which has no eternal existence.
Is it for the sake of these fleeting things
that you have forsaken the precious gem of Sri Ram's Name?

Consider this, O mind, the Lord is the source of all existence
– can you truly afford to forget Him?
Khalas is continually posing this profound question:
"When will you renounce your attachment to this world,
offering even your body and mind to the Lord,
depending solely on Bhagavan Sri Ram?

The Avadhut brought himself back from these powerful rumi-nations. It was time to sleep. Glancing at the village, he noticed that all the lamps had been extinguished and that everyone was asleep. The night had progressed to a late hour during his con-templations, but it mattered little. The spiritual wind called the Mahavayu blew across the inner landscape of concentrated awareness at this late hour. The Avadhut could never resist the tendency to immerse himself in it. Now, laying down on the com-fortable and accommodating sands, he closed his eyes, offered himself to the Divine Mother of the Universe, and was soon locked in a deep and refreshing sleep.

In the very early hours of the morning, the Avadhut experienced another powerful dream. He surfaced in the middle of an endless expanse of water. There was water on all sides and there was no land in sight anywhere. Strangely, though, he felt no anxiety at this whatsoever, and simply floated easily in the calm and bound-less waters. At a particular moment, a large fish with gold scales surfaced in front of him and circled him several times. After the fish had submerged, a feeling of holiness and sanctity came over him, as if he were an object of great veneration. Then, as if in an instant and in an inconceivable manner, all the water quickly got absorbed into his body and he was standing on dry land again.

When he awoke he lay still for a few moments. There was no sound anywhere and twilight was just beginning. The sea was so calm and silent that he finally had to sit up and see if it was still there. As he looked upon that great body of water he noticed that it was completely free of waves or ripples. It seemed as if the ocean had become a lake. He had never seen it so calm and the stillness of the waters added considerably to the clarity as well, affording the onlooker a clear view of reefs, fishes and ocean bottom for quite a distance.

Sitting for meditation, Ekanta enjoyed an undisturbed period of deep peace, both internal and external. He was roused out of his contemplative state by the sounds of the fishermen leaving their huts and heading for the boats which were beached on the sands a short distance from the village. When each boat was filled with hearty young men, they put out to sea with nets and poles to earn their day's bounty from the Mother Ocean.

A short while later, Ekanta noticed the elderly man who had asked him to be his guest for the evening, heading up the beach in the direction of the distant point. He was carrying a fishing pole and was walking at a leisurely pace. After the man had proceeded about halfway to the rock point, Ekanta gathered his belongings together and followed him at a distance.

When Ekanta arrived at the spit of rocks jutting out into the ocean, he saw that the fisherman had already made his way to the end of it and was busy fixing his line for the cast. Working his way up to the higher level of rocks behind the fisherman, Ekanta found a wonderful vantage point where he could see the entire scene in front of him without any obstructions. From this height, he could see everything in the ocean as well since the water was completely clear and exceedingly placid. Watching the fisherman as he cast his line into the ocean, he saw the end of the line with its hook, bait and weight splash down in the water and fall towards the ocean bottom which was not too deep at that point.

After a short wait, the fisherman suddenly reacted to a pull on his line and in moments he had landed a fish. Ekanta had been watching the area where the man's line had penetrated to the ocean bottom and had also witnessed the gradual congregation of fish around the bait. Other than that, the distance was too great to pick up details.

After the fisherman had baited his hook once again, he cast his line in a different direction, over towards the side of the point where the Avadhut was seated. When Ekanta saw the hook and bait splash in the water near his location, he stood up and slowly worked his way down the opposite side of the point where the fisherman stood so that he could not observe him. Arriving at the very edge of the rocky shoreline which was only a few feet above sea level, the Avadhut sat himself down with his eyes fixed on the line and bait in the water close by.

It was not long before a small group of fish had gathered nearby, attracted by the scent of the food and the sparkling lure that was attached to the line. Ekanta could see their shining bodies as they swam excitedly around the lure, each wanting to eat the bait but fearful to do so. The fish were of many different colors, sizes and shapes. Some were daring and others were more wary. Ekanta surmised that the older and bigger fish were generally cautious, and this was probably due to some prior experience with a deceptively easy meal. The smaller fish, some very tiny, were immediately around the bait, feeding off of it in quick motions, none of them substantial enough to cause any pull on the line.

As Ekanta watched, fascinated by the extraordinary view of the proceedings on this clear, calm day, he noticed that one fish was suddenly vaulted skyward, its colorful body penetrating the surface of the water before falling back into the ocean. Though it writhed and jumped in energetic fashion, it was inexorably drawn towards shore where the anxious fisherman waited with his small net for the capture. As Ekanta turned his attentions back to the community of fish below, he saw that life went on as usual. The fish were merely swimming around where the bait had once been, still attracted by its smell lingering there in the water.

This process, cyclic in nature, reminded Ekanta of the life and death drama above the surface of the water as well. In similar fashion, death was also casting his line into the world of mortals, waiting for the right time to take another human being out of the embodied state. In like fashion to the fish, human beings also went on with their existence in the same way that they had previous to the loss of one of their numbers. Death, then, was an unseen or barely discernible element in the lives of living beings. No one contemplated its presence other than as a passing phenomenon. To a being like the Avadhut, this was a curious fact. He found himself reciting a verse from Shankara's famous hymn once again:

Who is your wife and who is your son?
Where have they come from and where are they going?
The empirical process is always moving forward,
catching sleepers unaware.
Who are you and what is your origin?
Contemplate these perplexing questions now, in this very life.

On one occasion, Ekanta had asked his teachers about death and predestination. The situation at that time made the question imperative. A boyhood friend who lived in the village had suddenly passed away. The young boy's parents were grief stricken and Ekanta, too, was shocked and unhappy. Walking into the woods in the direction of the forest ashram with a view towards getting clarification and solace from his revered gurus, he came upon his two teachers walking slowly along the path leading to a nearby lake.

*"Ekanta, precious student,"* came the heartwarming words of his Mataji, *"where are you going? Have you come seeking us?"*

Distraught to a breaking point, Ekanta blurted out, "He was playing happily with me just yesterday! Now he is gone. Why? How can this happen?"

With the smiles quickly vanishing from their serene faces, the vanaprastin couple became silent. The three stood there on the path for a few minutes, Ekanta, with tears streaming down his face and his gurus with eyes closed, strangely quiet. Gradually, Ekanta felt his sorrow leaving him. The sounds of nature — the birds chirping sweetly, the humming of insects and the wind streaming in aromatic currents through the boughs of trees — began to fill his awareness and vaulted him into a high state of consciousness. After a while, he felt a gentle hand on his arm and words of confidence and concern washed over his ears.

*"Shanti, shanti, shanti,"* began his guru. *"Always be at peace while considering the problems of this earth. Your young friend is now all around us as well as within us as our very consciousness. He smiles upon you even now, for nothing is ever truly lost in Brahman. His form has been dissolved, that is all."*

"Thank you, dear teachers," came Ekanta's heartfelt gratitude. "I do feel much better already. It is my own attachment to my friend's form that has brought this state upon me. I have forgotten your precious instructions. It is hard to be calm in the face of such tragedy."

*"Yes, it is true,"* replied the Mataji, *"but it is also natural to the human condition to feel this way. Do not blame yourself, but at the same time attempt to temper your grief so that higher counsel and its healing effects can benefit you. Mindless grief is totally incapacitating and must be guarded against."*

*"What is more,"* stated Ekanta's Guruji, *"the Divine Mother who has fashioned this temporal state of existence is also guiding it and its many forms of expression. She has something else in mind for the evolution or existence of your friend. How presumptuous of us to think that we can stand in the way of another's destiny, what to speak of the Universal Mother's perfect will. If we believe Her to be omniscient, as we often affirm, then we must stand by our resolve and accept Her dictates. Otherwise, we may as well make our own mind and ego the supreme authority and follow accordingly."*

*"And this is precisely what most beings do,"* joined in the Mataji. *"The result is the world as we see it today, where the deluded masses are confused and the clever few are taking advantage of that condition. Rare is the one who rises to the ideal and refuses to pull the ideal down, who follows the instructions of the guru in complete trust and with adamantine faith. Truth is the criterion here, not one's personal assumptions or agenda. That is the true measure of what is real and what is not."*

*"So understand this thing called predestination, my son,"* said Ekanta's Guruji. *"She is Self-willed and knows all, yet Her spontaneity is legend."*

*"What She decrees and writes into the great document of destiny, Ekanta,"* the Mataji interjected, *"She can also erase. You will meet your friend again someday and the two of you will rejoice. Nothing is ever lost in Brahman."*

Ekanta returned his attention to the ocean. The fish had given up looking for the bait and were feeding along the bottom and on rocks in their usual fashion. There was plenty of food there for all of them. The Universal Mother had provided everything for all of Her creatures, even the aquatic ones. As the Avadhut sat ruminating, he saw a splash in the water in the same region where the last bait had landed. As the bait sank into the ocean, the fish came swimming hungrily towards it. This time, before it reached the bottom, many of the fish attacked the bait head-on and there was a general flurry of action around it, causing small waves and eddies on the surface. Ekanta saw that the fisherman had not yet cast his line and he wondered if the fish knew that there was no line attached to the recently thrown bait and that was why they were less cautious.

The next event was most interesting, for no sooner did the fish get accustomed to the free food floating there in their watery world, than another splash occurred. The fisherman had placed a perfectly executed cast right at the spot where he had just thrown the last bait. This was a neat trick, thought Ekanta, for the fish were now used to the idea that there was no danger in feeding. There was more likelihood of the fisherman landing a bigger fish with such a clever ruse.

Sure enough, as Ekanta watched with rapt attention, a larger fish, excited by the feeding frenzy around the unhooked bait and unable to get in close due to the many fish surrounding it, made a beeline towards the new bait and took it directly without any due consideration. This proved to be the undoing of this creature, for it was immediately hooked and drawn towards the surface where the fisherman eagerly awaited. Watching the lamentable fate of this beautiful specimen as it was pulled up onto the shore and seeing the fisherman's unbridled glee at having such great success, the Avadhut was plunged into a profound mood by all he had just witnessed.

Thinking back over the teachings he had recalled the previous evening having to do with attachment and greed, the Avadhut was struck by what he had just seen. Greed had been the final impulse that had doomed the large fish to capture and death. Losing its sensibilities and forgetting its prior experience due to one impulsive act, it was now food in the hands of death. How apt this illustration seemed to the Avadhut, and how applicable it was to many of the dealings that human beings perpetrated in the world.

Other than the many teachings which Ekanta had received from his gurus as a young boy, he had also learned the lessons of greed through his own experiences. At one time, he had been a party to a situation that had shown him the potentially insidious nature of human beings caught in the trap of greed and covetousness.

It had occurred between two brothers, both of them known to Ekanta and neither of them well-liked by him or the townspeople. When the mother of these two brothers finally died after a long illness, however, the entire village went to her funeral, for this woman was considered saintly among the people of the surrounding countryside. No sooner had this revered woman's ashes been spread across the fields then the two sons began fighting

over the family property.  Each was to be given an equal share and
there was nothing vague about the arrangement, yet they fell into
daily battles about the matter and caused all associated with them
undue discomfort and botheration.

One day, as Ekanta was working in the fields along with other
hired boys to prepare the field for a fence that would separate the
land into two equal parcels, Yogindra Yogi happened along the
road.  Seeing him, Ekanta ran across the field and called out to
him to stop.

"Dear sir," he breathed hard, as he drew near the holy man,
"please forgive my excitement but it has been so long since I have
seen you."

*"No matter, little Atman,"* replied the yogi, *"I am never in any
hurry and am always most happy to see and converse with the
likes of you.  What are you doing here in this field?  I hear the
saintly old woman has passed on to a better existence.  God rest
her soul!"*

"Yes, that is true sir," answered Ekanta.  "Now we are preparing for a fence to be placed here that will separate the land into
two parcels.  I have been hired to assist in this chore."

*"A fence?"* declared the yogi in a surprised voice.  *"Why in heav-
en's name would a fence be needed or wanted here?"*

"Those two brothers," explained Ekanta, "the two sons of the
saintly woman, are now arguing about how much land each one
should own and are eager to place a fence that will indicate and
declare the proper boundary."

The yogi was silent for a few moments, as if shocked to hear
this news.

*"Separations, divisions and lines of demarcation,"* said the
yogi by and by, *"ignorant human beings are ever placing such
obstructions in the way of unity.  In the name of ownership and
possessions, natural unity gets undone.  When that occurs, harmony falls.  With that gone, peace is the next victim.  In due
time, contentment, equanimity and justice disappear and the
natural order of things falls into chaos.  Don't these two brothers
know that they cannot own God's green earth?"*

"What causes beings to act in this way, revered sir?" asked
Ekanta.

*"It is greed, plain and simple, my son,"* replied the yogi.

*"Imagining themselves to be wealthy and respected, people grab onto whatever comes their way and cling to it until the last death gasp tears it away from them. In the meantime, they make no beneficial use of their properties and only gloat over them with a hideous pride of ownership that destroys their minds. This greed and the ensuing jealousy it fosters is the cause of war, is the cause of hate, is the reason that blood brothers, fast friends, devout sisters and close cousins fall at odds and will never talk to one another again."*

Another silence followed these words. Then, the yogi continued:

*"It is said that God laughs on several occasions. First, when a doctor tells the mother of an ailing son, 'Do not worry, madam, I will heal your son.' The Lord knows that he will take the life of this soul back into Himself. Next, the Lord laughs when two brothers put up a fence and declare, 'This side is yours and this side is mine. You do what you want over there but stay off of my side.' The blessed One knows that all land belongs to Him and He will dispense with it in whatever manner He chooses."*

Ekanta thought for a moment. "Will these two ever come to their senses about this matter?"

*"It is not likely, Ekanta,"* responded the holy man. *"They are caught in the grasp of greed and attachment. Who is to say, but it may be lifetimes before the needed lessons that they require will appear to them again. If that is the case, the open-mindedness necessary to bring such lessons to bear on their consciousness may not be present either due to negative karma, the type which is formulated by acts such as the kind we are witnessing here before us. It is a vicious circle, Ekanta."*

"One thing truly perplexes me, revered sir," Ekanta said.

*"And what might that be, little Atman?"* replied Yogindra Yogi.

"The woman was a saint, admired by all, yet her offspring show themselves to be greedy and jealous, indulging in all sorts of petty issues and illogical arguments. Frankly, they are not good people. How can this be explained?"

*"That is an odd situation,"* the yogi admitted. *"The saying goes that a good tree bears only sweet fruit. On the other hand, a pea falling in a dung heap nevertheless turns into a good strong plant. If this is true, the opposite must also be possible. Usually, like begets like, but sometimes the tree is good but the*

seeds are bad. Then again, fruit appearing from a good tree in the off-season is often sour. All things are potential in such a world as this. We are therefore very fortunate that we can recognize negative passions and take steps to alleviate them and strike them from our consciousness. This is the Lord's blessing upon those who love Him and who strive to do good to others and to make sense out of all such dilemmas. I know that if you or I were in the position of these two brothers, the entire situation would be different. If I owned such a field, may the Lord not saddle me with that responsibility just now, it would either be used to grow free food for the community or it would be utilized as a place for weary holy men to rest and recover during their pilgrimages."

The fish in the water where the bait had fallen were now pacified. Things were back to normal in that portion of the aquatic world. The fisherman, too, was casting his line in a different area in hopes of achieving success in a similar manner again. The Avadhut stood up and saluted the fish in the ocean.

"You have taught me a great lesson," he stated. "The dangerous and beguiling nature of greed has been duly demonstrated here today. You, the fish, have taught me once again the need for discrimination and caution with regard to matters pertaining to the world."

After finishing his salutation, the words of his Mataji came to mind once more:

"Greed is an unnecessary imposition, Ekanta. It wreaks havoc on every situation it touches. It is a bane on human consciousness and is the producer of selfishness and attachment in the human mind. May all beings be free of this treacherous passion. May it be replaced with generosity and selflessness in all peoples, all situations."

The Avadhut spent the next half hour in prayer for the good of all sentient beings. Then, he retraced his steps across the rocky point and returned to the wide sunny shoreline. Prostrating himself on the sands and offering his heartfelt gratitude to the Blessed Lord and Divine Mother, he turned his holy feet in the general direction of Maharastra and keeping the peaceful ocean with all of its living creatures on his left, disappeared into the endless miles of sandy beaches that lay ahead.

# — Chapter 11 —

# Teachings on Disgust Leading to Satiety

THE ELEVENTH GURU —*The Courtesan*

THE LESSON —*Expectation*

*rom the courtesan Pingala, well-dressed and seductive, I learned the meaning of disgust and satiation. For many years of her wayward life she based her expectations upon what lustful and manipulative men could give her, reaping in the end only disappointment and heartbreak. Finally, after a particularly harsh disillusionment, she gave up her ill-motivated ways and turned to the Lord, the repository of true wealth and satisfaction.*

It had been a long and wondrous journey along the coastline of Kerala and Karnataka, full of hidden teachings and divine associations. At one point, after bidding farewell to the beloved ocean, the Avadhut had turned inland to catch certain paths and roads known only to the solitary wayfarer that would more readily lead him to his next desired destination — the city of Bombay. It was not long, therefore, before the landscape began to reflect signs of condensed human habitation.

The large state of Maharastra was teeming with humanity.

292

Besides bordering the Arabian Sea on one side, it also acted as a connecting point between north and south India and the middle east. Traders, merchants, farmers and professional people of all types flowed through its well-equipped industrial centers, the most important of which was the port city of Bombay.

The Avadhut arrived at the outskirts of Bombay in the late evening. This was not a coincidence but was planned, for he wished to avoid certain unpleasantries of city life by this tactic. He also had friends in this city, which was one reason why he chose to visit it periodically.

The ashram of his friend, Pandit Pratapa, was located near the water in one of Bombay's less crowded, less noisy areas. The pandit was a learned man who had a wife and one son. Endowed with deep devotion to Brahman and a mine of wisdom besides, the Avadhut had met him during his travels to the Kumbha Mela, a holy celebration where thousands of Hindus met to bathe in the holy river at a particularly auspicious time of year. The pandit had attracted Ekanta's attention due to his unswerving devotion to God and his unyielding defense of the Upanishadic Wisdom and the Rishis who received it and passed it on so long ago. Wherever there was a debate about the authenticity of India's timeless philosophy, there one would probably find Pandit Pratapa involved, making his points of contention with the power, ease and grace of a mongoose defeating a king cobra.

The Avadhut, king of travelers, cut through the city streets like a hot knife through butter. The outskirts and suburbs, the trafficked thoroughfares, the ramshackle slums and the business district all fell behind him in a few hours as he headed directly for the sanctuary of the city ashram. Since he was coming from an inland route, he kept his eye out for the ocean and was soon rewarded by its vast, unlit expanse, standing out in stark contrast against the sea of city lights that distinguished Bombay proper. It was not long before he began to recognize certain landmarks that guided him onwards towards his safe haven in this maze of confusing streets.

As he entered the neighborhood where the pandit's spiritual center, the Advaita Ashrama, was situated, he breathed a sigh of relief. He knew that he would find rest and sustenance here, as well as that rare and welcome condiment to spiritual life called

holy company.  As he thought about this great boon, the words of
Sri Ramachandra, the Avatar of the Treta Yuga, came into his mind:

There are Nine Limbs to the tree of devotion, Truth seeker.
Holy Company comes first, like a flame that lights kindling.
Next, there is the intent and ability to spread the teachings.
Singing of My blessed Names and vast glories
and chanting the hymns of the eternal scriptures comes next,
followed by attention to the words of the illumined ones.
Service of the guru and the support of his cause is sixth,
while developing good habits through self-control
and devout and constant worship is seventh.
Serving the devotees and perceiving God in all is eighth.
while everything culminates with deep investigation
into the true nature of nondual Reality.
Though all of these limbs are important,
know that attaining the rare treasure of authentic Bhakti
all begins with holy company.

With these words fresh in his mind, Ekanta found himself on
the steps leading into the Advaita Ashrama.  As Ekanta entered
the hallowed precincts of the spiritual center, he noticed that
Pandit Pratapa was engaged in giving a class to students and local
townspeople.  When the pandit saw the Avadhut, he stopped in
mid sentence and stared.  As Ekanta started to take a seat on the
floor at the back of the gathering, the pandit stood and spoke
    "No friend of mine, let alone a wandering holy man of the high-
est order, will sit in the dust as long as I manage this ashrama!"
    This unprecedented pause and outburst from the highly
respected teacher right in the middle of the class caused all to
turn and look to see who was being referred to.  With all gazes
upon him and nowhere to retreat, the Avadhut rose and faced his
friendly antagonist, for he was no friend of false modesty.
    "The dust of this sacred hall is as good or better than any pil-
grimage sight I have ever visited," he spoke out boldly, "and I have
seen them all.  If I rolled my body here in this dust, I am sure that
the whole of it would turn golden."
    These words were all he was able to get out before the pandit
was in front of him, embracing him like a long-lost brother.  The

Avadhut too, laughing aloud and hugging his friend, was overjoyed as the two rocked back and forth in a mutual bear hug. This occurrence caused those present to gawk in shocked amazement and the spectacle was made all the more astounding when the pandit's wife and son entered the room in a hurry and rushed to take the dust of this new stranger's feet, bowing low before the respected Avadhut. To the audience, all that they saw was a dark and dusty stranger with unkempt beard and ragged clothes, certainly not the usual figure to which their revered guru and mataji would pay such high respect. This was only the beginning, as it turned out, for the night was still young.

Before the devotees were able to catch their breath, the pandit had taken Ekanta by the hand and led him up in front of the gathering. The pandit's wife had, in the meantime, run to get a suitable chair fit for the sacred guest and placed it next to the asana of her respected and beloved husband. As the Avadhut saw the reverence with which he was being treated, he almost balked. His natural inclination was to shrink from such honors, but thrust into this situation unexpectedly and being the recipient of his dear friend's attentions in front of all his students, he certainly could not let him down. Sitting himself down on the fancy asana, a beggar one day and an honored figure the next, he gratefully accepted a large container of fresh water from the pandit's son and quaffed it all down in a few moments, much to the added surprise of all present.

"Respected guests," the pandit announced. "I have the special privilege of introducing to you a rare personage, the likes of which India once had the great honor and blessing of seeing quite frequently. My friend, Ekanta, is a freely circulating member of that great lineage of Avadhuts which many of you have only heard about in stories and sacred scripture. As one sees a Brahman priest and thinks about the great Rishis of olden times, one can look upon an Avadhut and see there an illumined being representing everything that is holy in sacred Bharata. As long as he is here, I ask all of you to treat him as you would myself, for he possesses unique wisdom unrivaled by even the most well-known and knowledgeable pundits. This I say from direct experience rather than mere hearsay. We are fortunate to have him in our midst and I might add that as suddenly as he has appeared here, just as immediate will be his departure, so take advantage of his presence while you can. Now, I will ask him to speak."

Saying this by way of introduction, Pandit Pratapa turned to face the Avadhut, a huge smile spreading over his face. If the audience was expecting some grand words of wisdom, they were sorely disappointed. What they got instead was a loud and steady stream of laughter from the Avadhut. The pandit joined in too, and soon the contagion of humor shook the entire assembly. As the healing sound died down and trickled away, the Avadhut assumed an entirely different demeanor, though a good natured aura still covered him like some invisible cloak. Turning his attention upon the students and townspeople, he fixed them with a powerful gaze. Silence reigned for a full two minutes and no one stirred the entire time. All felt a palpable descent of grace into the assembly, attended by an indescribable peace and joy.

As soon as this blessed vibration was strong enough to be noticed by all present, the pandit stood up and spoke.

"You all now have a taste of the Avadhut transmission. If he were to leave now, saying no words whatsoever, none of you would be the poorer. So it is, in this day and age, that we all place the highest value on knowledge transmitted through words alone. The ancient ones, our distant ancestors, the Rishis, knew a wisdom that was beyond mere verbiage. They received God's grace directly into their hearts and minds on a daily basis. Some of them were munis, absolutely silent sages having no other teacher than their own radiant minds, which were informed by the Supreme Being Itself. Our friend here has now blessed you with a small sample of that ancient principle and has made our evening more fruitful than we ever could have hoped."

All remained silent after this grand statement. Soon, the voice of the Avadhut was heard for the first time that night.

"What my dear friend speaks is God's Truth. The ancient ones did have this power and stored it up over time from the austere practices they undertook. As for myself, I am the recipient of only a small modicum of God's Grace, having received that from my own hallowed teachers. If it did get shared tonight, it was not I but the Lord and Divine Mother of the Universe that allowed that to happen. All happens by Her sweet will, not by the exertions of the small and finite minds of human beings."

"This is exactly what we were talking about before you entered, my friend," the pandit joined in. "The subject of free will, karma and predestination was under study. Perhaps you can elucidate on this for us. It would be our honor to hear it from your lips."

"Only if you continue to offer your own insights," returned Ekanta.

"Agreed, my friend," replied the pandit jovially.

"The wise ones tell us that God's will is supreme," stated the Avadhut, "and that would cause us to think that everything is predestined. Taking this on a surface level, others have imagined this to mean that nothing that human beings do on earth matters in the least. These limited thinkers can cite plenty of examples in history to support their case: the endless wars that occur, despite all our best efforts to bring peace; the constant starvation that assails us even though we strive to procure food and distribute it justly and accordingly; the diseases that riddle our bodies in spite of all recent and ongoing medical advances.

"Yet, with all their support and citations, I call these limited thinkers timid and weak. They still, after listing all of these examples, fail to rise high enough out of their complacent gloom to perceive the uncompromising truth that the principle of predestination epitomizes. Only in Advaita, that verity upon which this ashrama is based and after which it is aptly named, do we find the true significance of what it means to know without doubt, act without fear, and live a thoroughly God-centered life."

At this point, a man in the group stood up and said, "Revered sir, I was under the impression that Advaita was a state beyond this world."

"Advaita permeates this world but is untouched by its appearances," replied the Avadhut. "It is a philosophy in name and word only. As a condition, if the definition can be allowed, it is the Lord's own atmosphere, His abode were He dwells in perfect bliss eternally."

"That is a wonderful description, dear sir," returned the man, "but I have a question. You have said that it is God that does everything, yet we hear from others that He is beyond action. Then again, some say that it is by our own efforts that we rise. In that case it is not God's will that accomplishes everything."

"Those are well thought out questions," stated the Avadhut, "and ones that have been proposed for eons. In this day and age, with such intense concerns due to over-population and rampant materialism, the answers become harder to access. Suffice to say that it is by the will of God that everything occurs, though He Himself is not involved. Like the air that allows us to breathe, but which is unseen, unheard and unaffected by anything that happens to us, whether it be by our own design or the effects of living in the world, the Blessed One pervades all but is ever free. As to your second question, it is the Blessed Lord that gives us the will to rise above our limitations. We think that we have accomplished this divine act by our own self-effort, but right timing and the Grace of the Universal Mother have played the essential part.

"Once, I had occasion to attend the courts of this land, accompanying a friend who was contesting a case. Throughout the day's proceedings as the judge heard each case, I noticed that the lawyers invariably had their say and took every possible occasion to give out extensive testimony and opinions. In the end, though, they always ended up stating something like, 'I have said everything that I have to say in the matter, Your Honor. The decision now rests with you.' I feel that this is exactly like the situation of karma and predestination which we are discussing here and now. The lawyers put forth great effort. In like manner, one cannot remain idle here on earth and must strive hard to rise to the level of God's ever-present Grace. After all is said and done, though, it is the judge, the Lord Almighty, that decides all things, draws all conclusions and bestows the final verdict. None can argue with that highest authority."

When the Avadhut had finished speaking, a buzz of excited talking ran through the crowd. This kind of example was exactly what the people needed in order to understand a little of the workings of the Divine Being. After letting them have their exchanges, the pandit brought the crowd back to order.

"Let us hear some more about this subject of predestination and karma. Please give the Avadhut your attention."

The Avadhut sat silently for a few moments. Then, a well-dressed woman, sitting a bit apart from the others, stood up and asked a question.

"Revered sir, if God decides our fate, how is it that so many striving and hardworking people fail to realize the goal of life and are reborn on earth amidst dire circumstances?  What do we have to do to receive His Grace and be relieved of suffering?"

"The inborn tendencies of past lives must be admitted," replied the Avadhut, "at least from the standpoint of relativity.  The world has a certain reality, though not an abiding one.  Here on earth, we reap the effects of our past actions, being convinced, as we are, that the body is real while clinging to the sense of individuality that we covet.  As long as we consider these things — body, ego and objects — most precious, placing them before the Lord, so long will we play the game of cause and effect, activity and retribution.

"I was once the guest of a powerful raja in northern India.  One day, while sitting with the maharaja in the inner courtyard, I observed the young prince and his royal playmates at play.  They were acting out fantasies having to do with power, prestige and leadership.  The young prince was, of course, always the prime player in these games.  The maharaja, looking up from his studies now and then, was noticeably proud of his son and he was, no doubt, a fine lad.

"After a time, the mood of the play began to change.  Abruptly, the prince exclaimed, 'Enough of these kinds of games.  We will play something different.'  Seizing the royal silks and expensive cloths that lay about the courtyard for the boys' amusement, the prince said by way of an order, 'We shall play a different game that I will make up just now.  I will lay here on my belly and all of you will beat me over the back with these robes and cloths, making a swishing sound in the air as you do so.'  The other boys were quick to comply, but the king, mouth open and obviously dumbfounded, just stared at the scene with authentic surprise combined with bewilderment.  When he looked over at me, I quickly averted my gaze.  How can one explain to a king that his princely son's previous lifetime was lived as the child of a washerwoman?  Who would savor such a task?  I left the place rather quickly at the first convenient opportunity."

For a few moments, there was silence in the room.  Then, gradually at first, but eventually in avalanche style, laughter started to permeate the room.  The pandit was the first to give way to it, in time holding his sides with an almost uncontrollable mirth.  After the uproar had subsided, it was the pandit who offered a question.

"Are we to infer by this unusual story about a washerwoman's son that what we do and say day-to-day, sometimes unexplainably so, is due to impressions from past lifetimes? If so, this is the most unique and apt illustration of that teaching that I have ever heard." Saying this, he gave way to more laughter, causing the others present to do the same.

At the appropriate time, the Avadhut continued.

"There is no doubt that this is true. Karma may not be the ultimate law and we should not limit ourselves to its control, but it is, nevertheless, a relative truth and the cause of most of what we perceive in this universe. Good and bad tendencies are all due to past actions. Looking at it from a higher standpoint, this is exactly why the Lord is beyond good and bad. He does not act, nor does the Mahashakti. She puts the wheels of the universe in motion and causes beings to jump about and perform various actions, but She remains absolutely aloof, perfectly uninvolved. She is the eternal Witness, the Sakshi Bhutam, aloof from all phenomena and their interaction."

"You may say this, sir," replied one man sitting near the front, "but I prefer to see Her everywhere, fully involved in the creation."

"In order to truly have such perception," stated the Avadhut in response, "one would have to have the very same detachment and lofty vision which She Herself possesses. If one had this, though, the world would seem an insignificant thing. The one cry of worldly people is that God is in the universe. He is not in the universe, the universe is in Him! There is a difference here, a subtle but important distinction. People want to embroil Brahman and Shakti in all manner of activity which they themselves cherish, even though they suffer repercussions from that activity. To insist in this folly is to say that God is subject to karma. He is not.

"To illustrate this, I can think of several examples. For instance, does a judge get down off of his bench and become involved with the proceedings on the floor? Furthermore, was he in any way involved with the actions of those who came to him for deliberation before the case commenced? No, he remains aloof and objective. The difference here, of course, between the Lord and a government official, is one concerning Omniscience. The judge presides only over a few matters of relative concern, while the Lord is the Witness of time, space and causation, the entire cosmic process. Therefore, place your faith in the Divine Couple, Shiva and Shakti, while remaining active and do all action without selfish desire."

A profound silence permeated the ashram as the sangha pondered the wise words and unique illustrations brought forward by the Avadhut. Everyone present knew that a direct experience of God was being bestowed upon them and no one stirred. Eventually, the Avadhut continued.

"There is another example that can be given in regards to this issue and this is from my own life experience. When I was a boy living happily in my village, an elderly matron who was a respected landowner in our vicinity announced that she would fund the entire festivities and worship for Navaratri, the religious festival of the blessed Divine Mother of the Universe, Sri Durga.

"As the days went by, she sent everything needed for the preparations. The workmen were paid to create special tirthas for the sacred images which were also newly fashioned by artisans who were well-compensated for their efforts. Modifications on the local temple of the Divine Mother were undertaken by masons and carpenters at the elderly matron's expense as well and a huge canvas to shelter the devotees was commissioned and sent for from the distant city. Chairs and tables were collected daily and brought to the auspicious site by servants and hired workers and much activity continued on around the clock.

"The preparation of the prasadam, which included many fine dishes to be offered to the Goddess and partaken of by the devotees was elaborate, expensive and time-consuming. Extra chefs and caterers had to be brought into the village to cope with the extensive burden and they cooked and prepared foodstuffs around the clock.

"Finally, though I could go on listing, well-known actors and musicians were hired from distant parts to present religious dramas and devotional music over the ten-day celebration. All in all, we villagers had never seen nor experienced anything like it. The expense must have been astronomical. A grand time was had by all and the worship of Mother Durga went off without a hitch, presided over by a well-respected pujari and several Brahmin priests from sacred temples out of town.

"What astounded me, however, is that though this rich matron planned for and paid for everything, giving unstintingly in the spirit of unselfish works to all involved, she herself was never seen at the celebration. It was rumored that she had pulled up in a carriage once at the entrance of the festival grounds to salute the Divine Mother from a distance and had simply observed the hundreds of devotees for a few minutes. Then she disappeared, unnoticed for the most part but highly acclaimed by all.

"I remember what Yogindra Yogi, a holy man of our vicinity, told me that night after the worship was over. Spying him from a distance and seeking him out after the puja was over, I told him that the matron was not present to enjoy the festivities. He simply stated:

"*How fitting. The Divine Mother of the Universe is just like that, too, my son. She provides everything for Her children, a whole universe of wonders and they enjoy it immensely, but She only watches lovingly from Her detached position. She acts not and receives not, being beyond all dualities. Praise and blame, success and failure, these things fail to touch Her. Victory to Sri Durga!*'"

After a moment's consideration, where one could almost hear the thinking process of those present, the same woman who had posed a previous question stood and asked another.

"From what you say, it sounds as if the Divine Mother is uncaring, revered sir, or at least uninterested."

"It is not to say that She is unconcerned about our sufferings, dear lady," responded the Avadhut, "but She teaches us the lessons of transcendence in no uncertain terms, for this is the only way we will see our way clear of this maze of limitation called the universe. We have, due to our own actions, created for ourselves a series or a sequence of repercussions. If a boy splashes about in a huge lake, the lake receives the effects, though the tiny waves are of little concern to the vast body of water. The Mother's creation is this lake, and we play about in it. No matter how much trouble we cause, no harm is done to Her or Her creation. In our vanity, we think that we should save the planet from all sorts of negative occurrences, but She has a universe full of planets. It may even be Her will to dispose of a few, like a child popping toy balloons."

"But sir," one man objected, "Her exploding of worlds is our death."

"And who are you, dear sir?" came the Avadhut's disarming reply. "Are you different from your Creator?  Perhaps you are but one of Her breaths that expanded the balloon in the first place.  Again, are we to attach to phenomenal existence and forget our true nature, falling again and again into the misconception that we are mortal, that we are physical matter, that we are bodies filled with blood, bones, excrement, puss and phlegm, that we are limited minds filled with selfish desires and a host of worries and incorporeal imbecilities?  I, for one, have left off with such nonsense. One's attitude should be, 'I will free myself with continual self-effort or die in the attempt.'  The Mother sees such commitment and adores the one who attempts it.  Those whom She adores become instantly immortal.  There can be no doubt about it.

"With regards to Her disinterestedness, as I have just pointed out, what is there here on this earth that the ultracosmic Divinity could possibly be interested in?  Do we expect Her to find any joy in the very things that cause us only misery and provisional happiness?  No, dear friends, do not make the mistake of projecting your own desires, attachments and conceptions onto the Mother of the Universe, thereby attempting to pull Her down into this maze of craving and confusion.  She allows us our fun and frolic here on this earth for a moment in time, but when we tire of the game, are threatened with dangers, grow old, diseased and face death, She brings us to our senses, so to speak, by reminding us of our true nature — That which She never forgets."

After a pause, the Avadhut went on.

"I mentioned that the Mother places the cosmic laws in motion and causes all beings to dance and jump about on the earth, as it were.  On different occasions, while traveling through the states of Bhutan and Tibet, I had the opportunity to see the old-style entertainment offered by the common people called 'shadow puppets.'  In the evening, when darkness has come, the puppeteers light lamps behind a constructed screen in the marketplace or neighborhood and bring out the various puppets.  Holding them on sticks at a length away from their bodies and between the lamps and the screen, they cause them to move.  To the children and audience on the other side of the screen, it appears as if the puppets have a life of their own.  It is all an appearance, though, for the puppeteer alone animates the figure and causes it to move about.

"In this fashion, spiritually speaking, it is the Universal Mother who actually animates all beings, for She exists within them as subtle unseen forces such as prana, thought and consciousness. She is the Master Puppeteer, the audience are Her companions and powers and the entire pantheon of gods, goddesses and illumined souls, the dolls she holds are living beings, and the projected shadow is a mere semblance of reality cast upon the screen of the material universe. After the evening's performance is over, She dismantles the screen, turns off the light, packs away the puppets and retires to Her own abode, taking everything with Her. She will set it all up again in the future, when it pleases Her."

After due consideration of this discourse on the ultimate will of the Divine Mother, another man stood up in the audience to question the Avadhut: "Forgive me for asking the inevitable, but are we then free from all responsibility for our actions, it being admitted that the Divine Shakti animates us?"

Smiling, the Avadhut answered, "That would be convenient, would it not?"

Laughter accompanied this statement.

"However," the Avadhut continued, "all individuals are parts of a whole. What we do affects that whole. A branch cannot bear fruit if it is not connected to the vine. Real fruit is grown by the consummate gardener, the Divine Mother, on healthy branches and limbs. The diseased limb is severed from the rest of the vine by the gardener. Those who go against the harmony of the whole sow no seed and therefore reap no beneficial results. Becoming separated from the vine, they are left with a limb barren of fruit and whithered as well."

It was at this point that the pandit intervened, though the group of devotees would have questioned the Avadhut all night.

"There will be more time to commune with our friend later," he said. "For now, let us adjourn and allow the Avadhut time to rest and eat. He has traveled days to reach our precincts. We will all meet at dawn tomorrow for meditation and at dusk for divine discourse. I expect to see all in attendance. Follow the tradition! Keep the spiritual life as your main focus and life will remain harmonious and fruitful. Protection also comes to those who take refuge daily in the Lord. May peace be unto us, may peace be unto all!"

Ending with a Sanskrit peace chant, the group broke up and went to their respective dwelling places. The Avadhut remained seated with his eyes closed until all had filed out of the small hall. As silence fell on the room, he felt a touch upon his feet accompanied by a slightly painful tingling sensation. Surprised by this, he inadvertently drew his feet back with a jerk and opened his eyes. The woman who had earlier asked him a few questions was at his feet.

"Forgive me revered sir," she said apologetically. "I did not mean to startle you. I wanted a brief word with you before you retire. My name is Pingala. I live across the street from this ashram and come here due to the grace of Pandit Pratapa and his kind wife. I am just a wretched soul and seek some solace from the wise. Would you be able to meet with me here in public, in this ashram hall to answer a few of my questions?"

"Dear lady," replied the Avadhut, "I am afraid that I do not have all the answers to your dilemmas but I would be glad to talk to you if it will help you in any way."

"Thank you so much," said Pingala. "I will contact you through the pandit over the next few days to find a convenient time to converse. In the meantime, please enjoy our city and the sacred atmosphere of this holy establishment."

Saying this, the lady withdrew quickly and the Avadhut was left alone.

"That was Pingala," said a voice near to him. He had not noticed that the pandit had quietly approached him. "She is a professional courtesan who entertains men who pay for her services, much to the disgust of the people hereabouts. With all of that, she is a sincere soul who has received a bad start in life. We allow her to come here though it causes some trouble with our more orthodox members."

"Now I understand why no one was sitting close to her earlier," said Ekanta. "I also understand my strange reaction to her touch."

"My friend," said the pandit energetically, "you must be tired and hungry. Marali has prepared food earlier today and is warming it up for you just now. Please come with me to the kitchen where we can converse in comfort. It has been a long time since we have seen each other."

The Avadhut enjoyed the rest of the evening immensely, conversing with his friends, eating sattvic food and resting his weary body. When the meal was over Pratapa and Marali, being sensitive to his need for rest, showed Ekanta to his favorite room facing the front street and sporting a balcony that overlooked everything from the second story of the ashram structure. Washing over the drain in his room's small washroom with some heated water that the couple's son brought him in a bucket, Ekanta was soon clean, well fed and lying on his bed, a luxury that rarely occurred in his life. Thanking the Blessed Lord for bringing him safely to his destination and offering himself to the Universal Mother before he closed his eyes, he then drifted off into a deep sleep.

The next morning, the Avadhut was awake before all others. The ashramites and devotees found him already seated for meditation as they began arriving in the early hours. The room seemed more spiritually charged than usual and all felt that the presence of this newly arrived holy figure had much to do with it. After the meditation, as the last refrains of the Gayatri-Mantra had drifted away in the fragrant morning air, the devotees left for their respective homes and duties, leaving the Avadhut still seated in lotus posture, lost in deep meditation on Reality.

Across the spontaneous and radiant mind of the Avadhut this morning came many spiritual teachings having to do with action and fulfillment. The last evening's discourse with all the different questions had left the Avadhut's mind pondering the nature of the world and its relationship with Reality. This field of activity, the realm of Karma Yoga, was an extremely complex one. How could the people of the world be lead along the right path in this regard? Blind and haphazard experience was a slow and frustrating teacher. As he mused upon this issue, the words of his illumined teacher came into his mind.

*"The greater percentage of people in the world proceed through life performing sakama karma, Ekanta. Do you know what that is?"*

"Revered sir," answered the boy, "that is work done based upon personal motives and for certain selfish ends."

*"Correct, dear student,"* replied the guru. *"Those beings who*

*labor under this limited mode of action are exactly the ones who
are bound by cause and effect. They sow and reap endlessly,
thereby relegating their precious life-energies to the karmic
stream which flows inexorably between the realms of birth and
death. This river runs fierce and swift, has no banks upon
which to gain a point of purchase, and involves the prisoner of
karma in an endless process of futile activity resulting in little
substantial gain. It negates the higher realms of liberating wisdom by focusing the mind upon work as the ultimate end. Rajas
and tamas are the alternating currents contained within it. As
long as beings are imprisoned by these two gunas, there is no
hope for freedom."*

"Blessed guru," the boy had asked, "in this world where all must
act, work and earn their keep, what is the way? Freedom seems
impossible of attainment here."

*"The way of niskama karma is open for those whose good
sense prompts them to it,"* replied the guru. *"Desire and attachment due to ignorance and egotism obscure the entrance to this
wisdom path. Thinking in a selfish way that the world is put
here for them, ignorant people disregard doing good to others
and never imagine that the path of unattached works can lead
to freedom. Therefore, few follow that noble and unencumbered
way. The result is the world as you now see it — a chaos of
confusion propelled mainly by self-motivated action."*

After due consideration of this information, Ekanta then asked,
"For those who do come to this level of understanding, knowing
bondage to be the result of greed and selfishness and freedom to
be connected to selfless service and compassion, what happens
to those who work without motives?"

*"First,"* replied the guru, *"in order to gravitate away from the
way of seeking after results for selfish ends, one must reach satiation with the things of the world. One sees this occasionally,
even among the young. Some children show little interest in
the world and have an entirely different set of priorities. Alas,
parents nowadays are inept at reading the inner nature and
samskaras of a growing child. They think, 'like father, like son,'
and force the poor youngster, who has his or her own dharma
and destiny to fulfill, into a life of pallid imitation resulting
in slavery to someone else's ideal. It is no wonder that adults*

*harbor all manner of distortions and perversions in their minds by the time they grow up."*

The guru paused to consider, then continued.

*"The point is that work, done in the right spirit, assists in the purification of the mind and this conduces to fulfillment. How can one who has transcended the world's petty temptations and pleasures, having had enough of its hard blows of suffering and pain, ever return to it in the same way? At that point, there remains one of two choices. The fulfilled individual can retire from the world and practice sadhana while living a reclusive life or can reenter the world as a teacher to help others destroy ignorance and attain fulfillment.*

*"Therefore,"* concluded the teacher, *"after the destruction of worldliness through the practice of niskama karma, one encounters a paradoxical place where the world is not desirable and God is not yet attainable. This void is characterized by the rising up of spiritual yearning. Such longing, say the wise, is like the glow of the rosy-red dawn. When one sees that, the appearance of the sun is surely not far behind. Similarly, for the aspirant who is through with the conventional world, realization and the vision of the Beloved is near at hand.*

*"I was once in the company of a mother and child for several weeks. Over that time, what I noticed most about the relationship was the absolute dependence that the young child had on its mother. The child was extremely restless if the mother was away for even a few moments."*

"Is that an example of the nature of attachment?" interrupted Ekanta.

*"Only those of immature renunciation would have seen that lesson in such a situation, my boy,"* answered the teacher. *"I saw it as an example of love and devotion manifesting as restlessness. When one yearns for God the way a small infant longs for its absent mother, it is a sign that one has become satiated with the small concerns and pleasures of the world. Imagine one who, finding no comfort or satisfaction anywhere around him, turns fully to the Divine Mother of the Universe and pines for Her with all his heart in such a fashion. Would not that one swiftly reach the goal of spiritual practice and receive the boon of Mother's Grace? Such intensity is what is missing in today's*

_world._ _Beings long for pleasures, pastimes, possessions and power with deep intensity, but no one longs for the vision of God."_

The Avadhut was awakened from his deep reverie by the touch of a small hand on his shoulder. Opening his eyes and looking over to his left side, he saw a small face peering at him through the soft light of the butter lamps.

"Badi," exclaimed Ekanta, looking at the son of his friend and host, "it is so nice to see you this morning!"

The boy's name, Badraka, which meant handsome and noble, was often shortened in an affectionate way so that most people called him by the abbreviated version. Badi's soft voice floated back to him, almost inaudibly.

"Mataji sent me to tell you that the meal will be served in the courtyard outside in the back. Will you come?"

"Tell your wonderful mother that I shall be there after washing my hands," affirmed the Avadhut

This reply was met with a slight but charming smile which flitted across the face of the youngster. Then, like a puff of incense smoke, he was gone.

The sun was shining into the small hidden courtyard of the ashram when Ekanta arrived there for breakfast. As he seated himself, the pandit gave the mealtime prayer and the little group ate their fill of chapatis and rice, supplemented by cauliflower curry. After the meal and some compelling conversation, Ekanta returned to his room to continue with his rest and meditation. These brief stays in more conventional living situations were both a luxury and a test for him, as well as a way to immerse himself in study of both scriptures and human nature. They provided an opportunity to see the divine manifestation in human beings up close in concentrated situations and this accented, enhanced and complemented his solitary times in nature.

As Ekanta settled himself on the little deck of his room which he remembered so fondly from earlier visits, he placed his attentions on the streets below and the flow of humanity going by in endless streams. To the Avadhut, a concentration of humanity bespoke of the presence of God just as certainly as the variety and wonders of nature. To him, it was the tendency to divide the two — human beings and nature — into separate entities, that signaled the beginnings of delusion.  In similar fashion, if any religious movement attempted to divide God and humanity, that revealed the same insidious ignorance.  To the knower of Brahman, balance, perfect harmony and indivisible unity were always present all around, regardless of what occurred in the external world.  In this sense, nothing had to be done except to fully realize the power and integrity of this Truth at every moment.  This was precisely what the Avadhut represented, and it comprised the only spiritual practice he still maintained.

As the Avadhut was naturally indulging in this spontaneous practice, he noticed a familiar face on the streets below.  After a moment, he realized that it was Pingala, the courtesan, whom he had met with briefly the night before.  As he watched, he saw her being approached by a middle-aged man.  After a little conversation, the two went inside the building directly across from the ashram.

It was only a few seconds before he saw them enter a room on the second floor which was evidently her home.  After a few minutes, the curtain on the street facing the window was drawn, but not before Ekanta witnessed a few affections that were lavished on Pingala by her companion.

The Avadhut was not a complete stranger to affectionate human relationships.  As a young boy of sixteen he had experienced a relationship with a young girl of the village in which he lived.  Sometimes, when circumstances allowed, the two went off together into the woods and spent hours talking and sharing stories and experiences of their respective lives.  As they got to know each other better, they became closer and enjoyed the amorous pastimes of the young on rare occasions.  Their friendship had been short-lived, however, for the girl had moved away with her family to another part of the country.  Ekanta always remembered her gentle smile and generous nature and he always associated them in his mind with the Divine Mother of the Universe.

Two years later, before giving himself to the life of a wandering monk in search of Truth, he had almost gotten seriously involved with a young woman of a nearby village.  It was, in the beginning, a matter of prearranged marriage as was common in India, for the parents of both were looking for suitable companions for their children.  At first, Ekanta had resisted the idea in his own quiet way, but had not said anything to his parents out of respect.  After meeting the woman, however, a friendship immediately developed and the two found that they were very compatible. As the months went by and as more frequent meetings between the two were arranged, it seemed a certainty that the marriage would be consummated at the first auspicious day convenient to both parties. It was at this time that the young woman had fallen ill with an attack of cholera. She never recovered and the loss of his beloved companion coupled with his own naturally evolving condition of renunciation, led him forcefully and with no misgivings into a life of asceticism. Thinking back, he remembered what his vanaprastin teachers had advised him after this dire blow to his future happiness on earth had occurred:

*"There is little that can be said that will comfort you now, my dear,"* said the Mataji one evening. *"You must now persevere, fall back on the teachings we have given you and attempt to rise above your sorrow. If you can master your emotions in this regard, right now, in the very thick of the mind's confusion and grief and in the face of the most dire of worldly losses, you will never again experience anything that will be able to dominate your Spirit."*

As for his Guruji, his male teacher, the teachings were, strangely enough, more empathetic.

*"Do not fight your grief, my boy, but let it wash over you. Feel it as you would experience a blissful sensation."*

After a pause for reflection, the guru continued.

*"Do you remember when we hiked to the snow line of the mountains in winter? The hot springs located there felt so wonderful. Then, after soaking for awhile, we would get out of the hot water and throw ourselves into the snow. Do you remember, Ekanta? Back and forth we went, from extreme hot to excruciating cold until we could no longer distinguish the difference between the two. Truly, hot was then cold and cold was hot, so heightened were our minds and so overstimulated were our senses.*

*"Here, my boy, is a similar experience, only joy and sorrow are the dualities instead of hot and cold. You know from the teachings that your companion, a good and spiritually oriented being, is now resting in peace — 'a peace that passeth all understanding.' Hers is not the sorrow, my boy. It is for you to learn this harsh lesson that the Mother has bestowed upon you and in*

*your case it is for a very definite and important reason. You are destined for great things, though the gross world will never see them and associate them with you. You are a rare being, Ekanta. The world will be a much better place due to your struggles and triumphs. You will not be the recipient or the bestower of individual or limited happiness upon others or for yourself. The collective consciousness will benefit from your singular experiences. I have this on the highest authority and tell you this in trust and confidence.*

*"On the other hand, your predestined companion has not left you, nor has your relationship with her changed internally whatsoever. Every god and goddess has their consort, though oftentimes they spend whole lifetimes apart to perfect themselves, be of help to others or to aid in the divine plan. She is there, even more intensely, within you. Feel her there and you will, in Truth, feel the Universal Mother."*

These bittersweet and potent memories were interrupted when, a few hours later, Pingala and her paramour emerged from the building across the street. From the animated conversation that ensued and the affected motions and glances that the two exchanged, it seemed as if great plans were being made. Ekanta wondered if Pingala had finally met someone who would accept her and take her away from the sordid lifestyle she was trapped in. He even faintly heard the final words which the man said upon parting with her.

"Yes, yes," the Avadhut heard him say, "I will be here tonight at the designated time. Do not worry in the least and do not fail to be packed and ready."

This occurrence caused a glow of happiness to suffuse the face of Pingala and Ekanta, too, felt a little elated for her.

That afternoon, Pingala came to the ashram to arrange a meeting with the Avadhut. Badi came to his room to announce that she was waiting in the teaching hall if the timing was convenient for him. He sent Badi back to tell her to wait a few minutes and he would come. When he entered the hall, Pingala bowed low in reverence before him.

"That is not necessary, dear woman," he said, motioning her to get to her feet. When she tried to take the dust of his feet in traditional Indian fashion, he allowed her, again indicating that it was not necessary.

"What have you come to tell me?" said the Avadhut. "Do you have some pressing problem or burning question for me?"

"The world is sometimes so cruel," said the courtesan, "and at other times it is so wonderful. I think that finally I am going to be happy, though, and live a decent life."

"The fluctuations of the world with regards to fate and karma go on inexorably, Pingala," came the sage counsel of the Avadhut. "One should be careful not to become too enamored of the world, for it contains both poison and nectar. Perhaps you have seen the jellyfish at the seashore in the water. It looks so gentle and is quite beautiful. One feels like taking it in hand to study its unique constitution. But no sooner is it touched, than it transfers a painful sting to the hand. The world is like this too. It looks and seems very nice but lands blow after blow on those who would try to possess it."

"What is one to do, then?" came the lamentation of the courtesan. "One is either a captive of the world or one makes the world a captive for oneself. I would choose the latter."

"There is another way," declared the Avadhut, "prescribed by the sages and illumined ones. It is the way of transcendence and its attainment confers true freedom upon the adept. One cannot be free if one is a slave to another, but the master is not free either, always having to keep an eye on his servants and possessions. Both ways bind, my dear woman, being bound or binding others. You have come to me to hear the Truth. I can say nothing but that in any case."

The courtesan thought for a minute. She looked at the Avadhut, sitting there at perfect ease, without a care or concern. He had, she thought, taken a very different route than any that she had seen before. He was neither in the world nor divorced from it, but instead seemed to be the very center of it.

"This transcendence that you speak of," she said, "it must be of the mind, for you do not show any outward signs of having transcended the world. I sense in you a kind of aloofness but it does not speak of rejection. It feels as if you are perfectly comfortable here. I'll bet that you are that way everywhere that you go."

"You are very perceptive and wise as well," stated the Avadhut. "True transcendence is of the mind. In the mind is bondage and liberation, pain and pleasure, virtue and vice and all other pairs of opposites. One transcends these opposites first and then goes beyond the universe as well. One even transcends the very idea of temporality, including heaven and all the gods and goddesses. Arriving at the essence of transcendence itself, the all-pervasive Atman, then only does one feel and experience bliss and freedom, but no individual awareness remains with which to measure boundaries and limits."

"This condition is for the enlightened, or possibly for the intellectual by way of attainment," said Pingala. "How is this possible for an ordinary person such as myself, one who is impure and has committed many reproachable acts?"

"There are many who are very intelligent who never perceive this Atman," stated the Avadhut, "being just as attached to their limited intellects as you are to your sense of impurity."

This statement brought a sharp breath from Pingala and tears formed at the corner of her eyes.

"Do you mean to tell me," she said, "that I do not need to carry the weight of these sins around with me anymore? Can I so easily shuffle off these many misdeeds and be pure just like that?"

"Why not?" affirmed the Avadhut. "Is anyone besides yourself so obsessed with them? Are others keeping these indiscretions and inconsistencies in you?"

"But I am worthless," cried the courtesan, "not fit to stand, sit and eat with others. I feel trapped by everything about my life and cannot see my way clear. Who is there to help such an inadequate person?"

"Who indeed?" answered the Avadhut. "Until you can help yourself you must call upon the Lord who is the very epitome of compassion. Can't you call on Him? Is that too difficult?"

"Despite my many shortcomings," said Pingala, "I do take refuge and solace in the Lord, even though I feel I should not bother Him with such small and insignificant matters like my sorrowful life. Also, feeling that my mind is impure, how can I approach Him, He who is purity itself?"

"This shows that you truly love Him," said the Avadhut, "and where there is true love without pretense and motive, the Lord abides. Therefore, I say that the Lord is in you and the Lord loves you dearly."

These words of sympathy and support brought a fresh wave of tears to Pingala's eyes. As she was wiping them away, the Avadhut told her a story.

"Perhaps you have heard of the great Avatar Jesus? After his passing, his disciples carried on his work, charged with the spirit of compassion and renunciation. Many were lifted up out of their gloom by these emissaries. One of those emissaries was Peter, a devoted servant of the Lord.

"Once, when he was doing the work of his Lord, there came word by messenger that a man named Cornelius was awaiting his visit and asking him for a private meeting. The coming of this man heralded the possibility of much benefit for Peter's mission. Cornelius, however, was of another caste, another race and considered impure by some. Therefore, Peter's friends advised him not to meet with him for fear of contamination to himself and his work. Before Cornelius' messengers arrived to ask Peter for attendance, though, Peter had a dream in which the Lord revealed to him the nature of all things as being equal in His eyes. In this dream, Peter saw a huge white curtain, like a sailcloth of infinite size, fall from the heavens, fastened on four sides as if by beams. Inside of this cloth, Peter beheld all manner of creatures, from insects to animals to men and women of all different races and colors. Every creature in creation was contained therein.

"He then heard a voice from on high which said, 'Eat, Peter, of this bounty.'

"'Lord,' Peter complained, 'I cannot eat impure things. How is it possible?'

"'Who are you to judge impure that which God has declared pure and wholesome, Peter,' came the reply.

"With this, the vision disappeared and Peter pondered it well.

"Impurity is of the mind, my dear woman," concluded the Avadhut, "and especially of the mind not given to God. Start today and surrender yourself to God, unreservedly. A noticeable change will come over you. It may be gradual at first, even unnoticeable, but if you persevere with longing and devotion, the Blessed Lord will attend upon you. This I promise."

After Pingala had left, the Avadhut returned to his room. As he sat on the deck overlooking the street, sometimes meditating, sometimes watching God go by in various forms, he thought of the courtesan and of all the miserable beings in the city. "Peace, peace, peace," came his prayer, addressed to all that suffered.

Throughout the day, he noticed that the curtain in Pingala's room remained closed and that she did not go out. As dusk fell, the Avadhut fell into a deep meditation upon the Self, relaxing into a state of unruffled calm. Like a candle in a windless place, he emerged now and again from his profound and prolonged state of mind to check his surroundings. Often, words of his teachers came to him during these shifts in conscious states:

*"The mind in meditation must be as peaceful as a clear lake, Ekanta. Ordinary beings, when they try to meditate, experience all manner of distraction. And what is it that pulls the mind towards earth, entrenching it in all sorts of worldly concerns? The base passions with some, worldly preoccupation with others. For the illumined one, however, it is only a natural flow of awareness that returns the mind to the world after meditative states, not bothersome weights. Herein lies the vast difference between the luminary and the unawakened soul."*

With these memories occupying his mind, a song from his boyhood surfaced:

My mind rests in a boundless sea of bliss beyond describing.
It soars into expansive skies of infinite awareness.
The limits of this realm are without measure,
free of boundaries.
Nothingness pervades It, full of everything I cherish.

But lo, a draft of stifling wind comes on to mar and spoil it.
Rising from the barren land of limiting desires.
A blast of hell's own wind which unexplainably assails me,
and drives my mind towards earth
and the concerns of mortal men.

Rise up, Oh king, rise up, Oh queen,
your rightful throne awaits thee.
Cast off this veil of sorrows with its weakness unbecoming.
Reclaim the royal land in which the mighty seers abide.
And drink the nectar filled with immortality and peace.

The Avadhut came out of his deep spiritual reverie. Darkness had fallen, the curtain on Pingala's window was open and a lamp within shed light about the interior of the room. From time to time, the courtesan could be seen pacing the room nervously. Up and down the floor she went, several times a minute, as the hour drew later and later. Finally, in exasperation, she seated herself on the bed. Soon, the Avadhut noticed that she was weeping, occasionally sobbing uncontrollably and he surmised that her potential suitor and beloved paramour was not going to show up. He felt extremely sorry for her and wondered what she would do next.

Exasperation and tears finally gave way to abject sorrow. In a torpid state, the courtesan lay back on her bed, suffering the ignoble effects of this callous rejection. Expectation had brought this on, casting her into a world more miserable than that which she had become accustomed to due to her chosen profession. As the Avadhut observed this pitiable condition, his mind went directly to the feet of his teachers who had warned him about the dangers of attachment and expectation:

"_Ekanta, dear student,_" came the voice of his beloved guru, "_just as one cannot dwell in the past, you must be wary of looking to the future as well. Expectation regarding what is to come is a subtle trap that depletes the life-energy that should be given to living in the presence of God at every moment of existence. Therefore, though expectations are many in worldly life, and whereas some get fulfilled and others do not, the overall tendency towards merely looking forward must be tempered in order that the true Self of humanity can be realized as it is, perfect and ever-present, not reliant upon time and its passing._"

"Dear guru," Ekanta had said, "is it impractical then to plan for the future and is it not wise to look back into the past in order to learn lessons from previous experiences?"

"_A wonderful point, my boy,_" replied the teacher. "_I do not mean to suggest that one abandon all other considerations with regards to living. Only, one must emphasize what is essential and keep that in mind so that distractions, of which there are many, will not upset the delicate balance of life in the world. To be spiritual does not mean that one must be a fool. Practicality is the mainstay of both spiritual and worldly life,_ *especially up until that time when there is no more distinction made between the two. However, a spiritual aspirant must guard against the impingements of impracticality masquerading as practicality, that is, what worldly people interpret to be practical as compared to what the sages tell us is truly so."*

"Revered teacher," said Ekanta, "since worldly existence is full of twists and turns, how can I distinguish between what is worthy of concentration and what is not? Surely, for instance, anticipation for spiritual realization is a type of expectation, as are hopes for the attainment of divine qualities?"

*"This is precisely what I have just mentioned, dear student,"* said the teacher. *"Whereas the peoples of the world, who are attached to it, will shun spiritual qualities such as renunciation and detachment, looking forward instead to pleasures and possessions that they deem will bring them happiness, the aspirant uses a well-honed discrimination to distinguish between what is substantial and what is ephemeral. In this way, they do not get trapped by the mind's penchant for surface attractions. In possession of this powerful type of introspection guided by the scriptures, the guru and God's Grace dwelling as the Self within, they find out quickly what is fit to be desired and what is vain and substanceless expectation.*

*"To conclude, one can say that divine qualities such as devotion, wisdom and Truth cannot be classed in the same category as superficial preoccupations such as land, power, wealth, fame and sensual pleasures. Expectation, then, is of two classes — one that leads towards satiation and fulfillment and the other that enmeshes one deeper in materialism and sensuality."*

The Avadhut stirred. A motion in Pingala's room had caught his eye. The woman was bustling about, piling things upon her bed in a rather haphazard fashion. Soon, it became evident that she was packing her belongings. Instead of an excursion with a paramour intended to end in some romantic fulfillment and a new life, it seemed as if she had her mind set on another type of voyage. The Avadhut was surprised to see this shift of energy, from lethargic and grief-stricken to active and determined. As he watched, a strange feeling came over him and he immediately stood up and headed for the street below, intent on having a conversation with Pingala.

When he reached the doorway, he saw that Pingala, too, had arrived in the street. As he stood there watching her, she emerged from her building and started across the street towards the ashram door. The Avadhut then stepped off of the porch and into the street. Seeing him, she bowed low.

As she rose to her feet, she said, "Revered sir, I was just coming to bid you farewell."

"Where are you going at such a late hour?" asked the Avadhut directly.

"A major crisis in my life has occurred," she related, "but after experiencing it I find that it is just what I needed to awaken me to an extremely important realization."

Pingala stopped for a moment to wipe a tear away. Looking up at the Avadhut and smiling, she stated her plan with a firm and inspired voice.

"I am leaving the city to seek that which I have always truly longed for but never had the strength and courage to go after. The Lord has always been my guide, my friend and my true love. All other attractions, I now see, have been only faint reflections of Him, most all of them insignificant and inadequate. Therefore, I bend my footsteps in the direction of the Jagannatha temple to the south. There I will take His prasad and beg His forgiveness and further guidance. I intend to take up residence as close to His sacred temple as possible, spending my remaining days in japa, meditation and singing his Holy Names. Please bless me, revered sir, so that I can attain this end, for there is nothing left for me to do in this incarnation other than this."

Without even thinking, the Avadhut placed his hand on her head and simply said, "Dear woman, the blessing has already occurred."

After she rose, it was all he could do to stammer, "This is amazing." Smiling at the recently retired courtesan, now a new woman, he bade her farewell then and there.

Turning on her heel with great self-assurance, she moved away down the street, but before she had gone a few steps she turned back and asked him for a favor.

"Please give my eternal gratitude to Pandiji and Maraliji. They have been true friends in this intense struggle called earthly life. I will pray for them and commend them to Lord Jagannatha. Allow me to say one more thing as well. You, revered sir, have been the impetus and final inspiration for this transformation I feel. This year I dreamed that a man would come who would signal an end to my torment and misery. I recognize you from that vision. Therefore, I offer you my most profound salutations, for you are His emissary. By doing what you do in this world, whether people realize it or not, they are benefited immensely. *Jai Sri Guru Maharaji ki Jai!*"

With these amazing words still echoing in his ears, the Avadhut watched as Pingala, a fresh acquaintance in his life, disappeared into the dark streets of Bombay at the dead of night. After comprehending what had just transpired, and before she vanished into the darkness completely, the Avadhut fell to his knees and saluted her with reverence, hands together in a symbolic gesture signifying the eternal union of all living things and the oneness of all existence.

"I salute you as my teacher of renunciation," said the Avadhut out loud, "and of the ultimate insubstantiality of expectations and desires. Furthermore, I acknowledge your teaching as a testament to the absolute truth of fulfillment in the Lord."

Rising, and reeling a little from the blissful reaction of his mind to this unexpected turn of events, the Avadhut returned to the ashram and to several more days and nights of holy company.

Late one night, not long thereafter, cloaked by pervasive darkness and completely unnoticed, another figure departed the city in the opposite direction that Pingala had gone. The Avadhut was on the move again, satiated with city life and longing intensely for the snowy heights of awesome majesty and splendor towards the north.

# ~ Chapter 12 ~

# Teachings on Stainlessness

THE TWELFTH GURU — The Wind

THE LESSON — Freedom

*Brother Wind also taught me well, O Prince. As I observed its freedom from all restrictions and impurities, despite obstacles and the presence of various pollutants, I learned that true freedom is based upon nonattachment, transcendence and responsibility. Air is all-pervasive. It naturally demonstrates the unbound and ever-free nature of the true Self. The powerful wind, I noticed, surmounts all barriers placed in its way and also performs the necessary function of purification for the world. Seeing the wind's sterling qualities brought me both appreciation and illumination.*

The Avadhut was high in the Himalayan mountains. Pausing in his ascent to Bhadranath, the holy pilgrimage spot that he was setting his sights upon, he drew in vast lungfuls of air, though not much oxygen followed. After he had caught his wind, he turned and looked behind him at the long and precipitous trail he had just traversed. The breathtaking view that he was now gazing upon in awe, to him, reduced to insignificance any and all attractions of the city life, no matter how enthralling or intriguing they might be.

Six weeks had passed since his sojourn in Bombay had come to an end, but he still remembered fondly his precious times with the pandit, his wife and child and all the members of the Advaita Ashram. Most of all, he remembered the singular boon of witnessing the renunciation of the world and its transient attractions by Pingala, the courtesan, who was by now probably partaking of the sacred prasad of the Jagannatha Temple in Puri while chanting the names of the Blessed Lord of the Universe. His mind rejoiced to think of her in this way and he hoped that all was going well for her by the Grace of the Divine Mother of the Universe.

The vista that spread out all around him — above, below and on three sides — was indescribable. Its beauty was surpassed only by the feeling of sacredness that permeated the surrounding landscape and atmosphere, for these were the Himalayas, the ancient and venerable mountains upon which numbers of pilgrims and holy beings had reverently tread with intense religious fervor for centuries, even thousands of years before the births of Christ and Buddha. On these hallowed leviathans of rock and snow, covered over with forests of indigenous trees and flowers and supporting myriad forms of life, had walked even the avatars. In its sublime waters, tumbling down steep cliffs and rushing through magnificent canyons, gods and goddesses had bathed, as well as countless illumined beings and wandering seekers. An endless march of devout parents had visited these shores to sanctify their babies in pristine liquids and the Ganges herself, queen of all rivers, flowed from the hidden precincts of these hoary mountains. Indeed, a multitude of holy rivers, so sacred that their names were obliterated in the distant reaches of time, flowed from the timeless snows that covered the dizzy Himalayan heights like a blanket of eternal and untouchable purity.

Here, then, was the crown of India, mused the Avadhut. The Shakti of the Lord had given form to powerful upsurges of divine thought when She gave birth to these mountains.

"Perhaps this is why I feel as if I am dying right now," the Avadhut told himself, speaking out loud.

The atmosphere is so rarefied, both physically and spiritually, that few can exist comfortably here, he thought, giving up speech in order to save his precious breath.  It is fitting, he surmised, that such an anguished condition should visit the mind in this hallowed place, for here the human being is reminded most forcefully that it is not human flesh, but something much more profound.  Even the mind's intelligence fails to function sharply here, he marveled to himself, and this emphasizes all the more that Absolute Existence is not of the mind.

Ekanta reached the top of the rocky slope that he had been climbing for several hours.  He collapsed atop the bluff like one occupying his last legs.  This was one more of many visits he had undertaken to the sacred Himalayas, each getting more difficult due to the advancing age of his body and the toll that was levied upon it by continual wanderings.  Still, he knew that he would return here as often as the Mother allowed him to and he felt in his soul that he would someday give up his body in this wonderful locale.  Let those who are afraid of karma, rebirth and imperfection give themselves up in Benares, he thought.  I will leave the human frame with my eyes feasting upon Mother's beauty and my mind in an elevated state of consciousness!

After a brief rest, the Avadhut sat up in a meditative position.  The broad openness all around him gave him vertigo.  He sucked in his breath and stared out into the vast expanse of space.  Before him was only air, stirred up occasionally by Vayu, the god of the wind, who also frequented these sacred heights.  All around him was one of the Mother's most subtle elements.  Whether calm or in motion and much like his teacher, the sea, the air was an unseen and often unappreciated blessing of life.  What is more, it represented the refined essence of its Creator like nothing else in creation.  Ruminating upon its unaffected condition, teachings from illumined beings he had met came rushing into his mind.

On one auspicious occasion, a young Ekanta had accompanied his teacher to the mountains to visit the ashram of the Giri sect of swamis, one of whom was a respected and revered guru.  This spiritual leader and Ekanta's beloved Guruji had been close friends all through the days of their early sadhana.  Many stories had been passed on to Ekanta about the swami's spiritual stature and experience.  While his Guruji had decided upon marriage after meeting his wife, the boy's revered Mataji, his friend had gone on to take monastic vows and was now the illustrious head of the mountain ashrama with its many branches throughout the world. Now, with heart beating both from the grueling climb as well as excitement and as they executed the last stretch of pathway leading to the ashram gates, Ekanta realized that he was going to meet this legend in the flesh.

The visit turned out to be unimaginably fortuitous for the young boy. For Ekanta, it had seemed almost mythological and the vibrations of the place were so peaceful and so blissful, so mentally austere and cerebral that he had forgotten his personal identity several times. Even now, when thinking back on those few days, he felt entirely new and fresh, as if he were an immortal god with none of the ordinary problems and concerns of humanity. After that journey, whenever the illumined ones spoke of enlightenment, Ekanta equated it generally to that feeling he had experienced in the mountain ashram and its sacred precincts. It was only in the Himalayas that this rare state of mind returned to him, which was one of the reasons why he came back again and again. Dwelling in the world of men, with their penchant for mindlessly neutralizing any and all heightened spiritual vibrations, he needed to refresh himself in the solitary and unsullied atmosphere of these holy mountains.

Now that he was here once again, happy and blissful, the words of the swami of the Giri sect rang loud and true in his sensitized awareness.

*"We live in the high regions and imbibe the elevated teachings of the ancient Rishis who went before us. Our health is good, our thoughts free from the worldly vibrations of earthbound souls who think themselves to be the body and occupy themselves with its concerns alone from life to life. Our water is pure and our heads are always in the heavens, surrounded by nothing but the invisible air which is our respected and revered teacher here."*

Looking at Ekanta, his dear friend's young disciple, Swami Anantananda, whose name meant the bliss of infinity, asked, *"My young friend, you have a question to ask, is it not?"*

With this queer expression, spoken in heavily accented English, the holy man smiled broadly and shut his eyes to look within, as if he had unlimited and eternal access to the essential meaning of his name at all times.

Exchanging a quick and amused smile with his guru, both of whom spoke a little English, Ekanta gave voice to his thoughts, emitting both words and foggy breath into the pure morning air.

"Revered sir, you have declared the air to be your teacher here. This is strangely wonderful yet also perplexing to me. Can you explain what teachings you receive from this most invisible of gurus?"

In lovely tones, permeated with both antiquity and sanctity, the holy one chanted in Sanskrit, vaulting the minds of all present into an inspired state and returning them once more to a primordial time when such excellent knowledge was evident and common to all:

*Agnir murdha chakshusi chandrasuryau*
*Vishah shotre vak vivritascha vedah*
*Vayuh prana hrydaya vishvamasya*
*Padbhayam prithivih sarva bhutantaratmam*

*"Do you understand the implications of this chant, my boy?"* asked the swami.

"I have heard it from the lips of my teacher, sir," replied Ekanta, "but I never tire of hearing it expanded upon by the illumined ones."

*"Here is a boy after my own heart, friend,"* said the swami to Ekanta's guru with a knowing and playful smile. *"Not only does he possess a thirst for Brahmajnana, but he calls me illumined as well. That makes me feel holy. Why not leave him with me for a time?"*

The vanaprastin guru saluted his monastic friend and said with a smile, "Alas, I have gotten used to having him near. It would be hard indeed to leave him behind. Who would I talk to in the wee small hours of Brahma Muhurta when lazy beings shut their eyes for eight long hours? As you can see, he is wonderful company."

*"Yes indeed, I do see your point and I appreciate what you say as well,"* returned the swami. *"I, at least have my many students here around me — but back to the point. The chant, my boy, speaks of air as God's breath. Of all the scents the wind carries from place to place, this aroma is the most intoxicating. It is not a scent that can be experienced using the olfactory sense, Ekanta. It is subtle, of the mind and intellect, having its origin*

*in the Cosmic Mind Itself. The air teaches us that Brahman is ever-free from all impurities, that even while bearing all the many conditions of relative existence within It, as it were, It never becomes restricted or conditioned by them in the least. Its essential lesson, then, is freedom and it renders this teaching accessible to us by demonstrating its unbound nature via the wind."*

"How marvelous," blurted out the young boy. "Here is another representation of Shiva and Shakti sporting in the universe. The air is the static Shiva and the wind is its Shakti power! We should add that to our list of expressions of the Divine Couple, revered sir," said Ekanta, turning to his guru.

As his teacher smiled and nodded his pleased assent, the swami continued on.

*"Yes, dear boy,"* he said, *"the Divine Couple are ever-free, never bound. They sport and rest interminably. Even Their work is play and Their play is the essence of inaction. In the case of the wind — one of Their powerful expressions — though many impediments, great and small, may present themselves from moment to moment, the wind is never thwarted or waylaid in the least. If it cannot blow over an obstacle, it blows around it. If this, too, is impossible, it finds a way under. When all avenues seem blocked, it will find a chink in the wall or even blow the impeding object over, all in its absolute determination to simply remain completely free and unencumbered at all times. You can see why we take it for our teacher. In a world that is so deluged by ignorance and fraught with seemingly impossible tasks and problems, our father, the wind, reminds us that we are supreme and encourages us to surmount every and all manner of adversity."*

"How else does it teach you, respected sir?" asked Ekanta breathlessly. "What other lessons does it transmit?"

*"I see that you are always on the trail of the essence, my boy, and without delay as well,"* said the holy one. *"I detect the influence of my friend here upon your thinking process. He has taught you well. As you are already practically comprehending, Ekanta, the teaching of surmounting obstacles is a secondary one, though very valuable in this relative world. The real teaching is that there are no obstacles, that all is eternally perfect, and*

*this can be understood from two standpoints.*

*"First, all so-called problems inherent in relative existence are placed there, as it were, by the Divine Couple. To know this is to possess a most important key to life on earth. These difficulties are removed by the Transcendent Two as well when the time is right. Shiva and Shakti constitute the essence of all that is. According to the Tantras, the jiva is Shiva, the Purusha is nothing other than Shiva enjoying itself in a projected realm of self-imposed limitation. This is accomplished using powers and vehicles such as the spandas or kanchukas. Maya, kala, niyati and all the rest are essentially distinctive wrappings constructed by the Shakti to allow and enhance the sporting of Consciousness. It is much like the case of an architect who constructs a huge and intricate maze for the entertainment of all the neighboring children and gets lost in it himself. At times, he may even become afraid and imagine that he is completely lost forever, but he himself fabricated the thing and has the blueprint for it in his own mind. All he needs to do is sit and meditate upon it and the way out will dawn upon him.*

*"Shiva is that one, my boy. The one who reigns supreme beyond the structuring of the kanchukas of pure and impure order and enters into them as the jiva as well. This is Their sport, the divine play of Shiva and His Shakti. Do not ask why. Rather, look to the ultimate solution. You are nothing less than the transcendent Shiva! How can you be other than He? This is the second perspective I mentioned.*

*"The air is ever-present, my boy, encompassing everything while remaining untouched and free. It is a metaphor for Brahman. In the static, immutable calm of unified Consciousness rests all Divine qualities such as peace, wisdom, love, truth, bliss and certainly freedom. No problems or impediments exist there. It is only upon entering the mode of expression, of manifestation, of creation, that troublesome considerations arise. The air, then, transmits at all times the message that true freedom is both beyond manifestation and is eternal. There are three choices here, which we like to call the witness, the warrior and the worker.*

*"As the witness, one should maintain the ever-unified position that Brahman is without attributes and free from modifications,*

*changeless, deathless and ever-blissful. The witness always remains merged with the eternal Source of all existence — the Parabrahman. This is the ultimate Truth, the Advaitic standpoint, the realmless realm where there is no duality whatsoever. The very thought of two or many does not occur. All is Oneness, indescribable and absolute.*

*"As the warrior, one must live in the realization that the entire creation is the mad sport of the Divine Couple, Shiva and Shakti, who create and destroy names and forms with an endless array of powers, manifesting and dissolving the universe as easily as a child constructs and destroys a sandcastle. What problem or impediment can persist in the mind of one who wholeheartedly enters the play, participating with the full capacity of life-force, mind and body in the chaotic fray and who realizes that all manifestation is ultimately insignificant, that nothing matters whatsoever! Let the many come and go, let life and death occur in turns, let earths, heavens and hells appear and disappear without number! The warrior participates in full awareness of the consequences, free at all times and unencumbered by whatever set of opposites arise in relativity. Every dragon that rises from the ocean of samsara gets its ugly head severed cleanly and neatly by the warrior's everready shining sword of nondual Wisdom.*

*"The third perspective is the worker's view. Whereas the witness is like the still air of heights, Shiva and Shakti in static equipoise permeating all as an immutable verity, and the warrior is the ferocious wind, the ultimate vehicle being driven by the twin forces of Shiva and Shakti as pure dynamism, the worker dwells in the world of clashing opposites and is like the low-lying air of a valley that is inundated by the smells and colorations of haze and smoke. This human drama, another sporting place for the Divine with all of its joy and pathos, proceeds under the heavy laws of karma — cause and effect — and operates within the tight and seemingly unalterable boundaries of time and space. Here, beings imagine that the world of relativity with its host of dualities is actually real. Their agreement on this matter actually gives such an idea validity, and they then begin to experience the effects of this weighty existence. One could say that the Divine Couple has, in this case,*

*placed masks over Their own faces and assumed the roles of countless unconscious and semiconscious living beings in all seriousness."*

"Can this be possible?" asked Ekanta, breaking in impetuously. "Can the Divine Couple take on such delusion in this fashion?"

*"Is there anything impossible for the Brahman, my boy?"* returned the guru. *"Whether one assumes the Vedantic position where all limitations are coverings superimposed over Brahman due to primal ignorance, or the Tantric view wherein the kanchukas are definite realms created purposely by Shiva for His sport, the end result is the same. The process may differ, however, and it is up to us, the embodied being, to figure out the maze with all its rules and laws and rise above it. Then we will know and unite with our true being.*

*"The Avatar, who returns again and again throughout the cosmic cycles, has given us many wonderful clues with which to make sense out of the creation. Among them, is this amazing statement: 'Even Brahman weeps, caught in the snares of His own Maya.' The Blessed One, then, has become all living beings and the universe of name and form, giving a solid form to what is essentially an inexpressible, eternal and infinite Truth. To do this, it became necessary to blind Himself, as it were, with His own power of distortion and obscuration. Then, with His essence well hidden, He participates in the creation by diving into the three rivers of time, space and causality, a trio of temporal flows created by Mahamaya, His eternal companion. The effect is what we see all around us, a magnificent projection replete with all manner of attractions and enticements."*

"Oh, I see now," stated the astonished young seeker, but his intended words trailed off as he became immersed in the depths of a mind captivated with this unique glimpse at Reality. The initial force of this realization turned him mute for a time. The external world simply disappeared, erased by the unique, primeval thought which prompted him to give up all other considerations so as to be able to ponder it with the full force of his awareness. It was blissful and freeing, this powerful descent of illumination, and Ekanta reveled in it on the spot, forgetting all who looked on. Ordinarily, he would never have disregarded the company of holy beings while in their proximity. Later, he wondered about his helplessness and had been abashed at his behavior.

Though unseen by Ekanta at that moment, tears of love and gratitude began to flow from his guru's eyes. Around the circle of devotees, smiles had appeared on many faces as the host of beings, gurus and disciples alike, had all experienced again the wonderful initial vision which each of them had received from their guru in days long past. Well they all knew what was passing through the mind of the young boy that morning, and all knew as well that the world of name and form would never appear the same to him again.

Finally, Ekanta emerged from his internal condition long enough to stammer, "Is it real then, revered sir? Does it persist? How does He break free?"

These terse, cryptic sentences worked their way to the surface of Ekanta's mind and spilled out with great difficulty.

Gazing at the young aspirant with compassionate intensity, Swami Anantananda answered the disjointed questions, knowing full well what the boy was experiencing.

"*I understand what you are thinking, dear boy, and have no fear. How do any of us break free from bondage and see through the Maya. Indeed, how have you just now gained a glimpse of Reality and created a hole in that tenuous substance? As our Bengali poet-saint has sung so brilliantly, 'Can anyone successfully hide a roaring fire in a cotton cloth?' In this play, called the Lord's Lila, are the roles to be considered ultimately real? In staged human dramas, the likes of which one sees in theaters and playhouses, do the acters and actresses permanently give up their real identities or do they do so only temporarily? No, my boy! In the case of the Divine Couple, it is all a mock drama. Only the dreamer is real, not the dream!*"

"Dear sir," asked Ekanta earnestly, his intellectual powers swiftly coming back to him, "what of the world and its peoples, of all the intense suffering and misery? Does the Divine being possess compassion? Is the creation not real to those living within it?"

"*Primarily and most importantly, who are these beings, Ekanta?*" replied the swami. "*Are they different than the Lord? Is not the creation an extension of the Creator? For those who perceive difference and insist upon their separateness from*

*Reality, strengthening the false sense of ego in them, suffering and misery pose considerable problems. Consider this though. The conscious life-force in each of us is a portion of that boundless ocean of immortality spoken of by the Avatars. Are we not cast in the same image of God? Listen to a poem, dear boy:"*

It is only those who are attached to the body
that piteously cry,
We are weak, we are lowly.
All this is atheism.
Now that we have transcended ignorance,
We will have no more of it
and will take our rightful places as world-renouncing heroes.

The boundless ocean of immortality,
into which the great Gods,
Brahma, Vishnu and Shiva have poured their strength.
From which emerged the eternal Vedas
and which is fortified by the life-force of the Avatars,
Divinity clothed in human flesh,
Into that nectar ocean, I offer myself.

*"Therefore, I say, that the drop of immortal nectar called the Atman dwelling within each of us is not different in essence from the boundless ocean called Brahman which permeates everything. In fact, the sense of division between the two is a mirage, is absolutely false. This line of demarcation is like a line drawn on water — it seems to separate one infinite body of liquid into two parts but in actuality quickly disappears leaving only one infinite and undifferentiated mass where two had once seemed to exist.*

*"As for compassion, Ekanta, is any such quality possible where there is the absence of two or many? Does the One, indivisible and infinite repository of all peace and bliss need to have compassion for Itself? Ultimately not, and the Ultimate is all that exists! Of course, in that ephemeral realm called relativity or the universe, where beings dwell in a false sense of separation from their source of origin and perpetrate ignominious acts that bring painful repercussions as a matter of course, the Lord*

*and Divine Mother exercise compassion. The lessons used to awaken ignorant beings to their inherent divinity though are not soft and easy. A strong remedy is needed where chronic disease has gained a foothold. In other words, Their compassion is not of a sentimental or pitiful variety. This is instanced by the powerful upheavals and intense ramifications that take place in the world when the acidlike nature of nondual Truth is applied to the ornery substances of ignorance, egotism and delusion."*

"Revered sir," said Ekanta. "This ignorance and delusion, what does the god of air, Vayu, teach us about that? Is there a correlation?"

*"Yes, there is, my boy,"* returned the guru. *"In the precincts of the huge metropolis lies the thick, putrid air of delusion. It obscures and pollutes the minds of living beings, allowing no clear view of Reality whatsoever. Those who choose to dwell there suffer the blinding effects of negativity, and their eyes burn and shed the tears caused by inadvertent bondage and slavery. The pollution that collects in the air about a city is nothing else but an indication of the ignorant acts that are continually perpetrated there, whether it be on the physical, mental or spiritual level. Therefore, the air and wind teach us in every possible way. I did not mention this last variety of air because it is essentially nonexistent. For those who choose to stay near to their Lord, such unsightly and unimaginable nightmares disappear with the dawning of awakening consciousness. Indeed, for the ever-perfect, Consciousness never sleeps. It is like the air in the Himalayas, always clean, clear and invigorating."*

The Avadhut opened his eyes from his delicious inner reverie and stared out across the vast open space. Standing up and bringing his hands together in formal salute, he turned in all the four directions, saluted up and down, and mentally paid his obeisances to the unseen regions as well, where akasha, subtle space, a more refined expression of air, existed.

Speaking out loud, he offered his salutations:

"Oh Vayu, exquisite subtle principle of Brahman, god of the air and the wind who purifies and liberates, I salute you as my teacher of freedom, in the original sense as eternal perfection and as the force that teaches us to overcome obstacles and impediments. To you, my eternal salutations."

The Avadhut turned and looked skyward.  Above him was one more cliff and he needed to scale it before darkness set in.  As the sun was already beginning an apparent descent towards the horizon, Ekanta, now rested and inspired with spiritual strength, began his assault on the rock face, his mind contemplating all the teachings which the Blessed Lord, in His endless Grace, had bestowed upon him.

Two hours later, he reached the summit and pulled himself over the edge of the cliff, breathing a sigh of relief.  A little light still persisted and the last hundred feet of the ascent had been precarious in the semidarkness.  Strangely enough, the Avadhut had not experienced any fear during the entire climb, his mind being overcome and absorbed in an unexplainable joy.  This was not, he affirmed for himself, climber's intoxication, that giddy faint-headedness which he had experienced early on in his mountaineering experiences.  Something almost palpable had taken up residence inside of him and was bringing him in and out of profound states of consciousness of Its own will.  Every time he thought that it might be his Beloved Lord, the experience became too intense and he pushed the thought away so that he could function properly in the potentially dangerous situation.

Gazing into the encroaching darkness, Ekanta made out a small game trail off to the left and immediately set his foot upon it.  As he penetrated the interior of the elevated plateau upon which he found himself, he made out a light in the distance.  What luck, he thought to himself, for he was gazing upon what could only be the dhuni fire of either a sadhu or a mountain tribe.  To have arrived at the peak of his climb so near to human habitation was too much to expect.  As he turned in the general direction of the distant light, he noticed patches of white standing out in the darkness here and there against the slopes.  This could only be snow, he surmised, and he knew that he was at the elevation where several of his holy destinations lay.  As it was late summer, the climate was not as foreboding as it had been on several other journeys he had taken in this area.  Nevertheless, he estimated that he was over five thousand feet in elevation and the evenings would be cold enough to warrant a warm fire.  Therefore, he set out towards the light like a moth drawn to flames.

As he had expected and hoped for, his walk brought him into

the campsite of a band of sadhus who were in the midst of visiting all of the holy sights in the area. A short conversation with them, facilitated in patches using several different languages, was enough to convince him that he had come upon a pious group of devotees. As was their unwritten but undying custom, the sadhus shared their foodstuffs with him, some of which had already been warmed over the fire, and after consuming some of the hot food and a little water from his own waterskin, Ekanta felt fully renewed.

As the sadhus were in a silent mood, the Avadhut withdrew a little distance and set up his asana for meditation. Sitting himself down in cross-legged fashion, he enjoyed the gradual appearance of the stars in the nocturnal firmament for a while and finally shut his eyes on the external universe. It was not long before the internal universe, subtle and infinite, opened to his inner gaze. No longer was he the name and form of Ekanta, nor the wise Avadhut who roamed relative existence perceiving only Brahman in everything. Something unspeakable had replaced those limited notions and was revealing that consciousness was infinite, unencumbered and simultaneously present in every location. Whenever his mind slipped into this formless mode, he knew he had momentarily merged with the Absolute Being. Afterwards only a sweet intoxication persisted, acting as an enticement to draw the soul back into the vast internal expanse which was its birthless, deathless origin.

The Avadhut had discovered over time and with experience that the intrepid inner voyager who plumbed the depths of nondual Bliss could not remain absorbed in Absolute Reality for long without giving up the body. Some he had known, who experienced such spiritual heights, had returned to consciousness of the world permanently, imagining that they had reached the goal of spiritual life and never again entered that profound bodiless state. Maya, being powerful, swiftly covered whatever realization their brief interlude with Reality had produced. Therefore, whenever Ekanta apprehended the earth before his outer gaze and entered into the body again after sublime transcendent meditation, he preferred to rest in the intermediary region, that unique level called Bhavamukha by the ancients, that perceived the world as an expression of the Supreme Being. In this way, he either spent his time transported into the highest realmless region through the will of his Beloved, or simply looked out onto the world possessed of a portion of that indescribable essence which painted everything the color of Brahman.

Tonight, the Bhavamukha condition, that intermediate territory between God and the Universe, was an especially pleasing place to be. From this position, the Avadhut began to think back and contemplate the experiences which he had recalled earlier during his ascent up the mountain. Swami Anantananda, the swami of the Giri sect, had proved to be a powerful figure, different from his own guru who was more subtle and presented the wisdom teachings in an extremely balanced fashion. The no-nonsense way in which the swami approached the explanation of Brahman, Shakti and the universe was unique and very attractive to Ekanta. Therefore, later on after consulting his guru about it and receiving his blessing, Ekanta had sought out and located the swami at the edge of a precipice where he was meditating and gazing out upon the lowlands below in turns.

*"Ekanta, my dear young friend,"* came the wise one's greeting, *"come and join me."*

"What are you doing, revered sir?" came Ekanta's reply. "Am I interrupting you? If so I can seek you out later."

*"No indeed,"* returned the swami. *"I am following my schedule as fits my own sweet will. Here, every evening, for several hours, I sit and radiate blessings to the world below according to my capacity, following in the way of the Buddha who transmitted peace and compassion to all sentient beings."*

Ekanta heard these words and was silent for a long moment. The swami too remained in silence, waiting for his young friend to speak his mind. After a time, Ekanta formulated a question.

"Sir, your teachings have caused a revolution in my very being. I just had to speak with you again before leaving tomorrow. I am not sure that I can even give voice to my concerns, let alone my profound appreciation."

*"As to your appreciation, my boy,"* said the swami, *"it all belongs at the feet of the Beloved One. I am both unworthy and incapable of receiving it."*

"But sir," protested Ekanta, "I have just found you sitting here transmitting blessings to others. How could an unworthy person accomplish that?"

*"That is a fair question,"* replied Anantananda, *"and follows upon what we were discussing this morning. You should know that of myself I do nothing. This is my firm resolve. It is the Lord who blesses all, though I am aware that he uses this vehicle for His purposes once in awhile. That much am I allowed to experience. If any sense of 'I' enters in, my Beloved flees, withdraws far away. I cannot bear this! Again, if too much God-Consciousness enters my being, I merge with my Beloved and remain at that time useless for any purpose in this world. What a predicament! All I can do is to serve according to my capacity, and even this is accomplished by His Grace."*

"Yes," responded Ekanta, "I now see the dichotomy of spiritual life in the world. This much I have understood this morning and that alone has brought me to the verge of tears several times throughout the course of the day. The Rishis have declared that Brahman alone is real and the world is unreal. Before, I understood that to mean that the world was an illusion. Now I see it from the higher standpoint — that Brahman alone is. The world is Brahman too, being an expression of That which is never nonexistent. Nothing can be taken away or added to That and all that is in That is Itself, eternal, being a part of That."

Ekanta stopped, realizing that he had gotten taken away by his own thoughts. A quizzical look must have passed over his face, for the swami then laughed out loud to see him. Ekanta too began to laugh and the sound of their combined mirth flowed out over the edge of the canyon and permeated the surrounding air, falling into the low-lying hills and farmlands far below as a blessing bestowed upon all sentient beings.

"I have heard my own guru speak in such riddles before," stated Ekanta after he had caught his breath, "but I never thought that I would be doing so as well! This is a little unsettling."

*"Now you can begin to comprehend the meaning of some of the crazy sayings of our tradition,"* replied the swami, wiping away a few tears. *"They say that the wise, full of realization and unable to contain themselves, go on prattling about the Truth. A pitcher indeed may stop gurgling when it is full, but some beings simply cannot remain limited within a pitcher's tiny confines and break that form to become vast receptacles of*

*infinite proportion. What else can they do? If they were to contain it, it would be too much to bear. Besides, it is for our own good that God bursts such boundaries and reveals profundities to us. He delights in tearing off the very mask that He has donned in order to conceal His own Truth from us. If all is Brahman, then His desire to sport provides the only answer for this strange creation while His infinite nature provides the only recourse. Back and forth He goes, hiding and revealing, and He has time on His side, which means that all beings swimming in that strange river will eventually forget where it began and will not be aware of its destination either. What a concept!"*

Ekanta smiled at this explanation and replied, "My guru once told me a story about knowing and not knowing. He used the example of a man who, while sleeping, is carefully moved from the room he fell asleep in to another room without knowing of it. Not only is he a bit befuddled when he wakes up but he has no knowledge of the transition which occurred during his sleep. Just so, apparently, do aspiring beings remain unaware of their own growth and realization which is all really accomplished by someone else, someone omniscient, gracious and beneficent. As you have said, revered sir, 'Not of myself do I do.'"

*"Well spoken, young man,"* responded the swami, evidently highly pleased. *"Would that all youth receive what you have been gifted by your Guruji, my good friend. Knowing what you know now, I clearly see and predict that you will be a light among lights, casting rays of sunshine upon the shadowy world of suffering humanity. Bring them this illumination the way you would bear a vessel of drinking water to a dying man or a precious medicine to a suffering patient. They are all God in human form, don't you see? How can we refuse to help them?"*

These were the last words that Ekanta had ever heard from the lips of Swami Anantananda, for after saying this, managed only through an emotionally cracked voice, the holy man lapsed into a profound silence, only his lips moving in constant prayer. Ekanta had harbored no doubt as to what the swami was praying for. He then left the revered being sitting as he found him after saluting him profoundly with a full prostration. Though a few days were all that Ekanta had been allowed to spend with him, he valued these precious moments above most other experiences and mentally held this man as one of his own gurus for all time.

The Avadhut stirred himself, allowing blood to flow back into his numbed legs once again. He had been sitting long. The fire was almost out and he stood up, walked carefully through the sleeping bodies and placed more wood on the flames. After warming his hands and feet near the fire's warmth, he returned to his asana and resumed his meditations. The night air, refined in the high elevation, was all around him. Thinking of it reminded him of the all-pervasiveness of his Beloved. As he thought upon this verity, the words of his Mataji, his guru manifest to him in feminine form, came to him out of the past.

*"Dear boy, everything proceeds from subtle to gross, not the other way around. It is only in this mirage-like world, with consciousness laboring under the heavy weights of the five elements and trying to perceive Reality with a dual mind, that it appears as though the process is reversed. Ultimately, there is nothing but Pure Awareness, timeless and deathless. This is the very Truth. This manifested world, indeed, the entire universe, is a preposterous and unfathomable appearance in time and space. Where it came from and where it is going is a supreme mystery which no one with any true sense would want to fathom. Yet beings attempt to do so, and get caught up in a trillion details as a result. Thus does the myth of evolution get perpetuated."*

After a time, during which Ekanta thought better than to interrupt her deep mood, she continued, much to his joy and satisfaction.

*"From gross to subtle is the way of those caught in the fundamental illusion of becoming, Ekanta, while those who know are ever resting in the abiding reality of Pure Being. One should be able to go from the Nitya — the Eternal — to the Lila — the play of the Eternal — and back to the Nitya, free of the fear of Maya — the Lord's dual power of veiling and distorting. Such a being is free and dwells only in the Atman at all times. If ever these wise ones deem it necessary to descend into the framework of illusion called the relative universe and get involved in the foggy and fleeting dreams of beings suffering from the delusion of individuality, this preoccupation with personality, this posturing and posing of the ego complex, this dangerous dalliance*

*with cause and effect, this vexing love affair with matter, they will do so by moving from subtle to gross."*

"Mataji," responded the young seeker, "can you explain this so that I can understand it better? What you have said has sent a powerful surge of energy up my spine just now. I feel that it is of great import for me."

Smiling graciously at her young charge, the guru replied, *"Breathe deeply my son and focus your mind on the higher centers of awareness, especially at the throat and third eye, but do not forget the heart which is your true home and your precious refuge while you are inhabiting the body."*

Saying this by way of instruction, the guru continued.

*"With regards to pure Awareness, Ekanta, there simply is no motion and no space through which to move, so speaking to you in terms of the movement of Consciousness will always convey a wrong impression. All-pervasive, timeless Awareness is completely other than the twenty-four cosmic principles with which my Divine Mother, the Mahavidya Mahamaya Bhagavati Durga Devi, has created this fantastic appearance called the universe. Still, as I have said, in order to free those who imagine themselves to be other than this all-pervasive Spirit, the Lord creates an adequate form and enters into it."*

Pausing a moment to consider, she then continued, *"My, this is difficult for an Advaitist to explain. It is all nonsense! Now I know why my teacher seldom broached the subject with me."*

Then, with an impatient wave of her arm in the air, she exclaimed, *"Oh botheration, may the Mother Herself explain it!"*

Continuing after a somewhat pregnant silence, she said, *"As I was saying, when the Lord creates a body for one of His children"* — again she paused, grasping for terms and seeking a way of explanation for the unexplainable — *"even though essentially there is no child for Him as He is ever one, He descends, as it were, from the extremely subtle conditionless condition of Pure Consciousness and enters this dreamlike world through the illumined intellect, called in a unified and collective sense, the Cosmic Mind, or Mahat. From there He can filter down into the universe and apprehend what others are thinking, what they are involved with and how they perceive things. The entire process occurs in four stages called Para, Pashyanti, Madhyama and Vaikhari. How painful it must be, in a way,"* she said aside, *"for this is a fragmentation, if that is possible, for One who is ever unified. This apparent movement constitutes the very heart of sacrifice on the divine level.*

*"Anyway,"* she said somewhat impatiently after pausing, *"along the way of this imaginary journey, as the world of name and form is encountered pertinent to the elements, it is the akasha or subtle space, sometimes called ether, that is perceived first. According to the Yogavashishta, everything manifest comes from the Jnanakasha — the space of knowledge. The jiva itself operates this Jnanakasha. Like an ocean that contains waves, ripples, foam and spray on its surface, the jiva creates all things in the universe with the help of Jnanakasha.*

*"We hear from the blessed Mother Sarasvati, the Goddess of Knowledge, that there are several types of akashas in this regard. I will enumerate them for you now before continuing on with the sweep of the five elements. She tells us of the Chidakasha, the Chittakasha and the Bhutakasha.*

*"The Chidakasha is spiritual space. It is the heart of Knowledge, the very essence of Wisdom. It could be described as the very atmosphere where the highest divinities abide. Space is an inadequate word in this regard, for this state is objectless except where wonderful realities are made manifest for the ecstatic enjoyment of the Lord's precious companions.*

*"Chittakasha is mental space, the world where ideas, concepts and divine plans are formulated. At its lower level, minds experiencing sankalpas move from one idea to the next, usually connected with the elemental akasha and enjoyments of objects existing there. When these desires die out, the mind can then rest in the Chidakasha.*

*"The Bhutakasha is physical space, elemental space. Here is where one finds the objects for enjoyment and where all the concrete laws of time, space and causality are operating inexorably. It is constituted mainly of the five elements. The first, ether, I just mentioned. Consciousness entering into form encounters that element first. After that, the other four elements — air, fire, water and earth — come into focus.*

*"So, Ekanta, if one analyses everything in the Jnanakasha — Cosmic Mind, its consciousness, individualized awareness, its*

*intelligence, dual mind, life-force and body — one finds the con-
stituents of the cosmic dream, further supported on the most
rudimentary level by the five elements from subtle to gross. All
this, along with the senses needed to perceive the gross universe
and the inner and external organs, make up this imposing
appearance called the universe, spoken of as a series of superimpositions over Brahman by the jnanis."*

Laughing suddenly and smiling broadly in drunken fashion as
she occasionally did, she added, *"This same series of manifestations is called an endless set of perceptions of Brahman by
the vijnanis."*

After a moment, the boy said, "Mataji, this subtle space which
you called akasha seems to be a fine example of God's unseen
existence. Air is all about us and though it is unseen, can be felt.
Space, however, is only inferred by the objects that it supports and
that only in a very abstract way."

*"Right, my dear,"* replied the guru. *"You are already catching
on here. Despite the difficulty of assuming name and form and
the problems inherent in determining and understanding all the
conditions of universal manifestation, everything here points
inexorably to the existence of a benign Creator. What fabric supports the lay of this universe? Upon what foundation does it
rest and how does it assume its position? Is it all just floating
on nothing? And where do all these objects that move across
its infinite expanse come from? What is more, who or what
created this perplexing and strangely wonderful human condition? Who put the sense of individual existence into creatures
and gave them intelligence and the power to reason? Has it all
come about in time according to the process of evolution, as the
scientist and the fundamentalist would have us believe?"*

The Mataji paused here, thinking over the subject.

*"Some would say yes, others, no, depending upon which the-
ory they propose and prefer. The truly wise would not venture
a guess, though, for they know what the Truth is and rest in It
eternally. Neither evolution nor the creation theory is adequate
to the task of revealing the Truth of Brahman, my boy. Subtle
to gross is the only way to explain it, though even this is secondary knowledge. Ultimately, as I have said, only Consciousness exists, which is why the Rishis of old proclaimed that*

*Brahman is the only Reality.  Secondarily, to explain the man-*
*ifestation of the many and the appearance of the worlds, they*
*presented us with a delineation and explanation of the layers*
*which the active principle of Brahman, called Mahamaya, deftly*
*weaves over the Reality, creating an appearance that is a net-*
*work of subtle deception.*

*"Oh, how incredibly perplexing this empirical process can be,*
*my dear.  Who, indeed, can see through it?  After many hun-*
*dreds of years of human existence and incredible austerity and*
*prayer combined with powerful devotion, the ancient ones*
*received a glimpse, imbibed a drop of wisdom nectar from the*
*primordial Mother of the Universe and were able to see through*
*the veils that Maya had constructed.  By Her Grace alone was*
*it possible — such is the magnificence of God's power!  There-*
*fore, Ekanta, we have unswerving devotion to the ancient ones*
*and the Vedas which came forth from them.  As the Avatar often*
*reminds us, the religion of the ancient ones — Sanatana*
*Dharma — is supreme.  It has been around forever and will con-*
*tinue to exist as long as beings draw breath and move about.*
*When the universe dissolves in Pralaya at the end of cosmic*
*cycles, the truths contained in the Eternal Religion will be auto-*
*matically stored in subtle form in the infinite mind of God.*
*Then, from subtle to gross, they will emerge again."*

Ekanta had never forgotten this unique expose on the extreme
subtlety of Brahman and the appearance of the world of name and
form.  Taking his opportunity as soon as it presented itself, the
boy had approached his male vanaprastin guru to get another perspective on this most engrossing subject.

"Revered sir," Ekanta asked, coming upon his teacher sitting on
a log in the woods near a quietly flowing stream of water.  "Mataji
has perked my curiosity by mentioning the akasha, the subtle substance that supports this relative universe.  Can you explain its
workings to me in terms of its relation to Brahman?  Is it similar
or different from prana, the life-force within us and around us and
what is its relation to air?"

*"That is a fine series of questions, my son,"* responded the
guru.  *"Let me see if I can shed any light on them.  First of all,*
*air and ether are interrelated, both being cosmic principles with*
*which the Mahashakti has formed this world and universe.  If*

*I know my beloved wife, she was speaking to you about subtle Reality, one of Her favorite subjects and one that she explains nicely. Possibly, what you are seeking to find out is how one can proceed from limited preoccupation with the gross physical world to the refined experience of subtle realms. Is that not so?"*

"That is it exactly." said Ekanta. "You have articulated what I could not for some reason."

*"Precisely so,"* returned the guru, *"for I myself remember experiencing the same quandary regarding this subject. This shows you to be one who is not only fond of hearing the truths of the scriptures, but one who perceives the absolute necessity of putting them into practice. Take thirst for example. I may be thirsty, but I will never receive satisfaction from this condition by simply sitting here and shouting, 'Water, water!' I must take the trouble to stand up, walk to the edge of the stream, get down on my hands and knees and drink. Then only will my thirst be quenched."*

The guru thought for a time, then said, *"As far as actual instruction regarding how to move your consciousness from gross to subtle, come tonight to the sacred grove and I will guide you. More generally, I can give you some instruction here and now.*

*"The yogi who contemplates Reality finds, as a result of inhabiting a body and working through the senses as well as finding himself in this relative world of name and form, that many obstacles are standing in his way to experiencing God-Consciousness, his true nature. Taking his mind off of one thing and placing it on another according to the instructions of the guru, soon rids him of these impediments and he then enjoys unalloyed peace and bliss which is his natural condition anyway. This happens over time and in a straightforward and deliberate fashion according to one's capacity.*

*"The first idea that must go, in no uncertain terms, is the fallacious assumption that one is the body made up of the five elements. Each of these elements can be meditated upon so that one comes to know that they are insentient principles used by a supersentient Being to affect a certain cause. This comprises, in part, the famous discrimination that allows one to know what is real and what is transitory.*

*"You know that our Mataji is like a tiger, devouring everything*

*that would get in her way on the return path to Absolute Reality. Therefore, she explains things directly, literally tearing the veils off of Reality. Sometimes, it seems that she is mad at God for placing obscuring ideas and coverings in front of her awareness. This is her way. But she also knows that one can also accept the world for what it is, an expression of Brahman. As long as one does not labor under or hold any misconceptions about the nature of the universe, knowing it to be essentially only a temporary appearance consisting of insentient principles, so long can one abide in peace with it as long as the Divine Mother keeps one in the body.*

*"One does not have to remain satisfied with this limiting condition though. As I was saying, by contemplating each of the five elements in turn and finding them to be lifeless without consciousness to apprehend them, one renounces each in turn and moves towards the Ultimate Reality. After earth, water, fire and air are transcended, the adept, coming to know the mysteries of each and placing them in perspective, the akasha, or ether, is taken up for internal study. This is a much more subtle area than the previous four, and the searcher finds that it has two divisions, actual physical space and a subtler mental space.*

*"The physical space is subtle enough. Beings dwelling here in this realm take it for granted and never look into its existence, its meaning, or its teaching. Imagine, Ekanta, all objects, from a tiny gnat to a massive planet are moving about and occupying physical space. We are not speaking of air or oxygen, for out in stellar space is there any such substance? This boundless physical space is subtle beyond normal thinking, then. It cannot be displaced like air, or contained like water, or consumed by fire or diminished by earth. It is no wonder that the timeless Rishis, blessed be the very mention of them, used it for a teaching to convey the subtlety of Brahman."*

Ekanta's wonderful guru paused for a moment to reflect. Then he began to recount the further steps of this fantastic inner journey.

*"If physical ether is so subtle, so refined, unseen and unknown, what of its more rarefied counterpart? The famous akashic records, where memory of all events are stored ad infinitum, are also encountered and plumbed by the yogi in deep absorption and transcended in typical fashion. Everything ever*

*known or to be known resides there in that infinite abstract space. It is no wonder that many beings get enamored with this region and return to normal consciousness blathering about Cosmic Consciousness, planetary configurations, the light of millions of stellar suns and all that. They have not even left the universal territories yet and already they are overwhelmed. You can see, Ekanta, what great preparation is needed before embarking on such a journey if one wants to go the distance."*

"What is the next step, revered sir?" asked the eager boy. "It seems as if this subtle akasha is the jumping off place for the heavenly lokas. Am I right?"

*"This is truly a pivotal position, my boy, but one cannot penetrate into the nether regions without the help of refined awareness. This demands a thorough purification of prana and manas — the vital and mental energy. With the knowledge that he is not physical matter firmly established, the yogi eradicates this notion from his mind and focuses on the life-force for a time. Perceiving the entire universe as a movement of prana, he is amazed and feels greatly illumined. Such a connection with all things is experienced that the yogi dwells in a unified state most of the time. It is easy to see how some can become convinced that this is, indeed, samadhi or nirvana. The guru, however, cautions the practitioner and also encourages him to move beyond this world of vital energy, for it is here that many beings get caught in the sensational realm of psychic phenomena, arcane sciences and magic, considering these to be the ultimate condition, just as they once thought the allures of worldly life to be so.*

*"Withdrawing the mind's awareness from prana, the yogic practitioner moves into the mind with its infinite array of considerations. Acquiring knowledge then becomes the main pursuit and one can get quite inebriated with this profound elixir. An entire cross section of secondary knowledge called aparavidya, a much more substantial and rewarding state than either the elements or prana can offer, is opened up. To such a one who has developed the powers of concentration upon the internal universe of the mind, a whole host of realizations emerge, get pondered and are then utilized.*

*"It is not until the intellectual sheath, the vijnanamaya kosha, is penetrated that more purely spiritual ramifications blossom.*

*It is here that the practitioner begins to perceive what an impo-
sition the sense of individuality poses. Coming up against the
mind/ego complex and being extremely restless for a freedom
which neither of these can give, the aspirant, through the guru's
insistent urging, achieves illumination of the intellect, giving
thought a truly spiritual turn.*

"*What results is a glimpse of Paravidya, attended by a long
look at the two higher worlds beyond earth and the physical universe. Celestial beings, semi-illumined beings and minor gods
and goddesses inhabit the first, while the major deities and fully
realized luminaries dwell in and around the latter. Here, a great
desire to enjoy the extreme pleasures of these worlds and the
subtle bliss of communion with the beings who dwell there comes
over the aspirant, who is by now an adept in a certain sense.
If the connection with the guru is strong, and the guru is masterful as well, this can be overcome and the vision of Brahman
can be attained, culminating in what the sages call samadhi or
nirvana. Once this is achieved, the fully illumined consciousness of any such being can go where it will and do what it
wants. Like the akasha, which contains all things physical and
subtle, this realization in samadhi holds and permeates all such
things, immanent, transcendent and absolute, while remaining
mysteriously and blissfully free of them simultaneously.*"

"Revered teacher," Ekanta had asked after this discourse, "you
have occasionally mentioned to me the seven upper worlds and
seven corresponding lower worlds. What are the names of these
worlds and is there a connection?"

"*Yes, Ekanta, that is a good thing to understand. The three
worlds I just mentioned — Immanent, Transcendent and Absolute, are given by way of an expanded or wide view, a sort of
general classification that covers the physical, mental and spiritual realms. Vashistha gives these as Chidakasha, Chittakasha
and Bhutakasha. These are the Three Worlds you often hear
about — the Triloka. What you are asking about exists within
these Three Worlds and are called the Fourteen Spheres of
Existence. Since all creation proceeds from mind, all of these
realms are actually states of mind. The upper realms proceed
from mind's radiance and the lower from its dark layers.*

"*From earth on up, my son, we find the seven planes of*

*existence.   Though Sage Narada, Yudhisthira and other lumi-naries had occasion to visit the seven below them, I trust you will never have to go there for any other reason than to liberate suffering souls.  Samkhya, Vedanta, the Puranas and other sys-tems mention these classifications and give varying names for these realms.  The most popular lists the first as Bhurloka, the realm of earth, of physical planets.  It is pivotal, is important, for there the interaction of polar opposites grind the aspiring soul into a diamond, as it were.  It is a perfect place for purifi-catory practices that conduce to perfection and transcendence. Blessings be upon it!*

*"The second higher realm of ascension is called Bhuvarloka, an intermediary realm, an astral realm where a mixed current of strong desires and passions interact.  In this interspatial region, the gods and goddesses have relations with human beings.  Many wise beings inhabit this realm, watching over the affairs of aspiring souls.*

*"Next in line is called Svarloka, the life-heavens where Indra and the gods preside over the lower two planes just mentioned. Remember that there are countless individual worlds inside of each of these realms, just as there are many planets out in space we notice as we gaze into the midnight firmament.  It should be mentioned that these three realms — Bhurloka, Bhuvarloka and Svarloka — are for souls that are evolving and this process of transmigration is associated with sojourns on earth and in the seven lower regions.  It is not until one transcends them and visits the four upper regions that freedom from birth in the lower worlds is attained.*

*"The first of these four upper realms is called Maharloka.  As its name suggests, it is a great world inhabited by illumined saints and sages in their subtle bodies.  Janaloka comes next, where the firstborn of Brahma throughout many cycles make their abode, also existing in their subtle bodies.  After Janaloka the aspiring soul encounters Taparloka, a realm where beings who have attained perfect desirelessness consisting of mature discrimination and dispassion reside.  They are called the Vairajas, the seven manes, and are filled with the spirit and essence of austerity.*

*"Finally, we find Satyaloka, also known as Brahmaloka.  What*

*can be said? Here the spirit soul communes with Brahman and encounters the highest condensations of pure spirit beings that are possible in subtlest form. From this lofty spiritual plateau, a final merging into Brahman is possible. Such bliss is there that it is indescribable. It is the crown of the Seven Planes of Existence."*

Not to be denied the full picture, Ekanta, by this time as happy as a tiny child listening to fairy tales, asked, "Guruji, please tell me of the lower realms. Light has its contrasting darkness. I am not afraid. I just want to know."

*"As I said,"* replied the guru, *"all worlds are states of mind. Beneath earth, we find the subconscious and unconscious mind reflected in seven divisions. Hear about them, then:*

*"The nether regions are frightful places, no doubt. In a world where negative actions are perpetuated daily and the law of cause and effect is operative, there must be a series of worlds that accommodate those unfortunate bits of transmigrating consciousness that are responsible for these acts. Remember, Ekanta, the Divine Mother has told us that we should never be a cause of suffering for anyone. Well, there are many beings that fail to heed this advice and instead are a cause of all manner of misery for living beings.*

*"In several of the scriptures, if one searches, there are listed a whole host of hellish worlds, hundreds of them, each with its own particular characteristic. Suffering is the norm there, Ekanta. A soul's own conscience, stored in the mind's memory, regulated by the overseer of all acts and deeds who looks on as the just Witness, records everything. None escape the effects of their deeds, especially those who fail to take refuge in the Blessed Lord, who is a powerful purifying agent for all and every karmic repercussion.*

*"These myriad of lower worlds fall under seven subdivisions according to the Puranas. There, they are called patalas, a word that translates literally as 'low-lying territory.' The first patala, lying just below the earth realm, is called Atala. The word means immovable and the beings sojourning here experience dense weightiness of body and mind. If the tamasic cycles of the earthbound souls are bad, Ekanta, imagine such a state intensified many times over. Suffering and despair in a long,*

*drawn out fashion, this is the everyday occurrence in Atala and one can assume that 'everyday' in this world means long and slow.*

*"Vitala is the second lower realm, characterized by desire as its name implies. We all know how depressing it can be when our desires are stymied. Every occurrence in this hell realm is accompanied by such disappointments. It is a world of smashed expectations and the continual surfacing of enhanced desires leading to no satisfaction. The beings attending there have perpetrated similar experiences on others and need to experience them intensely in order to be purged of that tendency. Insensitivity will thus be burned from them. This is accomplished by an emissary of Lord Shiva called Hatakeshvara, who rules over that realm. He is the lord of gold, of mineral wealth. Many of the inhabitants of Vitala are guilty of hoarding wealth and material goods, refusing to distribute it to others during their earthly lifetimes. This kept others from fulfilling their desires so that they could go forward to higher realizations. It is a great sin to stand in the way of others, my son. Such is the retribution.*

*"I hope you get the idea, dear student. The characteristics of these seven lower worlds match the various negative deeds of the perpetrator and each is presided over by a fitting teacher, an aspect that purifies in due fashion. The third nether world, for instance, is called Sutala, ruled by Bali, the emperor of the asuras. Where the asuras are, if one is subservient to them and their misguided powers, there can be no peace or happiness. Talatala comes next, whose overseer is named Maya. Incurable delusion marks the beings of this realm, delusions of a thousand kinds, each leading nowhere.*

*"Mahatala is the fifth hell realm. There, great serpents deal out deathless death in crushing coils and spewing poisons. The horrors there are unspeakable, but if the transgressor sinks lower, Rasatala is encountered. The overseers there are the daityas. We have all heard of them in the various stories of our culture. They are giant, ugly, ferocious beings. You would not want to come upon one in the forest at night, Ekanta, let alone be their slave in the Rasatala hell.*

*"The lowest hell is called Patala, proper. Its correlation is with the darkest reaches of the unconscious mind where any and all*

*dreadful dreams and experiences are possible. Imagine never waking up from a stifling and recurring nightmare, even while being conscious of its horrors and feeling it all to be real. Vasuki, the king of snakes rules there along with the nagas and naginis."*

After this discourse on the Three Worlds and the Fourteen Realms of Existence, the guru leaned back and stretched his legs. Returning to his former yogic position, he looked at his young charge and smiled.

*"What is it all about, Ekanta?"* he concluded. *"Freedom and bondage. True and lasting happiness, called contentedness and bliss by the yogis and eternal peace by the Rishis, is the natural condition of all beings, though many know it not. Vacillating away further and further from their inherent perfection within, either out of deluded thinking or misguided actions or both, they lose their precious freedom and the peace and bliss that go with it. So, never forget to remember, my dear student. Do not fall asleep in the river of time or get lost in the vast reaches of empty space. Do not get tossed in the ocean of cause and effect or circle in cyclic fashion on the Kalachakra, the wheel of birth and death. Realize your identity with Brahman and love and cherish the Divine Mother within you. She has placed the Atman in all things, all beings. As Ramprasad, the Bengali poet-saint, sings, 'You have only to open your foolish eyes and behold It.'"*

The Avadhut emerged out of his deep meditation, which had been both an inspiring remembrance and a fresh experience of the truths contained therein. The fire was almost out again and a faint trace of light was just beginning to appear over the eastern horizon.

Standing up straight, he saluted the vast space around him:

"Namo Brahmane! Namaste Vayo! Reverent salutations to the Indivisible One. Continual praises be unto Vayu, who is nothing less than the visible Brahman. I salute and honor you as my guru of all-pervasive Reality, ever-free and never bound. May I always remember your profound teachings, perceiving you always despite your subtle nature."

Wrapping his belongings in his blanket, the Avadhut placed more wood on the fire for the comfort of his pilgrim brothers and moved off into the dim light of dawn.  He wanted to be far away from all signs of humanity and well on his way to Bhadranath before the noonday sun reached its zenith.

When the group of pilgrims awoke and searched for the silent stranger who had entered their encampment at such a late hour, they found only a roaring fire over which they proceeded to cook their meager breakfast.  Wondering about the transitory nature of all phenomena and the fleeting interactions between all living beings, they too eventually packed their belongings and set off for the distant holy places, whose precincts were eternally hallowed by the Blessed Lord and all His noble spiritual children.

── Chapter 13 ──

# Teachings on Power, Compassion and Sacrifice

THE THIRTEENTH GURU — Fire

THE LESSON — Grace

*The presence of fire, O Prince, demonstrates so many virtues possessed by the Absolute. As I gazed deep into its mystical recesses, my mind realized the nature of sacrifice, of transmission, of purity and of concern. I also perceived the need for strength and power as well as the presence of Grace all about us. What else can I say? This teacher, fire, is my lifelong friend and companion.*

The Avadhut stared deeply into his own fire, hovering over it to shield himself from the extreme wind that blew ferociously at this extreme elevation. He had found the holy pilgrimage sight at Bhadranath in due time, with its age-old temple containing the sacred icon of the Divine Mother of the Universe. Now, he was camping nearby amidst the wisps of snow that surrounded the mountain village and was making daily and nightly visits to the living presence centered in the holy temple.

352

This evening, he had attended to his meditations after taking the darshan of the Universal Mother. During that time he had seen Her as a living presence, permeating the entire inner and outer regions completely and having no end. With his mind soaring in the aftermath of that experience, he was thinking back over his past communions with the Divine Mother and dwelling on the delightful internal feelings that this produced.

Tonight, the fire seemed to bear a powerful message. It appeared to be a living emanation of the precious Divine Mother, radiating the intense heat of nondual Wisdom. As he stared into its dancing flames and focused His mind on the Wisdom Mother, his mind began to dance, like the flames of his campfire, feeding on the limitless teachings that fueled his internal meditations.

Long ago, the Avadhut had accomplished his meditation on fire and had come to see it as an example of Grace. Though this seemed to him at the time to be an unorthodox interpretation, he had approached his guru about it and had received validation and encouragement for this viewpoint:

*"That is a remarkable insight, Ekanta, and one that I am glad that you have arrived at. The gist of the teaching is that fire, with its great power of consumption, devours that which it feeds upon. It accomplishes this by taking the form of that which it burns. After it has consumed any given object, it expires, leaving nothing but ashes behind. Can you explain to me what all of this indicates in spiritual terms?"*

Ekanta, then a young man of seventeen, pondered his guru's request for a few moments and then proceeded to answer.

"Revered guru, all that we see, feel, touch, smell and taste, as well as what we know or intuit through the mental faculty, is nothing less than Brahman. This, the wise ones of old hold to be essential. Accepting this after testing its validity, one begins to perceive that all the elements and the various objects that occupy this realm of name and form are representations of Reality in limited form, that is, they all transmit a message of import to those who have the eyes to see. I have understood, revered sir, through your gracious instruction and the tutelage of my revered Mataji, that if the senses are offered to the Divine, a transformation comes about which allows one to translate the messages of the earth realm into definite knowledge. From fire, I received a profound message, especially when I looked at it in relation to the Beloved Lord."

*"What did you receive from our Beloved One, Ekanta?"* asked the teacher, genuinely interested and temporarily stepping outside of the role of guru with his blossoming protégé.

"It was power, compassion and sacrifice, revered sir," came the answer, "all in accordance with the karma and suffering associated with this realm of existence. Fire proves that Mother's Grace is always upon us."

Here, Ekanta had paused, for devotion was beginning to well up in him, causing tears to form in his eyes and his voice to choke a bit.

*"Ah,"* said his guru, observing this delicate condition coming over his student, *"I see that you have been deeply affected by this teaching and have extracted the very essence of it in no uncertain terms."*

"I have no doubt of this," responded Ekanta, steadying his emotions. "What I have seen will never leave me and will bring me strength and solace even in the face of the worst calamities."

*"Deign to enlighten me as to this powerful insight,"* replied the guru, *"for to hear it fresh from the devotee's lips just after its realization is a great delight. Please continue with this discourse."*

Ekanta went on with his description, gathering his thoughts rapidly and in spontaneous fashion as he proceeded.

"It is the Divine Mother who bears all sufferings in this realm. There is no presence here other than She as She is one with Brahman. She is the ultimate fire that assumes the forms of all who are born here. Bodies, as it were, are nothing other than wood for Her, and She consumes them all in due time. Minds, to Her, are so many hearths and She burns brightly within them, casting forth the warmth of knowledge and the glow of illumination. Now do I comprehend more fully that powerful song by Ramprasad, the Bengali poet, who sings in an amazed tone:"

There yonder is the Black One, darker than the void,
Her hair a roiling tumult, like stormclouds in a hurricane.
Immediately She advances, with breathtaking speed,
and all forms in space and time are consumed entirely.

Take heart, She comes to reveal, not to destroy,
though all objects and projections must entirely disappear.
Subject and object and all other pairs recede,
as with Her fiery breath She causes a funeral pyre.

The guru sat still, his attention focused on his disciple. Ekanta could tell that what he was saying, as well as the potent song, had affected his master profoundly. Soon, the teacher spoke again.

*"So much for power, my boy. You need say nothing else on that score. But explain to me please the other two qualities that you mentioned — compassion and sacrifice — and tell me what fire has to do with karma and suffering."*

"Revered sir," replied Ekanta, "if one were to give fire human characteristics, one might think that it is a selfish element, for it consumes greedily what it invests. However, all objects which fire devours are insubstantial and will soon disintegrate, leaving fire without food, after which it will then die out. Therefore, it is more intelligent to conclude that fire is performing sacrifice, a service, as it were. It is not strange or even coincidental that many important rites and rituals performed by the ancients all involve the use of fire as their main component. To apply this to spiritual truths and the Mother of the Universe, it is the fire of Her austerities and the light of Her tejas which burns away all impurities in the forms that She inhabits. Beings imagine that the actions that they undertake to perform and the repercussions that result are all their own doing. As long as they maintain this misconception in their minds, so long does it hold true. However, they fail to perceive Her, lighting the inner path and burning away obstacles along it. What folly to retain the delusion of ownership and doership and what peace and bliss result from giving it up."

*"How true this is, young man,"* said his guru. *"To assume a form is serious business. The ego which covets that form or any form as its own, building itself into a conglomerate of self-centered ideas and concerns, suffers horribly in times of trouble and at the time of death. On the other hand, those who become pure by offering themselves to the inner fire of Mother's purification make all transitions easily and spontaneously. They realize Her Grace. But I am jumping ahead here. Please continue. What about compassion? Did you not mention that?"*

"It is a difficult topic, sir," stated Ekanta. "When an all-power-ful presence is perceived and admitted, and this presence is all in all, assuming all forms and bearing all sacrifices within Itself, where is the possibility for compassion? When all is understood to be ever unified, always one and indivisible, there is no second thing in existence for which to have compassion. Still, in this tem-porary mode called earthly life, where beings are convinced of their mortality and obsessed with the idea of limited individual existence, a need arises for an ultimate power which those who are suffering from the effects of temporal existence can turn to and who can enlighten them as to the nature of the world. This is where Ishvara or Ishvari enters the picture. The Absolute has provided for everything. Projecting the universe by the power inherent in His Mahashakti, the Supreme Being, essentially beyond the pale of relativity, enters into it as well, not just as the many elements, objects and living beings, but as the concentrated power of Consciousness which appears as Ishvara, as Avatara, and as the Nityasiddhas — the Ever-Perfect ones."

Here Ekanta paused and looked towards his guru for signs of acknowledgment.

*"Go on please,"* was the only response, and Ekanta knew that he had the full attention of his teacher.

"True service can only be accomplished under the influence of compassion blended with mature detachment. Since the Mother of the Universe is all service with regards to those who have taken refuge in Her, like a queen who dotes on her subjects and is full of concern for their welfare, She lifts suffering beings out of misery and trouble."

*"How does She accomplish this, Ekanta?"* interjected the guru.

"She does this by revealing to them their true nature as unified Consciousness," he replied. "There is nothing other than this, and I could stop with that statement."

*"I understand completely,"* responded the teacher, *"but indulge me a bit. What does the process of awakening entail?"*

"First, She slowly and in good time demonstrates to each soul that without a doubt the world is"....at this point Ekanta paused, searching for an adequate word..."a projection. Call it what you will — an illusion, insubstantial, ephemeral, transitory, unreal and fleeting or, on the other hand, just a secondary reality, an expression of Brahman, only real so long as the mind and senses behold it. A whole host of terms or viewpoints can be applied, but essentially it must be impressed upon the mind of living beings that the universe of name and form is unreal, or, if one is completely truthful, that it is real only due to the presence of Brahman, the sole Reality. As you have taught me, dear teacher, Brahman is eternal and the universe is the noneternal Brahman. Therefore, the Divine Mother awakens us to this fact."

*"Again, friend and student,"* interjected the guru, *"can you tell me how She accomplishes this task, given that beings are so addicted to relative existence and so enthralled and enchanted by God's Maya?"*

"There are eternal principles behind the appearance of the universe," replied Ekanta. "Not just cosmic laws within the universal scope, but underlying fundamental truths used only by the Supreme Reality. Brahman is one, Shakti is another. Ishvara, Maya, Truth, Unity and Grace are others. Again, there is one eternal principle through which She works most powerfully. That is called Guru."

At this point, overcome with fervent devotion for his teacher, Ekanta had fallen spontaneously at his feet, prostrating respectfully before him in traditional fashion. A few poignant moments passed after which Ekanta rose to sitting position to find his guru beaming with delight.

*"I understand once more,"* was his teacher's only response. *"Go on please."*

"When the aspirant, after tiring of the unfulfilling things of the world, begins to long or yearn for higher truth, the guru appears like clockwork. Depending on the amount of unresolved karma, upon the number of veils or thickness of ignorance that covers any given individual's perception of Reality, the guru is more or less effective according to time. A rare few recognize immediately, accept what the Mother says through the guru and awaken to Reality without delay. It may take a few months, a year or two, or a decade, but even one lifetime is quick when the heavy weight of accumulated karma is taken into consideration. The seeker has not only the upbringing amidst worldly circumstances to deal with and the ills of society and ignorant parents and family. He or she must also neutralize effects from past lives. The guru is a crucial link in this process. Those who deny the guru when he or she appears, either underestimating such a being or pushing this aid from Mother away, only postpone the inevitable. They are like the impetuous miner who overlooks the vein of gold above his head in the ceiling of the cave in his rush to get to a gold nugget lying on the ground underneath. The effects of worldly existence die hard."

There was a short silence as these words sunk in.

*"And fire, Ekanta?"* came the query.

"The guru, if such be authentic, represents fire of purification," came Ekanta's reply, "for many inconsistencies and obstructions get removed or destroyed through that medium. Fire burns without cessation and is completely devoid of any compromise. A sense of pity or weak concern is not present in it. The guru, too, is similar. The true preceptor, ever one while acting through different vehicles, is not there to coddle or baby the aspirant. There are certain sufferings which must be undergone if one is to get rid of ignorance and delusion and the guru will both prescribe the medicine and remain present as it takes effect, assisting in the entire process. All diseases in the mind will be burnt away, like wood in a bonfire, The Divine Mother is the bonfire and the guru is the one who tends it, determining what is to be consumed in its flames."

"Revered sir," continued Ekanta, after a few moments had elapsed, "the guru suffers for his part in this process. I am convinced, though, that it is the Divine who partakes of all the effects, like fire that consumes as long as the fuel persists and dies away when there is nothing left."

*"The Divine Mother's fire of purification may die out here and there,"* replied the guru, *"but it springs up in other locations. Not only that, it gets transferred in some cases, and this is one of them. What I have taught you has been realized through your own experience, Ekanta, and at a very young age. I now feel that you are ready to exude this knowledge to others. What I have heard today and what I have observed in you over the past year indicates both your readiness and your direction. Now all that is needed is a sign from the Divine. Be on the lookout for such a message, for it will not be long before it occurs."*

What his guru said that day actually came to pass soon after this conversation, for Ekanta thereafter responded to an inner call, leaving home after bidding good-bye to his parents and the revered vanaprastin teachers who had so cared for and instructed him. Now, as he sat near his campfire with the snows of the Himalayas all around him and the sacred temple looming nearby in the darkness, he was filled again with wonder at God's omnipresence and omniscience. Those words he had uttered in the presence of the guru were fresh in him at that moment, but their ramifications were infinite. Even after years of wandering and teaching, there still remained so much to do. It was all so vast. All that he could muster, being conscious of the Mother's all-pervasive presence and Her Grace upon him, was an intense gratitude and devotion that supplied him daily, moment to moment, with the extinction of his ego. Without the ego — the selfish I — in the way, his life had become an unending flow of peace and delight. He owed this in part to his wonderful gurus.

*"The key to success in spiritual life, Ekanta, is the effacement of egotism. The ego will remain in residual ways, no doubt, as long as the body idea exists, but life will be so much more fulfilling and blissful if one can diminish its hold over the mind."*

"What path is this, Mataji?" Ekanta had asked. "I do not find it mentioned often with any emphasis in the classical approaches, in the six darshanas."

*"That may be true in a sense, my dear, but it nevertheless underlies every system as a prerequisite. Little growth is possible without it, spiritually speaking. While ordinary beings are enamored of the world and before they are qualified to seek and realize the higher knowledge called Paravidya, the Divine Mother keeps this sense of individuality in them so that they can gain success in worldly endeavors. Unless they get this satisfaction, and this is particularly true of those who are still unawakened as to the ultimate purpose of existence, they will never be able to progress in sadhana."*

"Guruji told me that the ego is like the skin of a mango," responded the boy. "It must remain so that the fruit can ripen, but is discarded when the fruit is ready to be offered to the fire of Brahman within us."

*"Yes,"* replied the guru, *"that is a good metaphor in this context."*

"Another story he told me about the ego is that it is like an onion. One goes on peeling and peeling an onion and finds no end to its layers. In fact, it is found that it is all layers with no substance in the middle. The ego is like that as well."

*"It is true, my dear,"* agreed the Mataji, *"and what is more, peeling the onion makes one cry. The ego causes many tears too!"*

Laughing out loud at this development in the conversation, the two eventually fell silent and contemplated the radiant mind further. Soon, Ekanta pressed for more details about the ego.

"Mataji, can the ego's layers be defined or classified? This, it seems to me, would help us in this difficult process and possibly reduce all these tears that are shed."

*"Good thinking, my dear,"* she responded. *"Yes, there are some characteristics we can outline in this regard. The ego of wealth, for instance, which is centered around greed, covetousness and desire for power and possessions, this must be destroyed. When one's consciousness fastens upon objects, the objectless Reality fades from view.*

*"The ego of scholarship creeps into human consciousness too. It occupies the minds of those who assume that they are intellectually superior. Different than intellectual learning, Paravidya — spiritual wisdom — is a bonfire of eternal Truth that, unlike scholarly erudition, never diminishes and always satisfies. What is more, it enlightens. This is because it frees one from the feeling of my knowledge, my scholarship and my attainment through the realization that Wisdom — profound, infinite and supreme — is beyond the mind and abides forever in Brahman.*

*"The ego of old age, with its pride and shame, its delusion, its decrepitude, its mental anguish and its fear of death is another imposition on human awareness. One must affirm, 'I am not the body, its life-force, or its death.' Life-force moves, comes and goes. The Atman does not. The Atman is deathless, immortal Spirit. Therefore, detach from the body/mind mechanism and realize this.*

*"There is ego in everything, Ekanta. The entire creation is permeated with it. Division, duality, separate existence, these are nothing other than modes of the ego. It works on cosmic,*

*collective and individual levels, all three. You have asked me to*
*list a few of the coverings or layers of the onionlike ego, my dear.*
*That I have done. There are many more. See them and classify*
*them yourself as you go through life and then withdraw from*
*them and remain free. Teach others to do the same."*

The two remained quiet for a time, sometimes gazing into each
other's eyes. The Mataji finally broke the silence.

*"The destruction of ego with regard to a yogic path or method*
*can, as you asked for, be given a name, just like other systems.*
*It could be called, vinashahamkara-vada — the way of self-dis-*
*solution or, effacing the individual ego. With regards to the*
*already existing Yogas, it works like this.*

*"In Bhakti Yoga, vinashahamkaravada is attained through*
*self-surrender to God and guru. Its implements are devotion*
*and faith. In Jnana Yoga, vinashahamkaravada is attained by*
*perceiving the inherent primordial Wisdom in all things. Its*
*tools are insight and equanimity. In Karma Yoga, vinasha-*
*hamkaravada is attained performing all action not for oneself*
*or for others, but for the Self within. Its aids are inaction and*
*selflessness. In Raja Yoga, vinashahamkaravada is attained*
*through peaceful introspection. Its main qualities are contem-*
*plation on nothingness and the bliss and mastery that this*
*brings. In short, however, success in the path of ego effacement*
*is gained through heartfelt offering, selfless sacrifice and spir-*
*itual self-effort — all of the things that the ego hates. Follow*
*this system as a subtle practice in everyday life, my dear, and*
*the results will be both edifying and satisfying."*

Thus had self-surrender leading to a transparent ego played an
important part in Ekanta's spiritual development. The razor's
edge path of spiritual life had been much roomier due to his effective attainment of this prime attribute. From the standpoint of a
spiritual teacher, however, Ekanta had found it most difficult to
communicate the crucial nature of this practice of egolessness
to others, for the sense of agency was so strong in human beings.
After they had become accustomed to doing for themselves in the
difficult world of action and reaction, it was extremely hard for
them to surrender the lower self to a higher will. Yet, this act was
absolutely necessary in order to effect any substantial spiritual
growth.

Thinking about this dilemma, Ekanta's mind drifted back to conversations he had experienced with other teachers and colleagues in his life. Once, while visiting the forest ashram of a wise muni, a frequent stopping place for pilgrims en route to points both north and south, the Avadhut had received a wonderful spiritual experience. Over several visits, the muni and the Avadhut became good friends and though the muni was usually plunged into periods of deep silence, he put these austerities aside when Ekanta visited and the two talked about Reality into the late hours of the night.

*"One does not have to wait until one is perfect in order to begin the process,"* the muni told him one day. *"If one uses the excuse that one is not fit for spiritual practice and thereby puts it off until some future period, no appreciable progress will ever be made. In addition, we see that even in advanced practitioners, a little imperfection persists. In fact, man's nature, if you ask me, is imperfect."*

"What do you mean by that?" the Avadhut had responded. "Are we not cut in God's image?"

*"Yes indeed,"* said the muni, *"our true nature is Divine, but our human nature, by design, is defective. Otherwise, how could Mahamaya maintain the facade of this universe and convince us that we are body-oriented beings? The weaknesses and frailties of living beings are surmountable, to a great extent, but one will always find reason for complaint as long as the body persists, even so long as the mind continues its thinking process. I have observed great yogis and enlightened beings in their old age. Some cannot now even remember my name though I served them for years! Mind, as mind, as thought and memory, is certainly defective. One must make provision for leaving these tools of body and mind behind. If one is trapped in them, circling on the Kalachakra, the wheel of birth and death, a long train of suffering ensues."*

"What would be the solution, then, in your estimation?" asked the Avadhut. "How does one go about loosening the hold of body and mind in order to make ready for an unencumbered spiritual transition?"

*"By reducing the ego to its smallest and least meddlesome condition,"* came the muni's answer, without the slightest hesitation. *"If left to natural devices, installed subliminally in the heart and*

*mind-stuff by the Divine Mother of the Universe, the nature of human beings will spontaneously rise out of limitation and enter the divine status. However, the host of hindrances placed in the way by ego-oriented actions, desires and attachments are legion. Through surrendering the ego and offering it up for subtle surgery under the Divine Mother's wisdom sword, living beings effect the ultimate solution and open themselves up for the natural process of spiritual unfoldment. Through this they attain their respective swadharmas — their highest destiny."*

"Revered sir," pressed the Avadhut, "this is a very simple solution, at least by way of explanation. Though I am aware that the practice of egolessness is deceptively simple, what would you say about the many abstruse philosophical expressions which indicate various pathways out of ignorance. False superimposition, for instance, called vivarta in Sanskrit, is a way of explaining and transcending Maya. By seeing through the various coverings over Brahman, one thereby arrives at Absolute Reality. Is there a simple and direct way of actualizing the realization of this complex system?"

*"One can penetrate swiftly to the essence of the matter in this regard after certain prerequisites are satisfied,"* answered the muni. *"When a natural state is reached due to purification of the mind, self-surrender, devotion to the guru, study of the scriptures and the like, it becomes increasingly easy to behold the Beloved One. A being who lives in such a state is either in Jada Samadhi or Chetana Samadhi and as a result is continually communing with Brahman."*

"Muniji," inquired the Avadhut, "is it possible to state the difference between these two subtle perceptions of Reality? Can you describe it with words?"

*"A person under the influence of Jada Samadhi has no awareness of the outside world. By the way, after experiencing this, revered Avadhut, then only does one understand the Advaitic realization that the world is unreal and Brahman is real — not before. Jada Samadhi causes one to sit still, 'like a stone or an inert thing,' as the saying goes. The Christ experienced this. Birds perched in His hair at that time, while wild animals approached him without fear. We know the truth of this, that it is not an exaggeration. For instance, one of our Indian sages was in such a condition for so long that ants built an anthill*

*around him."*

A few moments passed after this description. Then, the muni continued.

*"A being experiencing Chetana Samadhi demonstrates some different characteristics. Perhaps that one has had Jada Samadhi already, but whatever the case might be, Chetana Samadhi is that state in which the mind is aware of the world while being simultaneously cognizant of the ultimate Reality which is experienced in jada and in other impersonal samadhis. Thus, a person living in constant communion with God that enables him or her to work in the world, for the good of the world, possesses the great gift of Chetana Samadhi."*

"Thank you, revered Muniji, for that explanation. You mentioned that there is a swift way of realizing the all-pervasive Brahman, even given the methodical path of purification of principles starting with Bhuta Shuddhi and the step-by-step neti neti process of the Vedanta. Is there a way of demonstrating this?"

*"By way of practice, revered Avadhut, I can show you this moment,"* answered the muni, emphatically. *"Please come with me."*

Leaving the confines of the muni's ashram, the two wise beings went outside into nature. The greenery of the forest and the distant mountains greeted their eyes, surrounding them on three sides. Behind them a lake, scintillating in the sunlight, lay pure and serene, nestled in the cradling hands of Mother Earth. The soft grasses underfoot, springing from the fertile ground, supported them and cushioned their steps as they proceeded to the center of the clearing in front of the dwelling. Stopping there, the muni took a deep breath and began instructing the Avadhut in the proposed exercise.

*"Kindly face the forest and the mountains. Stand on both feet with your weight balanced on each in equal proportion and with back straight. Now gaze upon the creation. Let your mind become still and quiet and simply look deeply into the appearance of things."*

Standing there with the muni, focused and keenly aware, the Avadhut gradually began to feel a falling away of weights and coverings. He felt like a ship eased from its moorings or a hot-air balloon that was being freed from the many bags of sand that held it down to earth. As he concentrated on the beautiful scene before him, he gradually became aware that the five elements and their various permutations were only apparent, that their existence was somehow lacking in both substance and reality. A feeling then came over him which convinced him that everything he beheld with his senses was illusory. Then, suddenly, all that presented itself before his penetrating gaze began to recede away from him into the background, naturally yet unexplainably, until he found himself witnessing a much subtler scene behind the grosser projected scene. The mirage-like nature of this appearance and its hypnotic hold over the senses was eventually dispelled and a new, more powerful insight dawned that allowed him an awareness of prana and its pervasive presence. This subtle observance of the profuse energy that was flowing in many directions all around him was wonderful, but it, too, seemed to be lacking. Temporal and phantomlike, it seemed to bespeak something more concrete or less incorporeal.

The next phase of this powerful movement of penetration came unexpectedly, yet with great assurance. Aum, the primal sound of creation, visited his awareness, Its welcoming vibration washing over his attuned consciousness like warm water or soothing, fragrant air. Continuing to look with intense gaze, the Avadhut watched with internal perception as the prana then merged with the Aum and the Aum dissolved into boundless Light. The earth with its soft grasses no longer supported him. Indeed, there was no support anywhere that he could see or detect. Only the vast living Light of pure Awareness surrounded him, infinite and indivisible, permeating everything and existing everywhere. Gradually, he became aware of the presence of his companion's voice, calling him back to limited awareness of the five elements and the senses once again.

"_Do not remain in jada forever, dear sir,_" came his friend's voice, "_kindly revisit the chetana condition._"

Slowly, the Avadhut became conscious of the outer reality once again as awareness flooded back into his physical senses.

"_Welcome back,_" stated the muni, "_O pilgrim traversing two countries. I only wish that my students were so apt as this and able to reach as deeply in such a short time. You have turned this rudimentary exercise into a full-fledged and successful_ *experience. God bless you, sir!"*

Somehow finding his voice, the Avadhut stammered out, "Blessed muni, only the training from my gurus has enabled me to perceive Reality in this fashion. I owe it all to them."

*"As well as to your own good karmas, inherent abilities and intense austerities, I might assume,"* added the muni. *"Whatever the case may be, you have answered your own question and have emphasized my point for me. What more can be said? Behind the five-fold curtain of nature lies the world of the multileveled prana with its various energies. Penetrating that, the yogi finds the Aum and all that it created, including mind and thought. With the dissolution of everything conceptual comes the advent of Brahman, if such an expression can be used, for Brahman is eternal and all-pervasive. It is ever-present and is the only Reality upon which all other provisional subrealities are superimposed. This is the simple Truth, Oh Avadhut, but in how many ways does our limited awareness attached to the physical form find to obscure It and run away from It? In the end, all will have to face It and in that moment every form, energy, and concept will become soluble, disintegrated, dissolved forever back into Its true Source of Origin."*

The Avadhut drew himself away from the fire. Earlier, while walking back from the temple, barefoot in the snow, his feet had lost their feeling and become numb. Now, he was having to draw them back to avoid burning them. The warmth of the fire had taken the numbness of cold away, though a painful and uncomfortable period of prickling sensations had passed in the interim. This reminded him of Yogindra Yogi's teachings and he recalled them from his past.

*"The misguided minds of human beings, due to wrong action and improper orientation, have become numb with the freezing effects of ignorance, young man,"* the yogi stated one evening as the two sipped hot tea in his dark mountain cave. The fire, warm and welcome, was casting weird, dancing shadows upon the uneven walls, lending a hoary atmosphere to the situation which Ekanta always cherished. As he soaked in the sacred vibrations of the place and its holy occupant, the yogi continued his discourse:

*"Only the fire of spiritual knowledge can cause that coldness*

*to seep out and return the mind to its natural alertness, its innate radiance. However, there are few beings in this day and age who can bear with the painful transition period and the discomfort that always accompanies spiritual practices at the outset of the early sadhana phase. What is more, even if the early stage is successfully navigated, there are many aspirants who balk along the way and fall back in the intermediate level. This faltering and the subsequent giving up of spiritual life makes it even harder to accomplish the desired and ultimate end in the future, even if the good fortune of a second opportunity comes along again."*

The Avadhut shuddered despite being warm and cozy. He could not bear to think of the suffering that beings let themselves in for due to their blindness and ignorance of spiritual matters. He had seen it firsthand, all over India as well as in other locations he had visited. Suffering was universal. Was this not what Sakyamuni Buddha had based his Four Noble Truths upon? Did not the Christ speak of the need to seek the kingdom of heaven before concerning oneself at all with the world? Suddenly, a saying that his teacher had been fond of flashed in his mind:

*"Rub your hands with the oil of the coconut before opening the jack fruit, Ekanta, lest they become stained with its sticky sap. What I mean is, it is only by first protecting oneself with the oil of discrimination and dispassion that one remains free of the sticky sap of worldliness leading to ignorance and misery."*

Ekanta tossed a few more precious pieces of wood on the fire.

"More beings for the sacrifice," he uttered.

Again his mind turned inward to access other wisdom teachings from his vast store of experiences.

*"Where is the Lord's compassion?"* his Mataji exclaimed one day. *"He enters into us as the eternal flame of existence after creating us from the dust of fires past. Then He burns in us as life-force until the organs and nerves can no longer bear His presence. Then He burns them with disease and exits without the slightest hesitation. Does that sound like compassion?"*

Ekanta looked at her with a startled expression, then the two burst into laughter.

After they had settled down, the guru said, *"It took fire to create this planet and fire will play a hand in destroying it as well. There are also other forms of fire, my boy. The prana, animating nature and all physical structures, is a wonderful blaze that lights the entire universe. Have you heard the story from the Prasnopanishad, Ekanta?"*

"No," Ekanta had replied, "I have not had the good fortune. Do you know it Mataji? Can you tell it?"

His eagerness was enough to bring it out of her in due fashion.

*"In the second prasna," she began, "a Sanskrit word meaning query or question, Bhargava, the son of a great saint, approached Pippalada, the enlightened rishi, to ask him about the various gods. 'What is the number of them?' he asked. 'How do they function for the good of living beings and who is the greatest of all of them?' In response, Pippalada told him the story of the god of prana. But first, he declared that all is Brahman, manifest in various forms and each with different intensities, as it were. He told Bhargava that ether, air, fire, water, earth, mind, speech, eye and ear — all were the omnipresent God, each expressing some inner presence and mystery of the ultimate and supreme Verity.*

*"These facets of Brahman, Ekanta, are physical representations of God's majesty and power, but there is an inner core to these principles called Indriyas, and these are the gods that control the outer conditions of God's universe. Of these mentioned before, it so happened that they all gathered at one time and began to tell each other of their supremacy over all the others. Water claimed its superiority of fire, air stated that it was by its power that both could operate, the eyes claimed higher qualities than the other senses and on and on so there was a big contest going on. You see, each thought that the power invested in them by the Creator was higher than any other, so pervasive is the sense of ego that penetrates every aspect of this phenomenal world.*

*"As this debate was going on, prana rose up and said assuredly, 'Do not harbor any doubt about who is supreme here amidst the present assembly. I alone have subdivided myself into the five senses and all other principles and support everything that you are and all that you do.' This statement, Ekanta, raised a great clamor, as all of the aforementioned components*

*of creation voiced their objections. Since they would not believe him, he became indignant and, thinking them all to be ungrateful for his life-giving force, raised himself up and out of the body, leaving it a lifeless husk. As he ascended, the five senses, the body, the elements and other functions found that they too were taken up and out as the prana moved."*

After consideration for a few moments, the guru continued telling the story from the ancient scriptures.

*"The upanishad uses the analogy of a queen bee in this instance, Ekanta, stating that as she comes and goes in and out of the hive, so too do the others follow her inexorably. When the five senses and the other principles found out that they could not even move without the help of prana, that they, indeed, moved when he did, they immediately accepted him as superior and settled down comfortably into the scheme of things."*

"What a remarkable illustration, Mataji," said Ekanta. "It makes it so easy to apprehend that there are subtle forces, unseen to us, at work in the universe and in the internal being as well."

*"Quite right, young man,"* replied the guru, *"and there is more. Shankara did his famous commentaries on the Upanishads, as we have told you. In the one concerning the Prasnopanishad, he declares:"*

As fire He burns
and He shines forth as the blazing sun in the heavens.
He rains as the cloud and rules over all beings.
It is He, as well, that kills all demons as Indra,
the lord of gods.

*"He is talking about prana here, the life-force in all things, and there is a cosmic aspect to this energy that is associated with the highest manifestation of the universe called Hiranya-garbha, or the luminous egg. The Cosmic Mind of God, then, is filled with this most excellent energy of prana. When Mahat is born, prana is present immediately."*

"What is the connection here with fire and sacrifice, Mataji, and with God's compassion which we just laughed about?"

*"Oh, my dear,"* replied the teacher, *"prana carries the energy of the gods, not to mention the five senses and the elements. This*

means that it allows all offerings to be brought before their respective enjoyers. To receive as well as to offer is a kind of sacrifice, is it not? He, the prana, is the vehicle for Mother's sacrifice. He bears the sun across the daytime sky, allowing it to shed its light and warmth on all. He bears the rain so that food can grow. Without Him there would be starvation. Importantly, as well, the individual mind, like the Cosmic Mind, functions on this prana. As blood carries all manner of nourishment and protection through the physical system, so too does prana carry essential ingredients throughout the universe as well as in the subtle arena of the mind and intelligence.

"As far as compassion is concerned, Ekanta, is it any fun to get into a body after enjoying the unalloyed and unlimited bliss of ultimate freedom beyond the form? To enter into a limited condition after experiencing the great heights of unbridled freedom in order to assist others would entail, I deem, a great act of compassion. In the end, my dear, it is only the Mother who bears all sufferings, bestows all fulfillment and accomplishes all ends. Though there is ever and always only One eternal and indivisible existence, and in that there is no thought of compassion, whenever beings experience the mode of separateness which is based on delusion alone, there the Mother comes and waits, working subtly to end this stunted condition and bring soothing and cooling relief. A little fire is necessary at first, though, to burn away impurities."

The Avadhut breathed a sigh of contentment and returned to outer awareness of the world. He turned around to give his back the benefit of the fire's warmth for a change. Stretching his legs, he detected a white rabbit at the edge of the light of his fire. Reaching over and pulling a piece of bread from his loaf, he gently tossed it in the direction of the animal. Standing on its hind legs, and taking the bread piece by piece in deliberate fashion, the rabbit ate it on the spot, entirely unafraid of his host.

The Avadhut rolled out his blanket, given to him by the temple priests when he arrived. All was provided by the Mother, he thought. There was not one thing that he did not think of that did not come to him in time. He had marveled over this before. It would be well if all beings would contemplate this verity every day of their existence. A host of complaints and troublesome desires would thus vanish and contentment would take their place. After placing a few last pieces of wood on the fire, he snuggled close to it and fell into a deep sleep.

In the very early morning hours, the Avadhut had a remarkable dream. He awoke while still in the dream in the hands of a wonderful being who was much larger than he and who held him in his grasp. Nearby, a huge fire burnt brightly, but no warmth came from it. Instead, its radiance exuded a feeling of heady ecstasy. As he wondered at his predicament, he thought to himself, Oh, this is what the gods receive from their fires. We get physical heat, they get bliss.

In his dream, the being then spoke to him in words that were not recognizable but which he nevertheless understood.

_"Worthy one, I am now offering you into the fire as a sacrifice to Brahman, the Highest. There can be no other offering that is better for this purpose than man, and you represent the best of human beings."_

Saying so, Indra — for this, Ekanta knew, was who he was having darshan of — cast him into the fire as if he were a piece of coal or wood. Flying through the air, the Avadhut saw planets flash by and the faces of celestials floating in the sky around them, looking on with interest. He felt not the slightest sense of fear, but only an unspeakable anticipation of being consumed in the fire of the gods. He awakened upon contact and continued to shake with the exhilaration of bliss for hours after.

During these few hours, as the aftereffects of the experience persisted, he thought that he could still perceive the faces of gods and goddesses hanging about in the air above him, though his rational mind would not accept it. Whenever he decided that there was no reason not to gaze upwards, he would look there and see only the ordinary sky of earth. Looking down or inward, there they were again, in the periphery of his vision as it were, most beautiful and enticing, beyond description.

Later, after the initial force of the dream vision had worn off a bit, the Avadhut pondered its meanings. So much of his thought on the previous day had been centered on and concerned with fire. It was no wonder that such a dream had occurred. But this was only a rational explanation. The mystical explanation was entirely different and the Avadhut was experienced at interpreting dreams. In fact, this was no dream at all, he surmised, but a dar-shan of the celestials, including the Lord of gods himself. That he was offered to Brahman could only mean the obvious and the only disbelief that the Avadhut harbored was that he had come back to the body at all after this intense occurrence. About this, he could only assume that there was some important work to be done yet and that His maker was not done occupying this partic-ular vehicle.

As the Avadhut contemplated this experience throughout the night, he remembered a forest fire that had swept through the region where he had been wandering one year. From a vantage point high atop a small mountain where he had scrambled in haste to escape the advancing blaze, the Avadhut witnessed a strange spectacle of destruction. Trees were utterly consumed by the dozens. Streams disappeared under a wreckage of blackened branches and ash while clouds and billows of endless smoke and steam colored the sky gray. Before the onrush of this living force, groups of animals ran helter skelter in a panic of fear. What was amazing to Ekanta was that the hunter ran neck and neck with the hunted, each putting aside their respective roles as predator and prey for at least as long as it took to reach safety. This mutual pact while under the pressure of strain and duress had revealed many interesting things to the Avadhut and had fueled many of his contemplations thereafter.

But the overriding focus of all this sporadic chaos had been the fire itself. There was no discrimination there, no compassion either. It burned and annihilated completely, without regard to what it encountered. No conscience kept it from its work. Indeed, it seemed to know what it was about and set itself to that pur-pose inexorably until everything was totally eradicated. Later, the Avadhut had walked through the devastation, observing the destruction with a queer mixture of loathing and admiration. The burned and charred carcasses of deer, squirrels and other forest dwellers were lying about, their death agony impressed upon their stiff remains.

It was his dream vision that had reminded him of the forest-fire experience, for as these creatures had been extinguished in the flames of conflagration, his own body had also been consumed in the dream. He wondered at the fear and pain of these body-bound animals and the great lesson was obvious. Death can come at any time, unheralded, unsuspected and without regard to one's earthly attachments and worldly considerations. All that was or seemed important to living beings was not so to the forces that be, whether they be of universal influence or of a more transcendent nature. Thinking thus brought a story to the Avadhut's mind, one that he had heard during his travels and associations with renunciate monks.

One evening, a particularly charismatic figure entered the campsite where the Avadhut was staying and had united the wanderers in mirth and discussion. This man was a Tantric sadhaka and a baul from Bengal. He practiced a strange blend of renunciation and affirmation and was very colorful, full of songs and stories. Stamped heavily with the markings and dress of his sect, he had engrossed the gathering in a series of wonderful stories from his tradition, causing riotous laughter amongst the otherwise contained and reserved group.

One story had stuck in Ekanta's mind, for it demonstrated how much the beings of the world were tied up in their belief that what they did and accomplished was of extreme importance. Before the baul's arrival, the Avadhut had been staring into the fire and contemplating its uncompromising power while simultaneously considering the evanescence of earthly existence. As he did so, teachings from his guru came to mind.

*"Everyone involved in work, dear one, seems to be under the sway of an egoistic assumption that the actions they are engaged in have the most extreme value, both to themselves and to others. In this vein, the worldly consider themselves and what they do to be important and irreplaceable. The world, however, its makeup and the powers that operate the universal process all indicate otherwise. To become aware of this ignorant behavior and annihilate the ego is to awaken to the actual reality of life and the temporal condition of human nature. This is both sobering and freeing."*

After the Avadhut had finished ruminating about these teachings, the Tantric sadhaka, Ramakrishnadas Baul by name, entered the camp and began his story.

*"There was once a man who, in his wanderings, came upon a nice hut atop a hill. It had obviously just been finished but*

*had also become deserted for some unknown reason. The man took this as a sign that he should settle down and take to living in solitude in one place. As he occupied the hut, a great wind began to spring up which eventually began to threaten the hut's existence. As it shook in the force of the gale, the man, having become accustomed to the hut, began to think of ways he could save it. All of a sudden he remembered that Vayu was the god of the wind, so he started praying fervently to Vayu, saying, 'This is Vayu's hut, oh wind, please do not destroy it.' After a while, when the wind did not subside, the man became despondent and had to think again.*

*"Next, he remembered that Hanuman was the son of Vayu so he began to pray to him to save the hut. The man prayed, 'Oh wind, this hut belongs to Hanuman. Please spare its existence.' This did not work either, so the man had to reconsider. Soon, as the wind reached gale force and the hut began to come apart, the man recalled that Sri Ram was the Lord of Hanuman, so he began to pray to the great Sri Ram, thinking that this would certainly do the trick. 'This is Ram's hut, oh wind,' he prayed. 'You had better not destroy it!' His disappointment was great however, when suddenly a great gust of air hit the hut and it began to come apart. In frustration, the man ran out of the hut to save himself, at the same time yelling angrily, 'This is the devil's own hut! The devil can have it!'"*

The assembled group of holy men laughed loud and long at this charming story, though there were a few younger and less knowledgeable sadhus there who did not get the message. To these, Ramakrishnadas Baul explained:

*"This story describes to us the ultimate futility of becoming engrossed in egoistic work and action. The hut represents the body and its actions, the wind is the force of death or, if one looks at it from a higher standpoint, the force of eternal life. With regards to the world, the wind symbolizes the undoing to all things — that which unties the energy in the body/mind mechanism from its occupations. The man who coveted the nice little hut is, of course, the embodied being who thinks, erroneously, that how he acts and what he does has great importance."*

After a little consideration, the baul from Bengal continued:

*"There is actually nothing here in this mode of existence that indicates to us that what we do has any lasting significance. History, as short as it is to us, bears this out. Before our recorded history, during the other countless cycles of manifestation and dissolution, did any word or deed have any lasting consequence whatsoever? Still, humans in everyday life get attached to the least significant detail or object and project a sense of extreme importance over them. The state of pride and self-importance that these beings exude would cause one to think that the worlds would fall apart if they did not exist.*

*"Again, the same thing applies to what people generally think of as important. The rise and fall of nations has been going on for centuries and men and women place so much emphasis on their respective roles, carrying out their positions of responsibility in governments with so much pretentiousness. They have no idea who runs the universe and think themselves to be a key force in the little game of world affairs. No one remembers that destruction is built right into the very fabric of this creation — that anything created must undergo decay and dissolution. In the end, then, it is the 'devil's own hut,' this work that we attach so much importance to, and no matter how much we may think that our work, action, career or duty is crucial to the operation and maintenance of the universe, we only delude ourselves."*

"Does this mean that we should give it all up then?" asked one young aspirant, sitting near the Avadhut.

*"Why yes,"* replied Ramakrishnadas Baul, *"that would be the wisest thing to do. However, there are different interpretations of what that entails."*

"What is best?" asked another aspirant.

*"In my opinion,"* returned the baul, *"one should do one's duty according to the injunctions of God and guru while always exercising detachment from the world and its considerations. It is a tinsel-town world, a mere trumpery of pompousness and self-aggrandizement. A wise person should have nothing to do with it. If one's dharma suggests that action in the world is necessary, that should be done after firmly fixing in the mind that only Brahman is real and that the world is illusory."*

At this statement, another sadhaka stood up and asked the baul a question.

"Sir, what if one perceives that there is no difference between the world and Brahman?"

*"If that is truly the case,"* stated the baul firmly and quickly, *"one will see nothing but Brahman. The world will not then be present, at least not in the usual sense."*

This logical but profound conclusion brought quiet and unanimous assent from all present, noticeable as a mutual nodding of heads and some reserved affirmations. Later, the Avadhut approached Ramakrishnadas Baul and the two talked late into the night about their favorite subject, Divine Reality. Thereafter, they became fast friends and mutual regard and respect grew up between them. Though a rather fantastic figure, the Avadhut had recognized him as an authentic luminary and one that had both feet in the world and his head beyond it.

The forest-fire experience had introduced the Avadhut to a force of the Universal Mother that he had never directly encountered before. He had heard of such a power, though. Thinking back on that experience now, the Avadhut listened again to the words of his enlightened guru, emanating from the recesses of his resilient intellect and memory.

*"Dhumavati is an aspect of the Mother that will entirely dissolve all attachment to name and form,"* came the cryptic words of his preceptor one evening. *"After Her work is done, no one and nothing will be left of this phenomenal universe. What to speak of the reality or unreality of the world, where is such talk when there is nothing substantial in relative existence in the first place — when manifestation is no more than an idea in the Cosmic Mind?"*

"Dhumavati," said Ekanta uneasily, "what does Her name mean?"

*"It refers to ashes, my boy,"* responded the teacher, *"for She destroys by smoke and fire. After Her flames rush across relative existence, all life is extinguished."*

"This is horrible then, is it not?" stated the boy, slightly perturbed at the thought.

*"To those who are attached only to phenomenal existence and earthly concerns it is, no doubt, a hard pill to swallow,"* returned the guru. *"Nevertheless, She is a fact of existence, a power of Durga, or of Shiva's fires of destruction. It would benefit all beings if they kept Her presence in mind."*

After a pause, the guru continued.

*"Do you know of the Mother's aspect as Rakshakali, Ekanta?"*

"Yes," answered the boy. "She is worshipped by the country villagers and placated by offerings so that She will not bring disease and pestilence upon them."

*"Exactly right, Ekanta,"* affirmed the preceptor. *"Is not disease and plague a fact of existence? Can we pretend them away? We must, no doubt, take precautions for our health, but even the hatha yogis who covet and achieve longevity have to suffer from various bodily ailments. If one analyzes and uses the powers of inherent intelligence, planted there by Mother Sarasvati, then transcendence, supported by discrimination and detachment, is the only option, at least for those who are more enamored of Brahman and Atman than with the earth and its fleeting pleasures and unavoidable pains. Therefore, my boy, I urge you to strive not for longevity, not for health, not for preserving the sense of individual existence or even for personal liberation. Get within your mental grasp the firm realization that you and everything around you is Pure Spirit, ever one with the Supreme Being. Dhumavati, Rakshakali, even Sarasvati bow to That and take refuge There."*

The Avadhut's awareness returned to his present surroundings. His fire was dying out and he had no more firewood.

"The process is over, the form is extinguished, the sacrifice has been made due to Mother's compassionate nature and Her Grace is all that now exists," he murmured to himself. These words, accompanied by the sight of his breath on the frosty night air, brought to mind some slokas from the Avadhuta Gita, a holy scripture of his order:

> The idea that reality exists or that unreality does not exist
> is foreign to me.
> I am ever-free and bondage is therefore nonexistent.
> My form has been extinguished forevermore.

> Purity and impurity, union and separation,
> such ideas are futile.
> This appearance called the universe does not affect me.
> My form has been extinguished forevermore.

I was never ignorant,
nor have I attained to a state of knowingness.
Both knowledge and ignorance are foreign to me.
My form has been extinguished forevermore.

The Atman is neither bound nor liberated,
neither virtuous or blemished.
It is neither divided or undivided.
My form has been extinguished forevermore.

That has no beginning, middle or end, has no friend or foe.
It is impossible to mention good and evil with regards to It.
My form has been extinguished forevermore.

Worship is pointless, for no form exists to worship.
Therefore, instruction and practice are useless.
How can one describe the Essence, which is infinite.
My form has been extinguished forevermore.

Neither have I conquered the senses
nor have I not conquered them.
Self-restraint or discipline never occur to me.
Friend, how shall I speak of victory and defeat.
My form has been extinguished.

As these verses rolled by in his mind's memory, the Avadhut slowly emerged from his internal contemplation. Looking around, he felt that he was coming out of Reality and revisiting a dream. Everything is a manifestation of the mind, an external rendering of what is within, he thought to himself. Looking deep into the fire, the words of his revered Mataji came to his mind:

*"The seed of the melon is more powerful than the melon, my dear."*

"How can that be," he had responded, for there are hundreds of seeds in each melon?"

*"Yes, but in each of these seeds lies the potential for hundreds of new melons. Of course, you can say that each new melon contains many new seeds, but the melon gets eaten or perhaps decays. The seeds inside do not suffer such a fate and bear*

*within them the power to create a whole new fruit, even if only
one of them comes to fruition.*

*"Similarly, the entire creation has proceeded from a tiny
thought-seed. What springs from it is subject to destruction
but the seed itself is indestructible. Lord Krishna says in the
Bhagavad Gita, 'I am the seed-bearing Father,' and 'I am the
Kutastha — the imperishable One.' From this changeless,
ever-present verity springs creation. Brahma, the creator, and
Sarasvati, his consort, preside over that. From them comes fire
and other elements. The essential Intelligence which is permanent is planted in the creation by them. It is the essential
thing. What exists before the creation appears and remains
after the creation is gone is this pure Intelligence, the pristine
state of Knowing. Thus, I say, the seed, the subtle Essence, is
most powerful."*

The last coals of the fire had long since faded away. All that
was left was ash. Having fallen to sleep for a few hours, the
Avadhut awoke at first light and arose to attend his meditation in
the temple. Noticing the fire was extinguished, he brought his
hands together in salute:

"I take thee, fire, as one of my great teachers. You teach multiple lessons. You are compassion, you are purification, you are
Grace. Strength and detachment are also reflected in you. Finally,
you reveal what is subtle by dissolving all that is material.
Reverent salutations unto thee."

Standing up at full length, the Avadhut stuck his hands in the
fire pit and smeared ash all over his body. Then, he turned and
walked towards the distant temple to offer his obeisances to the
Universal Mother and meditate upon Her constant and abiding
Reality. Later, with the sun still rising in the east, he returned with
more fuel and several hot coals to kindle a new fire and with it,
many wonderful teachings.

# Chapter 14

# Teachings on Attachment to the World

THE FOURTEENTH GURU — *The Pigeon*

THE LESSON — *Nonattachment*

*The pigeon was my teacher as well, O Prince,
and from it and its family I learned of the
dangers of attachment to transitory existence. The
poor pigeon family became slaves to the fowler,
snared in his net and caught unawares as they
sported amongst the pleasures of life. Similarly,
falling into a complacent mode with regards to
spiritual life and becoming preoccupied with worldly
activities, relationships and monetary concerns only,
beings run the risk of losing their center and balance
through inadvertent clinging to relativity. Thus, the
precious tool of nonattachment is of great importance
in both worldly and spiritual life.*

Gradually descending from the Himalayan heights after several
wonderful weeks of blissful worship at Bhadranath and other holy
places, the Avadhut came upon a beautiful meadow dotted here
and there by groves of trees. A stream of cold mountain water,
runoff from the Himalayan snows, fed the meadow on one side

while a small lake sheltered it on the east. An idyllic scene, it was covering the foothills of the hoary mountains like some unique hand-woven carpet. Ekanta stood and stared in wonder.

Birds of all sizes and colors inhabited the glade and a few friendly deer were seen peeking out of the shaded forest in curiosity at the newcomer's presence. As it was just dawn, the sun was shedding first light over the area and a few frogs about the lake were still singing in rhythm to nature's life-breath. Crickets were emanating a pulsating hum through the fresh morning air.

Below, on the plains, smoke was rising from early morning fires, prepared in stone and mud hearths within small huts of thatched cane and wood. The Avadhut took his seat to gaze in awe at God's pervasive presence as it spread itself out across the earth for miles in all directions. From this vantage point, he could watch the Lord awaken and observe as He rolled His apparently fragmented bits of human consciousness out of bed to begin the day. What mischief these particles of conscious light would get into this day remained to be seen, but one thing was certain. One undivided, eternal Being would see through all eyes, act through all bodies and think through all minds. A few would be conscious of this, the rest would not. Ekanta, in turn, would watch the watcher, for his great delight and preoccupation in life was to partake of the mood of the nondual witness of all phenomena and thereby learn valuable lessons.

Again, his mind turned to the problem of individuation. He could never stop thinking about this tendency in the human being. Following this trend in human awareness, whole civilizations lived and died in ignorance, never knowing the secret of the universe or what it represented. What an amazing facade the Mother had dreamed up! Here was life, generally considered by all to be a great gift from the Creator, a blessing to be utilized fully in light and love, yet partaking of it caused beings to assume the most banal and petty intentions unworthy of the noble Spirit within them. The width, breadth and depth of existence was thus left unfathomed, its physical proportions as well as its spiritual significance unknown. What was it that forced human beings into such narrow preoccupation with relativity? As he wondered thus, his mind recalled the words of his illumined teachers from days gone by. He again reflected upon their admonitions against attachment.

*"Dear boy,"* said his revered Mataji one evening, as he was plac-ing wood on the fire to cook their meager repast, *"the insidious nature of selfish clinging has worked its way into the vitals of human beings and is gnawing on their very bones, yet they know it not and remain unaware. It will not do to blame Maya for this tendency, or pass it onto the Divine Mother of the Universe out of ignorance. She did not intend for us to spend our days pursuing paltry possessions and coveting the petty pleasures that they bring. Such an idea is distasteful to Her."*

"I agree, Revered Mother," answered Ekanta. "This kind of pre-occupation is even boring to the likes of me. It must, then, be extremely disappointing to Her."

After a few moments of thoughtful silence, Ekanta posed a ques-tion.

"What is the way, then, Mataji? Why do beings continue in this folly and how may they be freed from this mundane habit?"

*"Would that it could be so easy to explain and follow, dear one,"* replied the teacher. *"There is no doubt that the Universal Mother gets some of Her work done through ignorant beings and that She covers and distorts Reality in order to preserve certain plans that She desires to unveil in the future. Still, She loves a struggle and She looks with favor upon those who fight to shat-ter limitations and see beyond relativity. Otherwise, why should She pit opposites against each other and join the fray? Where great battles that involve sacrifice, victory and surrender occur, there the awesome Mother dances and rejoices."*

Ekanta had drawn back a little to see the expression of inten-sity which had suddenly overshadowed his guru's face. Moods like this often came upon her and the boy was always aware of an extraordinary presence that entered her at these times. He never quite got used to it, though, and usually waited silently for her to break the powerful mood and speak.

This she did in due time, saying softly, *"Her presence spells death for all types of attachment. This is why the truly illu-mined, who want nothing less than Truth, Freedom and Grace, keep company with Her in their hearts."*

"Mataji," asked Ekanta, "what is the nature of attachment and where does it spring from?"

"It is the nature of narrowness born of fear," she answered. "It exists due to desire married to an unhealthy sense of insecurity. It thrives in egotism, the sense of separation from all that is naturally complete and full. It is fostered by repeated negative actions accomplished in error within the atmosphere of fragmented awareness. It recurs by the power of samskaras, seed impressions planted and nurtured in the mind over interminable periods of time." Saying this, the guru lapsed into deep silence.

After a time, Ekanta broke the silence.

"Revered Mother, from what you say, it seems as if this powerful bondage called attachment is impossible to rid ourselves of."

"My boy," returned the guru, "this is what weak minds think. Most beings fall into a complacent mode such as this, a kind of chasm that divides their understanding. They then lapse into the sleep of ignorance for lifetimes. I have spent my life in the company of the holy, who are like so many fires burning brightly and unceasingly amidst the darkness of this world. In their presence, I have warmed myself and learned to light my own flame of inner realization. I have awakened like fragrant spring from brooding winter. Knowing the bliss of this condition, I now strive to stir others from the pathetic state of worldliness and torpor."

Another silence followed these words. In due time, the Mataji graciously continued:

"A monkey clings fearfully to its mother. A kitten allows itself to be placed here and there but cries out for its mother from each location. A young bird, however, is pushed from its pleasant nest and learns to fly on its own wings and seek its own nourishment. Likewise, beings must raise themselves to a higher status and leave off this insipid preoccupation with possessions and pleasantries, with amorous pastimes and idle chatter. For instance, there is nothing so distasteful as to see a full-grown man clinging to his elderly mother. Both cling, one out of selfishness, the other out of fear. Fie on this loathsome predicament.

"Do you know what is sacrificed due to attachment, dear boy?" continued the guru. "Freedom! None knows the exhilarating bliss that proceeds from freedom, nor the deep and penetrating *peace of mind that manifests from it as well. Once, hearing me talk about renunciation of the world and the joy of transcendence, a woman said to me, 'But Mataji, I am perfectly happy here in the body. I feel at home in the world and want nothing else.' My response was quick and forthcoming. I simply said, 'That will pass.' These three words changed her in an instant. Her sudden grave demeanor gave her away. Evidently, she had experienced troubles before in life and they had left their mark on her. My direct statement brought it all back to her."*

After a pause, Ekanta's remarkable female guru continued to teach him.

*"You see, beings tend to forget their troubles when the mind is in a good mood, when a sattvic cycle is underway. Then, all that they recall is the happy times and pleasant experiences. The horror and pain of negative experiences recede quickly into the recesses of the mind. Instead of seeking pleasure and shunning pain, one should go beyond them both! It is only when one is free from attachments that life reflects what is ultimately good, what is spiritual, what is noble and uplifting. Otherwise, it is all bondage and delusion in so many forms.*

*"There are also teachers, gurus, who foster this deluded attitude in their students, Ekanta. They paint a pretty picture, describing life as a bed of roses without the thorns. Even spiritual practice is defined by them in these terms. This gives a wrong impression, my dear. Such so-called gurus outline the goal as being a life of leisure where others serve one's every need. This is slavery to name and form, both as nature and as human ego. Service for others is different than slavery to others. True service is powerful, sometimes intimidatingly so. It breaks through all such bondage of the mind. It gives what is freeing, not what is binding and it does so in an uncompromising fashion that does not so much consider feelings and fine sentiments but rather cuts to the core of all problems."*

Gazing at her charge with a look full of love and intensity, the Mataji continued.

*"You know, Ekanta, your Babaji and I have never coddled you or given you teachings watered down with weak sentiment of this type. We do not pander to that part of human nature which views life as an indefinite vacation in the sun. Gales and rain*

*clouds come uninvited and without warning across the sky of human awareness. What tools have we to deal with them if we are ill prepared for the storm? We must learn to not only survive such intensities, but also be able to live in the midst of these mental and physical hurricanes in total mastery over the various elements at play there. What is more, Ekanta, we should develop the ability to glean and comprehend the powerful lessons from these experiences, for mastery consists of this."*

Ekanta had never forgotten the Mataji's precious teachings on attachment and the no-nonsense approach she always took towards that and other barriers to living a divine life. As he sat thinking about the remarkable teachers he had been blessed with, a movement in the trees caught his attention. Another human being was present. As he looked closer, Ekanta saw a middle-aged man walking slowly and carefully amidst the shadows of the trees. He appeared to be outfitted with several nets and other accoutrements. In a flash, Ekanta realized that he was a bird catcher, out to capture a few of the wonderful specimens that frequented these groves in the early morning. With interest, the Avadhut looked on, waiting to see what the man would do next.

Soon, it became apparent that the fowler had his eyes on something. Ekanta quietly drew closer by walking around the edge of the hill on which he sat, remaining cautious lest he spoil the man's search. From a closer vantage point, he saw what the fowler was interested in. High up in a tree, several branches above the ground, some young pigeons were playing and flitting about, eating insects and calling out to each other but oblivious to the presence of imminent danger below. This easy prey was obviously what the fowler had been attracted to. Besides that, the male and female pigeon were nowhere to be seen, which made the young ones, who were not yet used to being cautious of humans, perfect targets. Quietly, the fowler unwrapped his net and made ready to cast.

With excellent aim speaking of much practice, the net hovered over the young pigeons and settled down in perfect position over the entire lot. As the young ones discovered their predicament and tried to fly to and fro, they only succeeded in trapping themselves further in the creases and folds of the net until each one was thoroughly bound in its meshes.

At this moment in time, from the recesses of the forest, another pigeon came on the scene. It was obviously the mother, for it was sorely distracted and flew by the net and its young ones several times, crying out in distress. In heedless fashion, it then plunged into the net, exerting its last strength to free its young and sacrificing its own freedom as a result.

The fowler, evidently pleased with the catch, started to make his way to the tree in order to climb its lower branches and reach the fruit of his work. Before he could set foot on the trunk of the tree, however, another pigeon was seen hovering over the net. The male pigeon had returned from gathering food in the forest and was now faced with the painful experience of seeing his family captured. Coming to perch on a nearby limb, it called to its mate, trying to get her to free herself before it was too late. Finally, in a last and futile effort, it too plunged towards the net to try and free the family and was thereby caught as well. The fowler, scarcely believing his luck, then climbed easily to the lower limbs of the tree and one by one, extracted the birds from the net, placing them in small wooden cages hanging from his belt. Then, with the capture complete and whistling a happy tune, he disappeared among the trees and headed down the slope towards the valley below.

The entire scene had taken only a few minutes. The Avadhut withdrew from the place of this little drama and resumed his seat on the edge of the hill overlooking the valley. Occasionally, he caught glimpses of the fowler as he appeared here and there on his winding course downwards. The birds would be sold in the marketplace, used for carriers and pets for children and maybe even eaten. The fate of these wild creatures played in Ekanta's mind, causing him to remember experiences out of the past that had affected him in a similar fashion.

"*You are young and free,*" came the words of his teacher one day, "*but can you remain that way?*"

"Why do you ask this question of me, dear teacher?" Ekanta had responded. "Do you see any danger of bondage in my future?"

"*You will soon be moving through the world on your own,*" replied the guru, "*this much I have come to know. I only wish to impress upon you that the training you have received, rare and given only to those whom God has chosen for a particular purpose, is being well utilized so that your life can reach its consummate fulfillment. Many others can also be benefited by seeing such an exemplary existence manifest before their eyes."*

"What else can you teach me so that I may always remain unfettered, revered sir?" asked the young man.

*"Have you ever seen the work of the fowler or the deer slayer, Ekanta?"* returned his preceptor. *"Clever is the movement of such beings and fatal the result for the unfortunate captives. The lesson of Maya and its insidious effects always comes to mind when I observe or hear of their exploits. Yet, Maya is more subtle than the dealings of these professional workers."*

"Why is this so?" Ekanta had asked curiously.

The elderly teacher leaned over and spoke almost in a whisper.

*"Because Maya binds by projecting a pervasive yet deceptive sense of well-being over the minds of human beings. The net or trap in this case is time and space, where beings rest comfortably amidst the allures of nature and become enamored of the many diversions that the world has to offer. Beings who become complacent about life and death and who take the world to be their home are in store for some unpleasant surprises."*

"Why should it be so, revered guru?" pleaded Ekanta. "Who has decreed this to be the case?"

*"The Universal Mother loves to sport in relativity,"* replied the teacher, *"and wants us to do the same evidently, but She does not want us to become attached to this physical world and She warns us in many ways if we forget. We are not born when the universe is created, Ekanta, nor are we actually present here throughout its interminable cycles. Having no birth, such as the appearance of the universe, we certainly do not experience death either. This is what the Advaita tells us and thank God for it too!"*

"This news is both wonderful and terrible, revered sir," stated Ekanta. "I need to hear more."

*"And so you shall, dear student,"* he said, *"both now and throughout your blessed lifetime and you shall repeat what I am about to say to others who are ready to listen as well. In this way, you and all that come into contact with you will be freed from the dangers of attachment to relative existence and will escape the fate of those who imagine themselves to be mere physical entities, trapped inexorably in the never-ending game of*

*universal projection.*

*"In earliest times, Ekanta, the Adipurusha, Sri Bhagavan, told us of the immortal nature of the Soul dwelling within us. He said that when the body is born, the Soul is not, and when the body comes and goes, the true Self within moves not. Interpenetrating everything, though completely free from all manifestation and its effects, the Atman, shining by Its own pure radiance, does not go to death, even when the universe expands or contracts in creation and destruction. Such is our nature, my son, that we, like our Beloved Lord, are indestructible. Many a saint and sage has wept over this realization and, truly, this Truth is the very essence of what realization consists of."*

Here, the blessed and wonderful guru paused, waiting for a response or a question. When he received none, he smiled approvingly and continued with his discourse and transmission.

*"We are beginningless, Ekanta, like the sky. Do you ever see the sky begin or end? It just exists. Nonorigination, then, is the recourse of the wise and all that they have to fall back upon. Thus says Gaudapada, the great Advaitan."*

"How did he explain away such things as old age and death, dear teacher?" asked Ekanta.

*"He stated it thusly,"* answered the guru directly:

All entities are by nature free of old age and death,
but by brooding on old age and death,
they deviate from their nature by the thought of them.

*"You see, Ekanta, the mind is everything. In its recesses exist creation, the sense of time and space, the presence of causality, the thought of dissolution and many other moods and attitudes. Stilling it, quenching its wayward movements forever, the wise realize what is beyond it, which is also that which gives it existence. Thus, the Ajativada, the knower of birthless, deathless Reality, is free from doubt and dispute."*

"Ajativada, dear teacher, that is an intriguing expression."

*"Indeed,"* came the reply. *"I remember that my guru translated it as 'The way of the unborn.' It is the belief in nonevolution. Jati means birth, so ajati is, literally, no birth. This does not pertain only to the perfected soul who refrains from*

*taking on a body. It goes further and affirms that even when such a one appears in a body, he or she is not truly born. Perplexing as it sounds at first, it is liberating and beautiful to contemplate. It can be understood better through analogies and metaphors. Take the sun, for instance. It projects its rays, but they are merely extensions of it. Though they appear and disappear, project and withdraw, this affects the sun not at all. In the same way, though bodies may appear and disappear, the Atman remains the same and the illumined one has realized this. They say, 'The Atman is without birth and death and I am That, so where and what is this body?' Of course, I am taking a few liberties here around Ajativada by talking about projection and so forth. In truth, projection and withdrawal are illusions. The nondual Advaita does not admit them. To go deeper, and this defies description and transcends logic, the Advaitic perspective sees both existence and nonexistence as another set of dualities. There can be no duality in That which is ever unified, always One."*

"What about the Lord in human form, dear guru?" asked Ekanta. "Is He also ultimately nonexistent? Is His appearance illusory, being that He has no birth in time?"

*"Why, dear student, Bhagavan Himself proclaims Himself to be unborn,"* replied the guru, *"and so puts an end to the matter. Unborn, however, does not mean nonexistent. It signifies what is eternal. It refers to what is truly existing at all times and what is beyond time as well. What is real is always and forever real, but what is fictional never really exists in the first place. A son of a barren woman, for instance, is only an illogical assumption, presented in sentence form. In actuality, such a being is an impossibility."*

"Revered sir," replied Ekanta, "speaking in terms of human attachments then — the object, the possessor of the object and the sense of ownership — are these all unreal?"

*"Ultimately, they are all unreal,"* stated the guru, *"in as much as they are all passing phenomena. Once, Sri Ram and Lakshmana were passing across land and came to the ocean. Since they were on their way to Sri Lanka to rescue Sita and the ocean barred their way, Lakshmana became angry and threatened to kill the god of the ocean unless he removed the*

*ocean from their path. Taking out his bow, he was about to shoot at the god of the ocean when Rama said, 'Peace, my brother. Your actions and words betray you. The ocean, your body and the god of the sea, all these are unreal. So too is your bow and your anger unreal. You cannot destroy that which is unreal by means of other unreal things.' Therefore, Ekanta, the wise are equal-minded and calm under all circumstances. Even their anger is calm, though it bears extraordinary power."*

"What of family life then?" Ekanta had asked. "Are those who enjoy life in the world deceiving themselves and endangering their existence due to attachments to family, children and friends?"

*"Not if they have renounced the world, my son,"* came the firm reply. *"Then, such preoccupations cannot harm them."*

"Dear sir," returned an amazed Ekanta, "I thought only monastics renounced the world. Are householders and those involved with relative existence also renunciates?"

*"If they are wise they are,"* the guru responded with certainty.

The Avadhut suddenly relived a taste of the same power of realization that had come upon him after hearing these words so long ago. With extreme clarity, he remembered his feelings and the conversation as if it were yesterday.

"Yes, of course," he had replied to his teacher, "you and Mataji have never taken formal vows of monasticism, yet you certainly epitomize all that is best in renunciation."

*"There you have it precisely,"* answered the blessed teacher. *"Formal vows are only for those who feel the need for them, either through preference, as a way of life or because they have something important to learn from them. Others need not take that course."*

After a short time the guru continued.

*"All should renounce the world, dear boy. They should give it up entirely. What does this mean? What does it entail? Desires and attachments mount up and breed more of the same. This is the nature of relative existence, of life in a physical body lived under the control of the senses. Observing this and taking note of the way this hampers spiritual freedom, one should take steps to give up every tendency of the mind and senses to grasp after things ephemeral. Only then will peace come to the mind and only then will true happiness prevail, for if one is bound by*

*anything external there will always exist the danger of entrap-*
*ment. True freedom cannot brook attachment to anything."*

As these words sunk into the Avadhut's awareness once again
after so much time had elapsed, he thought of the pigeons and how
they had met with disaster, their tiny and precariously balanced
world turned upside down by unexpected disaster. The guru's discourse on the ills of attachment and the efficacy of renunciation
continued in his mind's memory.

*"There is no happiness in this world, Ekanta. One should*
*understand this clearly and put all doubt to rest on that score.*
*Let no tendril of expectation for satisfaction in this world per-*
*sist in the mind. It will only bring disappointment and sorrow,*
*if not now, then in the future. Transcend all commerce with*
*the wheel of birth and death in bondage to nature and the*
*senses with firm resolve. Attaining freedom from all doubt and*
*attachment to the universe, then you may go about as both the*
*liberated and the liberator. Sri Ram, the very heart and soul of*
*India, put it this way to His brother, Lakshmana:"*

Observe the attachments of men and women, dear brother.
Fathers, mothers, children, wives and husbands —
their existence is as momentary
as the contact of pieces of wood floating down a river.
Fortune is as fickle as the position of your shadow
Youth slips by like a wave in a small pool of water.
Sense pleasures sap our vitality and become insipid as well.
Yet all beings run after these things!
Life is evanescent—like a dream castle in the air.
Death mars existence and strikes all to the quick.
Time rolls inexorably on as life-force leaks out of the body
like water from an unbaked pot.
Old age and disease attack at every juncture.
The body, another name for worms, dirt, and ashes,
eventually deteriorates and becomes despicable.
Yet, clothed within such a structure, a man thinks he is king
Attachment to the body causes one to think of it as the Self.
But how can the weak and destructible body ever be identified
with the all-powerful, immortal Atman, beloved one!
Reason well about this in your mind.

"Blessed guru," Ekanta replied. "This teaching is wonderful."

"*Of course it is, dear one,*" came the reply. "*Consider the source — Sri Ram.*"

After a short time had passed when both teacher and student pondered the teaching, Ekanta asked, "Is it possible then that even those who are involved in the business and duties of the world can live free and unencumbered while so conditioned?"

"*It is not only possible, my son,*" stated the preceptor, "*it is absolutely necessary. All those who have not accomplished this mental renunciation and who still operate in the world run a great risk of being bound into lifetimes of delusion. Attachment is insidious. It only conduces to more of itself. Own nothing, Ekanta, with mind, with hands or with heart. Covet no desire for future accumulation and do not regret the loss of anything in the present or in the past. Know that by all so-called loss, the Universal Mother is freeing you from so many chains. Be free, be naturally happy and rejoice forevermore in the bliss of your perfect nature!*"

The Avadhut was again soaring high in that very same blissful nature by the time he had finished recalling these thrilling words of his preceptor. He had, indeed, taken this advice to heart and had simply wandered the world, encumbered by nothing and with no ties. The joy of such an existence, which seemed austere and unimaginable to others, was indescribable. Freedom from the very attachments that others deemed acceptable and covetable was the way of the Avadhut.

Once, as he was traveling India's larger cities, he had come across a suspension bridge spanning a mighty river, linking one side of the metropolis to the other. It was magnificent and had hundreds of smaller chains fastened to the two mighty suspension cables that were holding it up, a few of which had broken and were hanging down here and there. As he reached the middle of the extremely long bridge, he paused to look down into the waters of the river far below. While gazing at the sight, a voice came to him from nearby.

"*This bridge speaks to us of worldly life.*"

Looking down, Ekanta saw a wizened old woman, stooped low amidst a few vegetables that she was selling on one side of the bridge. Squatting down near her, he purchased a couple of bananas and began to eat them.

"How is it that this bridge reminds you of worldly existence, Ma?" asked the Avadhut.

*"There are so many ties binding the worldly-minded down to terrestrial existence,"* came the answer. *"Even if a well-intentioned person desires for release from this kind of slavery, which occurs at a particularly rare moment in time, and takes the pains to free himself from the more noticeable ropes of attachment to worldly objects and relationships, still, there are many unseen bonds that continue to fasten him."*

"How does the bridge illustrate this, elderly mother?" asked Ekanta.

Looking up, the old woman answered:

*"Do you see all of those small chains which tie into the main supports of this bridge? Those represent the thousand and one attachments that trap the sojourning soul in this world of petty concerns, causing him or her to forget Truth-essence, their very nature. Just as these chains keep the bridge from falling down and allow endless activity to take place on its surface, so too do the invisible ties which bind perpetuate human work and toil and the misery it brings in its train."*

After a pause, as both were gazing up at the heights, the old woman continued.

*"Did you notice those few chains that have snapped and are hanging loose, my son? Those represent the few victories that man, in this life, has been able to achieve over things which enslave his consciousness. Things such as the giving up of immoral living and the chewing of betel nut and so forth. So much pride accrues in the minds of those who attain these small triumphs that they consider themselves to be reborn, to be new people. In fact, they have so many attachments left to break for, like this bridge, there are many chains left connected. No, the bridge of karmic bondage will not fall so easily!"*

The Avadhut sat for several minutes, marveling over the uniqueness of this teaching. Coming back to awareness of his immediate surroundings, he looked over to see the old woman but to his surprise found a young girl sitting in her place.

"Where has the elderly grandmother gone?" he asked the little girl.

The young one only pointed her finger into the distance, aimed at several possible locations. If Ekanta had trusted her sense of direction, he would have had to believe that the woman jumped off the bridge and into the river. As he made ready to leave, he gave the girl a few pice. Her smile, as devoid of teeth as the elderly woman, reminded him of her. Crossing the bridge and coming to the other side, he could not help being amazed at finding these refined teachings in such unexpected places.

The fowler had long since disappeared into the regions below. With him, he had the pigeon family, resigned to whatever fate that was in store for them. Perhaps the hand of grace would play a role and freedom would once again come their way. In the case of the pigeons, they would just return to their old life again. This was also the case with worldly people as well. After escaping the hand of death and destruction through the grace of a higher power, they would simply revert to old habits again and forget both their tragedy and their good fortune. It reminded him of a story that his father had told him one day.

"Once, Ekanta, there was a great archer from the country who joined the army of a powerful king. This archer practiced his art every day and never missed an opportunity to perfect his skills. Housed in military barracks in the city, however, he could find no place to fire his arrows for, unlike the country forests, there were no trees nearby onto which to nail his favorite target. One day, with a metal nail and a hammer, he was trying, with little success, to make an indention in the stone wall in the courtyard behind the barracks. A voice from behind caused him to stop.

"'It is more difficult to teach worldly people spiritual truths than it is to pound a nail into a stone wall.'

"Turning around, he found a wizened old sage with a staff looking on.

"'I am certainly learning the difficulty of the latter,' responded the archer, 'but I suppose that you may know about the former.'

"'Yes,' replied the sage. 'Going about through this city, where none are willing to pay heed, I have come upon you attempting the impossible. It reminds me of my own hard task. May we both find solutions to our respective problems and be free. What is more, may we never have to repeat futile actions again.'

"Saying this, the sage turned and was gone."

"Father," Ekanta had asked after the story's conclusion, "the story reminds me of deluded action and renunciation. I think about these two every day. I wonder where my own destiny will lead. I certainly want to realize the highest goal."

"I have no doubt that you will some day," replied his father with a smile, "for you are perfectly suited for spiritual life. Will you renounce the world, then, leaving your poor mother and I to take care of ourselves in our old age?"

"Yes," said Ekanta cheerfully, "as soon as I am able."

"That would be well, my son, and nothing would please us more than to know that you were free from the drudgery of life and helping suffering humanity along this ultimate course of action."

"Father," asked Ekanta, as the two stood looking off across the fields, "your story has reminded me of a question I have. Why is it that people do not learn from their painful lessons? Why do they not change? They always repeat the same actions that caused them to suffer in the first place. This happens in spite of the presence of teacher and teachings. None, it seems, will take recourse to these aids and attempt to change their detrimental habits."

"It is true, Ekanta," replied his father, "and no one can explain it. Yet, there are teachings even for this. Take the pigeon as an example. You can go on feeding it with peas and kernels of corn for hours. It gobbles them up and you think it has taken them into its stomach and digested them. Later though, you take the bird in your lap and handle it. It is then that you find that all those kernels have gone into its crop and are merely sitting there, undigested. It is the same with worldly people and the spiritual teachings given to them in the company of the holy. They appear to take in these lessons and act very piously while they are in holy company, but the result of the transmission goes only so deep, remains on the surface or in their crop, as it were. As soon as they get away from guru and sangha, they revert back to their old selves again, doing all the same things that they always did. Worldly people are simply unable to digest and act on spiritual teachings."

Yogindra Yogi had also instructed Ekanta on the ignorance of the worldly-minded.

"*You cannot penetrate the tough hide of a crocodile with a sword, my boy,*" he said one day, as they walked the high mountain passes together. *"The consciousness of ignorant and worldly people is thick like that. They are impervious to higher reason and even antagonistic towards spirituality. If you take them out of their pleasant confines and away from their attachments and place them at the feet of the guru in an ashram setting, they will cry out as if being tortured. It is like taking a worm out of filth and placing it in the purest rice. It will only die there."*

Reaching the floor of the high mountain pass, the yogi stopped to catch his breath.

*"Let us stop to rest here,"* he said, breathing hard in the thin oxygen of the mountain air. *"I am not the traveler I used to be."*

"Yogiji," responded the young man, "I am amazed that someone of your age is so mobile and strong. A worldly-minded person would not be able to attain a small fraction of what you have accomplished in this life. Tell me again what it was that caused you to renounce the world at such a relatively young age. I never tire of hearing it."

*"Oh, you have heard that story enough times, my son,"* replied the yogi. *"What I have not described in full to you is the great distaste for the world that arose in me on that occasion — an aversion that entirely took me over for months after. If I had been capable of it, I would have thought it to be hatred, but it was something less negative and much more healthy."*

"What could that be, revered sir?"

The yogi was silent for awhile. The two sat there, perched on the hard, cold stones like a couple of brooding vultures, high in the mountains amidst the early snows of encroaching winter. There were no souls around for hours in any direction and the biting winds of winter were already beginning to cast a cloak of chill across the higher elevations.

Ekanta loved this austere life, and the yogi welcomed such company, such acceptance of the stark realities of life in a young man. The two were really a pair from out of the ancient Vedic past, rare souls inhabiting a world of dying aspirations and hollow dreams — a world where most of its members had forgotten entirely the purpose for human existence and the Blessed One that gave them life.

*"My choice was based upon Truth rather than pleasure or*

intellectual refinement," the yogi finally stated. *"I can compare Truth to a substance of infinite power, an incredibly corrosive substance which eats through everything — through soft material quickly, through hard granite gradually but assuredly. The world of human convention, with its many shades of ignorance and deception, was not for me, my son. I simply could not make myself accommodating to every black falsehood that existed around me. I renounced it completely and I have since suffered for it all my life, but it is a type of suffering much preferable to that misery and deceit which inhabits the hearts and minds of worldly men and women."*

More silence followed these words as the old yogi and the young renunciate watched the quiet wind whip up little miniature tornadoes of snow about their feet. After a time, the yogi continued.

*"Here's a fine confession, my son, which I never told anyone, especially the companions of my early days of wandering and asceticism. Several times, I tried to return to the world when, driven by difficult circumstances such as illness and hardship, I thought I could not last in the wilderness. Upon entering the towns and villages, however, and seeing the ways of humanity, such an aversion seized me as to drive me almost screaming from the precincts of the worldly-minded. The Lord is great, Ekanta. He would not allow me to become a hypocrite. One cannot swallow the spittle spat out on the ground only yesterday."*

Ekanta sat spellbound to hear the admissions of the old holy man. Hardly stirring for fear of breaking the spell which had caused the yogi to pour out his heart in such a fashion, he remained still, waiting for more words to come from his revered and elderly teacher of renunciation. He had not long to wait.

*"So, Ekanta, I could not but be true to myself. What was inside had to emerge and the truth is that I hate this world, this dream, this horrible nightmare, with its judges and chicaneries, its spooks and blackguardisms, with its fair faces and false hearts, with its howling righteousness on the surface and its utter hollowness underneath and, above all, its sanctified shopkeeping. Indeed, to measure my soul according to what the bond slaves of this world say? They do not know the sannyasin! He stands on the head of the Vedas, say the Vedas, because he is free from churches, sects, religions and other things of that ilk.*

*No, Ekanta, in the end I could pay allegiance neither to the vain
and vexing pursuits of the worldly-minded nor the pompous
priests and the soothsayers of society with their blood-encrust-
ed holy books. Freedom, purchased even at the cost of health of
the body and loneliness of the spirit, was far more satisfying
and fulfilling. All the rest leads only to attachment, the enemy
of liberation. So, beware holy man!"*

The Avadhut gazed out over the valley below. Silently, he
began to examine his memory for teachings about attachment
contained in the sacred scriptures. Like clockwork, they began
to emerge while he relished them like savory food. Like clear,
sweet water from an enchanted mountain brook, the words of Sri
Krishna came into his mind, and they never failed to bring peace,
joy and inspiration.

> The fortunate and wise one delights in the bliss of the Self
> only after detaching from external objects, beloved one.
> Then, he easily gets into meditation on Brahman.
> For know this, Arjuna, attachment invites suffering.
> The wise withdraw from such poison.
> That one who succeeds in overcoming desire
> while occupying the body,
> that one attains peace eternal and happiness everlasting.

This detachment, Ekanta knew, was only the beginning of the
process. It was necessary to remove nonessentials in order to
get to what was truly desirable, like removing the uppermost
books from a stack so as to be able to get at the desired book on
the bottom of the stack. It was more a matter of practicality
than of fear of suffering, escape from the world or following the
moral rule. When withdrawal from objects, pleasures and habitual rounds of desires was finally accomplished and the mind was
once again master of its domain and focused on the Self, on
Reality, then truly spiritual life began.

Ekanta thought back on his travels of earlier years. On one
occasion, he had traveled extensively through Tibet and China and
had taken the opportunity to acquaint himself with the ancient and
venerable teachings of the Tao. The straightforward yet graceful
way in which the important messages of renunciation and free-

dom from attachments were woven gracefully into the Taoist teachings had impressed him favorably.

One day, as he was attending an outdoor class given by a Taoist master, mention was made of chen-jen, a teaching given by the great Chuang-tzu, a contemporary of Lao-tzu. Ekanta perked up to hear about the chen-jen, described as a true human being, reminiscent of the pure soul described in Vedantic writings. After the discourse, the Avadhut approached the preceptor and asked for more information. The Taoist teacher, looking him in the eye and obviously impressed by his presence, proceeded to recite some excerpts from an ancient text. A wonderful picture emerged and it was one that lived with Ekanta always and one that he never forgot:

> The chen-jen are simply true human beings.
> They are free from the calculating mind.
> They never work or act to procure results.
> Such beings never plan for the future.
> Failing, they have no cause for regret,
> succeeding, no need for compliment.
> The chen-jen are simply true human beings.
>
> The Tao wisdom is mature in such as these.
> They sleep without dreams, awake free of anxiety.
> They have no discrimination about diet,
> are unaffected by heat or cold.
> They breathe from their innermost Self
> while others breathe from the throat.
> The chen-jen are simply true human beings.
>
> Chen-jen describes the true human beings of old.
> They love not life nor rejoice in birth.
> They shun not evil nor shirk from death.
> They appear quickly and vanish completely,
> but forget not from whence they sprang
> They cheerfully play their allotted parts,
> waiting patiently for the end.
> The chen-jen are simply true human beings.

> Chen-jen unite the heart with the Tao
> and seek not to supplicate the divine.
> Their minds are free, their demeanor grave,
> though they are cheerful of expression.
> In winter they are warm, in summer, cool.
> Their passions pass like seasons and none can see their limits.
> The chen-jen are simply true human beings.

After this recitation, the teacher remained silent for a time. Then he spoke:

*"Our holy scriptures, the T'ai-ping ching, the book of Supreme Peace, states that the chen-jen are higher than the immortal ones, falling just below the gods themselves. They are birthless, deathless, have access to all powers while being free of attachment to them. They are not full, nor are they empty."*

"Revered sir," replied the Avadhut, "I see many correlations in this description with the writings of the ancient Rishis and other eastern scriptures."

"Yes," stated the teacher. *"Though I am not well acquainted with the Indian philosophy, I know enough to be certain that what is being transmitted there is similar in approach and identical is essence. My teacher, humble salutations be to him always, was a scholar of different religious systems. He admired the Vedas and Upanishads greatly and taught us some of the truths contained in them. Are you well versed in them?"*

"Since my boyhood I have been trained in them," answered the Avadhut, "but there is an infinite expanse of wisdom there. One could contemplate it to the end of time."

*"That is the preoccupation of the wise,"* returned the Taoist monk. *"Talking to you and remembering my teacher makes me long for such wisdom, in whatever form it takes and from whatever open channel it flows. Can you recite something from your tradition for me now, if it is not too much trouble?"*

The Avadhut thought a moment. Then from his radiant mind, given completely the Universal Mother, came a description of the jivanmukta, the eternal Soul liberated under all conditions:

> For the liberated, all pastimes exist in the Self.
> With a steady mind, they look on everything evenly.

Their word bears the stamp of Truth, which reason dictates.
They are always satisfied by what is obtained naturally
in due course.

The living liberated roam the earth unencumbered.
They offer all – food, water and thoughts – to the gods.
What is leftover they take for the maintenance of the body.
They never store up goods or thoughts for the future.

The living liberated have their minds purified by devotion.
The one indivisible Self is the subject of their meditation.
The pursuit of knowledge reveals apparent bondage.
Freedom consists of sense-control and yearning for liberation.

The living liberated beg food from homes and hermitages.
Humble forest confines are their preferred place of refuge.
Wild grains picked from fields satisfy their mild hunger.
Water from brooks, streams and rivers assuage their thirst.

The living liberated are done with body, mind and speech.
The visible world, to them, is unreal, for it perishes.
Brahmajnana is their only obsession,
detachment their one possession.
The essence of life is their only etiquette,
their one observance.

The living liberated move here and there over vast expanses.
Though wise, they seem like a child to others.
Though muttering like an idiot,
they are nevertheless quite erudite.
Well versed in scripture, still they have no code of conduct.

The living liberated are not bound by scripture
nor antagonistic towards them.
They neither dispute, discuss, refrain or take sides.
They do not disturb the beliefs of others,
nor do they vex themselves.
They bear all insult but never vilify anyone.

402 The Pigeon

The living liberated cause no injury to the living.
They know for certain that one Self dwells in all bodies.
Ever steady, no controversy ever affects them.
They die not when the physical sheath drops away.

The living liberated clothe themselves with what they find.
They eat to sustain the body, for God dwells within it.
They wash, bathe and observe cleanliness to honor the Lord,
and God inhabits their bodies and is well pleased.

The living liberated perceive no distinctions, no differences,
though as long as body persists
they retain a semblance of them.
This they bear patiently, tempered by their own realization,
until they finally merge with Brahman, the Highest.

The living liberated learn from and attend upon a master.
They realize that work inevitably produces pain.
Desiring peace of mind, they inquire into religion,
and seek out a sage to learn self-control.

Before the living liberated awaken fully,
they serve the guru with loving care and devotion.
Their faith in said teacher is unwavering, impeccable.
They never cause trouble by carping or complaining.

Thus, the living liberated come unto Brahman,
worshipping the Lord as a privileged duty.
Knowing completely the presence of God in all beings.
Endowed with realization and full enlightenment.

The Avadhut came out of his blissful reverie. Most of the morning had passed and it was approaching noon. This glade, the lake and its creatures had all taught him well. Picking up his meager belongings, he began the steep descent into the populated valley below, just as the birdcatcher had done hours earlier. The Avadhut, however was without possessions, without plans, and with no thought for the morrow. Meditating upon his freedom, enjoying the subtle bliss in his heart and possessed of a calm and contented mind, he picked his way slowly and deliberately down the slopes, heading for the distant flatlands where his Blessed Lord and Divine Mother dwelt in so many wondrous forms.

# Chapter 15

# Teachings on Nondual Reality

THE FIFTEENTH GURU — The Sun

THE LESSON — Unity

*he knowledge of absolute Unity is the
quintessential element to the wise ones,
O Prince. I learned it more fully through the example
epitomized by the sun. Though many suns appear in
the ripples of the mountain lake, they are all mere
reflections. Overhead shines the reality, the one
eternal sun. Through this illustration, one can
surmise that the many spring from the one which is
undivided and impervious to separation despite
appearances. Thus came my lesson from the sun.*

In the south of India, in midsummer, the sun beat down relent-
lessly on the dry earth. The heat was so intense during this
period that from early afternoon until early evening, no one stirred
or exerted much energy, but instead kept to the shade or remained
indoors, out of reach of the sun's direct rays.

The Avadhut had traveled across the breadth of India once
again. No matter how many times he did so, he never failed to
find more teachings reflected in the world's multifaceted drama.

His wonder for and awe of divine expression through the universal display of phenomenal existence never diminished. As long as the Mahashakti kept him in an embodied condition, he thought, he would rejoice in Her external manifestation and sport with Her in wholehearted abandonment through the marvelous mechanism of the body/mind complex.

The Avadhut was no dry ascetic. He did not plunge into spiritual practice and gain realization merely to turn around and look disdainfully upon the creation from some transcendent plateau. His renunciation was complete, no doubt, for he harbored no hope or expectation that the world would give him ultimate satisfaction. His teachers had seen to that.

*"Pretenders, glibly reciting the pithy phrase, 'All is Brahman' from the Upanishads, Ekanta, betray themselves by actions that run counter to their words. Be like the discriminating black bee, my son. Light on the flower but do not sip its nectar. This means that you should live in the world but never fall victim to it by coveting or desiring its many allurements. Your joy and fulfillment must consist of witnessing Mother's drama and of participating in a detached fashion. Never take to earthly ways in the manner that worldly people do. That is a type of spiritual suicide."*

With all of his detachment, Ekanta had never fallen prey to callousness or condescension the way many monastics did. His was not a withdrawal predicated on aversion or denial. Even in his discriminatory phase, he had retained his acceptance of everything as Brahman while finding and eliminating those illusory aspects that had no validity, no real existence. Appearances had never fooled him. Neither had negativities plunged him into depression or fear. Hand-in-hand with Reality, everything good and bad figured into the formula. Deliberately seeking out the phantoms and destroying them by the light of understanding, he had learned to perceive the Divine Being, undivided and eternal, sporting behind and inside of every portion and particle of existence. Thus he had drawn his own conclusions based upon experience.

Like the ancient Rishis, he realized that all is indeed Brahman. Like them, as well, he knew that Brahman had eternal and non-eternal parts, so to speak. Whereas some looked upon these two aspects as the real and the unreal, the Avadhut decided that they were the abiding Real and the transitory Real. The essence, the abiding Real, was supreme, no doubt — nameless and formless, unmanifest and absolute — but even the universe and its passing phases and the names and forms that inhabited it were real, since they sprang from Ultimate Reality itself. Thus he accepted Brahman and Shakti both, seeing Them as two modes of one all-pervasive, perpetual existence. Maya, he accepted as God's inscrutable power. Even personal delusion, that which Shankaracharya had called mithya, had its place. It was the Universal Mother who kept this covering in living beings until they either tired of it and struggled to be free of it, or She lifted it to show them the Reality within them.

The sun's heat was ferocious. Even the lizard sitting in the shadow of a nearby rock had not moved for over an hour. Extreme hot and cold, however, posed no problem for the Avadhut and were no match for his powers of forbearance and transcendence. From his storehouse of memories came the words of his vanaprastin teachers:

*"Uparati and titiksha, dear boy, these are the sadhu's powerful allies, while sama and dama are his best friends."*

"These are four of the six treasures, revered guru," Ekanta had responded eagerly, recognizing these attributes from his recent studies.

*"Yes, Ekanta, it is true,"* responded the guru. *"What are the other two?"*

The young boy had quickly searched his memory but, being under pressure, had failed to call up the remaining qualities listed in Vedanta sadhana.

*"Samadhana is one,"* his guru finally said, *"and shraddha is the other. These two — unique concentration and adamant faith — are the sadhu's pipeline to bliss, truth and freedom for, through them, a taste of liberation is experienced."*

"That is my favorite, called mumukshutvam," Ekanta asserted.

*"Correct,"* replied the teacher, *"and once having obtained the likes of these sterling qualities, both life and human nature will be duly transformed forever. But let us return to uparati and titiksha — self-settledness and forbearance. Can you remain immersed in ice-cold water all night or sit under the hot summer sun in south India all afternoon without flinching?"*

"I have never tried, revered sir," answered Ekanta. "Can you do these things?"

*"I can and I have,"* came the response. *"And you too will have to experience these in one way or another. I have no doubt that you will bear it all cheerfully and emerge triumphant."*

Ekanta had doubted these words of assurance coming from his preceptor, but later in his life he had encountered severe weather situations and had borne them easily due to his mind's capacity for detachment and transcendence. The highest Himalayan heights accompanied by the coldest evening wind, as well as the hot desert sun in summer had posed no great problem for him. Thus had he mastered the elements.

The mind and senses, however, posed a greater challenge and had turned out to be considerably more problematic. All aspirants and every adept that he met along the way agreed on this point. The mind, in which such ideas as wind, heat, cold, thirst and so forth had originally arisen in the first place, was a storehouse of potential trouble. Mastering that, controlling its penchant for all manner of diversions and aversions, was considered to be the supreme attainment. Coming to know this, the Avadhut then devoted his entire existence to this end. Now, at a relatively young age, though having lost track of how old he was, he felt completely contented and at home with his mind. All was Peace, Peace, Peace within him. Ruminating on this with gratitude, the Avadhut rose to continue on his way.

*"Purnoham, Purnoham!"*

These words found the Avadhut's ears late that afternoon as he wended his way over the flatlands towards the next watering hole or village. Following the sound of this oft-repeated phrase, he came upon an old man lying in a shallow indention in the earth, surrounded by a circle of four fires. The Avadhut was surprised to see this, but immediately recognized the Panchatapa ritual, the austerity of five fires, being enacted before his very gaze. At one stage of spiritual discipline, Ekanta knew, and in order to master one's fear and rise above weaknesses associated with suffering and discomfort, the sadhu builds four fires around himself and sits in the middle of them all day with the sun, the fifth fire, beating down upon him from above. As the Avadhut looked on, the old one spoke.

*"Come join me, young man,"* croaked the withered figure lying in the dirt. *"It is nice and warm here. The temperature is just right."*

Ekanta laughed in spite of himself and the old sadhu cackled along with him in unbridled glee.

"I am sorry to laugh," stated the Avadhut, "but you have caught me off guard."

*"Always expect the unexpected,"* came the reply. *"You of all people should know that."*

The Avadhut was intrigued again, this time by the enigmatic statement and, always alert for signs of mystery-mongering which occurred quite often among the company of certain types of ascetics, he confronted the sadhu.

"Do you know me then, sir?"

*"Only rarely have I seen your kind,"* answered the old one, *"but even so I could never forget you. Your very aura and atmosphere precedes and announces you. The question is, why have you come to this spot, illumined one?"*

Ignoring the man's reference to his spiritual state, Ekanta replied, "I heard your mantra ringing in my ears, even from a distance."

*"Oh that,"* came the old man's admittance. *"I seem to have acquired a powerful voice through the practice of certain austerities, though I never use it in public. They would make a circus exhibit out of me if I did. Could you see me spending my last days on display at the marketplace in front of gaping townspeople and curious children? I prefer to end it all here, in the warmth and radiance of my friends, the five fires."*

"My teachers performed this austerity," stated Ekanta, "and so I am familiar with it. I have never practiced it though."

*"Well,"* replied the old one, *"here is your chance. I am about through, having spent all day at this spot. There is still more wood leftover and I can act as your guide. Will you comply?"*

The Avadhut had been through his austerity phase in the past and did not relish such extreme practices anymore. Neither did he need them, but something about the way he was drawn to this spot, the old man's bearing and voice and, most importantly, his own inner prompting, caused him to reconsider. As he thought, the old man kept perfectly silent, and this too smacked of auspiciousness.

Finally, he said, "If you will instruct me and remain here until I have finished, I will undergo this practice for twelve hours, for I have never accomplished it and the Divine has guided me here at this point in time for a purpose. I feel the Mother's hand in this."

*"Done,"* replied the elderly sage. *"Now, you must help me up, for I am weak from hunger and loss of bodily liquids. We shall rest the night, eat and drink, and make ready for the sun's rising in the morning. Surya Narayan will be pleased to see another offering come first light!"*

Ekanta washed and fed the old man that night, giving him food and water from his own supply, for the old one had nothing. Ekanta suspected that if he had not come along, the old one would have given up the body. In fact, it seemed to have been in the plan, for no people, food or water were accessible for miles. The old sage would never had been able to survive a journey after his powerful austerity. Therefore, Ekanta surmised that it was all divinely planned. Now, he only wondered why the Mother had brought him here. It was certainly not to save him, for it was obvious that the old man's time for departure from the body was drawing near.

That night, as the sage rested, Ekanta sat under the desert stars and enjoyed the cool evening air. The night was dark, a new moon was upon them, and it was the Avadhut's favorite time of the monthly cycle. At this time, he could gaze deep into space, the surrounding darkness facilitating a glorious and mysterious view of the boundless universe stretching out on all sides. Shooting stars by the dozens streaked across the pitchy sky, an occasional one lighting up the entire area as it entered the earth's atmosphere in close proximity to his location. Such occurrences reminded him of spiritual illumination and the sense of indivisible Unity that accompanied them, for on more powerful occasions the mind got lit up in this fashion, momentarily catching a glimpse of its vast subtle interior expanse. As he ruminated on this rare experience, the words of his guru came to him in the night.

*"The sky of limited human awareness, as marvelous as it is, occasionally experiences a flash of God's infinity, Ekanta. At such times, all physical and phenomenal manifestation pale to insignificance. The eyes roll up in the head, the tongue cleaves*

*to the roof of the mouth, the body shakes and becomes immobile in turns, copious tears stream down the face uncontrollably and the fortunate recipient gazes inwardly into an inconceivable realm where all is an unbroken flow of pure Consciousness."*

Intrigued by this description, Ekanta, then a young boy, questioned his preceptor.

"How do these experiences come upon us, Mataji, and what are they like?" he had asked, full of curiosity.

*"There are many such experiences,"* stated the guru. *"One cannot easily categorize them, let alone describe what occurs. Words cannot convey what the mind cannot conceive of, dear boy, they being only an indicator of what lies beyond. Suffice to say that after five or more years of thorough sadhana have been carefully executed, this being the case for the dedicated seeker, sublime experiences begin to visit the mind. In order to recognize and fully assimilate what is happening, the presence of an authentic spiritual preceptor is necessary. This quickens the process and diminishes the chance that obstacles may thwart its progress. It is so easy, Ekanta, for the human mind to become sidetracked, both by pleasurable feelings and emotions as well as by negativities lurking in the mind. The purpose of sadhana is to realize God, not to wallow in self-pity and sorrow or to overindulge in lower emotional spiritual states that only drain one's energy."*

"I, for one, Mataji, would be pleased just to experience a little of what you are talking about, not to mention full enlightenment. Is that so bad?"

Laughing out loud, the guru replied, *"No, Ekanta, I suppose not, but in your case you have competent guides at your side almost continually. Your mother, for instance, will not allow you to eat only sweets all day, is that not the case? You will only get indigestion and will also then not have an appetite for food that will truly nourish and sustain you. In the same way, the guru will not let the aspirant fixate obsessively on the sugar cubes of preliminary devotional states that come and go during the process of spiritual discipline and awakening. The preceptor will instead drive the devotee onward towards consummate spiritual experience, for that is the ultimate goal. It is not only the remedy for all attendant ills in relative existence, it is also the natural fulfillment of all desires. It is the true Self that gets revealed in all its glory in this case. There is nothing that can compare to that revelation."*

"What is it like, revered Mother?" asked the boy tremulously, his awe evident in every word.

*"Descriptions are legion, Ekanta,"* she replied, *"but none are adequate to explain or describe. Words such as Truth, Freedom, Peace, Love and Unity, all to the infinite degree, have been utilized to impress upon the mundane mind, trapped in a limited mode of conceptualized thinking, the ecstasy of the consummate spiritual experience."*

"Pick an example and try to explain, Mataji," pleaded the boy.

The elderly woman was silent for a moment, then she spoke.

*"My own experience of It is indivisible Unity, Ekanta, an unbroken stationary flow, if such is possible, of infinite conscious Light streaming through all levels of existence yet remaining absolutely motionless. Perhaps pervasiveness would be a better term, yet it is not that It is just static or immobile. It lives...."*

At this point she could go no further and tears flowed down her cheeks.

*"I cannot describe..."* were the only words Ekanta could get out of her after that, so he went outside to attend to his chores, leaving her to contemplate the Infinite.

Later, he was called to her side. It was dusk and the colors were vivid as they walked by the rushing stream together.

*"I was thinking further on the subject of Unity we began to explore this afternoon,"* she said. *"I am afraid that the presence I was attempting to describe overcame me and spoiled our conversation. It is most rude in that way,"* she laughed. *"However, the aftermath of such experiences bring new clarity. That to me is an indication that God wants us to share what we experience in higher states with others, despite the difficulty involved in doing so. This is precisely why my revered husband and I remain in the world instead of withdrawing from it completely.*

*"In this day and age, Ekanta, worldliness is a chronic disease. Forgetfulness covers the minds of human beings resulting in dangerous ramifications. Even in spiritual circles, or*

*rather religious circles, beings are bound up in attachment to
their station in life, observing caste distinctions and the like,
and these act more as barriers to realization nowadays rather
than as aids. A new class of devotee is emerging. You, my boy,
have been groomed in that school with a view towards epito-
mizing something fresh and innovative. Actually, it is a return
to the refined condition of consciousness possessed by the
ancients. For this reason, we, the teachers, must find ways of
explaining or defining the unexplainable, the indefinable. This
kind of attempt resulted in the manifestation of the scriptures
of all religions in days gone by. We should never become complacent around this issue, for God has new and inspiring revelations for us every moment at all times."*

Pausing to pick a few wild flowers for the evening worship, the
Mataji continued.

*"Dualistic religion proposes to us that the word of God is
fixed, that all has been written. This is narrowness and shallowness combined, masquerading as religion, and it veils the
secret of Unity. It only gives rise to dogmatism and bigotry.
In truth, God is always adding to the scriptures, and he does
so by giving spiritual experience to human beings who seek it.
This, in turn, filters through the mind and emerges out of the
mouths of illumined beings as living realization. For this
reason, I must continue on in the vein of this afternoon's conversation. Whatever small amount of insight He has given me
must be transferred to others. This is the way of spiritual transmission."*

Ekanta's revered and beloved Mataji stopped before a lovely
tree and began to pick a few leaves from it.

*"These will do well for the worship of Vishnu, my boy. Here,
take these leaves and flowers and wrap them carefully in your
sacred cloth. Do not smell their fragrance. They are for the Lord
and are to be offered to Him first."*

"What if I catch the aroma anyway, Mataji? Will that be harmful?"

*"What comes about naturally is never truly harmful,"* replied
the teacher. *"In this case, the Supreme Lord, Paramatman, is
offering a trace of scent to the embodied Lord who dwells within
you, the jivatman. Just take care not to let the ego spoil it."*

"How am I to know where the difference lies in this instance?

Am I not to enjoy this offering?"

*"The unripe ego takes for itself and thinks not of others,"* came the guru's reply. *"It secretly enjoys and covets the offering, thinking itself to be the object of all worship. Simply keep your mind on God during all mental and emotional processes such as these, Ekanta. The ego will thereby come to understand that a higher power is in control. What is more, offerings made successfully to God increase a thousand times the enjoyment of the one who offers. The ego really cheats itself by its rash and ill-considered actions."*

Thus did Ekanta's precious training go on amidst every act of life under the preceptor's loving guidance.

*"So,"* the Mataji said, *"let us continue with this afternoon's subject, Unity. As I was thinking, the example of the sun came to me. Surya Narayan, the god of the sun, is both an anthropomorphic being and the very principle of light itself. This light is physical, mental and spiritual by degrees and according to subtle refinement. It is no wonder that all civilizations and cultures worship Him unanimously and in various ways. In our tradition, He is thought of ultimately in terms of Unity."*

Pausing to gather her thoughts, the revered Mother continued.

*"If one thinks of Unity, the thought of diversity must also surface. How the Lord maintains indivisibility while simultaneously creating the many lokas and the infinite number of beings who inhabit them is one of the great wonders of existence. It is the tendency of embodied creatures, though, to perceive and attach to the many, to the manifested portion of God's vast expansiveness. This is fine and, in fact, is what the Divine Mother intended when She created the universe. Obsession, covetousness, greed and delusion, though, is another matter. Actually, the presence of these things both spoils and spices up the play. The suffering and misery of karmic repercussions then occur. If beings want this constant pulling of good and bad, pleasure and suffering, then Mother allows them that for a time. But this is another aspect of the divine play. Let us focus, for now, on Unity and diversity."*

His teacher then sat with him beside the murmuring stream and began to discourse on Divine Reality through the mode of Unity.

*"Our scriptures state:"*

The Atman, like the sun,
appears multifarious due to what is attributed to it.
When It manifests itself through variety,
ignorant beings perceive it to be divided.

*"The idea here, Ekanta, is that the inseparable Atman, the core of existence, seems to be broken up into many parts, its living consciousness sporting here and there as different beings and objects. This is similar to the sun which, though ever one, appears to be many when it gets reflected in the tiny ripples of a lake's surface. This fragmentation is an apparent manifestation only, not the reality of the situation. In truth, the Atman never divides. The Lord is ever One, Ekanta. This is wonderful and points to the essence of Truth, the secret of Immortality and the Origin of all existence."*

"I know," broke in Ekanta, "that one cannot ask why with regards to the relative universe, revered Mataji, but it seems so obvious to me that God is ever One, even while He maintains this variegated creation. I wonder how people lose this knowledge and why it becomes a secret shared only by the devotees?"

*"This is one of the rewards of pure-hearted devotion, dear student,"* answered the guru, *"but we are not here to explain Maya and individual delusion. Let us continue on about indivisible Reality. Your other questions, indeed, all questions, will be answered in the interim, by exploring this eternal verity.*

*"Lord Krishna tells his beloved student, Uddhava, that though the yogi accepts what the senses receive by way of various objects, such a one merely experiences them without attachment and returns them to their source. This process is likened to the sun, that draws water from earth, lakes and oceans and gives it back in the form of rain and other forms of precipitation. Just so, the Atman distributes all forms of energy to the many levels of existence contained within It without ever changing in the least. Therefore, when it reflects in various beings and objects, it never changes, and when it radiates the Light of Pure, Conscious Awareness that gives all things their existence and ability to move and function, it nevertheless remains stationary and all-pervasive. This is what I tried to explain earlier when I compared It paradoxically to a 'motionless flow,' or an*

*'immobile stream' of Light.*

*"All things, then, Ekanta, are inseparable parts of an undivided or apparently divided whole. 'Purnoham, Purnoham,' say the saints and sages. All is complete. All is full. Even when described by mayavadins as illusion, by nihilists as nonexistent or shunyavadins as a void or an unending stream of mentation, they only end up confirming Its permanence and Its continuity. It is. What more can be said? As our revered Babaji, my blessed husband and your sacred guru, states, 'I do not know what God is, but whatever It is, I love It.'"*

Thoughts such as these occupied the Avadhut's mind until he went to sleep.

In the morning, the Avadhut awoke before dawn. A few hours of sleep were more than enough to refresh him. Beings sleeping eight hours every night not only wasted their precious time on earth, but fell prey to the misconception fostered by society that more sleep refreshed and vitalized the system. In truth, and as Ekanta had discovered through personal experience, too much sleep dulled the senses and actually allowed slothfulness and laziness access to the mind throughout the day. Just as too much eating slowed the system, so too did too much sleep hamper the body and mind's natural rhythm.

*"Try fasting, and sleeping less,"* his guru had instructed him. *"After weaning yourself off of the old habitual cycle of dependence on food and sleep for energy, you will discover vitality without limit. Happiness and peace follow as a matter of course."*

Ekanta mentally saluted his gurus and then bowed to the earth while keeping the Blessed Lord and Divine Mother in mind. As the sun's light illuminated the horizon, he reverently saluted it, for today the sun, when it appeared, would become his teacher. "Om Surya Narayan," came the words from his lips. The old sage was also up and came hobbling back from answering the call of nature.

After preparing a concoction within the circle of fires, which had now become smoldering coals, the old one began to prepare Ekanta.

*"Drink this water mixed with herbs, revered sir. It will sustain you through the ordeal."*

Ekanta did as he was told, but only after saluting the elderly one with folded palms.  The man merely stared ahead without moving.

Taking ashes from the fire pits on his hand, the old sage dropped his loincloth from his body and began to smear them all over his person.  Ekanta followed suit and was soon covered with grayish-white ash from head to foot.  Even his hair, matted and long, was permeated with ash.  Looking at each other, the salutations now became a matter of mutual regard.  Both immediately felt the increased presence of God as their minds opened to Divine Reality as pure Conscious Awareness, timeless and unbound.

As the old sage continued to work the coals once again, the Avadhut prepared himself inwardly for the next twelve hours.  From sunrise to sunset, he would sit, motionless, while the four fires burned around and the sun blazed down from above.  He became intoxicated just thinking about it.  At this point in his life, all fear and anticipation were absent.  He was not a novice anymore.  All was Brahman.

"What is the significance of the five fire ceremony, revered sir?"  Ekanta had asked his teacher one day after mention of it had been made.

*"The sun overhead, the fifth fire, is evident,"* replied the preceptor.  *"It is the eye of Absolute Unity looking down upon the devotee, burning away all impurities and witnessing the willpower, openness and devotion present there.  As a woman puts on a slipper, fitting comfortably and easily into its smooth interior, so too will God move into the human receptacle when all blocks and impurities have disappeared due to the intensity and power of the austerity.  Then, the human will become Divine, will see what God sees.  This is the essence of the Panchatapa, not to see how much stamina one has or merely to transcend suffering due to extreme conditions.  Those who have truly succeeded in this practice, not just put up with it as a necessity, have realized this.  They become Brahman.*

*"It is God who burns steadily in the five fires.  His constancy, power, grace and purity become visible and evident during the exercise, turning it from practice to presence, from austerity to sublimity.  What happens when opposites are transcended?  Few ever attempt to know.  The state of consciousness that is natural and spontaneous returns though, this we know, and what*

*that is like can be seen on the faces of those who succeed. Their actions, from then on, also reflect that in terms of more capacity and a certain imperviousness to both the world and its trials and sufferings."*

"Sir," Ekanta had asked, "I have heard that certain indigenous peoples of the western hemisphere practice a kind of austerity such as this that involves heat. They sit in an enclosure heated by fire and hot rocks for hours, chanting and smoking. They receive a vision of an animal spirit and experience other inner things as well. They also ingest a powerful substance from nature to induce these experiences. Have you heard about that?"

*"Yes,"* answered the spiritual preceptor. *"They have their own reasons for doing this, I am sure, but the Panchatapa is oriented towards the Highest. Ingesting something from nature, whether it be smoke or intoxicant, brings about an experience limited to nature and flavored by it as well. Why would we desire this, having had it for lifetimes? Neither is the Panchatapa practice accomplished for reasons of health for the body, for what is Absolute is beyond the body's ability to contain. Whether body lives or dies, gets sick or becomes healthy, that is not our concern here. Realizing our immortal nature is paramount, and knowing it to be free from the body condition and not predicated whatsoever on the thousand limitations of the mortal frame — that is necessary. Also, visions of the Absolute, whether in form or beyond form, is not the point of the Panchatapa. Such things may come and go naturally during such intense practice but the participant only witnesses them in a detached fashion."*

"What is the essence of this practice then, revered sir?" requested Ekanta.

*"Opening up entirely to the presence of the Divine after destroying all impurities that may be present; being able to receive that Presence without obstruction by any impediment including the limited will; realizing that a portion of Brahman is present within the individual; perceiving what it is to do away with what separates that particle of Divinity from the unlimited ocean of Consciousness existing beyond the body, mind and universe; and finally taking said realization and distributing its meaning and message to others — that is the*

*essence of the Panchatapa austerity."*

With this teaching fresh in his mind, the Avadhut watched the first bit of sun break the horizon. Under the supervision of the old sage, he then entered the arena of the five fires and sat himself down to meditate.

The morning passed uneventfully. If anyone had been present to witness the ceremony, that is how it would have appeared to them. On the inside though, and from the moment the Avadhut sat himself in half-lotus to begin the ordeal, his mind was in another plane of existence. Perhaps, he thought, I am really in a different state of consciousness. Whenever he looked out upon the world, it had transformed. The long, flat plains were an ocean of vibrating light and his guide appeared like a hoary sage from the ancient past, perhaps, Agni, the god of fire himself. The expanse of sky above lived and was full of beings, a field of celestials looking on and supporting him. This feeling lasted most of the morning.

About midday, the sweat had ceased to pour from his body, even though the heat was well over a hundred degrees. In late morning, the worst had passed, that being a sense of choking intensity that almost bested his resolve. He wanted badly simply to arise and leave the circle and almost did on several occasions, but at a particular moment his guide, nearly speechless for the entire day, passed a container of water through the flames and he drank. The water, though warm, was life itself. He remembered that it acted like a substantial meal given to a starving man. Thirst, his most difficult opponent, was not yet fully mastered he noted. As if to correct that thought, his guide spoke briefly:

*"You did not ask for water."*

Suddenly, his resolve came back and he whispered to himself, "I know this feeling of fear and confusion, of weakness. It belongs to the ego. It passes if one waits for a time. I do not have to move at all. I will become a burning pillar."

With this thought, his mind passed inwardly through time to an earlier day and his guru sat before him once again.

"I am having trouble meditating lately," Ekanta had admitted that day. "Every time I assume asana there comes an insurmountable urge to leave my seat. How has this happened, revered sir? I am aggravated at this."

Smiling, the guru responded to his plea.

*"Dear boy, you are out of harmony at this time.   Being out of harmony, can one be in Unity?   The cycle of your mind is experiencing a downward swing, a dive into tamas.   Now is the time, more than ever, to persevere.   If you do, you may succeed in detaching from the mind.   If you accomplish this but once, during this seemingly inauspicious time, you will gain the key to mastery of the lower self."*

Ekanta thought for a moment, then asked, "Sir, this low ebb of energy — am I weak or evil for experiencing it?"

*"Nonsense my boy,"* came the firm retort from his guru.  *"You should know that all beings experience this.   It is part of the embodied condition.   Jesus of Nazareth, Sri Krishna of Gokula, and even Lord Buddha himself bore this condition.   The difference between them and us in this regard is that they had wide open access to their Divine nature at all times.   This means that when their minds swung towards a tamasic condition according to the continual universal flow of the gunas, they would merely detach from the mind and abide in the Atman.   We are not the body or the mind, my son, you have heard us repeat this.   Those great ones fully realized this.   Abiding in the Atman, they were free from wasted energy, from depression and from karma.   What is more, their low cycle passed by more quickly due to their detachment from it.   This is like watering the flower instead of the weed."*

"That is amazing, revered guru," replied Ekanta.  "Does it apply to periods of sorrow and loss as well?  Can we, at that time, abide in the Atman and escape suffering?"

*"To a great extent, yes,"* answered the teacher.

"Sir," Ekanta said, "Lord Jesus suffered horribly on the cross. He is even said to have lost his faith by saying, 'O Lord, why have you forsaken me.'  Why did he not use this power and rely on it at that time?"

*"My boy,"* replied the guru, *"Jesus, the Avatar of that time, never lost his faith.   He was a Brahmajnani, a wisdom knower, an integral part of our Eastern heritage.  'O Lord, why have you forsaken me,' is the name of a popular hymn that was sung by devout people of that time.   By singing it out, even while his body agonized on the cross, he clearly demonstrated to us that the Soul of mankind is eternal, superior to body and sense life*

and that the world is not the ultimate Reality and can and should be transcended."

Silence followed these words. Ekanta was both inspired and awed.

Finally he said, "Revered guru, this message is wonderful and I have faith that it is true for it rings in harmony with my inner perception. However, I am not Jesus or Lord Buddha. How can I, at this time, solve my problem of restlessness and the inability to meditate on Reality?"

*"This is a most practical question, Ekanta, and I can help,"* came the reply. *"Prepare yourself for meditation instruction."*

What followed that day was a seven-point instruction which the guru called the "burning pillar." It signaled an end to all of Ekanta's problems with contemplation and meditation and vaulted him into the deeper levels of authentic spiritual life. In short, it established him firmly as an advanced practitioner. He left behind forever, the mode of beginner or novice. From then on he could always be quiet when he wanted. Restlessness, for him, died that day.

The Avadhut thought back on that wonderful day. Gone was the austerity of the five fires, retreating to the background of a mind that exulted in the word of God and guru.

*"Point one, dear student,"* his guru explained, *"revolves around the triple stance. The half-lotus is imperative. It is the only yoga posture one need be concerned with. Those of inferior orientation concentrate on multifaceted postures to gain longevity, health and psychic powers. This only increases identification with the body. You will never need to perform these poses, nor will you need to know many pranayama exercises. The breathing comes into control easily and naturally by that which I will teach you today, without the attendant dangers that physical exertion may bring to the mind and nervous system. So sit in half-lotus, Ekanta, and allow me to explain what it accomplishes. The Buddhists call it vajrasana. It takes up the energy associated with jealousy, covetousness and the like and utilizes it in the shushumna, the central channel."*

"How does this posture achieve that, revered sir?" asked Ekanta.

Patiently, the preceptor explained. *"We are talking about the*

*Muladhara chakra now, dear student. Listen carefully. At this lower center where, in a subtler sense, spiritual power is raw and unrefined, sleeping, as it were, the manifestation through human consciousness is at a gross level, associated with animalistic passions. Root selfishness and its attendant jealousies are operative here as long as consciousness remains asleep to its higher nature. Possibly you have noticed animals sniffing around fecal matter dropped by other animals. They are jealous of the territory. They know that others have been there, have enjoyed food and its energy. Desire for gross communion and domination occupies their ignorant minds. On the human level, some of this jealousy, pertaining to more refined objects and feelings, is operative. The half-lotus position affects the purification of this energy, takes jealousy into the central meridian while destroying its poisonous element and takes up the rest for sublimation. Point one, then, Ekanta. What is it?"*

"Revered sir," repeated Ekanta, "to assume the half-lotus position, to know that it affects the primal center of awareness associated with the energy of evacuation and to feel in one's meditation that the poison of jealousy is being taken up and transformed."

*"Excellent," affirmed the guru. "Let us proceed with point two. Fold your hands, palms up, the right over the left, and place them on your lap approximately a hand's width below the navel. Let them rest there with thumbs lightly touching, at the center of generation. Here, water energy, a wind of prana, is operative. Sexual expression is manifesting here at the second center. It is a kind of nectar, but where nectar lies, poison is also present. The poison potential here is anger, for lust and anger are intrinsically intertwined. Use the water energy to cool it. Therefore, as you assume this position, think to yourself that anger is being taken into the central channel and sublimated, its energy utilized as a force to help realize higher expressions. Repeat for me, dear disciple."*

"I am assuming the hands with palms up position, placed comfortably below the navel. Anger is being destroyed as I do this," stated Ekanta.

*"Destroyed in the sense that its negative element is being purified," corrected the teacher. "Its energy is being utilized."*

"Yes," said Ekanta, almost absent-mindedly, as he began to

experience a strange yet natural power flowing through him.

*"Point three concerns the posture of the back and the third center at the general vicinity of the stomach. Sit up straight to cause an open channel for energy to rise. Feel how the back must be straight, yet easy, as if the lungs have been filled with helium that always wants to rise. The shoulders must not be forced back, for that also impedes the channel in the opposite extreme. Therefore, as the Buddhists say, though the back be straight, the shoulders must be placed slightly forward, 'like the wings of a vulture.' Experiment, Ekanta, and you will find the exact dimension of openness that serves you. When you have, think to yourself that ignorance is being overcome, for the wind of earth is being activated."*

"Revered Guruji," asked the young man, "how is ignorance transcended in this manner and what does it have to do with earth energy?"

*"Think a moment, Ekanta,"* replied the guru, *"and you will come to know that ignorance stops knowledge from manifesting. Do you notice how normal people, unaware of their Atman, slump. They are always bent over, either with the torpor of inertia or by the slavery to frenetic energy used for selfish reasons. This is tamas and rajas. By sitting up straight and standing proud, the power trapped at the two lower centers begins its ascent to higher regions. Its immediate objective is the heart center, but that is getting ahead of our process here. Just know that the earth-bound consciousness is a friend of ignorance. There are much higher expressions to uncover. The straight back in meditation allows for a release of prana and spiritual energy into more refined states of existence. Ignorance thus gets transformed. This feels so good, dear pupil. You will never be able to make the comparison, for you have always been upright. I have taught other youngsters, though, and when the bad habit of slumping or bad posture is overcome, the effect on them is amazing. And this is only the physical manifestation. The spiritual is yet to express itself. Now, tell me what you have understood about this point."*

"The third point, dear teacher, involves taking the obstacle of ignorance into the middle channel using the energy of earth-wind by placing the back in a relatively straight position with shoulders slightly forward."

"*Fine,*" answered the guru, "*now sit in this three-pointed posture for a few minutes.*"

Those few minutes had passed by all too quickly for Ekanta, he remembered, for just these three basic aspects of meditation had awakened in him a constancy and a heightened feeling which he had never known before. All too soon, the guru's voice called him out of meditation.

"*You are picking this up swiftly, Ekanta. Now, stay attuned to what I am explaining further. The fourth point is subtle yet powerful. With half-lotus, palms faced up and back straight as discussed, you are now to bring the chin slightly downward and tuck it back inward. This small but significant movement rids one of desire by utilizing the fire-wind that takes the impetus of desire into the middle channel, purifies it, and allows it to rise to the heart center. From now on remain silent and I will answer your questions before they arise, for the terrain now becomes progressively internalized. How does this pertain and correlate? Physically, the straight back that facilitates an open channel must not get impeded by a crook in the neck. Adjust this and provide an opening. You will feel this as you experiment with subtle adjustments.*

"*Spiritually, the heart center represents awakening to higher Reality, especially to Ishvara, the personal God who grants salvation. Desire poses a substantial barrier in the way of this opening. This is due to the fact that one loves the small self, the ego, and gets used to its dictates. The ego loves to dwell in the atmosphere of ignited and satisfied desire and calls up more and more of this fuel for the fire in the process. In order to awaken love for God, the ego must become subservient to this higher power and, for that to occur, the Kundalini energy must rise to the heart center. When it does, spiritual life, per se, truly begins. Then, desire for relative existence, for sense-oriented life and for ego-gratification dwindles and desire for the presence and vision of God increases. So, think about this as you tuck the chin and offer desire into the central channel for sublimation.*"

The guru allowed this instruction to sink into his student's awareness. As he brought his chin down and in as directed,

Ekanta felt as if another key element had been put into place. His meditation was getting deeper, his restlessness was already a thing of the past. All too soon, once more, his guru called him forth to the realm of external consciousness.

*"Point five, dear student, has to do with the eyes, the gaze and, more importantly, the way our consciousness habitually follows the outer gaze. Kindly bring your gaze to the heart, dear one, and by the gaze I mean your attention and focus. Usually, the eyes are closed or mostly closed. Sometimes, you may have seen hatha yogis and other practitioners fixing their outer gaze on the tip of the nose, crossing their eyes and making horrible faces as a result. This is all outer show or misorientation, a lack of proper guidance and explanation. It misses the point entirely, as purely physical practice most often does. The process should proceed by a gentle and loving rolling of the eyes slightly downward in order to guide the human awareness to the chamber of the heart, the most excellent place to meditate."*

There was a short silence and Ekanta followed his guru's instruction not to talk.

*"Often,"* came the confident voice of the preceptor, *"one sees that the eyes of some practitioners are rolled up, searching the inner mind and looking up at the third eye center. Some of us have examined these beings and found that, in most, spiritual ego is strong in them. Pride is the obstacle in this case. This considerable impediment is linked with the desire for notoriety, fame and with a tendency to manipulate others and have them serve individual needs. It is made bereft of its sting if one simply focuses on the heart in meditation. Therefore, roll the eyes downward to the heart chamber by looking down the bridge of the nose and envision the form of the chosen ideal enshrined within. Humility will arise, for you are laying yourself low before Divine Reality. The personal God loves that selfless quality in His votaries. The poison of pride will thereby be taken into the central channel of the shushumna and be utilized, its negative element neutralized. When the time comes for the eyes to roll up due to the Divine Mother's insistence, it will happen naturally. One will not have to force it or make pretenses."*

Ekanta was now aware of two simultaneously existing realities.

They were both beautiful, both true, and he somehow floated between them, like a butterfly caught in the wake of two shifting winds.  Before he could concentrate upon them, the guru spoke again.

*"Not yet, my boy.  Stay focused here for a time.  The sixth point tucks in the last remnant of the blanket.  Place the tip of your tongue on the roof of your mouth, just behind the teeth.  This facilitates one-pointed concentration and also deals with egotism, the sense of individuation that maintains a sense of 'I consciousness' separate from Brahman."*

No sooner did Ekanta put this final element into place than he was gone.  Where he went in that timeless moment was hard to say, impossible to describe.  All he knew was that a new realm was accessible to him.  He dwelt in that place in bliss and contentment, free from concerns of all types.  He hardly noticed the passage of time and it was with difficulty that he drew himself into individual awareness to hear his teacher's words.  At first, he did not understand what was being said, nor did he know himself or his precious guru when he first opened his eyes.

*"Ekanta...Ekanta...are you here?"*

These words brought him slowly around and he stammered, "What happened?  Oh, Guruji!"

*"Do not try to talk or explain, Ekanta,"* came the soothing words.  *"Just rest in the knowledge that all is well."*

After a few minutes had passed, Ekanta was aware that his guru was rubbing his chest near the heart.  Tears welled up in his eyes.

*"Well,"* said the teacher, good-naturedly, *"what has happened to your inability to meditate?"*

At first, these words left Ekanta dumbstruck.  Then, he and his teacher burst into laughter.

After the laughter subsided, the guru said, *"You did not allow me the chance to give you the seventh point of this meditation.  You did not need it right away either, since you entered into that which I could have only described and instructed about.  For a moment in time, Ekanta, you became a burning pillar."*

"Please give me the seventh point, teacher.  I feel that I need it nevertheless."

*"Right you are,"* the guru affirmed.  *"By Mother's Grace you have encountered that which all search for by way of the spiritual*

*path. Now, and in the future, you will have to practice in order
to attain this priceless treasure. Restlessness, however, will not
torment you again. The pathway now lies open. Practice."*

Saying this, the guru now addressed the seventh point of the
practice.

*"The seventh point of this meditation pertains to the mind and
the seventh center of consciousness called the sahashrara. After
you have applied and assumed the six points prior to this, and
as you practice this mentally and physically leading up to direct
experience, you are to rid the mind of all thoughts such as 'I
am meditating,' or 'I am not meditating.' Whether you feel that
you are perfectly balanced or are out of balance, this should not
be given attention. In other words, do not enforce either position by affirming that 'I am having a good meditation' or 'I
am having a bad meditation.' Whether you are or are not, that
misses the point. Abiding calmly in the Self is what you are
after, if any goal is to be outlined. Thus, the burning pillar
comes into being, Ekanta, for if the meditation is not focused,
the power of this seven-pointed position alone will destroy this
imbalance, burning away personal delusions and impurities.
If you are focused, then the light of the pillar goes out to all
beings as pure spiritual radiance, like a roaring fire whose heat
destroys the cold numbness of universal suffering and illumines
the path to Truth."*

The Avadhut opened his eyes. He was staring straight into one
of the four fires. The sun was not beating down on him anymore.
Hazily he thought, What happened? The fire overhead has gone
out. My guide has become careless and fallen asleep. Then, he
realized that it was dusk. The afternoon had passed by unnoticed
and the oppressive heat of midday had never been experienced.
The calm, abiding seven-pointed burning pillar meditation had
stood him in good stead. Calmly, silently, he mentally saluted his
guru.

Looking around and stirring himself, Ekanta rubbed some feeling back into his limbs. As he looked around the circle of four
fires, now burning low, he saw the old sage lying flat on the
ground. All of a sudden he understood that the man was prostrating in his direction.

"Please sir," Ekanta called out. "Rise up and speak to me. What has happened here this day?"

Standing up slowly, the elderly one came close and addressed him with reverence.

*"You sir, have achieved in one day what I have taken a life-time to only approach. What type of samadhi you attained today I know not, but the fires had little to do with it. Can you tell me what you experienced?"*

"I became the fire, revered sir," answered Ekanta. "I was a burning pillar. More than that I cannot say just yet."

The old one gave Ekanta some water from a bowl which he drank with increasing gusto.

*"Come and eat something,"* said the sage.

"No, not right away," replied the Avadhut. "This is enough for now. I must walk a little to bring my mind back to the earth realm."

*"Yes of course,"* said the old one, and supported the Avadhut as he rose and took his first steps.

The darkness of evening was fast approaching. Neither sleep nor food was interesting to Ekanta, though he made himself eat a little rice with herbs. That caused him to settle into his body more easily as he began to feel the subtle after-effects of his ordeal. The cool evening air was like God's fragrant breath on his body. Without feeling blissful, he enjoyed a state of evenness that could not be described. Few words passed between the two sages and none were needed, for both felt an inner connection with Reality that was most superb and sublime. Late that night, both fell into a deep sleep, for both had kept vigil for an extended period and in similar ways.

When Ekanta awakened, he could not find the old sage anywhere. As he returned to the campsite, he noticed something inside the circle of fires, which had now turned to cold ashes overnight. As he drew near, he realized that it was the old sage. His body was partially covered in the ashes left over from the two Panchatapa ceremonies. As soon as the Avadhut saw him, he realized that the old one had given up the body during the night. As he drew near to confirm this fact, he noticed that the old one had drawn several sacred mystical diagrams, called yantras, in the ashes within the circle. Without disturbing these and after saluting them reverentially, the Avadhut checked the sage's body. It was a lifeless cage of bones and flesh, but the expression on his face was extremely peaceful.

The Avadhut spent the rest of the day gathering enough firewood for the funeral pyre. He then cremated the sage's body, chanting mantras the entire time. It was evening before the process was complete. During that time Ekanta knew that he had been led to this place for two powerful reasons. One was evident — to learn and accomplish the Panchatapa ceremony in the presence of one who was an adept in it. The other was less obvious, and that was to help in the process of dying and to perform the final ceremony over the body of this holy man.

At dawn the next morning, after a few hours of deep sleep during which he saw the old sage's smiling face in his dream, the Avadhut gathered some of the holy man's ashes in a small container for offering into the Ganges on his next visit there. The rest of the ashes he offered into the winds. They trailed off in an easterly direction. Minutes later, the Avadhut, too, was moving again, headed in the direction in which the ashes had blown, free and without cares.

# Chapter 16

# Teachings on Restraint and Discretion

THE SIXTEENTH GURU — The Bee

THE LESSON — Moderation

O Prince, many lessons were transmitted to me by observing the bee. Taking a little nectar from each flower it visits, the bee lives a carefree life which is nevertheless focused upon gathering essential ingredients. This is an example of how one should live, taking in moderation what comes one's way and seeking only the essence. The bee was a fine teacher for me in this regard.

The moon was rising over the sacred river. On its banks, hallowed by the footfalls of every divine personage who ever walked the timeless land of Bharata, Mother India, the Avadhut had made his campsite. The murmuring sound of the flowing waters soothed him and put him in an indrawn mood. His meager meal of precooked grains and puffed rice, gathered as alms in a nearby village, had satisfied him completely. The river water, boiled over the fire, had quenched his thirst and replenished his bodily fluids which had been sorely depleted from his long hike overland.

It had been several weeks since he had traversed the plains, heading east at first and then turning in a northerly direction to find Mother Ganga.  Now, on the holy banks of the Ganges River, somewhere east of Varanasi and west of Ratna, he had committed most of the ashes of the elderly old sage to its sanctifying waters.  With that objective accomplished, he was now free to trace the river to its source at Gangotri, for that was the inner prompting he had received in meditation.

The Avadhut slept on the banks of Mother Ganges that night amidst many other pilgrims.  He had arrived too late to find a suitable campsite far away from others as was his preference, so he simply joined a few sadhus, shared their fire and contributed a share of alms he had received to the communal store.  It was one of the few conveniences that this lifestyle offered, to be able to be accepted without question among other seekers and pilgrims, most of whom were simple souls with a genuine curiosity about him and a thirst for knowledge.  There were a few exceptions to this open-minded policy and also some narrow sects that most of the sadhus stayed away from, but in general it made the austere life easier.

In the morning, before others were even stirring, the Avadhut had finished his bath, meditated for an hour and was a few miles distant from the evening's campsite.  Following the river and keeping as close to it as the terrain would allow, he enjoyed a leisurely pace that bespoke of a man in no particular hurry whatsoever.  Whenever he encountered other travelers, he exchanged words and information with them, but generally, unless approached, kept to his own.  As the day drew to a close and dusk drew near, he began to look for a suitable lodging.

Securing alms in a few villages had provided him with several rupees along the way.  Therefore, as he came upon the outskirts of Varanasi just before dark fell, he began to inquire about a room, preferring to take private quarters for the night rather than to frequent the company of others.  This he found in a small group of huts owned and managed by a local landlord of the vicinity who was known to him.  The price was cut in half due to the man's good-hearted support of traveling sadhus, so Ekanta found himself housed in a quiet and reasonably comfortable lodging just after dark.

Dropping his bundle on the dirt floor, part of which had been covered with palm leaves, the Avadhut sat himself down to rest his weary feet and legs.  Before too long, a sound at the door of his hut prompted him to ask who was there.

"It is Varuni," came a young woman's voice, "come to ask if you need water for washing and charcoal for a fire."

"No charcoal will be necessary," answered Ekanta, "but please bring a bucket of hot water for washing."

The sound of her footsteps receding into the darkness convinced the Avadhut that she had understood and was complying with his request.  The thought of hot water, a luxury for him most anytime, was pleasing.  With it he would not only get a good bath, he would also soak his feet in the remainder of the water.  It was too bad, he thought, that he only had enough money for one bucket.

A sound at the door aroused him from his nap.  He had dropped off to sleep without even knowing it.  The journey over the past weeks had taxed his strength and taken a lot of energy.  It was good that he could spend a little time recuperating in this ideal atmosphere.

"I have brought your hot water, sir," came the voice of the woman.  "May I enter?"

"Yes, please come in and place the bucket inside," replied Ekanta.

The young woman who entered was carrying two buckets, both very hot.  Steam was rising from them.

"Dear girl," said the Avadhut, "I can only afford one bucket. Therefore I fear you have been put to inconvenience by having to bring two."

"Not so, revered sir," came the woman's slightly abashed reply, "I was instructed to double your request at no extra charge by Mr. Laha, the landlord of this place."

The Avadhut gave the young woman the allotted fee.  She would accept nothing more.

"It is my great privilege to serve a holy person such as yourself, revered sir," was all she said.  "Please excuse me."

With this, she was gone before he could speak, leaving behind two large buckets of hot water.  Ekanta drew near the buckets. As he looked into them he noticed that one had a small metal container inside.  Drawing it out carefully, he felt that it contained something.  As he unscrewed the metal lid while holding the container in his wearing cloth, the fragrant aroma of freshly brewed tea spiced with cardamom and flavored with milk and sugar wafted up to his nostrils. Breathing a deep sigh of contentment and approval, the Avadhut sat down on the spot and began to draw sips of the strong, refreshing brew straight from the container. The Divine Mother was definitely taking care of him tonight, he thought.

Not more than a few minutes later, Varuni returned with a bucket of cold water. She set it down before he could protest.

"You can mix this with the hot water to temper it and make it go further. There is a metal cup here for ladling as well. This too is a gift of this place."

Ekanta was too relaxed and tired to protest and Varuni seemed to sense it. Smiling, she turned and left the hut.

Outside, behind his dwelling place, Ekanta stripped off his clothes and began the process of bathing. The stars twinkled in the black evening sky, a million eyes of Goddess Kali set against Her dark, nocturnal form. Dust and dirt from long miles of Indian paths and roads were washed away that evening. The Avadhut washed all of his clothes as well, hanging them to dry inside his hut. Finally, with a half bucket of hot water left over, he retired into his dwelling and soaked his feet for an hour before falling into a deep and restful sleep.

Ekanta meditated early in the morning as usual but remained at rest for most of the early part of the day. Varuni brought him bananas, papaya, puffed rice and potato curry with rice which he washed down with yogurt and milk. By noon he was feeling like a new man and he packed his few belongings to make ready for his journey. As he exited the hut which had served his needs and purposes so well, Varuni approached and prostrated before him.

"Rise please," he pleaded with her. "I am not a traditional holy man that you must observe such formalities."

"Revered sir," Varuni answered, "I know this, and that is why I offer you my salutations. You are a true human being, not a pretentious person like some of our local Brahmin priests, filled with pride and vanity. I feel this in my heart. Therefore, I have come to ask you about the spiritual path. Do you have a few minutes for a simple village woman?"

"Of course I do," answered the Avadhut. "I have time for all beings who question me with sincerity about the nature of Reality.

Let us go over by the lake and sit under that tree."

With the formalities out of the way, the two sat by the lake and entered into a conversation about God.

"You are a holy person," began Varuni. "Please tell me, what is the way?"

"Do not think or act in the conventional sense, but merely abide in peace and contentment, despite any trials and in the presence of all dualities," came the answer. "Be a slave to no one but serve all as if you were their mother or sister and be a friend to those who respect your existence. As the Blessed Lord has said:"

> Be glad for all who succeed,
> rejoice for those who are happy,
> have compassion for all who suffer
> and remain distant from those who are under evil influences.

"Find a natural balance and dwell in it under all conditions. Make it your daily habit to love and seek the Lord and Divine Mother of the Universe and always acknowledge the presence of Them within yourself. If you can do just this much, personal impurities and the disturbances of relative existence will gradually dwindle away and an enlightened consciousness will abide in you."

Varuni was silent for a time. Finally she brought up what was on her mind.

"There is a man who wants me for his wife. I am torn, for though I love him, I cherish the Lord as my only intimate companion. I do not want to become caught between these two ideals. Can you advise me?"

"Here in India at this time, there are few provisions made for female monastics," replied the Avadhut. "Therefore, you may want to hold to both ideals and fuse them into one."

"Is that possible, revered sir?" asked Varuni.

"Why should it not be?" returned the Avadhut. "But it is only possible at an advanced level. A man reaches for a rose on a bush and also gets cut by a thorn there. Drawing his hand back, holding the rose yet bleeding, another man asks him if he is all right. 'Yes, it is nothing,' he replies. You see, though there is difficulty, one can hold two ideals if strength and resolve are secure. In fact, I would say that advanced spiritual practitioners must learn to

hold more than one ideal. Of course, they accomplish this by realizing Ultimate Reality first through one pathway, one chosen ideal,
and holding that as the firm foundation. Then, all else matures in
them naturally."

"So, what you are telling me is that I can marry my friend and
still hold God as my most intimate companion," said Varuni.

"I am bearing testament to the fact that all beings must learn
to see God present in each other," replied the Avadhut, "whatever
the situation. This can be done either from the standpoint of a
life given to a personal search for Reality or a life consecrated by
holy union between the male and female principles. In your particular case, since individual conditions and surroundings must be
taken into consideration, the Lord that you seek is present in your
friend. The love that you feel for each other, if it be true and sincere, is a sign of that. Authentic attraction between man and
woman is God recognizing God, is God seeking union with God.
Something gets fulfilled there and many circumstances get
worked out through such a divine relationship. This is sometimes
a more practical and expedient way of approaching Divine Reality
than through withdrawal from the world."

Pausing for a moment to consider, the Avadhut went on with
his train of thought.

"Surrender to God is really what is being discussed and considered here, for faith in the Absolute precedes realization. Self-
surrender can be attained only by offering the entire being to God.
This can be done through the union of Shiva and Shakti or
through merging the sense of individuality, the jivatman, into
Supreme Reality, the Paramatman. In truth, the two are never
really separate. The Lord maintains the sense of distinction so
as to heighten the experience of union. In both modes, the con-
secration of two into one is facilitated, whether the two be male
and female, as in the consecrated partnership which is the Tantric
way, or the individual and the Absolute, as in the immersion of
the sole seeker into Brahman which is the monastic way.

"There is no superior or inferior way here, though narrow-
minded beings in both walks of life may insist that theirs is the
best path. One may hear those who have selected the sacred relationship as their choice talking about the selfishness of the monks
and one may also notice the monastics looking down their noses

at those involved in consecrated union, but both are limited in their thinking. Pay no heed to either personal view but select your own ideal and go forward with positivity and sincerity. The Lord Himself is operating every aspect of the game. Give yourself to Him and swiftly reach the goal of human existence.

"Now, as to the difficulties of life," continued the Avadhut, "one must exercise restraint in all matters. The Buddha talked about it in terms of moderation. Those who join in sacred union must also practice some of what the monastics focus upon all their life. The monastics, through this one-pointed focus in the mode of negation, will eventually arrive at what the consecrated couple realizes through union and affirmation. One retains, the other moderates, but both must learn to direct and not squander, to sublimate. Moderation applies in all areas of life. Patanjali, the father of yoga, puts it in no uncertain terms."

Saying this, the Avadhut began to explain a few slokas from the yoga sutras.

"In the second sloka, Varuni, Patajali mentions the first type of control by stating:"

Yoga, union with Reality,
is aided by restraining the mind's consciousness
from assuming various forms.

"This is the principle type of moderation. It translates as the ability to control the mind and keep it from allowing negative and untoward thoughts to ruin one's spiritual equilibrium. If one can accomplish this, then detrimental patterns of thought will be destroyed at the source. What can ever again disturb the mind if this power is attained? Think well about this. All secondary practice that aspirants indulge in is only for the purpose of getting back to this pristine condition and realizing this one verity. The adept who wields this kind of restraint can send his mind-stuff wherever he or she wants. Think about it! Do you see the potential here?

"The second type of restraint, admittedly of a lower class than the first, is to struggle to effect control of a mind that has already assumed various forms and has therefore forgotten this natural power of primal awareness. Patanjali states:"

By continuous struggle,
the aspirant must control the waves of the mind
to attain equanimity.

"As the aspirant progresses, different kinds of results are attained according to the intensity of the struggle and level of commitment. After a time, when practice of this kind begins to bear fruit, restraint becomes second nature, rooted in the very being, and more positive approaches then begin to present themselves to the seeker. A refinement then takes place leading to the realization of a state without modifications. Fine impressions in the mind are destroyed and Ultimate Reality gets realized in samadhi. Within the perspective of practice, all this has been accomplished by restraint and moderation accompanied by discrimination.

"Therefore," continued the Avadhut without pause, "in your married life, if that is what you choose, do not forget to instigate these practices so that you will achieve balance and harmony in your relationship. Teach them to your children too, so that they will also be able to live happy and free of impediments."

Varuni had been much enlightened by the Avadhut's far-seeing advice and his explanation of moderation and self-control. After she had prostrated before him again, he said good-bye to her and went his way.

The Ganges river wended its way through the sacred land of India to empty out into the Bay of Bengal. The Avadhut traced his way up the sacred river in the opposite direction towards its source high in the Himalayas. Before he set his sight on that goal, however, he visited the auspicious areas in and around Benares, the holy city of Lord Shiva. Here, the blessed God of Wisdom breathed the liberating mantra into the very souls of those who were fortunate to pass from the body in this sacred place.

The semisweet scent and taste of ashes permeated the air as the Avadhut made his way along the river and past the ghats where lifeless bodies were being openly cremated. Taking out the last portion of ashes from the cremated body of the old sage who had taught him the Panchatapa ceremony, he distributed them into the river. Then he stood and gazed out over the expanse of waters, considered holy and auspicious by every occupant in India.

The Avadhut stayed in Benares well into the next morning.

After paying his profound obeisances to Mahadeva at the famous Shiva temple, he moved through the thick crowds of the city and reached the outskirts near the edge of the Ganges. Tracing the winding course of the holy river as best as he could and trying to stay as close to it as possible, the Avadhut walked all day. As he journeyed north towards the holy mountains, following the sacred river, his mind lingered on the conversation of the previous morning. The quality of moderation, he knew, was most precious and, if the truth be known, was instrumental in facilitating renunciation of the world. Not only did moderation lead to renunciation accomplished in the right spirit, it also contributed to a mature condition, even in the midst of the most exacting renunciation of the world. Teachings from his guru drifted back through his memory at this thought.

*"Lead a bee-like life, Ekanta,"* came the advice of his guru one day, as they stood gazing at a bee hive in a nearby tree.

"Can you explain that to me, Mataji?" asked the young man.

*"If one were to follow one of these bees individually, it would become clear that they attend on different flowers and take a little from each vessel. Just so, a wandering sadhu does the same, taking moderate amounts from each household he inquires at. This facilitates his vow of not storing up for the future and also causes him to maintain nominal appetites. A natural restraint of the senses then takes place which destroys expectation, attachment and other detrimental tendencies in the mind. He learns to live free and easy, not depending on anyone and accepting only his due when it comes naturally. This bee-like existence also fosters humility and does not tax the poor households that he frequents."*

"What else does the bee teach us, revered Mother?" asked Ekanta of his female guru.

After watching the bees for a time, she answered tenderly:

*"They are creatures that seek and gather only the essence. They extract only what is sweet and healthy and their entire existence revolves around that preoccupation. The wise ones, too, should follow this example, searching for and extracting only the essence of the teachings from the scriptures and from life, remaining focused on that. Remember the saying in our province, Ekanta? Even the common villagers know and repeat it."*

"Yes, Mataji," replied the boy, "it is that 'ants take only the sugar and leave the sand behind.'"

*"Precisely, dear student,"* affirmed the guru. *"If you utilize the example of the bee and the ant in this regard then life will proceed smoothly. Both moderation and knowledge of essentials are necessary."*

It was not long after this that Ekanta had witnessed the importance of moderation through an experience that happened to his family. One day, Ekanta's uncle visited the village where he and his parents were living simply and humbly. Entering the town in a drunken state, he had caused trouble and embarrassment to Ekanta's parents. The townspeople talked about this unseemly occurrence for weeks and Ekanta had wept to see the effect of this idle chatter on his mother.

One day, around the time of this occurrence, Ekanta's guru came upon him sitting on the stump of a tree in the woods near the little forest ashram.

*"What is the matter, son?"* asked the guru, seeing the boy's dejection.

After being told the story of the intoxicated uncle, the teacher comforted him:

*"Let us see if we can give this unavoidable incident a positive turn, Ekanta. It is not the end of the world. The lesson here is moderation, on all levels. You see, once, a drunken man came to the ashram of my teacher and began swearing and acting lewdly and finally fell down unconscious on the grounds of the sanctuary. We thought that the master would throw him off of the premises outright, but our guru took the man to his own quarters and gradually aroused him from his drunken stupor.*

*"I was present during this process, attending on the guru. First, my guru had rice water brought in several containers. When the man was conscious enough, he began giving him amounts of this rice water in small increments at regular intervals. I asked him why he did not just fill the man with the detoxifying liquid as quickly as possible but he only smiled and explained that an intoxicated man must be brought around slowly with small dosages of rice water lest he be physically upset and mentally hung over for days afterwards.*

*"'In the same way, precious student,' my teacher cautioned,*

*'be sure that you use restraint and moderation in all things, in much the same way that you see me exercising it here and now. You can learn from this incident in other ways, too. In the same way that I am bringing this unconscious man around with a detoxifying ingredient, the illumined teacher patiently applies the elixir of discrimination and dispassion into the ears of the worldly-minded so that they too will recover from the stupor of delusion.'* "Thus did I learn both compassion and service based upon knowledge from my revered guru. As well, I began to understand the wisdom of moderation in all matters."

"Revered sir," Ekanta then asked, "you mentioned moderation on all levels. In this situation that I am experiencing, how would you apply that?"

*"First of all,"* responded the guru, *"your uncle should have practiced it with regards to drinking, at least until he could give up the bad habit completely. Next, the townspeople should have used moderation in their talk and behavior, knowing that such idle chatter and unbecoming actions would reach others and cause more pain. Finally you, Ekanta, must now moderate the penchant of your mind to indulge in despondency and depression long after the incident is over. Lift your mind up and out by restraining it from lapsing into sorrow in the first place. Your grief will only cause your mother to remember this unfortunate matter. You must bring happiness and lightheartedness into her life. Therefore Ekanta, like Arjuna, who had much graver concerns than you, rise and destroy thy foes!"*

Teachings about moderation had also come from Yogindra Yogi, the holy man living in his vicinity.

*"Not only does one lose one's knowledge and discrimination by not heeding the wisdom of moderation and restraint, Ekanta, but danger also appears. Have you not noticed the unfortunate condition of the opium smokers? Day after day, their existence consists of apprehending more and more of the stuff and smoking it interminably. They are not content unless they are in a continual state of semiconscious torpor. They have absolutely no control, so they leave themselves open to robbers and disease which both inevitably come. Ruin and death are the result.*

*"Besides the obvious dangers of this horrible condition,"* the yogi continued, *"one should apply moderation in daily life to*

*insure the enjoyment of a balanced and happy existence. In spiritual life, too, Ekanta, keep the senses back and in check at all times when you are not directly involved in some act or deed. Detach and discriminate even when you are involved in action and contemplation. On other levels, one can even moderate the tendency to meditate too much so that one will not become irresponsible or mentally imbalanced before perfection is reached. In every regard then, Ekanta, and at all levels of existence, apply moderation."*

The Avadhut had swerved away from the river's direct path due to the terrain. Looking about, he found himself in a farm area and was suddenly seized by the need to simply sit and appreciate the scenery. He found a grassy knoll rising above a field of flowers and sat there in peaceful contentedness. Soon, he was humming to himself the melody of a song that had sprung into his mind. The words followed after:

> O seeker after Reality,
> place your mind on the very form of Peace.
> She, the Mother of the Universe,
> is the incomparable Essence that you seek.
> If you cannot perceive Her palpable Presence
> abiding in the Self,
> then restrain the mind from external stimuli
> and rest at Her Feet.
> When even this fails you and you fall into despondency,
> simply sing Her names and glories
> and peace will flood your being.
> This little I, who is no one, sings in rhapsodic delight,
> Call on the Mother, inaudibly or out loud.
> The treacherous ocean of the world will then become calm.
> In it, ply your mental craft consciously and deliberately.

As Ekanta's mind ruminated over the lines of this song, he fell into a meditative mood. Closing his eyes on the outer world, he spent the next hour abiding in the peace of the Self. After coming down from this highly sensitized state, he stood up and stretched his legs. Then, following the dictates of his mind, he made his way down the hill and into the field of flowers below.

It was late afternoon and a soothing languid quality had come over the land. The humming of the bees around him added to the intoxicating atmosphere as did the fragrance in the air. As Ekanta watched the bees take the essence from the flowers, he was reminded of the various wise beings he had met who had that wonderful ability to extract the essence from life and teachings. Some, those oriented more towards the wisdom path, were truly remarkable in that they could immediately perceive and understand what was being communicated in any passage of the scriptures, no matter how abstruse it might be. By keeping company with these individuals, Ekanta, too, had somehow imbibed this ability. That transmission, combined with the training he had received with his own gurus and the positive tendencies latent in his mind from past experience in other lives, gave him an innate gift for explaining spiritual teachings.

I am a bee, he thought to himself, and the wisdom texts of every religion are flowers containing the nectar of enlightenment. I need only fly here and there in order to draw from these nourishing sources of inspiration. This series of thoughts made him think again about moderation.

"Where is my moderation in this regard?" Ekanta asked his guru one day. "I do not have any restraint whatsoever when it comes to studying the scriptures. Sometimes I worry that I am becoming too wide, too open to the suggestions and teachings of all these religious approaches. Am I in danger of spreading myself too thin?"

*"You are almost twenty now,"* came the response from his guru, looking up from a text on the Diamond Sutra. *"This is a wonderful time for you. You are in possession of your youthful energy and you are oriented towards spiritual life. Therefore, absorb huge amounts of spiritual teaching, Ekanta, for you will not find any trouble in digesting them."*

After about an hour had passed, wherein the guru and the disciple both became absorbed in poring over the sacred books, the guru suddenly spoke:

*"Do not confuse your mind with limiting thoughts, Ekanta. Obsessing with worldly objects and concerns is vastly different than concentrating on Divine Reality. Reading insipid writings begets a mind stinking of worldliness. Placing the mind*

on God's word brings knowledge leading to enlightenment. Can there be any comparison?

"People who study secular subjects only are like vultures that pull strands of dead meat from a rotting carcass. The man or woman who indulges in stories about mundane existence or tales of evil, murder, sensuality and the like, resembles a crow who eats the filth of others. Take into your mind only that which will conduce to your spiritual health and stature and do not concern yourself with whether it will hamper your progress or not. Can the mind become inhibited by contemplating that which describes the very nature of freedom? Will one's consciousness become unconscious by meditating upon knowledge pertaining to the Source of unlimited Consciousness Itself?

"I know that some teachers prescribe devotional exercises only and ask their students to refrain from study and reading. This can be interpreted several ways. Perhaps these beings have no capacity for comprehension in the first place, having never developed that quality. Then again, it is sometimes better to put into practice what one has heard or read and that happens at certain auspicious times according to the mind's cycles. The temperament of the individual student must also be taken into consideration. Some are intuitive, others are psychic. Some are studious and others devotional or introspective. Knowledge is for everyone, though, and even those who are not intellectually oriented pass through periods of study. So go forward towards consummate understanding and pay little heed to what limited persons might advise.

"Small minds will never grasp the significance of higher wisdom and how important it is, Ekanta. Nor will these so-called teachers, who are like dogs that bark on the heels of elephants, know that there are some who must, as it were, know it all. These are the ones whom the Divine Mother intends to teach others. It takes only a razor knife to kill oneself, Ekanta, but to kill others one needs a shield and many weapons. In other words, learn every system as thoroughly as you can. It is a somewhat easy matter to destroy one's own ego, but to cause others to give it up is a difficult undertaking. Apply your moderation where it is most needed, in physical and sensual appetites and practical matters, but go full steam ahead where *spiritual advancement is concerned."*

The bees proved to be an interesting study. As he watched, Ekanta saw that it was true. Most of the bees lighted on flowers and extracted only a small amount of pollen, leaving the rest behind. Some did not take any from a certain flower after lighting there, though the next bee that came along did. Moderation, harmony, generosity, purity — these little creatures were fine examples of so many sterling qualities. The community of bees was even more interesting than that of ants, concluded the Avadhut, as he walked through the field in the general direction of the sacred river.

About dusk, the Avadhut met up with Mother Ganga once again. Repeating Her mantra, he walked as far as the waning light would allow and then simply settled himself down on a small cliff overlooking Her waters. The past few days had been amazing, he recalled, and filled with many teachings given through various creatures and situations. As the moon became visible over the horizon, the Avadhut contemplated another kind of bee, for in his innermost consciousness the sound of Om, like the combined hum of a thousand bees, seemed to emerge and soak the landscape with the bliss of perfect peace. With the accompaniment of the river's constant murmuring sound blending with the song of crickets, this made for an enchanting evening. Sitting still, a silhouette against the rising moon, the Avadhut plunged his mind again and again into the primal sound of Om, eventually merging into the Ocean of Pure Awareness from which it emanated.

# Chapter 17

# Teachings on Absorption

THE SEVENTEENTH GURU — The Brahmara-kita

THE LESSON — Meditation

*The brahmara-kita is a unique insect, O Prince, and by watching it seize its prey, the cockroach, I learned a lesson in meditation. The two, locked in what appears to be a life-and-death struggle, simply freeze and do not move for the longest time, or perhaps the brahmara-kita traps the cockroach in the wall of its nest. Either way, they become fixed, as it were, in meditation upon each other and in that meditation are fused into one being. This illustrates the essence of meditation, an absorption so deep that one forgets the world and the individual self, experiencing only Brahman. This was revealed to me in the example drawn from the brahmara-kita.*

Continuing his journey towards Gangotri, the source of the sacred Ganges River in the Himalayas, the Avadhut began to encounter rough terrain. One day, after taking a detour in order to skirt some impassable mountains, he came upon a glade of trees. Wending his way through these monstrous conifers, he came upon an odd sight. As he was resting, looking up at the tops of the trees in wonder, his attention was caught by the scurrying of an insect in his direct path. As the Avadhut looked down and in front of him, another insect came scampering in hot pursuit. The first, a cockroach, seemed deathly afraid and was rushing for its life, sometimes running and other times flying. It was of little use, however, for the second insect, larger and quicker, caught up with the cockroach and seized it. What happened next was remarkable.

The Avadhut had heard of the brahmara-kita, a large beetle-like insect, but he had never seen one. Now he conjectured that this was indeed one of them. As Ekanta drew near and knelt down to see the outcome of this struggle, he was surprised to see that there was no struggle occurring. Both insects were frozen in place. Bending down, the Avadhut tried to determine whether or not the brahmara-kita was actually eating its victim or was injecting the cockroach with venom. He soon found out that no such activity appeared to be taking place.

Ekanta sat himself down a few feet from the two who had become one. Is this another, though weird, example of Shiva and Shakti, he thought to himself, the active and static components of Divine Reality? As he watched closely for over half an hour, neither insect moved in the least but simply remained completely stationary. The Avadhut decided that this was something worth studying, so he laid out his cloth on the side of the path, took his drinking water out and sat down to wait.

Hours later, after he had napped, he sat up and looked over at the two insects, honestly expecting to see that they had disappeared. His amazement was doubled when he saw that they had not moved an inch. Taking a stick, the Avadhut carefully and deliberately drew a small circle around the couple in order to ascertain in the near future whether they had moved or not. Then, he sat himself down to meditate.

Thinking of the two insects, the Avadhut's spiritually active mind began to superimpose teachings over the incident. This is like pure and unadulterated meditation, he thought to himself.

"The meditator and that which it contemplates," he said, half out loud. "The two are united, as if forever."

As for the cockroach, which had at first been scurrying for its very existence, it was now calm and fixated on its captor. Ekanta wondered if this was fear, but it seemed to be more like self-surrender and even resembled one-pointed meditation. In a flash, he felt as if he were in the presence of his most excellent gurus once again, breathing the sacred atmosphere of the ashram of his boyhood days. As he exulted in this feeling, the guru's words echoed again within his radiant and retentive mind:

*"Meditation is feeling the presence of God, Ekanta. In essence, it is not an effort put forth by the individual will or a striving for powers and visions. These are mere by-products, hardly worthy of mention. You, at this moment and at every moment that you sit to meditate, have the unique privilege and the auspicious boon to place your mind in union and in holy company with the Divine Being. This is a rare thing, is it not?"*

After pausing for a few pregnant moments, the guru continued.

*"What is the meaning of this act of Grace called meditation, dear student? Do you remember Narada's prayer to the Lord or Radha's supplication of Sri Krishna? Were they of ordinary content? No, of course not. These were not beings who were enamored of personal desires or duped by the world's allurements or deluded by Maya. They asked only for pure Love, pure Knowledge and pure Devotion for the Lord. Does this not tell us something? When beings of this caliber stand in the presence of Divinity and ask for such things, are we to ignore them and what they say?"*

Again came the few silent moments. The sacred sound of Om filled the room.

*"God is the only Reality, Ekanta, the rest is all secondary. The rest is, at best, His expression and otherwise is His power of illusion called Maya. In the worst case scenario, it is all suffering and confusion. Therefore, when you meditate, even as you sit in the primary posture as I have taught you, your main concern should be how to make the body, mind and consciousness focus on God, the Reality, as a living, breathing presence."*

Ekanta moved a bit to assume a more comfortable position.

*"Why have you shifted, my boy?"* came the admonishment. *"Have you not assumed the burning pillar meditation of seven points as I have instructed you. Is your mind fully focused on what I am saying?"*

"Yes sir," came Ekanta's assertion. More powerful moments passed.

_"No trace of separation between God, the Reality, and yourself should occupy the mind's awareness anyway and if it does then you must efface it by drawing nearer and nearer to this eternal Subject. A rope is fastened to the top of the cliff. Hand over hand, slowly and deliberately, you are moving up the slope as if your very life depends upon it. The Blessed One awaits you up there, wondering where you have gone in the first place. You have only to keep moving upward, or inward, and you will see Him face-to-face."_

As the Avadhut remembered this particularly powerful session with his blessed guru, he also recalled the feeling he had suddenly attained. Light had absorbed him on all sides, rushing around him and enveloping him completely. At that moment, he felt absolutely taken over by another force and felt as if he were drowning in bliss.

_"Ekanta...Ekanta...,"_ the words seemed to come from another realm.

Opening his eyes, he saw his guru's smiling face. Ekanta's teacher looked deep into his eyes and after a few moments of silence, stood up.

_"Good,"_ was all he said as he left the room and disappeared into the interior of the ashram.

Ekanta had remained seated for a time, a little disoriented but simultaneously filled with a scarcely containable joy. He also felt that a great secret had become revealed to him and he began to understand the term spiritual transformation in a new light from that day forward. When he saw the Mataji later that evening, she only looked at him with a knowing smile. His whole world had changed and his outlook was never quite the same again.

The Avadhut set up camp that evening just a few paces away from the still united insect couple. He had taken a resolve that he would practice meditation until the two insects separated or some other movement occurred. When he got back from his short hike to the Ganges for water, there was barely any light left, but he could still see their silhouette. After taking a few morsels of food and a few drinks of water, he placed himself in meditation position. He intended to meditate until midnight, sleep a little, and awaken at first light to see if his fellow meditators were still at it. As he slipped into meditation, the quiet darkness surrounding him on all sides, he felt warm, protected and fortunate beyond comprehension. To be able to commune with the Self within without any of the usual mental, physical and emotional, encumbrances that the people of the world had to deal with was a great boon. Soon, after an hour of deep concentration had passed, the Avadhut brought his mind to the physical plane and began to contemplate the teachings. A favorite song next came to mind:

> Meditate, O mind, on Lord Hari,
> the pure, the ever-perfect eternal Consciousness Absolute.
> What incomparable radiance!
> How fascinating is His wondrous Form!
> How dear is He to all His devotees!
> Even more beauteous in fresh blossoming Love
> that shames the splendor of a million moons.
> Like lightning gleams the glory of His form,
> filling the soul with deep joy and sweet ecstasy.
>
> Worship His Holy Feet in the lotus of your heart
> and with eyes made radiant with heavenly Love,
> behold that matchless sight!
> Overpowered with devotion,
> immerse yourself forevermore, O mind,
> in that One who is pure knowledge and pure Bliss Absolute!

The memory of this song, implanted into Ekanta's mind at this moment by the Divine Mother of the Universe Herself, launched him into another two-hour meditation on formless Reality. As he emerged from this session, his mind went directly to the feet of his guru once again.

"On what do I meditate, revered sir?" Ekanta asked his guru one day. "I have an Ishta, a chosen ideal, yet when I concentrate within, that Ishta disappears and I am left with light or with wisdom. Is that a bad sign?"

The guru considered this question for a time:

*"Your Ishta needs only your devotion, dear student. If meditation upon that chosen ideal proceeds naturally, then by all*

_means, concentrate there. If, however, you directly go into a meditation on formless Reality, take it as a sign that your ideal has directed you there for a purpose, for truly 'form is emptiness and emptiness is form.' As the Diamond Sutra declares, there are no divisions in Consciousness when seen from the primal, original perspective."_

"Revered sir," began Ekanta. "What if I am not certain that what I am meditating upon is formless Reality or just a blank? Truly, sometimes I feel as if I have no point of purchase whatsoever and I am just drifting."

Laughing softly, the guru replied, _"A good question, dear student. What do you think?"_

"That is not a good meditation, sir, and I feel it. Having had a taste of what you have tried to describe to me, I know that I am just wasting time as it were."

_"Ah,"_ said the guru, _"now we get to the heart of the matter. This is called discrimination in meditation. What you have experienced in study and devotion, in work and in contemplation is an external discrimination. Now you must hone a more subtle type of that quality and apply it within, in the realm of divine form and Reality without attributes. This is where the practice phase of your meditation begins. It is not all a bed of roses, you know."_

"Why am I not surprised to hear that, Guruji?" Ekanta responded.

The preceptor laughed again, this time loud and long.

_"Yes, I empathize with you. Spiritual life is, especially at the outset, beset with challenges and problems which can only be overcome by perseverance and guidance. After one discriminates about the nature of Reality, withdrawing from external attractions and seeing through the Maya, then one has to condition the internal mind and consciousness in a different fashion. Inner realization must follow outer analysis. Having a glimpse of Reality is not enough. Hundreds of people get intimations of Divine Presence daily around the world, but few follow up and practice those prescribed disciplines that will allow the mind to conform to what they have perceived in a deeper state. Many never even come to know what these glimpses signify."_

After the guru had finished speaking these words, he stopped to consider. Ekanta kept quiet, watching the mind of his wonderful preceptor at work.

*"It is noticed that even after spiritual experience has dawned, that aspirants live in a way inconsistent with what the inner Self demands and not in accordance with Divine dictates. You will notice, Ekanta, as you go through life in the world, that there is a vast difference between a sincere aspirant and one who has only caught glimpses of Divinity."*

"Can you give me some examples, dear teacher?" Ekanta asked.

*"It will be obvious to the likes of you, dear boy, brought up by spiritually oriented parents and partially raised in an ashram atmosphere with illumined beings like our Mataji."*

"Still, revered sir," Ekanta pleaded, "I would prefer to hear this from you."

*"Very well then, you shall,"* came the answer.

*"How can we tell the difference between sincere aspirants and those either given to mere show or those entirely without a clue as to what is required for advancement? For one, you will see that the insincere and the unknowing never seem to grasp the art of service to others. The insincere always think of their own needs and concerns and expect others to entertain and serve them, whereas the unknowing need to be taken by the hand and shown every little detail over and over again. Both are worthless when it comes to doing for others, the former out of selfishness and pride and the latter out of ineptitude or inexperience. Whereas the latter can be trained and can begin to serve others according to inherent capacity, the selfish ones find it hard to break old habits and quite often remain self-centered throughout their entire life. For them, it takes a harsh blow accompanied by real yearning to change, and this is only the beginning. There is still the hard practice phase to deal with.*

*"Insincere spiritual aspirants usually have a good dose of worldliness in them which they take to be experience. In the spiritual setting, you will see them participating whole-heartedly in chanting or other pleasant and easy forms of sadhana but when it comes time to sit in meditation for an hour or two, or to worship the Lord who is other than their pathetic little egos, or study and listen to the guru's lucid discourse on practical application of spiritual precepts and verities, they quickly fall out.*

*You see, if others are not paying them attention, or if they are not able to express their ego-oriented actions and ideas, they become arrogant and rebellious.  Going about in a deceitful manner, they cause trouble at ashrams, laughing and joking in an unseemly manner, engaging in pastimes which they ordinarily indulge in at home or in town and speaking author-itatively with the sangha members behind the guru's back as if they were the teacher.  Possibly they behave lasciviously by trying to engage the attention of the opposite sex.  Though they are enamored of an inflated sense of their own self-worth and attainment, to those looking on they are mere fools and buf-foons."*

"Dear teacher," asked Ekanta, "you said that in the case of insin-cere aspirants, the hard sadhana phase is still waiting to be accom-plished.  Earlier in the conversation, you mentioned the need for more than just visions and glimpses of Reality.  I am beginning to get the gist of what you are leading towards."

*"Yes, I believe you are,"* replied the guru.  *"Everyone knows, or should know, that God exists.  It is a moot point to devotees, though an outlandish consideration to the worldly-minded.  I have often pointed out that Sri Krishna defines atheists or agnostics as 'those of deluded intellect.'  In this regard, and after acknowledging this wonderful truth, why is it that beings do not take steps to realize God?  It is shallowness, old habits, egotism, attachment to the world and the like but, whatever the case may be, those who do begin to practice discover how difficult it is to uncover, contain and express Divinity."*

The guru stopped and looked into his student's eyes.  Ekanta was all attention and waited with bated breath.  Gradually, the teacher looked off into space and then began to speak again.

*"Transforming human nature, to use the expression, into an image of the Divine, is no game and no picnic.  Along the way, a few patches of light called visions and spiritual insights visit the mind, and beings imagine that they are illumined thereafter.  However, their callous and insensitive actions, crass and worldly speech, their inability to serve, incapacity to grow and their dependence upon old ways and worldly habits prove oth-erwise.  Those who make the grade, Ekanta, who pierce through the egotistic tendencies of the mind and make a sincere effort*

to change, to live a spiritual life, they are true devotees. From such as these, the Divine Mother draws a few who can successfully guide others."

"Revered sir," Ekanta broke in. "Your words have given me a greater resolve to transform myself into a true devotee. I now see the tendencies and habits of those who are, as yet, still grappling with preliminaries. I see my own shortcomings as well. Can you now describe what a divine life is like and how those who arrive at such a wonderful style of living, act, think and speak?"

"This is a good question, my boy," responded the guru. "Such a one serves others, as I have said. Their first thought, whether they enter a monastery, an ashram, or a house full of relatives or strangers, is of how they can be of service to others. This service they accomplish without thought of recompense, a demeaning occurrence in the mind which always spoils any true act or deed. Next, such a one treats all beings, each situation and every environment with reverence, knowing that it is God that has appeared in body, object, or in energy form at that time."

The guru's own thoughts stopped him for a while. After due consideration as to how he could best express what was in his mind, he continued:

"Time is another factor, Ekanta. One who lives a spiritual life spends time meditating. First comes formal meditation so that one can exercise the discrimination of meditation and reach enlightenment. What follows is constant meditation under all conditions of life. Few can do this. The sincere aspirant also studies the word of God, both as direct transmission through the Avatars, Ishvarakotis, saints, sages and gurus and as philosophy which has come down through the Rishis and other illumined beings. Very few accomplish this either.

"There are many things that come to mind, Ekanta, with regards to a true devotee, one who lives and breathes spirituality. At an ultimate level though, and one of the supreme indications, is that such a one goes about with God in mind, in heart, and in spirit. Thoughts are always directed towards God or given a divine orientation. Feelings and emotions become thoroughly refined and reflect qualities like devotion, compassion and love. And the spirit in all, Ekanta, Oh the spirit!"

At this moment, the guru had begun to shine with palpable light.

*"Every word bespeaks divinity, every act is graceful and beneficent and all interactions with the world and human beings leave an indelible impression fraught with goodness and positivity. This is indescribable."*

"It may well be, revered Guruji," Ekanta replied, "but I will forever be indebted to you for trying."

Smiling at his protégé's gracious words, the guru went on:

*"Others, looking on, may criticize, calling such beings mad or accusing them of having a holier-than-thou attitude. In these cases, one may as well accept the truth. Such beings are, indeed, more holy than others, for they are meditating on what is undeniably sacred, the very concentration of holiness itself. The attitude problem, in this case, lies with the observer.*

*"The devotees, those who are allowing God to do His work through them, are not even aware of their holiness. They simply apply themselves to what the guru and the scriptures advise. You will see them meditating every day, participating in devotional exercises, studying the scriptures, reading about the lives of the illumined ones, chanting the names of the Lord and Divine Mother of the Universe and serving Them through all living beings. Finally, you will notice that they are always focused on God, upon spiritual life, while the others are forgetting and lapsing into unconscious behavior throughout the day. This, in fact, if you ask me, draws a definite line of distinction between those who are serious about spirituality and want to reach enlightenment and those who are half-serious and still desire the world and what it has to offer."*

"Guruji," asked the boy. "The list you just enumerated — meditation, study, devotions, and selfless service — do all sincere aspirants participate in all of these? It seems that different beings have various temperaments and that some are averse to certain kinds of spiritual occupation."

*"What you have asked me,"* replied the teacher, *"is to outline the qualities of those who are sincere and serious about spiritual life. That is why I have given this list with regard to the true devotees. They are matured in their practice. Their practice, in fact, has become their passion, their preoccupation. You see, my boy, somewhere along the path, they got the right*

*orientation, the right idea. When this occurred, they did not continue the discipline because they wanted to attain something. They did so because they fell in love with the Lord."*

At this juncture in the conversation, the guru had to stop, for Ekanta noticed that tears had formed in his eyes.

"I understand more fully now, revered sir," said Ekanta. "True devotees practice disciplines and seek God out of love, not out of any desire for what the Lord can give, not even for high attainment and full enlightenment."

The guru looked tenderly at his disciple.

*"I could not have said it any better, Ekanta,"* he replied. *"That is why even liberation is not the goal of the true devotee, though that comes in due time. If you have understood this subtle but important distinction between selfless practice and goal oriented practice, then all your spiritual efforts will bear fruit. The same distinction applies to work in the world as well."*

After a pause, while the two sat thinking, the guru added a few afterthoughts.

*"It is accurate, Ekanta, to say that different aspirants are given to certain disciplines and averse to others. This can, however, eventually turn into stodginess and habitual practice devoid of life and realization. This is why the consummate devotee dives deep into every aspect of the practice, the way an avid student takes to different subjects at a university. Only by this wholehearted and focused attention on all areas of spirituality will one comprehend the Eternal Subject in its entirety. Perhaps a story illustrates this best.*

*"Once, there was a devotee who attained the goal of all spiritual practice. Word got around the religious circles that he was an illumined person and as this occurred his fame spread far and wide. People would come to visit him from various places and would ask for instruction. After a time, news of his spiritual state reached an old friend of his who had known him in earlier days, before his enlightenment had dawned. Wishing very much to see his famous friend, the man traveled a distance to seek him out.*

*"When he arrived at the sage's residence, he entered and found his old friend busy with his devotions. In front of him was his guru's slippers and every so often the sage would place his head*

*on them in reverence.  Occasionally, he would offer flowers before
the images on his altar and chant hymns in supplication to the
Divine represented in all of them.  When the visitor saw this,
he was amazed.  After the worship was over, the sage greeted
his old friend as a long-lost companion and the two sat for tea
and prasad.*

*"'Why is it,' asked the friend at one point, 'that though you
have reached the goal of your sadhana and are enlightened, you
still observe these external formalities such as worshipping the
guru's slippers and performing puja?  You do not need these
things anymore and still you persist in them.  I do not understand.  Perhaps you can explain this for me?'*

*"'Why certainly,' answered the illumined one.  'I do these
things out of love, for, upon seeing the Lord after my practices
bore fruit, I could not help myself but had to express my love
for Him.  Besides, I continue to do everything else after illumination has dawned, such as walking, talking, eating and
keeping holy company.  Why not do devotional exercises as well?
Have you come to see me because I have grown two horns?  No,
you have heard of my spiritual condition.  A man's features and
actions are not what really changes when illumination dawns.
His internal nature gets transformed.'"*

After completing his story, the guru continued.

*"This thorough and ongoing approach to realization, Ekanta,
accomplishes the purification of the body/mind mechanism in
an easy and natural manner.  Some place their minds on their
many inconsistencies or transgressions, thereby giving strength
and energy to these negativities.  Keeping the mind on God
through practices prescribed by his emissaries and teachers
is entirely different.  One experiences transformation in due
course, usually much quicker.  This is the way of acceptance,
the way of the future vijnani.  It is a different way from concentrating on one's inconsistencies and imperfections with a
mind to change the self by one's own small willpower.  So do not
divide yourself, Ekanta, either in life or in meditation, but give
all authority and control to the Lord and follow the path with
sincerity and humility.  This will conduce to your own highest
good and will benefit others as well."*

Ekanta meditated for several hours after this contemplation on his guru's words.  Before he lay down to sleep, he checked the brahmara-kita and the cockroach to see if any change had occurred.  The two were still one, locked in an embrace of mutual meditation.  The Avadhut wondered what he would see in the morning as he closed his eyes in sleep.

In the night, a dream visited the Avadhut.  Actually, Ekanta knew, it was a vision, though not an ordinary one, if the term could be so used, but a living transmission.  One of his revered teachers from the past appeared to him and discoursed for a time on Reality.  The discourse was about meditation and its efficacy.

The mountain yogi, Yogindra, had disappeared out of Ekanta's life one day.  He had never seen the yogi again and it had proved a difficult and unexpected lesson in giving up attachment.  So many long years had passed since then in which he, the Avadhut, had left home and teachers and wandered away into the world.  In all his travels and pilgrimages, though, he had never forgotten to make offerings, both mental and physical, to the memory of Yogindra Yogi, his beloved guru of renunciation.

Upon beholding the yogi in his vision, Ekanta, nearly beside himself with joy, questioned him.

"Where did you go, revered sir?  When you did not show up at the village for so many days, I came looking for you but you were not to be found in or around the cave.  For days I hiked the distance uphill to find you and even searched the mountain passes for signs of you.  I never saw you again, nor did anyone in the vicinity.  It was one of the sore spots of my young manhood.  In fact, I left home and teachers myself after that and wandered over the land partly due to your disappearance."

*"And this was perfect, revered Avadhut,"* replied the yogi. *"Mother Reality does not waste anything, not the tiniest modicum.  She implanted this soreness in your heart due to my death to cause the final separation from your youthful surroundings.  That phase of your life was over, had reached its consummation."*

"Then you left the body at that time, revered sir?" asked the Avadhut.

*"Yes,"* came the reply.  *"I gave up the body into the rushing waters of the mountains we used to hike, dear one.  It was nearing its end anyway and was of no use to me or anyone else*

_except by this final act.   Therefore, I kicked the mortal frame_
_away from me and became myself again, my true Self.   It was_
_wonderful and I still remember the exhilarating feeling of free-_
_dom once again after experiencing the limitation of the physi-_
_cal condition.   People are silly to fear death."_

"Is the body truly a limitation then?" asked the Avadhut.  "What
I mean is, are you different now than when you were embodied
in terms of your realization?"

_"If you are referring to jivanmukti, revered Avadhut,"_
answered the yogi, _"you are better suited to answer that, for you_
_are in a more refined condition now than I was when I was in_
_the body.   I still had to observe such austerity in order to main-_
_tain awareness of the highest.   You have reached a supremely_
_natural condition and hardly even question it.   Perhaps, since_
_you are asking this question, this is the final answer you_
_require and, perhaps what I say will aid you.   It is certain that_
_Mother wants us to communicate like this, that is clear.   We have_
_a very close connection."_

"How true, dear sir," marveled the Avadhut.  "Here, in this
dream, which I am aware of, time is folded up, is practically
nonexistent except for my perception of it.   It is wonderful yet
perplexing, all in a perfectly natural way."

_"Yes, illumined one,"_ came the yogi's reply.  _"That is why I have_
_come.   Your austerity with regard to meditation has drawn me_
_here to give you this bit of teaching.   It is straight from the_
_Divine Mother, our wonderful ideal.   Remember how we used to_
_talk about Her in the cave at night?   She compels me to tell you_
_about meditation.   Listen for a time, and I bid you farewell in_
_advance, for once the message is delivered, I am absorbed once_
_again.   To say that we shall unite again would be incorrect, for_
_we are always together.   You know that."_

In a momentless moment, during which the vision of the yogi
somehow altered itself, the Avadhut became aware of an
increased clarity which occurred in both receptivity of the vision
and focus on his own part.  It was as if someone were adjusting
the fine tunings on a machine, the mechanisms in this case being
the two mind-streams of the yogi and the Avadhut.  Once this was
accomplished, Ekanta easily opened up and received the Divine
Mother's message to him through the yogi:

*"All is meditation. There is nothing in physical, emotional, mental, spiritual, celestial or causal realms that does not amount to the Divine meditating on the Divine. The subdivisions of these various states or conditions of consciousness are nothing but streams flowing from Reality, through Reality and returning to Absolute Reality, though to say that they return is inaccurate, for they never leave the proximity of the one, indivisible Divine Reality. This is the meditation of the Divine Mother, this total awareness of all realms and all that occurs in them. When beings meditate on Reality, from whatever perspective or orientation, it is the Divine Mother who causes them to do so. She is also the one meditating through them and the subject, object or verity upon which they meditate. To know this is what is called realization in all realms of existence.*

*"Furthermore, auspicious one, know that all beings who reach the plateau of spiritual comprehension which allows them to meditate upon Reality are, at that moment, no different than Brahman Itself. It is God, again, that affords all living beings the ability to destroy barriers and immerse themselves in the Infinite Being, for these veils obscure the essential connection between devotee and the Lord. Why else would such bliss come upon the meditator? Why else would Truth dawn on the consciousness of such beings? Why else would the desire for absorption into Reality, amounting to total freedom, possess the minds of aspiring beings?*

*"Meditation on death, beloved one, is the searchlight that illumines primal Awareness, so to speak, revealing It to be what It truly is. As long as fear, in any form, impedes the mind, so long will the embodied condition appear to be real, for insecurity will bind the mind to it. Lay yourself down then or enter a dark cave. Go within in whatever fashion you have become accustomed to and dive into meditation with a mind to break down all distinctions and strip Reality bare of its coverings. You will find, ultimately, that the coverings are all conceptions of the mind, that indeed, nothing but Reality exists. Let tears stream from the eyes due to this realization. Then you will live and breathe the atmosphere of Pure Conscious Awareness and not before.*

*"Become lifeless, simulate death. This is what my great sons*

*did, what the Buddha accomplished under the Bo tree, what the
Christ experienced in the wilderness, what Sri Krishna taught
in the Celestial Song.  The great ones die and come to life every
day, O seeker!  In Truth, all of my children experience this,
though they call it sleep and awakening.  Thus, they meditate
naturally every day, but do not awaken with ultimate knowledge.  Nor do they enter into sleep as if it were death, thereby
knowing death to be an illusion made strong by attachment to
the embodied condition.  Renunciation does not pertain to just
the world and its objects, beloved one.  The body, the life-force,
the mind and yes, even the Three Worlds are to be renounced.
Life itself, in all its multitudinous forms, must be given up consciously every moment, for only then will the truth of Eternal
Existence be realized.*

*"Come to know yourself as Consciousness and then realize
that Consciousness as Mine alone, ever-one with Me.  Thus, you
are eternal Awareness Itself.  Know that all forms are soluble
into Me, that I am the primordial solution into which beings
and objects, nay, entire universes, gross and subtle, get dissolved.  Thus will you know your Source."*

The Avadhut sat up, fully awake in one instant.  Or was he more
awake in the dream/vision he had just encountered?  Either state
seemed equally real at this point and he immediately closed his
eyes to survey again what the Divine Mother had transmitted
through the channel of Yogindra Yogi.  This was a powerful boon
he had just received.  Though it was not entirely different than the
words of the Avatars and prophets of old, their wisdom being also
what they had received from the Ultimate Source, it nevertheless
bore much more weight.  The words were spoken by Divine Reality
Itself and therefore had authority beyond description, able to
dissolve doubts and subtle misconceptions completely.  Ekanta
meditated on these words for two hours, running them through
his mind again and again.

After rising from his deep meditation, the Avadhut looked
towards the place where the brahmara-kita and the cockroach had
been locked in union the evening before.  To his amazement, the
two still remained as before, frozen in time, meditating, as it were,
on the reality of oneness.  Still in a very devotional state, the
Avadhut approached the brahmara-kita and bowed down before it.

"You are my teacher of meditation," he said, "for your meditation is eternal, deep and uninterruptable. As long as you remain in this condition, so long will I practice meditation as well, as is my vow."

During Ekanta's morning meditation, the teachings from the scriptures with regards to meditation occupied his internal thinking process:

> By meditating upon the unlimited Reality,
> posture becomes firm and natural,
> dualities cease to obstruct
> and breathing becomes regulated in natural fashion.

These words of Patanjali, the father of yoga, had always guided Ekanta beyond the tendency of the mind towards restlessness, beyond the tendency of the body to shift and obstruct and beyond the tendency of the breath to become arrhythmic or shallow. When others had put all their energies into postures, breathing and wrestling with the mind, Ekanta had, through guidance from his teachers, simply placed faith, devotion and attention on God. This was the secret to his success in spiritual life and it amounted to self-surrender, love of the Divine and knowledge of Its indivisible nature.

In the Avadhut's afternoon meditation, after he had walked to the Ganges and returned with water, he became absorbed in the various forms of meditation that his teacher had described to him from Buddhist texts.

"The first state of dhyana, meditation, according to this system, Ekanta, is the removal of unwholesome thoughts and bothersome desires through conceptualization and flow of thought. This meditation, a kind of absorption, is to be participated in with conscious effort, accomplished joyfully.

"The second stage of meditation brings an end to all thought and concept in general and creates instead a sense of well-being centered in evenness and internal calm. Joy continues to be a factor, dear student, and plays an essential part. The third stage, however, does away with feelings of joy or bliss and centers human awareness in a condition of equanimity called 'upeksha.'"

Ekanta loved this word and it had ever since characterized his meditations throughout his life.

*"Finally,"* the guru continued, *"the fourth state arrives and one feels equanimity mixed with total alertness. Such a one is awake and perfectly centered."*

"These are very helpful," Ekanta replied after the discourse. "Where do they come from?"

*"These are the Four Stages of Absorption listed in Buddhist teachings, Ekanta, dhyana according to Lord Buddha. One must relinquish base desire through vitarka, conceptualization, and vichara, discursive thought. Priti and sukha, joyful interest and well-being, then visit the mind. Next, one can concentrate on some divine object that results in calmness of mind. This joyful calm dissolves, however, and a state of evenness occurs. After that, in the last stage, one is simultaneously alert and equanimous. You are right, Ekanta, awareness of these types of teachings, when applied directly in practice, in spiritual life, can go a long way towards realization. It is strange that aspirants fail to implement such tools."*

Going through these stages one by one while remembering his guru's words, the Avadhut easily reached his mark that day and the afternoon slid by unnoticed.

At dusk, after an hour of rest and after saluting his meditation master nearby on the ground, Ekanta assumed half-lotus again and concentrated his attentions within. Dusk was his favorite time to meditate, besides midnight, and he intended to make the two time frames unite into one this evening. Coming out of meditation every few hours, the Avadhut spent the evening immersed in thoughts of the Divine. When thoughts disappeared, he contemplated formless Reality and occasionally attained annihilation of personal ego-awareness for long periods of time. Sometimes, a teaching would appear to his mind, propelling him on in his joyful exploration of the internal terrain of Consciousness.

*"Brahman is self-existent, self-effulgent,"* came the words of Sri Krishna to his mind. *"Hence, it is Brahman Itself that appears, assuming the many forms and vehicles such as organs, elements, bodies, minds and various attributes."*

Such teachings lifted the Avadhut's mental condition and plunged the mind over and over again into indivisible Reality until it no longer possessed a sense of individuality or any thought of separation from God. Thus did the austerity of meditation go on all evening and well after midnight.

As morning drew near, the Avadhut opened his eyes. He was not surprised to see that both the brahmara-kita and the cockroach were gone.

"I too disappeared after a long meditation," he said out loud to his tiny teacher. As these words lost themselves in the surrounding air, memories of his Mataji sprang into his mind with subtle force.

*"Indescribable nothingness and unimaginable fullness are present in deep meditation,"* she had said to him one day, *"but both are only appreciable if the sense of 'I' is either diminished or gone completely. Therefore, true meditation is not possible so long as one is bound to the senses, the mind and the body. On the other hand, when these things are realized to be insubstantial, limited expressions of Reality, then all transforms into meditation. Detach, O mind, give up desire for the world. Free yourself of doubts and minor considerations. Purify the senses and offer them as fuel for meditation. Heed Sri Krishna's words which declare:"*

Remove all doubts about the Atman.
Know it to be other than the body.
Turn away from sense objects
and dwell within with the bliss of the Self.

*"Become a true devotee, Ekanta,"* she said, gazing at him earnestly, *"a true devotee."*

— Chapter 18 —

# Teachings on Omniscience and All-Pervasiveness

THE EIGHTEENTH GURU — The Sky

THE LESSON — Transcendence

*What a teacher the sky proved to be, O Prince, for as I studied it I saw that it was simply reflective of its Creator, transcendent of all things and all-pervasive. Beings of the world are affected adversely by what seems negative and are overjoyed at what appears fortunate. Appearances, however, can be misleading. Teachers like the sky instruct us by example, revealing that we should rise above all dualities and be peaceful and content. By accepting the sky as one of my gurus, I learned all this and more.*

The Avadhut lay flat on his back looking straight up into the air. The infinite blue sky stretched out on all sides as far as the eye could see, decorated here and there by a few wispy clouds that added dimension to an otherwise boundless expanse. A few birds glided at high elevations, following the air currents that lent their wings the power of transcendence above the earth's solid mass and the onerous pull of gravity.  Like a flash, Ekanta's mind remembered an old teaching he had loved as a young man but had not thought about for years.  It had been given to him by his guru, his eternal companion.

*"If you burn a bird's nest, it will take refuge in the sky, Ekanta,"* said the teacher one day.  *"Such a teaching suggests both the possibility and necessity of transcendence, does it not?"*

Ekanta had not answered, for it was not the kind of question that ever elicited a response from him since he knew that none was expected.  That certain tone in his guru's voice provided this insight and also always prepared him for the series of teachings that would follow.  His teacher often warmed up to his topic in this manner and, on this occasion, it was no different.

*"Weak and jaded minds, Ekanta, either reject or fail to contemplate the need to transcend the body and mind.  The ignorant have not yet been awakened to that possibility.  You see, when a baby is born, it immediately needs mother's milk and is quickly placed on the mother's breast.  It is happy there for a time.  In the same fashion, when the first glimmer of awakening occurs in the minds of the ignorant, they must be given the essential knowledge so that they can contemplate it.  It is a shock, no doubt, to hear such powerful assertions, but it is also an absolute necessity.  We were not born for the purpose of merely enjoying an earthly existence while being a slave to matter.  We are born here to realize God and rise above the limitations that matter imposes upon us.  These limitations include the negativities of the mind that caused birth in relativity in the first place amidst the mind's mundane and habitual tendencies.  When this is accomplished, then only can we truly live.  All existence before this realization dawns, unless it is utilized for sadhana in order to destroy impediments in the way of enlightenment, is simply delusion and bondage, plain and simple.  It was to effect this twofold purpose that, in the ancient times of the Rishis, the children were given the perennial wisdom at a young age so they never suffered from bondage to root ignorance."*

A powerful silence followed these words.

*"What are the three axioms of Vedantic transmission, my boy?"* the teacher asked suddenly.

"That we must hear the Truth, contemplate the Truth and realize the Truth," came Ekanta's swift and decisive answer, "called shravanam, mananam and nididhyasanam by the ancient ones."

_"Ah,"_ replied the guru, _"it is inspiring to find this esoteric knowledge in the mind of a young boy. I am infinitely pleased. There is also another related triad in this regard, called shruti, yukti and anubhava — that is, taking recourse to the scriptures, reasoning on the precious truths they contain and then finally arriving, through practice and implementation, at direct spiritual experience. I am exceedingly happy to find that you, after spending several years with us as our student, are making use of all six of these fine Vedic principles."_

The two smiled at one another and the teacher went on.

_"The real devotee arrives at the third stage, realizing the Truth, through swift and decisive internal action, my boy. Approaching is not enough. The consummation of arrival must be achieved. Contemplation must lead one to the realization of that which one contemplates. Meditation must cause one to become absorbed in that which one meditates upon. This is yoga in action. Nothing short of this will do. All else is a masquerade, fraudulent appearances posing as the real thing. Such posturing and pretense is a bane on religion and philosophy and a blight on spiritual life. Never fall a victim to this, do you hear?"_

"Yes, revered sir," came the quick response.

_"Good,"_ was the only reply, and that was all that was ever said about the matter.

Ekanta reflected for a while, then he asked his guru, "After one realizes the Truth, is that it? What happens then?"

_"That is a simple but perceptive question, dear student,"_ answered the teacher. _"There is a fourth stage that is seldom talked about and that is expressing the Truth. Our transcendence of the body and mind is for the purpose of knowing the essence of Reality that is ultimately beyond life and mind, not limited by name and form. This Reality, however, also permeates life and mind and expresses itself through name and form. Few ever know the transcendent Reality, though, being enamored of the body and sense-life. These are the ones who complain whenever transcendence of the physical and mental condition is talked about and also balk whenever it comes time or appears_ *necessary to rise up and realize the Atman. These are precisely the ones who get trapped in the Kalachakra, the wheel of birth and death. Since many fail to realize the Atman, only hearing about it, illumined beings come back to teach them again and again. It is like blowing on the coals of a fire after morning has dawned in order to start the blaze up once again. Perhaps you have heard us chant from the Kathopanishad?"*

With this reminder, the guru recited some of the blessed wisdom teachings from the ancient scriptures:

*Shravanayapi bahubhir yo na labyah*
*Srnvato'pi bahavo yam na vidyuh*
*Ashcharyo vakta kushalo'sha labdha*
*Ashcharyo jnata kushalanushishtah*

*"Translated freely, Ekanta,"* the teacher continued, *"it reads:"*

Many there are who never hear of the Self.
Many others, though they hear of It, fail to comprehend It.
Wonderful is the one who speaks of It.
Wonderful the one who learns of It.
But supremely fortunate is the one, who,
having the good fortune to be blessed
with an authentic teacher,
is able to realize It in this life.

After this recitation, the guru stopped for a few moments to consider his next words.

*"As I was saying, the Atman pervades everything, therefore it is here in the body/mind condition. Its radiance lends life and animation to matter and thought, but It is never limited to them. It is with this in mind that the Kenopanishad states:"*

Indeed, that one attains immortality who intuits the Atman
in and through every modification of the mind.

*"Not only this, Ekanta, but the Atman is not subject to birth, decay and death like the body or bothered by the anxieties, doubts, lethargy and restlessness of the mind. Don't you see, by*

*identifying with body and mind as the true Self, one enters the arena of relativity and accepts it as Reality. Then a life of delusion begins, maybe many lifetimes. If one gives oneself to matter and thought alone, suffering is born. If instead, one realizes one's pristine, eternal nature beyond these modifications of consciousness, suffering is easily transcended."*

"Revered sir," asked the young man, "we notice without a doubt that the Avatars, those of divine descent, suffer the effects of relativity. Are they not well-trained in the art of transcendence?"

*"That is another good perception, Ekanta," replied the guru, "and one that many illumined beings have pondered at length. For one thing, all embodied beings who visit the earth must temporarily accept the burden of the six transformations — birth, growth, disease, decay, old age and death. This is the way of it. The Avatars are no exception. But since they do come, suffer, and show us the way to transcend limitation and misery, is this not ample incentive for us to emulate such an example? Should we emulate their suffering or their transcendence of it? If the question revolves around whether or not they actually do transcend suffering and the body/mind condition, there is positive proof in the teachings of the scriptures, particularly in the Advaitic Truths, but who will study them?*

*"Another wonderful proof is testimony as well," the guru went on. "I shall translate the actual words of the Avatar for you so you can better understand that perspective."*

Saying this, the guru closed his eyes and, after a time, uttered:

I would give thousands of bodies if by that I could help one single soul in the path of righteousness and God-Realization. I am now speaking and eating through many mouths. I am the Soul of all individual souls. I have infinite mouths, infinite heads, infinite hands and feet. My pure form is spiritual. It has neither birth nor death, neither sorrow, disease or suffering. It is immortal and perfect. All pain is in the body, all disease is in the body, but the Spirit is above pain and beyond the reach of disease. Any illness I undergo is to teach mankind how to think of the Spirit and how to live in God-Consciousness even when there is pain in the body, to set an example of mastery of the Spirit over matter.

After these words had come forth, Ekanta and his guru meditated for a while, lost in deep appreciation of the Divine Mystery. After a time, the guru spoke.

*"The Avatar suffers here in the web of time, space and causality too, Ekanta, but even in that state there is ecstasy most of the time. Coming down out of samadhi, such beings bear pain in order to teach the devotees and disciples and help suffering beings. In this event, the Avatar has to concentrate on the body in order to commune with those in the body. The Avatar can, though, at any time, rise to the realm of Spirit and only maintains the body for teaching others about the ultimate condition. After that, They pass from the body completely, though in truth, They were never really embodied since pure Consciousness is not present in time and space. Some remain here for a while in a subtle body and their presence is pervasive in the absolute sense. This is a great mystery, a wonder, and in accordance with that we proclaim, 'Jai Avatara Varishtaya,' 'Victory to the Supreme Principle.' That One even takes on a body for the sake of others!"*

The Avadhut focused his eyes outwardly again upon the blue sky above. Yes, those white birds high above seemed to glide around in substanceless space effortlessly, never coming to roost on the earth. The words of his Mataji came to his mind.

*"Great beings are like the eggs of the Homa bird that flies high in the sky, Ekanta. The Homa Bird lays her eggs in the sky, miles above the earth and they plummet for hours. Then, sensing the earth's atmosphere approaching, the chicks inside break their shells, see the imminent danger of physical matter coming upon them and soar back up towards their mother in the higher regions. Like this, my boy, the great ones only approach the earth. They never make their home here like ordinary deluded beings. They know that this world is the region of suffering and limitation. Why should they become comfortable here? Just to build a home, either of wood, flesh and bone, or concepts and have it destroyed? No, my son. Such as these do not fall victim to forgetfulness of their true nature by imagining themselves to be creatures of the body and the mind, and neither should you."*

Ekanta had heard the Mataji tell this story before, but at this moment in the evolution of his spiritual understanding, it struck him profoundly.  He had, at that instant, comprehended to a certain extent, the necessity of transcendence and the nature of enlightenment.  One night, later in his life, around the dhuni fire at a holy pilgrimage spot in the sacred mountains of India, he had instructed several sadhakas about this verity in inspired fashion:

"The Spirit which you seek, called Brahman by the ancients, the Father in Heaven by the Christ, Allah by the Muslims and Tathagatagarbha by the Buddhists, is anterior to life and mind.  It pre-exists everything experienced by the senses or known by the mind.  Can you expect to find this Eternal One, then, by searching the earth from one end to the other or by thinking any number of thoughts with the intellect?  No, you must seek that One within, the Self that is transcendent of body, senses, life-force, mind, intellect, ego and conditioned consciousness.  Then you will find It."

The Avadhut used to watch the birds for hours when he was young.  One day, the Mataji approached him quietly and seeing his fascination with them, spoke to him:

_"They are comfortable up there, my dear.  They need no foundation upon which to perch.  They could go like that for the entire day without resting for they have learned the art of negotiating the wind's currents with the least amount of expended energy."_

After a time, she added, _"The illumined ones are like that also. Bereft of attachments to house, food, companionship and all that comprises the worldly concerns of the earth-bound soul, these spiritual beings easily glide above all earthly affairs and are eternally contented.  Contemplate this spiritual facility of pure existence again and again, dear one."_

His two vanaprastin teachers, his Guruji and his Mataji, instructed him often in the Patanjala Yoga system during the course of his studies.  After the yamas and niyamas had been memorized and implemented into his daily life and the successive six steps had been explained, his gurus one day began to tell him of the condition of the yogi who had attained transcendence over mind and matter.

_"There are seven indications of the highest state of Consciousness according to this system, Ekanta.  Would you like to learn them?"_

"Oh yes, please," came the young man's response.

*"Good,"* replied his Guruji, *"then listen carefully and memorize. Patanjali calls them the 'Seven Stages of Advanced Knowledge.' First comes the realization that all knowledge is within. We see that illumined beings understand this while others do not. For instance, worldly beings, even those who are intelligent, go about the matters and concerns of relative existence in a mode of seeking satisfaction outwardly. Their enjoyments are sought externally. Their pursuits are all engaged in externally. Even their knowledge is sought for outside, never within, even though the Christ and others insisted that all true attainment resides within! This is a perpetual habit in this day and age. It is not that searching for knowledge outside is bad or totally fruitless, Ekanta. It is that all outward search will be meaningless, will amount to nothing without the spiritual orientation that reveals Reality to be an eternal verity that is beyond externals, ever residing within."*

*"Think about it Ekanta,"* the Mataji joined in. *"Does knowledge exist outside of you? If one considers this question, even if convinced that relative existence is the ultimate Reality one will invariably have to admit that all knowledge is within, that outer stimuli only prick the memory of it. Consideration, contemplation, meditation, all happen inside of us. This truth, taken to the ultimate position, reveals that the Source of all knowledge abides within. It is most definitely the natural and intelligent conclusion."*

Continuing his listing of the seven stages, the Guruji went on.

*"So, Ekanta, all knowledge resides within you. The reason that beings are unfulfilled and dissatisfied with their existence on earth is due to the fact that most of them cling to externals and seek consummation and knowledge outside of themselves. This can go on interminably and often does, but if one makes a subtle adjustment in the human awareness that perceives this hidden secret, then, suddenly, all outer action begins to satisfy. As a result, a natural detachment occurs that takes one beyond self-motivated work. The maturation of this detachment is what we see in the illumined ones who have realized this first stage of advanced knowledge."*

*"The second stage,"* said the Mataji, for his gurus often took

turns instructing him, *"is the cessation of pain, signaled by free-dom from attachment and aversion. We have instructed you on this before. It is not that the body and nerves cease to feel pain when injured or diseased, but that the mind has mastered the art of transcendence over the body and senses and can withdraw to a higher state of consciousness at will. I once saw my guru undergo a small surgery on his arm to remove a cyst. Before the doctor applied the scalpel, the guru said, 'Wait a moment.' Then he withdrew his mind from that part of the body and placed it elsewhere. He therefore experienced very little dis-comfort during the procedure due to his control of the mind's awareness over the body. I was a witness to this fact.*

*"So, Ekanta, when this power of transcendence is mature, the yogi can do amazing things. I am not speaking of those who walk on hot coals, manipulate their bodies into ungodly posi-tions and lie on beds of nails for show and monetary gain. This is all spectacle and pretentiousness for the sake of the ego. True luminaries realize the Spirit beyond the body/mind mechanism and set an example to us by placing their consciousness upon what is Eternal rather than on what is ephemeral. This is a profound teaching, and demonstrates to us the nature of pure Spirit."*

*"The third stage of advanced knowledge is the presence of real-ization through samadhi,"* said his revered male preceptor. *"Union with the Atman, that which is always present but which becomes obscured due to Maya and delusion, occurs at a par-ticular point in spiritual evolution. One experiences various bhavas, spiritual moods, and the different levels of supercon-scious Awareness. Basically, Patanjali categorizes these into two divisions which he indicates as Samprajnata Samadhi — that which is still conditioned by awareness of the relative universe — and Asamprajnata Samadhi called Nirodha, which is pure Consciousness free from any and all objectification or mentation."*

*"Tell him about the four types of Samprajnata Samadhi, revered husband,"* said the Mataji.

*"Please be my guest,"* he replied, smiling at her.

*"Samprajnata,"* continued the Mataji, *"is a concentrated state of mind that is one-pointed and destructive of all impediments. Its four phases are Savitarka, Savichara, Sananda and Sasmita."*

"Can you define these terms for me, Mataji?" asked Ekanta.

*"That is about all I can do, dear boy,"* answered the guru, *"and for the rest you will have to experience it for yourself. This description will act as a road map so you will at least know when such a condition comes upon you.*

*"Savitarka, the first of the four divisions of conditioned samadhi called Samprajnata, is a state where the highest logic and rationale are operative in the mind. Such a condition is, it must be admitted, still under the sway of the mental faculty, but very high experiences are taking place nevertheless. You might say that it and its mate, Savichara Samadhi, the second samadhi, are samadhis of the intellect. In the first, Savitarka, argumentation is going on, as it were, as the intellect strives to find the Source of this powerful light of Truth that is in the process of being revealed but that is ultimately beyond it. In the second, Savichara, argumentation turns into inquiry, that is, the intellect no longer doubts the existence of this Light of Truth but generally accepts It, though it wants to find a way of entering into It. Reason and deliberation thus take the place of argumentation and subtle skepticism. Thus, Ekanta, the first two conditioned states have been described to you."*

*"The third,"* his male preceptor joined in, *"is called Sananda. It is a wonderful experience and, as you might well assume from its name, heralds the rising of consciousness out of mere mind and intellect into a state of bliss that is not reliant on the thought process. This is the leap of faith that you have heard tell about, Ekanta. Fortunate indeed is the one who accomplishes this transition, for life and mind will never be the same again. In fact, Sasmita, the fourth kind of conditioned samadhi, proceeds from it. Sasmita, in Sanskrit, means, 'still with a feeling of individuality.' We are to conclude from this that all has been effaced from consciousness except the slight trace of ego. A person in this state proclaims joyfully, 'I am That,' or 'I exist.' All that he or she perceives is the Light of Truth, but a thin tendril of personal and possessive energy persists and restrains one from experiencing total immersion."*

Ekanta thought about this while his teachers remained silent for a time. Then he said, "I have memorized what you have told me. Now, can you tell me about Asamprajnata Samadhi?"

His twin gurus looked knowingly at each other, a look rife with significance.  Then, the Mataji continued:

*"What can we say, Ekanta?   It is the unexplainable, the Indescribable Itself.   It must suffice to say that Samprajnata Samadhi means 'with cognitive traces.'  It is a state wherein the triad of meditator, meditation and what is meditated upon persists.  It equates to Savikalpa Samadhi expounded in Vedanta Philosophy."*

"And Asamprajnata Samadhi?" came the voice of her student, meekly but persistently.

The Mataji laughed and said, *"My dear, you are always after the highest.  This is why we love you so much!"*

Pausing and looking at her husband as if for a sign, she then turned her attention to her beloved student.

*"If Samprajnata Samadhi pertains to a subtle trace of cognition with the mind, then Asamprajnata Samadhi would be a condition wherein that mental perception, no matter how high it may be, is totally annihilated.  In fact, that is what occurs, evidently.  The ego sense and the intellect are dissolved in Pure Conscious Awareness as ice dissolves into water.  The salt doll who enters the ocean with a mind to describe its contents and its depth will never be able to do so, for entering there, it will dissolve in its own element, its own nature.  This is about all that can be said.  Asamprajnata equates to Nirvikalpa Samadhi in the Vedanta system.  Notice that the Buddha described it as Nirvana and Patanjala as Nirodha.  All is 'blown out' in that experience, completely dissolved."*

After a short interval in which the gurus allowed Ekanta time for assimilation, the teaching continued:

*"There remains a difference of opinion among the seekers after Reality as to whether all seed impressions are destroyed in Asamprajnata Samadhi,"* stated his male preceptor.  *"Since some return from that state, there must be a motivating force that pulls one back.  Some insist it is the desire to do good to others in a spiritual sense, while others proclaim the presence of subtle seeds in the mental sheath.  Whatever the case may be, the stages of advanced knowledge that we are discussing may offer some clue.  So let us proceed.*

*"The fourth stage of advanced knowledge, according to*

Patanjali, is seeing all as God and acting accordingly with absolute freedom from bondage. After samadhi has been achieved, in whatever form and to whatever degree, the being transforms into an image of Spirit. The result is that all beings and the universe in which they live reflect the Light of Consciousness and the experiencer of this condition actually perceives this. What to speak of mere perception, though not a small attainment in itself, the ones who have realized the fourth state of knowledge act in this Light, think in this Light and meditate in this Light. This action, thought and meditation are accomplished in freedom and all dualities such as attachment and aversion, pleasure and pain and even life and death do not affect them. Thus does life go on in an entirely new and elevated awareness.

"As this occurs, the fifth stage of advanced knowledge is growing, maturing. This is freedom as well, but a freedom inconceivable to most. It is here where 'the men get separated from the boys,' as the saying goes. In the fifth stage, the mind gets freed from any notion that Consciousness requires a mind or a place to rest or exist. This means, Ekanta, that one realizes without a doubt that the mind is not the dwelling place of Consciousness and that heavens, earths and hells are not needed for the maintenance of Consciousness. Imagine then, if you will, a Consciousness so free that mental states, lokas, realms of being and cosmic imperatives are not required for it and, indeed, are insufficient to contain or limit its boundless expanse."

"What your revered guru is saying is profound, Ekanta," joined in the Mataji. "Essentially, what this means is that not only time and karma have been transcended, but that space itself, whether of a gross physical nature, a subtle ethereal nature or a realm of intellectual understanding, has been transcended, given up. This is the ultimate renunciation, is it not? The last vestiges of attachment or familiarity with relativity have gone. Where to rest, Ekanta, except in that which is the very essence of supernal Peace itself! It is like the Koa'e Ula bird with a long white tail that glides easily and naturally above high cliffs, transcendent of everything and perfectly content there. If it nests at all, it does so in pristine areas free of habitation, in *the walls of inaccessible cliffs and mountains. Similarly does the one of advanced knowledge abide as well, and if such a one visits the realms of relativity at all, he or she remains detached, experiencing a pure and natural existence, living only to teach and free others.*

*"It is at this stage, Ekanta, that subtle impressions in the mind get totally disintegrated. The sixth stage of advanced knowledge in a yogi is that of the destruction of the gunas and seed impressions called samskaras. If one is free from the gunas, then one must necessarily be free of the universe, of embodiment, of utilizing the mental sheath. So good-bye to relativity. If one exists in a body at all after the attainment of this stage, it is as a mere ghost, as it were. The illumined have described the bodies of such ones as strips of bamboo with pieces of cloth stretched over them, or puppets made of clear paper tied to transparent strings, or figures made of wax consisting only of one substance. The one condition here, of course, is Pure Existence. The one existing thing operative there is Pure Knowledge. The one experience present there is Pure Bliss. Thus, Satchitananda, the only Guru, takes a form, as it were."*

*"What Mataji describes leads well into the seventh stage of advanced knowledge, Ekanta,"* added the guru, *"and we use the term knowledge loosely here or only in the ultimate sense. Complete absorption is the seventh stage. Here, there is no more identification of the Atman with the mind, body or universe."*

"Asamprajnata or Nirvikalpa, revered sir?" came Ekanta's question.

*"Precisely, dear student,"* was the reply. *"The Atman is all in all, none else exists. There is not nor was there ever anything but That existing at all times and in all places. The superimposition of various coverings over Atman is called relative existence, life in the universe, body-oriented sense life and so forth. Look at it this way, Ekanta, from the standpoint of Truth first and knowledge second, then you will know the first stage, that all knowledge exists first within you — within the real you. Leave off this foggy and limiting notion that Truth is far off, or that the world is real and the Spirit an imagination. This is delusion, the beginning of misery and suffering and the cause for the continuation of many births in ignorance."*

The Avadhut was on his legs again and moving through the countryside. Recalling those precious and powerful teachings had inspired him in the extreme. It was no wonder that he had turned out to be a spiritually oriented being, conditioned by nothing save Truth Itself. Exposure to such teachings at a young age, transmitted by illumined preceptors, had been the cause of the destruction of root ignorance in his mind and the beginning of a life fully dedicated to living and emanating the highest Awareness. Now he was free and there was nothing so wonderful as spiritual freedom. All sterling qualities such as truth, unity, love, devotion, bliss and peace were contained and expressed there.

As he walked, night fell, first streaked with the many hues of dusk and then accompanied by the appearance of millions of bits of gleaming light in the night heavens. I am moving through the sky of Infinite Awareness, thought the Avadhut, as he walked on through the encroaching darkness. When he could go no further in the pitch blackness, he lay down and slept where he was.

Upon awakening in the early morning, he found that he was near a queer dwelling that stood just off in the distance. Approaching that hut with hopes of begging a few morsels for breakfast, he was greeted by an old hermit who smiled at him through toothless gums.

"Take prasad here?" said the old man in a cracked voice.

"Thank you kindly, sir," answered the Avadhut in the affirmative. Without asking Ekanta in, the old man disappeared into the hut and soon emerged carrying a bowl of water. Ekanta drank a portion of it and washed his face and hands in the remainder. The dirty water he used on his feet. As soon as this morning ritual was accomplished the old hermit was outside the door once again with a bowl of porridge and a few chapatis. The two ate in silence, sitting in the early morning sun outside the dwelling. It was Ekanta who broke the silence.

"You live in wonderful surroundings, sir," he said. "Here, on the flat highlands, one has earth, water, a temperate climate and an expansive view."

After thinking this over for a few moments, the hermit answered: "The sky is my teacher and companion here. It is boundless, so it reminds me that I am also infinite."

"That has been my meditation since I entered these parts," said the Avadhut. "It reminds me of a poem."

Saying so, Ekanta recited:

Have thou no home, what home can hold thee friend?
The sky thy roof, the grass thy bed
and food what chance may bring,
well cooked or ill, judge not.
For, no food or drink can taint the noble Self
that knows Itself.
Like rolling river free, thou ever be...say
Om Tat Sat Om.

The old man was delighted and cried out, "That is wonderful. Where did you get it?"

"I learned it from my guru," replied Ekanta. "It has inspired me all the time that I have been wandering. It is a poem of transcendent quality and I live by it and will never forget it."

The old man was silent for awhile. Eventually he also broke the silence. "The sky is my teacher, as I said, for it too transcends all things."

Saying this, the old hermit recited something as well:

Like the sky, that is never disturbed
by the presence of fire, water and earth,
nor even by clouds driven by the wind nor the lashing rains,
so must a man be untouched by things
that are the result of time, space and causation.

"This is all I know of recitation," he said humbly, afterwards.

"That, dear sir, is all you need know of anything," came the Avadhut's response.

After he had left the old hermit, he thought back on the saying that the old one had recited. Prompted by its timeless message, he suddenly fell to his knees and raised his voice and eyes to the sky.

"I salute you, Oh sky, for you teach one of the most profound of lessons. I accept you as my teacher of transcendence. Please accept my own sincere and reverent salutations."

That night, camping by the side of a small stream in the wilderness, the Avadhut fell into a deep sleep. Towards morning, he had a wonderful dream in which the sky took shape and talked to him.

Even with shape, the sky was boundless and the form which instructed him was translucent. From it issued a voice that reminded Ekanta of the winds that bathed the rock faces of the Himalayas with cold, fresh air.

"What have you to say to me, revered Father of the Sky?" the Avadhut asked humbly.

*"I am Vayu, revered sage, appearing to you in my gross form. The boundless space containing the stars and planets, the area that affords prana its free reign over life, the subtle ethers in which heavenly beings sport and even the mind's intellectual motion which gives room for thought and insight, all these are my realms. You have accepted me as your guru for rising above limiting objects and materials and realizing the subtle Reality. Though I am not the ultimate one in this regard, I represent that One. I am pleased with your offering and have come to give you discourse on a few more of my qualities. Therefore listen, for our time together in this mode of communion is limited.*

*"Transcendence is definitely my main teaching. Brahman, the Blessed One, created me to demonstrate this verity to those who would inhabit my various regions of gross and subtle space. You have the right idea, the correct orientation. Beings have fallen to sleep accepting only what they see with eyes, hear with ears and imagine with their dark minds. Everything here that they do perceive, with all the senses and body and mind, is a symbol for Reality. The Blessed Lord is telling them every minute of the day and night that He is present, and His votaries are present all of the time as well to instruct them as to the proper way of cognizing Him. Both of these powerful representations are ignored. The result is the suffering of human beings and the arrival of the age of darkness and ignorance. Seek the Divine Mother Shakti for the removal of both.*

*"But on to my other qualities. I am also revealing the Omniscience of Brahman, not only in the sense of a superior intelligence involved in the universe, but also as a detached and supreme witness beyond all that beings can conceive of. It is marvelous and awesome, though these are descriptive terms used by the mind. In the ultimate sense, then, my presence as sky suggests to all that Brahman is all-pervasive, another of my qualities. To be all-pervasive does not necessarily denote that I am*

*without modification, but since I am also transcendent, I am therefore taintless as well. Thus do the two qualities work in conjunction to give us a glimpse or insight into the nature of Brahman, the Absolute. Immanent, Transcendent and Absolute: in this way do the scriptures and the sages describe Brahman. Through all these three conditions, my all-knowing, all-pervasive and all-transcending Presence exists. Thus I have told you. Now be free forevermore."*

The Avadhut awoke practically on his feet. So swiftly and sweetly had the experience come upon him that he was loath to let it go. Perhaps if I act it will continue, his body and mind seemed to say, but his soul knew better and immediately he sat in meditation, reliving this wonderful boon given in sacred vision. As he contemplated the three aspects of the Father of the Sky, various teachings came back to him from the many illumined beings he had contacted.

"How can God be both present and transcendent?" came Ekanta's question one day, asked of the yogi who lived near his village in a mountain cave. Yogindra Yogi stretched his legs and sat back down to face his young friend.

*"You ask the most amazing questions for your age,"* said the yogi. *"I left the company of sadhus to be alone just because of such questions and the debates and discourses that accompanied them. Such a buzz and to-do over mere semantics. All I wanted was peace and quiet to meditate on Brahman. Now, you have found me to plague me once more. Is the Divine Mother pursuing me in this fashion to teach me something? I don't know, but I would not be surprised."*

Ekanta merely waited with a smile, unaffected by the yogi's rough exterior. In the presence of Yogindra, he did not have to act respectful. The man just had no sense of holiness about him, though the very ground he walked on was considered holy by others. He did, however, have the habit of speaking out loud about all of his thoughts, most of these coming in the form of complaints about being bothered. In a timely fashion, then, after the yogi had finished his usual process, he addressed the question in his characteristically astute yet straightforward fashion.

*"As to your question, why should it not be possible, Ekanta? Why should the Creator of a multifaceted creation, Who*

manifested three fantastic realms of being, each accompanied by thousands of worlds and lokas and each peopled with millions of terrestrial and celestial beings, be one-sided or two-dimensional? You tell me."

Ekanta burst out laughing to hear this.

"You put it so matter-of-factly, revered sir. I always fail to think in those terms when I begin to analyze or intellectualize things."

"*As do others as well, unfortunately,*" replied the yogi. "*We are either plagued with ignorant fools who want to know nothing of God or deluged by a host of intellectuals who have no connection with Him in their hearts but plenty of information to 'share' with us. Thus, I have retired into a cave.*"

After a futile attempt at trying to contain himself for a few terse moments, Ekanta gave up and laughed out loud. Recovering his composure a bit, Ekanta then pressed the yogi for more tidbits of wisdom.

"Explain to me what you mean by the three worlds, sir."

The yogi looked Ekanta in the eyes and stated firmly:

"*Consciousness is here, is it not — right here in this realm of earth which the ancients called Bhurloka. Again, Consciousness is beyond mere physical appearances and resides in transcendent form as well, both as the unseen worlds where the gods and their consorts reside and as the energy of intelligence coursing through millions of minds which are all expressions of the Cosmic Mind that conceived of everything manifest. Again, beyond what is both terrestrial and celestial and transcending the transcendent itself, Consciousness exists in its pure and unmodified condition as the Absolute. These are the three worlds and what lies beyond them and they are all filled with Consciousness. Now, hearing this, you should be able to answer your own question which I repeat to you now. Can God be both present and transcendent?*

"*Recently, I had a profound dream,*" the yogi continued after a time. "*Actually, it was more than mere dream. My body, seemingly solid, had the ability to walk through material objects and could float above the earth without any effort whatsoever. It was not wetted when I dove into the waters of a river nor was it overheated when I entered a fire. The wind blew right through me. I felt it, but it did not move me in the least. At the end of the*

*dream, I dissolved into thin air and awoke with a sense of calm
that never again left me. Meditating on that vision, I know it to
be a signal for the consummation of all my practice in yoga. It
is the affirmation of all that I have studied and experienced and
it is also the answer to all my prayers. I have never told it to
anyone, Ekanta. Now you have heard it from me and I declare
it to be the very Truth of life and existence. We are nothing less
than pure Spirit, my dear young friend, even when we are
embodied. You should come to know this and exult in it. May
the Blessed Lord and Divine Mother of the Universe, Who have
brought us together in this life, grant you this realization as well."*

This was the last time that Ekanta had ever seen Yogindra Yogi
in a body, save for experiencing his presence in a transcendent
sense and having vision of his ethereal form in a dream. That last
message, however, had moved and changed something in the
boy's mind and thereafter he had a sixth sense, as it were, about
subtle unseen things. Later on, Ekanta had become convinced that
the mere mention of this powerful experience in the presence of
the yogi who realized it had amounted to a transmission of what
it entailed directly into Ekanta's being. It was not strange at all,
then, that the Avadhut looked upon the yogi as one of his gurus,
always to be revered and never to be forgotten.

Coming out of his meditation on the appearance of Vayu in
his dream, the Avadhut saluted the god of space, of air, and of
wind once again and also mentally saluted the yogi. Standing
up and facing the west, he began moving through the all-pervasive presence of infinite sky once again, forever befriended, like
the hermit he had met, by this transcendent and subtle but
immanent Reality.

"I shall ever exist within the infinite sky of pure Awareness,"
he said out loud. "There is nothing but Brahman all around,
within and beyond."

With this powerful affirmation abiding within his mind as pure
revelation, the Avadhut gradually disappeared into limitless space.

# Chapter 19

# Teachings on Liberating Wisdom

THE NINETEENTH GURU — The Spider

THE LESSON — Bondage and Liberation

*The spider, O Prince, creates a web spun from its own person, constructs it and moves about freely on it. It can even take that web back into itself. This is a microcosmic illustration of how Brahman's Shakti power creates, preserves and withdraws the universe. This is very helpful wisdom. Additionally, what happens during the life of the web is instructive as well, for a dance of life and death is enacted there, indicative of bondage and liberation on many levels. The spider is a valued guru of mine in that respect who taught me many important and beneficial lessons.*

The Avadhut drifted down a wide river on a raft with several other wanderers. He had spent his last coins, received as alms, to secure passage in this craft which would take him across land to meet up with the Ganges once again. He had strayed away from his intended route up the sacred river out of necessity. Now, his intent was to make Gangotri, the source of the holy river, by the end of the month, for he wanted to go there and depart well ahead of the winter snows.

A song drifted to the back of the raft where the Avadhut lay with his hand trailing in the waters of the river. The atmosphere was perfectly relaxed, this mood broken only occasionally by a few minor rapids that appeared in the distance every once in a while. Since the Avadhut was fearless, knew himself to be deathless, he was not troubled by such things and spent his time in perpetual self-surrender to the Divine Mother's will which, to his illumined understanding, was supreme. The song was reminiscent of this verity.

> No matter where I go, I see only Mother.
> Looking up, I see the boundless sky,
> proof of Her pervasive presence.
> Looking down, I see Her feet treading the earth
> which She created.
> Cradled on the waters, Her murmuring voice calms me,
> high in a tree, Her wind-breath caresses me.
> It is She who stands before me as my beloved,
> She who tugs my hand as the child.
> The phenomenal world is Her playground,
> the empty void, Her silent meditation.
> Where is She not?
> Even this mind that perceives Her belongs to Her.
> No matter where I go, I see only Mother.

As dusk arrived, so did the pilgrims at their destination. It was too late to catch another boat to the Ganges from the point of landing so the Avadhut entered the little town. Sitting down near a cross street, he laid his cloth out and sat quietly with eyes closed. Opening them an hour later, he found a few coins, a banana and a small package of luchis, a type of fried bread, laying on his cloth. Taking these meager but appreciated offerings, he went to the river and selected a spot where he could both sleep and bathe. After prayerful offerings, he ate the sanctified food and curled up to rest.

In the morning, he was informed that no boat was available to travel the distance of three more miles to the Ganges River proper. Inquiring around, he found someone who could tell him how to journey there on foot. After memorizing the directions, he set out and soon found the trailhead he was seeking. Once inside the forest, he wended his way for several miles until he approached the Ganga, the Mother of all rivers. From a distance, high atop a hill, he caught sight of Her and bowed his head to the earth. Rising to a sitting position, he sat for a time, gazing at the wonderful sight.

Boats were plying up and down this endless stretch of water, held sacred in all of India. On both shores, pilgrims gathered and small dwellings and towns attended Her banks. Inspired by proximity to Her, the mantra he had received in connection with the goddess Ganga began flowing spontaneously in his heart and mind. After mentally reciting mantra for an hour, Ekanta went to look for a place to lie down in the nearby woods. Since the woods were at a relatively high elevation, he found several nice spots which were covered over with leaves and the needles of trees. Selecting one such area, he unrolled his cloth, lay down and closed his eyes.

In sacred dream, the kind which occurred often to Ekanta, the Avadhut was looking upon an aspect of the Divine Mother. He knew it was Her and he was also aware that it was just an aspect of Her, not a full manifestation of Her power such as Kali or Durga. As he watched, the goddess lay down, instantly became full with child and gave birth, all in what seemed to be an instant of time. Then, taking the babe in her arms and with infinite tenderness, the goddess suckled the newborn at her breast. After a few moments of this, the goddess suddenly became wrathful and, taking the little baby up to her mouth, devoured the infant in a flash. Then She too disappeared into brilliant light. Next, a voice in the form of thought echoed from within the Avadhut's consciousness:

*"Behold, sage, the cosmic process. All is Light, all is Pure Being. Nothing ever exists in time, for time is an illusion. Nothing ever ceases to exist in time, having never existed in the first place, so death is an illusion. As you are witnessing this play now, detached yet aware by your own consciousness, so too the Ultimate Reality is Self-existent, is eternal and all-pervasive. As a spider spins its web, moves about on it without getting caught and even draws the web back into itself, so*

*too does Brahman use His Shakti power to manifest, sustain and dissolve the universe. He is like a child on an endless stretch of beach who constructs, plays with and tramples down a sandcastle. Thus, time is like sand and God, a playful child. Infinity is His favorite plaything."*

When the Avadhut opened his eyes upon the phenomenal world once again, the voice was still ringing in his ears. Sitting up, he noticed that less than an hour had passed, for the sun was still high in the afternoon sky. As he went deeper into the woods to answer the call of nature, he reflected on the dream. His dreams had always seemed to have an inherent sense of naturalness about them. There seldom was much of a mystical aspect present. Thinking back, he remembered the first time he had experienced an opening of the Wisdom Eye at the sixth center of subtle Awareness. That too, had been extremely natural.

Cloudlike coverings had suddenly peeled back in animated, slow-motion fashion to reveal a perfectly cylindrical view into a beautiful Light. As the clouds parted within his inner vision, he had noticed that they were tinged with an effulgent pink color. This set off the radiant white light that formed the circle of the eye which, at first, contained blue flecks — lokas, floating like islands in a sea of pure radiance. As the fringes of the clouds pulsated and billowed, they finally turned effulgent black and framed that boundless expanse of living Light in a perfect circle.

This had occurred to the Avadhut one evening after a long trek through the Indian landscape. As he reached the top of a hill, this vision came upon him unexpectedly. The most wonderful thing about it was the unaffected yet tangible nature of the experience. To perceive this vision should have shocked him, but it did not. There he stood, on the crest of a hill, gazing in easy fashion into another realm, into a different state of consciousness. Whether he opened his eyes or closed them, the Wisdom Eye remained before him. He finally pinched himself to validate both his super-conscious state and his presence in the body. He then checked his breathing and found that he was aware of the vision whether he was focusing on the ever-present eye or upon the external world. However, the Wisdom Eye captured his full attention and he enjoyed that vision immensely for a time.

The experience lasted for a full five minutes, then it had slowly faded. As the Avadhut tried to maintain sight of it, colors danced within his inner perception and the eye half formed and faded from view in turns. Finally, only round blue tracers remained, a sort of residual effect and these had lasted over the next few hours as the Avadhut meditated on Reality. Throughout the years that followed, this appearance, the opening of the Wisdom Eye, occurred to him at intervals, especially when he entered water. Since there was no one around to explain or validate this experience for him, he thought of it as the opening of the Wisdom Eye spoken of in esoteric spiritual texts and understood it as a passageway for consciousness to exit the human form and the earthly realm. It became a natural and accepted part of his existence, given by the grace of the Lord on select occasions, free of but not dependent on any discipline or exercise to induce it. It was wonderful but did not elicit exuberance. It was powerful but easy to bear. Finally, it was ultrapersonal and never needed to be spoken of. It was the kind of thing that mystery-mongerers would have used for selfish and sensational purposes. The Avadhut, simple and humble, simply took it as an illustration of God's presence.

Coming out of his reverie, the Avadhut found himself looking at an intricate web, shining in the sunlight. On the edges was a spider, busy adding more dimension to its creation. With a smile the Avadhut thought of the voice in his dream. The Vedas, too, had used the illustration of a spider and its web in relation to the creative process of shakti. To know Her, be aware of Her power and to get into surrender and agreement with Her was to solve the problems of relative existence and reach a transcendent plateau of detached equanimity where true happiness and contentment reigned supreme.

The Avadhut was a lover of the earth, seeing it as a manifestation of the Goddess Herself. He lamented the opportunistic tendencies of human beings who misused and depleted its resources, but he did not waste precious time in mourning. Instead, he utilized his own precious energy to discover who the Source of the universe was and how She operated its laws. This path had led him to peace, balance and security. He had then uncovered some cosmic secrets through Her Grace, finding out that the world and, indeed, entire solar systems could disappear in a flash, but that the Source of these manifestations was eternal.

What was more, She could create an infinite number of universes with the subtle power vested in Her by the Absolute and this was only the physical aspect of Her Being. Celestial worlds and even subtler worlds also appeared and disappeared at Her bidding.

The result of knowing this was Peace, Peace, Peace. He therefore had reverence for the Earth Mother, the physical aspect of the Divine Mother's creation. He did not covet what she offered but only loved her. He did not seek to profit from plans and schemes, whether they were materialistic or altruistic, but instead, simply treated the earth and all its creatures with reverence. While others took her bounty for granted or wreaked havoc on her in a callous or disrespectful way, he did not grieve, for he knew that she was indestructible. Even the single planet on which he lived, if it were overrun with people and drained of all its beauty and resources, would simply regenerate itself over centuries as civilizations rose and fell like ripe corn. How well he remembered the words of the ancient Rishis in this regard:

> One should pay heed to how the ancients adhered to Truth.
> Notice, also, how the saints and sages of today do likewise.
> Mortal beings appear, ripen and fall like corn in a vast field.

In this regard he had no fear. He knew that everything around him, even bodies and minds, were transitory and insentient — only appearances. Their Source was the only Reality. Consciousness was eternal and stainless, he knew, and that was the Mother's essence and Her true gift to all living beings.

As the spider expanded his little web-world, extending it to each outlying leaf or twig, Ekanta watched with interest. The shining, gossamer web came out in abundant supply from the spider's body, providing everything it needed for the creative process. In similar fashion, using the primal vibration of Om existing within Her as creative potential, the Divine Mother fashioned the universe from unseen principles such as time, space, light, thought and other gross and subtle elements. It was a mystery only in as much as beings failed to comprehend its inner workings, but in actuality this process was completely natural. The One who wielded the ingredients for creation was the real mystery. As he thought about Her, a song came to his mind:

With a tiny portion of awareness in focus,
beings gaze upon creation and are amazed.
Enchanted, bewitched and wanting to possess,
they rush to unite with material principles.

The Mother, however, is not made of matter,
nor is She found in the physical universe.
She only guides it from Her transcendent view,
and remains unfettered by its imposing limitations.

Where are You, Universal Mother?
and why did You fashion this web of deception?
The five elements chain me, the body detains me.
The universe alone is more than I can comprehend.

This garden called earth that You have created,
lures us into submission and false security.
We taste the fruits, sweet and sour, growing here,
and react with joy or shocked surprise.

Suddenly, the Avadhut noticed another movement on the web. An insect flying by had not seen the transparent trap and had become entangled in it. Now, it was busy trying to free itself. It was not long before the spider, sensing the vibrations of the struggle transferred through the strands of its creation, moved quickly to the insect's location. Wrapping more and more web around it, the spider enmeshed it completely so that no hope of escape was possible. Then, the spider feasted on the insect, sucking the life-force out of it.

This tiny drama took all of a few minutes but already the Avadhut's mind was full of spiritual correlations, positive and negative. The lesson of entrapment by the allures of Maya was, of course, prevalent in the example, for many beings acted in just this sort of fashion with regards to the world, becoming entangled in various traps existing there. The way the spider sensed the vibrations through the strands of its web, however, interested Ekanta the most. This microcosmic view provided an apt illustration of the all-pervasiveness of Reality. The Divine Mother, too, was aware of all that occurred in Her creation. The web that She used, however, in the physical realm, was one of prana, the subtle life-force of the creation that was all-contained in Her. Consciousness was another far-reaching verity that She utilized. As he thought of these two principles, wielded by the Cosmic Creator, his mind drifted back to teachings he had received from his gurus.

*"Prana, the subtle life-force flowing through and animating all beings, and Chaitanya, Ultimate Consciousness, are two different things, Ekanta,"* his guru stated one day. *"Generally speaking, they are associated with different realms and functions, though they are also interconnected to a certain degree. Some beings actually think of their life-force as Consciousness, but prana is flowing always, permeating the entire universe, while Consciousness is only associated with the universe, or apparently so. In the highest state of spiritual awareness, prana is not present, it being a constituent of physical, astral and causal creations. Therefore, in the universe, prana acts like Consciousness and facilitates many of the commands and laws that Conscious Awareness dictates. Its all-pervasive nature with regards to matter allows it to be a sensor for the Divine Mother who, though She seemingly creates, preserves and destroys the universe in time and space, actually does not act or become involved at all!*

*"This amazing trick of Hers is accomplished, in part, by Her wielding of the subtle force of prana which is the Sanskrit word for vital energy and life-breath. The breath, however, which many confuse to be prana, is only a physical manifestation of prana which is an unseen and immeasurable energy flowing through the nadis or nerves of living beings. It is not limited to physical and vital sheaths either, but courses through the five elements of nature as well, providing them with their particular properties and imbuing them with vitality and energy. In short, prana is life. It even provides the brain its energy so that it can attune itself to thought and higher intellect. You see its essential function in the universe then, I assume?"*

"Yes, I am beginning to understand," answered Ekanta, gazing reverently at his guru. "But if prana is life itself, what is the Divine Mother of whom you speak? Is She not life?"

*"She,"* answered the guru firmly, *"is the Life of all lives. No,*

*Ekanta, She is not life as average humans think of it, but is beyond life and death. Many make this mistake. They do not understand Her essential nature and instead, if they are aware of Her at all, associate Her with the physical world, the body, the pranic life-force, the mind and the intellect. She is not any of these, and neither are you."*

Pausing for a moment while his student sat still, stunned to hear this precious truth, the guru went on.

*"Do you remember when we studied the Bhagavad Gita last year, Ekanta? In the latter chapters Sri Krishna explains to Arjuna that beings are ever mistaking Him for a human being, associating him with the manifest universe and overlooking His Avyakta nature — His unmanifest Essence. This is what I am speaking about here. The Divine Mother, the Mahashakti form of Brahman that provided Sri Krishna with His body, life, mind and appearance in the phenomenal universe, is never manifest in a relative sense. She is like the rich patron who provides all the food, drink, materials and monetary support for a huge gathering but who never shows up himself to partake or make merry with the guests. She is the Eternal Witness of all, dear boy, and the One whom all beings seek through various avenues. She is the Source of Origin without an origin. She is the Eternal Subject that reveals all objects. She is one with Brahman like the pattern of an intricately woven oriental rug is one with the rug. She is the gold in all gold ornaments, the clay in all clay objects. Know Her and be free. In the Rig Veda, the world's oldest sacred scripture, She states:"*

I spread the heavens over the earth.
I am the energy in Brahman and the Mother of all.
It is for Me that the Atman resides in all intellects.
It is I who have penetrated the many worlds with My power
and I am holding them in their respective places as well.
Yet, beyond the worlds, I remain ever the one primal force
and the single perfect Existence, unaffected by My magic creation.

Enchanted by the thought and description of the Mahashakti, Ekanta had pressed his knowledgeable guru for more details.

"She must be unknowable though, dear teacher," he said, "for

She sounds entirely beyond the worlds that Her powers create."

*"That is a good conclusion,"* replied the guru, *"and one that shows that you are understanding Her already, on an intuitive level. If a man is standing on his towel when he comes out of his bath, he cannot dry off. He must first step off and then only can he dry himself. In similar fashion, one cannot know the Mother if one is standing, as it were, firmly rooted in the world of name and form, for She is not found there. One must ascend in meditation to a higher, transcendent platform and then a glimpse of Her will be possible. In other words, Ekanta, one cannot know God with the finite and dual mind. One can only know God when one transcends name and form — body, mind, thought and ego. This is why so few actually have made Her acquaintance, why so few have ever glimpsed the Mother of the Universe. Attached to relativity indefinitely, they fail to perceive Absolute Reality."*

"Then what is life for, dear teacher?" Ekanta had asked, somewhat peevishly. "It all seems a worthless exercise in futility, an existence without a purpose."

*"Some would agree with you, Ekanta,"* the guru returned. *"And among them would be both the pessimists who are fed up with life, the cynics who are callous to it and the materialists who believe it to be the only reality. Even certain schools of Mayavadins might agree, thinking the world to be an absolute illusion. But we are not of that ilk, my boy. Mother has smiled upon us, as it were, and has revealed to us a higher purpose. Life alone will not satisfy, it is true, but Divine Life goes a long way towards that end. Divine Life, what we have described as having unalloyed devotion towards God, studying His word as scripture, chanting His names and glories, keeping holy company, meditating on His pure nature and serving all beings as expressions of Him, propels us towards spiritual consummation. This formula opens the gates of Truth and Its Light then shines fully upon us, dispelling the gloom of death, fear, doubt, darkness and delusion."*

The guru paused again to reconsider. Then, he continued:

*"Besides, Ekanta, life cannot be entirely futile. The Mother's Essence may not be obviously present here in relativity but there are plenty of indications of Her presence. When She is realized*

*as existing beyond the world of name and form, that wisdom, which comes as a result of illumination, opens up the secrets of the universe for us and we then behold Her everywhere. This is the last word in earthly and intellectual evolution and the beginning of true spiritual life. So do not despair, there is a purpose to existence."*

"Can you put it into words, revered teacher?" Ekanta had asked.

*"Some spiritual teachers say that life's purpose is for enjoyment,"* stated the preceptor. *"Others claim that happiness is the purpose. Both of these are partially correct, for if you seek life for life's sake alone, this will be what you get. However, the Avatar teaches us over and over again, throughout time, that the realization of one's divine nature is the purpose and goal of life in the world — what the illumined call God-Realization. Without that, life proves empty and fruitless. After realizing the Atman, one can then be truly happy and sport infinitely."*

"If we are divine by nature, dear teacher," asked Ekanta, "why do we need to seek at all? Can we not just abide in our true Self?"

*"Have you tried that lately, dear student?"* came the disarming reply. *"If you have and have succeeded, will you please teach me how to do that amidst the vicissitudes of the world and the limitations of the body/mind mechanism? One is not Divine until one realizes that one is Divine, Ekanta. It cannot be pretended. As well, one must come to accept all things, even what seems dark and evil, painful and negative, as part and parcel of Reality. Seeking pleasure and shunning pain will not work, for one accompanies the other in relativity."*

"Yes, I see what you mean," answered Ekanta. "That is why I love the Vedantic way. There is nothing concealed there and no hidden surprises. It is all laid out clearly and concisely."

After a brief pause, Ekanta asked another question.

"You said that the Avatar teaches us that God-Realization is the purpose of human existence, not happiness or pleasure-seeking. How did they state this?"

*"Some Buddhists say that happiness is the purpose of life,"* the guru responded. *"I did not get this from my studies of Lord Buddha's teachings. When life is a mixture of good and bad, bringing other dualities in its train such as pleasure and pain, virtue and vice, even life and death, can we ever be happy here?*

*Besides, the Tathagata further taught about the suffering inherent in creation, and through His boundless compassion sought and found a way out of that painful and limiting condition. No, of bondage and liberation, there is only the obvious choice and He illustrated it well both by example and through His teachings."*

"What were some of the Buddha's teachings, revered sir?" asked the boy.

*"Among the most famous, and formulated for the average understanding of human beings, the Arya Satya stands out clearly,"* answered the guru.

"What is that, dear sir?" Ekanta queried.

*"Ah,"* the teacher continued, *"they are called the Four Noble Truths. In them, Lord Buddha proclaims suffering, the origin of suffering, the cessation of suffering and the path that leads to this cessation of suffering. A spiritual seeker who accepts these gets greatly enlightened thereby while the worldly ignore them and live in ignorance. Here again, the purpose of existence comes to mind. Suffering drives us towards transcendence, so one could just as easily make a point that suffering is the purpose of life rather than terrestrial happiness. At least it delivers us into a higher understanding rather than a hedonistic and worldly existence.*

*"The Christ was also clear on the matter of the purpose of life,"* the guru said, returning to his original subject. *"'Seek the kingdom within you, first and foremost, and then all else will be added unto thee,' He stated. This may sound like one can reach God and then return to the world and enjoy it fully. True happiness, however, can never be based upon ephemeral existence. Bondage, that which is in the very nature of relativity, can only be subdued by liberation as ignorance can only be quelled by knowledge. After one acquires knowledge and receives the boon of liberation, one sees the Lord face to face. After seeing that splendid and awesome vision, will the paltry things of the earth ever attract one again? Therefore I say, liberating Wisdom is the fruit of spiritual life. We must deify the many aspects of life and thereby convert worldly existence into divine living. After this is accomplished, we strike off our bonds and fetters, no matter what they are made of or from where they originate.*

*We are then free, in a perpetually liberated condition."*

"Revered sir," asked Ekanta, "if liberation into God-Realization is the epitome of existence, then there must not be any illumined beings present on earth. Getting their enlightenment, they would never come back."

*"They are rare,"* admitted the boy's preceptor, *"it is true. Many of them, gaining such a condition for the first time as it were, merge into Brahman or attend on the life heavens above and beyond the pull of evolutionary gravity. Others, though, choose to come to the realms of Bhur, Bhuvah and Svaha, the three worlds of transmigration, to help liberate the bound. However, they swallow hard, so to speak, to make the journey, for they set themselves up for many difficult experiences, both with the limiting factors of the body condition and the narrowness and ignorance prevalent in the minds of beings ensconced in relativity. It is no picnic, that is certain, but beings such as these are the Divine Mother's true helpers. Thank God for them, Ekanta."*

"Yes," repeated the boy, looking lovingly at his guru, "thank God for them!"

As Ekanta returned from his visit to the past, he noticed that the spider was still draining the juice from its prey.

"Prana flows from one vehicle or container to another," murmured the Avadhut, "but the Atman pervades everything. It is the deathless essence, transcending even life-force and It is to be realized."

As he finished this pithy statement, some wise words from Yogindra Yogi echoed in his ears:

*"The Upanishads state, little Atman, that Brahman first manifested as the Purusha. After that, the kalas, or fifteen principles came into being. These are referred to in the Prasnopanishad and the Mundakopanishad, wherein they are termed 'the fifteen spokes of the wheel.' First among these is the prana and after that comes the mind, the five elements, the senses, their food and so forth. It is interesting to note, however, that all springs from the Purusha. That small bit of eternal Brahman then projects all It needs for existence by the power of the Mahashakti inherent in It. Second to note, is that the prana appears first among created principles. There must be space and energy, and the*

*prana sees to this. It flows out on many levels such as the space and energy of knowledge, of life-force, or ether and air. It fills the many created objects of the Bhutakasha with many sub-levels of prana. It is life itself by way of support."*

Thinking thus, the Avadhut lapsed into contemplation on the spider and its web once again. The web, after all, was a very tiny thing, a small trap that is easily avoidable. Even if one took all the webs and spiders on earth, the amount of free space still accessible would be monumental. Viewed in this fashion, the Avadhut surmised, the universe is a relatively small thing, especially next to the all-pervasive prana, what to speak of the boundless expanse of pure Consciousness.

Ekanta thought back on all the people he had known. He wondered how they had fared in their quest for liberation. He had no doubt that his revered twin gurus, the vanaprastin couple, were liberated while they lived and breathed. He felt that his parents were, by dint of their devotion to God alone, also liberated.

On one memorable occasion, the Avadhut found himself in the vicinity of his boyhood home. He had not, since wandering away into the world, ever visited the area again. On that occasion, he went back to the forest ashram where his beloved teachers had lived and taught. Upon arriving there, he found the place unused and run down. His revered female teacher, the Mataji, had given up the body in the forest, right at the ashram. This he found out from his elderly mother whom he visited. His revered Guruji simply left after the demise of his spiritual partner, to where, no one knew, wandering off into the woods to some unknown end. His father had passed away a few years earlier after providing for the care of his wife. This was not as difficult to accept, since Ekanta had fortuitously met him at several pilgrimage places during their mutual wanderings.

On that rare visit, the Avadhut accomplished many rituals at the old ashram and even cleaned it up and lived there for a few days. There was little sadness in him on that occasion, for the place, associated with so much of his youthful spiritual yearning and learning, still radiated a profound sense of peace. An atmosphere of freedom also shared that spot. The very trees and animals were, to Ekanta's eyes, manifestations of his teachers and their wonderful consciousness seemed to shine forth from everything present.

One night, while sleeping in the same room where his gurus had taught him, he had an amazing dream of the couple. They were changed, and since Ekanta had never known them when they were young, he imagined that what he saw in the vision represented their youthful forms.

*"You have come home at last,"* the Mataji said to him as he sat up in his dream. Looking down, he saw his physical form sleeping soundly. Speechless due to tears and emotions, the Avadhut only stared at them.

*"What we taught you,"* said his revered guru with a broad smile bordering on ecstasy, *"it was all true, was it not?"*

"Yes, it was," Ekanta stammered lamely.

*"You are one with us, always,"* said the Mataji. *"You know this, do you not?"*

"Yes," came Ekanta's short reply.

*"We will come again,"* said his male preceptor, and then they faded from his view.

When the Avadhut awakened later that night, the cloth that he used for a pillow was drenched with his own tears. He remembered being very affected in the dream and must have cried profusely while still sleeping. He wondered at the cryptic statement about their return and that caused him to stay there at the old dilapidated ashram for several more days and nights.

On the fourth night of his stay, much longer than he ever would have stayed in any location under usual conditions, the divine couple appeared to him again. This time, Ekanta was wonderfully mobile. His sleeping body lay before him on the floor of the old ashram but a body consisting of light walked the premises with his teachers. His joy knew no bounds at this and he was also not limited by the emotional state of the previous evening. The conversation that he held with his beloved gurus that night in sacred vision was easy and natural, as if they had returned just to teach him as they always had before. Later, he had recalled some of that precious dialogue and wondered at its profound significance.

"I heard that when Mataji left her body, you wandered away, Guruji," Ekanta said to his guru.

*"Her parting affected me deeply,"* the guru stated, *"and I could not bear the company of anyone or any familiar place at that time. With you and her both gone, I simply walked away and*

*journeyed until my strength left me. I could not make it as far as the Ganges but gave up my body in the company of monks who were students of my friend, Swami Anantananda, at the mountain ashram you and I once visited together. He had passed into samadhi earlier but do you remember that place?"*

"Of course, revered sir," Ekanta said. "I could never forget what I experienced there with him."

*"Our lives were blessed, Ekanta, as is yours. We have been following your journeys and experiences."*

"I have felt you both on many occasions and have known your combined presence in my heart and mind continually since my departure. But this experience is wonderful. I do not want it to end."

*"You still have work to do, things to share and experience,"* replied his beloved Mataji, *"and, as you say, we will always be within you as your very inmost Consciousness."*

Ekanta practically floated through the rooms of the old ashram, which were now strangely more spacious and filled with an ethereal light. The radiant forms of his gurus were almost too beautiful to gaze upon and a pervasive sense of sweet bliss combined with indescribable peace permeated the atmosphere.

After a time, he asked, "Mataji," for he still felt like a young boy in her presence, "where have you both gone? What is liberation like? Can you say?"

*"It is form that is out of place now, my dear,"* came her enigmatic answer. *"To become embodied in any concrete condition feels a bit unnatural, almost clumsy. Imagine, to move about in this limited condition and operate under sensual perception, whether subtle or gross! It is all a bother. Much better, it is, to move with the lightning swift ease of the Spirit in Consciousness. Still, Mother does like to sport, so She maintains this illusion of solidity to accommodate that, or because those individualized bits of apparently separated awareness called living beings still desire it. I could never understand it, even when I was embodied myself."*

*"Ekanta,"* joined in his Guruji, *"the freedom that embodied beings miss out on is indescribable. To covet a limited form of existence is to experience a living death. Think how it would be to try and fit into clothes that you wore when you were a boy. It would be painful if it were possible at all. As far as*

*where we are now, we are free to roam the three worlds but are not limited to their confinement. We can, therefore, attend on the most Beloved Presence of the Lord, both in form and as form-less Essence, in the company of our friends, teachers and the illumined beings from time immemorial. It is indescribable, so this tiny description will have to suffice."*

"Oh, dear teachers," Ekanta said with emotion, "the Lord with form and as formless Essence — can He, She or It be described a little as well?"

*"You have not changed at all,"* laughed the Mataji. *"Your inquisitive mind is still at work."*

"Well of course, dear teacher," smiled the Avadhut. "Can a lover of Divine Reality refrain from hearing about the Supreme Beloved when such an opportunity arises?"

*"No, I suppose not,"* she replied, *"and your point is well taken. In this accord, I can only say that what the scriptures state is true, Ekanta. What they say and describe, though, is but an infinitesimal part of the beauty and majesty of that Divine Personage. His appearance defies even the accounts contained in the various devotional hymns, the Vedas, countless spiritual poems and other forms of written or oral adulation."*

*"As far as the formless expanse, revered Avadhut,"* joined in his Guruji, *"that must be experienced to be understood. I can tell you that it is the ultimate fulfillment and experience all rolled into one. It is eternal and ongoing at the same time while simultaneously holding within it all possible sublime moods. Out of that boundless expanse of pure Consciousness, an infinite set of wondrous possibilities proceed while It remains poised and static, immutable and ever-pure despite the many various manifestations that take place. It is your Source of Origin, Ekanta, as it is ours and everyone's."*

"Beloved ones," the Avadhut continued, "my mind is full of longing to know about that One. Being here on earth, as you know, places a set of barriers between the devotee and the Beloved. It is a constant battle to remain in touch, to any great degree, with the Source of Origin. Therefore, answer my questions to the best of your powers of explanation."

*"We shall try, blessed Avadhut,"* came the response from both gurus at once.

"I long to know about God with form as opposed to and in conjunction with the formless Essence," continued Ekanta. "I believe I comprehend the intrinsic connection between the two, if They can be referred to in such dualistic terms, but can you describe the Lord when He enters His Vishnu form, His Krishna form, His Shiva form? What is He like then, how is it to gaze upon him and what about His Shakti?"

The two beings that had been Ekanta's vanaprastin gurus looked at each other. Then, the radiant form of his male guru said, *"Enter into me, Ekanta."* The Avadhut stared incredulously at him, then walked forward, somehow intuitively aware of what to do. As Ekanta's dream form entered into the form of his blessed guru, a great light filled his consciousness. The next thing he was aware of was the sweet presence of beautiful celestial music, the sounds of which seemed to rain down on his heightened awareness like honey. As he became accustomed to a higher perception, his eyes caught sight of a realm so splendid that his entire being was lifted up into rapturous bliss. Amidst that lovely and ecstatic place, Ekanta experienced the presence of thousands of joyful souls, all either dancing and singing, working happily, speaking words permeated with profound wisdom or sitting still in samadhi.

All of these beings circulated naturally around a central figure, like planets orbiting a brilliant sun. The beauty and majesty of this Being could not be described. He sat on a raised dais decorated with every imaginable jewel and gem. Elegant cloths and rugs of intricate design, each pulsating with living color, were draped around or in front in charming fashion, providing so much to look at that the eyes became dazzled. Flower garlands of unimaginable hues and fragrances bedecked Him on neck and limb and they were strewn all around His feet as well on all sides. Exquisite looking children played with more flowers, throwing them at each other and eating them with delightful expressions on their faces.

Hidden behind the Cosmic Being but strangely visible every now and then, as if appearing out of a wondrous mist, was a creature so enchanting that Ekanta concluded it could only be Narayani Herself. Well before he could drink in the scene to his satisfaction, there was an ecstatic outburst of divine music and a figure approached the raised dais and prostrated before the Lord.

Standing up, he began to sing and recite hymns to all the beings gathered there. Musical and poetic praises came flooding out of his being until all present knew that it was Narada himself that stood there, singing to his Lord who was none other than Mahavishnu Himself. As the Avadhut looked on, a thrilling hymn uttered by the ancient Devarshi entered his being, playing there as pure revelation:

> Behold this Divine vision, of thrilling dark complexion,
> wrapped in gold and silver garments
> and holding the mace of judgment and the conch of victory.
> Take refuge at His Feet!

> For He wears the Crest-Jewel of perfect mastery,
> exudes the fragrance of ecstatic Love
> and is adorned with all auspicious signs.
> Seek shelter there!

> He is the Lotus-eyed Lover who fascinates celestial beings,
> bewitches the gods and goddesses,
> and destroys the sins of mortals.
> Implore Him for His mercy!

> His beauty is unsurpassed, His posture all-attracting,
> and the sound of His flute transports one into ecstasy.
> He is Radha's Beloved and the favorite of the gopis.
> All rush to the sanctuary of His Feet!

> His beauty and charm are eternal,
> and He is forever worshipped by the gods,
> but knowledge of His identity is difficult to attain.
> Therefore, the wise ones seek His Grace!

> For, He is the Cosmic Enchanter, the mind-bewitcher,
> the God-intoxicated Lover, the Supreme Cause of Existence.
> May we all attain His Lotus Feet!

> He is the one upon whom all beings rely,
> who is steeped in Eternal Joy,

and who is the final beneficiary of ultimate praise.
May His Feet become our only treasure!

He is difficult to realize, even through intense disciplines,
yet He is the sole refuge of all beings
and the savior who grants immortality.
Fall at His Feet in reverence!

The darkness of ignorance vanishes in His Presence,
so He is an ocean of compassion to the helpless.
He is full of Awareness, the Lord of Lakshmi.
Supplicate Him for salvation!

He is the savior of the fallen,
the foundation of righteousness,
the pure and perfect one born of the highest status.
There is no better attainment than His Feet of Bliss!

Victory to Him, who reveals the Wisdom of Vedanta,
who is dear to gentle and simple souls,
and who is the Great Lord of Vrindaban.
Rush and take His Blessed Feet!

He is the upholder of Eternal Truth,
the dispeller of difficulties and obstacles,
abiding always in His own pure nature.
I take refuge at His Holy Feet!

Salutations to the Guardian of the Universe,
who is a boundless ocean of concern for everyone,
and whose Presence fills the mind with inspiration.
Abide at His Feet forever!

He is Supreme among Divine Beings,
the bestower of equanimity,
whose mind is always and ever immersed
in a pure stream of concentration.
Grasp His Feet of profound Peace!

O Jewel of the Holy City, destroyer of demons,
Thou art the all-pervasive one
who brings sentient beings to a transcendent condition.
Your Holy Feet are my sole desire!

For You are the Eternal Brahman,
the maintainer of the universal process,
and the one who grants union with Ultimate Reality.
I offer my all at Your Lotus Feet!

This ancient and divine hymn changed the condition of Ekanta's awareness completely. Suddenly, he was in a field, playing with dozens of beautiful boys and girls, all young and vibrant. A central figure predominated here too, and hardly daring to breathe for fear of losing this charming vision, Ekanta realized that he was in the presence of Sri Krishna. A song was being offered up to this Divinity as the group circled the enchanting figure before them, each completely fixated on uniting with Him. As Ekanta circled with the young men and women, another wonderful hymn inundated his consciousness:

To express Divine Love is the sweetest bliss, O Beloved.
I speak of Thee but You are indescribable,
I try to explain Thee yet You are indefinable.
Before my inner gaze You stand, with Radha and Balaram.
Your presence gives reality to creation, life to the gods.
Prostrate at Thy Feet I remain, O Beloved.

O Lord, accept my worship, hear my praises,
deign to grant sanctuary to your devoted disciple.
In humble service rendered selflessly, I long to be.
For, I have realized Thee dwelling in all hearts, all things.
Prostrate at Thy Feet I remain, O Beloved.

O Essence of the Vedas, Life of all dharmas,
extend to all the precious gift of safe refuge,
for attaining Thee is not possible without Thy Grace.
Always be my friend, guide and teacher,

and allow me to witness Thy Cosmic Dance of Creation.
Prostrate at Thy Feet I remain, O Beloved.

O Supreme Composer,
the Bhagavad Gita is Thy spontaneous song,
which bestows everlasting happiness upon all who listen.
Wearing celestial garments and handsome forehead marks,
You radiate tender love and concern upon all beings.
Prostrate at Thy Feet I remain, O Beloved.

Behold Shiva, Wisdom Lord, immersed in Thy worship.
Indeed, all who seek devotion lovingly remember Thee.
Thy enchanting dark form is impossible to forget.
Compassion is the root of Thy nature, O Lord,
and You bestow liberation at the appropriate time.
Prostrate at Thy Feet I remain, O Beloved.

Japa-mala in hand, You commune with the Inner Self,
yet Your Divine Sport continues
on the banks of the holy river.
Offering flowers, the devotees are dancing around Thee
as You grant them boons and fulfill their desires.
All are transported into higher consciousness.
Prostrate at Thy Feet I remain, O Beloved

The devotees await Thy sweet communion, O Lord,
Your Divine Play occupying their every thought.
This memory drenches all perceptions in the bliss of ecstasy
and makes sacred union possible.
Bestow Thy Grace upon them, O equanimous One.
Prostrate at Thy Feet I remain, O Beloved.

Renowned throughout the three worlds
and seven realms of consciousness,
You are the controller of the senses who grants dispassion.
The act of creation proceeds by Thy Will, O Supreme One.
Those possessing the youth of Timeless Awareness
take Thee for their eternal companion.
Prostrate at Thy Feet I remain, O Beloved.

Again, after the hymn had concluded and as swift as lightning, Ekanta found himself subtly transmuted into another realm. Gone were the prancing youths and the object of their longing and joy. Before he had time to regret this occurrence, he found himself within arms length of a powerful yet gentle figure. The words 'Hara, Hara' thundered in his consciousness and he knew that darshan with Lord Shiva was immanent. Realizing, to a certain extent, the implications of this meeting, the Avadhut fell to his knees and then prostrated fully before the Wisdom Lord. As he rose, Lord Shiva's incomparable voice reached his awareness.

*"What would ye have of me, great sage?"*

Hardly prepared to answer, the Avadhut, still on his knees, began to sing a hymn to Lord Shiva, his voice, memory and motions obeying some unknown, unsolicited power within him:

I pay heartfelt homage to Lord Shiva,
the ever-auspicious one who embodies all knowledge,
and who is ever united with His blessed Shakti.

O Thou of all-pervading presence,
who art endowed with innumerable sterling qualities,
bestow Thy compassion upon me,
Thou who art a boundless ocean of mercy.

O great Lord, who abides in sacred snow mountains,
the refuge of the gods whose very form is divine,
with crescent moon on Thy forehead,
kindly receive my salutations.

O bestower of boons, who art full of concern,
the Supreme Being
whose incomparable beauty enchants the mind,
please remove all fears and grant peace and contentment.

O beloved of Vishnu,
the One whom the Divine Mother holds most precious,
who is the refuge and hope of the lowly
and who personifies the sacred symbol Om,
to Thee, my eternal prostrations.

O Thou, who art all white,
robed in snow-capped mountains which are Thy garments,
whose voice is the primal Om, penetrating everywhere,
salutations to Thee.

O Lord of the Worlds, absorbed in nondual bliss,
pure and natural, who is the Master of Wisdom
who rescues all from worldliness and ignorance,
I salute Thee.

O enlightened Yogi,
ever-conscious of Thy indwelling divinity,
who is dear to the Avatar, whose renunciation is flawless,
I beseech Thee for your blessings.

O fully manifest Divinity, Brahman Supreme,
the all-pervading Lord
who is eternally and inherently perfect
and who abides fully in all things,
Victory unto Thee!

Ekanta suddenly found himself emerging out of the light form of his revered Mataji. He was still acutely aware of his three precious experiences and profoundly affected by them as well.

*"Now you know the true meaning of the word darshan, dear one,"* said the Mataji. *"For now, you must meditate on these experiences and cherish them in your heart, as well as in your mind's eye."*

*"When you wake up,"* came the words of his Guruji, *"you must not move for an hour and when you finally rise you must take water and refreshment and remain still for the entire day until dusk. This is for two reasons. One, you must retain and digest the experiences given to you by the Lord's Grace and, two, you must not strain your subtle body and mind for it has borne much this evening. We would say good-bye to you but that would amount to a ridiculous concept, would it not? Peace be with you, my student and spiritual son, who is the revered Avadhut."*

The Avadhut did not wake into the relative world at once, but remained in a sort of spiritual hibernation, assimilating the experiences he had received. When he finally did open his eyes just after dawn, the instructions of his teachers dictated his morning and afternoon activities. Barely moving about, exerting only enough to bring food and drink to his mouth, Ekanta rested throughout the day. He did not feel tired whatsoever and actually felt quite exhilarated, but whenever he expended more energy than usual at this slow pace, he did feel the effects in the form of subtle strain to his being.

When dusk arrived, he walked slowly out into the evening and enjoyed the soft, fragrant breeze blowing across his bare body. The stars appeared from their hiding places and glittered with new life, as if they too were privy to all that Ekanta had experienced. Gradually, as the evening progressed, Ekanta felt the increase of a full and complete joy that spread through every part of his being like some rare form of celestial nourishment. Inebriated by the onrush of this stream of bliss, he duly selected a seat for meditation and was soon sitting motionless, contemplating the vision of the Blessed Lord that appeared to him in a triple aspect.

The night passed in this fashion and Ekanta opened his eyes only as the first birds sent their thrilling calls across the sweetly scented air of morning. Rising to his feet, he wondered at his condition. All traces of fatigue were utterly gone from mind, body and nervous system. He had never felt more integrated and complete in his entire life. Everything, including and especially his own person, was radiating light and love. Though he waited for this feeling to leave him or diminish, it persisted throughout the day and for days thereafter.

A week later, after he had packed his meager belongings and prostrated in the dust of the holy old ashram, the Avadhut was still flying high, supported by a spiritual current so sweet, so powerful, so elevating and heavenwards, that he thought he might leave the body at any time. It was in this same lofty condition, weeks later, that the Avadhut arrived, one fine summer day, in Gangotri, at the source of the mighty and sacred Ganges River.

# — Chapter 20 —

# Teachings on Sanctity and Holiness

THE TWENTIETH GURU — Water

THE LESSON — Purity

I stand in awe of my teacher, water, having learned valuable lessons from it. Its homogenous nature bespeaks of the indivisibility of Brahman while its two modes, stillness and motion, indicate the Creator's divine plan. Even more, I observed its wonderful quality of purity, both as a physical element and as a container of sanctity and holiness. It cleanses the earth and its beings of impurities of body, mind and spirit. Exhilarating, congenial, vital, sweet and powerful, it is truly an amazing phenomenon.

Ekanta stood and stared in amazement. The water that flowed from the source of the Ganges seemed to emerge from out of the very bedrock of the Himalayas. There was no waterfall, just water appearing, as it were, from the mountain itself. The clarity of the water too, was overwhelming. Just gazing upon that primal gush of life-giving liquid vicariously quenched the substantial thirst he had built up along the long and arduous hike into these high elevations where the Ganges River maintained its home ground, both physically and spiritually.

The Avadhut had arrived at Gangotri after hiking almost the entire length of the mighty Ganga River. This journey had taken him on a few circuitous sidetracks but had finally culminated in a successful and long-awaited arrival. That he had never been on pilgrimage to this location at the source of this marvelous river was surprising considering his widely traveled status and the fact that he had visited nearby Kedarnath, the blessed pilgrimage site, several times in the past. Now, however, he was here and he meant to stay for several days.

Against the canyon wall, a short distance away from the surging waters, the Avadhut unrolled his small pack and set up camp. A few other pilgrims were located here and there in the vicinity, at times just sitting, at times meditating and occasionally making ablutions in the healing and auspicious waters of Mother Ganga. After the Avadhut had set himself up for the evening, he too went forth towards the flow of liquid spirituality to immerse himself.

Standing on the banks for a short time, just feeling the aura of holiness emanating from the sacred river, the Avadhut finally reached down and dipped his hand reverently into the pure and holy waters. Then he brought the anointed hand up to his heart, forehead and crown of the head in turns. Repeating the sacred Sri Gangaji mantra taught to him by his blessed gurus, he reached down again and took a handful of water and poured it slowly over his entire head. A thrill of joy passed through his body and he stood stock-still, feeling the full extent of that blessing. After this initial meeting had taken place, indicative of the powerful union of Shiva and Shakti, he slowly slipped his entire body into the cold river, feeling months and years of wearisome travel and worldly impositions dissolve completely.

After a time, when his mind had descended somewhat from spiritual heights, the Avadhut opened his eyes and stared out across the expanse of flowing waters. Somehow, the austere temperature of the river, extremely cold even in this warm season, did not bother him. His mind remained above any limiting contact with the body and the senses were elevated to a very heightened plateau. His mind, however, was becoming very receptive to lofty spiritual teachings and as he observed this change in his mental faculties, memories of teachings received in the past came fully to bear on his sensitized awareness.

*"Immerse your mind continually in the presence of God, over and over again, like you would your body in the holy river, until all traces of mundane consciousness have been effaced."*

These instructions had come from the mouth of his guru on the eve of Kali Puja as the two sat for an extended period of meditation intended to last well after midnight and towards dawn.

*"It is in that same mind, purified by inner austerity, that you will then behold That which you are seeking in this lifetime. The Divine Mother Herself, if you study Her many manifestations and Her sublime teachings, is seen to be ever engaged in such powerful undertakings. She accomplishes two major things by this strong spiritualized effort, Ekanta. First, she breaks down barriers with Her austerities and allows Her votaries to become free and gain higher vision. These barriers are twofold: barriers that She Herself maintains for certain reasons as well as those constructed by the evil and ignorant actions of others. Both are torn down by Her concentrated effort during this time, especially in association with the auspicious times of Durga and Kali Puja. Secondly, She illustrates the all-important need for us to struggle against Maya, to accomplish sadhana in order to remain free at all times so that we will never forget Her and always remember our true nature which are one and the same thing."*

"Revered teacher," Ekanta said respectfully after a short time had elapsed. "This great Mother whom the scriptures and the luminaries call Bhagavati, whom our beloved Mataji refers to as Mahavidya Mahamaya Bhagavati Durga Devi, where is She and how does She work? Why can I not see Her and fall at Her feet? The ten-day Navaratri worship for Sri Durga has recently ended and we are on the verge of Kali Puja. My devotion for Her is greatly intensified yet I have no place to direct it. I feel as if I may explode if I do not see Her. Can you help me?"

*"Dear boy,"* answered the guru, *"you ask the impossible. You cannot see Her because She is beyond the senses to perceive. First, explain this to your mind and get its agreement and consent on this matter. Consciousness connected to the body and senses gets accustomed to experiencing everything via the eyes,*

*ears and other physical instruments.  Then, it takes this faulty experience for Reality.  It also begins to form the habit of assuming that transcendental principles can also be understood and experienced with the senses.  This twofold delusion must be corrected if any true spiritual life is to be established."*

A short silence ensued.  Then, after due consideration of Ekanta's series of questions, the teacher continued:

*"What to say, dear boy?  You cannot see Her with these eyes because she is essentially formless.  Her formless Essence is the Reality, but it is That which gives power to the prana so that the eyes gain their ability to see.  Is it possible then that such gross organs, initially lifeless and insentient, could ever see the subtle power that animates them, let alone perceive that which animates animation itself, which gives consciousness to the mind?  Listen a moment to the Hasta-Amalaka Stotram, dear one, for some comprehension of what I am saying may come to you through that."*

So saying, Ekanta's wonderful guru launched into a wonderful rendition of that ancient and time-honored hymn of enlightenment.

> I am not a human, a god,
> or a being inhabiting celestial realms.
> Neither am I a priest,
> a warrior, a merchant or a menial worker.
> I am neither monk, householder, hermit, or wanderer.
> I am the ever-conscious eternal Self,
> infinite and pervading everything.

> Without the sun, no terrestrial actions are possible,
> Yet the light of Timeless Awareness allows
> the sun its moment of glory.
> That inner Radiance, vast and conditionless,
> illumines the corridors of mind and senses.
> And That Light am I, pure and boundless,
> attributeless and free.

> Comforting and life-giving,
> like the quality of warmth in fire,
> Whose nature is always awake, all-abiding,

and one without a second.
Who animates inert objects, mind, and senses,
and engages them in action.
That Self-aware entity am I, sublime and indivisible.

As the reflection in a mirror is identical
with the object reflected,
So is the universe identical with the Self,
revealed in the mirror of pure mind.
Thus are living beings perfect images of the eternal Subject,
the undying Self.
And that limitless Self am I,
identical with the Supreme Being.

Remove the reflective surface and the form disappears,
What remains is the formless essence, the objectless Reality.
Like this, when the external mind is stilled
and focused on Reality,
What is left is oneness, the eternal abode, my true existence.

Even bereft of sense experience, mental cognition,
and vital functions,
That internal Reality continues to exist,
relying upon nothing.
It is That which animates the senses, impels the life-force,
and awakens the mind.
That perpetual Being am I, Self-effulgent,
illumining the cosmos.

Absolutely unique, the ineffable essence
which is the source and origin of all.
The primal Purusha,
playfully manifesting Itself in Pure Mind,
Who is the one impartial sun,
reflecting in the different waterpots of various intellects.
That One and I are identical, nondifferent, inseparable.

It is one homogenous presence that causes all eyes to see.
It is one omniscient entity

which graces all minds with thought.
It is like unto the sun
which reveals the world of name and form for perceiving.
That One and I are nondistinct and form one cohesive unity.

The eyes see, the ears hear, all due to the presence of the Self.
The sun becomes manifest due to That effulgence
which imparts the ability to see to the eyes.
If not for It, darkness and ignorance would prevail at all times.
The Self and I are one and the same, free of divisions.

One transcendent sun becomes many,
reflected in the ripples of a lake.
One indivisible Being appears multiple,
animating many bodies.
But relativity ever fails to divide It,
ignorance only momentarily obscures It.
It is undeniably whole,
which is the pervasive condition in all.

The ignorant and naive, beholding clouds,
deem the sun to be nonexistent.
These same beings, perceiving nightfall,
imagine the sun has expired.
Ever-present, always shining,
this is even more true of Brahman, the ineffable.
This Self and Brahman are one, not two or many,
and none else exists.

There is only this One, existing in all beings
and all existing in It.
It filters down and touches all hearts and minds,
yet nothing can touch It.
It is like the sky, pure and serene,
subtle and impossible to taint.
That One am I, I am that One, there can be none other.

After that marvelous moment in time had passed, Ekanta breathed a sigh of combined relief and admiration. Looking longingly at his guru, tears began to stream from his eyes. With a gaze of tender love mixed with beneficent concern, the guru broke the silence:

*"Now have you gained an idea or attained a glimpse at That whom we call the Divine Mother? If so, you have begun to cross over and rise above that tendency of the human mind to concretize Divine Reality into limiting concepts and gross objects. Therefore Ekanta, turn your mind's desire to know Her and your heart's longing to see Her inwardly and gain Her full vision, unlimited by impediments such as the senses. You will thereby turn from a dualist into an Advaitist and will then come to know Her secrets. Water lays still, it also flows in fluid motion. The Mother accomplishes all through these two modes as well, yet She remains formless throughout."*

"Dear teacher," Ekanta asked, "what is this earth, this universe spread out on all sides? Who are all these beings? Are they the Divine Mother's creations and is She separate from them? You said that She is the true nature within all. How am I to understand this?"

*"This cannot be truly understood by the ordinary mind, Ekanta, any more than an object can be truly experienced via the gross senses. When something is truly still, it tends to blend and disappear, like the deer we saw in the forest yesterday. Though we saw it move from time to time and our eyes knew exactly where it was, whenever it remained motionless it blended with the background so perfectly that it became as if invisible. Mother's nameless, formless essence, is static, is motionless. Only upon this totally immutable backdrop can such a variety of energies find full expression, playing on and on until they inevitably sink and merge into Her, their Source, once again. Thus, though Her creatures seem separate from Her, they are never truly so. They spring from Her like plants and trees from the soil. They live on and in Her like ants on an anthill, bees in a hive or fish in a river. Ultimately, they dissolve into Her like hailstones into an ocean. Nature describes Her secrets to us daily, but beings fail to comprehend due to their attachment to insipid pleasures and mundane pursuits.*

*"As to your question about the appearance or temporary existence of the universe, my boy, it is merely Mother's instrument*

*on which She plays and sports. It has no lasting existence so
the wise place it second to the Reality, which is primary and
permanent. Thus comes Her name, the Adishakti, Ekanta, the
first, foremost and original Being from which all others have
sprung. Oh, She is beautiful, my dear! Much more so than any
form the mind can conceive of."*

When Ekanta's mind came down from these exalted memories,
his body was wonderfully numb. The cold waters that gently
swirled around him provided a reminder of the Divine Mother's
sport. Though his teachers had been uncompromising as to their
insistence on apprehending the Adishakti as subtle and formless,
he had also learned from them of Her Immanent Reality. These
teachings regarding Her all-pervasiveness had stood him in good
stead and had been reinforced by his experiences in nature. That
Her Essence was reflected in every little thing, in every event, in
every action, provided continual inspiration for him. From the initial movement of discrimination that signaled the beginning of
spiritual effort to the all-affirming resolve and realization that perceived Her throughout and beyond the creation, Ekanta had been
a party to it all. Now he merely dwelled silently in the Self, Her
Light, and watched Her amazing mechanism, the universe, move
forward. As the Avadhut climbed out of the cold mountain waters
at the source of the Ganges, more teachings entered his mind.

*"The Mahashakti?"* came the question from the great savant's
lips, *"well, She is the totality of everything. As the queen has
access to every room in the castle and is also intimate with the
king, so too does the Universal Mother command power over
every aspect of creation while simultaneously resting eternally
with Her Divine Husband. They, the Parabrahman and Parashakti, are not two, though they often appear as two."*

Ekanta had been attending the divine discourses of Ramakrishnadas Baul whom he had met with several times in the course
of his wanderings over the sacred land. He had come to love this
colorful, gentle, yet enigmatic holy man, knowing him to be a cut
above many others who possessed spiritual knowledge. Now, in
a huge tent spread over several acres at a holy gathering of pilgrims and sadhus, the Avadhut sat quietly and enjoyed the host of
questions and answers being taken up for consideration.

As the crowd buzzed with quiet conversation, a turbaned sadhu stood up and hastily rattled off a statement.

"In many of the teachings of sacred India, sir, we find no mention of the Divine Mother. Why should we believe in such a Being?"

*"My friend,"* came forth the reply from Ramakrishnadas Baul, *"the scriptures represent a very tiny portion of eternal Truth and can by no means describe even a modicum of Her glory. You remind me of the fellow who, waking up one night with a momentary loss of memory, forgot the existence of his father and mother lying in the next room."*

A few laughs came forth at this statement. After they had subsided, the seer went on with his discourse.

*"The Mother's wisdom is always obscured. She intends for this to happen. If She were to reveal it, beings would awaken swiftly from the Maya She projects to sustain this dreamlike world of relativity and the universe would disappear in the upheaval which followed. In addition to the illusion She projects, though, there is the quagmire of delusion that individual beings create. Turning us loose across the face of this earth and allowing us to sport here, it soon became clear that mischief is a companion to human nature. Previous to that, She thought Herself to be the great Enchantress, conjuring up all manner of deceptions and ruses through which to continue the sportive play of the Absolute in relativity, but when she saw mankind get ahold of this world and observed what outright insanity reigned after that, She stood back in amazement. We have definitely taught Her a few new things about trickery, deceit and madness."*

A rash of conversation burst forth at this statement, accompanied by laughter and general consent. When all this died down, the seer continued to make his point.

*"I say this partially in jest, of course, but the point is dead serious. To awaken from the slumber of delusion is to escape from the trap of Avidya Maya with its binding double strand of tamo and rajo guna. In the Kali yuga, it is the work and duty of those who still recognize and cling to dharma to act as beacons of light for those who are confused as to the path and the way. Without acknowledging the Universal Mother, such work proves fruitless, for She is the driving force behind this*

*appearance called the universe. Propitiating Her is the recourse of the wise."*

"Who is it that we propitiate, revered sir?" came the question from a voice in the crowd. "Tell us of Her."

Without even pausing to consider, the baul plunged onward.

*"Jnana Shakti, Kriya Shakti, and Dravya Shakti — if we understand these three dynamic principles to any degree then we have a grasp on what She is about in regard to the seven-tiered cosmic structure. They are the principles through which cosmic Ahamkara gets produced and appears in this relative world of creation, preservation and destruction. First, as Jnana Shakti, She is the very force of intelligence called Medha in the scriptures. Intelligence is the active force which absorbs and digests the field of mental sustenance called knowledge. Both are based in Truth, the static and ultimate Reality. Jnana Shakti produces the sattvic ego, just shy of Nirguna Brahma. In this mode She is the power by which knowledge is both produced and obtained. The five main presiding rulers of the internal organs are produced out of this sattvic power as are the four presiding rulers of the fourfold antahkarana called mind, intelligence, ego and chitta. So you can see how important is the One who wields this power.*

*"Kriya Shakti is incredible. Operating this aspect of Her Ahamkara, the Divine Mother not only places into motion the seven worlds and all that occurs there, She also allows for a spontaneity that at once provides the foundation for all acts, thoughts and insights to occur, both simultaneously and inde-pendently of each other. Many dimensions get superimposed over one another and this multilevel existence interacts with karma, predestination and the urge towards absolute freedom from manifestation. The result is the infinite sport called Mahalila. This rajasic activity called Kriya Shakti, placed in motion to accomplish all of this, produces the five senses, the five motor organs of the senses and the five organs of action. The cosmic Maya continues easily due to this fifteen-part cause.*

*"Dravya Shakti is a producer of substances. The Queen of cre-ation is at work in exquisite fashion here, fashioning the very building blocks of the phenomenal existence. The atomic struc-ture itself, whether of a gross nature or a subtle contingent, is*

*manufactured by Her in this mode. Out of Dravya Shakti of the tamasic condition proceeds the five qualities of sound, touch, form, taste, and smell which in turn produces the five elements of ether, air, fire, water and earth, the five tanmatras. Have you not heard, dear friends, the scriptures and what they declare regarding this matter? I quote, 'These ten gross and subtle elements, at the bidding of the Mahashakti, when combined, become endowed with the power to shape whole worlds and entire solar systems by generating material substances.' Now, revered sirs, can you see a bit of what Mother is? Does She come forth and reveal Herself to your minds?"*

"Respected Baul," said one elder, standing and speaking, "for those of us that have seen Her or have become acquainted with Her before, your words act as a sobering and inspiring reminder of what is so often easy to forget. But what of those who have not yet gained intuition or direct insight? Will they not, upon hearing such words, simply tend to perceive the three aspects you have so wonderfully put forth as products of mind and matter alone? Where is the proof in all of this for an independent force other than that of mere kinetic energy, what to speak of a Divine Being?"

*"That is a good question, dear sir," replied the baul, "and one that I have previously anticipated and have been forced to answer before. There is another aspect of shakti in this way of thinking. She is called Iccha Shakti. Creative energies are Her various tools. She is the One who started the initial and primal movement towards original manifestation and She watches blissfully as it burgeons and develops while entering into all living beings as awareness in order to experience the cosmic play."*

"What are some of Her characteristics, respected teacher?" the Avadhut asked. Though his tone was low, the voice penetrated and carried with it an air of intensity and poise. Ramakrishnadas Baul knew that his learned friend, far from needing to know such information, was leading the conversation and the crowd both towards an enlightened conclusion. Smiling upon his compatriot, the baul continued his exploration of the many aspects of shakti.

*"Iccha Shakti is pure Divine Will. She is not at the beck and call or under the control of anything that She creates, sustains or destroys. She is independent and self-willed, like an*

*irresistible Cosmic Force that wraps Itself with many infinite layers of perpetual existence while adeptly wielding the myriad forms of energy that come forth from them. None can oppose Her, as is seen by the subservient positions which all demonic forces arrive at when they attempt to do battle with Her. This is related in symbolic fashion in the Devi Puranas and in our Divine Mother scriptures. It would behoove us all to recall, remember, contemplate and invoke the power inherent in us as the Mahashakti. Then, after this primal connection is made, let us go forth and be about the business of awakening others to their divine heritage. No regeneration for the world or for our beloved Mother India will be possible without first awakening and worshipping the primal shakti power within us. Let us not delay then! All beings have a primordial Mother. Let us speak of Her to everyone!"*

Stars were beginning to twinkle in the early evening sky. The Avadhut was wrapped in his blanket and sitting before the flames of a small campfire. Wood in the area was scarce, but with a little kindling gathered along the way together with a few pieces of coal gifted to him by an admirer at the nearby village he had passed through, his fire was soon hot enough to boil water. After the soup was ready, the Avadhut enjoyed his light meal under the stars at the source of the holy river at the base of the sacred mountains. Under the spell of this enchantingly beautiful place it was not long before he placed his mind in meditation, enjoying the Peace, Peace, Peace of the ancients.

The sound of the Ganges flowing nearby easily placed him in a deep, introspective mood. Contemplating the wonder of water, with its homogenous nature and healing vibration, the Avadhut suddenly recalled a discussion he had with a Brahmin priest at a certain temple along the Jamuna River. Ekanta had been attending the temple worship while on pilgrimage. The priest had befriended him and the two had quickly become friends. As they were relaxing on the banks of the river after the evening worship of the Lord, the priest spoke, breaking the silence.

*"Simply by observing water, friend, many of the most precious attributes of spiritual life can be apprehended and understood."*

"How so?" came the Avadhut's query.

*"It is inherently pure,"* returned the priest, *"so it confers*

*holiness in a most natural way wherever it is found and when-*
*ever it is used. It tends towards homogeneity, always blending,*
*joining and unifying. In this regard it reminds us constantly*
*that God is eternally one and undivided, even though apparent*
*separation into parts seems to occur. It is soothing and heal-*
*ing, whether it is still or in motion. This indicates that, like*
*Brahman and Shakti, the static and dynamic modes of Reality,*
*peace and well-being always exist and can be enjoyed despite*
*interchangeable periods of activity and inactivity.*

"What do you know of this divine element, respected Avadhut?"
came the priest's question after a short and pregnant silence.

"Like Brahman and Shakti again," replied the Avadhut, "it satisfies thirst like no other thing in existence. This fact carries a
profound lesson. It is not just to slake our thirst for water that
this element is granted to us by the Universal Mother. Primarily,
to my way of thinking, water exists both to remind us of the sanctity of life and to reinforce our resolve that a burning desire for
God-realization constitutes the main reason for our existence here
on this earth. It is the thirst of longing for God which gets implied
by seeing water."

The priest, obviously impacted by such a powerful insight,
remained quiet, thinking. Minutes later, as the two watched the
river flow by in the light of dusk, he ventured to ask the silent
Avadhut more about the teachings of water.

"Other than this powerful reminder," came the Avadhut's response, "water has taught me lessons of equanimity and has awakened me further to the actual purpose and innate secret of the
Divine Couple's blissful presence. Everything, whether it be gross
or subtle, manifest or held in abeyance, hidden or exposed, all is
One and that One is holy, is purely and pervasively sacred by
nature. Who does not experience awe and anticipation even upon
just perceiving water, and who will not feel trepidation, excitement and heightened emotions at the thought of immersion into
that liquid body? No, forgive me, but I say that even the heights
of nondual unity are not sufficient if the Divine Presence is not
felt and known there as a palpable verity."

After a few moments, the Avadhut went on.

"What is the amorphous mass of light without its radiance?
What is the ocean without its sound? How nondescript the sky

without clouds. In much the same way, unity without the sacred presence of God is undesirable. Water and the wonderful feelings that it confers upon us when we are in and around it speaks to this crucial fact.

"I want to have God on all levels brother," stated the Avadhut, turning an intensely smiling face upon the priest. "Every feeling, every divine emotion and intense mood that crosses my being as I approach Him is essential for full communion, just as the feelings and experiences that we pass through on the way to our sacred ablutions are integral to consummation. After I plunge into water, whether it be a mountain lake, a boundless sea, a private bath or the source of the Ganges, may I sit silently and absorb to the fullest level of my capacity the meaning of this blessed boon and may the Mother grant that I abide in that highest of experiences at all times, never coming down from such heights again to mundane awareness."

The Avadhut was wide awake all of a sudden. The river still flowed nearby, its waters making a soothing, rushing sound that bespoke of holy communion. Ekanta had fallen asleep while remembering the conversation so long ago with his friend the priest on the banks of the Jamuna River. In that sense, he mused, water in a river was an apt example of the flow of time. Thoughts and words shared before had resurfaced here, at the source of another river. The flow never ended. *"Like the river, everything returns,"* came the old saying to Ekanta's mind.

Standing up, the Avadhut felt drawn to the Ganges once again. After finding it, sparkling in the moonlight, he followed it downstream for awhile, captivated by its graceful movement. Soon, in the soft light, he could make out a figure on the opposite shore of the river, immersed in it up to his head. The sight was eerie. It was as if a decapitated human head had caught on a submerged branch jutting out of the shallows of the shoreline and was floating there. Finally, the Avadhut called out across the waters in order to get some satisfaction for his curiosity.

"Hello! Is someone there?" came the Avadhut's question.

At first there was no stirring, but soon the head seemed to turn in the semidarkness and Ekanta could dimly make out a pair of shoulders rising out of the water amidst small amounts of steam. The figure next produced an arm from out of the waters as well and that arm beckoned to Ekanta to advance across the river.

Though the spectacle before him was eerie and the figure fantastic, Ekanta set out bravely into the current. Sometimes swimming, sometimes walking on shallow sand bars and rock, the Avadhut crossed the river and approached the mysterious figure. As he did so, a wonderful thing happened. The water, so cold at first, became gradually more and more temperate until, as Ekanta neared the direct vicinity of the bather, the water turned actually hot. Enjoying this feeling immensely, the Avadhut forgot to greet his new-found companion. This oversight, combined with the look of pleasure and surprise which must have inhabited Ekanta's features, brought forth some laughter from the stranger. Ekanta then responded sheepishly.

"Excuse me, Brother," came his apology. "I was caught up in amazement at this wonderful phenomenon. This is, indeed, a welcome occurrence. Imagine, a hot spring near the source of the Ganga. I had never heard of such a thing!"

The stranger merely nodded his head in affirmation.

"It is not always present they say, but only occurs at certain times of the year," he finally replied. "We are fortunate to be here at this auspicious time. The Mother, in the form of thermal energy, has seen fit to warm our bodies here at this high elevation in the cold of night. When I saw the steam rising from across the river, I swam over and found this delightful spot waiting for me. I am also happy to have someone to share it with. Can I know your name?"

"I am called Ekanta," answered the Avadhut, getting his first close up view of this man. "I am pleased to find another nocturnal explorer who is wide awake and seeking intense and unusual experiences in the dead of night. It is lucky that I saw you in the dim light and called out to you. I was sure that I saw a human head over here."

"Yes indeed," returned the bather, "and this head is still attached to a body, not yet taken by the sword of the Goddess."

"I am sure that this is true in a physical sense only," said Ekanta, "for your presence here, late at night and in the face of substantial dangers and the hardships of the pilgrimage and the path, certainly speaks otherwise. Those who have not offered themselves to the Divine Being would hardly be in such a location as this, let alone practicing spiritual disciplines in a rushing river at midnight. They would be home indulging in various comforts and leisures or slaving away for lust and lucre inside the yoke of worldliness. The only yoke you seem to bear is that of yoga."

"You are observant, sir," replied the man. "My name is Manksha and I have come here from far off Meghalaya. Once in my life I had to see the famed and auspicious source of the Ganges and bathe in her waters. So I have come, even through many obstacles."

"You are well-named," responded the Avadhut. "Your name means longing. You have fulfilled that longing for communion with the liquid Mother by traveling across the entire subcontinent. Your longing is purely spiritual as well, for your practices are both intense and unique, given your presence here tonight. Therefore, I am glad to make your acquaintance and share this experience with you."

"It is surely a twist of fate that has brought us together during this brief moment in time and under these circumstances, is it not?" said Manksha.

"Truly," replied Ekanta. "One can only wonder about such momentary meetings. Sometimes, the most profound things happen around these occurrences. Tonight, we are on the verge of such auspiciousness merely by proximity of circumstances and surroundings alone."

The two men fell silent for a time, each enjoying the combination of cold air and hot water, experienced in the rarefied atmosphere of the Ganges River and the Himalayan mountains. Occasionally, they would climb out on the shore to cool down in the brisk mountain air before plunging back in the hot upsurge of water rising from below the surface of the river. No one else appeared and the two enjoyed uninterrupted communion in silence with the Self and the primal elements. Just before dawn the two separated, each telling the other of the location of their respective campsites so that they could meet and talk some more in the days to come.

Ekanta slept the morning away and rose near noontime. His store of foodstuff, as rudimentary as it was, would suffice to keep him satisfied and healthy throughout his stay. He finished the last of his puffed rice that afternoon, eating it while dipping his feet in the waters of the Ganges in childlike fashion. Later that afternoon, he found a place where he could climb the rock cliffs to attain an altitude suitable for meditation. There, overlooking the valley below, he sat for three hours, absorbed in loving attention on the guru, the Divine Mother and the precious Self. While thinking about his revered gurus, memories of a conversation with them regarding meditation recurred in his mind, even after so many years had elapsed.

Ekanta had approached the simple yet wonderful vanaprastin couple one day while they were relaxing by the river near the forest ashram. All around were colorful songbirds and forest creatures and the place verily exuded the peace of the ashrams of old in the times of the ancient Rishis. The place lived in Ekanta's mind even now and it would continue to do so as long as memory had existence. It was a state of mind, he realized, an eternal and elevated vibratory realm, not merely a transitory place in time.

*"Ekanta,"* came the greeting from his Mataji. *"You have found us! How wonderful to see you. Please be seated and converse with us. We are always here for you."*

The boy sat himself down at their feet after prostrating in respectful fashion. Losing no time, he launched into verbal communion with his knowledgeable gurus.

"Revered teachers," came the question. "Is meditation necessary for enlightenment?"

*"What is enlightenment, dear boy?"* came the return question from the Mataji.

"I do not know," answered Ekanta.

*"Then you had better meditate to find out,"* stated his Guruji.

For a few seconds, seriousness played across the faces of his preceptors, then they both burst out laughing. Ekanta too, was swept into this mirth, which was characteristic of both his teachers in certain moods.

After the laughter died away, his male guru spoke:

*"True meditation and true enlightenment, both are unknown, Ekanta, being impossible for the ordinary mind to comprehend. By starting into the practice of formal meditation, however, after being initiated and guided by a spiritual adept, the nature of enlightenment gets revealed by degrees. One then opens to plateaus of spiritual perception unbeknownst to worldly minds."*

*"It is all subtle,"* continued the Mataji without pause. *"As one*

*cannot explain the personal joys of married life to a small child,
so too is it impossible to explain meditation and all its wonderful results to the beginner. On faith and personal resolve
alone one must proceed at the outset, leaving the rest to fall into
place later. The experience will eventually mature under the
influence of perseverance."*

"Does it help to contemplate God with form and feel reverence
for that ideal in meditation, dear teachers?" Ekanta had asked.
"My friend's older brother is practicing meditation without any
object. His meditation is devoid of emotion and devotion. He says
that this is the superior way of practice and that those who take
to other types are mere beginners."

*"This is a serious charge,"* returned the preceptor, *"obviously
made by one who is still in the beginning phases of the practice himself. Imagine, one knows next to nothing about spiritual life, yet still makes such sweeping declarations. Do not
listen to this type of nonsense but rather follow your own way.
Each seeker has a path best suited for him or her according to
their nature. Judging spiritual progress is nothing but vanity.
Never indulge in it or give voice to such ideas but go forward
along your own lighted path. That is what the Lord intends for
you in order that your own highest good becomes manifest and
operative. As regards to devotion, reverence and other forms of
spiritual sensitivity, our experience is that these are great aids
to success along the Raja Yoga path. Those who feel them and
exercise them naturally have actually been blessed by the Lord.
In fact, past karmas would have to be positive in order for such
a boon to occur at all. Therefore, take it as a sign of God's Grace
upon you that you are able to enjoy those qualities, thereby making the road smoother and the goal more accessible."*

"Ours is a yogic path then, dear sir?" Ekanta ventured.

*"Generally speaking,"* replied the boy's male guru, *"there are
three main paths beings here in the relative plane of existence
proceed by. There is the terrestrial path, the ritualistic path
and the transformative path. There is also the transcendental
or perfect path, if it could be called such. But concerning the
first three, which are those taken by most beings experiencing
the embodied condition, they equate to the world, dualistic religion and the sincere seeker. In the first, beings live a deluded*

*or a limited life, either indulging in evil pastimes or making sensuality their preoccupation while pursuing wealth through the acquisition of lower or secular knowledge. In the second, beings dabble in the surface level of religion, emphasizing ethical and moral existence and either assuaging their guilt or remorse thereby or satisfying themselves with only an occasional thought of God, once a week or at meals. Lastly, there is the transformative path called yoga. The word can be used either in the religio/cultural sense relating to a system of Hindu Dharma or can be used broadly to mean any and all paths which proceed through the utilization of spiritual disciplines, called sadhana."*

The guru paused for a moment. When the instruction proceeded, it was the Mataji who spoke.

*"It is in this last way that true liberation occurs, for one is finally about working out one's own salvation instead of either pursuing it wrongly by catering to the world or by relying on religious institutions, their often distorted message and their puritanical or money-minded priesthood. The pursuit of this pathway, an eternal and blessed road to Reality, signals the approach of apparently individualized awareness towards the unified position of nondual Awareness. This is the Satchitananda you have heard about, Ekanta. It is the truth of life and existence Itself, the very foundation, and if you ask me it is not possible to perceive It or come into contact with It without feeling extreme reverence, for It is the intrinsic nature of holiness. Sanctity is Its very fabric. So, my dear, do not vex your mind with other people's opinions but rather find out for yourself what God is and move towards It, either gradually or, ideally, with swift progress. Godspeed to you in crossing over the sea of samsara and reaching the distant shore of Divine Existence."*

Ekanta slowly emerged from his meditation. Darkness was beginning to fall so he decided to make his way down the cliff while he could still navigate his footing. Descending swiftly but carefully, he reached the valley floor and started again towards the source of the river nearby. On the way he met Manksha who was in a rather excited state.

"Come friend," he blurted out, "there are some new arrivals this day into our midst and a satsang near the river under the stars has been arranged for this evening. We should attend, for there will be much wisdom shared this night."

"Wonderful," replied the Avadhut. "I am in the mood for this. Let us take a little sustenance at my campsite and join the holy ones under the stars."

So saying the two returned via Ekanta's camp where they took a few mouthfuls of food and water before seeking out the newly assembled congregation.

The new arrivals were already in place when the two men approached the small group. Several mountain yogis, a few renunciate wanderers, some pilgrims from distant points of India, the Avadhut, Manksha and the newly arrived monks made up the gathering. All in all, there were about a dozen beings on the banks of the sacred Ganga that evening and a few more arrived throughout the night. Numbers, however, were unimportant, neither was time a factor, nor did thoughts about food, sleep, family responsibilities or morning schedules hamper the proceedings in the least. The mart of joy began to flow immediately.

Tea made the rounds quite often, prepared over a fire which burned brightly in the encroaching darkness, providing the group with mystical glimpses of each other swathed in the light of dancing flames and bursts of exploding sparks. Serious conversation mingled with peals of laughter but the focus always and ever remained upon the Blessed Lord. Formless Reality, Divine Mother Reality, Shunyata, Ishwara — many aspects of Reality and the truths that supported them were discussed at length. At times the exchange became so involved and profound that gasps of surprise or exclamations of delight emitted from the fully concentrated participants. All in all, it was one of those special times when everything was in harmony. Even the arguments and disagreements were illuminating and nonthreatening to anyone's preferred spiritual position or religious belief.

Ekanta became involved in the ongoing discussion only late in the evening, after listening carefully to everyone's wisdom and assessing everyone's chosen point of view in characteristic fashion. In due time, one of the monks who had been observing the Avadhut turned to him and spoke.

"Tell us the way, wise one. Do you think that we will just allow you to sit idly by, noting everything we say while remaining mute?

You will not escape so easily."

The Avadhut did not at first respond, having been singled out in such a manner, so the monk ventured a question along philosophical lines.

"Tell us then, is the world an illusion, God being the only Reality?"

The Avadhut smiled momentarily. All became silent as he spoke.

"The Self is God, the universe is a creation of mind."

These words broke upon the group with a subtle force that bore amazing spiritual weight. As heads nodded in assent to this profound but cryptic statement, the monk pressed for elucidation from the Avadhut.

"Is that not the same as saying that God is real and world is unreal, as the Vedanta proposes?"

"In part, depending on how one interprets," replied the Avadhut, "but what I have said leaves nothing to chance. If the world is an illusion as the Mayavadins say, if the mindstream is merely a constant flow of conceptualization as some Buddhists believe and if the ultimate state is void of all qualities or attributes as the nihilists assume, what of Supreme Reality? Something cannot come from nothing so what is this world that appears before us and from whence has it come? The denial or affirmation of any state, idea or concept inevitably points to the existence of an entity that is doing the affirming or denying, so Who is That? What is more, who are you and who am I?"

This tact, a unique slant on the inquiry into Reality called Atma Vichara, took the entire assembly off guard momentarily and before they could catch their breath or formulate thoughts, responses or questions, the Avadhut plunged onwards.

"What I have proposed ascends beyond the realm of mere speculation. It is Atma Vichara, inquiry into the Supreme Nature of Reality and it rests in Truth alone, undeniable. The Sanatana Dharma which we adhere to is not hazy with regard to the existence of Divine Reality, nor does it conveniently hide this essential Being by not speaking of It or by denying its existence. There can be no creation without a Creator. Those who propose the idea that no such Being exists, either out of atheism or agnosticism or to prove some nihilistic theory, have only come half way. God exists here and now as the sculptor of the phenomenal universe, the mastermind of its divine plan and the wielder of its many powers and energies. Even if one believes that the universe is ultimately unreal, there is still the position that it is real so long as it is perceived.

"As Dravya Shakti, the Ultimate Being fashions the universe, manifesting all gross and subtle materials from within Its own boundless expanse. As Jnana Shakti, the Supreme has conceptualized the entire framework of this immense and many-faceted creation, including its wonderful animal, human, and celestial dramas with all their joy and pathos. As Kriya Shakti, the Supreme Being manages a whole host of powerful and minuscule powers, animating the universe with energies too diverse to imagine. Finally, as all these three cosmic powers combined and more, the Absolute Brahman appears as Iccha Shakti, whose indomitable Will foresees, outlines and facilitates everything that occurs, past, present or future. This puissant Will also decides the time when every soul awakens to its inherent divinity and lays open the path for transcendent realization, such be Its grace and mercy."

The Avadhut paused, both for impact and to let this wisdom sink in. Then, he proceeded with the full attention of the assembled group.

"This awakening and final journey, though, is truly only a remembrance of That which is always within us. The universe is, then, all a manifestation of the Cosmic Mind while we, as apparently and temporarily individualized bits of consciousness sporting in that realm of expression, are the essential ingredient. As pure and indivisible Consciousness Absolute which is the Divine Self of every existing thing, we are undeniably and irrevocably fused with Brahman, identical with It, nondifferent from It. We can and must, then, if we are true human beings cast in His image, play this game of cosmic permutation without ever becoming disassociated whatsoever from our true nature. Have you not heard the song sung in my area of this holy land?"

Saying so, the Avadhut charmed everyone present with a powerful wisdom song:

Once, in a timeless state past remembering,
I heard your voice, O Mother,
speaking to me as my own indwelling essence, sublime.

You bade me descend into the realm of space
and the whirlpool of time
to sport amidst the many expressions of manifest thought.

But lo, dear Mother,
I did not understand Your immaculate intent,
the smile on your face and the wink of your eye
and now I am captive here, bereft of your stunning vision.

This game called life is marvelous, no doubt,
but there is an invisible thorn
in the clothing of temporal existence,
an irritating grain of sand in every bed
which ruins our sleep as we toss and turn.

Ramprasad can only surmise
that it is You, O Wisdom Mother,
who has placed this inconceivable twist in every mind,
who maintains this uncomfortable condition throughout
so that we may be forced to recall our true identity
and recognize all as nothing other than Brahman.

After the tones of the song had died down there was a short period of appreciative silence. Then, the Avadhut went on.

"Notice how the composer of this song, itself a miniature testament to Divine Reality, constructs the message around Truth. First of all, there can be no breach in the perfection of Unity in God, that intrinsic Oneness with Brahman which forms the essence of the Advaitic knowledge. Without that, beings are set afloat on the ocean of religion and philosophy with only speculation for a boat and doubt as a paddle. Nicely does the singer of this song affirm that before time appeared and anterior to life, mind and the universe in space which it created, the Soul Eternal called the Atman rested in total oneness with That which is Its primal essence which we call Brahman. That is why I stated that the universe is a manifestation of mind while the Atman is God. No lasting peace is possible without this realization."

After this had sunk in for a few moments, the silence was broken by the inevitable question.

"This is wonderful, no doubt," said a sadhu who had been silent up to this point, "and we may or may not believe it according to our capacity and predilection, but the question still remains as to why the Mother sent us here in the first place. If we understood this then our problems would be solved."

"Indeed," stated the Avadhut, "would that really be the case? Would it not make more sense to know Her, the Supreme One, first and foremost? Then, knowing that which creates the cosmic plan, we would know the intent of the plan. The difference is that in one way we render ourselves helpless by sitting and crying 'Why are we here, why are we here,' while in the other we take steps to know based upon acceptance of and faith in our intrinsic connection with the Divine Being. The confused cry out 'Why are we here,' but the wise ask 'Who am I?' The bird, which enters unsuspectingly into the room of a house, flies first from one side of the room to another looking for an exit in utter fear and confusion. When at last it does not find one, it simply sits quietly in a corner and waits for the hand that will free it. In this way, we must accept our situation, have faith, be silent and go within to find the answers. Only by this bold act will the ultimate knowledge come to us and, in truth, it is not really courage, but practicality mingled with natural progression. When we have a toothache, we find a dentist. This is not an act of courage but of course."

The Avadhut paused to examine the group momentarily, then he continued.

"Looking at this from another perspective, why must there be a purpose to this creation? Perhaps it is purely by an act of the Divine Will that this creation in time and space appears and continues, or maybe it is not really here at all, being a dream of the Absolute. Either way, let me be one with that Supreme Will. May Thy will be my will and may I have intimate knowledge of the Divine Dreamer. The dream will therefore either come true or dissolve. Otherwise, what will be the result of existence? Beings spend countless hours, days, decades and even lifetimes searching for the answers to the purpose for this creation but they never locate and consult the Creator. Is this not strange, seeing that the ultimate Being abides within every other living being as the Self? Listen to a story.

"After living many lives and gaining illumination, a sage came before the Lord and fell at His feet. 'I have finally found you,' cried out the sage, 'after searching the seven worlds over, after many births, deaths and rebirths, after indulging in many spiritual disciplines, austerities and much reasoning. The purpose of my existence is fulfilled as I stand before you now, gazing to my heart's content! Thank you for awakening me to your divine purpose and guiding me through the maze of the worlds.'

Amazed, the Lord looked at the sage and responded:

"'What you see before you is still a figment of your mind. I exist here in this form to satisfy the longing of those who want to see me in form, but my Essence is formless. That Essence permeated completely the seven worlds you searched through. It was there within you while you struggled and practiced disciplines. That Essence remained constant while you went through the illusory process of birth, death and rebirth. It forms the foundation for the seven worlds which you have called a maze. To know that Essence as your very own Self is the Truth. Truth has no purpose, It just is. Nor does the universe have a purpose, other than for the pure sporting of indivisible Consciousness.' The sage then saw it all and was silent."

After this story, the Avadhut looked around, sweeping all present with his gaze. Then he reiterated his original statement.

"This, again, is why I say that the Self is God and the universe merely a projection of His power. It is true as long as it appears, as long as Consciousness desires to sport in it, but ultimately there is nothing but the Self. To emphasize and conclude, I offer the following song for your enjoyment and consideration."

With his discourse over, the Avadhut sang:

I have finally understood, O Lord,
that everything exists in Thee.
Every heart is ultimately united in Thee.
Nothing exists but Thee!

O Beloved, Your Grace has returned me to my eternal abode
and Your Love has permeated my heart,
Indeed, is there a heart which exists

> that is devoid of Thy Love,
> when nothing exists but Thee!

> God and Goddess, man and woman,
> Hindu, Mussalman, Christian –
> all are brought into existence by Thine own inscrutable Will.
> What are these beings without You? They all exist in Thee!

> Churches, Temples, Kaaba – all places of worship;
> You fashion them and cause all beings to bow down there.
> You have become the worshipper, the act of worship
> and the place of worship.
> Nothing exists but Thee.

> From the life heavens, throughout the boundless universe
> and even into the dark nether regions,
> wherever our souls journey we find only Thee –
> for nothing exists but Thee.

> Matchless is Your Presence, O Lord,
> I have found nothing which compares to it.
> Contemplating it, this humble singer, Jafar,
> has become illumined,
> and this simple Truth has dawned upon his understanding –
> that nothing whatsoever exists but Thee!

This song had a salutary effect on the assembled group. After its positive tones had died away and the full impact of its timeless message had percolated into the awareness of everyone present, all were plunged into different spiritual moods. Some meditated deeply, some wept tears of joy. The Avadhut, however, was not finished speaking on Divine Reality.

"The universe and the seven worlds are the passing Reality — Consciousness vibrating, as it were — but the Supreme Being is vibrationless by nature. Manifestation becomes extinct in It. Why else would the deep thinkers of all philosophical systems use the Sanskrit root 'Nir' to describe It? It is Nirbija in Yoga, Nirguna in Vedanta, Nirvana in the Buddhist view, Nirvikalpa in Advaita. Truly, It is the all in all, saturating all states, modes and instruments like sweetness permeates sugarcane juice, but it is beyond all of these concepts and mechanisms as well. As the Upanishads state, 'It is to be known.'"

The satsang let out well after midnight. All were extremely elevated yet fully satisfied. Manksha and Ekanta then went downriver and found the hot pool again, staying in it for several hours. After Ekanta had returned to his campsite, he still could not sleep. His own discourse had awakened in him similar profound teachings that were given to him at a young age by his gurus. Sitting and contemplating the evening's activities and conversations, he reflected back on some of them.

*"There are positive and negative poles at opposite ends of the earth's axis, Ekanta,"* stated his Guruji one day. *"There are positive and negative forces at work in the universe as well. There are also positive and negative ways of describing Reality. In fact, the positive way describes the negative and the opposite is also true. For instance, when we behold the Blessed Lord as the repository of all beneficial qualities, as the Deva Devi Svarupaya, we find Kala or Kali, who are predominantly powers of negating and destroying. Thus does the affirming, positive force bring us to that which dissolves and merges. The opposite is also true."*

"Revered sir," Ekanta had asked, "how then does the negative force reveal what is positive?"

The guru thought for a moment, then answered:

*"Take the Sanskrit root 'Nir,' for instance, generally associated with what is attributeless or what has been extinguished. Though a prefix denoting what is negative, it describes Divine Reality perfectly."*

After Ekanta had thought about this for a brief time, he asked, "Can you give me some examples of this, dear guru?"

Smiling, the guru said, *"Why am I not surprised to hear such a request coming from you, my son? Put your mind in a receptive and retentive condition and I will relate to you some of what my teacher once told to me on a similar occasion."*

Saying this, the guru lapsed into thoughtful silence for a time. Emerging from his contemplation, he began to enumerate several wonderful examples pertaining to the exposure of Divine Reality using the Sanskrit root 'Nir'.

*"Divine Reality is everywhere, my boy, and can be experienced — must be experienced. It exists on all levels of manifest being. The pujari stands before the image and performs Nirajana, the burning of camphor which exudes light. What does this signify? Is it merely a ritual with no meaning? The camphor is extinguished with nothing left, is it not so? As this occurs, radiance emits from the offered materials. Similarly, the desires, attachments and limitations of the offerer are also burnt away and while this process goes on, light is revealed within the human heart and mind, the light of pure Consciousness. Is this not a fine multidimensional example of the negative revealing what is positive? The devotee divests the self of everything. The camphor evaporates completely leaving no trace. What is left is magnificent."*

The guru continued after a brief pause.

*"Now, on a completely different level, Ekanta, let us look at another powerful example. The scriptures and the sages describe Brahman as supportless, that is, not requiring any foundation upon which to rest or exist, yet providing that same function for everything else. In this case the terminology used are words like Niradhara, Niralamba, Nirashraya and others. If something needs nothing, has no resting place, no requirements in order to exist, then that thing is self-sufficient and self-supportive. Being such, it is perfectly at peace and therefore eternally contented and blissful. This is an extremely positive condition and therefore again reflects how nothingness is conducive to and even identical with fullness.*

*"Niramaya, Niranjana and Nirmala: these words suggest something that is without imperfection or blemish, either of a physical nature such as illness, a mental nature such as negative samskaras or a spiritual nature such as subtle or sattvic obstructions to ultimate realization. Taking away, being without, becoming bereft of, giving up, all these and other ways of expressing emptiness or voidness, whether on an individual level or a collective or cosmic level, point to and even emphasize what is purely positive, always complete, eternally full. Thus is renunciation the mainstay of those who seek everything, and that particular everything represents and epitomizes that which is eternal and ultimately fulfilling.*

*"So, Ekanta, Brahman is full and complete but cannot be known in Its formless mode without a stripping away of coverings and attributes. So Brahman is described as Niravarana, without veils or coverings, and Niravayava, deplete of arms or limbs. It is also Nirupadhika, without limiting adjuncts of any type. If no obscurations, limitations, or modifications are present in It, Ekanta, what would be its state?"*

"Extremely blissful," came the boy's quiet and awe-filled response.

*"Yes,"* was all the teacher said, in a long and drawn-out tone, his eyebrows rising dramatically.

*"Do you require more of this, my son?"* asked the guru after a few moments had elapsed.

"If you do not mind, dear sir," answered Ekanta.

*"Very well, then. There are some descriptive words or phrases that relate out-and-out positive affirmation, even though their Sanskrit roots are still negative. Take for example the word Nira-vadhiatitaram which translates as complete or profuse. Now, how can something totally without, be fully complete? If it has nothing, how can it possess or reflect abundance? Well, we are learning about that here today, are we not?"*

A smile passed across the boy's face at his guru's playful attempt to lighten a serious and abstruse subject.

*"Nirbharata is a good expression of this anomaly as well,"* the preceptor continued. *"It translates as excessiveness or fullness. Now, are we to believe that nothingness can even be taken to an extreme in a positive or affirmative direction — that it is actually full? Where is the limit to Brahman, you tell me! Yet, though this is often said of the Absolute, at the same time It is called Nirvishesha, without any special characteristics. You begin to see, I hope, why the illumined have given up trying to describe Ultimate Reality at all, so contained, diverse and enigmatic is that One, and this only after exhausting every possible attempt in that area.*

*"Attachment is a deadweight upon spiritual life, robbing it of its buoyancy. In this regard the Absolute is described as Nirlipta, ever unattached and as Nirmoha, free of delusion. Thank God that there are double negatives here, wouldn't you say, for we are taught thereby that one can use the power of*

negation to get rid of negative impositions. *Another quandary presents itself here though. Brahman is described as Nirvedya, undisturbed by knowledge or, if you prefer, unknowable. Either way, the presence of knowledge is revealed to be a possible impediment to consummate Knowing. Such a concept hurts those of us who have both reverence for and attachment to knowledge, but we are thereby forced to see the necessity of rising beyond the mind in order to attain Nirvikalpa, God-realization in samadhi.*"

After a short silence, the guru continued.

"*And, my dear boy, at the highest level of existence, where the infinite Parabrahman and Parashakti reside in nondual bliss, there is the ultimate negative positive as well. She is called by the most mind-boggling name in this respect. Her name is Niratishayaghanibhutashakti. Hers is a power that is infinite and limitless but which is so condensed and concentrated as to be all but nonexistent. In this aspect She is subtle in the extreme.*"

"How can I take advantage of such power for the good of my spiritual life and to benefit others, dear sir?" Ekanta had asked at this point.

"*By maintaining and intensifying your sadhana, Ekanta,*" came the firm reply. "*At this juncture, this is what you need to be about doing. Of course, in the realm of sadhana we find helpful negatives as well. Take Nirodha, for example, a type of restraint or suppression that detains and then destroys sins and transgressions at their source. In that regard, may the Lord give us unlimited access to such a cleansing and purifying bath. Additionally, after such a cleansing, one can expect to be Nivritti, free from longing for the waves of existence. One no longer desires to take the plunge into the waters of relativity. The calm, unruffled ocean of Absolute Existence is then the best and only recourse.*"

The Avadhut opened his eyes from his late night ruminations to behold the early dawn. Internalized meditation in the form of inspirational thought and spiritual transmission had brought him into the morning hours. The thought of water remained with him all that day, for its presence at the source of the Ganges, its divine association linked irrevocably with the gods and goddesses, its healing powers and thirst-quenching qualities and its direct correlation to everything that was sacred and holy seemed so intertwined with all of his remarkable experiences at Gangotri.

So it was that dusk found him bowing down at the source of the sacred river, tears of devotion in his eyes, his belongings packed and ready for the journey, his good-byes completed and his heart full of gratitude.

"I salute you with reverence, Oh Goddess of the holy river," he whispered quietly. "You are the profound teacher that reminds me of all that is holy, sacred and pure. May your healing qualities enter into me and manifest throughout my travels to benefit others."

Falling to his knees, the Avadhut took out a small clay container, filled it with the sacred water and placed a cork in it. Turning to follow the river in its course, the Avadhut then continued his extraordinary odyssey, making his way along the banks of Mother Ganga and across the sacred earth — the realm of pure Consciousness alone.

# Chapter 21

# Teachings on Covetousness

THE TWENTY-FIRST GURU — The Honey-Gatherer

THE LESSON — Avarice

In my wanderings I came upon and watched the
honey-gatherer, O Prince, and learned the lesson of
noncovetousness. Avarice is a horrible thing! After
storing up for the future by hoarding wealth and
supplies in massive amounts, beings think that they
are quite safe and secure. But alas, monetary and
material wealth is inevitably sapped, squandered or
lost due to ill health, court litigations, selfish relatives
and thieves. In the case of the honey-gatherer, it was
the bees that suffered loss and grief as their precious
and hard-earned store of sweet nectar was uncovered
and swiftly carried away to be enjoyed by others.
Anger and confusion was all that was left behind.
From this uncompromising teacher I learned the folly
of amassing wealth and the wisdom of being free
from the tendency of covetousness.

The Avadhut opened his eyes and looked out on the field of flowers below.  A motion to the left of his view caught his attention.  Crouching low and creeping slowly towards a small structure at the edge of the field, he saw a man dressed in beggar's clothes.  Rushing upon the structure, the man knocked the top off of it and plunged both hands inside.  In a flash, the Avadhut realized that this man was a thief and that his present object of desire was the store of honey gathered by the bees dwelling in a beehive that a farmer had installed at the edge of his field.

The Avadhut could see the cloud of bees as they literally burst from the hive, buzzing angrily around the intruder and trying to penetrate his covering with their stingers in order to dissuade him from his task.  The honey-thief, however, was practically impervious to them as he scooped out handfuls of dripping honeycomb, permeated through and through with the sweet, sticky liquid.  The man worked methodically but swiftly, occasionally glancing around for signs of the farmer or other onlookers.  He did not notice the Avadhut above him, observing the entire drama with detached and meticulous attention.

After the hive had been cleaned out completely, the man placed his container in a pack and slung it over his shoulder.  As he exited the scene, a stream of bees could be seen following him as he disappeared into the outlying woods while others hovered helplessly over the ravished hive, confused and enraged.  As the Avadhut witnessed these final moments of the nature drama, his mind began to extract the essential teaching inherent in it.  It was not long before an apt lesson revealed itself, coming to him in the form of teachings he had received in days long gone as a young boy in the presence of his parents.

"Why have you taken to storing up for the future, dear boy?" came the admonishing tones of his mother's voice.  "Did you not know that loss follows gain and that suffering follows both?"

Ekanta had been keeping annas and silver coins in a jar buried under the earth near his house.  Upon this particular day, he tried to recover his little fortune and found that someone had already unearthed it and had made off with the bounty.  Tears came to his eyes as he looked upon the scene of the crime, searching the empty tin container again in disbelief.

"Mother," came his pitiable words, "I wanted to buy you

something for the holy days and was saving for that end. Now look what has happened."

The young boy's mother was speechless for a short time. Looking at him tenderly, she then spoke to him about some of the harsh realities of life:

"I have no doubt that your intentions were pure, Ekanta, but the lesson stands nevertheless. About one's possessions, including one's own precious body, the wise tell us to develop detachment. This is due to the harsh fact of existence in this world that declares an end to all created things. The scriptures warn us that the body will eventually perish and when that happens all our so-called belongings will no longer be accessible to us. Shockingly, the body will then be enjoyed by others, either the flames will devour it or worms will infest it or scavengers will take it for themselves. Are we then to make such a big concern of this physical structure which will end up as no more than a few pounds of ash or a mass of decaying matter returning to the five elements? It is much better to set the mind at rest on this matter and use the body for the realization of the Atman within while awareness still inhabits it. We should, as well, assume the same attitude with regards to material objects and earthly wealth."

Looking at his beloved mother with renewed respect, Ekanta asked her a question.

"All around me, dear mother, I see beings working for money and security. The villagers seem to spend their entire time obsessed with day-to-day concerns surrounding the accumulation of money. Yet we are different in this regard. Why should we be any different from them?"

"My dear," returned the saintly woman, "this family and a few others too in and around the village have a different orientation in life. Faith in the Blessed Lord of the Universe is our chief wealth, our only true treasure. Others may work for material gains but we work to serve the Lord. Abiding contentedly in peace while working for what comes naturally due to His Grace is our way, Ekanta. This way begins with peace, exists in peace and ends in peace. No worries or insurmountable obstacles are possible within this atmosphere, for desire and attachment have gone by the wayside. It is a subtle thing to understand. The worldly-minded will hardly be able to comprehend it."

"Mother," replied Ekanta, after a few moments of silence had passed, "I find my mind in perfect agreement with what you have said. I understand it completely. It makes perfect sense to me."

"Of course it does, dear one," returned his mother. "You are born of pious stock, with auspicious markings as well. Before you entered this world, and while I still carried you in my womb, Yogindra Yogi had a dream and came to our house to tell us of it. While in the dream state, a messenger from the realm of the sun god, Surya Narayan, paid him a visit and told him that a manifestation of pure light would be born in the nearby village at the home of some devotees he knew. Indicating your father and I to him, the messenger disappeared. Yogindraji then came here and told us of his vision and we were thus prepared for your coming. Your father and I, independent of the yogi's insight, also knew that a special child was on the way. Therefore, we are looking for you to do wonderful things."

"I do not feel special, mother," admitted Ekanta.

"Contact with the world and your own growth and experience will reveal this to you in time, my precious son. The knowers of Brahman do not say that they know Brahman, for they know that God cannot be known with the mind. The mind can only intuit the presence of God. Of course, when mind becomes pure it can know Brahman, but at that time it becomes something else, something other than ordinary mind. From what I understand, the possession of this pure mind is the goal of all spiritual practice. As possessions go, then, the devotees have that one thing that they pursue and, once having It, covet It and nothing else, for pure mind is one with Brahman. So, my dear boy, do not store up for the future while here on earth. If you are to store up anything, accumulate good merit by doing selfless actions for the good of others. This, my guru tells me, leads to a sattvic condition of mind through which you can get at the supreme attainment. May the Lord and Divine Mother bless you in that endeavor, my son."

The Avadhut arose and walked down the hill to the beehive. It lay as the thief had left it, on its side with a swarm of angry bees still buzzing around it. Keeping his distance, the Avadhut drew a little nearer to watch the activity. The hum that rose into the air and the swift motions of the bees in their orbit around the damaged orb told the entire story. As he watched, Ekanta heard more voices speaking to him in his head, coming from a time long ago when he had taken refuge at the feet of his vanaprastin gurus, a divine couple of incredible spiritual attainment.

*"Arise, dear boy."*

Ekanta had risen to his feet after a long and reverent prostration before his newly acquired gurus. The ceremony of initiation was over and the cycle was consummated. This particular cycle had begun several months earlier when the boy stumbled, as if by accident, onto the sacred grounds of the forest ashram. A swarm of bees from a tree stump had taken exception to his presence and began to sting him as he lay nearby. Jumping up and heading for a nearby stream with the bees in hot pursuit, Ekanta dived into the stream and thereby deterred his attackers. Then, having run much farther and penetrated far deeper into the forest than usual, he had come across the holy ashrama of his destined gurus.

As he stood at the edge of the ashram grounds examining his arms and legs, the Mataji had noticed him and, taking him into the confines, treated his stings while drying his clothes over the fire. The male teacher of the ashrama, whom he later referred to as Guruji, had met him later that day while the boy wandered around the place in happiness and peace. It had been a momentous occasion.

Now, he had received formal entrance into spiritual life and was extremely pleased with this chain of events. He was also anxious to begin the training that would shape his mind and character. As he was thinking about this, the Guruji had approached and took him aside.

*"You are already well named by your earthly parents, therefore we need not give you an additional name. You have now completed the preliminary practices and have received initiation into formal spiritual life. From now on your life will vibrate in tune with higher attainment. We now offer you, like a beautiful flower, on the altar of the Blessed Lord and the Divine Mother of the Universe. May they be pleased to accept this offering and take full responsibility for your spiritual unfoldment. We, too, shall be here to assist in that auspicious task."*

From that day on, indeed, Ekanta's life had vibrated more fully. His gurus often teased him about the fate which brought him to them saying that Mother Kali's own bees, which swarmed about

Her in constant bliss, creating the primal sound of Om, had taken a short leave of absence at Her behest and hidden in the stump to await his coming.  Then, they had literally driven him towards his swadharma, his highest destiny, by chasing him to the vicinity of the ashram.  Now as the Avadhut watched the swarming bees in the damaged hive, all of these memories surfaced in his receptive and inspired mind.  As he stood there, lost in his own reverie, a voice suddenly resounded behind him.

"What are you up to there?"

Ekanta turned around to find an elderly man, obviously a farmer, standing there with hands on hips in an angry fashion.

"I merely watch the bees, sir, and ruminate as to the loss of their precious nectar," stated the Avadhut.

"And you, I presume, have no idea what happened to the honey?" came the accusational response.

"On the contrary, I was witness to the entire occurrence," replied the holy man, disarmingly.

This answer caused the farmer to consider the Avadhut more closely.  After a short time, the farmer spoke again:

"Yes, I see that you are obviously no thief, but a wandering holy man.  Please excuse my rash speech earlier.  This is the second time I have found this hive robbed.  It is disturbing."

"Please sir," came the Avadhut's response, "you need not apologize for I understand completely.  If I had not been so far away at the time perhaps I would have intervened, but as it is, the damage has already been done and there is nothing to do about it.  Please accept my condolences for this loss."

The farmer laughed and began to explain himself.

"It is not really my honey after all.  I only constructed this hive and the bees came of their own accord.  I have enjoyed their bounty on several occasions since they allow me to carefully reap a little of the fruits of the hive at times.  This rascal thief, though, if he be the same one who came before, is insensitive and careless.  However, I have more hives near my farmhouse.  Perhaps you are in need of a meal and a place to spend the night?  I would love to share my humble abode with you if you desire."

"That would be very appreciated at this time," returned the Avadhut, who had been traveling great distances and subsisting on very little food.

"Then come with me, revered sir," said the farmer, "and we will repair to the vicinity of the farmhouse."

Ekanta and the farmer walked a short distance, penetrated a stand of trees at the periphery of a clearing and came close to the farmhouse situated at the far edge of the field. Skirting the field, the two drew near to the house and washed their feet in a small trough of water at the front door. Entering the nice-sized dwelling, Ekanta immediately appreciated the earthy and rustic atmosphere of the place. As it was beginning to get dark, the farmer lit oil lamps in two of the rooms. These cast a soft light over the dwelling, bathing it in a pleasant glow which contributed to the feeling of peace and well-being already present there.

Without speaking much, the farmer indicated a small room where Ekanta could place his belongings. After doing this, the Avadhut returned to the kitchen where the farmer was preparing vegetables near a pot of water which was already beginning to boil over the wood fire that had been lighted underneath it in the hearth. Looking at the abundance of foodstuffs on the table, Ekanta knew that he would eat well that night. Sitting himself down at the wooden counter near the farmer, he began a conversation.

"Have you no wife then, sir?" Ekanta asked.

"I had at one time," replied the farmer, "but she is no more in the body, having left me earlier in life to return to the Creator. Since then I have maintained this farm on my own, without wife or children, abiding peacefully and contentedly with what I have been given until my own time to depart this earth arrives."

"I hope that I am not intruding on this privacy and peace," replied the Avadhut.

"By no means," responded the farmer, "and please make yourself feel right at home and stay as many days as you like. Company, to me, is a great rarity and one that I enjoy immensely when it occurs."

"I will stay only one night as is my custom," the Avadhut responded, "unless you have some work in which I can assist you. I am most happy to work for my food and lodging."

"Let me consider that," responded the farmer. "For the meantime please relax and rest yourself."

The two men were silent for a time.

Finally, the farmer continued the conversation. "From where do you hail? You look as if you are far from home."

"My home is everywhere, dear sir," answered the Avadhut, "though I spent much of my boyhood in parts further east of here. For many long years I have led the life of a wanderer and have been much gratified by it."

"Yes, I can imagine," said the farmer. "I, too, desired to lead such a life at one time, but the management and custodianship of this farm fell to me and my lot. So, I have lived here very well for years."

"Truly," the Avadhut remarked, "a sedentary life is much better for the contemplation of Brahman, generally speaking. One has all the conveniences at hand so that spiritual life can go forward smoothly and without breaks or hitches."

"That is true to an extent," responded the farmer, "except a problem often occurs in this regard. Beings who have everything close at hand begin to spend all of their time in daily mundane pursuits and tend to forget about God. Such is the curse of the householder."

"Nowadays," offered the Avadhut, "the curse of the monk's life is much the same. Many of them live at monasteries, have everything taken care of for them by others and fall into a complacent lifestyle. Thus they are unable to call up any of the intensity that is needed for realization or, at least, constant remembrance in the form of purifying sadhana."

After a brief silence, in which the two considered what had been said, the Avadhut went on.

"What has been your sadhana over these long years, dear sir?"

"After completing some of the prescribed disciplines advised in the scriptures and after neutralizing the ill-considered actions of my youth, I began to partake of a kind of sadhana that utilized every moment of the day as a way of living consciously. After my wife passed, I was still relatively young, so I merely continued to live in the moment. Does this make sense to you?"

"Certainly," replied the Avadhut, "I know exactly what you are referring to. My own ongoing practice, if such it could be called, has been concerned with just that kind of moment-to-moment awareness. I am very glad to hear you articulate that as a way of being. For you, then, what has this practice or process entailed?"

"Mainly, it consists of listening intently and being sensitive to my own inner Self," answered the farmer. "I am not really the orthodox type, I must admit. The gods and goddesses do not appeal to me, nor is the formless Brahman my only goal, since That is the permanent abode for all beings rather than a destination. I just love to consult with and abide in my inner Self. Does that sound blasphemous?"

The Avadhut laughed out loud.

"No indeed," he replied. "Were that more beings were so tuned into their true nature and less dependent on names and forms, whether they be physical or celestial. The wisest woman I every knew stated that as one goes higher and higher in spiritual life, finally reaching the loftiest heights, the more the gods and goddesses recede and fall away. The seven levels of consciousness and the many lokas contained therein are all formed out of thought, albeit refined and subtle in nature. Beyond the power of thought, of conceptualization, is the Self, the Atman, and it is That which is one with Brahman. So I say, more power to you in this quest, in this abidance. More power to you!"

After a short pause, Ekanta pursued his line of questioning further:

"What else does your unique practice entail?"

"It consists of being free from all negativities of the mind," replied the farmer, "that is, rooting them out and destroying them as they occur in an uncompromising fashion. In addition, and since I am a landowner, if such a thing is really possible, I consciously draw each breath and live each moment in the awareness that I own nothing, possess nothing. Therefore, I keep myself free of covetousness which, I have found, is an insidious tendency of all embodied beings that robs them of their ability to dwell in the divine atmosphere of spirituality. As the old song goes, they then 'imbibe earth instead of nectar.' They overlook the feast of divinity that sits before them and instead consume delusion. I will never give in to this impulse as long as I live."

As the farmer continued to cut vegetables, the Avadhut's memory penetrated into the past in swift and direct fashion. The last words of the farmer had prompted his mind towards a time when many wonderful teachings such as these had been an everyday occurrence in his young life. Closing his eyes and smiling inwardly, the words of his guru came fully into his memory once again.

*"Anger, lust, greed, jealousy, covetousness and desire — these are the six passions. The sons and daughters of the six passions are also present in the human condition. These are such things like the eight fetters with their various combinations and offshoots such as caste, pride, shame, hatred, fear and others. According to the Upanishads, there are also the six 'billows,' namely, hunger, thirst, grief, delusion, decay and death. The pairs of opposites exist here in this relative world as well, like pleasure and pain, heat and cold, good and bad, success and failure, virtue and vice, life and death, bondage and liberation and more. When all these are present, are we to claim this realm as our own and desire to dwell here?"*

"Dear guru," broke in the young boy. "If it is God who created the worlds, why did He introduce all of these poisons into the creation? Why would anyone want to be here considering this tainted condition and sordid state of affairs. I would want a place where all is perfect, without these dread impositions."

*"Such a place exists, Ekanta,"* replied his guru, *"but it is not this world. It is your Source of Origin, your true nature. It exists at all times and so it is anterior to both life in the universe and the thinking mind. The creation is only possible when the perfect equilibrium of undifferentiated Consciousness is broken, just as activity on the surface of the ocean occurs when wind breaks forth and causes waves. Either transcend these waves of suffering on the sea of samsara or learn to sail through them, or both. Those who can do both are the consummate devotees. The Divine Mother loves them very much!"*

"Revered guru," Ekanta ventured, "how can we give up the desire to take for the self? Gathering and coveting things seems to be a natural part of the creation. The animals gather for themselves. Some of these even store up for the future."

*"My boy,"* came the response, *"the consciousness of plants is different from the consciousness of animals. Similarly, human awareness differs from that of the animals. We were not born to covet, to store up, to take to the self what belongs where it is. We have a God-given right to sustain ourselves on what is here, but even this type of gathering must be done in the spirit of true*

*human values utilizing yajna, a sacrifice of consciously offering all back to the Source of Existence. The human, originally conceived, is Divine if you ask me. Our natural condition is pure and innocent. Taking just what we need is a part of that divine nature. Hoarding and storing up is an impulse of distorted human nature. Learn this well and live in your true and perfect condition. Even when the society around you declares that such behavior is okay, be willing to go entirely against such assertions and the behavior that follows and instead maintain the true path."*

"Am I to be entirely without then?" asked the young boy?

*"Learn to live without anything is my advice,"* replied the guru, *"for when hard times come upon you, you will be able to persevere and exist without any undue suffering. The difference between a renunciate and an impoverished person is mainly one of attitude. When abundance comes to you unasked, then you can partake of it, but take only what you require at any given time and that only after checking to be sure that those around you whose need is greater than yours are satisfied first. If this is done as a rule then you will find that, yes, indeed, you are living without anything of your own. This is first and foremost, and with regards to practice, a very beneficial attitude. Eventually, it becomes a state of mind, one shared by the devotees of the Lord who know it to be a divine attribute cherished by Him very highly. Ultimately, it is an undying facet of freedom. You, Ekanta, will exemplify this and other qualities in your life. There can be no doubt about it."*

"Revered sir!" The farmer's voice brought the Avadhut back to the kitchen where a wonderful aroma was filling the air. That nominal but righteous share of bounty that was gifted to him as life-giving food was about to become his indeed.

"I am ready," replied the Avadhut to the farmer, who was now aware of the thoughtful nature of his guest, having watched him enter a deep state while he cooked the meal.

"Then come to the table, please," said the farmer. "Soup and bread is our fare, and a little kichuri is there as well. Sweet pudding will end the meal."

After a prayer, the meal was enjoyed in silence, an atmosphere in keeping with mindfulness and spirituality. After eating, the farmer, whose name was Kuntala, prepared tea and the two sat for a time and spoke on spiritual subjects.

"There are those who have and hold," stated Ekanta, "those who have and hold not, those who have not but want and those who have not and desire not. In other words, whether one owns things or not, the true renunciation is in the mind and the subtle secret about it depends upon complete nonattachment. Therefore, one should not covet and store away. This basic precept is found in the original tenets of every religious approach or philosophy. Yet, man-kind forgets this and turns towards accumulation and amass-ing wealth and materials. Thus it goes, and this tendency, among others, is the death or obscuration of spirituality among the masses."

"Revered sir," said Kuntala, "what of those who, as Sri Krishna mentions in the Bhagavad Gita, seek the Lord through wealth? It is stated in the scriptures that one of God's glories is Sri, opulence. How does this fit in with what you are describing just now?"

"Those who approach God for wealth belong to the various classes of devotees, no doubt," replied the Avadhut, "but they have Spirit in mind, not matter. Having known God to be the only Reality, they then proceed along their destined path. The Lord in His Grace bestows all abundance upon them and they become sat-isfied and fulfilled by what He gifts to them. This is far different than the person who gathers habitually with no sense of who is supplying these bounties and then obsessively grasps those things in a condition of inordinate attachment. These two instances are entirely opposite of each other. The subtle key that reveals the distinction here is acknowledgment of and faith in God."

"That is nicely put," sighed Kuntala, "and is, of course, believ-able and understandable. It is plain to see that those with the divine orientation reach the goal of human existence not only easily, but blissfully. The highest state is then attainable to them. On the other hand, those who do not adopt this purely practical stance suffer from the dangers of rampant egotism and adverse karmic repercussions. Faith in God is required in order to rise above the impulse of ownership, for selfish grasping is based upon fear of not having. Since all things come from and exist in God, it stands to reason that I should naturally turn to Him for all my needs and live happily thereafter in the knowledge that I am protected forever."

That night, the Avadhut could not sleep and went for a walk under the moon in the fields and forests surrounding the farm. His stroll took him past the beehive, now broken apart by animals and invaded by insects. Despite this and upon closer inspection, the Avadhut could still detect some buzzing sounds in portions of the hive, revealing that some of the bees were loath to abandon it even in its damaged condition.

This reminded him of the difficulty involved in breaking old habits. Covetousness, then, was not necessarily limited to physical and material things, but also involved habitual tendencies in the mind. In fact, the mind's attachment to old, worn out and outdated ways of thinking was the real cause of inadvertent clinging to various objects. Like the bees adhering to the hive out of habit, security and tenacious attachment, human beings acted in similar fashion in life. This limiting tendency not only brought about anguish and suffering, it stood in the way of beings enjoying the natural flow of boons coming from the Universal Mother's bounteous Grace. As the Avadhut contemplated this unfortunate fact, his mind tapped into various practical teachings given to him by his earliest gurus—his father and mother.

"There are two acceptable ways by which it is okay to increase one's income," Ekanta's father had declared to him one day. "First, you may unhesitatingly do so in order to maintain a religious family. Secondly, you may legitimately do so in order to support holy causes. But one should always remember that an object kept near a mirror reflects in it. This means that as long as you have contact with money and what it represents, it will leave its impression on you. That impression is a kind of taint, even for the religiously-minded. You, Ekanta, will not have to worry so much about this issue in life, for your destiny lies predominantly with other concerns. You will, however, need to counsel others on this point. Therefore, take a word to the wise and be free of avarice and advise others to do the same. You will be very happy as a result."

One day, Ekanta had visited Yogindra Yogi in his mountain cave, high above the village precincts. As he was sitting in the cave with the ascetic holy man, he suddenly thought, How can one live in such austere conditions and be happy?

As if on cue, the yogi looked at the young boy.

*"I am old, Ekanta, otherwise, I would still be wandering far and free. It is not easy to live without even the basic amenities of life, even for an ascetic. The condition of my life at present demands a certain stability. I take it in this cave and the villagers such as yourself and your family provide me with alms upon which I can survive. This allows me to remain free of encumbrances to wealth and other materials as is my preference."*

"Revered sir," Ekanta asked, "why did you give up the world? What was the reason? You could have been a great scholar or statesman."

At this, the yogi laughed derisively. *"You see, my young friend,"* he said, *"I was adverse to the glitter of the world from a very young age. My parents tried to enamor me of wealth and fame, themselves being fully given to this kind of existence. Due to their insistence, I was almost convinced to lead a worldly life when, one day, a dreadful yet wonderful thing happened.*

*"I was on my way to the marketplace to make a few purchases for my mother. Soon, I noticed that a crowd had gathered and that there was some excitement. Wending my way through the congregation, I saw that a merchant had fallen down on the street and was obviously suffering from some malady. He had his goods with him, consisting of a satchel of rich brocades and satins and his bulging money pouch was plainly visible in his clothes due to the way in which he had landed on the ground. The mental condition of the crowd at the time of my arrival on the scene was teetering somewhere between pity and avarice. As I arrived, two men had drawn near and were trying to question the merchant as to his home location. One of these was casting sidelong glances at the money purse and occasionally reaching out as if to grab a hold of it. The second man was questioning the half-conscious merchant and fending off the other's hand at the same time.*

*"I thought that this second man was good-hearted, but as it turned out he only wanted the goods and money too, for when the first man finally laid his hands on the money pouch, the second man grabbed it also and a fight ensued. In the interim, the pouch, pulled at from two sides, split open, spilling silver and gold coins and paper notes of large denominations all over*

*the street. This, of course, was all the brooding crowd needed and a free-for-all developed in a fashion too swift to comprehend. I remember crying out in indignation but my well-intentioned words were swept away in the rush and conflagration. The people virtually fell on the merchant, each grabbing for the clothes and money like beasts of prey tearing at a dying animal's throat. In horror, I heard the merchant's screams as he must have realized what was happening. These were the last sounds he ever made, for the milling, pushing hordes literally swept over him again and again, killing him in a crush. Minutes later, as the last of the crowd hastily dispersed, and as a few officials came on the scene, all that was left was a dead man's torn and lifeless body."*

Silence followed as Ekanta, suddenly noticing the fearful shadows dancing on the walls of the dark cave, shivered in dread at the telling of this story. Drawing nearer to the fire, he waited for his teacher to continue. After a time, as if recovering from the memory of this unfortunate incident, the yogi went on with the story.

*"I never went home after that occurrence. My father was a merchant and I could not help but hear his daily remonstrances to me as he repeated, 'Work hard, learn this trade, sell many items and eventually take over my business. Then you too will truly enjoy life and be respected by others. Wealth and fame will be yours and you can choose from all the good things of the world.' Those words haunted me as I gazed upon the poor cloth merchant lying dead in the road, forgotten and stripped of 'all the good things of the world.'*

*"Departing the city, I only stopped long enough to tell my guru of my intentions. He knew my inner feelings anyway, but seeing the intense look on my face and hearing the resolve in my voice was all it took for him to give his blessing on my undertaking. He even offered to tell my parents of my decision the next day after I had departed.*

*"I have never regretted that decision, Ekanta. Truly, I believe that if I had remained at home in the family business, regret would have haunted me all the days of my life. You see, dear boy, vultures always gather around the carcass of a cow. From the relative standpoint, one must see that this is the way of the*

*world and learn to give it up completely.  From the ultimate standpoint, though, and more importantly, both vultures and carcass are unreal.  Nothing exists but Brahman.  This truth, supreme in nature, is what I have gleaned from my experiences as a wandering sadhu after renouncing the world.  It comprises my only wealth and is my greatest treasure.  It would have been extremely difficult, no, well nigh impossible to gain such real-ization while living the worldly life.  It is that which makes it easy for me to live here in this cold, dark cave without any pos-sessions or relations."*

With tears in his eyes at this poignant memory and its profound lessons, the Avadhut turned his steps away from the deserted bee-hive and made his way through the darkness back towards the farmhouse where Kuntala lay sleeping.  In his room, Ekanta con-templated another memory from his past:

*"Beings who covet wealth become puffed up with pride, Ekanta,"* his guru said to him one evening.  *"The peacock proudly displays its feathers but its feet are always filthy, since it walks in its own excrement.  This illustrates the nature of the wealthy who flash their money around vainly yet use it for petty and selfish ends.  It reminds me of a young man who used to live in our neighborhood.  Once, he acquired some money and he immediately went out and bought himself some fancy clothing.  Then, he would walk up and down the street wearing a pleated shirt covered over with an expensive shawl.  Every now and then he would stop, take the shawl off and expose his pleated shirt for all to see.  Then he would look around to see if anyone was noticing.  Even with all this ostentatious show, it was seen, much to the humor of all watching, that when he walked away, he was knock-kneed.  This spectacle was the cause of much mirth amongst the villagers."*

Ekanta laughed to hear this story from the lips of his guru, told with such a particularly special combination of mockery and seriousness.

"Please, dear Guruji," he had pleaded, "tell some more of your experiences in this regard."

Smiling, the preceptor complied.

*"Once, a beggar women in our village acquired some expensive trinkets.  As soon as she put these on she became an entirely*

*different person. She began pushing her way through crowds and lines, showing the bracelets on her arms by waving them in the air so that they would make noise. One day she even snubbed the Brahmin priest who visited weekly to perform puja for the village. At this, the elders informed her that she must leave the village if she could not control her vanity. This stopped the old woman from causing any more trouble, though she still maintained a haughty and superior attitude towards everyone. The ownership of these few insignificant articles turned her into a demon, as it were. It is said that at the time of her death, she shrieked horribly when her relatives tried to take the bangles from her and insisted that she be buried with them. Such delusion!*

*"You see, Ekanta, the camel is extremely proud, yet it is ugly. What has it got to be so proud about? It will even spit at you if you venture too close. If such an attitude persists even in a camel, think of what this type of delusion turned loose in the human mind is capable of. It pains me to think about it. May we never be exposed to this kind of vilifying behavior. Men and women degrade themselves through such actions, all for the sake of superficial attainments and material wealth. Be free of the untoward passions and never frequent the vicinity of these kinds of people. Thus will you be content and blissful, living a life of innocence and purity."*

The Avadhut spent two days with Kuntala, the farmer, helping him with some two-man chores around the farm. Kuntala also demonstrated how to take honey from the beehives without disturbing the natural harmony of the nest and even taught Ekanta how to gather the honeycomb. With bees all around him, lighting upon him as well, a profound sense of harmony with nature visited Ekanta's mind. These bees were not angry. They seemed to understand that a redistribution of wealth was necessary in order that the process of natural accumulation and dispersion might go forward again in unimpeded fashion and without greed or avarice.

As he stood there with his small insect friends humming softly around him, the words of his teacher came to him clearly and distinctly from a time long past:

*"Spiritual seekers are like honey-gatherers, my boy, extracting only the essence. Wise, they resemble those who mine for*

*gold or silver, overlooking the few nuggets that lay strewn around the floor of the cave in lieu of the major vein that runs through the entire length of the mountain. Therefore, Ekanta, be like the man who stops not until water fills the well he has dug, the engineer who drills long and hard until oil gushes into the sky or the excavator who ignores semiprecious stones in his search for ancient fossils which hold the amazing secrets of the past. With regards to human beings and other creatures of this realm, my son, be an ideal beekeeper, for they tend the hive, revere the occupants and take only so much as will satisfy their basic need."*

When the time came for parting, the farmer extended his invitation for Ekanta to stay at his home whenever he wanted and for as long as he desired, anytime that he passed through that part of the country. Their short time together had been rich beyond expectation. In Kuntala, the Avadhut had found an exemplar of living in the world without being tainted or attracted to it whatsoever. The farmer, in turn, had seen this quality in the Avadhut but had also come face to face with a being whose every action, thought and word reflected absolute purity of purpose married to intensity. Since this corresponded so well to what the farmer had been practicing for so many years, Kuntala felt, as he watched the Avadhut cross the field and disappear beyond the woods, that he had finally found a guru worth contemplating.

Unbeknownst to the Avadhut, the farmer fell to his knees after he had vanished into the woods bordering the property and sent heartfelt salutations in his direction along with prayers for his continued well-being. Minutes later, after entering the small woods, the Avadhut, too, offered reverent salutations. Coming upon the beehive, now completely in pieces and well into the process of decomposition, he paused. Bowing to the earth, he saluted the honey-gatherer, both in the form of the farmer who was free from covetousness and in the form of the thief who stole what was stored up by the efforts of others.

"May all gather nectar in the right spirit," prayed the Avadhut softly, "using it for the common benefit of all living beings."

Turning in the general direction of the farmer's land, the Avadhut placed his palms together and saluted his teacher of non-covetousness:

"I offer my heartfelt salutations to thee, oh honey-gatherer, for you have taught me recondite lessons on the ills of covetousness. What is more, I now rejoice in the deeper understanding that those who seek for the Essence of existence are the ones who become truly happy, truly contented. May those worthy ones find and enjoy the inexpressibly sweet nectar of bliss in freedom."

Mentally acknowledging the sixteen directions, the Avadhut emanated a blessing upon the earth and chanted a benediction from the most ancient scriptures of the world:

*Om tacchnio ra vrini mahe*
*Gatum yagynaya gatum yaynapataye*
*Daivi svastirastu naha, svastir manuse bhyah*
*Urdvamjigatu bhesajam*
*Sang no astu dvipade sang chatushpate*
*Om Shanti, Shanti, Shantih*

May we ever delight in offering all into the great Self.
May we rejoice in sacrifice
and always acknowledge and revere the Lord of sacrifice.
May divine blessings be upon us,
may peace be unto the entire human race.
May health, well-being and prosperity abide among us.
Om Peace, Peace, Peace!

# — Chapter 22 —

# Teachings on Self-Reliance

THE TWENTY-SECOND GURU —The Snake
THE LESSON —Solitude

*M*y guru, the snake, taught me several fine lessons. Seeing it occupying the dens and holes made by other animals, I learned not to become attached to a permanent dwelling place. From the snake, I also learned that a person should not betray his real worth by his or her actions, for by merely looking at a snake one cannot rightly ascertain whether it is poisonous or not. Finally, the snake's contentment with a life of solitude reflects the efficacy of a quiet and unostentatious existence. Knowing the Atman and depending upon It for everything forms the recourse of the wise. Like the free-roaming snake, such beings form no attachment or dependence on external things and abide always in peace eternal.

The Avadhut stood staring into a deep hole in the earth. Minutes earlier, he had observed a large snake slide into the opening and disappear. This same snake had traveled for some distance, being followed by the Avadhut, and had, it seemed, selected this burrow for a home.

Saluting the snake he said, "You and I are much alike in that we have no permanent home. Anywhere and everywhere is our home. I salute you, my guru of solitude and self-reliance, for reminding me once more of the efficacy of this, my chosen lifestyle."

*"Have thou no home!"* These powerful words echoed over cycles of time to find a response in the fertile and spontaneous mind of the Avadhut.

*"That is the credo of the ever-free, my boy,"* stated his guru one day. *"This means that one should not burden the mind with the erroneous idea that this earth is one's home. The only true place of residence is and has always been the Atman. By accepting a permanent external location as one's home, we impose a great limitation over our personal consciousness. This attitude is an invitation for all sorts of adverse circumstances to develop, whereas the attitude of a freedom-loving wanderer is not encumbered by these."*

"Revered teacher," the boy questioned, "you make this sound as if it is the mind and attitude which is important rather than the actual act. Am I understanding you correctly?"

*"Yes, Ekanta,"* replied the guru. *"I am pointing out that whether or not one lives in or actually owns a permanent dwelling, it is the attitude which claims it for one's own that is detrimental. Most anytime that we utter the words 'me and mine' we transgress one of the natural laws of the universe. Such utterances mount up and interact with our everyday awareness. They eventually and mistakenly convince us that we are actually what we are not and cause us to covet those things which cannot be owned. Those beings who, though they may or may not be granted material wealth, do not consider house, goods and objects as personal possessions and maintain the stance that all things belong to God and are given and taken away by Him, live freely and happily under all conditions. They never suffer from the ills of greed, anger, covetousness, envy and the like. Worries, depressions and momentary elations also never plague them. They enjoy the bounty of the earth but never agonize over gain and loss since they never fall victim to misguided orientation."*

After a moment of consideration, the guru continued.

*"Take this ashram and its grounds and surrounding forests, Ekanta. Your Mataji and I never claimed it for our own. Neither do we consider it ours. We caretake it by the grace of the Lord and will eventually leave it, one way or another. In the meantime we live here contentedly. We are like the snake who, never staying in any one hole or burrow for any length of time, goes from one place to the next devoid of both longing and expectation, satisfied by what comes naturally. In this way, we abide in our true abode, the Self, the Atman."*

"Revered sir," pleaded the young boy, "how does it feel to abide always in the Self? What do you experience in that state and how is such a condition maintained?"

*"First of all, there are certain requirements that have to be satisfied in order to approach this great Self. The Self never presents even a thought of Itself to those who are preoccupied elsewhere, let alone reveals Its Essence. As the wise say, there is a tree called the achina tree, but most have never seen it and only know of its existence by hearsay. Many more have never heard it spoken of at all so have no idea of its existence whatsoever. The same holds true for the Atman. When, however, by the Grace of God or guru combined with good samskaras created by clean living and devotion to the Lord, the auspicious time for spiritual awakening arrives, these qualifications arise and get fulfilled through intense spiritual effort on the part of the aspirant. Then the Self is ready to stand revealed. Only a special manifestation of Grace still needs to happen."*

"Guruji," the boy asked at this point, "can these qualifications be enumerated or are they hidden and unseen?"

*"At one point in time they were guarded and protected Ekanta,"* answered the preceptor, *"reserved only for those who were ready according to the assessment of the guru. As to what they are, you have heard of them already. In recent times they have become known as the four jewels while in the times of the ancients they were the four qualifications or four disciplines, the Sadhanachatushtaya. They are called viveka and vairagya, the six treasures of sama, dama, uparati, titiksha, samadhana and shraddha, and the fourth jewel, mumukshutvam. Without these — discrimination and dispassion, the six treasures of*

*inner peace, self-control, self-settledness, forbearance, concentration, faith and finally an intense desire for liberation — it is highly unlikely that the Atman will become noticed, let alone realized. So you can see that it is no small task to become qualified. Such qualification confers upon an aspirant the level of adhikara.*

"What is more," continued the guru, "*these jewels, after being attained, must be made manifest. Herein lies the answer to the next stage of your question about how it feels to be abiding in the Self at all times. When these attributes become like second nature, that is, when discrimination between the unreal and real is automatic, when detachment from what is unreal is mature, when inner peace is a natural condition of mind, self-control is effortless, contentment is second nature, forbearance is easy and spontaneous, concentration is fully focused at all times and faith is unshakable, and when the desire for true freedom occupies every waking moment, then does the Self emerge from Its subtle hiding place like the sun breaking forth in all Its splendor from a bank of dark clouds.*"

This description inspired Ekanta greatly. He immediately pressed for more details.

"Dear teacher, what could be higher than this? Is there a stage beyond what this entails?"

"*Sthiti prajnasya, my boy,*" came the words from his preceptor's lips," *steady wisdom. Not mere knowledge of systems of philosophies and abstruse truths but an actual dwelling in the core of Reality where all these wonderful flows of wisdom energy exist. Thus, an abidance in the Truth actually occurs which not only signals an end to all ignorance and delusion, a wonderful state in itself, but also equates to an unending immersion in the supreme state or condition Itself.*"

"Is this Nirvikalpa, Guruji?" asked the boy.

"Yes and no," the teacher answered. "*That is, Nirvikalpa is there should the Atman desire to manifest that condition, but other wonders are experienced there as well. Where is the limit? How to explain? Have you seen the sand crabs at the seashore? They have amazing eyesight, an unerring sense of direction and feed on small insects and other inert and living things which the waves wash up on shore. They have their holes in the sand*

*and take refuge there in an instant at the hint of any movement nearby. Sometimes the ocean waves wash over their holes, obliterating them completely from view. Soon though, the crabs pop to the surface, throwing sand here and there to uncover the opening to their little homes.*

*"My point is, life for these creatures consists of sand. Life is lived on sand, food is procured on the sand, refuge is in the sand. Like this, Ekanta, the realized being is fully immersed in and dependent on the sand of pure Existence. Nothing, no act, word, thought or realization is apart from that Essence, that stable and immutable foundation of pure Being. Like crabs sporting on endless stretches of beach, experiencing life amidst innumerable grains of sand, this is what it is like to perceive Divine Reality. To dwell in It, too, is equally indescribable and indeed, perception and experience are merged there into one ultimately satisfying and interminable existence. Additionally Ekanta, and in keeping with the beginning of our conversation, the sand crabs do not become attached to any one home. The waves see to that. Instead, they stand ready to create or occupy any new dwelling place as conditions demand, for they know that nothing but sand exists below, above and all around them. They are good teachers, are they not?"*

After a pause, the guru concluded his description.

*"I can say little more about this, dear boy. From what I have said you will have to draw your own conclusions, but do not forget to bend all your efforts towards realizing what has been revealed in these precious moments. The sincere aspirant wastes no time in getting out of the condition of ignorance, the same way that a woman with a child does not hesitate to swiftly abandon a house on fire. When delusion is gone, what is left is ineffable, indivisible and indescribable. Satisfy all conditions of entrance into that wonderful state and then experience it for yourself. Then abide in it forever."*

The Avadhut left the hole in the ground where the snake had disappeared and went his way, fully inspired by the thoughts occupying his mind. Nearby, a village stood. Entering it, the Avadhut found where water was available and then sat in the streets, his cloth laying open beside him. As he watched the pulse of village life vibrate around him, several items began to collect on his cloth.

After an hour had passed, a few rupee coins, a small bunch of bananas and a few luchis were granted him by the grace of the Lord dwelling in the villagers as the energy of generosity. These he took to the edge of the village and making a spot to spend the night, ate his alms and lay down to sleep.

That night, snakes occupied his dreams. He found himself in a huge cave, lit in certain areas by several torches stuck in notches in the stone walls. A huge congregation was present and they were all chanting in unison. The sound reverberated throughout the massive cavern and caused goose bumps to appear on Ekanta's skin. As the dream continued to unfold, Ekanta could make out a huge image in front of the assemblage, whom he now realized were mostly monks. The image was like a large statue showing the intertwining of many snakes. The dancing flames from the torches lent the statue a life of its own as the snakes seemed to dance and writhe of their own volition.

When the Avadhut awoke from this dream it was still dark. Stillness lay over the land and the nearby village like a blanket. Only occasionally, the sound of a cricket broke the somber silence. Sitting up, Ekanta contemplated for a while, thinking back on his dream and its possible significance. As he did so, the words of Ramakrishnadas Baul came into his memory. The two had met together late one evening after one of the baul's informal public discourses. Kundalini Shakti was the topic under discussion for most of the evening and the Avadhut had been very attentive to all the insights and questions posed that night. Later, when he met with the baul in private and as the two sat under the stars, the conversation had continued on in a similar vein.

"Revered Baul," the Avadhut began, "what is the significance of the snake in association with Kundalini?"

"*Oh, my friend,*" replied Ramakrishnadas Baul, "*there are so many facets to this auspicious image. The snake is an important companion of Vishnu and, split into several reptiles, provides the very bed upon which the Great One rests at times of universal dissolution. This signifies that the sleep of the Lord is in terms of manifestation only and that the Essence of existence never sleeps. What is ever-watchful, ever-aware, is that primordial One who, by Its very nature, is supremely intelligent and all-knowing. Does something that is Omniscient ever fall into an unconscious state?  Therefore, what better form to represent this fully awake condition than the snake.  Its eyes are always open, even when it rests.  Besides this, it coils itself before releasing its energy in a strike.  In similar fashion, the spiritual energy at the base of the spine lies coiled up as well, apparently sleeping, but holding potential for releasing the true essence of human existence into an arching spiral that culminates in the highest union with Brahman."*

After some time, the baul went on.

*"One does not rightly know by merely looking at the snake whether it is poisonous or not.  The same is true regarding the spiritually awakened one; that is, what kind of character he or she has is unknowable by a mere gaze.  Has the snake of subtle spiritual power opened its hood and risen up to light the fourth, fifth, sixth and seventh centers of conscious awareness?  Only by inquiring and remaining near for some time is it possible to get a substantial answer to this question.  It is like tracking the snake and watching it for a long time until its peaceful or dangerous nature is known through observation and direct experience.*

*"So, I say, that the entire nature of Kundalini Shakti is extremely subtle and practically unknowable by the usual or conventional methods of analysis and observation.  Even the systems of philosophy are powerless to reveal any more than just a glimpse of Her, albeit an important one.  This is why so many misinterpret Her, misunderstand Her and become misinformed as to Her nature."*

"Friend," said the Avadhut, "you may be referring to the many beginning and intermediate seekers who claim to have experienced this Kundalini power firsthand.  They, I deem, are quite transparent with regards to their claims.  Although it is difficult to immediately spot an illumined being due to his or her subtle state or condition, it is easy to spot these pretenders."

*"Yes,"* returned the baul.  *"Such as these posture and pretend in many ways, feigning the effects of Her transformative presence in various ways.  With tongues protruding, bodies gyrating and minds in a comically ludicrous state of pretense and confusion, they make both a show and a mockery out of something which is both precious and extremely subtle."*

"We have seen these circus acts around the width and breadth of this country," stated the Avadhut, "so we are used to ignoring them. However, the other extreme, those who have this energy awake and rising upwards through the higher centers, what are the characteristics of those beings?"

*"They vary with differing temperaments,"* replied the baul, *"but certain constants are noticeable."*

The baul sat still for a few moments, contemplating his next response.

*"When my brothers, the Bauls of Bengal, get together and dance, sing and turn in circles, we are, in effect, either asking Her to rise within us or enjoying Her pristine and powerful essence bubbling up inside and feeling it course upwards. There is a state of ecstasy upon us and it manifests outwardly in noticeable ways. However, after She rises to whatever position She decides to assume at any given time, a period of deep absorption or introspection occurs. It appears as a sort of internally concentrated dwelling on the outwardly invisible spring of spirituality that She embodies. It is like a hypnotized snake dancing gently to the charmer's intoxicating music or an inebriated hemp smoker sitting by the side of a waterfall, mesmerized by the various sounds and patterns in the cascading waters.*

*"In others, this fantastic power causes an increased ability to accomplish beneficial work with far-reaching ramifications. I have known a few who, after their spiritual energy has reached a zenith, continue to work in the world and produce a wealth of inspiring material in various areas of the Mother's concern. Some I have seen and known direct this energy into the minds of aspiring students, thereby creating more avenues for this divine expression to surface and affect the world in exceedingly positive ways. No, it is certain, whenever you see a great manifestation of unusual power, the type of which has little or no connection with the ego of show and pretense, you can be sure that Mother Kundalini is at the root of it. I see Her in you, revered Avadhut, and hear of your travels and deeds wherever I go. I see nothing but Her in you and in your divine thoughts and actions, yet no one knows of you or recognizes you when you are near. It is all Her work and Her will, is it not?"*

The next day, the Avadhut begged his meager breakfast at the village. Papaya and puffed rice was his morning fare and he gratefully thanked the Mother for this gracious offering. Setting off for parts unknown, he entered the forest once again and was thereafter lost in the cool shade and wonderful aromas of the dense foliage for some time. Later, after penetrating deep into the woods and selecting an ideal spot for meditation, he sat for his noon worship which consisted of contemplation of the teachings and meditation on God with and without form. The powerful image of the snake was still occupying his mind so he let his memory glide back over a rich and varied pool of life experience. As he did so, his mind settled on a conversation he had with a unique Vaishnava saint in Bengal one day as he was passing through areas sacred to the memory of Lord Chaitanya on his way to pilgrimage in Bodhgaya.

*"On the thousand-headed snake named Ananta,"* the old saint, Sripada Vishnutirtha, stated to him at the time of their brief meeting, *"whose very name suggests the infinity of God, the entire superstructure of the three worlds and seven levels of existence rests interminably. The lower realms also operate and pay obeisance to the great serpent. Like Vishnu, the master whom this powerful reptile serves devoutly, Ananta appears as many but exists ever as one undivided substratum. If you could look closely at the root of Ananta's being, behind the apparent and into the subtlest level, you would see that all of the many reptilian heads and bodies start from one massive tail. You mentioned, dear Avadhut, that you are on the way to the sacred holy place of Lord Buddha. That primordial reptile was the very one that protected the Tathagata Buddha as he sat in the forest meditating. Such an unusually powerful symbol of Divine Reality is scarcely seen in any of the religious traditions of the world."*

Somewhat intrigued by Vishnutirtha's openness to other spiritual traditions, given the very orthodox and even fundamentalist leanings of some of the Vaishnavas he had met, Ekanta had explored the old saint's outlook on these matters.

"Revered sir, I am most interested in the many religious traditions of the world in as much as they are all connected in absolute Unity. You seem to speak from that standpoint as well. With regards to the sacred symbol of Ananta and what it signifies, are there correlations from other paths or approaches that you can cite?"

The old saint thought for a moment, then replied:

*"Sometimes overlooked in our tradition is the essential principle of the Divine Mother. Due to the widespread acceptance of Tantra, the Mother has made Her mark and revealed Herself to us in this age, as in other ages. Imperialist and fundamentalist factions in religion tend to fixate on one very clear and well-marked path. This is good, but the negative side of this is that other paths, all leading to the same goal, are denied. This weakens the rich tradition of Sanatana Dharma into which we all are born. Furthermore, it would be well to point out to all narrow-minded persons that our broad and revered scriptures contain eighteen Puranas — six to Brahma, six to Sri Vishnu, and six to Lord Shiva. If this is not a universal testament then I am greatly mistaken and deluded.*

*"As far as the great holy reptile of Sri Vishnu is concerned, the Devi Bhagavatam mentions it with regards to being the very basis for existence. Since the snake also symbolizes the Kundalini power in humanity, dormant in deluded beings and rising in all who have awakened from illusory projections of various types, it is easy to find the intrinsic connections existing there."*

"Excuse me revered sir, but did you say that the Divine Mother scriptures speak of Ananta and the Blessed Lord, Sri Vishnu? If so, could you give a rendering of that wondrous reference, for my ideal is the Divine Couple whom I see at work everywhere I travel. I am ever eager to hear of such things."

*"Certainly, revered Avadhut,"* the old saint replied. *"It is the idea of many of the greatest pundits that the Supreme is One. This One is, to use the simplest of terms, force. In this regard, there is the force of Brahma that creates, the force of Vishnu that sustains and the force of Shiva that dissolves. Without their force, however, these three greatest of beings would be unable to perform their functions. This primal Force is stated by the Vedas, Puranas and Agamas to be the Essence of all existence. Some, they say, may worship the sun, the various devas, Indra or Varuna, but the Maha Rishis point to the great Force, the Primordial Mother, using the illustration of Mata Ganga, the holy river, who is none other than the liquid form of radiant Mother Reality. It is She, they unaniminously proclaim, that*

*though One, is always expressing Herself through various chan-*
*nels. Thus is the point brought to bear.*

*"Other great luminaries point out that both Kurma, the*
*ancient tortoise, and Ananta, the great and powerful snake of*
*a thousand heads, who are both seen as the supporting foun-*
*dation of celestial and earthly existence, are given their power*
*of position by the subtle force existing in and through them. To*
*condense this view, if Shiva Mahadeva himself, the incompa-*
*rable power of dissolution, were to be deprived of this Kula*
*Kundalini Shakti, he would become a lifeless corpse — he would*
*himself dissolve."*

Here, the old one stopped and gazed at the Avadhut.

*"You have as much or more knowledge about this ancient and*
*auspicious subject as I, revered sir,"* he stated. *"Now you please*
*share some of that with me."*

"Ah," replied the Avadhut with an endearing smile, "you are right
about my interest in the Goddess. She is essentially formless but
we never tire of hearing of Her sport — Her Mahalila. Suffice to
say that even Sri Suta, of unsurpassed wisdom, bows his hoary
head to the Goddess and reveres the very mention of any of Her
ignorance-dispelling, boon-bestowing names. In the scriptures of
the Goddess he says:"

The Devi Puranas, whose incomparable Subject,
the Divine Mother of the Universe,
is mentioned as early as the Vedas,
indicate Her as the secret of all the Shastras.
At Her gentle Lotus Feet I bow my head eternally,
She whose nectar-bearing and bliss-filled Names such as
Sarvachaitanyarupa, Brahma Sanatani Devi, Bhuvaneshvari,
Mahakali and others, is the presence upon which
the munis meditate as the Source of their liberation.

At this moment, Sripada Vishnutirtha raised an old, trembling
arm. The Avadhut ceased to speak and waited. With tears gathering in his eyes, the old sage said in a tremulous voice:

*"As the Source of their liberation, that expresses it perfectly."*

"Yes, revered sir," returned the Avadhut. "I too have always
thought so. In addition to this, Sri Suta says:"

> Daily, I call to my mind the Mother of all the worlds
> who creates this universe. who is both real and unreal
> and who, taking Her sattvic, rajasic and tamasic qualities,
> resolves them into Herself and sports alone,
> independently, at the time of universal dissolution. –
> At that time may I remember my Mother of the Universe.

The old saint was now weeping profusely. His attendants immediately entered the hut and, giving Ekanta a scalding look, tried to get Sripada to leave and take rest.

*"Get out of this place,"* he roared at them, his mood taking an amazingly swift turn, sending them scrambling out of the door in a hurried departure. Then, as if nothing had occurred whatsoever, he turned his attention back to the Avadhut.

*"Forgive them. They are afraid that your talking about the Absolute will send me into samadhi and out of the physical frame. They do not know that it is not quite my time to depart yet, even though I have told them time and time again. So let them live with that fear. I can not dispel it for them, it seems. Please go on with your rendering of the Devi Puranas."*

"Do not let me dominate this topic, revered sir," replied the Avadhut. "You please kindly continue on."

*"Oh, this communion with Her devotees,"* said the old one, *"it is the very essence of what I desire most now, at the end of this incarnation. She, the Divine Mother of the Universe, whom I have known as Sri Radha, She is the Ultimate to me. My mantra, called the Mahamantra by the Vaishnavas, has everything to do with Her, I have found."*

At this point, the Avadhut felt impelled to speak out a spontaneous desire that had risen in his heart.

"Revered sir, I know of this mantra and use it often, but if you know of the mantra to Sri Radha given in the Srimad Devi Bhagavatam and can confer it on me, I would be blessed to receive it from you."

The old one considered this request for a time. Finally he gave his consent.

*"This is highly unusual and under normal circumstances I would have to put you under a period of waiting and practice. But this is not a normal situation and I know of your own lofty*

*spiritual caliber. Therefore, I give you this mantra of Sri Radha, for your own best good and the good of those who are fortunate enough to come in contact with you."*

Saying so, Sripada Vishnutirtha did what he seldom had done before in such a situation in his long life. He conferred the mantra of Krishna's Beloved on someone without the usual preliminary instruction and the traditional formal period of waiting and practice. The Avadhut, though no ordinary practitioner, was nonetheless very fortunate, benefiting from the old sage's gracious nature. After this profound moment had passed, the old one spoke again.

*"I will also tell you a secret about the Mahamantra which you use. It represents the powerful attraction of the Divine Couple for each other, an attraction based in Prema Bhakti through which the three worlds and seven levels of Consciousness have originated. Such intensity of Love has gone unprecedented in the history of the cosmic cycles."*

The old one paused for breath, for he was extremely inspired by the Avadhut's presence, the transmission of the Radha-Mantra and the subject under discussion. Ekanta took this moment to dig deeper into the old sage's knowledge of the Divine Couple through the Vaishnava way of viewing.

"What then is this secret of the Mahamantra, revered sir?" he asked. "We know the literal meaning and the philosophical implications, but what is the essence?"

*"Ah,"* replied the old one, *"you too, I see, are a lover of Essence. I have done right by transmitting the mantra this day. The secret can be explained in the following simple terms, so listen well and comprehend, for this is my own realization, gleaned after many years of contemplation on Them in this and other lifetimes."*

So saying, and with the Avadhut completely focused upon his words, Sripada Vishnutirtha gave out the esoteric teaching.

*"You know that the Mahamantra starts with 'Hare Krishna, Hare Krishna, Krishna Krishna, Hare Hare.' 'Hare,' as spoken here, is an essential name for Radha. Thus, you see, Krishna, in longing to attract His companion to Him, calls out with such sweet love 'Hare.' Then, in passionate response, dearly hoping to hear His voice again, Radha, the treasure of Vrindaban, answers 'Krishna!' Govinda, now even more enamored of the*

*thought of Her imminent presence, calls again 'Hare.' Sri Radha,*
*now beside Herself with desire for union, swiftly and enticingly*
*answers 'Krishna.' Receiving no immediate response and in*
*dire fear of losing immediate contact, She then cries out with*
*all the naked abandon of her longing soul 'Krishna, Krishna,'*
*to which He, now sure of getting into ecstatic union with Her,*
*replies 'Hare, Hare.'"*

At this point, the old sage could speak no more because his
voice was cracking with emotion. All that he could manage after
that was, *"It is so beautiful!"*

After this novel interpretation of the Mahamantra, the two wise
beings sat for some time in a deep state. Soon, after returning to
normal consciousness and having recovered his composure, the
old one spoke:

*"Now, what else can you tell me about the Divine Couple from*
*various other standpoints?"*

Ekanta thought for a time. Eventually, some more teachings
came to mind.

"About the snake, Ananta, he provides the bed for Vishnu to
recline upon at times of universal dissolution. However, what
many do not think about is that there are primal waters by which
Ananta is supported. That ethereal ocean is called Ekarnava, the
one, fresh and original liquid foundation. But water needs some
vessel, revered one. It is the Divine Mother Reality about which
we are speaking today that provides the support for what appears
supportless. It is in these kinds of ideas and explanations, given
to us by the Rishis and Maharishis, that we find just how subtle
the Mother truly is."

*"That is so true,"* responded the saint. *"In these great Agamas,*
*in fact, reference is often made of the procession of spiritually*
*illumined beings through which this otherwise incompre-*
*hensible knowledge comes down to the world. May we always*
*acknowledge and have faith in the great ones through whom*
*these highest teachings emanate."*

Ekanta came out of his contemplation on the wisdom teachings.
Hours had passed by unnoticed, for the ambiance of dusk was
beginning to spread across the land. Walking out of the denser
part of the forest, the Avahut found a trail and followed it until
absolute darkness inhibited his movement further. It was at this

point that he came across a small hut at the edge of the forest.  A young boy sat near the front door and when he saw the Avadhut approaching, he swiftly disappeared inside, emerging a few moments later with an older man.  This man, with the boy hiding behind him, came near the Avadhut and asked him a question in a language which he did not readily understand.  After groping through several different dialects, the two finally found one that could suffice for basic communication.  Using that form of speech, Ekanta found out that the man was asking him to take a meal and stay overnight in the hut as a guest.  The Avadhut gave his consent to this proposal and the three entered inside leaving the darkness behind.

Within the hut, a lantern lit the interior and by its light Ekanta noticed that the dwelling was of the most rudimentary kind.  Laying his meager belongings down against a wall, he turned and looked upon his hosts who were already busy preparing the meal.  Since the two were not taking any interest in him and were focused on their task, Ekanta sat down on the dirt floor and closed his eyes in meditation.  Remembrance of the time with Sripada Vishnutirtha still occupied his memory, as did the powerful symbol of the reptile.  Thinking again of the snake and its unique teachings, Ekanta thought back to a time when his own guru had taught him in this regard.

*"The snake is an enigmatic figure in the history of our spiritual heritage, Ekanta,"* his guru replied one day in answer to Ekanta's question.  *"In other parts of the world and, indeed, among the masses, it is regarded with suspicion and fear.  In some Christian sects it is seen as synonymous with negative forces.  Whatever the case may be though, the fact remains that the snake is perfectly suited to represent certain mysterious facets of spirituality that are not ordinarily dealt with in mere religious life that deals mostly with ethical living alone."*

"What are some of these representations, dear guru?" asked the boy innocently.

*"Ananta, or Adishesha as he is often called, is the foundation of the worlds and, speaking in philosophical terms, is the very space supporting the universe and the heaven realms.  Thus is the snake seen as a representative of the subtlest element.  Remember that Ananta rests on Ekarnava, the ocean of*

primordial etheric substance. These primal waters are a spiritual archetype of the very streams, rivers, lakes and oceans that the nagas and naginis, those powerful reptilian gods and goddesses, occupied in ancient times. Therefore, all the treasures held by these bodies of liquid and the healing power inherent in them is directly associated with and pertinent to the form of the snake. These watery worlds are their domain.

"Next, Valmiki states in his Ramayana that Adishesha was a mind-born son of Brahma who acted as Prajapati or chief spiritual instructor for the world at its beginning. This is a powerful position and indicates the unique nature of the reptile figure in general. The reptile, then, is an ancient teacher, a being that informed the likes of the firstborn children of Brahma. Spiritual knowledge, called Paravidya, is there in Ananta in a potent form. In correlation to this, my boy, it may be mentioned that, in mythological renderings, the nagas and naginis had a jewel in their heads. The symbolic meaning of this is that the priceless jewel of Self-Realization in the form of the Atman, that which Buddhists refer to as the Diamond nature or Buddha nature, is fully imbedded in these auspicious creatures. This wonderful story is so ingrained in our Eastern culture that even now some of the simple folk of our country believe that every snake has a stone or jewel in its head.

"Furthermore, it is said that Balarama and Lakshmana were incarnations of this special being. Indeed, Ananta, as a name, has become associated with such august personages as Brahma, Shiva, Krishna, Shesha, Vasuki and even the Supreme Being as nameless, formless Reality. In the case of Balaram and Lakshmana, it is easy to make the correlation of the Vishnu and Ananta couple with regards to manifest Divinity and its support when one explores the auspicious lives of Sri Ram and Sri Krishna, for Balaram and Lakshmana were, indeed, important supports for these two Incarnations. They were quite often in the background and performed many amazing feats in conjunction with the wishes of the two Avatars. In other ways, too, Ekanta, we see the actual divinity of the reptile representation like Lord Shiva wrapped with snakes and the Blessed Mother Kali with reptile anklets and bracelets. There are many such examples one could give."

Ekanta listened to all these teachings with great interest. When his guru had finished, he asked a question that had been on his mind for some time.

"Guruji," he said, "what of the snake symbology with regards to Kundalini Shakti, the coiled up and sleeping spiritual energy abiding at the base of the spine?"

"*Oh,*" replied the teacher, "*you have heard of that subtle mystery have you? Well, the nagas and naginis act as guardians to all of the seven portals of consciousness through which this subtle power flows. They are in an unseen and invisible condition, of course, but are there nevertheless. The very symbol of a compacted reptile, ready to spring forth at the auspicious moment and rise to the crown at the top of the head, is indicative of shakti power present throughout and beyond the creation.*

"*Have you seen a snake move, Ekanta?*" asked the guru after a short pause.

"Yes, I have," replied the boy.

"*Then you may have seen that with no arms or legs, the snake still has great powers of mobility and possesses extreme speed. This points to the qualities of omnipotence and omniscience, absolute power and absolute wisdom. Also, its movement suggests both immobility and effortlessness, for in its hypnotic and recurring series of cyclic motions it often appears stationary even while moving. 'It moves but moves not' — is that not what the Upanishads say about Atman? The snake seems to epitomize action in inaction. A more fitting representative for the many divine mysteries present within spiritual awakening can hardly be found, is it not true, my boy?*"

"Revered sir...revered sir! Your food is now ready. Will you eat?"

These words brought Ekanta out of his contemplation and into the present, where he found two strangers looking at him curiously.

"Yes," he replied quietly. "I am now ready. Excuse me for delaying you."

The three ate their meal in silence after a blessing had been said over it. That night, the Avadhut remained awake for many hours, sketching a diagram on the dirt floor of the hut. Then he slept soundly for two hours, awakening before dawn to make his way into the forest surroundings once again. When his hosts awoke, they found only an imprint of the Avadhut's body on the dirt floor where he had spent the night. Next to it, curiously, was an intricate drawing of a many-headed snake, resting in quiet waters and sheltering a divine being with four arms. The drawing was so engaging that the two sat and studied it for some time. They never did remove it. Long after the unique drawing had faded away, the man and the boy remembered the strange but endearing man who had visited them late one night, sitting still for hours, his gaze fixed within upon some unseen Reality.

# — Chapter 23 —

# Teachings on the Dangers of Attraction

THE TWENTY-THIRD GURU — *The Deer*

THE LESSON — *Delusion*

*In the forest, gazing upon the gentle deer, I became more aware of the dangers of delusion, particularly in association with attraction and allurements. The hunter sets a trap for the deer using the soft and enticing sounds of music. The deer, simple-minded and naive, seeks out the source of that compelling sound and thereby meets with death. How strange that something so pleasant can become the source of agony and annihilation to something so gentle! Such too is the nature of relative existence, O Prince. The wise do not indulge in worldly preoccupations such as feasting and making merry, sensuous music and amorous company and other things coveted by high society. Otherwise, they too would meet with foul death and abject suffering at the hands of delusion.*

A weird and faraway sound wafted by on the gentle air and the Avadhut, fresh from his sojourn in the plains, stopped still in his tracks. The forest was silent, basking in the mild heat of the midday spring sun. Various sounds of nature gently entered his ears, putting him into a semiblissful state. The ecstatic Lord and Mother of the Universe, taking the many forms of creation, greeted him on all sides, filling him with love and devotion. Savoring this wonderful feeling, Ekanta allowed himself to drift into spiritual reverie, the kind of which was seldom utilized by ordinary people but which the Avadhut enjoyed often. As he gazed inwardly, a familiar voice entered his mind from far off in time. It was the voice of the Mataji.

*"Ekanta,"* came the voice of his beloved Mataji one day, drifting to his ears over the murmuring sound of the large brook he was swimming in, *"where are you?"*

"I am here," yelled the boy, emerging from the stream that flowed near the ashram.

*"Please come,"* came the Mataji's voice once again.

Ekanta hurriedly put on his clothes, not even bothering to dry himself. Then he ran swiftly in the direction of the ashram. As he approached he slowed down to a reverential walk, for just ahead was the Mataji, his holy female guru.

*"There you are my boy,"* she said with an endearing little laugh that always made him feel good. *"We have guests for lunch. Hurry and help Guruji with the preparations."*

Inside the ashram, the smell of Indian bread filled the air. A hot and sweaty Guruji knelt by the little oven, retrieving pieces of the stuff from the fiery heat for consumption. Already at the table were two figures, sitting cross-legged and still. A regal air seemed to exist around them, blended with an earthy and natural wholesomeness.

*"Ekanta,"* said his guru, turning away from the earthen oven and facing him, *"meet our guests, Chinmaya and Bhalendra. They are Tantric adepts, worshippers of the Divine Mother of the Universe, traveling to faraway places. Bid them welcome and serve them well."*

Turning to his guests, Ekanta's guru said, *"this is my chela, Ekanta."*

Ekanta saluted the pair who merely smiled and stared at him. Ekanta, too, gazed upon the pair with interest, for they exuded a palpable vibration that was somewhat exhilarating. Not forgetting himself completely, Ekanta busied himself around the kitchen in preparation for the meal, but he kept his eyes on the two guests nevertheless.

When the meal was ready, the Mataji entered the room as if on cue. Chinmaya and Bhalendra stood up and saluted her. She, as if indifferent to their reverence, simply seated herself at the table and asked Ekanta to begin the service. The meal was eaten in silence after the blessing was given. Afterwards, however, the five retired to the sitting room and a conversation soon sprang up.

"How do you worship?" asked Ekanta's guru, breaking the silence. "What form does your worship take with regards to the Divine Mother of the Universe?"

*"What can I say?"* responded Chinmaya. *"She is our all in all. We have no specific rites through which to pay deference to Her. Instead, we see Her everywhere and hear Her always. This alone constitutes our worship."*

"If you see Her everywhere, then," joined in Ekanta, "She must have a form, and if you hear Her, She must have a voice."

Both Chinmaya and Bhalendra turned their gaze upon the boy. Ekanta felt a tingling sensation go up his spine.

*"Yes, what you have just uttered is the very Truth,"* returned Chinmaya. *"She is not only formless but acts through us and speaks through us as well. The entire creation is Her sport, Her play of Consciousness. Millions of bodies encase Her blissful essence and a boundless multitude of sounds comprise Her voice."*

There was a short silence. Then Ekanta spoke again.

"A play has its problems and sport often results in injury. In this game of Hers, why do beings suffer and get hurt?"

Chinmaya considered the boy's question, then replied:

*"We do not pretend to know Her will in this matter, but rather turn to the scriptures for elucidation. Anything that enters the body and sports in time and space is subject to dvanda mohena — the many pairs of opposites in creation. That is a fact plain and simple. There is no explanation for the question 'why' in this regard. There is this much that we know of. Through personal delusion, beings suffer unaccountably. Were they to listen to the inner Self which is a glint of Her golden nature placed within them through Her grace, they would enjoy bliss rather*

*than suffer ignobly. Speaking for myself, my entire life was misery until I was awakened to Her, by Her Grace. Since then I have never known what suffering is. As an impediment, it has disappeared entirely from my existence."*

"Sir," said Ekanta incredulously, "that is a remarkable statement. What do you mean, 'as an impediment?'"

*"I mean,"* replied Chinmaya, *"that any suffering that now comes my way is both greatly alleviated by my closeness to Her and seen as a gift from Her meant for my own benefit. I accept everything as Her Will and Her Grace. Thus I live happily under all conditions."*

Later that night, Ekanta sought out Chinmaya and his silent partner outside under the stars. The two were sitting quietly in yogic fashion, staring up into the sky and meditating with closed eyes in turns. The boy sat still with them for some time, then broke the silence with a question.

"I know very little about the Divine Mother," admitted Ekanta. "In fact, I know practically nothing about the opposite sex. Some say that they are goddesses walking the earth and others that they are demons put here to ensnare man."

Both men laughed at this statement and Ekanta breathed easier. It was the first sound he had heard Bhalendra make.

*"Both are partially right,"* replied Chinmaya. *"The Vidya Shakti aspect of Mother is nothing short of the Divine Mother appearing on earth in certain forms to aid the evolutionary process. The Avidya Shakti, however, is nothing less than ego gone mad. Such as those can injure and even destroy men. It is not hard, however, to tell the difference between the two, that is, if one is awake to Divine Reality. If one is asleep to higher things, the entire world represents danger."*

After a short silence, during which the three gazed at the stars, Chinmaya spoke again.

*"The enigma of personal delusion with regards to enlightenment is explained nicely by this example. When the coconut is still unripe, it is all one thing, that is, the outer shell, the husk, the meat and kernel are inseparable and form one solid mass. When the coconut is ripe, though, one can pick it up, shake it and hear the kernel rattling around inside. It has become separated from the other layers of the fruit. This is precisely the*

*state of the jivas, the embodied beings, when they are in awak-
ened and unawakened conditions. The spiritually unawakened
ones in their delusion perceive the world and God all as one
thing. They think that the world is God and nothing exists outside of it. The illumined, however, know without a doubt that
Brahman exists beyond the world, that only Brahman exists and
the world is His expression. In that way and in that way only,
the world is not different from Him. The view is only slightly
different here, the emphasis shifted ever so little, but what is
achieved is vastly different by way of clarity and understanding.*"

"That is amazing," replied Ekanta after thinking a moment. "It
describes the condition of many people I have met who talk one
way and act the other. Their religion is as you have described
and amounts to materialism and sensuality. They do not perceive
the Divine here and instead just enjoy the world without paying
allegiance to anything. It is a kind of oneness but it is devoid of
anything sacred."

"Yes," replied Chinmaya, *"that kind of oneness is a kind of
deluded unity with something ultimately unreal. People, so
long as they are spiritually immature, think everything is one,
but their realization of this is materially and sensually based.
It is, as I have said, like the coconut which is all one thing
when it is unripe, but which has many distinct layers — outer
shell, husk, inner shell, meat, milk and kernel — when it is ripe,
all intrinsically connected but separate as well. Therefore, lip-
service affirmation with regards to oneness is inadequate. A
life lived in the pale of such a philosophy amounts to nothing.
You have much substance in you,"* said Chinmaya admiringly,
*"and you do not fear to speak your mind. What else do you want
to know?"*

"In this Avidya Shakti aspect," asked Ekanta, "is the Divine
Mother actually present? How could She be there when ignorance
predominates? It would be a contradiction in terms."

"*Ultimately,*" replied Chinmaya, *"She is not present in either
the Vidya Shakti aspect or the Avidya Shakti aspect. She is ever-
detached and always in witness mode, yet She perceives through
these conditions. The ocean is not fully contained where every
wave breaks but it is still connected and present on that occasion nevertheless. One can see a glimmer of the power of shakti*

*in the deluded feminine mechanism. The only problem is, it is a power that will blast and destroy, like an explosion going off near a child without any conscience or regret. Beware of Avidya Shakti throughout your life, Ekanta. Steer clear of such manifestations, for they will lure you deftly, only to ruin you without the slightest care or concern."*

A few minutes later, Chinmaya continued:

*"It is not just a feminine form that contains avidya. The creation is composed of portions of it as well. Avidya Maya rages through the demonically possessed man and every deluded person regardless of gender or body type. Sometimes it is masked, lying in wait as it were, while at other times it is blatantly exposed and actively destructive. It takes a discriminating person to avoid its allures and negative effects. Take refuge in Vidya Shakti, though, and there will be no danger for you. That is the secret."*

That curious sound reached Ekanta's ears again, awakening him out of his spiritual reverie and bringing him back to awareness of the physical world. This time, he recognized it as a few distant strains of music and he turned his footsteps in its general direction. Soon, he came to the edge of a clearing. Stopping there, he surveyed the surroundings carefully, eventually finding what he was searching for. At the other edge of the small clearing, a hunter was sitting well-hidden behind a tree and some tall bushes, bow and arrow poised in readiness. Every once in a while, the hunter turned his attention to an instrument placed on the ground near him and played a few notes. The vibrations caused by the musical instrument wafted up and were carried by the wind across the meadow. It was not long before the Avadhut noticed movement in the bushes.

A deer appeared from the forest, its brown fur still camouflaging it well against the backdrop of trees and leaves. The experienced eye of the hunter did not miss it though, Ekanta noticed, for he was immediately on his feet, though crouching low to avoid detection. The deer eased itself out of the trees slowly as the music emitted again from the direction of the hunter's position. At first only its head could be seen, but gradually it came slowly and carefully into the clearing. Every time the luring sounds of the music became audible to its heightened senses, the deer came a little closer, drawn by that invisible enticement.

When the gentle animal was halfway across the small clearing, Ekanta half expected to see an arrow lodge itself in the deer's body, as if springing straight out of the flesh. He was surprised, instead, to see the deer disappear before his very eyes with a crashing sound. The hunter then jumped up and, emitting a shout of triumph, went quickly to the pit he had dug and swiftly dispatched the deer with a well-placed arrow. After this sequence of events had played out, the Avadhut once again entered the woods and went along his way. Later, over an evening fire, he mused about the day's occurrences and the lessons that they reflected.

*"Danger attends upon everyone, Ekanta,"* came the voice of his friend, Yogindra Yogi, one night near the cave dwelling of the old sage, *"but it is greatly alleviated and even neutralized in the presence of God. This is a great secret. Even the warrior, pressed on all sides by a dozen enemies and faced every second by life-threatening circumstances, escapes danger due to his faith coupled with his skill. So, too, does the spiritual aspirant avoid grave danger in the form of personal delusion and the ills of relative existence by resorting to refuge in the Lord and adept manipulation of the many tools which the Divine Mother has given him."*

"Can you give an example of delusion, revered sir?" the boy had asked.

*"Of course,"* returned the holy man. *"Delusion, another word for ignorance, is threefold. There is, to start, the collective delusion and the individual delusion. An example of collective delusion would be waging war in the name of God and forcing everyone into one religious perspective. Individual delusion centers around the wayward thoughts and misconceptions a being labors under that causes him or her to perform deceitful and malicious actions. There are subtle levels to both of these types of delusion as well. When a society acts out of good intention but for the wrong reasons it is a case of subtle collective delusion. So, too, does an individual commit such acts when, for the sake of personal comfort or pleasure, he or she convinces himself or herself that what they are doing is for their own benefit while in reality they are deceiving themselves."*

"Sir," broke in Ekanta, "you said that there are three kinds of delusion. What is the third?"

"*The third is cosmic, my son,*" returned the yogi, "*and since it is surprising to think that the Cosmic Being can be capable of delusion, we call it illusion in this case rather than delusion. The Creator takes an entire host of universal principles with names and forms and projects them over the nameless, formless Reality, thereby covering up and apparently segmenting that Sublime Being. The universe then stands before us in all its external glory and we think it to be the most wonderful thing and take it for Reality. This is a deception on the grand scale of things, is it not, for Truth eternal gets veiled from view. It reminds me of a song. Have you not heard it?*"

So saying, the yogi placed his old voice into operation and sang.

O blessed principle of eternal Truth,
forgive me for these transgressions of which I am guilty.
First, I have sought you out across the face of the earth,
longing with my entire being to gaze upon Thy face.
But Thou art essentially formless, homogenous and free.
Therefore, forgive me for attempting to solidify Thee.

Again, I have indulged in the ultimate folly.
Time after time I have called upon Thee
with innumerable names,
ascribing to Thee magnificent titles without number.
Thy many qualities have I praised unto the skies,
celebrating Thy many glories with elated heart and mind.
But now I realize that Thou art beyond description,
that names and qualities only tend to limit Thee.
Therefore, forgive me for this, my transgression.

Birthless and deathless art Thou, O Supreme One,
yet repeatedly I imagine Thee to be born and pass away.
Inseparable and indivisible, eternal art Thou,
still, I fragment Thee and conceive of your end.
Beyond the mind art Thou, to be sure,
while I, deceived, attribute thought to Thee.
Therefore, forgive me, Beloved, for my transgressions.

I run here and there, visiting every sacred place,
worshipping Thy presence in nature and stone images.
You are here but not over there, I say,
as my mind, deluded, divides Thee.
But every wise one knows, Oh precious Essence of Being,
that Thou art everywhere and all-pervasive.
Forgive me, then, gracious Lord and Mother,
for these and other transgressions.

After the song, a long and deep silence ensued.

Finally, Ekanta asked the yogi another question.

"In the case of the cosmic delusion, the power of illusion, is there a subtle aspect of that as well?"

*"It is all pretty subtle, Ekanta,"* replied the yogi, *"though it is simultaneously grandiose. Some aspects of it are more sublime than others, however. Take for instance the power of attraction. There is a purpose to the power of attraction. The divine aspect of attraction is known as Yogamaya, the compelling force that calls forth and merges diverse principles and properties into a unified state. It, too, has apparent and subtle functions. The constant deteriorating force that is always breaking down names and forms is an example of its apparent workings. It is not necessarily either good or bad but just goes on merging opposites. Through it, many things get returned to their Source of origin.*

*"On the ultrapersonal level, God delights in the ecstasy of Love. Graciously, compassionately and with extreme sensitivity, the Beloved One absorbs all beings into an intense internal communion with Itself. The extremely blissful power of Yogamaya in this mode is an example of the subtlest ecstasy of attraction. All names and forms will dissolve in unity in that ocean of immortality. The illustration that comes to mind is of the ship that sails past a mountain of magnetic iron. As it nears, all the screws throughout its hull and timbers are loosened and pulled out of their grooves. The ship then falls apart on the spot and sinks into the ocean."*

"Oh," Ekanta exclaimed, "that is a delightful example. I am both awestruck and puzzled though. With this vision of Divine Love before us, why do we not take recourse to it? Where are all of those who love so intensely and who are experiencing such bliss?"

*"That is a fair question,"* replied Yogindra Yogi, *"and one that many of us who love the Lord have been asking ourselves all our lives. To answer it in part, I must explain to you the other extreme involving the power of attraction, one of negativity and utmost delusion. When this type of delusion is involved, the force of attraction becomes distorted, dwarfed and personalized and used for selfish ends. Its effects are then negative with regards to human existence and experience. Attraction then becomes a tool for passion-based pleasure and greed. Let me tell you a story.*

*"When I was younger I had a friend. Unlike myself, who was always averse to the ways of the world, my friend, though a good person with many fine qualities, pursued life with an eye to getting and possessing all the finer things coveted by society. Time and time again we would argue about the nature of relative existence, myself opting to explain things in terms of temporality, cause and effect and the various vicissitudes of life and he always overlooking my explanations and calling me morbid and pessimistic.*

*"During the year just previous to my final renunciation of the world, my friend became enamored of a beautiful young woman who had a reputation for using men to gain her own selfish ends. Though proof of her insincerity was apparent and many of her potential suitors had suffered along the way, still I could not convince my friend of the danger of courting her. She, too, urged him along as an angler would play a fish or a hunter would systematically stalk a deer. He was adamantly committed to his course of action and fully taken by her charms. I could see that he was mesmerized like a mouse before a cobra.*

*"The courtship went on for a year until finally, one day, she announced that she would marry a nobleman from a nearby township. The callous way in which she informed my friend revealed her cold and calculating nature. She even delighted in the pain she caused him. This, Ekanta, is an example of Avidya Shakti. There are many of these inhabiting the world, both male and female. They are a godless people, brutish and insensitive, wholly bereft of higher virtues and fully given to the world and*

*its affairs. You must always beware of the likes of these. Do not get attracted to outer show, ostentation, the glimmer of earthly beauty and external radiance.*

"*This type of person is clever. You will see them in high positions of society such as law and politics. They occupy positions of power and prestige in circles of piety as well, in churches and religious organizations. Through the power of subtle deception and the name and fame allotted to them by deluded followers, they rise to the top like a crow flying over other animals to perch and feast on a mountain of trash. They shine with external light and thereby entice sincere seekers to a life of servitude and personality worship but the end result is deception and a preoccupation with lower ideals.*"

After considering these words for a time, Ekanta asked the yogi for more details. "Revered sir," he stated, "whatever happened to your friend, the one who fell in love with the Avidya Shakti?"

The yogi became silent and a dark shadow seemed to pass over his face. With tears in his eyes, glinting in the firelight around which the two were seated, he answered slowly:

"*I helped to cremate this dear friend of my youth the very next week. So distraught was he over the entire affair and at the loss of his beloved, that he took his own life.*"

Ekanta was stunned to hear this. "This occurrence probably caused the woman great remorse and many misgivings," he said. "Possibly she even repented of her cruel ways."

The old sage looked at the young man and stated matter-of-factly, "*She did not even show up to pay her respects at the service, Ekanta. Word came later that she had immediately married the nobleman for money, position and power and was living a life of pleasure and ease. Now do you fathom the insipid nature of deception and delusion and perceive the ways of worldly attraction? In truth, my young friend, beings like these are to be pitied. In the case of my friend, a lesson was learned and utilized somewhere along the way, but this deluded woman has no such recompense. The suffering that accrues through deceiving others is substantial. I shudder to think of it.*"

As the Avadhut lay down to sleep that night, the forest and its creatures resting around him, he wondered at the power of attraction that his gurus had advised him about. The entire universe, he knew, was existing due to this intense force. The greatest beings he had heard of declared that it was intense love that was the cause of the creation. Why then so much of suffering he thought, as he fell off to sleep.

In the morning he sat for meditation just before sunrise. After an hour of formless meditation, he entered a mode of contemplation. The recollections of Yogindra Yogi's teachings the night before still lingered in his mind. He recalled the following day when, as a result of thinking over the yogi's words, he had approached his Guruji for further clarification.

"*Ekanta,*" said his guru jovially as he beheld the radiant countenance of his student. "*Where have you been these past few days?*"

"At home helping my mother and father with chores," answered the young man. "Last night, though, I made the hike to the high places beyond the village and the mountain yogi and I sat up late around the fire and discussed the aspects of Avidya Shakti and Vidya Shakti with regards to individual and collective delusion."

"*Indeed,*" came the response from the teacher, "*that must have been most edifying.*"

"Yes, it was," replied Ekanta, "but the subject is abstruse and complicated in some ways. There are facets of it that escape me entirely it would seem, especially those associated with ignorance in relation to the force of attraction. According to Yogindraji, there are many levels regarding this subject."

"*That is true,*" responded the guru, "*as is the case with any spiritual topic. Some say that Truth is simple, but that is a misleading description. I would say that it is simply profound. What is meant by simple is that Truth always rings clear in human awareness. It is recognizable by this unerring trait. Truth is not, then, always easy to understand. If it were simple in this way then normal, everyday people could easily grasp it and all would be enlightened. This is obviously not the case judging by the state of affairs in the world today. One must stretch and expand one's understanding to be able to comprehend the profundity of God's Truth. When one rids the mind of root ignorance, then Truth becomes less and less obscure of meaning and more clear and precise. But tell me, what are these obscure areas that you speak of?*"

Ekanta gave thought for a moment before replying:

"Where does ignorance enter into consciousness and how does it get a hold there? Then, if Maya is controlling deluded beings, how do they get free from that influence?"

*"Very well put,"* responded the boy's preceptor. *"Let us look at these issues more closely under the microscope of the scriptures and the teachings of the illumined ones.*

*"First of all, from our perspective, that is, the outlook of Advaita Vedanta, there is no ignorance in Consciousness, ever, and by Consciousness here I mean primal Awareness in its pure, unadulterated condition. Pure Consciousness does not occupy time and space. If one knows oneself to be That, that is, knows the Atman, the immortal spark of Divinity in each and every being, then no ignorance is possible. This must be stated out front so that all who study our Sanatana Dharma will know for certain where we stand. Whether they accept it or not is another matter and entirely up to them.*

*"From a secondary or relative position, that of dualism rather than nondualism, consciousness identified with the sheaths of body, life-force, mind, intellect and ego, the five koshas spoken of in Vedanta Philosophy, is in ignorance of its true nature. Where this delusion begins is hard to say, though the enlightened ones have proposed that as soon as the very first act of creation takes place, there the equilibrium of perfect Being is disturbed and ignorance is immediately operative."*

The guru thought for a moment. Then, with a smile he continued:

*"Take, for instance, the case of a man resting on his favorite and most comfortable chair. Fat and happy, his work put aside, he is sleeping peacefully in midafternoon on his day off. Perfect silence reigns in his sitting room where he is reclining with no worries or cares. Suddenly, his five children burst into the room, screaming loudly and running and tumbling over one another, accompanied by their dog who is barking ferociously. They are quickly followed by his wife, yelling at them for interrupting their father's repose. The poor rotund father is instantly on his feet, rudely awakened out of a deep sleep, filled with confusion as to his identity and location and plunged unwillingly into the surrounding chaos. This is an adequate description of the difference between the state of pure, timeless Awareness and the condition of universal manifestation."*

This story brought laughter bubbling out of Ekanta in waves. The two enjoyed a short period of mirth and after it had subsided the preceptor continued.

*"For whatever reason, Ekanta, call it the will of the Creator if you want, creation takes place and with it comes root ignorance. The sages call it Mulavidya, for it permeates the universe of name and form like syrup soaks a rasagola. All beings are then plunged into delusion as to their Source of origin, born into the realm of relativity housed in a body/mind mechanism which is itself incapable of perceiving Absolute Reality, let alone ascertaining the reason for relative existence.*

*"It is a game of hide and seek, my boy,"* continued the guru after a short pause. *"Mankind is the seeker, the universe of names and forms are the hiding places and God is the one apparently hiding amidst them. Then again, sometimes God is the seeker and mankind is hiding, refusing to accept the Truth. In truth, it is just Consciousness seeking itself. Have you ever had the experience of putting something away and then later forgetting where it is, possibly even failing to remember that you packed it away in the first place? It is a case of unexplainable forgetfulness, yes? Life in the world is somewhat like that. The real prize, your true nature, is elsewhere, but there you are, participating in all the diverse activities of the world as if they are most important, even crucial. In this externalized state, the world is real, your body is real and your thoughts and actions, all real. This is root ignorance, Mulavidya. Avidya Maya has gotten a hold of you, pure and simple."*

"Revered sir," Ekanta replied, "what you are telling me is that delusion permeates the creation and that God, the remover of delusion, is in disguise here in a purposeful manner."

*"Yes,"* the teacher agreed, *"and importantly, when you recognize the situation this delusion vanishes. Such recognition consists of ultimately realizing your divine nature, your identity with Absolute Reality. Until that happens, again by the will of the Absolute, one must exercise all the tools placed here for that purpose. They are like clues to ultimate understanding. It is like introducing helpful hints into the game of hide and seek. From this we can conclude that God is a serious player, has a sense of humor and loves to sport. By the word God, here,*

*I mean the dynamic principle of the Absolute, that aspect that decides to create and enter into the universal play, not the static aspect that remains always in an unmanifest condition beyond the play of opposite forces and diverse principles."*

"But sir," Ekanta complained, "this game that the dynamic aspect of Reality is perpetuating is filled with suffering for us and we are mere pawns."

*"That,"* the guru replied, *"amounts to a matter of perspective and is potentially under your control. Who are you really? Are you that body, subject to death and filled with filthy stuff? Possibly you are the life-force, coursing through the nervous system and depleting itself with the passage of time. Then again, do you believe yourself to be a mind, a physical organ called the brain, caught in the fundamental illusion of primal ignorance, happy one moment and depressed the next? If you labor under these fallacious beliefs, Ekanta, then Avidya Maya, the illusory power, is in full control and God is in successful hiding."*

At that moment, Ekanta breathed a sigh of relief.

"Thank you, revered sir, for reminding me of what you began this conversation with — the truth of Advaita Vedanta. I have just learned something very valuable."

*"Yes, I can imagine,"* responded the guru, *"but it is the most enigmatic piece of essential wisdom that you will ever attempt to possess. Remembrance of the Self is a subtly illusive practice. Realization of It is much more difficult. That leads us to the last question that you raised."*

"Yes, dear teacher," Ekanta agreed, "the matter of how one releases this apparently bound self from the clutches of ignorance."

*"There are many ways, Ekanta,"* the guru continued, *"all connected to the clues I mentioned. God hints at His presence continually. In fact, the very Maya with which He hides Himself is the greatest hint to His existence! You know that Maya is His power. Unlike dualistic thinkers who assign ignorance to a specific location by personifying it in the form of a demon or a devil, we know that it is God Himself, clothing His presence in various obscurations, who appears to us under the guise of good and bad. In this regard, and for one who has this key and uses it boldly, it becomes easy to see that even the negative experiences which happen to us are brought about by His will, all*

*ultimately for our best good. This healthy understanding, in turn, leads to freedom from the impositions of suffering and misery because the mind grows strong and resilient through trials and tests that it consciously knows spring from the Beloved.*

*"This is the beginning of being able to perceive all as Brahman. Very soon, the mind becomes extremely adept at locating what is Divine in any given situation under all circumstances. As to the ways, Ekanta, they are legion, but the same old standbys are always there, invaluable, time-tested principles such as discrimination, detachment, patience, perseverance and faith. The old witch, Avidya Maya, cannot stand the penetrating searchlights of discrimination and detachment. Their opposites in the world of human relations, promiscuousness and inadvertent involvement, rob human awareness of its ability to focus."*

"Guruji," Ekanta broke in, "that reminds me of some confusion I had in talking to Yogindraji. He was using the term Avidya Shakti and you are emphasizing Avidya Maya. I take it that one is cosmic and the other personal or individual?"

*"Generally speaking, yes,"* replied the preceptor, *"though they can be used interchangeably. In terms of human relationships which, I presume, perked your question, the term Avidya Shakti applies well. In these cases, negativity does get personified, though often the person conditioned by ignorance and delusion is not aware of himself or herself as being deluded. This is a case of ignorance being unaware of itself as ignorant,"* laughed the guru. *"In this way, Avidya Maya runs rampant across the face of the earth and many misguided individuals commit all manner of nefarious deeds through her influence. Truth seekers must beware, then, and never fall under the control of this force."*

"Are we not faced with this condition at birth then, revered guru?" asked the young man innocently.

*"Yes, in many ways, Ekanta,"* replied the guru, *"but the slate has been wiped clean to a great extent in the case of a baby. There are, to be sure, hidden impressions lying dormant there in the infant's mind, as any parent knows who has raised a child and been faced with both positive and negative results. Those are there due to repeated actions performed in past lives. Therefore, another tool comes to light. During this very life,*

*Ekanta, we must be about refining our individualized human awareness and cleaning the mind of its negative impressions. By neutralizing samskaras, those potentially dangerous seed impressions occupying the subconscious and unconscious mind, and refraining from the repetition of similar negative tendencies during this present existence, we will be born in a predominantly pure state, free of these inhibiting factors. I have seen such children before. Their existence is exceedingly happy and they live a blessed life."*

"Revered sir," pressed Ekanta, "you mentioned that dualistic thinkers personify this negativity into certain forms instead of recognizing it as the Divine playing through a restricted or alternate mode. You also admitted that Avidya Shakti in human vehicles is a type of personified evil. Is there a conscious evil in the world?"

*"Conscious evil is a contradiction in terms, my son,"* replied the teacher. *"As far as one personified conglomerate of evil is concerned such as the fundamentalist Christians of the West believe in, no, there is no such being in existence. There is no ultimately good being in creation either. There is just One, indivisible and impeccably pure Consciousness, beyond both good and evil and transcendent of every other duality or mental concept as well. When this Ultimate Being projects and enters the arena of the created worlds, whether they be celestial, earthly or the nether regions, It becomes apparently modified by the existing principles around It. In a heaven sphere, it sports as both god and goddess and the mighty asuras who contain both good and evil traits. On earth, it appears as both a world-preserver like the Buddha and a world-destroyer like Attila the Hun. In the nether regions it is both sufferer and savior, depending on its selected role. Yet, all of these realms are but dreams to It. You see, It is indivisible and ever-perfect. It never really becomes involved in the first place. It only appears to act, move and think, and that only through its many vehicles. It is ever the Supreme Witness of all phenomena. All salutations belong there!"*

"Revered guru," Ekanta stated breathlessly. "I understand! There is no God and there is no devil. There is only the Great Self!"

Ekanta's guru said nothing, but simply stared intensely at the boy. Then, placing his hands together in a profound salute, he reverently bowed low before his student. Ekanta knew he had spoken words of Truth for such a response to come forth from his teacher. After this precious moment had passed, the guru continued his talk with a story.

*"You see, Ekanta, once several Christian missionaries came to our ashram with a view towards converting us. They are a bit like the radical sect of Muslims, spreading their message by force, either subtle or violent as their history reveals. In this case, of course, these deluded missionaries tried the subtle methods which are, for all intent and purposes, equally insidious. Your Mataji and I greeted them cordially and listened to their words courteously. Essentially, their message was dualistic, ultimately based upon the acceptance of a Divine personality for redemption and salvation, much like the fundamentalist Krishna sect here in India."*

Ekanta's wonderful guru remained silent for a few moments, thinking. Then he continued:

*"What was most objectionable, though, was their insistence upon mankind being sinful by nature rather than Divine as we would insist. Inquiring deeper with a somewhat feigned interest, we saw that they are really materialists. They told us that their scriptures state that the soul is nothing in the beginning, that it is created from dust, is basically a physical entity and returns to nothingness after it experiences one life. Thereafter, it is resurrected at the judgment day, either given salvation or doomed to eternal damnation based upon its one life. Nothing before this life or after it accounts for this decree for it was nothing in the beginning! Needless to say, Mataji and I were dumbstruck, not only due to the narrowness of their religion and the cruelty of their God but also that human beings would fall so low as to believe such a distorted doctrine.*

*"What is more, their first man, called Adam, committed a heinous sin. He ate an apple off of a forbidden tree, as was explained to us. Due to this sin, the entire human race was deemed to be sinners with no other recourse than to accept their fate and turn to a benign savior. Therefore, as these missionaries told us, all of the suffering that the human race experiences is not due to past actions which we ourselves have committed but falls on Adam due to his imperfection. His flaw is inherited by*

*the whole human race.  Finally, death itself neutralizes a person's sins for he or she returns to nonexistence.  Abiding as either dust or nothingness, we could not make out which, that nonsoul then awaits resurrection and judgment at some future date.*

*"As if this were not enough to turn our insides, these missionaries then proceeded to give us the lowdown on the devil, an evil being that presides over the entire world because the Lord abandoned it and gave it over to him.  The good news was not long in coming, however, although it was not very cheerful to your Mataji and I.  After the resurrection, beings who are not cast into hell to burn forever, receive their place in paradise which is not even a heaven but rather a paradise on earth, replete with a body that does not get sick or die or even suffer anymore.  Imagine, a place where happiness based on physical living is the norm and one must remain there forever.  To us, Ekanta, that sounded like hell, for we are free beings that have realized our inherent perfection by trial and error and have transcended both the joy and sorrow of relative existence to reside in the true equanimity and peace of transcendent liberation.  What could beings such as us possibly want with a place of continual physical happiness?  We want nothing less than immersion in Brahman which is our true nature.  Even in the embodied state, without some contrast, such a realm would turn insipid in no time.  No, the Peace of the ancients is far beyond streets of gold running with milk and honey.*

*"Later, Ekanta, we learned that these missionaries represented the fundamentalist sector of Christianity and that there were others that followed the true way of the Christ rather than the distorted word.  Since then, I have met and spoken with a few of these and find much more sense to the symbology present in their teachings.  Also, there is more of a focus on God in these more practical Christians and less of a dependence upon a human personality.  God appears on earth as a divine personality, no doubt, but that is so that, as Christ said, we can all learn to be perfect even as the Father in heaven is perfect.  By such a divine example, we learn what is right and what is wrong, what is beneficial and what is nonessential.  The work, however, is to be done by our own self-effort, though guidance from on high is constant.  Self-effort and Grace then constitute*

*the path leading to Truth and there are many ways and an infinite expanse of time with which to accomplish that goal. But this is all put in terms of secondary concerns applicable to relative existence. Far beyond such considerations is the Ultimate Reality where birth and death, bondage, salvation and liberation and even God and man have ceased to be. No distinctions exist in That. Such is the beauty of the Advaitic Reality."*

After the Avadhut had brought himself out of his spiritual reverie, he sighed loud and long. He had been blessed in the extreme, he realized, to have come to such illumined gurus at so young an age and with so much acceptance and openness. Looking back over his entire life, he could not perceive one rift in the perfection of it. Breaking camp after packing his few belongings, the Avadhut saluted the spot upon which he had sat for meditation. As he left the locale, he came across a herd of deer just on the other side of the forest enclosure within which he had camped. The deer looked up, startled a bit to be approached so easily, and then retreated slowly, sensing no danger from the Avadhut.

Following a whim, the Avadhut stopped and began whistling a tune similar to the one that the hunter had played the day before. To his surprise, a few of the deer began to draw near him with curious expressions on their docile faces. As he waited, one deer actually came up to him and sniffed his clothes. Taking a morsel of bread out of his pocket, Ekanta fed it to the deer. After this, several deer began gathering around him and a few nuzzled his pocket in hopes of procuring more food. The Avadhut enjoyed their company immensely and stood among them for a few minutes.

As he was leaving, he turned and faced the beautiful animals. Bringing his hands together in a profound salute, he bowed his head and offered his respects:

"I salute you, the deer, who have taught me both the danger and meaning of attraction. Through your example and your sacrifice, beings can see that they must not be enticed by the superficial things of the world, falling into the many traps of delusion."

Then, shouldering his small pack again, he turned and disappeared, as lightly and as easily as a brown deer, into the deeper recesses of the dense forest.

# Chapter 24

# Teachings on Guilelessness

THE TWENTY-FOURTH GURU —The Child

THE LESSON —Innocence

*O great prince, one of my greatest teachers is
most small and humble.  Observing the child at
play and speaking with her from her own innocent
understanding is much like being in the presence of
God.  From this little girl I learned how to live
unattached to everything, transcendent of all that
may cause pain or sorrow and fully present in the
moment at all times.  The obvious absence of
jadedness in the child that fills the minds of the
worldly, who are wholly preoccupied with selfish,
mundane matters, made her the perfect study of what
it means to be truly free and happy.  From her I
learned that authentic freedom and abiding
contentedness are based upon innocence and purity.
Therefore, I salute her profoundly.*

Tears of joy welled up in the Avadhut's eyes.  The face he was
looking into reflected similar sentiments and was completely

taken over with a huge smile as well. It had been several years since Ekanta had seen Dharman, the arrowmaker, at whose house he had stayed and whom he had accompanied to the city on that memorable occasion. He had cherished this man in his heart and recalled him to mind often along with his pious wife and their daughter whom he had never met. Now, out of the corner of his eye, he saw Gramani, the arrowmaker's wife and behind her, peaking around her mother's skirts, a little girl not yet ten years old.

The two men embraced each other as long lost brothers. After this bear hug ended, the two paused for breath and stared at each other unbelievingly.

"I knew you were in our part of the country," Dharman spoke first, "for I dreamed about you just the other night. Were you going to visit us at the cabin?"

"Dear Brother," the Avadhut replied, "it is so good to lay eyes on you. I have just come from the city where I had hoped to see you first at your shop, for I had a few bits of business to attend to in town. I found your shop closed and was therefore going to try and see you both at your cabin. I was just heading that way on this old familiar trail and here you are, appearing out of nowhere as it were! I am so happy that we did not miss each other somehow."

"The Mother of the Universe has decreed otherwise, thank God," returned Dharman. "But here, please greet Gramani and my little daughter who was not present at our first meeting."

Turning to see the two, Ekanta found that Gramani was already taking the dust of his feet in typical and reverent Indian fashion.

"Please," objected the Avadhut mildly, "there is no need for this." But he was too late for Dharman's little daughter was already following her mother's example, placing her sweet little head on each of the Avadhut's feet in turn. Ekanta felt a rush of subtle energy from that contact which was at once warm and healing. As the two rose, Gramani spoke.

"Namaste, revered sir. I did not get to give you this salutation at the time of our last parting so now I have satisfied that need. Please do not be angry with us on that account. Your teachings and presence have lived on with us and have helped to transform our lives as well, even as short and condensed as that auspicious time was. We are fortunate to see you again."

"Revered Mother," the Avadhut replied, "it is I who gained benefit from the two of you, representing as you do what it is to live perfectly in the world as an example of piety and goodness while serving others unselfishly. The both of you have lived on in my store of cherished memories all these days."

"And you," said the Avadhut, turning his attention on the young girl, "I have heard so much about you. That I failed to make your acquaintance was a great loss. Now, may I know your name?"

Though bashful in some respects, Dharman and Gramani's daughter was also spirited and outspoken. Ekanta could see that a special emanation of the Goddess resided in her just by merely looking at her form. Her eyes bore the look of one who was fresh from the Divine presence and always accustomed to living easily and naturally in that sublime atmosphere. As she spoke, a few wisps of hair fell into her radiant face.

"My name is Puspi," her little voice rang out softly but clear and true in the forest confines. "I heard about you too."

"Indeed," Ekanta replied. "I hope that what you heard was good."

"Oh yes," the little girl returned in a naturally affected voice. "I have heard that you are my dear uncle, too. Are you?"

"With your permission and the approval of your mother and father, I would be honored to be your uncle."

"Can I call you Dada, then?" she asked innocently, using the word for uncle in her part of the country.

"That would be nice," said the Avadhut with a smile, charmed by Puspi's endearing ways.

"Okay," she said with a smile of her own, and that officially ended the matter, for she turned abruptly away and began playing with a grasshopper that caught her eye.

Dharman smiled in obvious approval of the first meeting between these two precious beings and in anticipation of what it promised for the future.

"Revered Avadhut," he said. "We have a dilemma and I believe that the Mother has proposed a solution in Her own insightful way. We are on the way to the city, as you know, and you are headed for the cabin. In the city, we mean to visit a friend who has a mild but contagious case of cholera. It is both inconvenient and discomforting to leave Puspi anywhere there and we do not want to expose the child to the disease. She did not want to leave her home anyway and wants to go back as soon as possible. You have come along at this moment and we hope that you can take Puspi back to the cabin with you and stay with her until we return in three days' time, maybe sooner. Will you do this for us or is it asking too much?"

"Why, I should be most happy to tend to the child," replied the Avadhut, "though I do not know much about taking care of her. You will have to instruct me in that."

"Even this will not be necessary," returned Dharman, "for she is able to accomplish most everything on her own and what she cannot do she will tell you herself how to complete. She has proven herself to be an amazingly able child at a very young age and is already surprisingly knowledgeable about life. You will find many occasions to marvel about this, I have no doubt."

"Nor do I doubt it," replied the Avadhut, "even having seen her for this very short time."

"Then it is all settled," said Gramani. "We will leave her in your capable hands."

Calling her daughter, Gramani said, "Puspi, come and stay with Dada. He will take you home as you wanted. We shall be back to see you in two or three days."

Though Ekanta thought that the child might balk or make a fuss, he was surprised to see that she complied without hesitation. Coming to his side and taking his big hand in her little one, she smiled up at her parents and simply said "good-bye." Dharman bent down and gave her a kiss on the cheek. She pushed his face away in embarrassment but a second later her mother followed suit and the child did not flinch. Turning away after saluting the Avadhut, the couple walked slowly to the next bend in the trail, turned and waved, and were gone from view in a second.

Ekanta stood for a few seconds with the girl holding his hand. As he looked down at her, a tear rolled down her cheek.

"Baba, Mata," she whispered in a heart-rending voice. Then, wiping her face with a sleeve of her dress, she looked up into the Avadhut's face and said, "Let's go home now. They will come back soon."

A few minutes later, as they walked the return trail towards the cabin and even after the tearful and poignant moment, she was laughing and smiling in turns, chasing the butterflies and hiding behind trees to try and scare Ekanta, whom she acted towards as if they had always been together. The Avadhut occasionally feigned a scared demeanor at which she laughed with childlike abandon and the entire walk back to the cabin was spent in frolic and play.

The Avadhut reached the cabin just at dusk with Puspi in tow. After a few hours she had gotten tired and despite his encouragement to keep walking, had simply lain down next to the trail and fallen asleep. He then carried her the rest of the way home and, arriving there, placed her in her little bed while he looked around the kitchen area for food. There was, of course, no short supply and soon Ekanta had tea brewing, chapatis baking and a vegetable curry simmering over the hearth. The smell of food must have been more enticing than sleep, for just as the meal was ready, Puspi poked her head out of her little room.

"I'm hungry," was all she said.

The Avadhut placed two metal plates on the table and began to dole out small amounts onto them. Puspi took a chair at the table and waited silently and patiently for him to finish.

As he sat down, she asked, "Do you bless the food regularly like we do?"

"Oh yes," he replied, "most definitely. We must always thank the Lord for what is given to us out of His Grace."

"Yes," she agreed, and bowed her head.

The Avadhut bowed his head as well and after a few moments of silence, offered the blessing:

> May the good Lord and Divine Mother of the Universe
> bless our house, our home and our ashrama,
> our body, life, heart, mind and soul,
> our work and our spiritual efforts.
> Grant us pure love, pure knowledge, pure devotion,
> and bless this food. Om Harih Om Tat Sat."

After the prayer, Puspi looked up and smiled.

"That was nice," she affirmed.

Then she fell to eating and the Avadhut, hungry from his travels, did the same.

Puspi washed her own bowl after the meal.

"Will we meditate tonight before bedtime?" she asked.

"That is a wonderful idea," he replied. "Let us meet in the shrine before the altar in a few minutes."

Flashing another brilliant and momentary smile, she disappeared quickly into her room. Minutes later, the Avadhut and the little girl were seated in silence before the images of divinity on the family altar. After about fifteen minutes, the Avadhut heard the little girl stirring and opened his eyes.

"Are we done?" she said sweetly.

"Since we have traveled long this day," responded the Avadhut, "we shall conclude early tonight. Is there anything else?" he asked, anticipating her mood.

"Yes," she replied. "Baba always tells me a story about the saints, sages and Avatars and the rich kings, queens and princesses that they meet. Do you know any stories like that?"

The Avadhut sat still for a moment. Then, to her absorbing delight, he turned his attention on the little one and began to relate a story from the ancient scriptures.

"Have you heard of Hayagriva, little one?" he asked Puspi.

Wide-eyed, she only shook her head to mean no.

"He is the horse-faced god. Do you know who he is and how he got that way?" came the next question.

Somewhat anxiously and already entering into the spirit of the pending story, Puspi shook her head again.

"Well then listen closely," said the Avadhut, "for Hayagriva is none other than Bhagavan Himself, Lord Vishnu the Supreme!"

Puspi was now all ears and, having her full attention, Ekanta began to relate the somewhat obscure but famous story.

*"The Adideva Jaganath, Lord Vishnu himself, whom all the scriptures praise, who is stated to be the cause of all causes and upon whom all the devas depend, this very one lost His head one day!"*

A giggle escaped from the attentive Puspi at this beginning but a mock, semiserious look from the Avadhut silenced her quickly.

*"Yes,"* he continued, smiling, *"it is true, and the wonder of it is being related to you this evening as it was to the entire assembly of auspicious personages throughout history who love God as their sole refuge.*

*"After a ten-thousand year battle in which Vishnu destroyed*

*two evil daityas, the Lord became very tired and desirous of rest. Seating himself in a lotus position on a patch of soft grasses, he rested his head on his powerful bow, placing it on the front of the weapon with the bowstring lying flat but taut along the ground. In this secure position he soon fell fast asleep for what he thought would be a short nap. Of course, and as you probably know, when Vishnu sleeps, even for a day, it is a very long period in human reckoning, even lifetimes."*

Puspi nodded her assent and knowing that he still had her full attention, he went on.

*"Now, it seems that while Vishnu napped, and at that very moment, Indra Brahma, Shiva and other gods were commencing a sacrifice and became deeply involved in the ritual before too long. Realizing eventually that they would need Janardana's blessing on this sacrifice...*you do know that Janardana is another name for Vishnu, do you not?" Ekanta asked the girl.

"Yes," said the girl, decidedly.

"Very good," he replied.

*"Well, these gods journeyed to Vishnu's realm in Vaikuntha to consult the Lord of all sacrifices. When they arrived, however, they did not find Him there and were thus stymied in their purpose. Meditating deeply for a time, they came to know of His presence through their inner powers and went directly to the spot where He was sleeping.*

*"When they arrived, though, they were again perplexed to find the Lord in deep sleep and thus unavailable for consultation. Indra then said, 'Revered gods, if we do not finish this sacrifice there will be great and powerful negative ramifications. We must awaken the Lord Vishnu and get his blessing.'*

*"Lord Shiva then stood and spoke, saying, 'None of us must wake the Lord, for His anger will be swift and awful.'*

*"Hearing the words of his friends, Brahma, coming up with an idea, bent down and, saying some primeval mantras, created some white ants named Vamri and strew them on the ground. He then explained that he would have the white ants eat through the bowstring of Vishnu's weapon and, when it snapped, the Lord would naturally awaken from his slumber due to the noise."*

When Puspi heard of this plan in the story and imagined it in her mind, she could not hold herself back and burst forth in laughter.

"What is so funny?" the Avadhut asked.

"It is so funny," she countered. "They are funny and what they are planning is funny. But go on, Dada," she pleaded "tell some more."

Complying with her request, the Avadhut went on with his tale:

*"The gods approved of Brahma's plan and he then turned to the Vamri and ordered them to carry out his devising. But the king of the Vamri balked at this plan and said, 'Revered creator, we dare not do this thing. To awaken the Lord from his much needed rest is neither wise nor advisable. Besides, there is no gain in this for us. If there were some tangible advantage to this act then we may risk it since we are tiny and practically beneath Janardana's notice.'*

*"At this, Brahma said, 'We are performing a great sacrifice in the heavens. If this is successful then much Soma nectar will emerge. If you perform this act to our bidding, then you will receive a portion of this blessed nectar. Do you agree?' At this, the Vamri began hurriedly chewing on the bowstring in anticipation of their share of the bliss-filled nectar.*

*"After a short time, an amazing event took place. As the ants were chewing, gathered together on the Lord's mighty bow, they reached the last strand of the bowstring and it suddenly gave way with a sound that shook the three worlds. At that moment, the very ground upon which the devas stood rocked ferociously as the horrific sound reverberated across the vast spaces, sending all beings residing throughout the many lokas into a peak of fright. In the physical universe, the planets got extremely agitated and suns exploded. On earth the seas became swollen and overflowed their shores while huge waves pitched to and fro in a roiling tempest. Aquatic animals were terrified and land animals thundered across the various terrains in bewilderment and chaos. Winds surged and turned into tornadoes and hurricanes and the mountains shook and rained boulders in avalanches onto towns and villages. A dark haze immediately covered the sun, which sank quickly and unexplainably below the horizon. Everything in all the three worlds then turned to darkness.*

*"As the devas saw all of this, they became dumbstruck and confused. When the darkness passed and the air cleared, the*

*poor gods had more to worry about, for there, seated where he had been all along, was Vishnu, but his topmost portion — head, hair and crown — had completely vanished into thin air and none could see where it had gone. This extremely perplexing development threw the gods into an even more agitated condition. They, being bereft of their highest Lord, began to weep and wail and thereafter fell into a despondent mood. Bhrihaspati, the great teacher of the gods, seeing them in this state said, 'There is no use in this behavior. Instead, gather yourselves together and we shall use our intelligence to locate a solution. Success does not proceed through luck, but through one's exertions. Come, let us consider this situation.'*

*"Hearing this, Indra said in a fatalistic tone, 'What! Our Lord lies here in a headless condition and you are talking about luck and intellectual prowess! This is our fate and fate is superior over intellect, effort and exertions. We are lost due to our thoughtless actions and are doomed.' Brahma, listening to all of this and feeling greatly responsible, then became inspired and spoke with a view to harmonize these views.*

*"'Yes,' he said, 'it is true. Fate is inexorable. In days long gone and through the decrees of fate, Shiva once severed my own head. Again, you dear Indra, due to your fate, were once expelled from heaven and had to live in watery worlds amidst the lotuses, suffering miseries untold. What was it, though, that brought us relief from these various calamaties? We suffered but we also persevered and through our self-efforts in the form of austerities, we united with that which is superior to both exertion and fate. Do you remember, revered ones, what we have always done in times like this? Think and recall well! It is that which we must do now.'*

*"These words of hope from an inspired Brahma awakened the gods from their depressed stupor. With voices united they began to recite the names of the Divine Mother of the Universe called Mahamaya, Brahmavidya, Paraprakriti and others. Then, taking their seats in an auspicious circle, they began to call up the Vedas who were embodied amongst and between them, being parts of their inmost being. When the Vedas were then manifest there in that august assembly, the gods commanded them to recite the beneficial hymns of the most high Devi out loud*

and in praise of Her.   The Vedas then sang out these powerful hymns."

Eternal salutations to Thee, O Devi Bhagavati!
Thou art the animating power
behind the creation of the universe,
being beyond its triple-guna constituency.
You grant to the gods all that they desire
and guide the actions of human beings in the world .
Being the giver of all auspicious things
and the receptacle that contains them,
You are therefore present everywhere.
Thou art prana and the ruler over its movements.
Thou art also buddhi, shobha, kshama, shanti,
shraddha, medha, dhriti, smriti —
the essence of intelligence, abundance, splendor,
forgiveness, peace, faith, intelligence, resilience,
remembrance and many other qualities.

Besides this, you are the hidden subtle principle
residing in all the bija mantras
and the gracious force that benefits the three worlds.
The five elements, the creation and the gods
and goddesses that preside over it,
all are Thy parts while only You are the whole.
Though You comprise all parts,
You are also transcendent of the creation.
What a wonder You are, O Mother of the Universe.
No one can enumerate Your names and powers.
Therefore, with all our hearts as one
and our minds directed towards Thee,
we pay our obeisances to Thee eternally.

"After this potent hymn had risen up from the heart of the Vedas, embodied there amongst the gods, this ultimate repository of the sacred word began to offer up a plea for the granting of favors.   The Vedas therefore said, 'Oh Mother of the Universe, we, Thy votaries, know next to nothing.   Please notice our dilemma then, which is the loss of Sri Hari's blessed head.

*Are you testing Lord Vishnu? Is there something He or we need
to learn through this predicament? Did Janardana incur some
sin or is He working out some karma? Truly, Thou art the most
insightful One who can see into all causes. We make continual
pranams to Thee and ask Thee hopefully to reveal the solution
to this situation and return Vishnu's head to his body.'"*

Puspi stirred and the Avadhut looked over at her to ascertain
her state of alertness. She merely smiled at him and looked on
with her big eyes.

"Please tell me some more," she said endearingly. Ekanta then
went on with the conclusion of the story of Hayagriva.

*"When the great Devi heard these wonderful Sama hymns,
along with the pleas of the various gods, She became gracious
and thereafter a wondrous voice came forth, from where, no one
knew.*

*"'Oh gods, be free of fear. Come to your senses. You are immor-
tal parts of Me, why should you worry then? As far as the
reason for Vishnu's head disappearing, you may now hear.*

*"'Once, in the presence of His consort, Lakshmi Devi, Lord
Vishnu laughed for no particular reason. The beautiful Devi,
wondering at this, came to the conclusion that he had seen something ugly on her face. She could not understand the reason but
argued in her mind that possibly he had tired of her, or that
some other consort, more pleasing to him, was occupying his
mind. As she brooded over this small thing, she slowly became
angry and tamo guna possessed her.*

*"'When she next saw her Lord, and at that time being very
influenced by a fierce tamasic condition, she snapped at him,
exclaiming the words, "Let thy head fall off!" Though she said
this unthinkingly and while bereft of her proper senses, the
curse, spoken by one so intrinsically pure and perfect, could not
but come true. Therefore, by the womanly qualities contained
in the mode of tamasic shakti such as falsehood, false modesty,
craftiness, stupidity, impatience, greediness and harshness, this
horrible condition has come about. Lord Vishnu's head is now
lying at the bottom of the vast salt ocean, but do not worry. I
will retrieve it and affix it to his body once again.'*

*"The gods stood in awe of this powerful presence who was all-
knowing and all-seeing. As they listened further, the Supreme*

*Devi spoke again.*

"'There is another reason for this predicament. Listen and hear! In ancient times there was a powerful daitya who practiced austerities on the banks of the Sarasvati River. His name was Hayagriva, for he had a face that resembled a horse and looked unlike any other being in the three worlds. His practices were so powerful, being maintained for a thousand years, that I, Myself, went to him and appeared before him, attracted by his devotion. As he beheld Me, he prostrated and then with tears in his eyes, circumambulated Me fully chanting a hymn of praise. Pleased with this offering, I granted him any boon of his choosing. "Grant that I may be an immortal yogi," he asked Me, "invincible to both suras or asuras."*

"'Death is certain to all that are embodied,' I assured him, 'and that is the order of things in the universe. The violation of this inexorable rule never occurs. Therefore, Hayagriva, ask some other boon of Me.' Thinking well in his mind, he then said, "Oh Devi Bhagavati, if you will not grant me physical immortality then grant that I may never be killed by any other being than one whose face looks like mine." Hearing this strange request, I complied and gave him his wish and sent him home to his kingdom.*

"'Now, over many of these past ages, this daitya has become bloated with pride at his nearly deathless state. He has been causing much suffering and trouble to the gods and the sages as well. There has been no one in the three worlds who can kill him until now. From what I have said, do you see My plan?'*

"The gods stood dumbfounded at this turn of events and began to see the workings of a higher power in their present drama. As understanding dawned on their minds and faces, the Devi spoke out again, addressing the great Visvakarma.*

"'Visvakarma, you now cut the head from a horse and place it on the headless body of Vishnu. He will then rise up and destroy this evil demon for the ultimate good of the three worlds and all creatures dwelling there.'*

"Visvakarma did as he was told, encouraged by all the other gods present. A few days later, Bhagavan Vishnu in his Hayagriva form with a face like a horse, descended upon the evil daitya and slew him dead along with his entire army.*

*Afterwards, by the grace of the Divine Mother, Vishnu's origi-*
*nal head was restored and the gods completed their important*
*ritual. Therefore, this is the story of how Vishnu acquired the*
*name Hayagriva, the horse-faced one."*

The Avadhut looked over at Puspi, fully expecting her to be
asleep. To his surprise she was completely awake and smiling
brightly.

"That was so wonderful," she drawled, being fully delighted by
the story. "Do you know other stories like that one?" she asked.

"Oh yes, a whole host of them I expect," replied Ekanta.

"Then you can tell me more tomorrow."

Concluding the conversation in this fashion, she ran over to the
Avadhut and hugged him tightly.

"You are the best uncle I have ever had or that can ever be. I
knew you were coming, too, and I am so glad that you are here."

Saying thus she ran off into her little room and was soon fast
asleep.

Ekanta sat for a time, thinking back over the events of the past
few days. It had been his great good luck to be able to meet
Dharman and his family on the trail. The present situation was
truly a gift from the Divine Mother, for he was now able to
observe, firsthand, a child born of an illumined couple and raised
in an atmosphere of sanctity and spirituality. This was something
that was close to his heart for he had always believed that many
of the ills of the world would be naturally resolved if children were
given and taught the truths contained in the ancient scriptures.

As he thought about this issue, he remembered Puspi's cryptic
words regarding his coming. He wondered at the natural psychic
abilities of this child and her spontaneous spiritual demeanor. She
had no vast erudition and was completely artless. Her guileless
nature, completely untouched by the world and its jaded tendencies, was an inspiration to him already and reminded him of
teachings he had received when he was not much older than she.
Thinking back, he could still hear his mother's words in this regard
after he had visited the house of some local people who owned
and ran a business suspected of illicit dealings.

"Son," his mother told him seriously one day, "never frequent
the house of those people again. Merely by contact you may absorb
some of their bad habits, their insincerity and will thereby become

insensitive to and even intolerant of spiritual matters like they are."

"But Mother," he had complained, "I am not like them. How is it possible that they can influence me simply by going to their house?"

"You will have to trust my judgment in this matter, Ekanta," she responded. "We have seen what the vicissitudes of the world can do when they act on people's hidden weaknesses, not to mention young, impressionable minds."

After a short pause, she continued:

"I can even cite examples. Listen to me. The officer at the police station last year, after taking simple payoffs for personalized protection over certain properties of the outlying areas of the village, was then caught red-handed dealing with known dacoits of the province and got swept into a life of crime. Again, one local politician, previously known to be honest and forthright, was convicted of accepting bribes and was sent to prison after he began mixing with other corrupt officials. One vacillates towards what is represented by the company one keeps, Ekanta.

"You must retain your childlike innocence throughout your life, my son, and remain pure in the face of all the corruption that the world throws at you. Otherwise your spirituality will suffer and will not be given the chance to emerge and develop. Many people suffer this horrible malady without ever knowing the cause. I have seen it happen often. This lack of spiritual light caused by unsavory company is similar to a house that is poorly lit. If you walk about the village at night you can tell those families that are impoverished due to the dim light in the house. They are burning very little oil and have the wick on their one lamp trimmed to the extreme. Other houses are well lit and shine forth beautifully. Like this, a person who labors under the weights of the effects of bad influences has no inner light. They even look dismal and drab and their actions reflect this condition as well. In contrast, a person in possession of his or her true nature shines brightly. They have protected themselves from jadedness and worldliness. They are guileless and pure and their entire life is one continuous flow of balance and serenity."

Ekanta had listened well to his mother's advice. Shortly thereafter, he began to notice examples of what she spoke of that day. A friend of his, usually friendly and quiet, had begun to hang around some of the old men who frequented the more undesirable spots in the village.  Over the weeks that this occurred, Ekanta was surprised to see that his friend seemed to reflect many of the mannerisms and habits found in these men.  His speech turned coarse, his motions became abrupt and impatient and his actions were unbecoming of a boy from a pious family.  Once, when Ekanta had caught himself mimicking a particular mannerism of this boy, he became shocked at himself.  After that he began to avoid his old friend completely.

One day, he found his father alone and began to speak of this newly found awareness with regards to innocence and jadedness.

"Baba," the boy said, "Mother has opened my eyes to the dangers of frequenting bad and undesirable company.  It seems that, as we grow, certain influences are not good for us.  It is painful, though, to leave off contact with people who I used to care for and who change for the worse.  In fact, I am having a hard time finding truly good people now.  They all seem to have been tainted by the harsh ways of the world."

"Ah, my dear boy," the father commended, "you are learning the hard lessons of growing up at a very young age.  It is good.  Protect that small spark of purity inside of you with devotion, for it will grow into a bonfire of realization.  You will never regret detaching from people who sacrificed this spark of divinity in them for the allurements of the world.  In fact, you will be exceedingly glad that you took the pains to refrain from such company and engendered instead a taste for what is subtle and refined by way of spirituality."

"Father," the boy then asked, "where can I find people worth meeting and mingling with, who are pure and who have kept their spirituality alive?"

"Why," replied Ekanta's father, "that sounds like holy company.  In that case I want to introduce you to our local holy man, Yogindra Yogi, who lives in a cave in the mountains above our village.  You have seen him occasionally in town.  I have talked with him and we have agreed that when the time is right, you should hike up there and speak with him.  He will give you some training in the spiritual arts and merely by being near him you will get something tangible."

"Father," Ekanta had asked, "then this influence of company

also acts in the opposite way?"

"Yes, my boy," replied the father. "In those who have engendered the spirit of sanctity we find a power of purity that affects others. They can transmit some of what they have to us. It is a rare thing to find such a person and a great blessing to learn from one. In the case of the mountain yogi, he has not mingled with society for a long time. He has, therefore, awakened the sacred power within him, charged it with various spiritual disciplines, reserved it for spiritual purposes and stored it up over time. It comes out of such a being in the form of the light of refined intelligence, intangible to the senses, but nevertheless a palpable force."

"Is this the energy that I have heard speak of that illumined beings use for transforming the world, Father?" asked Ekanta.

"My son," replied his father, "the world does not need transforming, being exactly the way it is supposed to be. It is the Lord's own projection, His manifest power. Can there then be any flaw in it whatsoever? No, it is limited human consciousness under the influence of immature ego that needs this healing. The yogis, therefore, use this energy for transforming limited human awareness. This power has its gross and subtle manifestations. A person's state of purity and their inherent innocence or guilelessness has much to do with how this energy is managed throughout one's lifetime. But son, please go to the yogi and ask him for details. It is his special area of expertise."

Following his father's wishes and very much intrigued himself, Ekanta hiked to the low-lying hills the very next day. Starting at noon, it was three hours before he arrived at timberline and encountered a little snow. Following his father's directions, he traced his way to a particular mountain, higher than the others and found a huge cave there. Signs of a fire were to be seen near the mouth of the cave and Ekanta decided to sit there by the hot coals and wait. He then smeared some of the ash across his forehead in three streaks and sat patiently, awaiting the yogi's return.

He did not have long to wait, for within the hour an old, bearded man emerged from the cave. Catching sight of the young boy he stopped still and glared at him for several long moments. Then his external demeanor softened and an expression of pleasure came over his features.

*"You are the son of Aryaman and his pious wife Svarmani, are you not?"* he said in a deep and powerful voice which at once demanded respect.  The boy was amazed to hear these accurate words about his parents.

"Revered sir," he replied, "how did you know?"

*"I know all and see all,"* came the reply with all grandiose overtones.

"Truly?" returned Ekanta with awe and incredulity.

The yogi then laughed out loud, much to the surprise and chagrin of the young boy.  After he had stopped laughing, he stated:

*"Now, how can a mere man equipped with only five senses, a body and a brain know everything and see everything, especially when these vehicles are all inherently defective by nature?  Are you so gullible, boy?"*

Ekanta was caught somewhere between shame and laughter, for the yogi's presence was intimidating and his mirth was contagious.

Seeing the boy's dilemma, the old sage introduced himself.

*"I am Yogindra Yogi, but even you are all-knowing with regard to that information, is it not so?"*

Smiling, Ekanta said, "Yes sir, I do know that, but there is much else I am unconscious of and so I have come to you for greater clarification."

*"Then let's get started,"* said the yogi.  *"Here, break this wood into pieces for the fire.  The day is advancing and night will soon follow in due course.  We must be prepared for the sudden onrush of cold temperatures at these heights which come before dark falls, even though this is the temperate season."*

After the two had prepared the fire, they sat down cross-legged and faced each other.

*"First,"* the yogi said, *"I want you to meditate here, in this atmosphere, free of the world and its many distractions.  Close your eyes to earthly sights and shut down your thought process.  Dwell close to the Atman in your heart region for a time in this way and feel Its subtle power."*

As dusk fell around the two meditators, stars began to twinkle and the colors of sunset bathed the ethers in a glorious day's conclusion.  Ekanta was called out of his meditation by the crackling of wood being devoured by flames.  Warmth from the fire reached him and he drew closer to thaw out his backside and feet which had become cold from contact with the ground and exposure to the mild evening wind that raced up the slopes. After the fire was well underway and burning brightly, the yogi sat down again and gazed upon the young boy. Ekanta felt that he had been transported to some ancient and primordial time when illumined beings populated the earth in great numbers, inhabiting the mountains and forests to meditate on Absolute Reality.

*"What has been occurring in your mind of late, Ekanta. Your father told me that you were an introspective young man given to periods of deep thought and naturally disposed towards discrimination and solitude. Tell me what has brought you here today, for I am sure that this is the first of many meetings we shall enjoy."*

"I certainly hope so," replied Ekanta, "for I feel very elevated here."

*"Oh, you are,"* replied the yogi, tongue in cheek. *"You must be at least four-thousand feet in the air tonight!"*

The boy laughed, more at the yogi's expression than his jocular remark. Still, this light joke relaxed the atmosphere and put Ekanta at ease. He was then able to articulate his question more readily.

"Revered sir, recently I have had some awakening about the effects of company, both good and bad, on the people of the earth. One of my friends, by frequenting a place of ill-repute, has been transformed into an unfortunate example of what is said and done there. I knew him as an innocent and sweet boy. Now, he is changed. My father and mother, however, are unlike anyone I have ever met or seen, being entirely holy and pure, yet they have brushed up against the world for several decades. My first question regards how to account for this difference and further, I want to know how the transmission of spirituality occurs through contact with illumined beings and how it can be utilized? Why are some beings holy, some beings insensitive and others completely unholy? Can you answer these questions for me please?"

Yogindra Yogi smiled broadly to hear these astute queries come from the mouth of such a young boy. Inside his mind that night, he thought that his many years of silence and withdrawal from the world were now being rewarded in the form of a young boy who could comprehend and utilize the special teachings meant for those who had grown tired of and transcended the mundane matters of relative existence. Now that he had ascertained the level at which this new charge of his was operating, he could begin to fill him with some of the beneficial teachings he had gleaned over so many long and fruitful years of sadhana.

*"Innocence is corrupted by two main things, my boy,"* came the yogi's answer. *"The recurrence of past impressions and exposure to the world without the protection of a spiritual discipline that reveals Truth. In obverse terms, innocence is retained by those who successfully locate and destroy negative samskaras in their subconscious mind and who remain in touch with their inner Self despite all of the impositions of relative existence. In the case of your friend, he was led into contact with jaded people in an unsavory atmosphere. This has triggered his own buried memories which have influenced him in an adverse way. Perhaps, through contact with the good impressions that are also there in his mind, he will perceive his misdirection and place the boat back on course before it sinks in the ocean of worldliness. Otherwise, this is precisely what happens in the case of evil and corrupted beings.*

*"You yourself could act as a medium for his resurrection in this matter, but you must be careful not to take in the negativities existing there yourself. You see, mental samskaras are like germs. They can get transmitted. Therefore, before you deal with such people who are afflicted with the disease of worldliness, you must inoculate yourself with the medicine of holy company and sadhana. Then you will contract no ill effects.*

*"With regards to good impressions, the force that causes that is the goodness in others which comes into contact with the inherent good that is already there within those who have garnered positive thoughts and deeds in the past, both in respect to this lifetime and others. This is a relatively simple matter of cause and effect. There should be no confusion in it. It follows a natural course of like attracting like."*

After thinking for a moment, the yogi added drew another correlation:

*"In the case of your parents, a twin force of good has come together, making the outcome all the more powerful. They are remarkable people and their uniqueness is accented all the more*

*by the unfortunate condition of those around them. For those with eyes to see, that is, for those who are jewelers, such a diamond is of considerable value."*

"Revered yogi," said the boy, "you have explained how both these positive and negative forces get born and have their outcome. Is there a way by which you can describe how the energy of positivity can be brought to bear on human awareness? I want to purge myself of imperfections and help others as well."

*"That is a wise choice, my son," replied the yogi. "This is a delicate matter though. Be patient and I will attempt to explain a bit of the art."*

The yogi closed his eyes for a time and was lost in thought. Soon, he came out of his short reverie and became somewhat animated.

*"I know what it is that you are seeking. You need to find out the intricacies of the merging of pairs of opposites, especially pertinent to spirituality. It will be a great tool for you in times to come. Remember that I said that your parents combine a dual force of positive samskaras in their relationship in this incarnation. Well, the result, in an external sense, is you! The child is the result of merging the dual forces residing in male and female principles. In another way, though, with regards to their own realization, that light which shines through them is the internal manifestation of the same force. Allow me to explain.*

*"Within every man and woman is a powerful spiritual force. It both indicates the presence of Truth and allows for the revelation of It through the process of evolution. Its external manifestation, called Vindu, is twofold, and they are called shukra and maharaja, the male semen and the female fluid discharged from the ovaries. Males contain the female force of maharaja in them in an undeveloped condition and females also have the male shukra in them as potential. When these two are combined and the energy sent forth, a child is produced and this is the external result of union. When any being, refraining from releasing these fluids, stores up the energy and sublimates it within, a state of blissful transcendence occurs. This is called Soma, which has been mentioned by the ancients with regards to that sublime nectar that comes from sacrifice and, when imbibed, causes ecstasy. This is a subtle internal effect of the energy of refined Vindu.*

*The blessed scriptures state:*

'This powerful Vindu is of two types, Shukra and Maharaja.
Skukra is white, denoting Shiva,
and Maharaja is red, symbolizing Shakti.
Shukra is the moon, Maharaja the sun.
Through their combining within by yogic practices,
union, though difficult, is attained
and one experiences the soma state leading to samadhi.

"*So, my boy,*" stated the yogi after his short discourse. "*You can see how subtle and mysterious is this inner realm of practice and transformation.   That same uprising of sublimated current, on its internal pilgrimage to the crown of the head, produces an emanation that radiates from the very person of an illumined being.   Different beings, due to their good merit and positive karmas, then experience contact with such a person and receive a transmission.   Some see an aura of light around the luminary and are amazed and inspired.   Others behold that being as an embodiment of divinity and experience visions. Others are transported within themselves and have spiritual moods while some are lifted to the portals of transcendence through an inert state of meditation.*

"*The emanation that arises from the pure yogic state is called tejas, a subtle light that transforms.   Ojas is another name for the stored up power which effects the release of Mother Kundalini into higher regions.   The experience of temporary bliss which comes just before this release is called udghata.   It is a precursor to true spiritual awakening.   When a man or woman is thus awakened, they act as blessings on the entire world.   Most of them are not even aware of their power and just radiate naturally.   When we come into the presence of such as these, we feel blessings, grace and upliftment without ever knowing how it happens.   If beings knew the process of awakening and also understood its natural progression, there would be less mystery-mongering in the field of spirituality and fewer charlatans to confuse and distort public awareness.   You shall hear more about this later in your training.*"

As it turned out, Ekanta had indeed learned more on the subject, but not from Yogindra. Soon after this, additional holy company was granted to him through the Mother's boundless Grace in the form of the two vanaprastin teachers who became his formal gurus by initiatory rites. The Babaji and the Mataji instructed Ekanta in many of the secrets of spiritual science and Kundalini Shakti was no exception. One night, while remembering his earlier conversation on the subject with Yogindra Yogi, Ekanta had asked his guru for more information about it.

"Revered sir, I have been informed about the Vindu, its two types called shukra and maharaja and its sublimation to higher centers. The resultant light of refined energy that emanates from the illumined ones has also been explained in part to me as an effect of this called tejas. I sometimes see this light in you and Mataji, or feel a palpable energy coming off of you that is most wonderful. I am attracted by it and love you both even as I treasure my parents. Still, I do not understand what it entails and how it works, though I do desire to know. What can you tell me about it?"

"*My dear Ekanta,*" his guru explained, "*there is much to know in this life and you are young. What to speak of the vast worldly knowledge, this subtle spiritual wisdom is unknown to most, and Kundalini Shakti, the most enigmatic and refined of energies that is the matured result of successfully combining the four main yogas, is even more perplexing to understand.*"

"Guruji," Ekanta had pleaded, "surely you must know something of it, for you shine with its light! Therefore, do not hold this knowledge back from me due to my young age or for any other reason, but tell me what you know."

Smiling on his sincere young devotee, the teacher complied:

"*Much of what we know of this sacred phenomenon has been lost in time, Ekanta. Now, in some regards, we are rediscovering what it is and rewriting the information for those who desire to know. This process will take several centuries, especially in the spiritually arid climate of this particular age. I can only relate to you what I and the Mataji have gleaned from many years of practice in a science that demands lifetimes of study to appreciate, let alone fully comprehend.*"

"Dear sir, that will suffice and I will be so grateful to hear it."

"*Very well, dear boy,*" stated the guru, "*listen well and I shall try to describe concisely what I understand.*

*"The emanation of tejas from the holy ones is a vibration. This vibration, too, has its external and internal energy, just as Vindu does. What we feel from those high beings as outward spiritual force is only a fragment of what is there and that they use, both consciously and naturally, to inspire and uplift those who strive and who suffer. The inward part of that force gets utilized too, both for their own continuing realization and for training others who may be able to imbibe much more than just external tejas.*

*"You see, Ekanta, many come in contact with the holy and that is their good fortune, but what they get from those meetings is enough for them and they vacillate away from these profound centers of light and use what they received for various purposes. This type of transmission wears off and only goes so deep. There is, on the other hand, a type of aspirant that commits fully to spiritual life and, after selecting an appropriate guru, settles in to learn the powerful inner secrets that this supreme lifestyle can offer. Herein is where we find spiritual transmission in its fullest manifestation, among those who can inject Brahma-jnana and those who are making themselves fit to receive It."*

The guru paused again, as he often did when considering an abstruse subject. Then he continued on, much to the young aspirant's satisfaction.

*"When Kundalini is fully awake and active, speaking in limited human terms, She appears in Her four aspects called Kriyavati, Varnamayi, Kalatma and Vedhamayi. These are contacted and known through the three avenues of bhakti, jnana and yoga. The manifestations of these yogas can be subcategorized into four other divisions of hatha, mantra, laya and raja yogas. Kundalini covers them all and is therefore often called Mahayoga. Perfection in this comprehensive endeavor requires the practice of all the yogas and comes to fruition through the help of an adept — the guru. What is seen in such a wonder is a combination of Vedic Truth, Tantric practice and Yogic realization. Such a teacher will engender love or devotion in the student, for it is the bhakti path blended with the transformative path of yoga that assists towards Self-realization. Knowledge, or Jnana Yoga, also proceeds smoothly with the aid of devotion to God and guru and the final grace of meditation*

*signified through the practice of Raja Yoga is not far behind in this series. The powerful Shakti courses upwards naturally in the compelling atmosphere of this combination of practices."*

"Revered guru," Ekanta broke in, "you mentioned the four aspects of the Mother Shakti. I would love to hear more about them."

*"And so you shall, my thirsty student,"* answered the preceptor. *"Along with this mention I also included the four subcategories of yoga. The four aspects correspond to the four subcategories as follows.*

*"Kriyavati is the aspect of Kundalini Shakti that manifests on the physical plane. Therefore one can see the connection with the hatha element in yoga. 'Ha' denotes the sun and 'tha' the moon. These two symbolize the union of the ida and pingala nerves. It is not physical exercises in the ordinary sense that are involved here. The illumined one who knows the force of Kriyavati does not practice exercises but instead manifests all the usual results of hathayoga such as asana, mudra and pranayama in a spontaneous fashion. It is therefore that we see great spiritual beings manifesting and expressing powerful truths far beyond the realm of self-effort.*

*"Those who practice asana and breathing exercises with a view to awakening Kundalini, then, do not comprehend the system rightly. Devotion and Wisdom are Her all-attracting desires. All manner of twisting and turning of the body or the bellowslike huffing and puffing of the lungs may very well bring some minor occult powers into possession, but they will accomplish nothing to attract Mother Kundalini upwards to the crown chakra. More often than not, a preoccupation with asana and pranayama accomplishes little more than dizziness and perspiration, which are then mistaken for spiritual states engendered by intense sadhana. Only love combined with Brahmajnana can affect Mother's appearance, for the Divine Mother is a fully conscious spiritual presence, not a being attracted and attached to the body and the vital force like limited human beings.*

*"The three following subyogas aid greatly in awakening. Varnamayi is the appearance of Mother Kundalini in the realm of speech. Therefore, mantrayoga is utilized to effect spiritual*

*awakening and ascension. Truly, it is Kundalini Shakti sport-
ing as Sarasvati through the marvelous illumined yogi that
accomplishes success in mantrayoga. The one in whom Varnamayi is awake has great knowledge of the sacred word in terms
of scriptural wisdom. Mantras are also known to such a one
and can be transmitted to others effectively. Divine discourse
is always flowing from this luminary and hymns, sacred music
and devotional songs are ever in the mind and on the tongue.
What is more, the sounds of nature, including insects and animals, are clear and understandable in their root meanings to
the mantrayogi or mantrayogini. This yoga is also often called
Shabda Yoga. The comprehension of the sacred syllable Aum and
all of its significance is also part and parcel of this realization.*

*"Kalatma, Ekanta, is connected with the psychic center on
the plane of the mind. She is greatly internalized and deals
with the dissolving of external manifestations into a more
subtle state. Therefore, we have the layayoga phase of Mother
Kundalini's ascent and sport. Whereas Varnamayi is concerned
with the names and forms of the sacred word, Kalatma is
involved with the various phases of time and the subtle principles of the creation and the different lokas. It can be seen that
Kriyavati prepares the body mechanism for the upward rise of
Mother Kundalini and detaches the prana and mind from the
physical sheath while Varnamayi and Kalatma then aid in the
realm of the mind and intellect.*

*"The fourth shakti, Vedhamayi, is transcendent and works in
the realm of peace and light. After layayoga has occurred, that
is, the dissolving of the mind's thoughts and concepts, the
rajayoga stage is attained which is the highest place of ascent
where Mother Shakti meets and merges with Her Lord Shiva. All
six spheres have then been pierced and the subtle Kundalini
energy then merges in the crown at the top of the head called
Sahashrara. Great ecstasy is experienced — true love, authentic freedom, absolute knowledge — proceeded by one or several
of six conditions. Blissful pleasure, trembling of the body, fresh
power, intoxication, sleep and the merging of consciousness into
Itself, these are the results of the newly awakened Kundalini
sporting as Vedhamayi.*

*"Now, Ekanta, you have a short description of this most*

*involved and complicated of spiritual sciences. There is an infinite amount of other information but one should always be about trying to please the Divine Mother so that She will rise up and sever all the bonds of Maya. She is the ultimate transformational power. It is She who shines through the illumined. It is She that transmits and She is also transmitted from the guru to the disciple. She is the consummate holy company, therefore the yogis always meditate on Her in their hearts, allowing no one else to enter in.*

*"Therefore, know that when you receive something from your associations with illumined beings, that you are getting the transmission of the Mother Kundalini Shakti and that it is coming through a primary and secondary vehicle. Her aspects are the primary transmitters and the pure, innocent and radiant mind of the guru is the secondary channel. One cannot get the wine to one's lips without the vessel. The gurus and enlightened beings are very great, therefore, and all that they have gone through to receive God's Grace, including their trials, strivings, insights and realizations, radiate from them with tremendous power and enter into the sincere seeker who loves and serves devoutly. One should never take them for granted, then, and must be very careful not to offend them. It is therefore that Sri Krishna states in His celestial song:"*

You will receive enlightenment by bowing before your guru,
inquiring of him the secrets of spiritual life,
serving him faithfully and assisting all living beings.
It is the wise, beloved, who will transmit the essence to you.

Seeking and possessing this precious treasure, Dhananjaya,
you will never again stray from the true path again.
Ignorance and delusion will become a thing of the past,
From that moment onward, the entire creation will be yours,
and you will perceive no difference between us.

The Avadhut awoke the next morning to soft fingers playing on his face. Opening his eyes he saw Puspi, entirely naked and innocent of the fact, gazing down at him. As he raised his hand to scratch his face where she had tickled him, she giggled and smiled mischievously.

"Where is my breakfast?" she said suddenly, a look of serious-ness quickly transforming her features.

"It will not be long in coming," replied the Avadhut. "Why don't you get ready and I will call you."

Scampering away to her room, she disappeared inside and Ekanta rose to prepare their meal.

Two days passed by in relative bliss. The odd pair — wandering renunciate and life-loving child — enjoyed each other's company immensely and became fast friends. Each night the Avadhut told Puspi another story from the wealth of tales contained in the Mahabharata, the Ramayana and other spiritually-based texts. In the daytime, the two would walk out in the woods, the very forest through which the Avadhut had passed to arrive at the cabin of this remarkable family, and at the edge of which he had once seen Puspi playing with flowers.

Ekanta found Puspi to be entirely fearless and free of all sense of time. She truly did not know her own limitations and though still a child, understood everything she was told on an intuitional level. This astounding fact endeared her to the Avadhut all the more until he found himself entirely dedicated to her, not just in the sense that a father might love and protect a daughter, but also out of reverence and worship. The more he saw of her, the more he realized what a pure and powerful manifestation of the Goddess was residing in her.

One afternoon, as she sat in the forest, winded after running around for hours and with her mind in a slightly abstracted mood, Ekanta felt compelled to prostrate before her and to offer flowers at her feet. She smiled shyly but offered no resistance or com-plaint. After he was through she took the flowers in her little hand, smelled them and then tied them into her hair. Moments later she had entirely forgotten the incident and was running to play in the stream that flowed nearby. As she waded out into the water, the Avadhut, watching from a distance, saluted her.

"I pay my obeisances to you, the child, who has taught me in the most unassuming and natural way the secrets of purity and inno-cence and of their intrinsic connection with true spirituality. You are truly a teacher of a very high order, never to be forgotten and always to be cherished. Victory to the Mother Shakti, forevermore."

It was during the next afternoon that they caught sight of Dharman and Gramani coming out of the woods and into the clearing near the stream. The Avadhut pointed them out to Puspi.

"There are your parents, do you see them?"

With a shriek of joy and excitement, the little girl vaulted to her feet and within seconds was running full speed across the field towards her parents. Ekanta smiled broadly to see this demonstration of love and affection and watched until he saw her melt into their arms. Minutes later, the three came near to the cabin and Dharman and Gramani saluted the Avadhut.

"You have come at last," he said to them as they embraced. "It is good timing, for I have just finished preparing the meal and it is nearly ready to eat."

"Praises be unto the Divine Mother," replied Dharman. "The long journey has made me hungry."

"We are so grateful for your presence, dear friend," said Gramani. "Without you here I do not know what may have transpired."

"The pleasure and privilege has been all mine," answered Ekanta. "No thanks are necessary. Puspi and I have lived these past few days and nights in subtle bliss, have we not?" he said, turning towards the little girl.

"Yes Mother, and I have some stories I want to tell you that he told me," she replied excitedly.

She did not wait until the three grown-ups were settled either, but began to relate the story of Hayagriva, the horse-faced god, as they went into the cabin.

The Avadhut stayed for three more days due to the special circumstances. Then, he felt the urge to be moving on. Dharman and Gramani, though disappointed to see him go, knew of his life and how he lived. Puspi, however, would not hear of his going and raised a horrible fuss, the first sign of any unhappiness Ekanta had ever seen in her.

After she had calmed down a bit, she went to her room and wept silently. Ekanta was grieved to see this and he too was not fond of the idea of being without her. He wondered at this condition in himself and was careful to examine it for signs of inadvertent attachment. He concluded that it was a kind of attachment, that he had fallen under the influence of deep affection for her but that his yogic training could easily handle this. Besides, he thought, she is both a manifestation of the Goddess and my teacher as well. Thinking thus, he went to her room and called her to him.

After saying farewell to Dharman and Gramani and promising them another visit within a year or two, the Avadhut took Puspi by the hand and the two childlike beings walked together to the edge of the forest. All across the field, Puspi acted as though they were going on one of their walks together. She talked as if nothing was going to change, pointing to the deer and the birds and keeping up a continual stream of conversation. As they neared the edge of the forest, though, she became pensive, as if mentally pushing away something that she did not want to face.

The Avadhut felt this mood coming over her and finally stopped and turned to her.

"Dearest one, it grieves me to have to part with you."

At these words, Puspi burst into fresh tears.

"Why do you have to go?" she pleaded. "She said you would come and now you are going. I cannot stand this."

"I know," the Avadhut tried to console her, "but I will be back in a year's time. We shall then continue our sport. Besides, I must go forth to different areas of this country and collect more stories for your little ears. You have literally sucked me dry of them."

This promise brightened Puspi's demeanor and she giggled.

"Really," she said, "you will tell me more stories about the saints, sages, gods and goddesses?"

"Surely I will," affirmed the Avadhut. "I will make it a point to gather them in great abundance on my travels and I will have some stories of my own to relate as well. We shall then have such fun and laughter together."

These statements changed the girl's mood entirely so that another amazing transformation came over her. Ekanta saw light coming off of her face and body and felt something akin to bliss radiating from her person. She then ran to him and hugged him tightly. The feeling that came over him at her touch on this occasion was indescribable. Before he could determine what was occurring, she had let go of him and was running away across the field.

She never stopped to look back until she had reached the door of the cabin. Then, with the Avadhut gazing across the field at her, she raised a small arm and waved her hand at him slowly and deliberately. Ekanta felt it as a sign of benediction and saluted her profoundly. It was the Divine Mother of the Universe standing there in Her aspect of the innocent child, blessing him. At that moment in time, the words of the Mataji, his female vanaprastin guru, echoed in his consciousness.

*"Spirituality is everything, my dear. It is true life to those of us experiencing this apparent reality called earthly life. Our true nature, Ekanta, is pure and perfect and the teachings of God, guru and scripture confirm this. We are like the child who is sometimes delighted, sometimes despondent, but never attached. Our Divine Mother dwells here in us as our true essence, but ultimately is transcendent of this earth and of time and space. There are those who vainly strive to trap Her in this constricted plane of life and death, but She is ever uninvolved. Dwelling as the substance of Pure Consciousness, untainted by any and all of the many diverse aspects of relativity, She is Supreme, always one with Brahman. She has, though, left many wonderful reminders of Herself here in this realm. Of these, living beings are the most precious. If we know our own essence we will see that same essence in others. Then, balance and harmony will prevail and we will remain in constant communion with the Blessed Lord and Divine Mother of the Universe."*

Moments later, Ekanta was once again lost in the deep, dense confines of the forest with trees surrounding him on all sides. Though he missed his three friends, it felt wonderful to be moving across the face of the sacred earth again. Hiking all day, he camped that night in silence and solitude at the edge of a bluff. As evening, with its encroaching darkness, swept over everything, drawing him into a realm of peace and mystery, he thought back on all the teachings and gurus he had been fortunate enough to be blessed with. Minutes later, infinitely inspired, he was immersed in deep meditation, poised on the brink between the Absolute and the relative, his deepening mood gradually obliterating all such distinctions to finally rest, peaceful and serene, in the perfect equipoise of yoga.

# Appendix

# Guru Tattva

As was mentioned in the introduction of this book, the Avadhut's twenty-four teachers in nature were not formal gurus. They were not the traditional kind that accept disciples and undergo the rigors of tending to spiritual organizations in order to bring uplifting teachings to the public. However, as can be seen, Ekanta's formal gurus are all-important and intimately present throughout his life. A traditional religious teacher instigates positive change in individual and collective human awareness and we can see from this basic sketch of Ekanta's life what great importance the formal guru plays in awakening the mind from the sleep of ignorance by eradicating delusion. After this preliminary work is accomplished, which amounts to an end of suffering in ignorance, the disciple can get down to the business of living a divine life while the guru can give further and higher teachings according to the growing level of comprehension in the disciple. With this in mind, the following insights into the nature of Guru are given.

Guru Tattva, the very principle of wisdom transmission in the universe, and Guru Yoga, adherence to the instructions of the beloved guide with surrender, self-effort and devotion, lead the student to a deeper understanding of just who Guru is and what Guru represents. Moreover, one uncovers and recognizes that eternal presence in oneself and learns to follow the dictates of the infallible Guru principle within, spoken of by all great luminaries. This conduces to peace and bliss for, knowing that the Lord is present in the universe of name and form as an eternal companion in the sport and as compassionate guide through all trials and tribulations, a sense of subtle bliss and calm equanimity descends. From a calm, detached and contented state of mind, clear vision proceeds and applying that clarity to the presence of God as Guru, we glean many valuable lessons that have been forgotten or overlooked in today's polluted spiritual climate.

The problems facing the world today with regards to spiritual life — which the great luminaries believe to be the solution to all of life's problems—are legion. They can be classed, however, in relation to Guru Tattva, into two basic subdivisions. First, there is the problem of worldliness, a term used to denote materialism, complacency, jadedness, insensitivity, mundane convention and a whole host of other descriptions. This is the Vyavaharika path spoken of by Vedanta teachers and is the way followed by most beings in this age. In it, there is little or no room for God, unless God is seen as secondary to pleasure, security and individual concerns. For the most part, this path and its adherents perceive the physical universe along with the present lifetime as the only Reality, disregarding any thought about past or future existences or other realms or states of being.

Secondly, there is the outright antagonism of egocentric beings full of pride and lust for power. These asuric (demonic) beings, temporarily under the destructive influence of negativity, eschew what is good and spiritual and go out of their way to cause havoc among the ranks of those who are engendering peace, love and goodwill in themselves and in others. Guru Tattva is, to them, an evil that must be either destroyed or held at bay for as long as possible in order to enjoy dominion over the world of name and form.

Strangely enough, though anything is possible in this age of spiritual slumber, these two paths are not so clear cut or distinct from one another as they seem. The former seems to be comprised of people who simply prefer to live their lives without acknowledging a Creator or a Divine presence. They simply ensconce themselves in all that the material world has to offer with no thought for the morrow and have no desire to contemplate a deeper meaning or purpose of life. The beings following the latter way have similar characteristics, but have an actual aversion to the idea of God and Guru.

Where these two "paths" blend, we find an intermingling of

disturbing patterns  that undermines much of the potential good that spiritual beings attempt to do for us.  Our political leaders, for instance, seem to be adherents of the first path, having little or nothing to do with anything resembling spiritual life as the illumined see it.  That is, they profess to be pious or "God-fearing" but their lives and actions reflect a sad condition that is spiritually undernourished and immature.  Even if dualistic religion were enough to sustain a healthy spiritual life which, as practiced today, it is not, these beings would not be able to live up to the relative truths and practices contained therein and would simply continue to involve themselves with fame, power, money and sensual satisfaction for personal or ulterior motives.

Even more deplorable and frightening is the wayward tendency of such beings, placed in positions of power, to be seduced by the dangerous enticements of relative existence so that, in actuality, they begin to be secret exponents of the negative path.  In other words, they are not just worldly beings pursuing material comforts and benefits in simple and naive fashion, but become addicted to such things and begin to grasp after them and take to covetousness as a rule.  At the level of world politics, this creates beings who, though they outwardly profess to be law-abiding and moralistic members of society are in actuality, nothing less than negative forces acting for selfish and corrupt reasons.

This pretension, being an effective facade that covers all nefarious doings, is a most dangerous deception.  From positions of power, and these are operative in both church and state, beings of deceived and demonic influence masquerading as beneficent leaders in religion and government, can effectively control the influx of that which influences the public life in general.  They also distort and deter specialized or esoteric information destined to be given to the masses for their worldly and spiritual benefit.  This information is actually spiritual transmission in the form of subtle vibration which is a sort of mental composite of all that illumined beings have accomplished and realized in life.

It may be asked how these beings resist the positive forces of beneficent beings and obscure the presence and emanation of subtle spiritual vibrations.  These negative powers, like the asuras of ancient Vedic religion, have mixed qualities.  Unlike the incarnate evil called the devil proposed by contemporary fundamentalist Christians, the asuras are possessed of some good attributes as well. Since they have focused their awareness on certain attainments, this very concentration has brought them certain abilities which they use for selfish purposes. These abilities are called occult powers in spiritual circles and their effects have a distorting influence on individualized consciousness. Statesmanship, politics, the military, corporate business — these areas of worldly existence provide fit vehicles for the amassing of power and wealth and are therefore perfect for the exercising of an asuric being's powers. These powers are detrimental to the way of spirituality taught by Guru. Therefore, a profound difference is noticed between Guru—the Wisdom power manifesting in dedicated human teachers—and so-called world leaders or teachers.

Before delving deeper into the eternal and ever-blessed subject of Guru, a few more mentions should be made about God and the world. In essence, the two are not different, yet to hear some spiritual teachers talk about the world, one would think that the two will never meet. In the Sanatana Dharma of the ancient Rishis, an eternal and illustrious pathway to Divine life and Ultimate Reality, we find some definite answers to the problem of duality in all its aspects. The Rishis held two ideals simultaneously: one, that of the common good for all living beings with regards to material well-being and bodily and mental health and the other, admittedly the most prominent and of the utmost importance, the realization of Atman and Its intrinsic connection with Brahman. The Peace Invocations of the Vedas are replete with sacred assertions to this effect.

> There is peace in the sky, there is peace on earth.
> There is peace in the heavens, there is peace in the world.
> There is peace in the waters, there is peace on land.
> There is peace with the plants,
> animals, flowers, insects and herbs.
> There is peace with men
> and peace with women and children.
> There is peace with the gods and peace with the goddesses.
> May this all-pervading peace enter into us
> and permeate us to the very core of our being.
> Om peace, peace, peace.

O gods, may we with our ears hear what is auspicious;
may we with our eyes see what is auspicious.
While praising the gods with perfect health
may we enjoy a life that is beneficial to ourselves
and to others.
Om peace, peace, peace.

May we chant in praise of sacrifice
and sing in praise of the Lord of sacrifice.
May divine blessings be upon us.
May peace be unto the whole human race.
May healing, well-being and prosperity abide among us.
Om peace, peace, peace.

May all the gods and the all-pervading Vishnu
be propitious to us and grant us earthly welfare
and spiritual bliss.
Reverent prostrations to Brahman,
to Vayu who is verily the perceptible Brahman.
Thou art what is right, what is true, what is best.
May the Universal One preserve me.
May that One preserve my teacher.
May Brahman protect me and my guru.
Om peace, peace, peace.

O Supreme One, grace my limbs with strength.
May my speech, vital force, eyes, ears
and all my senses expand in capacity.
The Upanishads rightly declare that all existence is Brahman.
May I never deny Brahman
and may Brahman never deny me.
Let there be no rejection of Brahman by me, ever.
May all the virtues cited in the Upanishads
reside within me,
I who am devoted to the Atman.
Om peace, peace, peace.

It is encouraging and inspiring to know that there was a period
in human history where these two ideals — earthly success and

spiritual attainment—were realized and enjoyed. We should not, however, make the mistake of thinking that it was easy of attainment. The foundation of this twin ideal was based upon living a spiritual life in the world. This requires sadhana, spiritual practice and mental discipline and the Rishis exerted such self-effort for hundreds of years in order to purify the mind and realize That which is eternal. Here, an interesting and crucial distinction comes to light.

The universe, relatively speaking, is not eternal, but passes through changes and upheavals that mark it as a transitory or ephemeral realm. What is more, it is insentient, not imbued with Consciousness but is instead a derivative of Consciousness. What is eternal, then, according to those who have effected sadhana and come to realize the nature of all things, is Brahman alone—Pure Consciousness, Absolute. As a reflection is not different than the medium that it is reflected in, but is nonetheless a passing phase of that, so too is the universe a reflection of or a superimposition over Brahman and one with It.

In the final evaluation, the universe has its own reality. It is real only as a facet of Brahman, a finite expression of Its infinite expanse. The Peace Invocation before the Ishavasyopanishad clarifies and explains this nicely:

> What is visible is infinite.
> What is invisible is also infinite.
> Out of the infinite, the finite has come,
> yet being infinite, only infinite remains.
> Om peace, peace, peace.

Knowing all of this in proper perspective provides an important key for opening the many multidimensional doors of homogenous existence. At every door there is a guide, all of which are expressions of one, all-pervasive Guru. The universe would have neither sentiency nor order without the inherent presence of Guru in and throughout everything. The person or persons that deny this principle suffer in body and mind, going round the wheel of birth and death inexorably, in ignorance of their true nature and unaware of their underlying and essential relationship with Brahman.

This is, of course, their choice. In a world where relative free will is operational and where the sense of separation from God is strong due to the prominence and pervasiveness of the unripe and immature ego, beings go forth into life uneducated and uninformed about Guru within. As a result, the maladies of life, many wrapped up with the seed-forms contained within the sprouting layers of the unillumined mind, emerge and cause havoc and suffering. The manner in which unenlightened beings, both individually and collectively, as a society and its members, deal with these unwanted problems, often creates more of the same, compounding an already volatile situation. Far from finding solutions to the original root discrepancy and ending its repetitive cycle, most beings waste precious time fighting an unending series of secondary and related problems. Instead of the divinely oriented existence that God intended, then, human beings experience a caricature of true life. Thus does worldly life gain prominence over spiritual life in the minds of living beings.

The divinely intended life mentioned here, proceeds under the guidance of Guru, always and ever. Even those who are spiritually oriented, if they denounce Guru and opt to follow their own way, are still dependent on the inner guide which is simply Guru in another form. Guru is not merely a person of extraordinary capabilities or even God in human form. Guru is not found only in Ishvara, the Cosmic Being, either, unless one defines Ishvara as the totality of all created things.

In actuality, Guru is there from the inception of the creation and is anterior to it as well. As the energy that guides and facilitates —God's own presence in subtle form—Guru is there in the seed of a tree, guiding it to its fullest growth and expression. A flower opens at the proper time and with all inherent portions intact and operable due to Guru's guidance and overseership. What to speak of the minute phases of the creation, the cosmic laws themselves are put in place and made functional because of Guru. Even without the parents, the child would eventually walk on its own and that is due to Guru dwelling within the child as its own Atman. Nevertheless, Guru is there in the parents too.

With these few examples, though more could be cited ad infinitum, it is important to find out what obscures or alienates the awareness of Guru within us. Due to the prominence and popularity of the two paths listed earlier — the worldly and the demoniacal—this pristine principle gets apparently tarnished and misused. Charlatans and opportunists abound in religious life as well as in government and business. Since Guru can never truly be sullied or destroyed, being an eternal principle, It only gets submerged under the heavy weights of egocentric motive and action. The deep waters of samsara are a fit place for the forgetfulness of one's inner guide—that which God placed in the human heart and in everything, sentient and insentient, from the beginning of time.

Even this submersion, though, is only apparent. Acting in every aspect of life, Guru witnesses the entire drama in all its phases, from the corrupt on up to the exalted. The harshest of lessons as well as the most sublime boons are bestowed by Guru. In short, balance is maintained by Guru, while chaos is kept in check by the same principle.

It is helpful to look into that aspect of Guru which manifests as human being. A stone contains powerful Guru principle, being the best example of still and silent meditation one can find. A silent lake is inspiring as well, but it cannot explain the intricacies of the human heart and mind. Thus, those who take nature as their teacher make some progress, but when it comes to dealing with the world in all its phases and in particular that semidivine and bittersweet drama called human life and existence, nature remains detached and unable to assist. Herein we find the human guru on the scene and if such is authentic, i.e., unattached to name and fame, above desire for power and its manipulation and not attracted by wealth, lucre and personal gain, there is hardly a more worthy and beneficial ideal to be found.

In this day and age, Guru is not popular. Nevertheless, It permeates every aspect of life. Whereas the most traditional and classical approaches to religious life place Guru on a par with God Itself, the world will not accept the same. There is little wonder in this, for when beings realize that they are in dire need of a guide, either due to their own lack of direction and insight or because of the untimely fructification of their distressing and incapacitating negative karmas, they turn to that guide that most suits their own level of understanding, especially with regards to motive. If the intention is to supplicate the Divine for all manner of selfish ends, the teacher that is in accordance with the substance of such a lowly motive appears before them and, together, they play the game of victor and victimized.  After the fallacy of such interaction is realized, there is little chance that Guru will be sought after again, at least for some time.

In the case of those whose intentions are somewhat sincere and whose motives are of a higher caliber, there are a host of teachers ready to guide and direct.  These, like the aspirants that attend upon them, are of a mixed nature and reflect limited facets of the ultimate Guru.  Some growth can be attained here, though the attraction towards occult powers and sensationalism often persists amongst these and some of this gets passed on to the disciple if it did not already attract the student in the first place.  In short, like attracts like and one gets what is in line with what one desires and seeks after.

It is only amidst the pure teachers, rare as they are, that true spirituality is found.  They are rare because they do not seek accolades or notoriety as the others do.  This keeps them invisible to those who seek after the sensational rather than the spiritual and thereby endears them to those of pure motive.  Due to this, the two — bona fide guru and sincere disciple — easily recognize one another while others seek elsewhere according to a more inhibited capacity and limited insight based upon impure or mixed motives.  This moment in spiritual life represents the very height of all human relationships.  Suffice to say that where the authentic guru is present and the disciple is completely sincere, there occurs an implosion of such subtle and powerful ramifications that it turns the course of the aspirant's entire existence, changing it forever.  Instead of the usual evolution in time and space, the disciple's direction reverses and involution occurs, entirely independent of the world, its creatures and the trajectory along which they are heading.  This amazing process happens swiftly or more slowly according to the practitioner's capacity and inherent karmas and here again, where worthy teachers are concerned, guidance is both patient and infallible.

At this point, the qualities of Guru could be listed, but there is neither enough time or paper in the world for such an undertaking.  A study of the Avadhut and his many gurus can suffice for this purpose in the meantime.  However, many of the fine attributes of the Satguru, the world teacher, emerge as we look at the Guru/ Shishya Dashangika — the ten conditions of the teacher/ disciple relationship mentioned by Sri Adishankaracharya.

1) The first condition to be satisfied in the spiritual aspirant's earnest drive to attain enlightenment is Sruti/Shravana, that is, the seeker needs to hear the fundamental truths stated in the sacred scriptures from the lips of the beloved spiritual preceptor. This is a main facet of the all-important tenet of Holy Company mentioned by saints and sages in every sacred religious tradition of the world and must be accomplished both in one-on-one communion between instructor and instructed and in classes and discourses given by the teacher among those of like mind. Thus, the Truth is heard and understood through the medium of a direct transmission that carries with it not only the original revelatory power of the ancient seers but also the inherent comprehension and realization of the guru. Such profound spiritual weight impresses the intrinsic meaning of the teachings deep into the devotee's thought processes where it will gradually release both intellectual and intuitive forces. These destroy ignorance and delusion and prepare the heart and mind of the student for the advent of the light of pure Conscious Awareness. Therefore, the crucial nature of hearing the precious truths of the scriptures through the person of the preceptor is of the utmost import.

Further, the truths which are initially conveyed are the essential messages of nonduality which form the basis for all authentic spiritual transmission. The truth of the indivisibility of Consciousness, Its eternal and undying nature, Its all-pervasive presence and Its pure and taintless condition count as the most important. In addition, the guru reveals the secret of the presence of the Atman or Immortal Nature/Soul existing within the inmost being of the seeker and affirms Its identity with the infinite expanse of Conscious Awareness called Brahman or Absolute Reality beyond name, form, time, space and creation. This welcome news immediately awakens a strong and intense inner desire for freedom and compels the aspirant to embark upon the transformation of human nature that will eventually culminate in total illumination.

All of this proceeds from the rare and precious boon of Holy Company which itself is a blessing that comes about through one's good thoughts and deeds from previous lifetimes. These positive effects arise and get combined with the gracious concern and compassion of the Blessed Lord and Divine Mother of the Universe, called Shiva and Shakti — who are none other than the Atman within, the Antaryami, or the inner Ruler Immortal enshrined within the heart.  The guru's presence and bestowal of teachings are extremely efficacious, then, and amount to nothing less than beholding the Divine Being face-to-face and receiving immeasurable Grace.  Hearing the Truth from an enlightened being, Sruti/Shravana, is not to be underestimated.  During that one intrinsically real moment in time, from the blessed lips of the guru, through the precariously balanced medium of the tiny human frame, proceeds such power as will change forever one's various broodings on mortality into revelations of the Immortal Self within.

2)  Yukti/Manana is the second condition of this special relationship.  Here, it is up to the student to put forth effort, both in the form of quiet study and reflection as well as in daily actions, moment-to-moment thoughts, conversations and in service of others.  This alternating combination of inward contemplation of spiritual truths and careful application of them into everyday existence plays a key role in fusing all aspects of life together into one healthy and cohesive divine expression.  This is where the Four Yogas—the paths of knowledge, devotion, action and meditation —begin to be successfully integrated, which in turn leads to a peaceful and joyful existence.

It is crucial that the disciple spend time reflecting on the transmission from the guru.  Not to do so is likened to the difference between merely looking at food and actually consuming and digesting it.  Ongoing nourishment of one's spiritual life is the result of the latter while weakness, stagnancy and confusion in alternating cycles is the outcome otherwise.  It can therefore be said that being near the guru is one form of receiving, hearing the guru speak is another, while acting on the guru's instructions insure the optimum result.  The three together comprise the highest wisdom-level transmission.

It is at this juncture that the aspirant begins to feel the movements of inner intuition and hears the subtle spiritual voice of the higher element of mind with its call to action.  It does not take long for the powerful elixir of Truth and its acidlike effect to penetrate deep into subconscious layers of the mind.  Purification on this deep level leads to the uncovering of That which the disciple has been searching for.  Spending time in contemplation upon what has been given by the guru—that esoteric knowledge that few in the world are fit to hear and act upon—the aspiring student begins to understand that all knowledge lies within. The meanings to all teachings as well as the solutions to all problems then lie within reach and are accessible to the calm and reflective mind that gains inner vision. With open, single eye, the seeker observes the mutable nature of all phenomena while simultaneously beholding That which is changeless and eternal. It is through deep contemplation on spiritual matters that one rids the mind of the habit of brooding which causes the mind to become heavy with laziness and despondency and lose its natural spiritual buoyancy.

3) Anubhava/Niddhidhysanam, the third condition of the guru/disciple relationship, brings multifaceted experiences. Initial realization occurs at this auspicious level, for the student has fulfilled the prerequisites of approaching the teacher, listening closely and acting upon spiritual instruction. Through a thorough reasoning-out process that utilizes logic and rationale, the aspirant arrives at the pinnacle of the illumined intellect where, with specific meditation instruction, again given by the adept guide, the light-filled nature of the spiritualized mind rises spontaneously and naturally, giving birth to various sublime experiences. Thus, the infinite nature of Awareness is brought to bear upon the aspiring intellect.

One important occurrence that emerges during this phase of spiritual experience is the knowledge that the Atman is different from the universe of name and form. The astute and persevering aspirant is then able to perceive the distinction between what is mutable and what is immutable and this wisdom both increases inspiration and heightens the desire to behold the Eternal Being face to face. Coming to know that the intellect is different from the Immortal Self within, that it only reflects a minute portion of that ineffable Verity, and that only if the intelligence is purified of egotism and other impediments, the aspirant places more attention and concentration on the Atman, seeking the source of that great wonder. This gives rise to the fourth stage of guru/disciple relationship.

4) The well-known principle of Atma Vichara — inquiry into the nature of the Atman — is the fourth step along the Brahman way and the guru still plays an important part in it. It is nothing less than the essence of Reality that is being encountered in this

process, but first, the devotee must complete the discrimination process that matures the ability to clearly perceive what is real and what is unreal, what is eternal and what is transitory. In addition, the devotee must then learn to live in that transcendent essence of Pure Being, abide in Absolute Reality more and more, and this is to be accomplished in the midst of life and in the company of others who may or may not be awakened or empathetic to such inner realizations.

All the while that this internal analysis is taking place, the mind is receiving an intense makeover of the most exacting degree. Subconscious and unconscious layers of mind with their recurring thought patterns, preferences and aversions, existing concepts, old habits and latent impressions are gradually becoming exposed to the light of intelligent Awareness radiating from the still distant Atman. Recollections of past existences surface in the mind's memory at this time as well, and the devotee is amazed to see the record of such lifetimes and notice their effects. Realization takes on a twofold significance here, for along with the comprehension of something subtle, eternal and sublime existing within, comes the additional realization that much inner work must be accomplished before the radiant sun of Atman will fully emerge from behind the clouds and shadows of the curtain-like nature of the mind.

As the process of inquiry into the nature of the Atman goes on, the devotee feels more and more that the Atman is a completely distinct Reality from life and mind and begins to realize Its eternal nature. It is noticed that as the various elements of the mind such as ego-sense, variegation, apprehension and the thinking process rise and fall, the Atman remains constant. While the changing attributes of the mind such as perception, awareness, intelligence and determination dance within the inner vision of the awakening aspirant, the Atman remains still and pervasive. Also, when the cognitive powers of the mind perceive the five elements through the five senses and react outwardly to their stimuli, the Atman stays detached and aloof, uninvolved in the play of life and death, poised above all dualities.

As the devotee moves nearer to this undying Source of existence, the Atman's all-supportive yet transcendent nature fascinates and inspires all the more. Keenly aware of the difference between created things and That which is, as Swami Vivekananda has stated in his writings, "uncreate," consummate Wisdom, which is beyond the triple distinction of knower, knowing and that which is known, dawns on the aspirant's mind. Then, an experience of union beyond all diversity permeates existence and a clear view of Reality is attained. This ushers in the fifth stage of this rare, sacred relationship.

5) In the fifth stage, called Vivarta Nirodha — the destruction of what is unreal — the seeker comes to know without a doubt that Ultimate Reality is different from the Universe and all created things. The guru affirms this truth by continuing to guide the aspirant into deeper levels of communion with the Atman while leading the student around various obstacles and impediments that crop up due to the mind's negative propensities and inconsistencies.

Vivarta, false superimposition, the projection of appearances, coverings, or secondary realities over Brahman, is the result of the illusory power of Maya which veils Reality. Maya is neither good nor evil, neither positive nor negative, neither real nor unreal nor both real and unreal. Yet, it is a fact of existence whose very presence indicates the possibility for creation and expression. Through its tenuous though pervasive substance, the universe appears and the march of time and events go forward. With Its force, It projects coverings over the Atman which obscure Its nondual radiance. This projection is called vivarta. Body, life-force, mind, intelligence and ego—these are some of the obscurations that veil Reality from view. From mind, in the cosmic sense, proceed other concealing elements, such as thought, whose conceptual vibrations produce time, space, the three gunas, nature, the five senses and other phenomenal principles.

All manifestation is ultimately an appearance, a phantasmagoria projected by the inherent power in Brahman called Mahashakti, who wields the power of Maya in a similar way that a magician enchants an audience with various optical illusions. Thus, the aspirant who has seen the glory of the Atman seeks to shatter this illusion completely, see through the play of universal manifestation and go beyond name and form. As Swami Vivekananda has written, "We will crush the stars to atoms and unhinge the universe." Great gurus like he, though rare, demonstrate in their own lives, in plain view for all to see, that the destruction of such appearances is not only possible but extremely desirable, for it is only by this powerful act of internal sadhana and austerity that Maya will recede and enlightenment dawn.

Exercising discrimination and detachment and the twin modes of adhyaropa and apavada which help reveal the presence of cosmic illusion and individual delusion, the aspirant, under the guidance of the illumined preceptor, tears away the superimpositions from in front of Reality and achieves a vision of the Absolute. Such a glimpse changes the mind forever and brings about the ultimate renunciation that is so often mentioned by illumined beings. Such renunciation often reaches outward as well, and the aspiring devotee becomes indifferent to externals such as home, family, food and worldly attainments. This heralds the sixth level of the guru/disciple relationship.

6) Mithya-Tyagi, the sixth stage of the interaction between guru and disciple, compels the aspirant to relinquish social formalities and human conventions. Personal habits, as well, get a transformation. Seeing the guru and other illumined beings living a life of equanimity and balance, unattached to self-motivated works and undisturbed by rounds of distracting activities that take precious time and energy away from the true goal of human existence, the seeker follows suit and gradually or all at once gives up the desire for satisfaction in the world. This wise observance is for all, not just for monastics or ascetic wanderers. Having come to know that the world is a temporary state of existence, in actuality a projection of the mind, the aspirant no longer hungers after sensual pleasures or the attractions of name, fame and power. To abide continually in the highest condition of purified awareness, with Its bliss, peace and all-attracting light, is far more appealing and irresistible.

It is at this stage that the disciple begins to lose the sense of separation from others and from all created phenomena. All manifest phenomena now become friendly portions of one indivisible Reality. Even the guru is seen as nothing less than the Self in all. Therefore and oddly enough, it is while finally giving up all attachments to the external world and its various beings that one finds ultimate union with them. In this sublime state, there is none to love and none to hate for all are part and parcel of the true Self which is one and inseparable. It is not hard to imagine, then, how bliss comes upon the aspirant, leaving him or her with a profound and unending sense of peace.

Though some find it difficult to conceive of, after beholding the Atman, external objects and the stimulations they produce seem insipid. It is not that one becomes lifeless and devoid of drive and passion. It is that all energies, desires and ambitions get fused into one force that is directed towards the ultimate attainment of God-realization. What joy to behold the Source of creation and what relief to be free from the limitations of creation, which includes in it destruction as well. Renunciation finds its fullest expression here, in the perfectly natural and fully mature atmosphere of one-pointed focus upon the Atman. What follows such singular concentration is equally blissful.

7) In the seventh stage of Guru/Shishya relationship, called Brahma-Shuddhi, the devotee becomes pure by meditation on Brahman. Perceiving the Atman within gives way to entering into It fully and tracing Its pathway to the formless Brahman, the Ultimate Reality. As longer periods of immersion into that radiant effulgence ensue, more and more of the deeply buried impressions of the mind get unearthed and purified. As this process goes on, the mind is transformed into something other than mind, for all of its contents get emptied and thoroughly cleansed. This is why Sri Ramakrishna stated that "pure mind is God."

At this wonderful plateau of spiritual experience, meditation finally gets defined. It is no more a withdrawal of the mind from externals through self-effort or a mere attempt at concentration with varied results. Steady and constant, the mind focuses naturally and easily, like the cobra upon a snake-charmer. What is more, the devotee begins to meditate in all that he or she does. Whether eyes are closed or open, the Reality is nonetheless ever-present and all-pervasive. This Reality is not merely apparent either, but is obvious and thrilling to behold. All of life gets transformed in Its peerless presence.

8) Atma-Jnana, direct experience of the true Self, comes next. In the previous stage, as well as in this one, the guru has melted into boundless light. That is, though the provisional guru may still be present and accessible, the eternal Guru, the Atman within, is so brilliant and arresting that one naturally refrains from seeing

that omniscient principle of guidance in any one location. In truth, there is nothing but Guru all around and within. Guru-bhakti becomes, as it were, a contradiction in terms, for where there is only one effulgent radiance lighting the way, what becomes of darkness and of losing the way? In addition, who is there that is distinct from oneself towards which one may exercise devotion?

Atma-Jnana has been described by many as the ultimate stage of realization, but the mind and its impressions from many past lives as well as the ego sense that occupies it, struggle to stay alive up until the very last moment. Consciousness which is in the habit of perceiving duality everywhere and that has accumulated fear-laden impressions is tenacious and stubborn. Doubts continue to rise and must be effaced completely. The penultimate stage sees the destruction of these subtle impediments.

9) Vinasha Samskara, the ninth stage, involves the detection and dissolution of detrimental impressions in the mind. Here, the aspirant faces and does away with the final vestiges of subtle seed desires which hamper final immersion into Brahman. As the consummate vision of the Absolute presents itself, trepidation born of tiny residual waves left over from past desires and fears interrupt the flow of Conscious Awareness towards its intended goal. By proximity to Brahman alone and through elongated periods of meditation along with encouragement from the guru, the devotee finally succeeds in transcending the fear of leaving behind temporal existence and moves beyond both attachment to joy and refined pleasure and the desire for bliss in an individualized state of consciousness. The portals of relative existence are broken down and all boundaries are destroyed. The illusion of separation from Brahman fades away and one, boundless ocean of Light-filled Awareness remains.

10) The final stage of the precious communion between teacher and disciple culminates in an uninterrupted experience of union with Brahman called Sthiti Samadhi. This steady and balanced conditionless condition is peace-filled, bliss-filled and full of Truth and Wisdom as well. Freedom is Its atmosphere and Consciousness its only substance. Guru and Shishya are merged in It. All distinctions are effaced, all boundaries and divisions, dissolved. Eternity, infinity and indivisibility are natural to It. All is Peace, Peace, Peace.

To those four types of beings who have accepted the spiritual preceptor's timely assistance — the suffering, the seeking, the aspiring and the liberated — the attributes of Guru are well-known and appreciated. To the rest, it is a moot point and this brings up another issue for consideration. To the illumined ones, Guru is within. Seeking outwardly, the uninitiated and the unenlightened never understand Guru with any precise clarity. The condition of most seekers, those of mixed or impure motive, is such that the principle of Guru becomes a fad, a sensation and something to be bantered about and gossiped about. Those who title themselves gurus are, more often than not, deceitful, pretentious or deluded about their own spiritual status and this makes for more confusion among the seeking masses.

A secret emerges due to this, however. The realization of God is, as the poet stated, "The Pearl of Great Price." It is neither cognizable nor attainable to those of immature intellect and insincere devotion. The truth of this fact is a natural safeguard against all who would "defile the temple," so to speak, for God, the very essence of purity and excellence, is accessible only to those who are themselves pure and of excellent character. That is why, in this day and age, one finds so few authentic teachers and aspirants. Rare are those who are willing to follow the true teacher's instructions, what to speak of taking the considerable effort needed in finding and recognizing such a being in the first place. As Sri Ramakrishna has stated, "It takes a jeweler to recognize the value of a diamond."

Besides this important point, there are other insights and lack thereof which figure into the picture, as the case may be. Personality worship, for example, is best left amidst the exponents of the Vyavaharika path, among those who seek entertainment, pleasures, fun, glamour and the like. The constituents of this worldly path mimic the words and actions of others who, having forsaken the true purpose of life, leave the field of the soul untended and instead seek name, fame and wealth — that which is of no lasting value or benefit. Speaking about the worldly-minded, the poet/saint, Ramprasad sings, "Don't you know that all are lost here? Everyone lives in pallid imitation of everyone else."

In the spiritual realm, that is, where true spirituality is fostered and appreciated, the personality, rather than being the point and

essence of existence, is eschewed for the most part and egolessness is the ideal.  It is not that the personality is not appreciated,
for many of the saints and sages of the past were great characters, but it is the Divine Being which takes prominence and those
who have been seeking That for lifetimes take this as a welcome
change.  The Divine Being is not without personality either.  Its
ultimate nature is formless, but where the universe of names and
forms is concerned and where the spiritual well-being of precious
sincere seekers is at stake, It assumes the form of its own nature
and appears before the world's awestruck eyes as Avatar, the messenger of Ishvara.  Those who have the great good fortune to
behold this auspicious manifestation of Divinity, witness a transcendence of what is usual or normal in mundane life and perceive
the Lord sporting in the universe for the good of all beings.  This
is an especially powerful aspect of Guru.

The personality of a man or woman of lesser stature, however,
can only reflect so much of this form-effacing divinity.  This truth
is a direct indication as well as a dead giveaway.  That is, it reveals
those whom the Lord would make His true representatives and
betrays those who hide behind the facade of opportunism and
pretension.  If a person pretends to be spiritual, the ego-oriented
tendency there will emerge in stark contrast to the pure and humble condition that a holy man or woman exudes.  Conversely, if
someone wants to ascertain if another is holy, an examination of
the person's character under all conditions of life will bring this
to light, for the lack of certain known distortions found in the egocentric person will be noticed and noted.  Therefore, one of the
accepted and crucial practices a seeker undertakes is the intense
scrutiny and examination of the teacher which leaves by the wayside all doubts pertinent to the situation.  One who does not apply
this practice deserves the teacher he or she accepts and, as a
result, suffers the consequences.

All legitimate preceptors point towards the formless Guru
within.  They do not, unless to effect certain beneficial ends, position themselves in such a manner as to appear as the only teacher
or the ultimate guru.  Still, those who have realized the inner
guide cannot but reflect what It entails and begin to radiate those
excellent qualities associated with that Eternal Principle.  Such
mysteries are known only by those who experience the blessing

of intimacy between guru and disciple.

Along with the absence of ego and the lack of desire for worldly goods and attainments, the true preceptor takes seriously the charge of helping others out of the darkness of ignorance and delusion. Whereas fakes and frauds put on a show and enjoy all that comes from being worshipped and admired, the true spiritual teacher works hard for the benefit of the students, showing them how to remove certain blocks that are in the way of spiritual advancement and realization of the Atman within. This is a lifetime's preoccupation with them and it is difficult terrain where only patience, perseverance and reliance on God prevail. Such austerity would cause the charlatan to "flee with the money, the girl and the car," as they say, and many in this day and age have been caught doing just that. Such aberrations occur often in today's spiritual marketplace, but it does not open the eyes of the deluded. They remain duped, as dull as ever and accept the imitation while overlooking or denying the authentic.

One can only stand, bow and lovingly salute true Guru. Soon, after certain disciplines have been exercised, the Atman chooses to reveal Itself, both in the preceptor and in the disciple. This is the point and purpose of all life, both worldly and spiritual. This moment is brought to bear by the presence of Guru. With reverence mixed with awe, the beholder of such inner radiance and excellence can only prostrate and praise the human guru, seeing that one, in fact, as nothing less than the ultimate Guru. In this realization there is much less aggrandizement, adulation, personality worship and the like and all reverence appreciation and love instead. It is with this in mind that the Kularnava Tantra states:

Following the instructions of Guru is more beneficial
than study, knowledge, offerings, sacrifices charity and worship.

Further, it is said therein:

Guru is higher than friends and family,
more efficacious than mantra.
Meditation is, itself, the form of Guru
and by Guru is liberation gained.
All holy actions are facilitated by Guru,

all fulfillment granted thereby.
Fear, distress, grief and other pains
disappear through Guru's Grace.
Wandering in the trackless wastes of Samsara
is brought to an end by Guru.
When Guru gives Himself to the disciple,
sins drop away and peace descends.
Brahma, Vishnu and Shiva bestow their Grace
when Guru is pleased.
Through Guru's direction alone,
karmas are transcended and freedom is attained.

# Sanskrit Glossary

**Abhava Yoga** —A highly realized stage of yoga wherein the Self is meditated upon as formless essence, characterized by a practice and realization that is attained primarily through negation.

**Abhaya Mudra** —A sacred hand position or gesture that indicates the boon of fearlessness.

**Abhyasa Yoga** —The path of constant and dedicated practice, well defined by Lord Krishna in the Bhagavad Gita.

**Acharya** —Teacher; preceptor who guides one in study of the scriptures and spiritual life in general.

**Achina Tree** —A tree, possibly of mythological reference, which some claim to have seen but which no one can find.

**Adbhutananda** —The bliss of experiencing great wonder; a swami who was a friend of Jagachakshu Muni and whom Ekanta heard stories about from his guru.

**Adharmic** —Going against dharmic path through deluded or wrongful action.

**Adhyaropa** —A mode of discrimination used by the jnanis which aids in the detection and removal of false superimposition and mental delusion.

**Adideva Jagannatha** —Lord of the Worlds; Vishnu as the Lord of the Universe.

**Adipurusha** —The original and authentic primordial Soul of souls.

**Adishakti** —The Mother of the Universe as the first and foremost of all powers.

**Adishankara or Adishankaracharya** —A name for Sri Shankaracharya, the great Advaitan. See Shankara.

**Adishesha** —The primal serpent who is seen as the support of the universe.

**Advaita Ashrama** —A spiritual center in Bombay which the Avadhut visited occasionally that was managed by his friend, Pandit Pranath.

**Advaita Vedanta** —Nondual philosophy of absolute unity without compromise, well defined by Gaudapada and brought into prominence by the great philosopher Adishankaracharya.

**Advaitan** —One who follows the Advaita Vedanta. A nondualist.

**Advaitananda** —The bliss of Oneness; the swami who befriended the Avadhut after witnessing his divine state.

**Advaitic** —Having to do with Advaita Vedanta. Nondual by nature.

**Advaitic Truths** —Eternal principles which are based upon Absolute Unity.

**Advaitist** —Same as Advaitan.

**Agamas** —Auxiliary texts such as the Tantras which deal primarily with the eternal principles of Shiva and Shakti and Their union.

**Agastya** —Literally, "one who levels mountains", he was a revered rishi of the Vedic period, the preceptor of Drona and the husband of Lopamudra.

**Agni** —Fire; the name of the god of fire in ancient Vedic tradition.

**Agni-hotra** —An ancient Vedic ceremony involving offerings into the fire which is symbolic of the purification of all aspects of the being and the attainment of divine qualities.

**Aham Brahmasmi** —"I am Brahman." One of the four Mahavakyas or sacred declarations of Advaita Vedanta.

**Ahamkara** —The sense of individuality or tiny personal self which is a condition of limited or congealed consciousness characterized by narrowness and possessiveness; one of the four aspects of the mind according to Samkhya and Vedanta, along with mind, consciousness and intellect.

**Ahimsa** —Nonviolence or refraining from harming living things; one of the ten yamas and niyamas of the Patanjala Yoga system.

**Ajapa-Mantra** —The sacred mantra, Soham, which arises naturally from the incoming and the outgoing breath; breathing exercises prescribed in Hatha Yoga.

**Ajati** —Unborn.

**Ajativada** —The view of nonorigination often used to proclaim the birthless, deathless nature of the Soul; theory of nonevolution.

**Akasha** —Subtle space, in any of its modes such as intelligence space, knowledge space, energy space, material space (chitakasha, jnanakasha, pranakasha, bhutakasha); ether, one of the five elements of nature.

**Akashic Records** —Memory of all occurrences taking place in time that are imprinted on the Cosmic Mind, which Itself is the container of the akashic records.

**Akushala** —Negative and detrimental tendencies such as the passions and various delusions of the mind; unwholesome tendencies.

**Anadi** —Of untraceable or indeterminable origin; without beginning.

**Ananda** —The transcendent bliss of Pure Consciousness which is the very nature of the Self.

**Ananda-mayah** —Being full of transcendent joy.

**Ananta** —Without end; infinite.

**Anantananda** —An infinite repository of bliss; full of the bliss of infinitude; the swami of the mountain ashram whom Ekanta visited as a boy.

**Anapanasati** —Preliminary breathing exercises prescribed in Buddhism.

**Anavasthi-Tattva** —A condition of spiritual stagnancy associated with the false and egoistic assumption that spiritual realization has an end.

**Anima** —One of the eight siddhis or occult powers which enables the seeker of lower ideals to reduce physical matter to nothingness or to attain weightlessness.

**Antahkarana** —The internal organ or fourfold mind. It consists of manas, the basic mind which considers, chitta, the mind's contents, buddhi, the intellect that determines and ahamkara, the ego or sense of individuality.

**Antaryami** —The "Inner Ruler Immortal" seated in the heart.

**Anubhava** —True Being; the direct perception of Divinity which is the result of self-effort and Grace; after shruti, hearing the Truth, and yukti, contemplating the Truth, it is the third of a succession of Vedantic practices which allows for the direct perception of Reality.

**Aparavidya** —Lower or secondary knowledge, usually pertaining to secular or worldly subjects but sometimes even associated with mere scriptural knowledge as compared to direct experience of Reality.

**Aparigraha** — Defined as nonreceiving of gifts, it is one of the ten yamas and niyamas of Patanjala Yoga which brings freedom from the double-edged problem of ownership and expectation. It is a prerequisite to the successful practice of yoga.

**Apaurasheya** —Not of human authorship, used often in reference to the scriptures of Sanatana Dharma.

**Apavada** —A discriminatory power that, in conjunction with its partner, adhyaropa, recognizes and destroys delusions of the mind and false superimpositions over Reality.

**Arati** —Devotional ceremonial worship, usually performed at dusk or dawn, using fragrances, lights, and devotional music.

**Arhat** —Literally, "worthy one"; a realized Buddhist holy man whose enlightenment culminates in Nirvana.

**Arjuna** —One of the five Pandava brothers who was a great devotee of Lord Krishna and who received the great Avatar's discourse and message of the Bhagavad Gita on the battlefield at Kurukshetra.

**Arya Satya** —The Four Noble Truths, taught by Lord Buddha.

**Aryaman** —Literally, of noble descent; surrounded by enlightened beings; aspiring towards Truth; the name of Ekanta's father.

**Asamprajnata Samadhi** —Described by Patanjali in Yoga Philosophy as a superconscious state of pure Awareness where all cognitive traces of the relative universe and the individual self are obliterated completely. It is generally synonymous with the Nirvikalpa Samadhi of the Vedanta school.

**Asana** —Seat used for formal meditation; basic posture recommended by Patanjali in his Raja Yoga system to facilitate a strong and steady foundation for the body so that it will remain stationary and still, allowing the mind to concentrate on Reality.

**Asanas** —A complicated and potentially injurious series of postures in the Hatha Yoga system which exercise the body and nervous system but which often lead to heightened desire, pleasure seeking, a thirst for power, the pursuit of longevity and occult attainments – all impediments to spiritual realization.

**Ashram or Ashrama** —A spiritual center where ongoing sadhana or spiritual disciplines are practiced under the guidance of a guru.

**Ashramites** —Members of an ashram who undergo spiritual discipline.

**Ashtavakra** —An enigmatic holy man, great sage and rishi of the Vedic period, who was born deformed due to a curse from his father while in the womb but who later saved his father's life and had the curse reversed. He is the author of the Ashtavakra Samhita.

**Ashtavakra Samhita** —A Sanskrit text concentrating on nondual Wisdom that is one of the finest scriptures of Advaita Vedanta.

**Asta Siddhis** —The eight occult powers, proclaimed by enlightened beings to be detrimental sidetracks along the path of spiritual realization.

**Asteya** —Noncovetousness. One of the ten yamas and niyamas of the Patanjala Yoga system, it is a prerequisite to the practice of yoga and an important implement for the destruction of selfishness.

**Asura or Asuras** —Powerful beings and demonic forces who vie with the gods for supremacy; negative forces or demons.

**Atala** —One of the seven hell realms lying below the earth plane.

**Atma Vichara** —Inquiry into the nature of the Divine Self within.

**Atma-Jnana or Atmajnan** —Absolute Knowledge of the Immortal Self, the highest knowledge knowable to the human mind, knowing which will lead the aspiring soul to spiritual realization.

**Atman** —The eternal Soul residing within every being and permeating creation, which is birthless, deathless, pure, and perfect by nature.

**Aum or Om** —The primal vibration which is the sound symbol for Brahman, Ultimate Reality, and which is an essential element in all systems of Hindu Philosophy. From this primal sound come all aspects of the creation, yet being beyond the manifest universe it is the bija or sacred symbol for formless Reality Itself.

**Avadhut** —A wandering ascetic belonging to the class of Avadhuts who represent a high state of sannyas.

**Avadhuta Gita** —A sacred scripture focusing on nondual Wisdom which, besides addressing the nature of Reality, also describes the condition and philosophy of the Avadhut, a wandering holy person.

**Avatar** or **Avatara** —One who descends; the appearance of Divinity in human form; an incarnation of God.

**Avyakta** —Unmanifest; undifferentiated; transcendent of the three gunas.

**Avidya** —Ignorance; nescience.

**Avidya Maya** —The deluding power of Maya that leads away from illumination and towards ignorance.

**Avidya Shakti** —The deluding power of shakti that restricts rather than aids in the attainment of enlightenment.

**Ayamatma Brahma** —"This Self is Brahman." One of the four great declarations (Mahavakyas) or nondualistic statements given in the Vedas.

**Babaji** —Revered spiritual father; a term of endearment and respect used by Ekanta for his male vanaprastin teacher.

**Bala** —Omniscience, which is one of the powers of the Supreme Being.

**Balarama** —Literally, "abode of strength"; older brother of Sri Krishna; incarnation of Vishnu.

**Bali** —Monarch of the asuric beings who was defeated by Vishnu when the Lord incarnated as a dwarf.

**Baul** —A sect of colorful wandering holy men, usually centered in Bengal, who sing songs of devotion to God.

**Benares** —A city in India which is holy to Shiva and which is a place of pilgrimage for devout Hindus.

**Bengal** —A province in India made famous by such Divine Incarnations as Lord Chaitanya and Sri Ramakrishna.

**Bhadi** —Short form for the name Bhadraka.

**Bhadraka** —Handsome; noble; a young boy, son of Pandit Pratapa, whom the Avadhut saw on his visits to Bombay.

**Bhadranath** —An important pilgrimage spot in India situated high in the Himalayas.

**Bhagavad Gita** —The quintessential sacred scripture of the Hindus containing the comprehensive message of Lord Krishna.

**Bhagavan** —An especially sacred name for God which implies the Supreme Being who is endowed with the six divine attributes – power, virtue, fame, glory, detachment and freedom.

**Bhagavata** —Refers to the Purana, the Srimad Bhagavatam, which is sacred to Vaishnavas.

**Bhagavati** —A sacred name for the Divine Mother of the Universe; the Supreme Being in feminine form.

**Bhaja Govindam** —Literally, "worship the Lord, Govinda;" the name of a famous devotional hymn by Sri Shankaracharya.

**Bhajan** —A devotional song offered to any of the aspects of God.

**Bhakta** —A devotee of the Lord; a follower of the path of bhakti.

**Bhakti** —Love and devotion to God.

**Bhakti Sutras** —Devarshi Narada's authoritative expose on the path of devotion.

**Bhakti Yoga** —The path of devotion leading to union with God.

**Bhalendra** —Literally, God of Fortune, it is a name for Lord Shiva and the name taken by a silent holy man whom Ekanta met at his ashrama.

**Bharat or Bharata** —Literally, "supported by God" and "the Realm of Fulfillment," it is an ancient name for the sacred land of India; the name of a great sage worshipped in India.

**Bhargava** —The son of a great saint who approached Pippalada for clarification in the Prasnopanishad.

**Bhavamukha** —A high spiritual condition in which the illumined one experiences awareness of both the transcendent and phenomenal realms, in turns or simultaneously.

**Bhavas** —Devotional moods or spiritual feelings associated with the awakening of God-Consciousness.

**Bhrihaspati** —Literally, "Lord of prayer and devotion"; a grandson of the creator, Brahma, who is also the preceptor of the gods.

**Bhur or Bhuh** —The first of the three worlds; the physical plane; the universe; the earth; the first word of the Gayatri Mantra, which when uttered by the firstborn of Brahma, created the physical universe.

**Bhurloka** —Same as Bhur.

**Bhuta Jaya** —Victory over the physical elements. The first stage of purification of the mind prescribed by Tantra, particularly the path of Kundalini Yoga, wherein the aspirant trains the mind to acknowledge fully that the true nature of awareness is not dependent upon the physical universe.

**Bhuta Shuddhi** —Purification of the gross physical world and its elements and aspects attained by directly perceiving that all such things are mutable.

**Bhuta Yajna** —Offerings made to the animals and lesser lifeforms.

**Bhutakasha** —Physical space, wherein are contained all manner of bodies and objects.

**Bhuvah** —The realm just beyond the earth called the astral realm and the second word of the Gayatri Mantra, which when uttered by the firstborn of Brahma, created the atmospheres.

**Bhuvaneshvari** —Literally, "Mother of all beings, all realms"; a sacred name for the Divine Mother of the Universe.

**Bhuvarloka** —Same as Bhuvah.

**Bija** —A seed syllable which forms an essential part of a mantra and which invokes the presence of God through a particular mode or aspect.

**Bodhgaya** —A city in India where Buddha attained His enlightenment.

**Brahma** —The first aspect of the Hindu Trinity who represents the power of creation; also, the term occasionally refers to Brahman Itself, beyond the acts of creation, preservation and dissolution.

**Brahmacharya** —Continence, not just in the physical sense but also as a way of remaining constant in devotion to the highest ideal. It is also one of the ten yamas and niyamas and a prerequisite to the practice of yoga which allows the aspirant to access the essential purity inherent within.

**Brahmagni** —Literally, "the fire of Brahman"; one of the names of Death cited in the Yamastakam, a hymn citing eight names of Yama.

**Brahmajnana or Brahmajnan** —The knowledge of Brahman, used in the sense of that which is to be known about Ultimate Reality.through direct experience

**Brahmajnani** —A knower of Divine Reality who possesses Brahmajnan.

**Brahmaloka** —The highest of the realms of existence, sometimes called Satyaloka, where enlightened souls live in the company of the Supreme Being; the realm of Brahma, the Creator.

**Brahman** —The Absolute; the Ultimate Reality; formless Essence; pure Consciousness.

**Brahmara-kita** —A large beetle-like insect; a silk worm; a wasp.

**Brahma Muhurta** —A special time late at night which is best suited for meditation and spiritual practice. It occurs approximately after midnight until just prior to sunrise. The yogi easily detects the sound of Aum at this time, feels the upward movement of the Mahavayu – the subtle spiritual "wind" – and communes with the Kundalini Shakti.

**Brahma-Shuddhi** —Attaining again to one's original purity by meditation on the formless Brahman.

**Brahma Sanatani Devi** —Literally, "The Eternal Goddess who is One with Brahman," it is a sacred name for the Divine Mother of the Universe.

**Brahma Sanatani Devi** —A name for the Divine Mother of the Universe which describes Her as the "Eternal Principle of Brahman."

**Brahmin** —A member of the priesthood; the fourth and highest caste of Hindu society responsible for matters of religion.

**Brahmopanishad** —One of the minor Upanishads belonging to the Atharva Veda which gives a clear rendering of the nature of the Atman and its four states, four tirthas and four locations for meditation.

**Buddha** —An enlightened being, generally considered to be an Avatar, and the founder of the religion that bears His name.

**Buddhi** —Intelligence; one of the four parts of Antahkarana, the mental sheath or thinking mind according to Samkhya and Vedanta.

**Buddhism** —The truths of religion and philosophy as propounded by Shakyamuni Buddha, born in India in the sixth century B.C.E.

**Cardamom** —A spice used in Indian cooking.

**Chaitanya** —Consciousness fully aware of Itself; a great God-man of 14th-century Bengal, considered by some to be a divine incarnation of Radha and Krishna conjoined.

**Chaitanya Shuddaham** —"I am Pure Consciousness."

**Chakra** —A subtle center or vortex of spiritual energy, sometimes referred to as a lotus, through which Kundalini Shakti flows on its ascent to the crown of the head. There are said to be seven such lotuses from the base of the spine to the crown of the head and twelve more in the brain.

**Chela** —Student; disciple.

**Chen-jen** —A Chinese term for an illumined being who lives a natural and spontaneous spiritual existence.

**Chetana Samadhi** —A very elevated kind of spiritual experience characterized by simultaneously knowing God while perceiving the true nature of the world.

**Chetana** —Intelligence; pure Knowledge.

**Chetomukhah** —mouth of knowledge or opening of knowledge.

**Chidakasha** —The boundless space of pure Spirit which is a realmless realm occupied by nothing other than pure Conscious Awareness, timeless deathless and unlimited.

**Chinmaya** —Pervaded by and being full of pure Consciousness.

**Chit Mudra** —A mystical symbolic gesture of the hands affected by the bringing together of the two palms in salutation.

**Chit Shakti** —The Divine Mother as the power of pure Intelligence.

**Chitta Shuddha or Chit Shuddhi** —Purity of thought, of mind, of intellect.

**Chit or Chitta** —Pure knowledge; one of four constituents of the antahkarana along with manas, buddhi and ahamkara.

**Chittakasha** —The space containing thoughts, ideas, concepts, etc.

**Chang-tzu** —An important Chinese Zen teacher.

**Dacoits** —Thieves or ruffians.

**Daityas** —A class of mighty asuras.

**Dama** —Self control; one of the Six Treasures contained within the Four Jewels of Vedanta practice.

**Dardadhana** —Upholder of justice; destroyer of mortal sins; a name for Death in the Yamastakam.

**Darshan** or **Darshana** —Literally, to see clearly; referring to the six darshanas, which when studied under an authentic teacher, enable the aspirant to be free from bondage and limitation and behold inherent divinity; direct association with a divine being.

**Darshanas** —The six orthodox systems of Vedic Philosophy, namely Samhkya, Patanjala (or Yoga), Uttara Mimamsa (or Vedanta) Purva Mimamsa, Nyaya, and Vaisheshika.

**Devarshi Narada** —A luminary who wrote the Narada Bhakti Sutras which are definitive texts of Bhakti Yoga. Sage Narada appears throughout the many scriptures of Hinduism where he was privileged to have the darshan of Lord Vishnu and many other gods and goddesses. Sri Ramakrishna mentions him as a holy man of the highest order.

**Devarshi** —An illumined sage who is a teacher of the gods.

**Deva Yajna** —Offerings made to the gods and goddesses in higher worlds.

**Deva** —A word for a god in the Hindu pantheon; a title for the highest divinity in human form.

**Devi Bhagavati** —A reference to the Divine Mother of the Universe.

**Devi Puranas** —Those scriptures that pertain to the work, actions and worship of the Divine Mother of the Universe in Her many forms.

**Dharana** —Concentration; the sixth limb in the eight-limbed system of Patanjali's Yoga which allows the aspirant to access deeper states of meditation.

**Dharma** —Proper and balanced living and thinking according to the scriptures; righteousness; virtue; one of the four fruits of life (Purusharthas) granted by the Divine Mother.

**Dharman** —One who follows and epitomizes dharma – righteous action and spiritual living; the name of the Avadhut's dear friend, the arrow-maker.

**Dharmarajan** —Literally, "the king of righteousness"; one of the eight names of Death in the Yamastakam.

**Dharmic** —Having to do with or pertaining to righteous thought and action.

**Dhriti** —Resolve; firmness; patience.

**Dhumavati** —An aspect of the Goddess, one of the ten Mahavidyas whose name, which refers to ash and smoke, implies the eventual or immediate destruction of all names, forms and ideas. As with all the workings of the Goddess, Her destruction is for a higher purpose.

**Dhuni fire** —A sacred fire around which the yogis, pilgrims and ascetics sit to meditate and listen to divine discourse.

**Dhyan or Dhyana** —Meditation; the seventh limb in the eight-limbed system of Patanjali's Yoga which leads to Samadhi.

**Diksha** —Initiation into serious and dedicated religious life by a spiritual teacher, ususally accompanied by the giving of a mantra.

**Dravya Shuddha** —Purity or purification of place and object.

**Dravya Shakti** —An aspect of the Divine Mother Shakti who aids in the creation of the phenomenal universe; the producer of substances.

**Dristi** —What is seen, perceived or revealed; false view, called ditthi in Buddhism.

**Dristisristivada** —The view, upheld by some and denied by others, that what is seen and experienced is real, at least so long as it appears before the eye of the beholder.

**Durga** —The Divine Mother of the Universe; the ten-armed Goddess who is the essence of all gods and goddesses; the firstand foremost of five main aspects of the Universal Mother (Prakriti Panchaka) according to the Srimad Devi Bhagavatam.

**Dvaita** —Dualism, whose main exponent was Madhva. The view that God is separate from the world and human beings which are dependent on God for their existence.

**Dvandva Mohena** —Delusion arising from the incorrect view which accepts multiplicity and diversity to be real and which fails to perceive Unity in everything; the infinite sets of pairs of opposites in relativity.

**Dvapara Yuga Avatar** —Sri Krishna, the full manifestation of God who appeared in the Dvapara Yuga.

**Ekanta** —Devoted to one thing; of single solitary motive; solitude; the Avadhut's given name.

**Ekarnava** —One formless, boundless ocean of Consciousness in which the potential for manifestation of future creations is contained.

**Ganapati** —The elephant-headed god who grants success and good fortune.

**Ganesha** —Another name for Ganapati, the elephant-headed god of the Hindu pantheon.

**Ganga Ma** —The Goddess of the sacred river, Ganges.

**Ganga** —The sacred river which runs practically the entire length of the Indian subcontinent. It is considered holy and auspicious by the Indian people and the faithful believe that it removes all manner of defects from the body and mind.

**Gangotri** —The source of the sacred river, Ganges.

**Garuda** —The great dragon bird who is Lord Vishnu's celestial mount and who makes auspicious appearances throughout the Vedic scriptures.

**Gaudapada** —An illumined rishi who was a major exponent of the Advaita Vedanta. He is said to have been the guru of Shankara or possibly the guru of Shankara's guru.

**Gayatri Mantra** —An extremely important mantra from the Rig Veda chanted several times daily by devout Hindus; a particular rhythmic meter.

**Gerua** —A shade of orange which is considered auspicious and used to color the wearing cloths of those who take monastic vows in the Hindu religion.

**Ghanananda** —Literally, "mass of bliss."

**Ghat** —A place of access on a lake or river where people bathe and draw water.

**Giri** —Mountain; title of reverence given to certain Rishis; a sect of ascetics belonging to the mountain ashramas.

**Gokula** —A district in India made holy by association with Sri Krishna during his boyhood days; a herd of cows.

**Govinda** —Literally, knower of creation, referring to Sri Krishna as the master of the earth and the senses; cowherder.

**Gramani** —Village woman; a celestial being that attends on Shiva and Surya; the name of Dharman's wife who was a friend of the Avadhut.

**Gudakesha** —A name for Arjuna used by Sri Krishna in the Bhagavad Gita which means, "one who has conquered sleep."

**Guna** —Trait or attribute of nature; quality born of nature of which there are three – sattva, rajas and tamas – balance, frenetic activity and inertia.

**Guru** —Satchitananda or Ultimate Reality appearing as the Atman or true nature of every living being; the revered spiritual preceptor who is the provisional guru.

**Guruji** —Revered teacher; a term of respect used by Ekanta for his male vanaprastin teacher.

**Guru-Shishya Dashangika** —The ten steps of attainment in the guru/disciple relationship as cited by Sri Shankaracharya.

**Guru Tattva** —The essential principle of guidance, elucidation and enlightenment inherent in every atom of the creation and existing eternally beyond the creation as the Ultimate Guru.

**Guru Yoga** —The path of union with God through following the illumined preceptor and his instructions with one-pointed devotion.

**Hamsa** —Literally, "I am That"; the outgoing breath of the ajapa mantra.

**Hanuman** —Also known as Mahavir or "Great Hero," he was the monkey-god and a great devotee of Sri Ramchandra who aided the Lord in regaining the beloved Sita from the hands of the asura Ravana.

**Hara** —Destroyer; a name for Shiva Mahadeva.

**Hasta-Amalaka Stotram** —Literally, "Fruit in the Palm of the Hand," it is an ancient writing of nondual content meant to convey the nearness and immediacy of the Atman.

**Hatakeshvara** —Literally, "Lord of gold" who is an aspect of Lord Shiva in a wrathful form.

**Hatha Yoga** —A stage of Kundalini Yoga associated with natural and spontaneous expression of asana, mudra, pranayam and kriyas; a system of body postures undergone for health of the body, longevity and the attainment of occult powers.

**Hatha yogis** —Those who follow the prescribed exercises of Hatha Yoga as their primary discipline.

**Hatha** —Literally, "ha" – the breath of the sun, and "tha" – the breath of the moon, to be united by asana, sitting still in one prescribed posture, and pranayama, breathing naturally. When single posture and single breath become one, control of the senses, called pratyahara, becomes possible; desire.

**Hayagriva** —A powerful horse-faced asura who presided over the realm of Narakasura; an incarnation of Vishnu who temporaily sported a horse's head in order to kill the horse-faced asura, Hayagriva.

**Himavat** —A name for the divine presence of the Goddess associated with the Himalayan Mountains; personification of the Himalayas as a god.

**Hindu Dharma** —Sanatana Dharma, or Eternal Religion, of India which includes all the various and sacred yogas, darshanas and philosophies and the texts containing their teachings.

**Hiranyagarbha** —The cosmic egg, meaning the matrix of creation from which all things come forth. It is also synonymous with Mahat or cosmic mind, Brahma, the god of creation, pranakasha or subtle space, and Karya-Brahman.

**Homa Bird** —A mythological bird who lays her eggs miles high in the sky so that they hatch in mid air before touching the earth. It is used as a metaphor for the illumined being who is not really born of matter and only briefly sojourns on earth with the purpose of helping others realize their divine nature.

**Iccha Shakti** —The power of indomitable will inherent in the Divine Mother by which She accomplishes all manifestation, all action and all conceptualization – Dravya, Kriya and Jnana Shakti; Divine Will.

**Ida** —In Vedanta, the Goddess of speech and sacrifice who brings refreshment and vigor; in Kundalini Yoga, a subtle nerve and its current associated with the left nostril and left channel of the spine which, when open and flowing, brings a cooling effect to the body/mind mechanism.

**Indra** —The Lord of the gods; the foremost among the celestial powers of the Supreme Being.

**Indriya Jaya** —Victory over the senses. The second practice of purification prescribed by Tantra wherein the aspirant comes to know that the senses are limited and unable to give any complete rendering of the nature of Reality.

**Indriyas** —The subtle power inherent in the senses by which the eye sees, the ear hears, etc.; minor gods who receive offerings through the five senses.

**Ishavasyopanishad** —Also called the Samhitopanishad because, unlike other Upanishads, it is found in the samhita portion of the Vedas, in this case the White Yajur Veda. Its teachings revolve around pious and unpious works, the realization of the Atman and the transcendence of death.

**Ishitva** —One of the eight occult powers by which those attracted to lower ideals attain domination over beings and situations.

**Ishta** —The chosen ideal; that which the devotee accepts as the highest standard in spiritual life.

**Ishta-nishta** —One-pointed devotion to a single ideal.

**Ishvara** —The supreme and most comprehensive aspect of Divinity residing within the universe who oversees its various lesser powers and their functions.

**Ishvarakotis** —A class of illumined beings who are perfected in spiritual life and who usually attend on a Divine Incarnation.

**Ishvara-pranidhana** —Literally, self-surrender to God, prostration before God. It is an important prerequisite for the practice of yoga and one of the ten yamas and niyamas without which all efforts by way of sadhana will prove ultimately unsuccessful.

**Ishvari** —The Divine Mother as Ishvara; the supreme power of the universe manifesting through a feminine aspect.

**Jada Samadhi** —A high spiritual state wherein the aspirant becomes still or inert for long periods of time.

**Jada** —Stationary; insentient.

**Jafar** —A devotee of God who wrote devotional songs blending Hindu and Islamic ideals.

**Jagachakshu Muni** —An illumined holy man whom the Avadhut encountered and whose ashram he visited.

**Jagad** —The world; physical universe.

**Jagadguru** —World teacher; one who is divinely empowered and capable of transmitting the highest spiritual teachings to humanity.

**Jagannatha** —The Lord of the Universe; a temple in India which is a main pilgrimage point for all seekers of Truth.

**Jai or Jaya** —A divine exclamation which means victory.

**Jai Avatara Varishtaya** —Victory to the Avataric descent.

**Jamuna River** —A sacred river in India associated with the childhood of Sri Krishna.

**Janaka** —A famous king, the father of Sita, who attained both lordship and enlightenment. The famous rishi, Yagnavalkya, was his court priest.

**Janaloka** —The fifth of seven realms of higher existence where the first-born of Brahma make their permanent abode during cycles of existence.

**Janardana** —The fulfiller of desires; an epithet of Sri Krishna.

**Japa** —The efficacious practice of silently reciting the sacred mantra or names of God while turning the holy beads (mala).

**Japa-mala** —A string of beads used for repeating the mantra; rosary.

**Jati** —Birth; creation.

**Jiva** —The embodied soul; transmigrating soul.

**Jivanmukta** —An illumined being who is liberated while living, enlightened while still residing in the body.

**Jivanmukti** —The state of liberation attained by fully illumined beings.

**Jivatman** —The individual soul or jiva. It is known to be identical with the Supreme Soul after realization dawns.

**Jnana** —Spiritual knowledge.

**Jnana Shakti** —A power of the Divine Mother used for sustaining knowledge and wisdom; force of intelligence.

**Jnana Yoga** —The path of Wisdom leading to union with the Supreme Being.

**Jnanakasha** —The subtle space which supports intelligence and wisdom.

**Jnani** —A practitioner of the path of Jnana Yoga; one who has spiritual knowledge.

**Kabir** —Poet and spiritual luminary who lived in India in the fifteenth century. His songs/poems blend Hindu and Muslim ideals.

**Kala** —Time; a name for Yama, the god of death; a name for Shiva.

**Kalachakra** —The wheel of birth and death into which unawakened beings are born, experiencing various dualities such as good and bad, pleasure and pain, etc. according to their karmas until enlightenment dawns.

**Kalas** —Principles such as prana, mind, the senses and the elements; in Tantric systems, kanchukas or restricting sheaths which apparently condition and limit the limitless Reality.

**Kalatma or Kalavati** —One of the four Goddesses or aspects of Kundalini Shakti who, when awakened, presides over and directs the force of Kundalini into the higher centers of awareness, breaking down all impediments and all attachment to name and form.

**Kali** —The Divine Mother of the Universe in Her four-armed form, worshipped by Sri Ramakrishna Paramahamsa; the consort of Lord Shiva from the Tantric viewpoint.

**Kali Avatar** —Sri Ramakrishna Paramahamsa, the Divine Incarnation of Kali, the Divine Mother of the Universe.

**Kali Puja** —A profoundly intense and auspicious ceremony performed on a prescribed day sacred to the worship of Mother Kali, the Divine Mother of the Universe, Who is the essence of all gods and goddesses.

**Kali Yuga** —The present age characterized by a prevalence of ignorance and loss of spiritual awareness.

**Kama-vasayita** —One of the eight occult powers which allow those who seek lower ideals to thoroughly enjoy all desires which come to mind.

**Kanchuka** —In Tantra, a word used to describe any of the many principles through which Consciousness as Shiva or Shakti can manifest; divisions of apparently conditioned Reality; covering; armor.

**Karma Yoga** —The path of selfless service and divinely oriented action.

**Karma** —Good and bad action and its results; residual effects appearing in the life of embodied beings due to past and present activities.

**Karnataka** —Referring to a specific race of Indian people.

**Karya-vibhavaka** —The Supreme agent of all action; he who acts in accordance with his highest dharma.

**Karya-vibhavini** —The Divine Mother as ultimate cause of all activity; she who acts in accordance with her highest dharma.

**Kashmiri Shaivism** —A well-developed philosophy emphasizing Shiva as the ultimate ground of existence which declares the identity of the individual soul, jiva, with the Supreme Soul, Paramashiva.

**Kathopanishad** —An upanishad sacred to the Vedic tradition in which Nachiketas, a young man, journeys to the realm of Yama, the god of death, to uncover what lies beyond death and learn what is the essence of life.

**Kedarnath** —A sacred pilgrimage place high in the Himalayas.

**Kenopanishad** —A short but powerful scripture which concentrates upon the transcendent and all-pervasive Atman and which includes a story about the gods and their encounter with the Absolute Brahman. In this upanishad, the Divine Mother of the Universe also makes a rare appearance.

**Kerala** —A province in India.

**Khalas** —A devotee of the Sri Ramchandra who wrote endearing songs.

**Kichuri** —A tasty Indian food preparation.

**Keshava** —A name for Lord Krishna meaning long-haired; slayer of Keshi.

**Kilesa** —Pali for klesha used in Buddhism to describe certain impediments to the attainment of enlightenment.

**Kleshas** —The five obstacles to spiritual advancement according to Patanjali, the father of yoga, which are ignorance, egotism, attachment, aversion, and clinging to life.

**Kosha** —Sheath or covering. The term is used in Vedanta to indicate those aspects of creation – namely body, life-force, mind, intelligence and ego – which obscure or apparently condition pure Consciousness called Brahman; a small metal container used for water offerings in sacred puja.

**Kritanta** —Literally, "end of action," it is a name of Yama, the god of Death, who takes away all acts, words and deeds as well as plans and intentions.

**Kriya** —To act; in Tantra, spontaneous divinely-oriented action; internal rising of Kundalini Shakti which produces certain external effects on the body and mind; practice aimed at higher understanding with regards to spirituality.

**Kriya Shuddha** —Purity of act and intention.

**Kriyavati** —One of four Goddesses or aspects of Kundalini Shakti that, when awakened, grants detachment from the body and fulfills all aspirations associated with the physical realm, allowing for the transcendence of matter and revelation of higher awareness.

**Kshama** —Of the earth; enduring.

**Kularnava Tantra** —One of the Tantras which, among other teachings, upholds and praises the qualities of the guru.

**Kumbha Mela** —An important religious festival held in India where thousands of aspirants and spiritual beings gather to bathe in the confluence of three sacred rivers during an auspicious cycle of time.

**Kundalini or Kundalini Shakti** —The powerful yet subtle spiritual force that when awakened brings illumination to all levels of the being.

**Kundalini Yoga** —The path of union with God that concentrates upon the union of Shiva and Shakti through the awakening of the spiritual power inherent within. It is said to incorporate and contain all other Yogas. For this reason it is often called Mahayoga.

**Kuntala** —Master farmer; plough; a farmer whom the Avadhut met and stayed with during his travels.

**Kurma** —The great tortoise which was Vishnu's second incarnation and whose exploits are listed in the Kurma Purana.

**Kurukshetra** —A famous location in India where the great war spoken of in the Mahabharata took place and upon whose field Sri Krishna gave His inspirational discourse on yoga and the Atman to a confused and dejected Arjuna.

**Kutastha** —Immutable; imperishable; firm or rock solid.

**Laghima** —One of the eight occult powers by which those who seek lesser attainments become light and are said to defy gravity.

**Lakshmana** —Literally, "bearing auspicious marks"; the devoted and illumined half-brother of Sri Ramachandra and husband of Sita's sister.

**Lakshmi** —The Goddess of Fortune who is listed as one of the five main feminine divinities in the Srimad Devi Bhagavatam.

**Lao-tzu** —Literally, "ancient master," he was a contemporary of Confucius and taught in accordance with the Tao, living an unpretentious but prolific life.

**Lopamudra** —Literally, "of extremely subtle form." The illustrious wife of the renowned sage and rishi, Agastya, she was said to have written a portion of the Rig Veda.

**Laya** —Dissolution; immersion.

**Layayoga** —The merging of the individual soul into the Supreme Soul; a stage of Kundalini Yoga associated with refining the mind and intellect, dissolving mental barriers and merging consciousness into its Source.

**Lila** —Play or sport, especially associated with consciousness appearing in the universe.

**Loka or Lokas** —Literally, world or realm; world of names and forms.

**Luchi** —A Indian bread that is usually fried and sometimes sweet.

**Madhya Pradesh** —A province in India.

**Madhyama** —The third phase of the manifestation of pure knowledge from the primal sound vibration wherein thought and meaning are formed and fused; subtle sound.

**Mahabharata** —Literally, "Great Land," which is an epithet given to Mother India; an epic divinely-oriented story which forms a part of the secondary scriptures of India called Smritis.

**Mahadeva** —Literally, "Great God," which is a name for Lord Shiva.

**Mahakali** —A most powerful aspect of the Divine Mother in Her formless, transcendent nature.

**Mahalila** —The great play or sport of Consciousness; the cosmic theater with all beings as actors and actresses and the Divine Being as the writer, producer and director.

**Mahamantra** —An important mantra for Sita, Radha, Rama and Krishna which is essential to the worship and spiritual practice of the Vaishnavas; a mantra of divine origin associated with the Avatar of any given age or yuga.

**Mahamaya** —The grand illusion; the superimposition of the universe and its constituents over Brahman; the One who conjures up the grand illusion.

**Maharaja** —In Tantra, the female fluid discharged from the ovaries and its inherent power and potential for spiritual awakening; a name of reverent respect given to an illumined swami; great king.

**Maharloka** —The fourth of seven higher realms of existence beyond the nether regions or transcendent of the physical universe.

**Maharastra** —A province in India.

**Maharshi or Maha-Rishi** —A great soul or seer of ancient times. Though there are many Rishis, there are seven predominant ancient ones, one of which, according to Sri Ramakrishna, has recently reincarnated in this age as Swami Vivekananda.

**Mahashakti** —The Supreme power inherent in Ultimate Reality which causes the powers of creation, preservation, and dissolution to formulate and activate the worlds of name and form.

**Mahat** —Cosmic Intelligence; the first principle of creation according to the Samkhya Philosophy of Kapila.

**Mahatala** —One of the seven hell realms below earth or beneath the physical universe with regards to evolution.

**Mahavayu** —Literally, "Great Wind," referring to the rise of Kundalini Shakti, the spiritual energy which ascends up the spinal column and opens the spiritual centers of higher awareness.

**Mahavidya Mahamaya Bhagavati Durga Devi** —A name for the Divine Mother of the Universe resplendent with all power and glory, cited in the Srimad Devi Bhagavatam.

**Mahavishnu** —Literally, the "Great Worker," who is Lord of the Worlds presiding over their preservation and overseeing all other functions.

**Mahayoga** —The highest aspect of yoga where through the power of pure affirmation within the context of realization, all is seen as Brahman.

**Mahayuga** —The combined time span of the four yugas: Satya, Treta, Dwapara, and Kali.

**Mahima** —Greatness, glory; one of the eight occult powers which bestow upon those who seek lower pursuits the ability to become radiant, impressive or suffused with light.

**Mahuts** —Elephant drivers.

**Maitreyi** —One of the most virtuous and learned women of India who was also the wife of the great rishi, Yajnavalkya.

**Manana or Mananam** —Utilizing the mind for spiritual studies and pursuits; the second of three stages of spiritual progress in Vedanta where one contemplates the Truth with an open and receptive mind in the proximity of guru and sangha. It must be preceded by hearing the Truth from a competent preceptor and followed by realizing the Truth through direct experience.

**Manas** —Mind; one of the four aspects of antahkarana according to Samkhya and Vedanta, the other three being ego, consciousness and intelligence.

**Manasa** —A powerful manifestation of the Goddess with great intellectual prowess and characterized by austerity and renunciation.

**Mandukyopanishad** —A major upanishad made all the more important by Gaudapada's karika or commentary on it. Its teachings explain the four quarters of the sacred bija Aum and transmit the essence of nonduality called Advaita Vedanta.

**Manksha** —Longing; to long for or desire intensely; a fellow sadhu whom the Avadhut met in Gangotri.

**Manojavittvam** —Victory over the mind and its various powers. The fourth practice of purification prescribed by Tantra wherein the aspirant gains control of the mind and can move easily throughout the three worlds.

**Mantra or Mantram** —A powerful formula consisting of seed syllables and Holy Names that the initiate uses to purify the mind and invoke the presence of God.

**Mantra Yoga** —A stage in Kundalini Yoga associated with phonetics, bijas, and mantras.

**Marali** —A female swan; Pandit Pratapa's wife, friend of the Avadhut.

**Mata Ganga** —Literally, "Mother Ganga." A name for the sacred river Ganges and particularly the Goddess who resides in it as its various spiritual and healing properties.

**Mataji** —Revered Mother; a term of endearment and respect used by Ekanta for his female vanaprastin teacher.

**Maya** —Illusion; the projecting and veiling power of Brahman which causes the appearance, existence and disappearance of the universe; in Tantra, the basic fabric which underlies every created realm and thing and which is an essential power of the Absolute called Paramashiva.

**Maya Shakti** —The Divine Mother as the power of illusion and obscuration and as the One who removes these from human consciousness at the auspicious time.

**Mayavadins** —Those who prescribe to the theory that the universe and its various aspects are an illusory appearance over Reality with no existence whatsoever. They are sometimes mistaken for Advaitists.

**Medha** —Intellect and its power of retentive memory; the goddess of intelligence.

**Meghalaya** —A province in the northeastern part of India not far from Bengal and bordering Bangladesh, heavily populated by tribal peoples.

**Milarepa** —A luminary of the Mahasiddha lineage of Tibet who was a fine songwriter and an uncommon and unique teacher. He was a student of Marpa who brought the yoga-based teachings of the Mahasiddhas to Tibet from India. His songs communicate the essence of enlightenment and are a living transmission even today.

**Mithya** —illusion, unreality.

**Mithya-Tyagi** —Literally, "renunciation of delusion," it is also the sixth stage of progression in the guru/disciple relationship.

**Moha** —Delusion; false identification; infatuation.

**Mohur** —A monetary denomination.

**Moksha** —Spiritual emancipation, or freedom from the rounds of birth and death due to karma.

**Mudra** —Mystical hand gestures symbolizing various expressions of divinity and spirituality. Some are used for purification, some for transmission and others for conferring boons and blessings.

**Mukti** —Spiritual emancipation similar to moksha.

**Muladhara chakra** —The root chakra located at the base of the spine where Kundalini Shakti lies coiled up and sleeping until it is awakened by spiritual disciplines.

**Mulakleshas** —According to Buddhism, any of a set of ten or more unwholesome tendencies which attend the unillumined human mind such as hatred, pride, desire, misconception, etc.

**Mulavidya** —Root ignorance or primal ignorance. It is the same as mula-jnana in that all potentialities, positive and negative, spring from it.

**Mumukshutvam** —A strong desire or longing for liberation; the fourth of the Four Jewels of Vedanta sadhana and spiritual attainment.

**Mundakopanishad** —Literally, the "cutting edge of a razor," this Upanishad gives teachings designed to cut away ignorance from the mind. Its profound authority comes from the fact that its wisdom, a direct transmission from the god Brahma, is given by the great rishi Angiras to the famed disciple Saunaka.

**Muni** —A wise person or sage, often one that observes mauna – silence.

**Mussalman** —An adherent and follower of the Muslim religion.

**Nachiketas** —The bright young aspirant of Kathopanishad fame who transcended death after thoroughly questioning Yama, the god of death, about Reality.

**Nada Brahman** —Like Shabdha Brahman, a path to Brahman, the Absolute Reality, through the sacred sound Aum and its many expressions such as wisdom based devotional music, the scriptures and the refined life-force.

**Nadis** —Subtle nerves or channels which conduct life-force and psychic current.

**Nagas and naginis** —Reptilian gods and goddesses imbued with great spirituality, who are guardians of the watery realms.

**Nama-rupa** —A cover-all term for name and form, applying to the world of created things that are transitory and impermanent.

**Namaskar** —A term of reverence and respect in Bengali.

**Namaste** —A Sanskrit term of reverence used as salutation.

**Narada** —The great sage and Devarshi who was associated with many Divine Beings and who was an authoritative commentator on the path of Bhakti Yoga.

**Nara yajna** —Offerings given to all human beings in the form of various types of service, which also includes sacrifice for the common and individual good.

**Narayana** —A name for God; God manifest in mankind.

**Narayani** —A name for the Divine Mother of the Universe.

**Navaratri** —Literally, "Nine Nights," indicating the nine-day festival of the Divine Mother of the Universe celebrated in India and around the world, usually during October. On the tenth day the sacred image of Sri Durga, the Universal Mother, is immersed in the Ganges River.

**Neti neti** —"Not this, not this." A Vedantic practice of the Jnana Yoga school which proceeds by negating all phenomenal things until the Ultimate Reality stands revealed. The practice culminates in iti iti – "all this, all this" – which declares that all is indeed Brahman.

**Nididhyasana** —After shravana, hearing the truth, and manana, reasoning about It, it is the third and highest level of comprehension in Vedanta sadhana which involves realizing Truth. Its attainment signals enlightenment while lack of its attainment shows the need for deeper insight. Those who have merely heard the Truth are novices and beginners. Those who reason about Truth are sincere aspirants and, at a higher stage, jnanis or wisdom knowers. Those who have experienced what Truth epitomizes are the true luminaries and are rare.

**Nine Limbs of Bhakti** —A complete and beneficial system of devotional and wisdom practices transmitted by Sri Ramachandra in the Adhyatma Ramayana.

**Niradhara** —Depending on nothing for support.

**Nirajana** —Burning of camphor and incense before the sacred image on the altar.

**Niralamba** —Without support; needing no foundation.

**Niramaya** —Free of taints and diseases.

**Niranjana** —Immaculate; spotless.

**Nirashraya** —Supportless.

**Niratishayaghanibhutashakti** —Massive power; intense potency; concentrated force.

**Niravadhiatitaram** —Complete; constant, profuse.

**Niravarana** —Revealed; without veils.

**Niravayava** —Devoid of limbs; without attachments.

**Nirbharata** —Fullness, even to an excess.

**Nirbija** —Free from mental impressions called samskaras; without potential for imposed manifestation.

**Nirguna** —Formless; completely devoid of qualities or attributes.

**Nirlipta** —Totally unattached.

**Nirmala** —Free of impurities.

**Nirmoha** —Free from delusion.

**Nirodha** —Literally, destruction or suppression; the absolute extinction of all adjuncts or conditions resulting in the highest samadhi.

**Nirupadhika** —Free of limiting adjuncts or conditions.

**Nirvana** —Literally, "Free of desire," it is the direct experience of freedom uninhibited by any condition or limitation; spiritual emancipation.

**Nirvedya** —Unknowable.

**Nirvikalpa Samadhi** —Direct nondual experience of the impersonal or egoless type; the highest Samadhi; immersion into formless essence.

**Nirvishesha** —Devoid of characteristics.

**Niskama Karma** —Work or actions performed without any desire for personal gain or recompense. It is the kind of activity, transcendent of any karmic residue, that enlightened beings engage in.

**Nitya** —Eternal; permanent; a phrase used to affirm the eternal nature of the scriptures as the word of God.

**Nityasiddhas** —A class of ever-free beings who are always aware of their inherent perfection.

**Nivritti** —Renunciation; freedom from worldly vibrations.

**Niyamas** —Five preliminary exercises from the Raja Yoga system which prepare the aspirant for spiritual life, namely, tapas, svadhyaya, ishvara-pranidhana, santosha and saucha – austerities, study, devotion to God, contentment and purity.

**Niyati** —In Tantra, one of the kanchukas or wrappings over Reality which creates the relationship between cause and effect and is therefore crucial to the process of creation; religious duty; a name for the Divine Mother Durga in the Devi Purana.

**Ojas** —Spiritual force developed from sublimation of the sexual energy in human beings that is then used to realize one's inherent divine nature and to teach others about the eternal principles of spiritual life.

**Om** —Same as Aum.

**Om Namo Narayana** —A greeting of great respect and reverence used among those who recognize God dwelling in each other.

**Om Surya Narayan** —Salutations to the Light of Pure Conscious Awareness; a reverent salute to the god of the sun.

**Paddy** —Unhusked rice processed under a mortar or husked by hand.

**Pakoras** —Vegetables, dipped in spicy batter and deep fried.

**Panchatapa** —The ritual of the five fires, an austerity undertaken for spiritual benefit.

**Pandava** —The dharmic family of Panda and Kunti who gave birth to the five Pandu brothers, including Arjuna and Yudhisthira.

**Pandit** —A scholar; an erudite thinker.

**Para** —Supreme; the first stage of manifestation of highest knowledge through the primal sound vibration. It is an undifferentiated state where no concepts, thoughts, meanings or words are yet manifest.

**Parabrahma or Parabrahman** —The Ultimate Reality or Supreme Being as formless essence or Pure Consciousness.

**Paramahamsa** —Literally, 'Great Swan.' A title referring to the highest class of sannyasins.

**Paramatman** —The Supreme Soul.

**Paraprakriti** —The Supreme One, the Mother of the Universe, who presides over the powers of nature.

**Parashakti** —The highest aspect of shakti.

**Paravidya** —Supreme knowledge associated with the direct experience of Brahman; sometimes used to indicate the distinction between knowledge of the truths of the scriptures as opposed to secular knowledge.

**Parvati** —An aspect of the highest shakti, the Divine Mother of the Universe, spouse and consort of Lord Shiva, who was daughter of King Himavata of the great snow mountains. Therefore comes Her name which means "mountain-born" or "of the mountains"; the cashew nut; flax plant and seed.

**Pashyanti** —The second stage of manifested knowledge through the primal sound vibration where undifferentiated Wisdom begins to condense and form in order to manifest as conceptualized thought on the cosmic level.

**Patala** —Nether regions; the seventh and lowest of the hell realms.

**Patanjala Yoga** —Called Raja Yoga and Ashtanga Yoga, it is the classic yogic pathway with eight progressive but interconnected practices, namely: yamas, niyamas, asana, pranayama, pratyahara, dharana, dhyana and samadhi. It bears little resemblance to, nor should it be mistaken for what passes for yoga in present times, which is often just Hatha Yoga, a series of body postures practiced merely for gaining health, longevity and the occult powers which are potentially detrimental to the attainment of true spirituality.

**Patanjala** —The eight-limbed Yoga Philosophy named after its founder.

**Patanjali** —The founder of the Patanjala Yoga system and author of the Yoga Sutras.

**Pice** —A monetary denomination roughly equal to a penny.

**Pingala** —Golden or tawny-colored; in Vedanta, a demi-god who is an attendant of the sun; in Kundalini Yoga, a subtle nerve and its energy associated with the right nostril and right side of the spine which brings radiance and power.

**Pippalada** —An enlightened rishi of ancient Vedic times best known for his appearance and discourse in the Prasnopanishad.

**Pitru yajna** —Offerings given to the pitris or respected ancestors.

**Pradhana Jaya** —Victory over the force of initial conception. The sixth practice of purification in Tantra wherein the aspirant gets control over the very first power of creation – the Mahat or Cosmic Mind. After this realization, full enlightenment dawns. This consists, in part, of the comprehension that the Atman is both beyond and superior to the process of evolution and is the only true and abiding Reality.

**Prajapati** —Literally, Lord of creation; the first-born of Brahma and teacher of gods and human beings.

**Prajna** —Pure Intelligence; Conscious Awareness; a name given to the causal state of consciousness by Vedanta philosophy which is the third condition of awareness correlating to deep sleep.

**Prajnanam Brahma** —"Brahman is Pure Consciousness;" one of the four Mahavakyas or divine declarations of Advaita Vedanta.

**Prakamya** —One of the eight occult powers which allows those who pursue lower ideals to become free willed with regards to fulfilling any desire or wish.

**Prakriti** —Nature; causal matter; the universe of name and form and those ingredients which comprise it; the pradhana of Samkhya which corresponds to the Maya of Vedanta with these main distinctions – it exists independent of Spirit and it is considered real.

**Prakriti Jaya** —Victory over the modes of nature and the cosmic laws. The third practice of purification prescribed by Tantra wherein the aspirant realizes that the Self is not subject to either the forces of nature or the cosmic powers which operate those forces.

**Pralaya** —Dissolution of all material forces, energies and substances into their immediate cause after cycles of manifestation are over. Pralaya is of four types: Nitya, Naimittika, Prakrita and Atyantika. The first three denote dissolution back into a cosmic source while the fourth is dissolution to the Ultimate Source.

**Prana** —Subtle energy; life-force; vital being; the subtle force from which all mental and physical energy has evolved.

**Pranam or Pranams** —Reverent salutations, usually by way of prostration.

**Pranayama** —The fourth stage of Patanjala Yoga involving the control of the various energies in the vital being; breathing exercises, which when used carefully under the direct supervision of an illumined preceptor, help still the mind for meditation.

**Prasad** —Sanctified food, either blessed during a religious ceremony, blessed at mealtime or blessed by the hand of the guru. Such food is essential to spiritual life and unfoldment due to its purified condition.

**Prasna** —A question.

**Prasnopanishad** —One of the sacred scriptures of Vedanta which forms a part of the knowledge portion (Brahmakanda) of the Vedas, concerned solely with the realization of the Soul (Atman). The Prasnopanishad revolves around the rishi Pippalada's answer to six questions by six different aspirants.

**Pratapa** —Majesty; brilliance; warmth; the name of the Pandit whom the Avadhut used to visit in Bombay at the Advaita Ashrama.

**Pratipakshabhavanam** —Raising an opposite wave; a Vedantic spiritual practice of the individual will that substitutes a positive tendency for a negative one, i.e., courage for fear, love for hate, etc.

**Pratyahara** —Withdrawing the senses from their objects; the fifth limb in the eight-limbed system of Patanjali's Yoga.

**Prema Bhakti** —The highest kind of devotion, beyond Vaidya and Raga Bhakti, which involve ritualistic devotion and the various devotional moods. To paraphrase Sri Ramakrishna, Prema Bhakti is that purest of Love which makes one forget all personal considerations – even the body that is usually so dear to human beings.

**Priti** —Joy; love.

**Puja** —Ceremonial worship attended by offerings, mudras, mantras and devotional music.

**Pujari** —One who officiates at a puja, usually an ordained priest or trained assistant.

**Punyamitra** —Literally, "bestower of merit," it is a also name for Yama, the god of death; virtue.

**Puranas** —Ancient scriptures illustrating the lives of the gods and Avataras and their relations with saints, sages and human beings. They are eighteen in number: six to Brahma, six to Vishnu, and six to Shiva and they take the form of dialogue or discourse between guru and disciple. There are also a set of Upapuranas and some Sthulapuranas.

**Purna** —Fullness; completeness.

**Puri** —A holy city that is one of the four cardinal pilgrimage places in India, the other three being Dvaraka, Kedarnath and Rameshvaram. The Jagganatha Temple is in Puri and attracts thousands of pilgrims.

**Purnoham** —Literally, "This Self is full, complete," indicating that the true Self of all beings has no wants, needs or desires.

**Purusha** —Divine indweller in the heart; the Supreme Soul; in Samhkya Philosophy, the Supreme Self as opposed to Prakriti, the insentient nature principle.

**Puspi** —Like a flower; tender, fragrant; the young child, daughter of Svarmani and Dharman, whom the Avadhut came to know and learn from.

**Radha or Sri Radha** —The Divine Mother of the Universe in Her form as selfless, all-pervasive Love; The divine consort of Sri Krishna.

**Radha-Mantra** —A sacred mantra invoking Sri Radha, the divine consort of Sri Krishna; the Mahamantra.

**Rahu** —A mythical demon that was believed to dwell in the sky and which devoured the moon over cycles and at the time of lunar eclipses.

**Raja Yoga** —The royal path, in reference to Patanjala Yoga which facilitates control of the mind, mastery of meditation and attainment of samadhi; a stage of Kundalini Yoga associated with penetrating and ascending above the lower centers of awareness and merging in samadhi.

**Rajarshi** —A learned king or kingly figure who is also versed in the scriptures; a teacher of kings.

**Rajas** —Rajo guna, the mode of Prakriti that, on a cosmic level, places all things in motion and on an individual level, induces beings into all manner of activity, usually of a frenetic variety.

**Rakshakali** —A terrific aspect of the Divine Mother who is worshipped for protection from all negativities.

**Ram or Rama** —The Divine Incarnation of the Treta Yuga whose heroic actions and superior teachings appear in the Adhyatma Ramayana and other scriptures.

**Ramachandra** —Same as Ram and Rama.

**Ramakrishna** —The great God-intoxicated holy man of nineteenth-century Bengal who was the guru of Swami Vivekananda and the husband of Sri Sarada Devi. Accepted by many as the Kali Avatar, the Divine Incarnation of this age, He came with a host of Ishvarakotis and illumined followers who founded the order named after Him and whose followers sustain it in the present day. His advent has been responsible for the reemergence of the Divine Mother path.

**Ramakrishnadas Baul** —The holy figure of the baul sect whom the Avadhut met and exchanged wisdom with occasionally in his travels.

**Ramakrishnadas** —Servant of Rama, Krishna and Sri Ramakrishna.

**Ramayana** —The famous epic Hindu scripture detailing the events of the auspicious life of Sri Ramachandra and His divine consort Sita, replete with well-loved characters such as Hanuman and Lakshmana.

**Ramprasad** —The well-loved poet/saint of eighteenth-century Bengal whose wisdom songs to Mother Kali, the Divine Mother of the Universe, inspired a nation and are still inspiring the world today.

**Rasagola** —An Indian sweet.

**Rasatala** —One of the seven hell realms.

**Ratna** —A city in India.

**Ravana** —A powerful and arrogant asura who abducted Sita and was finally destroyed by Sri Ramachandra.

**Rishis** —Illumined beings from ancient Vedic times who practiced extreme austerities in order to receive the truths contained in the Vedas and Upanishads. Most were married, of both sexes and passed their wisdom orally to their children.

**Rishi yajna** —Offerings of reverence and respect given to the ancient teachers who disseminate spiritual truths to the peoples of the world.

**Rudra** —Shiva in His wrathful form as the destroyer, who destroys both the universe at the time of pralaya and the ignorance and transgressions of His votaries.

**Sadanga** —Literally, six-limbed; used in reference to Patanjala Yoga with regard to the final six limbs of that system since the first two, the yamas and niyamas totaling ten different practices, are often seen as a system of their own and worthy of intense effort. Without learning and practicing the ten yamas and niyamas under an adept guide, an aspirant should not even begin the basic posture and breathing exercises prescribed in the third and fourth limbs of Patanjala Yoga. Otherwise, attachment to the body and sensual pleasure will occur and impede the practice. This oversight is a cause for the gross misuse of the yoga system in the world today.

**Sadhak or Sadhaka** —One who practices sadhana, or spiritual disciplines.

**Sadhakas** —A group of practitioners undergoing spiritual exercises.

**Sadhana** —Spiritual disciplines undertaken to realize God.

**Sadhanachatushtaya** —The Four Jewels and Six Treasures of Vedanta: viveka, vairagya, sama, dama, uparati, titksha, samadhana, shraddha and mumukshutvam – discrimination, detachment, inner peace, self-control, self-settledness, forbearance, one-pointed concentration, faith and a desire for liberation or enlightenment.

**Sadhu** —Same as Sadhaka.

**Saguna** —With attributes; with form.

**Sahashrara chakra** —The highest center of awareness, called the crown chakra, located at the top of the head.

**Sakama Karma** —Work or action done with desire for results or personal motive. It is karma-producing whereas niskama karma, action done as selfless service of God in all beings, does not create new karma.

**Sakshi Bhutam** —The Supreme Witness of all phenomena.

**Sama** —Inner peace; one of the Six Treasures of Vedanta practice.

**Samadhana** —One of the Six Treasures of Vedanta, it is a kind of concentration that, at early stages of sadhana, saves against the danger of the mind drifting back to sense objects and at advanced stages of sadhana allows for one-pointed concentration in meditation.

**Samadhi** —Literally, "to make immovable," steady and impervious to external conditions. Any of the various kinds of spiritual moods or states of Consciousness brought about by meditation upon Reality, either with form or without form.

**Samana** —Seeing all as equal; one of the names of Yama, the god of death, in the Yamastakam.

**Samasti** —Macrocosm; collective experience; one of the two modes of Maya, the other being vyasti – individual.

**Samhita** —One of the four sections of the Vedas which deals with sacred hymns and mantras; a collection of verses contained in a religious text.

**Samkhya** —One of six orthodox systems of philosophy in Vedic culture which astutely outlines the various principles that comprise the universe. Its widespread acceptance is noted in both Yoga and Vedanta.

**Samprajnata Samadhi** —A high state of Awareness mentioned by Patanjali in the Yoga Sutras which is still accompanied by traces of individualized consciousness. In it, an awareness of the triad of meditator, meditation and that which is meditated upon still remains. It is generally synonymous with Savikalpa Samadhi in the Vedanta school.

**Samsara** —Life lived in ignorance of one's true spiritual nature, the effects of which cause repeated births and deaths in ignorance.

**Samskaras** —Positive and negative latent impressions in the subconscious and unconscious mind that shape human character and which are caused by repetitious actions through many lifetimes.

**Samvit** —Highest knowledge; pure Consciousness; a name for the Divine Mother of the Universe.

**Sananda** —Literally, 'with bliss'; a blissful state of awareness which is one of the four lesser states or conditions of Samprajnata Samadhi.

**Sanatana Dharma** —The Eternal Religion of the ancient Vedic culture; eternal Truth which is never conceived of or non-existent but is ever-existent.

**Sangha** —Literally, 'in good company,' the term is used to denote holy company, particularly with regards to the spiritual family of seekers with which the devotee associates.

**Sankalpas** —Thoughts, imaginings or fantasies which occupy the mind and keep it from one-pointed concentration and meditation on Reality. They are potentially positive whereas vikalpas, doubts and misconceptions, are detrimental and must be eliminated. Both sankalpas and vikalpas are overcome by the consummate Yogi.

**Sannyas** —The vow of renunciation bestowed upon one who gives up the world and takes fully to spiritual life.

**Sannyasin** —One who takes a vow of renunciation of the world and enters spiritual life.

**Sanskrit** —Literally, "perfect." The ancient language of the Vedic culture.

**Santosha** —Contentedness. One of the ten yamas and niyamas of Patanjala Yoga which provides for balance and peace of mind.

**Sarada Devi** —The Divine Mother in human form manifesting in this age, also known as the Holy Mother, the spiritual consort of Sri Ramakrishna Paramahamsa. She lived from 1853 to 1920 and was the inspiration and spiritual leader of the Ramakrishna order after the Master's samadhi, initiating hundreds of devotees into spiritual life.

**Sarasvati** —The Goddess of art and learning who is listed as one of the five main aspects of the Universal Mother (Prakriti Panchaka) in the Srimad Devi Bhagavatam.

**Sarvachaitanyarupa** —Literally, 'the form of all Consciousness' or, 'Whose form is all Consciousness,' it is a name for the Divine Mother of the Universe listed in the Srimad Devi Bhagavatam.

**Sarveshvarah** —Lord of all beings.

**Sasmita** —Literally, with I-sense; one of the four stages of Samprajnata Samadhi in which a tiny presence of the individual persists, maintaining a transparent barrier between the devotee and Absolute Reality.

**Satchitananda** —Pure Being, pure Consciousness, pure Bliss Absolute; a name for the formless Brahman.

**Satguru or Sadguru** —A world teacher such as Krishna, Christ, Buddha, Mohammed or Sri Ramakrishna and other founders of the world's great religious traditions.

**Satsang** —Literally, 'In the company of Truth.' A gathering together for informal spiritual talk and discourse with guru and sangha.

**Sattva Purusha Nytakyati** —A realized condition described in the Tantra Philosophy experienced by the illumined ones, the main characteristic of which is the absolute knowledge that the Atman is the only unchanging principle in existence.

**Sattva or Sattvas** —Sattva guna. The mode of Prakriti that, on a cosmic level, fills the universe with peace and unity and, on an individual level, induces balance and equilibrium in human action and behavior.

**Sattvic** —Being in a balanced and positive condition where sattva guna is predominant.

**Satya** —Truth; truthfulness in thought, word and deed. It is one of the ten yamas and niyamas of Patanjala Yoga and a mainstay of spiritual life in general.

**Satyaloka** —Literally, "Realm of Truth," it is synonymous with Brahmaloka.

**Saucha** —Purity. One of the ten yamas and niyamas of Patanjala Yoga which allows the aspirant to experience higher states of Consciousness.

**Savichara** —Literally, "with inquiry"; one of the four stages of Samprajnata Samadhi in which the intelligence is fully refined but still operative, therefore causing a subtle distinction between Brahman and the jiva through awareness of individual knowledge.

**Savikalpa Samadhi** —A very high state of Consciousness wherein Brahman with attributes is experienced through the refined mechanism of the detached and ripened ego/mind complex.

**Savitarka Samadhi** —Literally, with logic and reason; an exalted state of mind which is one of the four stages of Samprajnata Samadhi. It is reached by taking logic and reason to their highest expression.

**Shabda Yoga** —A path to God utilizing sacred and universal sound such as Aum and its transforming power which is an expression of Brahman. The shabda, or sphota, infers a world of sound that has two aspects, gross and subtle. When these two are comprehended and fused in understanding, a great force called shakti is released and through Her Grace and Presence, enlightenment dawns on the mind.

**Shaivism** —The philosophy which stresses the worship of Lord Shiva, it is ancient and Tantric in nature and has many different schools of thought. It is one of the four main religious approaches of the Tantra, the other three being Shaktism, Vaishnavism and Ganaptya.

**Shaivaite** —A follower of Shaivism.

**Shakti** —The creative force of the universe which is the active principle of Brahman yet identical with It. It is different and more subtle than prana, which is a force that it uses to create. As the Mahaskati or Universal Mother, it is also the wielder of the forces of Maya and Prakriti.

**Shankara** —The great exponent of Advaita Vedanta who brought it into prominence and spread it broadcast throughout India and the world. He authored such important texts as the Vivekachudamani and Atma Bodha among others; a name for Lord Siva.

**Shankaracharya** —See Shankara.

**Shankari** —The spouse of Shiva; a name for the Divine Mother of the Universe; Uma; Parvati.

**Shantadasya** —Servant of peace; two of five moods through which a devotee looks upon God as chosen ideal called Ishta-devata – with a peaceful attitude (shanta), as master (dasya), as child (vatsalya), as friend (sakhya) and as beloved (madhura).

**Shanti** —Eternal Peace, sublime and inexpressible, precious to the Rishis of Sanatana Dharma and to all aspirants and luminaries.

**Shantoham** —Literally, "His name is peace," indicating that the Lord is of the very nature of deep and profound peace.

**Shastras** —The scriptures; spiritual teachings given with authority.

**Shesha** —The one-thousand headed serpent who supports Lord Vishnu and who symbolizes eternity, from which comes his name, Ananta.

**Shiva** —The third deity in the Hindu Trinity; the God of Wisdom who dissolves the universe of name and form at the end of cosmic cycles.

**Shiva-lingam** —The sacred symbol for Shiva worship which signifies the all-pervasiveness of Reality. There are twelve natural lingams in India where Shiva is said to dwell more intensely.

**Shobha** —Lustrous; radiant; brilliant.

**Shraddha** —Faith; one of the Six Treasures of the Four Jewels of Vedanta practice.

**Shravanam** —Hearing the scriptures; listening to God's glories daily, one of the eight devotional practices according to Narada along with smaranam, archanam, kirtanam, vandanam, sevanam, bhajanam and sharanam – remembering the Lord, adoring Him, singing His glories, worshipping Him, serving Him and His devotees, fostering devotion to Him and taking complete refuge in Him.

**Shruti** —Listening to Truth; divinely revealed scripture; the highest scriptures of absolute authority such as the Vedas and Upanishads; the first of three practices in Vedanta called shruti, yukti and anubhava – hearing the Truth, reasoning about It and realizing It.

**Shuddha** —Purity.

**Shukra** —The male semen and its powerful subtle energy which can be sublimated and utilized for spiritual awakening.

**Shunya or Shunyata** —Void; nothingness.

**Shunyavadins** —Those who subscribe to the belief that all phenomena is without substance; a follower of the Madyamika school of Nagarjuna.

**Shushumna** —A subtle nerve channel and its current that runs between the Muladhara chakra to the Sahasrara chakra and which acts as a channel when Kundalini Shakti awakens and rises.

**Siddhas** —A class of perfected beings; a class of beings attracted to the attainment of limited powers.

**Siddhis** —Perfections, as in the authentic qualities and attributes of an disciple or luminary; occult powers that are detrimental to spiritual advancement and realization.

**Sita** —The Divine Mother of the Universe in Her aspect of immaculate Purity who manifested in the Treta Yuga as the divine consort of Sri Ramchandra.

**Skandha** —A portion, paragraph or sentence of a scriptural work.

**Sloka** —A Sanskrit phrase.

**Smriti** —Retentive memory; remembrance; secondary scriptures of Hindu tradition such as the Code of Manu, etc.

**Soham** —Literally, "That am I"; the indrawn breath of the ajapa mantra.

**Soma** —A type of divine elixir made from the soma plant and used in Vedic ritual. Mentioned often in the Rig Veda, it was coveted by the gods and goddesses for its pleasurable effects and was thought to confer supernatural powers.

**Spandas** —Vibration; movement; subtle principles above the twenty-four tattvas of Samhkya listed in Shaivism and other Tantric paths.

**Sri** —A name for Lakshmi, the Goddess of abundance, a term of respect for a holy being.

**Sri Bhagavan** —A reverent name for the Blessed Lord.

**Srimad Devi Bhagavatam** —One of the essential scriptures of the Tantra, particular to the Divine Mother Shakti tradition.

**Sri Durga** —The Divine Mother of the Universe in Her ten-armed aspect, worshipped reverently as the first and foremost Goddess of the Prakriti Panchaka, the five main root manifestations of Divinity.

**Sri Gangaji mantra** —A powerful healing mantra invoking the goddess of the sacred river Ganges.

**Sri Hari** —A name for Lord Vishnu.

**Sri Krishna** —See Krishna.

**Sri Ram** —See Ram, Rama or Ramachandra.

**Sri Ramakrishna** —See Ramakrishna.

**Sri Sarada Devi** —See Sarada Devi.

**Sri Sri Ma** —See Sarada Devi.

**Sri Suta** —A renown disciple of Vyasa and son of a great rishi.

**Sripada Vishnutirtha** —A Vaishnava holy man whom the Avadhut had darshan with during his travels.

**Sthiti Prajnasya** —A person of steady wisdom or a knower of Brahman who attains equipoise.

**Sthiti Samadhi** —Steady condition of samadhi.

**Sukha** —Happiness; a condition of fleeting enjoyment or temporal happiness always followed by its opposite, duhka – sorrow.

**Surebha** —Possessing a fine voice; singer; the boatman who helped the Avadhut and who in turn received spiritual instruction from him.

**Surya Narayan** —The God of the Sun, used as an epithet in both a physical and a cosmic sense.

**Sutala** —One of the seven hell realms or nether regions below the earth plane.

**Sutra** —A Sanskrit phrase, sentence or verse with profound meaning.

**Svadhyaya** —The act of engrossing oneself in an in-depth study of the scriptures, particularly the Srutis, with a view towards comprehending Truth. If this prerequisite, one of the ten niyamas of Patanjala, is not satisfied, no appreciable success in yoga is possible.

**Svarloka** —One of the seven higher realms above the earth plane, it being third in a gradated succession.

**Svarmani** —Jewel-like; bedecked with gems like the nocturnal sky; the name of Ekanta's mother.

**Svarupaya** —Essence, used in relation to the Essence of Consciousness or the highest aspect of pure Spirit.

**Svayamjyoti** —Inner Light, shining by its own inherent power, referring to the light of the Atman. Through analogy, the Vedanta Philosophy compares the light of the sun to the Atman and the light of the moon to the mind. The sun shines by its own light while the moon shines by borrowed light.

**Swadharma** —One's true and destined spiritual path leading towards full enlightenment.

**Swaha or Svaha** —An offering to the gods; an exclamation used in sacred ceremony during oblations; a bija; an aspect of the Divine Mother of the Universe.

**Swami Vivekananda** —The foremost disciple of Sri Ramakrishna Paramahamsa, he lived from 1863 to 1902. Considered to be an emanation of Lord Shiva, he was also the first to bring the spiritual teachings of Vedanta and establish them in the West.. He is also credited with giving lucid contemporary interpretations to many ancient scriptures. His auspicious appearance and august presence at the Parliament of Religions in Chicago in 1893 is a major spiritual event in the history of the Western hemisphere with profound significance.

**Swami** —A reverent title given to a spiritual teacher of the Hindu faith who has taken monastic vows.

**Taijasa** —The second of four states of consciousness described by Vedanta, called the dream state.

**Talatala** —One of the hell realms or nether realms below the earth plane.

**Tamas** —Tamo guna. The mode of Prakriti that induces slothfulness and inertia.

**Tamasic** —Being of the condition of tamas, slothful and dull.

**Tamboura or Tanpura** —A four or six-string drone instrument used to accompany Indian classical and devotional music.

**Tanmatras** —The five rudimentary elements, the essence of sound, touch, color, taste and smell; an atom, or an infinitesimal measure.

**Tantras** —Scriptures concentrating upon living a divine life in the world through the balancing of the Shiva and Shakti energies within the human being. Though they are considered by the orthodoxy as secondary scriptures, there is reason to believe that they are as old and as important as the Vedas since many of the Rishis were Tantric practitioners. Also, the worship of Shiva and Divine Mother Shakti probably predates the Vedas which suggests that the Tantric stream is extremely ancient.

**Tantric** —Having to do with Tantra, the ancient philosophy which stresses direct experience of spirituality while living in the world.

**Tantric sadhana** —Any of a plenitude of spiritual disciplines associated with the attainment of enlightenment in the Tantric tradition.

**Tao** —or Taoism, it is 'the way of man,' an indescribable path that means both way and teaching. It is mentioned in Confucian teachings but the Tao-te-ching of Lao-tzu is its main text.

**Taoist** —One who follows Taoism and who strives to become one with the Tao through emptiness and spontaneity.

**Taparloka** —One of seven higher realms beyond the earth plane, it is sixth in succession, just below Brahmaloka.

**Tapas** —Austerity. One of the ten yamas and niyamas of Patanjala Yoga which allows the aspirant strength and resilience and the ability to bear all problems and extremes which emerge in both worldly and spiritual life.

**Tathagata** —Literally, "which appears, vanishes and enlightens," referring to a thoroughly illumined being; a name associated with Lord Buddha which He used in reference to Himself and other Buddhas.

**Tathagatagarbha** —True inner being; the transcendent conscious Awareness that is the true nature of all things, all beings.

**Tattva** —Cosmic principle; in Samkhya Philosophy, a term for twenty-four constituents of Prakriti which make up the universe of name and form.

**Tattvamasi** —Literally, "That thou art," in reference to the apparently individualized soul and its connection to the Supreme Soul.

**Tattva-Shuddha** —Purification of principles.  A method in Tantra Philosophy by which the aspirant identifies each ascending principle in mind and nature in order to reveal them as being mutable and other than the immutable Atman.

**Tejas** —The fire of austerity; inner power which comes from intense and continual sadhana; subtle energy obtained from sublimated lifeforce which radiates from illumined beings and thus aids in conferring spiritual transmission to others.

**Thakur Sri Ramakrishna** —See Ramakrishna.

**Theravada** —Literally, "The Path of the Elders."  Called the Hinayana, or lesser vehicle, it is Buddhism as followed by those who focus upon the early and fundamental sutras uttered by Lord Buddha and who view him mainly as a great teacher rather than a divine transcendent Being.

**Tirtha** —Place of pilgrimage; place where divinity dwells; holy seat or throne containing the energy of the gods; holy waters.

**Titiksha** —Forbearance and patience in spiritual practice; ability to bear all extremes, whether of a physical or mental nature; one of the Six Treasures of Vedanta practice.

**Treta Yuga** —In connection with the doctrine of evolution, after Satya and Dvapara Yuga, the Treta Yuga occurs, followed by the present age called Kali Yuga.  In each succeeding age or yuga, awareness of one's spiritual nature gets more and more obscured.  After the Kali Yuga, pralaya occurs, which is the dissolution of the universe of time and space.  The passing of all four yugas is called a Mahayuga, after which the cycle begins again.

**Triputi or Triputa** —Any of a set of three principles which have an intrinsic connection and profound meaning such as the seer, what is seen and the ability to see or the knower, what is known and the act of knowing.

**Trishna** —Thirst, especially with regard to sensual craving and desire.

**Tulsi Ma** —An aspect of the Goddess associated with the natural healing power inherent in plants; a divine consort of Narayana.

**Turiya** —Literally, "the fourth," referring to the fourth and highest state of consciousness beyond waking, dreaming and deep sleep.

**Uddhava** —Literally, "one who uplifts"; a member of the Yadava clan who was a great devotee of Sri Krishna.

**Udghata** —The early awakening of Kundalini in the root chakra, Muladhara which affects higher centers.

**Umavati** —Friend of creation; a name for the Mother of the Universe, especially in Her aspect as Uma, eternal companion of Shiva.

**Upadhi** —A limiting adjunct; body; vehicle; a veil that obscures the true nature of a thing.

**Upakleshas** —Various negative elements which spring forth from the Mulakleshas with regards to the effects of pride, desire, greed and other passions.

**Upanishadic** —Having to do with the Upanishads and its Wisdom.

**Upanishads** —The Brahmakanda portion of the Vedas dealing with the knowledge that confirms Truth and reveals the Atman.

**Uparati** —Self-settledness or contentment, it is one of the Six Treasures of Vedanta practice which keeps the mind from drifting back to old habits and actions.

**Upeksha** —Equanimity; detachment; indifference.

**Uttar Pradesh** —A province in India.

**Vaikhari** —The last and grossest state of manifest knowledge through the primal sound vibration wherein words are formulated from and associated with thought and meaning and connected to their specific objects.

**Vaikuntha** —The celestial abode of Lord Vishnu.

**Vairagya** —Detachment. Also defined as dispassion, it is one of the Four Jewels of Vedanta practice. After discrimination is applied revealing what is real and what is unreal, detachment supplies the necessary power to withdraw from what is unreal.

**Vairajas** —Illumined souls occupying a high realm of existence who are perfect in detachment.

**Vaishnava** —A follower of Vishnu, devotee of Krishna and Ram; one who follows Vaishnavism.

**Vaishnavism** —The philosophy which stresses the worship of Vishnu, especially through the incarnations of Sri Krishna and Sri Ram. It focuses on the Bhakti Yoga path as the essence but favors elements of Jnana Yoga as well.

**Vaishvanara** —The first of four states of consciousness described by Vedanta associated with the waking condition.

**Vajrasana** —A posture ideal for sitting in meditation in that there is perfect ease and little strain on the body, which allows the aspirant to concentrate the mind and meditate on Reality instead of being preoccupied with the body.

**Vak Devi** —Goddess of the word; a name for Sarasvati, the Goddess of knowledge and learning. It is She who connects the thought, the sound, the word and its meaning together and it is She who is inherent in all four as the very power of comprehension.

**Valmiki** —Best known as the author of the Ramayana, he is also credited with writing the Yoga Vasishta. Venerated as a sage, he was not always so. It was he, in his life as a thief, who attempted to rob Narada but Narada reasoned with him and Valmiki repented. Entering spiritual life, Valmiki is said to have remained so long in meditation that an anthill (valmiki) rose up around him. Thus, his name.

**Vamri** —White ants. In one story, Lord Brahma used them to eat through the bowstring of the bow that Vishnu was sleeping against in order to wake him up, but when they succeeded the force of the string breaking severed the head of the Lord. It was replaced temporarily with a horse's head by the Divine Mother so that Vishnu could then kill the demon Hayagriva who could die only at the hand of a horse-headed figure.

**Vanaprastin** —The forest dweller who retires from the world and practices spiritual disciplines in solitude; the third stage of life according to Hindu Dharma, the first being the celibate student, the second being the married householder and the fourth being the renunciate or sannyasin.

**Varnamayi** —One of four goddesses or aspects of Kundalini Shakti that, when awakened, lights up the heart and throat chakra and infuses the being with love, devotion, and wisdom resulting in increased powers of speech, music, mantra and intelligence.

**Varanasi** —The holy city of Shiva, also called Benares.

**Varuna** —An ancient Vedic god whose powers are all pervasive, traditionally associated with the earth, the heavens and the elements, especially water.

**Varuni** —Waterlike; consort of Varuna in his aspect as the overseer of lakes, rivers and oceans; a village woman whom the Avadhut instructed about marriage and spiritual life.

**Vasishtha** —The great rishi, one of the seven great original Rishis according to Manu, who is said to be the author of the Rig Veda. The Yoga Vasishtha of Valmiki consists of instructions given to Rama by this great sage, for he was also the family priest of Ram's father, King Dasharatha.

**Vashitva** —One of the eight occult powers which allows those in pursuit of lower ideals to draw others to them.

**Vasuki** —A huge snake of great repute, king of the Nagas who supports the earth. He acted as an arrow for Shiva's bow, the axle for His chariot and his bracelet as well.  He was used by the gods and asuras as a rope with which to turn Mount Mandara in the churning of the nectar ocean.

**Vasundhara** —Literally, abode of wealth; the goddess of the earth; a name for the earth.

**Vayu** —The god of the wind, of air, of atmosphere; vital breath; prana.

**Vedamayi** —One of four goddesses or aspects of Kundalini Shakti which, when awakened, enlightens all levels of the being and brings about bliss and nondual realization.

**Vedangas** —The six limbs of Vedanta, namely shiksha, kalpa, vyakarana, nirukta, chandas, and jyotisa – pronunciation, ritual, grammar, etymology, prosody and astronomy.

**Vedanta** —One of the six traditional philosophies and orthodox darshanas of India, also called Uttara Mimamsa.

**Vedavyasa** —A name for Vyasa, who gathered the Vedas into a collection, thereby preserving them for our times.

**Vedantic** —Pertaining to Vedanta and thus being Vedantic in nature.

**Vedas** —The ancient and eternal scriptures of India which are without beginning, eternal and not ascribable to human authorship.  They are the Rig, Atharva, Yajur and Sama Vedas.  They are generally divided into four parts called the Samhitas, the Brahmanas, the Aranyakas and the Upanishads.  In addition, two other subdivisions occur called the Jnana-kanda and the Karma-kanda – the knowledge portions and the ritualistic portions.

**Vedic** —Pertaining to the Vedas and their wisdom.

**Vibhishana** —An asura who was the brother of Ravana but who was nevertheless devoted to Sri Ram.

**Vichara** —Inquiry into the nature of any aspect of Reality such as the Atman or a Mahavakya.

**Vichikitsa** —Perplexing; variegated; in Buddhism, the tendency towards skepticism that impedes the acceptance of spiritual truths.

**Vidya** —Higher knowledge, usually associated with spiritual wisdom.

**Vidya Shakti** —The positive aspect of Divine Mother's creative power that leads towards God and away from ignorance and delusion; the Universal Mother's transmission of spiritual wisdom.

**Vijnanamaya kosha** —The sheath of the intellect; the intellectual body as a covering over Reality.

**Vijnani** —One who has gone beyond the duality of knowledge and ignorance.  To paraphrase Sri Ramakrishna, in a spiritual context, an ajnani is ignorant that there is fire potential in wood; a jnani knows that there is fire potential in wood; but a vijnani knows how to kindle that fire in wood and can therefore cook his meal and receive nourishment.  This demonstrates the difference between a worldly person, a wisdom seeker and an enlightened being.

**Vikarana Bhava** —The power to abide in a conditionless state beyond the senses and the universe; the fifth practice of purification prescribed by Tantra wherein the aspirant realizes that Consciousness is not dependent upon anything manifest for its existence.

**Vinashahamkaravada** —The way of self-dissolution or the effacing of the limited ego in order to attain identity with Absolute Reality. In a positive sense, ripening the ego so that it does not act as a barrier to enlightenment.

**Vinasha Samsara** —The destruction of ignorance which allows the aspirant to transcend rounds of birth and death in suffering and ignorance.

**Vindu** —In Tantra, the twofold power called shukra and maharaja that is associated with sexual energy and procreation, which when sublimated, acts to aid the process of enlightenment.

**Vishnu** —The second deity in the Vedic Trinity; the God of preservation and the one from whom the Avatars emanate.

**Vishnutirtha** —Throne of Lord Vishnu; any place where Lord Vishnu resides.

**Vishva** —The Universal Soul; the cosmos; a name for the individual soul in the waking state.

**Vishvakarma** —Literally, "accomplisher of all actions"; the divine architect, weapon maker and charioteer for the gods who was also a son of Brahma.

**Vishvarupa Darshanam** —Literally, "direct perception and communion with the Cosmic Form"; a chapter in the Bhagavad Gita wherein Arjuna beholds the Supreme Form of God.

**Vitala** —One of the seven hell realms or nether regions below the earth plane.

**Vitarka** —Debate; discussion; in Buddhism, doubts which arise that threaten to undermine one's balance and which, if unchecked, bring violent thoughts.

**Vivarta** —False superimposition; a term Vedanta teachers use to indicate the unexplainable appearance of the unreal over the real, especially with regard to matter and Spirit

**Vivarta Nirodha** —The destruction of false superimposition which reveals Reality and leaves the mind clear and radiant.

**Vivekachudamani** —Crest Jewel of Discrimination; a profound text by Shankaracharya citing the value of spiritual life and containing deep philosophical teachings.

**Viveka** —Discrimination, of the type that allows one to see through all personal and collective delusions and penetrate the coverings over Reality.

**Vrindaban** —The holy city in India associated with the life of Lord Krishna.

**Vyapti** —One of the eight occult powers which allow those who are attracted to lower ideals to increase in size and weight or appear bigger.

**Vyasti** —Microcosm; individual experience; one of the two modes of Maya, the other being samasti – collective.

**Vyavaharika** —Pertaining to the world of relativity; empirical process; worldliness as a path as opposed to spiritual life.

**Yadu** —An ancient hero mentioned in the Vedas, he appears in the Uddhava Gita as a prince of the Yadava clan who approaches an Avadhut for spiritual instruction.

**Yagnavalkya** —An ancient rishi of great repute who authored portions of Upanishads and who was the founder of the school of the White Yajur Veda. His discourse to Maitreyi, one of his two wives, forms an important part of the Brihadaranyaka Upanishad.

**Yajna** —Sacrifice; spiritual practices done in the spirit of dedication to achieve beneficial results; rites and rituals to the gods accomplished for the sake of heavenly attainments.

**Yama** —The god of death in the Hindu pantheon, whose function is not only to bring an end to life and action but to guide aspiring souls in the afterlife on the path that they have chosen, whether it be Godward or towards the nether regions. His most prominent appearance is in the Kathopanishad where he instructs Nachiketas in sacred ceremony and discourses on the truth of the Atman.

**Yamas** —Five preliminary exercises which prepare the aspirant for the practice of Patanjala Yoga, namely, satya, ahimsa, brahmacharya, asteya and aparigraha – truthfulness, peacefulness, continence, non-covetousness and nonreceiving of gifts.

**Yamastakam** —A hymn composed in honor of Yama, lord of death, in which eight of his many names are listed and honored.

**Yantra or Yantras** —Mystical diagrams, said to be Vedic in origin but developed and used in Tantra, designed for meditation and the visualization of certain aspects of Reality. The deities associated with any particular yantric symbol can work through that medium to destroy the ignorance and impediments of the votary and can also manifest their form and powers through it.

**Yashodhara** —The wife of Lord Buddha.

**Yoga** —Union; yoke; one of the six orthodox systems of philosophy in Vedic culture, founded by Patanjali, which outlines a well-developed path of spiritual disciplines designed to help unite the seeker with Supreme Reality.

**Yoga Vasishtha** —A sacred text of spiritual teachings and stories written by Valmiki. The transmission takes place through the rishi Vasishtha who instructs a world-weary Prince Rama on the eternal nature of Consciousness as well as the value of selfless action in the world.

**Yogamaya** —The Divine Mother as Vishnu's cosmic dream-play; the power of attraction, specifically that of disciple for guru, devotee for God.

**Yoga Sutras** —Written teachings on the philosophy of yoga, especially associated with the eight-limbed Yoga of Patanjali.

**Yogi or Yogis** —Beings who have attained perfection through yoga.

**Yogindra Yogi** —An ascetic who lived in the mountains behind Ekanta's village during his boyhood and who instructed him in spiritual life.

**Yogindra** —One lost in yoga, in constant communion.

**Yogini** —A woman who has practiced yoga and who has achieved union with Reality.

**Yogins** —Same as yogis.

**Yuga** —One of four ages or divisions of time, called Satya, Dvapara, Treta, and Kali, each consisting of thousands of years, which together make up a mahayuga or chaturyuga.

**Yukti** —Adeptship in yoga; skillfulness; one of a succession of three practices by which the aspirant comes to realization. They are shruti, yukti and anubhava – studying the scriptures, reasoning about the truths therein and gaining direct spiritual experience.

## SRV Associations of Oregon, San Francisco, Hawaii and New England
## Other Books By Babaji Bob Kindler

Advaita Vedanta Series

*Strike Off Thy Fetters!* – Commentary on Swami Vivekananda's Poem, the Song of the Sannyasin

*Hasta-Amalaka Stotram* – A Hymn of Eternal Enlightenment (translation and commentary).

Sword of the Goddess Series

*Twenty-Four Aspects of Mother Kali*

*The Ten Divine Articles of Sri Durga*

Poetic Verse

*We Are Atman All-Abiding* – 108 Verses on the Atman

Future Releases

*The Nine Limbs of Bhakti of Sri Ram*

*A Complete Anthology of Sri Ramakrishna's Stories* – In Categories, Numbered, and each with Commentary

*Visions of the Goddess* – Commentaries on the Ecstatic Songs of Ramprasad

*The Sword of the Goddess*


Inquire at:

SRV Association of Oregon

P.O. Box 14012

Portland, Oregon, 97293-0014

or

SRV Association of Hawaii

P.O Box 380

Paauilo, Hawaii, 96776

# Instrumental and Devotional Music by Babaji Bob Kindler

## Bhajans, Chants and Stotrams

Bhajans of Love and Wisdom
Shakti Bhajans
Guru Bhajans
Bhajananda
Hymns to the Master and the Mother
Hymns to the Goddess
Kali Bol
Universal Aspects
Avatar Bhajans
Hari Om Ramanam
108 Names of Sarada
Deva Devi Swarupaya
SRV Puja and Arati Hymns
Sarada Ramakrishna Name

## Songbook for Bhajans, Chants and Stotrams

Jai Ma Songbook

## Devotional Songs in English

Worlds Unseen

## Poetry with Music Background

Ecstatic Songs of Ramprasad

## Instrumental Music

Wingspan
Music from the Matrix I – Infinite Space
Music from the Matrix II – Sacred Earth
Music from the Matrix III – Waters of Life
Tiger's Paw
Ever Free, Never Bound

Inquire at:
  SRV Oregon
  P.O. Box 14012
  Portland, Oregon, 97293-0014
         or
  SRV Hawaii
  P.O Box 380
  Paauilo, Hawaii, 96776